American Adventures

Scholastic

American

Adventures
New Edition

**by Ira Peck, Steven Jantzen,
and Daniel Rosen**

Historical Consultant:
Joseph F. Wall, Ph.D.
*Chairman, Department of History
State University of New York at Albany*

Scholastic Book Services
New York Toronto London Sydney Auckland Tokyo

**Teaching Consultants for
AMERICAN ADVENTURES, New Edition:**

John B. Bastolich, Ph.D.
Consultant, Department of Social Studies
Minneapolis, Minnesota

Florence A. Jackson
Director, Center for the Humanities and the Arts
New York City Board of Education
New York City, New York

John W. Larner, Jr., Ph.D.
Klein Independent School District
Spring, Texas

Debbie Leidner
Social Science Resource Teacher
Los Angeles Unified School District
Los Angeles, California

**Staff for
AMERICAN ADVENTURES, New Edition:**

Project Editor: John Nickerson
Editor-in-Chief: Sturges F. Cary
Editorial Director: William F. Goodykoontz
Teaching Guide Editor: William Johnson
Contributing Editors: Elizabeth Dowling,
   Jonathan Landman, Norman Lunger,
   Frances Plotkin, Carl Proujan
Editorial Assistant: Elvira Pedernales

Production Editor: Nancy J. Smith

Art Editor and Designer: David Rollert
Art Director: Irmgard Lochner
Maps: Wilhelmina Reyinga
Illustration Research: Elnora Bode

On the cover: *Daniel Boone (center) leads
American settlers on their way west. Detail is
from a painting by George Caleb Bingham.*

For reprint permission, grateful acknowledgement is
made to:
American Heritage Publishing Company, Inc., for
"Legend of the South" by Cornelia Barrett Ligon from
the June 1956 *American Heritage*, copyright © 1956 by
American Heritage Publishing Company, Inc.
Citadel Press, a Division of Lyle Stuart, Inc., Secaucus,
New Jersey, for the excerpt from A DOCUMENTARY
HISTORY OF THE NEGRO PEOPLE IN THE UNITED
STATES FROM COLONIAL TIMES TO THE FOUNDING
OF THE N.A.A.C.P., edited by Herbert Aptheker.
Joan Daves, agent for The Estate of Martin Luther King,
Jr., for the excerpt from I HAVE A DREAM by Martin
Luther King, Jr., copyright © 1963 by Martin Luther
King, Jr.
Doubleday & Company, Inc., for the excerpt from
FOLLOWING THE COLOR LINE by Ray Stannard Baker,
copyright 1907, 1908 by The Phillips Publishing
Company, copyright 1908 by Doubleday & Company,
Inc.
The Emporia (Kansas) Gazette for the editorial by
William Allen White. Copyright 1920 by The Emporia
Gazette.
Fortune Magazine for the tables from YOUTH IN
TURMOIL, copyright © 1969 by Time Inc.
Harper & Row, Publishers, Inc., for the abridgement of
"Life in Bomb Shadow" from THE SECOND TREE
FROM THE CORNER by E.B. White, copyright 1951 by
E.B. White. This originally appeared in *The New
Yorker.*
Alfred A. Knopf, Inc., a Division of Random House,
Inc., for the excerpt from IN SEARCH OF LIGHT: THE
BROADCASTS OF EDWARD R. MURROW, 1938-1961,
by Edward R. Murrow, edited by Edward Bliss,
Jr., copyright © 1967 by The Estate of Edward R.
Murrow; and for "Mother to Son" by Langston Hughes
from SELECTED POEMS, copyright 1926 by Alfred A.
Knopf, Inc., and renewed 1954 by Langston Hughes.
David McKay Company, Inc., for the excerpt from
THE LONG SHADOW OF LITTLE ROCK by Daisy Bates,
copyright © 1962 by Daisy Bates.
Meredith Corporation for the excerpt from Carl
Sandburg's article describing the first jet passenger
flight across the U.S., copyright © 1959 by Meredith
Corporation.
Newsweek, Inc., for the excerpt from "The 100-Year-
Old-Woman," copyright © 1976 by Newsweek, Inc.
Pantheon Books, a Division of Random House, Inc., for
the excerpt from HARD TIMES: AN ORAL HISTORY OF
THE GREAT DEPRESSION by Studs Terkel, copyright ©
1970 by Studs Terkel.
Twayne Publishers, a Division of G.K. Hall & Company,
for the excerpt from NORWEGIAN-AMERICAN STUDIES
AND RECORDS.
Warner Bros. Inc. for the lyrics to "Blowin' in the
Wind" by Bob Dylan, copyright © 1962 by Warner Bros.
Inc. All rights reserved.

Contents

MAPS

CHARTS, TABLES, GRAPHS

To the Reader:

This book is about people — all kinds of people — who made history. It is about a woman who, in wartime, made bullets out of spoons. It is about a child who died in a covered wagon and was buried on the Oregon Trail. It is about decisions of Presidents and debates in Congress. It is about people who came from all over the world seeking opportunity in America. It is about freedom — and slavery. It is about good times — and bad times. It is a history of the United States.

The book is divided into four parts. In the first part, the United States is born. In the second part, the nation is torn by war — and then rebuilds. In the third part, Americans move onto the world stage. In the fourth part, the U.S. fights wars all over the globe — against Germany and Japan, in Korea and Vietnam. Of course, that is not all that happens; there is much more.

There are special sections in the book called "Looking Ahead" and "Looking Back." The "Looking Ahead" sections describe a period of time in a general way. The chapters that follow go into detail about the period. The "Looking Back" sections conclude the study of each period. They remind you of all that you have learned. They also help you to practice old skills and learn new ones.

You should also be aware of special materials in the back of the book. There is a chart that gives facts about all the Presidents. Another chart gives facts about all the 50 states. Here too you will find our country's two most important documents, the Declaration of Independence and the U.S. Constitution.

The history of the U.S., as presented in this book, is not complete. In some ways, it never can be. For people alive today — including you — are making history. Right now our country is changing for better or for worse. This is why you need to learn what Americans have done in the past. You will then be better prepared to guide our nation in the years ahead.

Book One

A Nation Conceived and Dedicated

11

1 THE FIRST AMERICANS

The manner of their fishing.

Looking Ahead: A Journey of 21,747 Years

Scene one. It is summertime. The sun burns hot in a clear blue sky. A small group of men, women, and children move swiftly but steadily across a grassy field. They wear animal skins around their waists. Some of them carry long, heavy sticks with pointed stones at one end. Others have just the branch of a tree to use as a weapon. Several dogs run at their feet.

These people are looking for food. If they are lucky, they will find a herd of wild horses. They will then chase the horses and kill them with their spears. If the hunters fail, however, they will have only fruits and berries to eat. They know no other way of obtaining meat.

Scene two. A 15-year-old boy is seated at a table. Two logs burn and crackle in the fireplace. The boy opens a small book and begins to copy from it. He dips the tip of a feather into an inkwell and writes these sentences:

Keep your Nails clean and short, also your teeth clean.
Sleep not when others Speak, Sit not when others stand.
Cleanse not your teeth with the table-cloth.
If you Cough, Sneeze, or Yawn, do it not Loud but Privately.

An old man enters the room. "Master Washington," he says, "your horse is ready." The young man stands and puts on a long coat held for him by the old man. He looks in a mirror, straightens his coat, and walks out of the house.

Both of these scenes are imaginary. Yet both are based on clues that have been put together from the past. What

How do we know how the first Americans lived? A few Europeans drew pictures that tell us. In the painting at left, a 16th-century Englishman, John White, shows what Indians in Virginia ate. How did they catch food? How did they keep warm?

13

do the two scenes have in common? At least one simple thing. Both are set on the same continent — North America. But many thousands of years apart.

The first scene is based on some careful guesses. It shows the way experts think people might have lived some 20,000 years before the birth of Christ. As far as experts know, Americans of those days did not have houses to live in or horses to ride. Like most humans of their time, they lived off the land as best they could.

The second scene is based more closely on known fact. It shows the way George Washington might have spent a day at his home in Virginia in 1747 A.D. By that time, many changes had taken place in the way some people in North America lived. Some of these changes can be seen in Washington's boyhood notebook. It contains the sentences about tablecloths, coughs, and sneezes.

What happened in North America between scene one and scene two? That is the subject of the first part of this book. In moving from one chapter to the next, the part sometimes covers thousands of years. How is it possible to keep track of all the changes that are taking place? It helps to keep the following three periods in mind:

The Pre-Columbian Period (about 20,000 B.C. to 1492 A.D). In these years, people in America knew little or nothing about the rest of the world. And the rest of the world knew little or nothing about the people in America. Groups of people now called *American Indians* developed their customs slowly — and by themselves. These groups learned to make tools out of stone — axes, spears, arrowheads, knives. Later some groups invented calendars. A few of them created their own form of writing. As time went on, some groups developed very advanced cultures. A few of the main "events" in the history of these groups are covered in Chapter One.

The Age of European Exploration (1492-1600). This period began with one of the most famous sea voyages in history. In 1492 three small ships from Spain landed on an island near North America. The voyage was led by an Italian sailor, Christopher Columbus. It touched off a race among European nations for the riches of the New World.

In the beginning, America was just an obstacle in the race. European sailors kept bumping into America on their way to East Asia — that is, to China and Japan. Soon, however, the Europeans found gold in the New World — in Mexico and Peru. They also stumbled upon large supplies of furs, fish, and other items that could bring wealth. European explorers were lured by such riches. Again and again, they set out to find more.

Most of the earliest voyages came from Spain and Portugal. These two nations led the way in exploring the New World. But the English and French did not want to be left out of the race. As time went on, they put more and more of their own ships to sea.

Europeans drew maps of the lands they had visited. Before long, they knew how vast these lands were. Some of the European voyages of exploration are described in Chapters Two and Three.

The British Colonial Period (1607-1775). These were the years when British families came to America

The moon, stars, trees, and people are all about the same size in this Indian painting on doeskin. Indians considered themselves one small part of nature — no more important than any other part.

to start a new life. The British were not the first people to set up colonies in the New World. The Spanish had already done so in Central and South America; the Portuguese, in Brazil. But the British colonies were to become a starting point for the European settlement of *North* America. It is from the British settlements that the young United States drew its language, some of its customs, and most of its laws.

The first British settlement in North America was a failure. It was planned by a bold fortune-seeker, Sir Walter Raleigh (RAWL-ee). Raleigh sent out his first group of settlers in 1585. Twice, bands of British people tried to make a home on Roanoke (ROE-uh-noak) Island off the coast of what is now mainland North Carolina. The first group ended up returning to Britain. The second simply disappeared.

Not long afterward, however, British settlers did succeed in building colonies. They did so first in Virginia, and a little later in Massachusetts. A century passed. In 1732 a British colonist named George Washington was born. In the same year the British king created the 13th and last British colony — Georgia. By this time, the English language and many British customs had been brought to the New World.

The story of how this happened is one of high adventure. It is the story of thousands of British people, carried across the dark Atlantic Ocean and put down in a strange land. And not all the settlers of the British colonies were British. Some were French and German, coming to the New World in search of religious freedom. Some were Dutch and Swedish, interested in building settlements of their own. Some were African, forced to endure the hardships of the journey as slaves. Parts of this story are told in Chapters Four, Five, and Six.

One of Columbus' sailors drew this map of the New World in 1500. He thought Cuba was an island. But Columbus himself was not so sure.

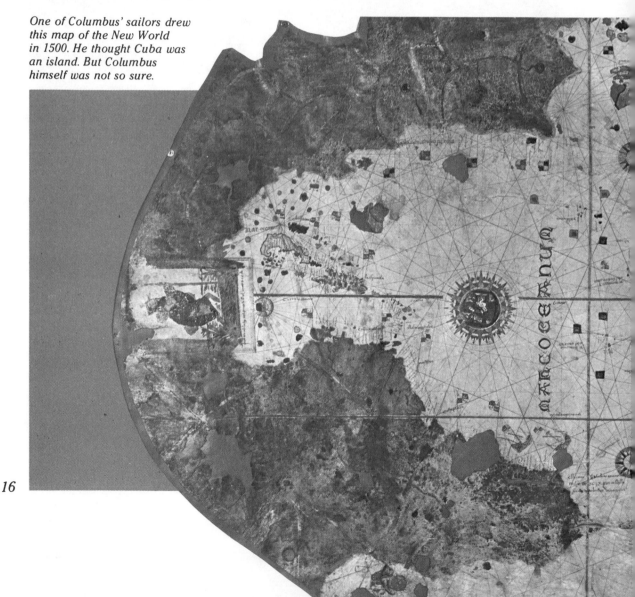

Chapter 1

Earth Mother, Sun Father

The ground under their feet was more than just grass, rock, and dirt to them. The sun in the sky was more than just a ball of flaming gas. To the American Indians we now call *Pueblos* (poo-EB-lows), the earth was like a mother because it fed them. The sun was like a father, giving warmth and light.

In the springtime, Pueblos thought of the earth as a woman pregnant with new life. For this reason, they were careful about the shoes they wore and the tools they used. They did not want to hurt their "earth mother" by wearing hard heels. They did not want to cut into the soil with sharp farm tools.

The Pueblos thought of themselves as part of nature. They usually tried to live with nature as it was. In this way, they were much like other groups who made their home in the Americas. Respect for nature was common among nearly all the people we refer to as the "first Americans."

Why "first"? Because ancestors of these Indians are thought to have been the first people to "discover" America. Scientists disagree about the date they arrived on the continent. Some say it may have been 20,000 years ago. Others say it was much longer ago than that.

But most scientists agree about how the first humans came to America. They came from Asia, crossing over a narrow strip of land that no longer exists. Now that land is under water. The Bering Sea that separates Asia from Alaska covers the route once taken by these people.

The earliest travelers were hunters from Asia. They wandered almost everywhere in search of animals to kill and eat. They made knives and spear points out of stone. With these they would kill wild horses, bison, and mammoths (early elephants with long tusks). Thousands of years passed in this way. Groups of hunters spread out from Alaska all the way to the tip of South America.

These groups differed greatly from one another. In fact, the Indians were many different people with different beliefs and languages. In most cases these different groups did not think of themselves as being related to any other group. Each group called itself by a certain name. Often the name was the word for "the people" in that group's language.

Then, approximately 2,000 years

ago, something very important began to happen in America. Certain American tribes learned to grow corn and beans. They were becoming farmers, instead of hunters. Instead of wandering from place to place, they were beginning to settle in villages.

Routes to America

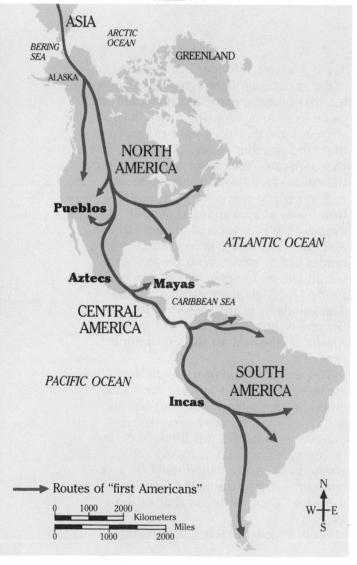

Routes of "first Americans"

0   1000   2000
Kilometers
0   1000   2000
Miles

N
W E
S

Hundreds of years passed. In Central America, one of the greatest of all Indian empires rose and fell. This was the empire of the Mayas (MY-uz). The Mayas developed their own system of picture-writing. They created a calendar at least as accurate as our own. In some ways, the Mayas were ahead of Europeans of the time.

The Golden Age of the Mayas ended around 900 A.D. In the next few hundred years, two other great Indian empires sprang up far from one another. One was the empire of the Incas (ING-kuz), centered mainly in what has now become Peru. The Incas were great engineers. They built a road system that ran for hundreds of miles. The other empire was that of the Aztecs in what is now Mexico. The Aztecs built a capital which, by 1600, held more people than most European cities of the time.

North of Mexico lived the Pueblos. At first they made their homes in giant cliffs of reddish brown rock near the Grand Canyon. On the tops of some of these cliffs, the brick houses where the Pueblos once lived still stand. Sometimes old Pueblo villages can be found in deep caverns right in the middle of a cliff.

The houses are more like apartments than separate dwellings. In fact, one Pueblo village — Pueblo Bonto in New Mexico — was once the biggest "apartment house" in the world. A thousand people probably lived in it. They lived there for about 200 years.

In the hot, dry lands of the American Southwest, Indians we now call Pueblos *built some of the world's most unusual homes.*

Rule by the people. Every apartment was about the same size as every other apartment. No Pueblo family was wealthier or more powerful than any other. The Pueblos also divided responsibilities equally. Half the citizens of the village were known as Summer People. They would run the village government during the summer months. The other half of the citizens, the Winter People, would run the government during the winter months. A Pueblo village in the year 1200 was a fine example of a *democracy* (rule by the people).

The Pueblos were also a peaceful people — one of the most peaceful in history. Unlike the Aztecs, they fought only when they were attacked. They did not think much about war. Instead, they cared most of all about planting and harvesting corn. Prayer to their nature gods was an important part of almost everything they did.

Around the year 1300, the Pueblo people began to leave their apartment dwellings on the red cliffs. Perhaps they were attacked by the more warlike Apache (uh-PATCH-ee) and Navaho (NAHV-uh-ho) peoples. Or perhaps their villages had grown too big to support their way of life. Scientists are not sure why they left. But scientists do know that the Pueblos moved south across Arizona. They moved onto lands where another Indian people, the Hohokams (ho-HO-kumz), lived. The Hohokams were also peaceful. The two cultures lived side by side for 100 years. There was no warfare between them. Neither people tried to conquer the other.

But these peaceful peoples were not prepared for what happened next. No Indian peoples anywhere were really prepared for the foreigners that came after 1500. The foreigners were warlike. They had metal weapons that nobody on American land had ever seen before. They also brought horses, cows, pigs, and other strange animals. They worshiped a single God — not the many gods of sky and earth that the Indians knew. They called themselves Spaniards, Portuguese, English, Dutch, and French. They did not believe in sharing land with other peoples. They believed in conquering it.

The Pueblos and other Indian peoples tried to preserve their cultures and their beliefs. But after 1500 their lands were taken from them by the foreigners from Europe. Never again could they live in peace in the old way.

A Second Look. . . .

1. *How did the Pueblo culture differ from the Aztec culture? How did it differ from the culture of Europeans?*

2. *The Indians of North America were divided into many different groups with different languages and beliefs. Yet we now refer to all of these peoples as if they were one. In your opinion, is this fair? Why or why not? How would you defend the use of the term* Indians *if you had to?*

3. *Divide a map of the United States into four roughly equal parts. Call one part the Northeast; another, the Southeast; a third, the Southwest; and a fourth, the Northwest. Find a book about North American Indians in your school or public library. Study one group from each of the four geographic areas. Write a report comparing the four peoples — their religions, foods, clothing, amusements, and dwellings.*

Chapter 2

Across the Sea of Darkness

A man riding a mule moved slowly down a dusty road in Spain. He wore an old and shabby cloak over his shoulders. Though his face seemed young, his red hair was already turning white. It was the winter of 1492, and Christopher Columbus was leaving Spain.

Twice the Spanish king and queen had refused his request for ships. He had wasted five years of his life trying to get their approval. Now he was going to France. Perhaps the French king would give him the ships he needed.

Columbus heard a clattering sound. He turned and looked up the road. A horse and rider came racing toward him. The rider handed him a message, and Columbus turned his mule around. The message was from the Spanish king and queen, ordering him to return. Columbus would get his ships. At last he would get his chance to sail to Asia. He would be the first person in history to reach Asia by sailing west across the ocean.

At least that is what Columbus thought. He was sure that his ideas

Christopher Columbus thought he could find a shortcut to Asia by sailing west from Europe. What he did find was as interesting as Asia.

about the world were right. First of all, he believed that the world was shaped like a round ball. Most mapmakers and scholars thought so too. Columbus also believed that the world was fairly small. He thought that Asian islands were only 2,600 miles (4,100 kilometers) west of Spain. Most mapmakers disagreed with him. They thought Asia was many thousands of miles from Europe. No ship could sail that far, they warned. They believed that any sailor foolish enough to try would surely starve to death. But Columbus thought he knew better.

Then, the Spanish queen Isabella decided to let him risk his life. Let him try to cross the Sea of Darkness, as the western ocean was called. If he succeeded, Spain would become rich from shipments of Asian spices, silks, and gold. This trade would make *any* nation rich. Spain's hated enemies, the Turks, now controlled these riches by controlling the land route to Asia. Spain's neighbor, Portugal, was also very close to becoming rich from the Asian trade. Portuguese ships had already sailed to the tip of Africa. Soon these ships would probably reach India by sailing south and then east.

But Spain might get there first if Columbus could sail west across the Sea of Darkness.

And what if Columbus were wrong? What would the Spanish queen lose? She was risking three ships — the *Santa María*, the *Niña*, and the *Pinta*. She was also risking the services of Christopher Columbus and 90 other sailors. But these were fairly small risks compared to what might be gained.

Columbus' journey. Columbus' three ships sailed from Palos, Spain, on August 2, 1492. They stopped at the Canary Islands for repairs and then started off again. Now they were moving through uncharted waters. Columbus was an able and experienced sailor. Under his command, the ships moved rapidly through peaceful seas.

Even so, his crew became nervous. They had been at sea for one whole month without seeing land. They demanded that Columbus turn back, but Columbus persuaded them to be patient a few more days. Finally, before dawn on October 12, a crew member shouted from the tallest mast: "Land! Land!" They had arrived.

But where was this? Who were these people who greeted them on the shore? They were practically naked. They were not dressed in fancy silk robes and jewelry as wealthy Asians were supposed to be. Columbus was puzzled. But he was certain that he had landed in the Indies — islands that now make up part of Southeast Asia. Surely, he thought, these people must be Indians. He captured a few of them so he could show them to the Spanish queen and king.

Columbus made three more trips across the Sea of Darkness. He spent the rest of his life trying to prove that he had found a sea route to Asia. On his death bed, he still believed that Asia lay just beyond the islands he had explored. Columbus was wrong, of course. But it took many more voyages by other sailors to prove that he was wrong.

Cabot and Magellan. Another Italian sailor, Giovanni Caboto (joe-VAH-nee kah-BOH-toe), had ideas much like Columbus'. He too thought he could reach Asia by sailing west. He too

To 16th-century Europeans, sailors who ventured into the Sea of Darkness were great heroes. One artist showed dangers he believed awaited brave Magellan (below). Explorers received heroes' welcomes when they returned to Europe. So Europeans assumed that welcomes must have been as warm on the other side of the ocean (above).

found a foreign country that would help him. He went to England where he dropped his Italian name and became "John Cabot." With only one ship and 18 men, Cabot sailed across the Sea of Darkness. He landed somewhere on the coast of Canada; nobody knows exactly where. This was in 1497, only five years after Columbus' first voyage. The English later believed that Cabot's discovery gave them the right to settle in North America.

But what were these lands that Columbus and Cabot had discovered? Were they part of Asia? Or were they a new continent — a whole new world? Europeans learned the answer in 1522. In that year, a ship carrying 18 sick and hungry sailors arrived in a Spanish port. The sailors had an amazing story to tell.

They and their captain, Ferdinand Magellan (muh-JELL-un), had left Spain

three years before. Magellan had led them through stormy waters around the southern tip of South America. He had led them for thousands of miles across the Pacific Ocean. Finally they arrived in Asia. Here, in the Philippines, Magellan got caught in a local war and was killed. The 18 sailors then went on to India, Africa, and finally home.

By accident, they had taken the first trip around the world. Now everybody knew that America was far from Asia — much farther than Columbus thought. Yes, Columbus was wrong about the size of the world. But we might never have known the size of the world if he had not dared to sail across the Sea of Darkness.

A Second Look. . . .

1. Columbus, Cabot, and Magellan all wanted to find a water route to Asia. Why was this goal so important to them?

Which of them succeeded in reaching his goal?

2. A Viking named Leif Ericsson (leaf ERR-ick-son) sailed along the coast of North America around the year 1000. Columbus sailed more than 450 years later. Why, then, do you suppose that Columbus usually gets credit for "discovering" America? Should the Vikings share some of the credit? Why or why not?

3. The map on this page shows the routes of the first voyages of Columbus, Cabot, and Magellan. Using a piece of tracing paper, copy the outlines of the continents on this map. Then refer to a map of Columbus' three later voyages — which can be found in most books of historical maps. Draw these routes on the map you have traced. Did Columbus ever actually land on the mainland of North or South America? If so, where?

Routes of Exploration, 1492–1522

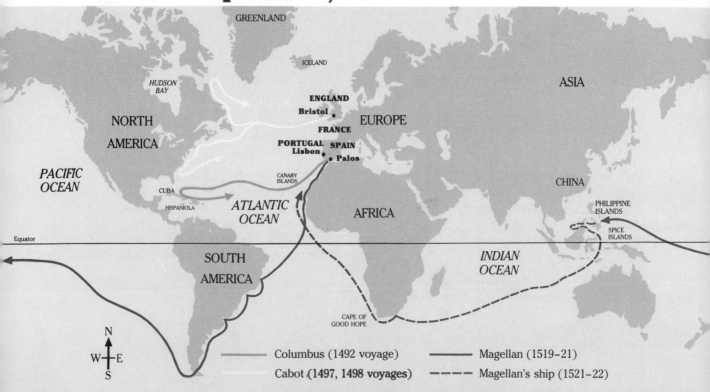

Chapter 3

Opening the Wilderness

People in London had never seen so much wealth. It gleamed and glittered along the city's cobbled streets. A long parade of horses and carts carried it in front of Londoners' wondering eyes. There were exactly 27 chests filled with bars of solid gold. Then came 99 carts heaped high with gold and silver coins.

What a wedding gift this was! Spain's Prince Philip was showing off his country's great wealth to his new bride, England's Queen Mary. The year was 1554. The gold and silver came from Spanish mines in Mexico and Peru. Thousands of Indians had been put to work digging it up for their Spanish conquerors. But what did Prince Philip care about how the gold was mined? He and his country were now the envy of all Europe. Most of the New World and its riches belonged to Spain.

That, in any event, is what the Spanish believed. But not everyone in Europe agreed. The English, French, and Dutch also wanted some of the American land and gold. Many people in England and France hated Spain. They had fought wars with Spain in the past. They expected to fight more wars in the future.

Spain, after all, was a Roman Catholic country. England was partly Protestant. In those days, Catholics and Protestants feared each other. Each thought the other was serving the devil. In England, therefore, many Protestants were

unhappy that Mary, their queen, had married Philip of Spain. They were overjoyed when this Catholic queen died. Her half sister Elizabeth, a Protestant, now became queen. Elizabeth was a proud and independent Englishwoman. She too wanted gold and silver from the New World. She wanted whole ships to be loaded with it — *English* ships. The French king meanwhile had the same ambition for France.

War at sea. Ships from England and France kept sailing for America. Many of them were well equipped for a fight on the high seas. Cannons were aimed through square portholes on both sides of a ship. Soldiers on board were armed with swords and muskets. From the tallest masts, sailors could look out over the dark blue water. The ships they saw on the horizon were often Spanish ones, loaded with treasure from New Spain. English ships then prepared to attack.

The attack often went like this: After an hour's chase, the English ship pulled alongside its target. The captain gave the order to fire. Boom! The Spanish ship fired back. Boom! A cannonball ripped into the side of the English ship. The English captain shouted: "Sling a man overboard to stop the leaks!" A man climbed over the side of the ship. Hanging from a rope, he plugged the hole with tar, then climbed back to the deck.

25

Now the ships were so close they touched each other. With shouts and curses, the English leaped into the Spanish ship. The Spanish were outnumbered. Their ship was slowly sinking. They surrendered. The English grabbed all the Spanish treasure they could and carried it home.

Such attacks on Spanish shipping happened again and again. The English captains who led the attacks became known as "sea dogs." They acted no better than pirates. But the English people loved them. So did their high-spirited queen, Elizabeth the First. To Elizabeth the attacks seemed a clear threat to Spanish power on the high seas. Besides, much of the treasure stolen in the at-

Europeans didn't come to the New World for fun — they came for gold. When they arrived, they put Indians to work, as this engraving shows.

tacks went to support the English queen.

Of course, Spain fought back. It was especially worried about Spanish ships sailing from Mexico to Cuba. To protect them, the King of Spain sent several hundred soldiers and sailors to Florida. Their commander was Pedro Menéndez de Avilés (PAY-droh muh-NAIN-dez day ah-vee-LACE). He was instructed to start a Spanish colony. In August 1565, Menéndez built a fort out of wood and mud in northern Florida. He called the place St. Augustine (AW-gus-teen). This was to become the first permanent settlement in North America.

Farther north along the coast, French Protestants had built another settlement. This was Fort Caroline, and it was a threat to Spanish shipping. Soon after arriving in the area, Menéndez led his small army to the French port. They arrived at the fort early in the morning when all the French were sleeping. The French didn't have time to reach for their weapons. In less than an hour, all of them were dead.

But the French did not give up. Neither did the English. Both groups still hoped to share the riches of North America. French explorers were most interested in lands far to the north. The English seemed more interested in the lands we now call Virginia and Maryland. They tried several times to set up villages in North America. But as late as 1592, 100 years after Columbus' discovery, their efforts at starting colonies had failed.

Jamestown and Quebec. Success came finally — in 1607 for the English and 1608 for the French. One spring day in 1607 three English ships carrying 100 passengers sailed up Chesapeake Bay.

Their type corned

Their greene corne

Corne newly sprong

Their sitting at meate

SECOTON.

A Ceremony in their prayers w strange gestures and songs dansing aboute posts carued on the topps lyke mens faces.

The howse wherin the Tombe of their Heroundes standeth

English artist John White drew the Indian village of Secoton in what is now North Carolina in about 1590. White showed many kinds of activities. Hunters in woods (top left) are searching for food. Figure in hut (top right) is waiting to scare birds away from a cornfield. Figures in circle (bottom right) are performing a religious dance in a sort of open-air temple. What other clues can you find to how these Indians once lived?

One of their leaders was a young, bearded soldier named Captain John Smith. On a low, marshy strip of land they started building a town. They named it Jamestown after the English king.

A year later, on a summer day in 1608, another bearded soldier climbed up a steep bank overlooking the broad St. Lawrence River. He raised the French flag high in the air and named the spot Quebec (kwih-BECK). The soldier's name was Samuel de Champlain (sham-PLANE). At Quebec, with the help of 32 men, he built a trading post and started a new French colony.

Both Champlain and Smith were unusual men. They wanted to build colonies that would last. Many of their companions wanted only to dig for gold, strike it rich, and go home. But the colonists soon learned to value food more than gold, health more than wealth. At Jamestown few of the colonists were

27

skilled laborers who knew how to work with their hands. The first winter was a hard one, and many fell ill and died. After John Smith took command, however, he set a new rule: "No work, no food." For many months after that, matters improved.

Most of the earliest European settlers of both colonies were men. But as time went on, some women also traveled from the Old World to the New. In 1619 Helen de Champlain, the young wife of Samuel, came to Quebec to live for several years. At about the same time, larger numbers of women also arrived in Jamestown.

The first black settlers also arrived on the North American mainland. They came to Jamestown on a Dutch ship in August 1619. The ship's captain sold 20 of them to the colony, probably as *indentured servants*. (These were servants who agreed to work for another person for a certain period of time. In America the period usually lasted two to seven years.) Many white colonists were also indentured servants in those days.

As the colonies grew, each became known for a special product. Quebec survived by selling the hides of beavers and other animals, trapped and traded by the Indians. These skins were shipped back to France and sold to French hat-makers. In this way they made money for Quebec colonists.

In Jamestown colonists turned to another kind of business. From the Indians they had learned to grow and smoke tobacco. Soon London taverns were filled with the smoke of tobacco grown at Jamestown. The colonists there did not exactly strike it rich. But tobacco helped their village to survive.

The first settlements at Quebec and Jamestown were very small beginnings. But they did make one thing clear: North America no longer belonged only to the Indians or the Spanish. The French and the English had arrived on the continent to stay.

A Second Look. . . .

1. *Is it true that American Indians helped Spain to become wealthy? That they helped colonists at Jamestown to survive? That they contributed to Quebec's success? Explain each answer, using evidence from this chapter.*

2. *Some of the earliest warfare among Europeans in North America grew partly out of religious differences. Why do such differences sometimes lead to fighting?*

3. *St. Augustine, Jamestown, and Quebec City all began as tiny villages. Which of them has grown the most since 1619? You can obtain this information by consulting an almanac or encyclopedia.*

Tobacco became Jamestown's leading product. It started a new European habit — smoking. Tobacco was sold in Europe under labels such as this one.

28

Chapter 4

They Were Free at Last

"Land ho! Land! Land ho!"

The men, women, and children on the little ship looked up. They saw a sailor on top of the tallest mast, waving and shouting. They could hardly believe what he was saying. They rushed to the side of the ship. It was true. There was land ahead.

The Mayflower *sails stormy seas.*

The trip from England had been terrible. The travelers had been at sea for 65 days. Great storms had shaken and tossed the ship. Huge waves had crashed down on it. But now, on November 19, 1620, land was in sight. The people on the ship cried with joy and gave thanks to God. At last they could see the shore of the New World.

Who were these people who had made such a dangerous trip? Why had they left their homes to settle in a wilderness?

They had come to America because in England they were outlaws. The laws of England said that there could be only one kind of church. This was the Church of England, and it was ruled by the English king. What if you wanted a different religious service? What if you and a group of friends worshiped in your own home? Several groups of English people tried this. Many of them were thrown in jail. These people were called *Separatists* because they wanted a separate church — a church of their own.

At first the Separatists thought of going to Holland where the Dutch were allowed to worship freely. Many of them packed up and moved there in 1608. But after a while they became unhappy with their new home. They did not like to see their children speaking Dutch, instead of English. The Separatists wanted to keep their religious freedom. But they also wanted to be English. Now they began to think about starting over again somewhere else — in America.

The English government allowed people such as Separatists to move to lands it held overseas. It did so to encourage the growth of colonies in the New World. So, one autumn day in 1620, a group of Separatists met together on a dock in Plymouth, England. They crowded onto the deck of a little ship called the *Mayflower*. For two long months at sea, they suffered terribly from storms and sickness. Then at last, they reached the edge of North America. 29

Settlers at Jamestown feared the mysterious forest. Puritan settlers in Massachusetts feared other things more. A New Englander drew "The Progress of Sin" in 1744. Notice that he has put "Sion" — the Puritan colony — in a wreath to shield it from those things he thinks sinful.

The English government had given the Separatists a charter to settle in Virginia. But perhaps by accident the captain of the *Mayflower* had taken them far to the north, outside of the Virginia territory. Even so, the passengers were eager to go ashore. They decided to settle where the captain had taken them, in New England, near Cape Cod. While still on board ship, they signed a compact, or agreement. They agreed to obey all laws that were made for the good of their settlement. This *Mayflower Compact* marked an important step toward self-government in the New World.

Settling in Plymouth. Now the ship's passengers would have to build a village. But where? They looked up and down the coast of Massachusetts. After a month of searching, they found a good place to start building. They named it Plymouth, after the town they had left in England.

The first winter in Plymouth was very hard. The settlers had never known such cold in England. About half of them died of hunger and disease. But in the spring, help came. A tall Indian named Samoset walked into the little village. He was a quiet, helpful man, as were many of the other Indians who lived in the area.

One of them, named Squanto, came to live in Plymouth. He showed the English how to plant corn, pumpkins, and beans. He also showed them the Indian ways of hunting and fishing. The Plymouth colony might not have lasted if it had not been for Squanto.

At Plymouth, the Separatists — or *Pilgrims*, as we now call them — found what they had come for. They were at last free to build their own church and worship in their own way. English laws did not bother them in the American wilderness.

Back in England, meanwhile, laws about religion were getting even more strict. More and more people were being punished and even tortured for their beliefs. One group, called *Puritans*, were fighting to change the English church. They thought the church put too much stress on ceremony. For example, they disliked the costly robes worn by ministers of the church. They thought a minister should dress more simply. Just for speaking their minds about this, Puritans could be whipped and jailed. Like the Pilgrims, they too began thinking of escaping to America.

Hundreds of them finally decided to make the dangerous voyage. In 1630, 17 ships landed in a harbor several miles north of Plymouth. On board were about 2,000 people — 20 times the number of people carried by the *Mayflower*. Some were Puritans; most were not. But a Puritan, John Winthrop, was governor. Other leaders were also Puritans. They set to work building a new English colony to the north of Plymouth. They called this colony Massachusetts Bay.

Puritan leaders decided where towns should be built. They named one town Boston, another Salem, and a third Newton. The Puritans believed that only they could understand the true meaning of the Bible. At first they thought that only they could make the proper laws for Massachusetts Bay.

But John Winthrop was a fair-minded man. He could see that more and more settlers were coming to the colony. He thought that the views of these newcomers should be taken into account. So, in 1630, he and other leaders worked out a plan for holding some elections.

Most early Puritan churches were very humble. Worshipers sat on hard benches in cold rooms (above). Puritan painters — called limners *— limited themselves almost entirely to portraits such as this one of a woman named Ann Pollard (right).*

This was the first step on the road to democracy in Massachusetts Bay.

In other ways, the Puritans were less fair-minded. They forced everyone to live according to Puritan teachings. Everyone was required to go to Puritan churches. People who fell asleep in the Boston church could be whipped at the town whipping post. Puritans thought such punishments were needed. They believed strong religious laws would make people respect the Bible.

Puritan critic. One young minister, however, began to wonder about all these laws and punishments. He began to ask hard questions. Was it right, he asked, for people to be forced to go to church? Could people who were wicked at heart be saved simply by sitting in church every Sunday? Did the English colonists have a right to take land away from the Indians? The young minister, named Roger Williams, answered all his own questions. No, said Williams, many Puritan practices in Massachusetts Bay were wrong.

Williams' ideas were dangerous. They threatened everything that the Puritan leaders were trying to do. The Puritans demanded that Williams stop criticizing the church officials. Williams refused. Puritan leaders tried to place him under arrest.

But in the middle of winter, 1636, Williams escaped from the colony. With the help of Indians, he started to build a new town southwest of Massachusetts Bay. He called it Providence. His friends from Massachusetts joined him there. This was the beginning of a new colony, Rhode Island. Here anyone could attend any church at all. Williams promised that his government would not interfere with religion. In Rhode Island, people could go to church or not, as they wished.

The Pilgrims at Plymouth and the Puritans at Massachusetts Bay had found religious freedom for themselves. Now they would give it to nobody else. No Catholics or Jews could worship in Massachusetts. But because of Roger Williams, there was one place in America where everyone could worship freely.

A Second Look. . . .

1. *In this chapter, you have read about the beginning of three British settlements in America. In the previous chapter you read about a fourth settlement. What were the four settlements? Why was each of them founded? Why were the four located where they were?*

2. *Roger Williams believed that Puritan leaders in Massachusetts Bay were wrong about some of their ideas. What were these ideas? Do you think Puritan leaders were right or wrong in trying to arrest Williams? How else could they have dealt with his criticism?*

3. *Imagine that you are a Pilgrim. You have been given the job of planning the village of Plymouth. How many houses need to be built? (The* Mayflower *carried 98 passengers when it landed at Plymouth.) How will the houses be built — of wood, brick, or stone? How long will it probably take to build these houses? Where will people live in the meantime? What can be done to protect the village from outside attack? Should animals be kept inside the village? (How Plymouth was actually built is described in the teaching guide which belongs to your teacher.)*

Chapter 5
So Wise a Ruler

"My prison shall be my grave before I will budge one bit. I owe my conscience to no man."

These words were written in 1668 by a "born fighter" named William Penn. He wrote them while he was in jail in the Tower of London. His cell was a tiny, bare room under the roof. It was icy cold in the winter. It was steaming hot in the summer. Bad prison food made him thin and weak.

Penn didn't have to be in prison. He could have had a soft life. His father was a British navy hero and a rich man. His home was a castle with servants and many acres of land. His father had sent him to a famous English college, Oxford University. Many of the students there were the sons of noblemen. Penn was friendly and good at sports, and he had soon become popular.

But after a while, Penn began to question an English law. The law said that all English people had to belong to the Church of England. Puritans and people who belonged to other churches were often beaten. Sometimes they were put in prison, and even hanged. Penn saw many college students beat up Puritans, Separatists, and Quakers in the streets. He tried to defend the people who were beaten, and was called a "troublemaker." Penn and some of the other college students stopped going to the Church of England as a protest. Then

Penn was forced to leave college.

Penn's father was very angry with him. At first he threw his son out of the house. Later he felt sorry and took him

The portrait below is the only one known to have been drawn of William Penn in his own lifetime.

back. Then he sent the young man on a trip to France and Italy to make him a "gentleman."

Penn did become a gentleman. He wore fine silk clothes and a sword. In London he met the king and many great noblemen. Then in 1665 a terrible disease hit London — the plague, or "black death." Many thousands of people became sick and died. Others ran away from London to save themselves. But the Quakers stayed to take care of the sick and the dying. Penn liked these brave people. Before long, he became a Quaker himself.

Quaker beliefs. What were the Quakers like? They lived simply and wore plain clothes. They did not have churches or regular ministers. They met in plain buildings called "meeting houses." Any member could speak at meeting when he — or she — felt moved by the spirit of God. The Quakers believed in strict honesty in business. They were against violence and war. They would not serve in the king's army. They were against any kind of unfair treatment of one person by another. They also believed in helping the sick and people in jail. They called themselves "Friends."

William Penn became a leading Quaker. He was thrown into jail in the Tower of London for nine months. He was told to give up his Quaker beliefs. His answer was to refuse to budge. Later Penn was sent to prison two more times.

Penn began to feel that freedom of religion was impossible in England. More and more, he thought of starting a colony in America. In this colony, men and women would be free to worship in whatever way they wished. Men would

also be free to vote as they pleased.

The king owed Penn's father a lot of money. Penn's father was now dead. So Penn asked the king to give him, instead of money, a grant of land in America. The king was glad to give Penn some land — anything to get rid of this Quaker troublemaker. He gave Penn the land that is now Pennsylvania. The name means "Penn's woods."

Charter of Liberties. In 1681 Quakers from England and other countries set sail for Pennsylvania. Penn wrote a *Charter of Liberties* for the new colony. Many years later it became a model for the U.S. Constitution. The Charter said: The lawmakers of the colony would be elected by the citizens of the colony. Every male citizen of the colony could vote. There would be freedom of religion for all. There would be freedom of speech for all. There would be trial by jury for anyone accused of a crime.

Thomas Jefferson, who wrote the Declaration of Independence in 1776, called Penn "the greatest lawgiver the world has produced."

Penn was also a good friend to the Indians of Pennsylvania. He was honest and fair, and the Indians respected him for it. Penn once told a group of Indians: "All will be brotherhood and love. I consider us all the same flesh and blood, joined by one heart."

Penn agreed to several treaties with the Indians. At these times, the Indians replied that they and the colonists "must live in love as long as the sun and moon give light." The treaties were not broken in Penn's lifetime.

Penn made Pennsylvania "a free colony for all mankind." It was free not just

There is no minister at a Quaker meeting. Each person who attends a meeting is free to remain alone with his or her thoughts. An American artist recorded this meeting-house scene in the 1700's.

for English people or Quakers, but for people of all nations and religious beliefs. One colonist said this about Penn: "He is loved and praised by all. The people have never seen so wise a ruler."

A Second Look. . . .

1. *Why did William Penn want to start a colony in America?*

2. *William Penn treated the Indians of Pennsylvania with great goodwill. How* *did Penn's attitude help Pennsylvania in his lifetime? If Penn had been cooler toward Indians, do you think they would have reacted the same way to him? Give reasons for your answers.*

3. *Imagine that you have been asked to write a charter of liberties for your community. Look very carefully at the five points Penn included in his charter. Then make a list of the liberties you would want to include in yours. In what ways do the two lists differ?*

Settlement of the 13 Colonies

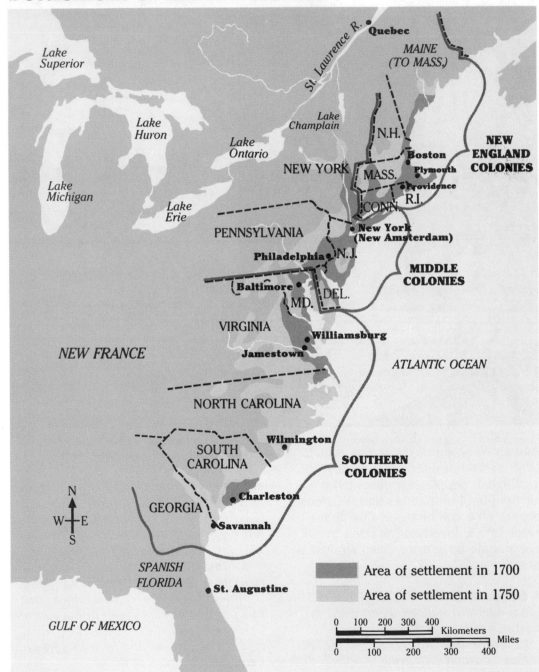

Lake Superior

Lake Huron

Lake Michigan

Lake Ontario

Lake Erie

Lake Champlain

St. Lawrence R.

Quebec

MAINE (TO MASS.)

N.H.

NEW YORK

MASS.

Boston

Plymouth

Providence

CONN

R.I.

New York (New Amsterdam)

PENNSYLVANIA

N.J.

Philadelphia

MIDDLE COLONIES

Baltimore

DEL.

MD.

VIRGINIA

Williamsburg

Jamestown

NEW FRANCE

ATLANTIC OCEAN

NORTH CAROLINA

Wilmington

SOUTH CAROLINA

SOUTHERN COLONIES

GEORGIA

Charleston

Savannah

NEW ENGLAND COLONIES

N
W E
S

SPANISH FLORIDA

St. Augustine

GULF OF MEXICO

Area of settlement in 1700

Area of settlement in 1750

0 100 200 300 400 Kilometers

Miles

0 100 200 300 400

The Impossible Dream

In 1728 an Englishman named James Oglethorpe (OH-gull-thorp) visited a friend in a London prison. Like many other prisoners, the friend had been put in jail because he could not pay his debts. The prison was damp and dirty and overcrowded. Oglethorpe was shocked by the filth and suffering that he saw.

Not long after Oglethorpe's visit, his friend became sick and died. This only made Oglethorpe more eager to correct conditions in English jails. Oglethorpe was a member of Parliament, England's lawmaking body. He had power and influence. He worked to free thousands of people who were rotting in jail only because they were debtors.

But where were these people to go after getting out of jail? There was not enough work for all of them in England. That much seemed clear. The problem troubled James Oglethorpe until he came up with a plan. "Why not send some of the poor to a new colony in America?" he asked.

In 1730 Oglethorpe and some friends began working on the idea. They proposed calling their new colony Georgia in honor of their king, George II. They asked the king to grant them land to the south of South Carolina for starting the new colony. The king agreed in 1731 and signed a charter the next year. He gave the power of making rules for Georgia to 21 men, called Trustees. One of the Trustees was James Oglethorpe.

The Trustees went about their work very seriously. Unlike others who organized British colonies in America, these men did not promise any profit from their plan. They acted unselfishly. They wanted their colony to grow strong. They knew that such growth would depend on the settlers themselves. For that reason, they chose their settlers very carefully. They tried to make sure only trustworthy people were selected.

Trustees' rules. By late 1732 the future settlers were ready. Oglethorpe and 38 poor families sailed to America to make a new home. The other Trustees stayed in London. They had never seen America. Even so, they gave very detailed orders for the running of the new colony. From London they decided exactly how much cheese and soap each settler would need. They planned to allow each just enough to live on — and no more. They also made three very unusual rules for Georgia. No other American colony had rules like these:

1. Nobody in Georgia would be allowed to drink rum or brandy.

2. Nobody in Georgia would be allowed to own a slave.

3. Anybody who owned 50 acres

37

An English prisoner kneels and tells British lords about harsh jail conditions. The lords created a new colony for debtors — Georgia.

(20 hectares) of land would have to plant 50 mulberry trees on it.

The first rule was meant to keep settlers hard at work and out of trouble. Then as now, some people who drank rum or brandy at night did not show up for work the next day. Nor were rum-drinkers always dependable soldiers. This worried the Trustees, who wanted to be certain that Georgia's borders would be defended.

The second rule made Georgia a very different colony from its neighbors. To the south lay Spanish Florida, where Indians had been enslaved for many years. To the north lay North and South Carolina and Virginia. In these colonies, slave-holding had recently become much more popular. The reason had to do with farming. Many farms in the South were growing very large at this time. These farms, called *plantations*, raised crops such as tobacco, rice, and indigo. They could make big profits if they had cheap labor.

So more and more plantations used black *slaves* shipped from Africa or islands in the Caribbean Sea. These newcomers faced a much harsher future than the black people who had arrived in 1619. The first black people in America had probably been indentured servants. Unlike them, black slaves had no term of service for their work. They were supposed to remain slaves for their entire lives.

Slavery was not, of course, limited to the South. By 1732 it had spread into nearly every colony, becoming the cruelest practice ever to take root in American soil. As early as 1688, some white people in Pennsylvania had spoken out against it. Some Trustees of Georgia also opposed it on moral grounds. But they mostly opposed it because it went against their plans.

Their plans were to make Georgia a land of small farmers. Slavery, they feared, would destroy the whole idea. If a white farmer owned a slave, they believed, he would be less likely to work himself. He would have to spend much of his time "watching against any danger ... from the slave."

The third rule was supposed to make money for England. The leaf of the white mulberry tree was the favorite food of silkworms. Mulberry trees seemed to grow very well in Georgia's hot climate. It seemed that Georgia would become a great silk-growing colony. Therefore, the Trustees required every Georgia farmer to plant mulberry trees.

Why the rules failed. But none of the Trustees' rules worked out very well. The English were used to drinking rum.

They could not imagine living without it. It didn't take long for Georgia settlers to find ways of breaking the Trustees' rule. Soon they were making rum in their own houses and drinking it as freely as if there were no rule at all.

The settlers also discovered that silk did not grow on trees — at least not *their* trees. They had trouble getting healthy silkworm eggs from Europe. Even if the worms lived, few people knew how to get the silk from them. The

Englishman Mark Catesby was one of the first artists to paint wildlife. He did this watercolor of an American woodpecker on a trip to Florida and the Carolinas in the 1730's (right). Another English artist showed the half-built city of Savannah in the new colony of Georgia (below).

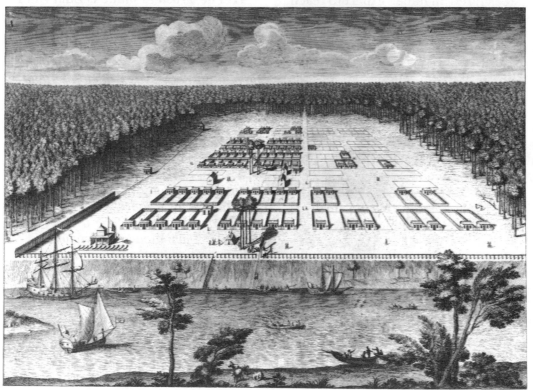

39

James Edward Oglethorpe

Trustees hired an Italian expert to teach the colonists. But he was not a good teacher. One day, in a fit of anger, he smashed his special tools and equipment and sailed for home.

To many settlers, the rule about slavery seemed least practical of all. They saw their neighbors in South Carolina planting rice on huge plantations and getting rich. But the rice crops planted in Georgia usually failed. Why? Because, the settlers argued, slaves were needed to do the hot, tiring work. Some settlers felt so strongly about this that they moved to South Carolina, where they could own slaves.

As time went by, the Trustees granted land to settlers in larger parcels. But every time they did, demands for slave labor increased. Finally, in 1750, the Trustees allowed the settlers to use slave labor in Georgia's rice fields. Two years later the Trustees gave their charter for the colony back to the king. The Trustees' plan had failed, but not

for lack of planning. If anything, the Trustees had come up with a plan so detailed that it could not be carried out. Their failure showed that rules for the opening of a new colony could not be set, with any success, from Europe. To be successful, these rules, whether good or bad, had to be laid down in America by Americans themselves.

Georgia survived the failure. After 1752 it became a royal province, governed in much the same way as Virginia. Over the next 20 years it grew very slowly in population. At the time of the American Revolution it was one of the smallest of the 13 rebelling colonies.

A Second Look. . . .

1. *The Trustees made certain rules for Georgia that did not work well. Name two of these rules and explain why they failed.*

2. *The English founders of Georgia thought the best way to help the poor was to send them to America. Do you think this was a good idea? Why or why not? How else could the government have helped the poor? How are poor people in the U.S. being helped today?*

3. *You have now read about the beginnings of five colonies — Virginia, Massachusetts, Rhode Island, Pennsylvania, and Georgia. Make a chart that shows: (a) when each colony was founded; (b) who founded it; and (c) why it was founded. With the founding of Georgia, there were 13 British colonies in all. The eight not mentioned in this part were Connecticut, Delaware, Maryland, New Hampshire, New Jersey, New York, North Carolina, and South Carolina. You might add to the chart by finding out how four of these eight were begun.*

Looking Back: The First Americans

	A		B		C		D		E		F	
1450		1500		1550		1600		1650		1700		1750

Putting Events in Order

Chapters One through Six have shown how Europeans discovered and colonized America. Ten events in this history are listed here. Your job is to match each event to the correct period shown on the timeline above. On a piece of paper, number from **1** to **10**. After each number, write the letter of the period in which the event occurred.

1. The first permanent English colony is begun at Jamestown.
2. Sailing from Spain, Christopher Columbus makes his first voyage across the "Sea of Darkness."
3. Samuel de Champlain explores the St. Lawrence River for France.
4. One of Ferdinand Magellan's ships completes a voyage around the world.
5. James Oglethorpe founds Georgia, the 13th British colony.
6. Roger Williams promises religious liberty in Rhode Island.
7. The first black people arrive on the North American mainland.
8. William Penn receives a grant of land to start a colony.
9. Pilgrims leave the *Mayflower* to build a new colony at Plymouth.
10. John Cabot explores North America.

Interpreting a Source

The passage below has been adapted from the writings of Gustavus Vassa, a black American. Vassa was born in Africa in 1745. He was only 15 years old when he came to America on a slave ship. This is his description of what he and other Africans suffered.

At last, the ship's hands made ready with many fearful noises, and we were all put under deck. The hold was so crowded that each of us scarcely had room to turn himself. The stench was so loathsome that it was dangerous to remain there for any time. The closeness

41

of the place, the heat, and the number in the ship almost suffocated us. The air soon became unfit to breathe, and brought on a sickness among the slaves. Many of them died. The shrieks of the women, and the groans of the dying, made the whole a scene of horror.

One day, when we had a smooth sea and moderate wind, two of my wearied countrymen who were chained together somehow made their way through the nettings and jumped into the sea. They preferred death to a life of misery. Immediately another fellow also followed their example. I believe many more would very soon have done the same if they had not been prevented by the ship's crew.

Two of the wretches were drowned. But the crew got the other, and after-

Poster below advertised one of the cruelest businesses in history — trade in black slaves.

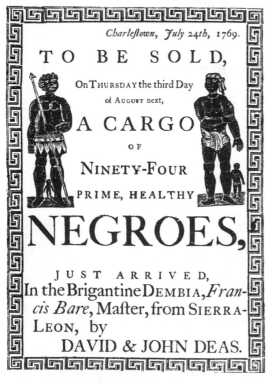

ward flogged him unmercifully for preferring death to slavery. In this manner we continued to undergo more hardships than I can now relate.

1. *Africans on slave ships died from many different causes. What two causes of death are mentioned by Vassa?*
2. *Why did the white slave traders rescue a drowning slave and then flog or whip him?*
3. *In your judgment, were the slave traders guilty of any crime? Suppose you had been a lawmaker in colonial Virginia. What law concerning the slave trade would you have tried to pass?*

Sharpening Your Skills

In 1750 the American colonies depended upon the heavy wooden ships that sailed in and out of their harbors. Where did the ships go? What goods did they carry? Find out by studying this map.

1. From Newport, Rhode Island, a ship carrying rum sailed for Africa's Guinea Coast. What was this ship likely to carry back to the West Indies? What was it likely to carry from the West Indies back to Newport? Why is this trade often called the *triangular trade?*
2. Besides the primary triangular trade route with Africa, there were two secondary trade routes. Describe one of them.
3. Where did the American colonies get most of their manufactured goods?
4. A ship from Charleston usually traveled either east or north. With what country was it likely to trade if it went east? With what cities was it likely to trade if it went north?

Triangular Trade Routes

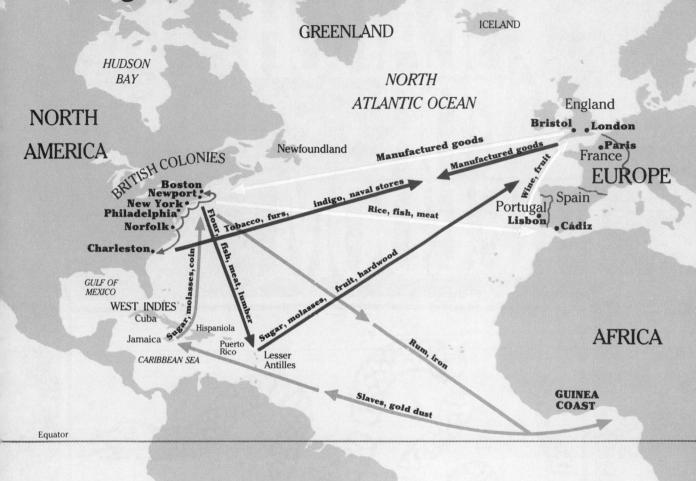

GREENLAND

ICELAND

HUDSON BAY

NORTH ATLANTIC OCEAN

NORTH AMERICA

England

Bristol • London
• Paris
France
EUROPE

Newfoundland

BRITISH COLONIES

Boston
Newport •
New York •
Philadelphia •
Norfolk •

Charleston •

Manufactured goods

Manufactured goods

indigo, naval stores

Rice, fish, meat

Wine, fruit

Portugal   Spain
Lisbon •
• Cádiz

Tobacco, furs,

Flour, fish, meat, lumber

Sugar, molasses, coin

GULF OF MEXICO

WEST INDIES
Cuba

Jamaica

Hispaniola

Puerto Rico

Lesser Antilles

CARIBBEAN SEA

Sugar, molasses, fruit, hardwood

Rum, iron

AFRICA

Slaves, gold dust

GUINEA COAST

Equator

SOUTH AMERICA

PACIFIC OCEAN

SOUTH ATLANTIC OCEAN

N
W + E
S

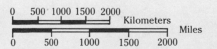

0 500 1000 1500 2000
Kilometers
Miles
0   500   1000   1500   2000

2 SEARCH FOR FREEDOM

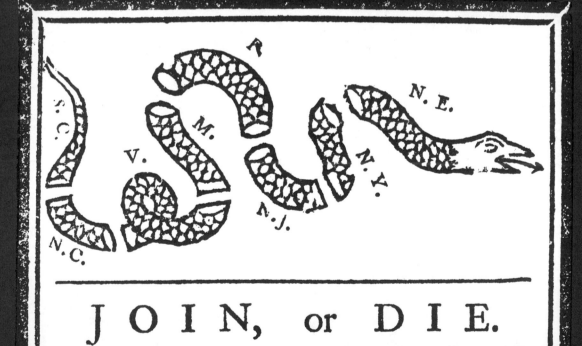

JOIN, or DIE.

Looking Ahead: Changing Loyalties

In 1750 a teenager named George Washington felt quite proud to be an Englishman. True, he lived about 3,000 miles (4,800 kilometers) away from London. But his older brother had gone to school in England and had worn a British army uniform. Young George greatly admired his brother. He too wanted someday to be an officer in the British army. Like most colonists in 1750, he expected to be a loyal British subject all his life.

At least that was George Washington's thinking as an 18-year-old. Yet, only 25 years later, he became a leader of a revolt against the British king, British laws, and the British flag. What happened? What changed the minds of Washington and thousands of other loyal British subjects?

By 1754 British colonists had found that they had to be able to defend themselves. So Ben Franklin printed the first political cartoon in America.

The answer is not simple. Scholars still argue about what really caused the American Revolution. Who was to blame for it? Was it the fault of an ambitious king and his foolish advisers? Was it the work of a few angry and determined Americans? Or did the Revolution just naturally happen? Did Americans wake up one morning and discover that it made no sense to be British any longer?

There is no single explanation of how the American Revolution came about. There were many causes such as the following:

Roots of independence. American colonists had long been an independent people by nature. Many of them had left Britain to escape rules they did not like. In America they had been joined by restless people from Scotland, Germany, and elsewhere. In time they had been made more independent by the hard life of the unsettled frontier.

For most of the 18th century, Britain

had ruled the 13 colonies with a light hand. In fact, the colonies had enjoyed more self-rule than any colonial people anywhere. Most of the colonies had the same kind of government. Under this system, there was a governor chosen by the British king. There was also an assembly elected by voters in the colonies. The assembly had most of the power for making new laws.

Problems of defense. By 1750, then, colonists had learned how to run their own governments. They had also learned how to fight and survive in a wilderness. What did people who had mainly lived in Britain know about surviving in a wilderness? Not very much, as George Washington sadly discovered in 1755.

In that year, a war was being fought between Britain and France. A British army had come to America to fight the French and their Indian allies. In America this conflict was known as the French and Indian War. George Washington, now 23, became directly involved in it. He and a group of colonists joined the British army in a march through the western woods. Washington warned the British general about fighting in American forests. He said it was very different from fighting on a battlefield in Europe.

But the British would not listen. They marched right into an Indian attack. Several bullets ripped into Washington's coat and hat. The British soldiers panicked. They did not know what to do. Only the colonists stood and fought. Washington was lucky to escape with his life.

After this, Washington and other colonists began to think that they did not need the British to defend them. The colonists, it seemed, could take care of themselves better than any troops from England.

New policies in Britain. After seven years of bloodshed, the British won the war against France. A victory at Quebec in 1759 gave Britain control of French Canada. A treaty of peace signed in 1763 made the victory final. Most of North America east of the Mississippi River now belonged to the British.

At this point, the British government decided it must get more serious about governing its huge American empire. It decided it must stop ruling with such a light hand. A new king, George III, was on the throne. He was young and unsure of himself. He became nervous and upset if people seemed to challenge his power. He and Parliament worked together to change the rules for governing the colonies.

First, in 1763, they decided that colonists should not be allowed to live west of the Allegheny Mountains. The British drew a line on the map. "West of the line," they said, "nobody shall be allowed to settle. It is for your own protection. It will prevent any more trouble from Indian raids." But the colonists wanted more land. They screamed with anger when they heard about this new rule.

Second, the British government decided to station British troops in the colonies. It did so to guard its empire. The colonists did not want these rough and brawling soldiers in their towns. But they were forced to receive them anyway. And they were required to lodge them in their inns and taverns.

Third, the British government needed

help in paying the expenses of the empire. The French and Indian War had been costly. The British thought it only natural that the colonies help to shoulder some of the debt. As a result, Parliament passed the Sugar Act of 1764. This act put a tax on molasses and other goods bought by colonial merchants outside the British Empire. The next year Parliament passed the Stamp Act, which created another tax in the form of a stamp. The stamp was to be placed on "every piece of paper" used in the colonies — even playing cards.

British leaders meant business. They were going to run the colonies now. They were going to make the rules and see that people obeyed them. At least that is what they *thought* would happen. What actually happened next surprised almost everyone.

Opposition. Many colonists refused to pay the new taxes. Their assemblies had not voted on the Sugar Act or the Stamp Act. Therefore, the colonists were being taxed without their consent. Many of them thought that a king who tried to make them pay such a tax was a *tyrant*. (A tyrant is a cruel and unjust ruler.) "No taxation without representation," they cried.

For a short time, the British appointed officials to collect the new taxes. These people soon received notes, threatening them with death. Their houses were torn apart by angry mobs. They were covered

In the 1760's, most American colonists were loyal to the British king. But many objected to having to pay new taxes to Britain. Bostonians rioted in the public square in 1765 to protest the Stamp Act (above). Such protests greatly angered the king, George III (shown at right about 1770).

with tar and feathers, and driven out of town. Finally, the British *repealed* (took back) the Stamp Act. Not even this ended American opposition.

Organization. As we have seen, America was broken up into colonies. Each colony was jealous of its neighbor.

The colonies had rarely united in the past. But now Britain's hated laws and taxes brought the colonists together. In Boston, a skillful leader, Samuel Adams, made sure that all Americans knew about the latest "danger to their liberties." Committees that he organized sent letters to all the towns of Massachusetts. The letters suggested ways to oppose British "tyranny." Soon other colonies organized letter-writing committees of their own.

Clash of arms. By 1775 only 10 years had passed since the first trouble over taxes. But enough had happened in this time to make some Americans think that British soldiers were their enemies. Colonial farmers and British soldiers prepared for a fight. It happened early one April morning, 1775. The British tried to march through two Massachusetts towns, Lexington and Concord. The result was a clash of arms. It was one of the most important turning points in the Americans' struggle to win their independence.

In the humorous British cartoon below, Boston patriots have tarred and feathered a British tax collector. They are forcing him to drink boiling tea. A final threat awaits him — hanging from the "Liberty Tree."

The·TIMES are Dreadful, Dismal Doleful Dolorous, and DOLLAR-LESS.

of the STAMP

An Emblem of the Effects

O! the fatal Stamp

Thursday, October 31, 1765.   NUMB. 1195.

T H E

PENNSYLVANIA JOURNAL;

A N D

WEEKLY ADVERTISER.

EXPIRING: In Hopes of a Resurrection to LIFE again.

Philadelphia's William Bradford closed his newspaper because of the stamp tax. He said he couldn't afford the stamps. "The times are dreadful," Bradford's newspaper moaned. "O! the fatal stamp."

Chapter 7

If This Be Treason

He was lazy and good-for-nothing. That was what some people said about young Patrick Henry. It was a waste of time sending him to school. He didn't seem to learn anything. All he wanted to do was go fishing or hunt in the woods. Patrick's father, a Virginia farmer, didn't know what to do with the boy. Sometimes he whipped him and other times he prayed for him. But nothing seemed to help.

Finally Patrick's father took him out of school. It was a happy day for both Patrick and his teachers. At home Patrick's father taught him the Bible, math, and Latin. Patrick really wasn't stupid. He could learn — when he wanted to. The trouble was he did not like school. He liked being out in the woods.

Patrick's father worried about the boy. How would he ever earn a living? The older Henry decided to start his son in business. When Patrick was 16, his father bought him a country store to manage. But Patrick was no business-man. On nice days, he would just close the store and go hunting. There were many wild animals in the forests of Virginia in 1751, and Patrick knew

49

how to use a rifle. After a while, Patrick's father had to close the store for good.

At 18 Patrick fell in love with the daughter of a poor farmer and married her. Now he tried to make a living by raising tobacco. But he had no luck at farming and soon had to give it up. Then he started another store, but he had to close this one too.

By this time, Patrick Henry had three children as well as a wife to support. He knew he had to make a living in *some* way. There was one thing he did well — he was a very good speaker. So he decided to become a lawyer. He studied law books night and day for six weeks. Then he took a test and passed. At 24 Patrick Henry began to practice law.

Questioning the king. Henry's gift for speaking helped him win many cases. His first important case came when he was 27. It had started out as an argument between the Virginia legislature and some church ministers. Virginia at that time had a church supported by public taxes. Many people thought that the ministers of this church were overpaid. So the Virginia legislature passed a law that cut the ministers' salaries.

The ministers were angry about this. When King George III heard about it, he was angry too. He threw out the Virginia legislature's new law. Then the ministers went to court. They wanted all the money they had lost since their pay had been cut.

This was where lawyer Henry stepped into the case. He stood for the idea that Virginia didn't owe any back pay to the ministers. Nobody thought he would win. What jury would dare go against the

king? But when Henry got up to speak to the jury, there was magic in his voice.

What right did the King of England have to throw out a law passed by the people of Virginia? Henry asked. The voice of the people, he said, is the voice of God. When a king throws out a law passed by the people, the people do not have to obey him anymore.

This was pretty strong talk in those days, when kings were very powerful. Some people in the courtroom were shocked. But Patrick Henry won his case.

Questioning a tax. The young lawyer was now a hero in Virginia. He was especially a hero to the small farmers and the woodsmen. They elected him to serve in the Virginia legislature in the town of Williamsburg. Soon after, Henry really gave the people of Virginia something to talk about.

This time his subject was King George's Stamp Act. The act had put a tax on "every piece of paper" used in the American colonies. This meant that any business paper or legal paper had to have a stamp on it. Not even a marriage license would be any good without a stamp. Many Americans were angry about this. They didn't want to pay for a stamp every time they signed something. Besides, they believed that only their own legislatures had the right to tax them. But few people were brave enough to protest out loud.

Then, on May 29, 1765, Patrick Henry got up to speak in the Virginia legislature. The stamp tax was against the law, he said. Under the law, the people could be taxed only by their own representatives. The colonists had no representatives in the British government. So how could the British government place a stamp tax on the colonists? It couldn't, Henry argued — unless it broke the law.

Henry said that nobody in Virginia should obey the Stamp Act. What he said next really shocked many of his listeners. He compared King George to a tyrant. And he warned the king that tyrants were sometimes killed.

Suddenly there were shouts of "Treason! Treason!" from those who were loyal to the king. Henry waited until the shouting died down. Then he said, *"If this be treason, make the most of it!"*

Word of Henry's speech traveled fast. Before long, Americans in all the colonies refused to pay the stamp tax.

Patrick Henry's fighting words helped stir colonists to revolution. "Give me liberty or give me death," Henry told Virginians.

Sometimes they burned stamps and beat up the tax collectors. In Boston there were riots against the tax.

Did the British learn anything from the uproar over the stamp tax? Some people thought so. The British repealed the Stamp Act in 1766. But at the same time they passed another law — the Declaratory Act. This act said that Britain had full power to make laws for the colonies and the people of America — "in all cases, whatsoever."

These were fighting words.

A Second Look. . . .

1. *How would you describe Patrick Henry? Was he a good student? A successful businessman? An exciting speaker? A talented lawyer? Give reasons for your answers.*

2. *If Patrick Henry were alive today, which of the following taxes do you think he would be most likely to refuse to pay? (a) A $100 tax on tobacco voted by members of Congress. (b) A $50 tax on playing cards voted by the lawmakers of Virginia, Henry's home state. (c) A $10 tax voted by the government of Canada. Explain your answer. Which of these taxes would you be most likely to refuse to pay? Why?*

3. *Patrick Henry protested the Stamp Act in the town of Williamsburg, Virginia. Williamsburg had become the capital of Virginia in 1699. By Henry's time it was the social center of the colony as well. Look at the map of the 13 British colonies at the beginning of Chapter Six. What other colonial capitals can you identify? Choose one of them and go to the library to find out more about it. Report to the class on when the town was founded — and why.*

Chapter 8

Blood on the Snow

It was a cold winter night in Boston. The moon was shining brightly over the snowy streets. A British soldier stood guard near the Custom House, where British records were kept. The soldier had already been in an argument with several young people. Tension was in the air.

Suddenly an icy snowball flew past the soldier's ear. Another nearly knocked his hat off. A third caught him right in the chest. The snowballs were thrown by a group of boys across the street. Soon the boys began to yell at the soldier. "Lobster back! Lobster back!" they shouted. British soldiers wore red uniforms in those days. Americans often called them "redcoats" or "lobster backs."

There had been many fights between British soldiers and Boston people in those years. What were the fights about? The British had backed up their Declaratory Act. They had placed several new taxes on the colonies. The people hated these taxes. In Boston there were riots against them. The people hated many of the other laws made for them in far-off England. "Why should we obey these laws?" many colonists asked. "Especially when we had no part in making them."

King George III of Britain became angry. In 1768 he sent 4,000 soldiers to Boston to stop the riots. The people of Boston hated these soldiers even more than the taxes. They had to make room for the soldiers in inns, taverns, and other privately owned buildings. Some of the soldiers were put up in people's homes. And that wasn't all. Many of the soldiers took off-duty jobs that the colonists themselves needed. Tough dock workers often attacked soldiers who were off duty.

Screams from a crowd. On this night, March 5, 1770, the British guard was nervous. A bell had rung from somewhere. A number of men and women had joined the shouting boys. Soon there was a large crowd. The soldier then fixed his bayonet on his rifle. The crowd nearly went wild. "Kill him! Kill him!" they screamed. A group of dock workers and sailors joined the crowd. One of them was a giant of a man named Crispus Attucks. He was part black, part Indian, and part white.

The British guard called for help. Seven redcoats led by a captain came to his aid. The captain told his men to load their rifles, but he ordered them *not* to fire. He tried to get the crowd to break up, but it was no use. Soon the crowd began getting out of hand. A British

Paul Revere drew and engraved this print of the Boston Massacre to turn colonists against the British. The original included a poem in which the British were called "savage bands."

The BLOODY MASSACRE perpetrated in King Street Boston on March 5th 1770 by a party of the 29th REGT

Engrav'd Printed & Sold by Paul Revere Boston

Unhappy Boston! see thy Sons deplore,
Thy hallow'd Walks besmear'd with guiltless Gore.
While faithless P—n and his savage Bands,
With murd'rous Rancour stretch their bloody Hands;
Like fierce Barbarians grinning o'er their Prey,
Approve the Carnage and enjoy the Day.

If scalding drops from Rage from Anguish Wrung
If speechless Sorrows lab'ring for a Tongue
Or if a weeping World can ought appease
The plaintive Ghosts of Victims such as these:
The Patriot's copious Tears for each are shed,
A glorious Tribute which embalms the Dead.

But know Fate summons to that awful Goal,
Where Justice strips the Murd'rer of his Soul:
Should venal C—ts the scandal of the Land,
Snatch the relentless Villain from her Hand,
Keen Execrations on this Plate inscrib'd,
Shall reach a Judge who never can be brib'd.

The unhappy Sufferers were Messrs Saml Gray, Saml Maverick, James Caldwell, Crispus Attucks & Patk Carr
Killed. Six wounded; two of them (Christr Monk & John Clark) Mortally
Published in 1770 by Paul Revere Boston

guard was knocked down. Suddenly someone shouted, "Fire!" No one ever found out who shouted it, but the British soldiers began shooting.

When the smoke cleared, Attucks and two other men were dead. Two more lay dying in the snow. This was the *Boston Massacre.*

The angry crowd charged forward again. Soon other soldiers turned out to halt the rioters. War against Britain might have started right then and there. But Governor Thomas Hutchinson of Massachusetts rushed to the scene and made a speech to quiet the crowd. He promised the people that the soldiers would be put on trial.

Speeches from a patriot. The next day Samuel Adams spoke out. He said the "redcoat butchers" had to be punished. But others felt that the crowd was partly to blame for the "massacre." Little doubt existed that the first argument had been started by young people, not the British troops.

John Adams, who was a cousin of Samuel Adams, agreed to defend the soldiers in a court trial. John Adams was an excellent lawyer. (He would one day become President of the United States.) As a result of the trial, the British captain and six of his men were freed. Two others got mild punishment. They were branded on the thumb with a hot iron.

But Samuel Adams kept making speeches about the bloody "massacre" and the courage of the men who were killed. Before long, many people were thinking of Attucks and his friends as heroes and great *patriots* — lovers of their country. And they were thinking of the British as murderers — and enemies.

A Second Look. . . .

1. *What set off the Boston Massacre? How was the rioting of March 5, 1770, finally brought to an end?*

2. *In your opinion, who was most responsible for the "massacre"? The boys who threw the first snowballs? The British soldier who fired the first shot? Bostonians for suggesting that British laws not be obeyed? The British government for sending soldiers to Boston? Why?*

3. *Study Paul Revere's famous print of the Boston Massacre, pictured in this chapter, very carefully. Remember that Revere meant the print as a way of turning public opinion against the British government. In designing the print, Revere "made up" several of the details. The English Custom House, for example, had no sign reading "Butcher's Hall." Compare the print with the story of the "massacre" given above. What other inaccuracies can you detect?*

The label beneath the coffins on this Paul Revere poster reads: "On the Death of Five young Men who was Murthered, March 5th, 1770. By the 29th Regiment." The fourth coffin from left bears the initials "CJA" — for Crispus J. Attucks, one of the first Americans to be killed in the struggle against the British.

54

Chapter 9
Tea, Taxes, and Trouble

Three ships with a dangerous cargo were anchored in Boston harbor in December of 1773. The cargo was a shipment of tea. But it might as well have been gunpowder. No one dared to unload it. What were they afraid of?

The tea had come from warehouses in London. The warehouses were operated by a British trading company, the East India Company. The company had too much tea to sell — and too few buyers. The British Parliament had therefore allowed the company to sell its tea in the colonies at a lower price.

This meant that colonists would be able to buy tea more cheaply than before. In fact, they would have to pay even less for it than they had been paying for smuggled tea. But the new law also meant that some colonial merchants would lose part of their business. These merchants were worried. "If Parliament succeeds," they asked, "might it not try to control all colonial trade?"

Other colonists objected for a differ-

Patriots wished this fate on Thomas Hutchinson, Massachusetts' governor.

ent reason. The fact was that the East India tea carried a tax. The tax had not been set by the colonies. It had been fixed by the British Parliament across the sea. Many colonists now believed they should have a voice in deciding what taxes they should pay. They were determined not to buy any goods that carried a British tax.

Some colonists took immediate action. In October 1773 the people of Philadelphia held a mass meeting. They condemned Parliament's law allowing the tea to be sold. In November New York City refused to allow ships carrying the tea into its port. In December Boston leaders also tried to prevent the tea from being unloaded. Samuel Adams asked Governor Thomas Hutchinson to send the ships back to Britain. Hutchinson refused.

Committee work. Hutchinson was on shaky ground. Several months earlier Boston patriots had held a town meeting. At the meeting a committee had been formed to spread word of Boston's

55

Bostonians, dressed as Indians, hold a "tea party." British soldiers scream idle threats from the dock.

position to nearby towns. The patriots had called this group the *committee of correspondence*. The committee had taken charge of the patriots' activities in Boston. Now it was stirring the anger of the townspeople to a fever pitch.

Similar committees had also sprung up in other colonies. By the middle of 1773, the committees existed in Virginia, Rhode Island, Connecticut, New Hampshire, and South Carolina. These committees added to the danger of armed force. For they could be used to unite the colonies against the mother country (Britain).

Now it was the night of December 16, 1773. Governor Hutchinson was in his country house outside Boston. There was a knock at the door. A wet and tired messenger from Boston stepped in.

In the name of the people of Boston, the messenger begged the governor to

send back the tea. Again Governor Hutchinson refused. "The ships will never leave Boston with the tea on board," he is reported to have said. "The king's laws must be obeyed."

Protests from a crowd. In Boston a large crowd of angry people waited for the messenger to return. They had been listening to many speeches against British taxes. "Whoever drinks tea is a traitor!" they shouted. "We will not sell our rights for tea leaves!"

Just then the messenger returned. He rushed up to Samuel Adams with Governor Hutchinson's answer. Adams was on the speaker's platform. He turned and told the meeting: "The ships stay. This meeting can do nothing further to save the country!"

A moment later wild war cries were heard outside. A troop of about 150 Boston men were parading in the street.

They were made up to look like Indians. They carried clubs, tomahawks, and knives. "Make Boston harbor a teapot tonight!" they shouted.

The "Indians" rowed out into the harbor. On the dock a big crowd of people cheered them. The "Indians" then boarded the tea ships. The British soldiers did not try to fight them. Soon the "Indians" were dumping big chests of tea into the harbor. When they finished, they lined up on the dock like soldiers and marched away. No British soldier made a move to stop them.

The Boston "tea party" shocked Britain. Many Americans were shocked by it too. King George III was filled with rage. He ordered the port of Boston closed. He sent more soldiers there to keep it closed. No ships could enter or leave the port. Many businesses in the city came to a halt.

News of the king's acts ran quickly through the colonies. It fed the anger of committees of correspondence up and down the Atlantic coast. These committees, in turn, persuaded many colonists to think again about their ties to Britain. Once most colonists had hoped only to declare their rights as British subjects. Now many of them talked openly of settling matters by force. The colonies were beginning to unite against Britain.

A Second Look. . . .

1. *Why were three ships of tea sent to Boston? Why did the people of Boston refuse to allow the ships to be unloaded?*

Why did Governor Hutchinson refuse to allow the ships to return to Britain?

2. *News of the "tea party" enraged King George III. What did he do to show his anger? Put yourself in his place. Bear in mind that you need to protect your power as king. What would you have done? Would you, for example, have apologized for sending the tea against the wishes of the Americans? Punished all the people of Boston for the deed? Or punished only those who participated in the "tea party"? Give reasons for your answer.*

3. Propaganda *is the spreading of ideas to influence someone else's opinion. How good are you at writing propaganda? Imagine that you belong to a committee of correspondence in Virginia in 1774. You have heard about the Boston "tea party" and the king's harsh methods of punishing Boston. Write a letter to other Virginia colonists telling them what has happened. Your letter should use words that alarm readers about the new danger to their liberties.*

A patriotic New York barber sends away a British captain, after giving him only half a shave. This print was made in London by British people who supported the colonists against the British.

Chapter 10
Father of Liberty

"Quick! Wake up Mr. Adams and Mr. Hancock. The British are coming!"

It was Paul Revere talking. He had just made his famous "midnight ride" from Boston to Lexington. "The British are coming!" he had warned the people along the way.

What did the British want? They were out to grab the guns and gunpowder stored by the *Minutemen* in Concord. The Minutemen were farmers who were training to fight the British if war came. The British also wanted to arrest John Hancock and Samuel Adams, who were staying in Lexington. Hancock and

Adams had been stirring up the people against British rule. That had not been a hard thing to do after the king ordered the port of Boston closed.

Soon Hancock and Adams came downstairs. "You must leave at once for Philadelphia," Revere told them. "The British want to send you to London — to hang you as criminals. Redcoats are on their way here right now."

Hancock was easily excited. At first he didn't want to leave. But Adams told Hancock it would be foolish for him to stay. Hancock was too important to let himself be captured.

Paul Revere's "midnight ride" to Lexington remains an important symbol of the American struggle for independence. Grant Wood, one of America's finest artists, painted this version of the ride in 1931.

58

Patriots escape. It was dawn when Adams and Hancock drove away in Hancock's carriage. Suddenly shots were heard coming from Lexington. British soldiers and Minutemen were firing at each other. The fighting which both sides had feared had finally broken out. The date was April 19, 1775.

John Hancock was 38. He was a rich merchant and had fine clothes and manners. Samuel Adams was 53. He was a poor man and looked much older than his age. His head sometimes shook. His voice was not always strong. Yet more than any other man, Adams had fanned the flames of rebellion against the British. He was known as the man the British most wanted to hang.

Samuel Adams was born in Boston in 1722. He was the son of a brewer who had done very well in business. But when Samuel Adams went into business, he failed. He owed lots of money. His children often wore clothes given to them by friends.

Soon Adams turned from business to politics. At politics he was a master. He was elected to the Massachusetts legislature. He fought hard against British taxes. He was a leader of the Boston men called the *Sons of Liberty*. They tarred and feathered tax collectors and stirred up riots against the British.

Adams attacked British rule every chance he got. His speeches and writings whipped up the anger of the people of Boston. Adams formed the first committee of correspondence in his city. Later he gave the signal for the "Indian raid" on the tea ships in Boston harbor.

After King George III closed the port of Boston, the city's trade and shipping came to a stop. Then Adams called for a

American militiamen send British forces into retreat. The artist shows what he thinks of British soldiers. Look closely at their faces.

meeting of the leaders of all the colonies. This became the *First Continental Congress*. It met in Philadelphia in 1774. The angry colonial leaders sent the king a long list of complaints. The king paid no attention to them. Meanwhile, the Minutemen began to train.

Redcoats march. On the night and morning of April 18-19, 1775, the redcoats marched on Lexington and Concord. They burned whatever ammunition they could find. Then they ran into the Minutemen. On the march back to Boston, the Minutemen fired on them from the cover of trees, walls, and houses. Two hundred forty-seven British soldiers fell dead or wounded.

Warned by Paul Revere, Adams and Hancock were already on their way to Philadelphia. By the time they arrived, the Continental Congress was in session again. Adams gave some fiery speeches before the Congress. He called for liberty for the American colonies. A little more than a year later, the Declaration of Independence was signed. Then Adams' job was done — he had given Americans the courage to fight for their rights. Patriots honored him as the "father" of their liberty.

A Second Look. . . .

1. *Why did the British march on Lexington in April 1775? Who were the Minutemen who stood guard against the British? What happened when the two sides met?*

2. *In 1775 Americans argued with one another about how to deal with British "tyranny." Some Americans were moderates. They wanted to keep the peace as long as possible. They opposed the idea of declaring independence from Britain. Others, known as radicals, were impatient for change. They thought war with Britain could not be avoided. Do you think Samuel Adams was a radical or a moderate? Why? If you had been an American in 1775, would you have been a radical or a moderate? Why?*

3. *Samuel Adams was known as the man the British most wanted to hang. Do you think they would have hanged him if they had captured him at Lexington? You and your classmates might try writing and acting out a five-minute skit built around this question. The skit should point out Adams' importance as a leader of the patriots.*

John Singleton Copley finished this portrait of Samuel Adams in 1772. Copley was one of the best-known artists of the time. He painted portraits of many leaders of the American Revolution.

Chapter 11

Letters from a Patriot

"Take the spoons. Let's throw them in the kettle there and melt them down into bullets. We surely need bullets now more than spoons. Put more wood on the fire, Johnny. Your uncle and I are making bullet soup."

A woman took a dozen large spoons from their hooks and dumped them into a large black kettle. The man she was speaking to was her husband's brother, Elihu Adams. The eight-year-old child at the fireside was her first-born son, John Quincy Adams. The woman herself was Abigail Adams.

As usual, her husband John Adams was away from home. He was the lawyer who had defended the British soldiers after the Boston Massacre. This time he had gone to Philadelphia to meet with other colonial leaders. The year was 1775. A few weeks before, the Battle of Lexington and Concord had taken place only a few miles from the Adams' farm in Braintree, Massachusetts. In Braintree and many other American towns, people were getting ready for war. There seemed to be no way of avoiding it.

In Braintree the young men were leaving their farms to join a new American army. The British camp in Boston was only a few miles away. From the hill of her farm, Abigail Adams could see Boston in the distance. Her neighbors feared that the British in Boston would soon attack their town. Many mothers of young children planned to leave Braintree and move to other towns far from danger.

Abigail Adams, however, was not easily scared. After Lexington, British troops had been penned up in Boston. New England troops had occupied Breed's Hill in Charlestown across the river. Abigail would wait to see whether the British attacked Braintree. If they did, she was prepared to deal with them.

Thoughts on politics. In some ways, Abigail Adams was like most women in colonial times. Like them, she had never gone to school. She had never held a job. She had never voted in an election. Unlike most of them, however, she loved books as much as her college-educated husband. She was as good a writer as he was, perhaps even better. And she had strong opinions about government, law, and politics.

She was not supposed to think about such things. In colonial America, a woman was supposed to think only about her home and family. No woman was permitted to vote or hold office. Women such as Abigail had been given lessons at home in reading and writing. But they were never expected to take books and ideas as seriously as men did.

Abigail Adams accepted the role of wife and mother. At the time, she really had no other choice. She had the same talents as her husband, but she could

Abigail Adams

not hope to become a lawyer like him. How then did she express her interest in law and politics? She did it by writing letters — long, thoughtful, witty letters.

Abigail saw with her own eyes how the Revolution came about. In her letters, she described men being tarred and feathered by Boston mobs. She wrote about British soldiers marching and drilling on the streets of Boston. In the winter of 1770, she saw the children of Boston throw snowballs at the soldiers' red uniforms. She heard the names that the soldiers were called — "lobster backs, bloody backs."

She feared what might happen when three British ships carrying tea arrived in Boston harbor. Could the British king make the people of Boston pay the tea tax against their will? Abigail did not think so. She wrote to a friend: "The tea is arrived. I tremble when I think what must be the direful [horrible] consequences." Eleven days after she wrote this, the tea was dumped into Boston harbor.

Her husband was home with her in Braintree on the April day when the British marched through Lexington. Together Abigail and John gave food and drink to young Minutemen who stopped at their farm to rest from the battle. Shortly after that, John left for Philadelphia. Abigail stayed home and made bullets out of spoons.

Sounds of war. One morning in June, just before dawn, Abigail was awakened by a terrible noise. It sounded like thunder. Indeed it was the sound of British cannons far in the distance. They were firing at the harbor of Charlestown, near Boston. With one hand, Abigail grabbed a spyglass. With the other, she grabbed her boy Johnny. Together they marched up a nearby hill to see what was happening far in the distance. "They're burning Charlestown!" Abigail gasped. She and Johnny watched the smoke and fire rise up into the summer air.

Hours later they finally learned what had happened. The British had tried to take Breed's Hill from the American troops. Twice the Americans forced the British to retreat. But the third British charge was too much for the Americans. They gave up Breed's Hill — and then another, Bunker Hill. Even so, Abigail was proud of the American effort in what is now called the Battle of Bunker Hill.

On June 17, 1775, the British attacked American positions on Breed's Hill in Charlestown. British took this hill, then nearby Bunker Hill as well.

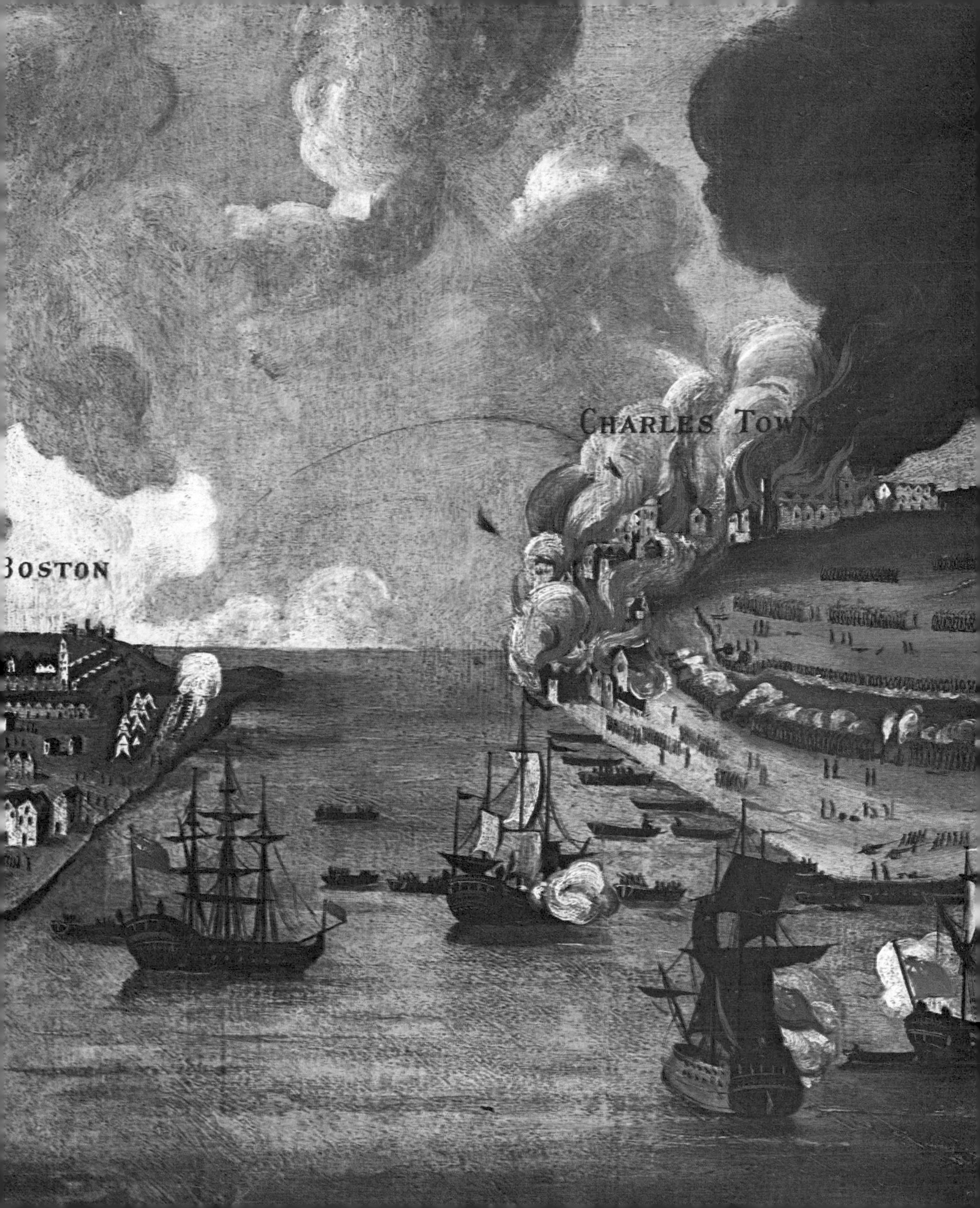
CHARLES TOWN
BOSTON

She wrote to her husband in Philadelphia: "Figure to yourself the town in flames all around them, and the heat from the flames so intense as scarcely to be borne. The day was one of the hottest we have had this season. The wind was blowing smoke in their faces. Then consider that we do not count 60 men lost. Every account agrees in 1,400 or 1,500 slain on their [the British] side."

After this event, life would never again be the same for Abigail Adams. Already she was finding it harder and harder to think of herself as a loyal British citizen. Soon she would be calling herself an American. She and her husband John would be working to break the ties that bound the colonies to the mother country. The American Revolution was about to begin.

A Second Look. . . .

1. *Name three important events that happened close to Abigail Adams' home. Which of these events did she describe at greatest length in her letters?*

2. *Why do you suppose no women went to Philadelphia to meet with colonial leaders? Do you think women should have been represented in these meetings? Would Abigail Adams have done a good job repre-*

senting *American women at Philadelphia? Why or why not? How would you compare the role of American women in Abigail Adams' day with the role of women today?*

3. *Abigail Adams lived long before there were any radio talk shows. But suppose there had been such shows. Imagine you have been given the job of interviewing Abigail Adams on the radio. Draw up a list of three questions you will want to ask her. Then write some of the answers you think she might give, based on what you know about Abigail Adams and what you think she would be likely to say.*

The cartoon at right may seem to be poking fun at women's hairdos. In fact, it is criticizing the British government's attempts to make light of losses suffered at Bunker Hill. At the top of the hairdo is Charlestown. British and American troops are firing on one another.

64

Looking Back:
Search for Freedom

	A		B		C		D	
1756		1761		1766		1771		1776

Putting Events in Order

Chapters Seven through 11 have described the major events that led to the American Revolution. Ten of these events are listed here. Your job is to match each event to the correct period shown on the timeline above. On a piece of paper, number from **1** to **10**. After each number, write the letter of the period in which the event occurred.

1. The first shot is fired in the Battle of Lexington and Concord.
2. Patrick Henry makes a speech comparing King George III to a tyrant.
3. The First Continental Congress meets in Philadelphia.
4. A peace treaty ends the French and Indian War.
5. News of the Stamp Act angers American colonists.
6. Colonists destroy British tea in the Boston tea party.
7. Victory at Quebec gives Britain control of French Canada.

8. The British close Boston harbor.
9. Five Americans are killed by British troops in the Boston Massacre.
10. British and American armies clash at the Battle of Bunker Hill.

Interpreting a Source

The song on the next page became popular in America after 1773. The "rich lady," of course, is not a lady at all — but a nation. Read the lyrics of the song, then answer the questions below.

1. *Who is the rich lady? Who is the rich lady's daughter?*
2. *What event is being talked about in the next to last verse: "But the bouncing girl poured out every pound on the dark and boiling tide"?*
3. *The rich lady says a daughter has a duty to obey her parent's commands. Do you agree that this daughter did? Why or why not?*

65

The Rich Lady over the Sea

There was a rich lady lived over the sea,
    And she was an island queen;
Her daughter lived off in the new country,
    With an ocean of water between.

The old lady's pockets were filled with gold,
    Yet never contented was she;
So she ordered her daughter to pay her a tax
    Of thruppence a pound on the tea.

"Oh mother, dear mother," the daughter replied,
    "I'll not do the thing you ask;
I'm willing to pay a fair price on the tea,
    But never the thruppenny tax."

"You shall!" cried the mother, and reddened with rage,
    "For you're my own daughter, you see;
And it's only proper that daughter should pay
    Her mother a tax on the tea."

She ordered her servant to be called up
    To wrap up a package of tea;
And eager for thruppence a pound, she put in
    Enough for a large family.

She ordered her servant to bring home the tax,
    Declaring her child must obey,
Or, old as she was, and woman most grown,
    She'd half whip her life away.

The tea was conveyed to her daughter's own door,
    All down by the oceanside;
But the bouncing girl poured out every pound
    On the dark and boiling tide.

And then she called out to the island queen,
    "Oh mother, dear mother," called she,
"Your tea you may have when 'tis steeped* enough,
    But never a tax from me."

---

*To steep something is to soak it. *Steeped* tea is tea that has
soaked long enough in water.

Sharpening Your Skills

Chapter 10 makes mention of Paul Revere's famous "midnight ride" on April 18, 1775. Exactly what route did he take? How far did he ride? This map gives you the answers.

1. About how many miles did Paul Revere have to travel between Charlestown and Lexington? In which direction was he headed when he was captured?

2. Which forces crossed the Charles River? For what purpose?

3. Did the Minutemen stop fighting after British troops came to the rescue of retreating British soldiers? Give a reason for your answer.

Battle of Lexington and Concord, 1775

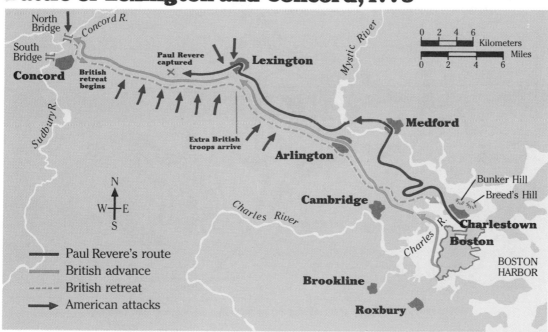

3 FIGHT FOR INDEPENDENCE

THE HORSE AMERICA, throwing his Master.

Looking Ahead: Gaining the Edge

It was very late at night on August 29, 1776, but the American troops were not sleeping. They were climbing into rowboats and barges as quietly as they could. A tall man on a horse signaled for the boats to shove off. Everybody was tense and nervous. If there were any noise, all might be lost.

The British were only a few hundred yards away. Earlier that day they had beaten the Americans — beaten them badly. They were only waiting until morning when they could attack again and force the Americans to surrender. If they had known what was happening now, they would surely have marched on the Americans and crushed them.

The Americans were stranded on the western shore of Long Island. Their only hope was to try secretly to cross over a

river to the island of Manhattan. Luckily the river was unusually calm. A thick fog concealed any movement. Nine thousand American soldiers made the trip that night across the dark waters of the East River.

When everyone else was safely across, the tall man dismounted from his horse and got into the last boat. He was George Washington, commander of the American army. He was completing one of the most brilliant retreats in American military history — and barely saving his troops from disaster.

Washington had now been the commander of the American army for more than a year. He had taken charge on July 3, 1775, two weeks after the Battle of Bunker Hill (see Chapter 11). In Washington's first year as commander, there had not been much fighting. A small force of Americans had marched through the northern woods in a daring attempt to capture Quebec. The attempt

The British cartoon at left is called "The Horse AMERICA, throwing his Master." Britain's enemy, France, watches the ride.

69

The British took New York City in 1776, driving out George Washington's scattered army. Washington and his men almost had to surrender.

had failed. British ships had attacked Charleston harbor in South Carolina. But they had been badly damaged by shells fired from American cannons.

The biggest event in the first year of war did not involve armies. It was a decision of the American leaders who attended the Second Continental Congress. Early in July 1776, they declared that they were no longer British subjects. Instead they announced that the 13 colonies were now "free and independent states."

After this, Washington's job was to win American independence on the battlefield. He just barely succeeded. The war for American independence lasted for seven hard years. Many times the British had a chance to crush Washington's army. With a little luck, they might have trapped Washington at the Battle of Long Island. Not many people gave the colonies much chance

of winning a war against Britain. After all, the British seemed to have most of the advantages on their side.

For one thing, they had a better army. The men in it were all professional soldiers. They knew how to march together in perfect order to the signal of a drum. They were trained to load and fire their guns together as if they were machines. This army was assisted by another strong force at sea. The British had the largest navy in the world.

The colonies had no warships. Their army, the Continental Army, started out with part-time fighters. Most of the men and boys who fought and died on Long Island were poorly trained for battle. They had a lot of courage but little skill. Many of them did not understand how to use their bayonets. They were not used to obeying orders. The captains who tried to lead them often did not know what they were doing.

At first, American soldiers provided a further problem. They would sign up for a few months of service, then quit and leave for home. In the winter of 1777, most of Washington's army disappeared. He had only 3,000 men left, while the British had 20,000.

It costs a lot of money to feed and equip an army. Here too the British had a big advantage. They had enough money to pay thousands of German soldiers to fight with them in America. Washington, on the other hand, had a very hard time raising money. The Continental Congress had practically no power to collect taxes. State governments could raise taxes, but they usually failed to raise enough. The paper money that Washington used to pay his soldiers was almost worthless. One group of soldiers once showed how much they thought this money was worth. They made coats and pants out of it and wore it as a joke.

Without enough men or money, Americans could not defend their cities. They had trouble in Boston in 1775. They lost New York in 1776 and Philadelphia in 1777. They had to give up Savannah, Georgia, in 1778 and Charleston, South Carolina, in 1780.

And yet the Americans finally defeated a superior British army. How? They were able to win for four main reasons:

Because they had something to fight for. A writer's pen is sometimes more powerful than a soldier's sword. Great words and ideas can move people to keep fighting even when all seems lost. Powerful words came easily to two American writers, Thomas Paine and Thomas Jefferson. In 1776 they persuaded thousands of people that America had a right to be independent. Americans understood that they were fighting for their lives and their liberty. Why was the British soldier fighting? Mainly because fighting was his job.

Because they were fighting on home ground. North America was a vast continent. It was almost too big for foreign troops to conquer. The British could not be everywhere at once. If they won a battle in the North, they still had trouble in the South. If they marched to the South, Washington's army was still a threat in the North. American troops lost more battles than they won. But they always managed to slip away from final defeat. One American general, Nathaniel Greene, explained how his troops just wore out the British. He said: "We fight, get beat, rise, and fight again."

Because they had determined leadership. Some of the British generals were lazy. They made foolish, careless mistakes. After winning a battle, they often relaxed, allowing the Americans to escape. But the American leader, George Washington, stayed with his job through victory and defeat. He knew

This British cartoon was printed with a verse about some men and their goose. The goose laid a golden egg each day. But the men wanted two golaen eggs. When the goose couldn't lay two, the men killed it. The men represent the British. What is the goose?

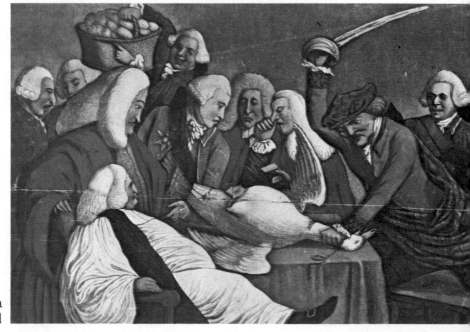

when to attack the enemy and when to retreat. Even more important, he worked day and night with his soldiers. He got them to drill and fight. He won their respect and admiration. He was able to keep an army together even in the cold winter months when everyone wanted to quit.

Because the French helped them. Americans fought alone for only a short time. After 1777 they were joined by England's old enemy, France. The French gave ships and money. They also sent many soldiers, including the remarkable Marquis de Lafayette (mar-KEE duh lahf-ay-ETT). This young man had been inspired by the ideals of the American cause. He arrived in America in July 1777 and offered his services to Washington. He fought bravely with the Americans for the rest of the war. The help given by Lafayette and other French people gave the Americans new hope. Partly because of this help, the United States is now an independent nation.

These were not the only reasons why Americans won their war for independence. They were also lucky. For example, fog covered Washington's troops as they retreated from the Battle of Long Island. On a clear night, the British might have seen what was happening. And that probably would have been the end of Washington and his army.

Americans needed some luck to win. But they also needed great courage and determination. They had plenty of this, as you will see in the chapters that follow.

Here is "Poor old England endeavoring to reclaim his wicked Americans." England will try to give them a whipping if he can. But England, once strong, is too old and weak to pull his "children" over to where he can reach them. This cartoon appeared after American victories at Trenton and Princeton.

Chapter 12

Liberty's Penman

Tom Jefferson might have cried once or twice as he rode through the woods of Virginia. After all, in 1745 he was only two years old. He was seated on a pillow close to the horse's neck. The large man in the saddle held him firmly with one hand. The boy probably did not know it at the time, but the man holding him was his father's slave.

After Thomas Jefferson had become famous, he wrote about this ride through the woods. He said it was his earliest memory. He remembered that he and his older sisters were being moved from one house to another. The house they were leaving was just being built by his father. It was a wooden farmhouse — large but not fancy. The house they were going to was a huge and splendid mansion, one of the finest in Virginia. It belonged to a friend of the Jeffersons who had recently died. The Jeffersons had agreed to look after the friend's three children. Each of these children was cared for by three slaves.

The idea of slavery bothered Thomas Jefferson all his life. As an adult, he himself owned many slaves. He depended on their labor for raising tobacco on his plantation. Yet he understood that slavery was wrong, terribly wrong. It was the opposite of the thing he valued most in life — freedom.

Some people can go through life without thinking much about right and wrong or good and evil. Thomas Jefferson was not one of them. Even as a youth, he thought deeply about the ideas he found in books. His father, Peter Jefferson, liked to see him read and study. Peter never had much time to sit down with a book. His whole life was spent in the Viriginia forests looking for new land to clear and a new house to build. But Peter Jefferson respected books and learning. He thought his son should be better educated than he was.

Tom was 14 when his father died. Three years later, the young man entered William and Mary College in Williamsburg, Virginia. At the age of 16, he was tall, thin, and awkward. But he could charm people with his pleasant laugh and intelligent talk. His teachers noticed his ability right away and made him their friend.

Ideas about liberty. Jefferson especially admired George Wythe (pronounced "with"), the professor who taught him law. Wythe was a genius, one of America's greatest lawyers. Jefferson worked hard to please this man. Fifteen hours every day, he studied books about law and politics. He would start studying at dawn. Often he would not stop until two o'clock the next morning.

The books that Jefferson read talked about morals and ideals. They talked about the right to liberty that belonged

Portrait shows Thomas Jefferson in 1775. It was drawn by Pierre Eugéne Du Simitiére in the year Jefferson went to the Continental Congress.

to every person from the moment of birth. They also talked about the tyranny of kings who tried to take people's rights and liberties from them. Jefferson took these ideas very seriously. He enjoyed talking about them with friends and with his teacher, George Wythe.

After leaving college, Jefferson never forgot the books he had read. Ideas about liberty, tyranny, and human rights were as much a part of him as the blood in his veins. They were part of the arguments he made as a lawyer. They were part of the speeches he made when his

county elected him to sit in the Virginia legislature. They were part of his conversations when he sat down to dinner with his young wife, Martha.

For 10 years, Jefferson watched the growing conflict between Britain and the American colonies. By 1774 he was certain that the rights of all Americans were in danger.

A warning about rights. Finally he put these beliefs in writing. In the summer of 1774, he wrote down the thoughts that filled his mind. He wrote about the colonists who first settled in

America. Who had helped these people to make a living out of the wilderness? Nobody had helped them, Jefferson wrote. Their own toil and their own blood had made America what it was. The British government had only begun to care about America after the hard work was finished.

Americans had a natural right to make their own laws for their own land. But the British government, Jefferson said, was now trying to take away this right. In fact, the British seemed to have a "plan of reducing us to slavery." Jefferson admitted that Americans also made slaves of other people. But whose fault was that? The British king's, not the Americans'. After all, the Virginia legislature had once passed a law that would have made the slave trade illegal. But the king had not allowed the law to go through.

Jefferson accused the king's government of other mistakes. Then he concluded with one of his favorite ideas: "The God who gave us life, gave us liberty at the same time."

Jefferson put down his pen. A messenger carried what he had written to Williamsburg. Friends of Jefferson were excited by it. They printed copies of it and gave it a title: "A Summary View of the Rights of British America." More copies of it were made in Philadelphia. A ship carried a copy to London. More copies were printed there.

The king was furious. He ordered the arrest of the young Virginian who wrote so boldly and so well. The name of Thomas Jefferson quickly became famous in all 13 colonies. He was only 31 years old. But no one wrote more impressively than Jefferson about human rights. This gift was an important one in 1774. For the American colonies were moving toward war with England over this very subject.

In the spring of 1775, Jefferson attended the Virginia legislature. There he listened while another Virginian, Patrick Henry, spoke in defiance of the British king. "Is life so dear or peace so sweet," Henry asked, "as to be purchased at the price of chains and slavery? . . . I know not what course others may take, but as for me give me liberty or give me death!"

Less than a month later fighting broke out at Lexington and Concord. On June 21, Thomas Jefferson arrived in Philadelphia as a delegate to the Second Continental Congress. He was the third youngest member of the Congress, but his age mattered little. For now he was at the center of events. A year later he would be chosen to write the key document of the American Revolution. And he would base his ideas on the books he had studied, books deeply concerned with human rights.

A Second Look. . . .

1. *What was the name given to the essay Thomas Jefferson wrote in 1774? What was the main point of the essay?*

2. *Jefferson was served by slaves all his life. Yet he said that he hated slavery. Does this seem strange? How would you explain it?*

3. *Jefferson used to keep a record of the books he read. His lists have helped later scholars understand what ideas influenced him the most. What book or film or TV show has made the greatest impression on you this past year? Be prepared to name it in class and tell why it impressed you.*

Chapter 13

A Dangerous Declaration

"We ... do ... declare, that these united colonies are ... free and independent states...."

These words are part of America's Declaration of Independence. They were dangerous words at the time they were written — June 1776. The colonies had been in rebellion against Britain for a little more than a year. The Americans had scored some victories in this struggle. But so had the British. It was much too early to know which side would win.

Many Americans were not really sure of what they were fighting for. Were they fighting to make Britain take back its unfair taxes? Were they fighting for the right to make their own laws? Were they fighting to throw off *all* British rule — to be free and independent?

American patriot leaders had been arguing this question for months. Many of them had been meeting in Philadelphia almost since the fighting had started. This meeting was the Second Continental Congress.

Most members of the Congress were strongly in favor of independence. Even some who had been against it at first had later changed their minds. By this time, several battles had been fought. Many American lives had been lost. It now seemed as if independence were the only goal worthy of this bloodshed.

But some members of the Congress were still against declaring independence. They believed that too many Americans remained loyal to the British king. They also feared that a declaration of independence would turn the rebellion into all-out war. They felt that the colonies were too weak to win an all-out war.

There were many arguments on both sides. But while the arguments were still going on, a group of men was chosen to write the Declaration of Inde-

Thomas Paine

pendence. The group gave the main job of writing the Declaration to one man, Thomas Jefferson.

Jefferson knew that such a declaration was dangerous — especially while some colonies were still against it. But he also knew that other colonies were not willing to wait any longer. They might declare independence on their own, even if others held back.

A famous little book. Jefferson sensed that a great change had come over America since the fighting had started. Few Americans now drank to King George's health in taverns. Instead they talked about a little book written by Thomas Paine. Paine was an Englishman who had been in America for only a short time. In his book *Common Sense,* Paine called King George "the royal brute of Britain." He said it made no sense for Americans to bow to a tyrant. Across the last page of *Common Sense* were the daring words "The Free and Independent States of America."

Paine's book had been bought and read by thousands. Jefferson himself had read it, and he agreed with what it said. Its words influenced him as he began writing his Declaration of Independence.

By July 1, 1776, the Continental Congress was listening to the last arguments on the question: Should it take a stand for independence? Should it hold back?

The arguments went on for nine hours. By this time, no one was against the idea that the 13 colonies should be independent. But some members were against *declaring* independence. They said it was too early. One said it would be "like destroying our house in winter, before we have got another shelter."

Other members gave strong speeches in favor of declaring independence. They seemed especially upset by the actions of the king. The king had never sent an answer to the long list of complaints that the First Continental Congress had drawn up. The Second Congress had sent him another list of complaints. It had also tried to explain to the king why the colonists had taken up arms against his troops. But again the king had sent no answer. Instead he had issued a statement saying that the colonies were "in rebellion."

Now the fighting had been going on for more than a year. Those in favor of independence argued that the fighting was no longer a "rebellion" against Britain's unfair laws. It had changed into an all-out *revolution* against the British government itself — a fight for complete separation and independence from it. One member said that this change had already taken place "in the hearts and minds of the people." How could the Congress hold back?

A vote on independence. The Congress met early the next day, July 2, to take its vote. The vote came out strongly in favor of declaring independence. The members knew that this was one of the most important decisions they would ever make. Now the true goal of the fight against Britain had been set.

Many thought that July 2 — the date of the vote for independence — would go down in history as America's Independence Day. But that was not to be.

For the rest of July 2, and on July 3 and 4, the Congress looked over the Declaration of Independence that Thomas Jefferson had written. Was this the Declaration the Congress should adopt? Many members asked for

77

In the 1700's, town leaders often read the news aloud to citizens. Many Americans heard the Declaration of Independence before reading it.

Now the "united colonies" of America were the *United States* of America. Americans were no longer the "subjects" of a faraway king, but *citizens* of a nation of their own. The Declaration's words are still fresh today:

"We hold these truths to be self-evident: that all men are created equal, that they are endowed by their Creator with certain ... rights, that among these are life, liberty, and the pursuit of happiness."

A Second Look. . . .

1. *In the spring and summer of 1776, colonial leaders gave much thought to declaring independence. Give two arguments of those who favored the idea. Then give two arguments of those who opposed it.*

2. *According to the Declaration of Independence, governments get "their just powers from the consent of the governed." In other words, the only "just" governments are those approved by the people. How do Americans now give their consent (approval) to their government? Must they give such consent every day? Once a year? Once every two years? Once every four years? How does the American system allow you to give consent to new laws even though you are not yet old enough to vote?*

3. *The Declaration of Independence says that people have a right to "alter" or "abolish" their government. Under what circumstances? (Consult the text of the Declaration at the end of this book.) Do you agree that people have a right to change their government under these circumstances? Why or why not? Write a short essay answering these questions.*

changes. About one quarter of the writing was scratched out. But most of it was left as Jefferson had written it.

July 4 was a hot day. The members of the Congress wiped their foreheads with their handkerchiefs. One by one they voted "yes" to Jefferson's Declaration. Then the Declaration was delivered, scratches and all, to a nearby printing house to be printed. July 4, the day Jefferson's Declaration was dated, has been celebrated as Independence Day in the United States ever since.

Soon the Declaration appeared in many newspapers. At last Americans understood what they were fighting for.

Chapter 14

A Needed Victory

It looked like the end for General George Washington's army. Unless he got more men, he said, "the game will be pretty near up."

Washington and his army had been driven off Long Island and out of New York. They had fallen back across New Jersey. Then the British had chased the Americans across the Delaware River into Pennsylvania. It was now December 1776. Washington had fewer than 3,000 men left out of about 20,000. The rest either had been killed, had been taken prisoner, or had deserted.

Many American soldiers had no shoes, shirts, or coats. Winter was closing in, and the men were freezing. At the end of the year, their terms of service would be up. Then most of them would leave the army and go home. Washington badly needed a victory just to keep up the fighting spirit of his restless troops.

Across the Delaware River, in Trenton, New Jersey, were 1,500 enemy soldiers. They had come from the small German state of Hesse, and they were called Hessians (HESH-uns). They had been hired by the British. The Hessians had chased Washington's army across New Jersey. Now they were enjoying their victory and the coming of Christmas.

Washington sent a spy, John Honeyman, among the Hessians. Honeyman told Washington that the Hessians were planning a big party on Christmas. There would be lots of eating — and drinking. The Hessians would be in no condition to fight.

Crossing the Delaware. This was the chance Washington needed. He planned an attack on the Hessians. If the attack succeeded, he might be able to make a dash to nearby New Brunswick. New Brunswick was where the British were keeping their supplies.

On the night of December 25, Washington's men began to cross the Delaware. They used 40-foot rowboats. The river was flooded and full of ice. Huge chunks of ice crashed against the boats. But somehow 2,000 men and 18 cannons were rowed across. The men split into two columns and headed for Trenton, nine miles away. One column took the river road. The other took an inland road. Snow, sleet, and hail fell upon the soldiers.

Both roads to Trenton were covered with ice and snow. Men slipped and fell along the way. Men in bare feet or torn shoes made a trail of blood on the snowy roads.

About 7:30 A.M., a sleepy Hessian guard thought he saw men moving on the inland road. He called out a warning — too late. Shots rang out; men ran and shouted. Down by the river, the second column of Americans was charging with bayonets. Cannons began to open fire.

79

Defeating the Hessians. Colonel Johann Rall, the Hessian commander, was awakened by the noise. He was still dazed from the Christmas party. Probably he had a bad hangover. But he dashed bravely into the streets between the stone barracks. He cursed and called his sleepy, tired men out to fight. Most of them couldn't even get into action. The American rifle and cannon fire was too heavy.

Finally Colonel Rall was hit by a bullet and fell wounded. The frightened Hessians threw down their rifles and surrendered. Rall died after giving up to Washington. More than 1,000 of the enemy were taken prisoner. Only two of Washington's men were killed and three were wounded.

After the battle, Washington retreated back across the Delaware. A few days later he set out again, this time doing battle with British troops. At Princeton, Washington's army put some of these troops to flight. But Washington decided against attacking New Brunswick. His troops were too weary to attempt it. Instead he moved his command to Morristown in the hilly area of northern New Jersey. There he spent the next six months.

The Americans were amazed by their victory at Trenton. They wore rags — but they had beaten a tough, trained army. As a result, many Americans signed up for more service. The British

gave up all hope of ending the war in the winter of 1776-1777. Washington's army was saved. It would fight on until help came from France.

A Second Look. . . .

1. *In the winter of 1776, Washington's army was small and weak. Yet it defeated a superior force of Hessians at*

At the Battle of Princeton, George Washington took notice of the brilliant work of Captain Alexander Hamilton. In this painting of the battle, the general is talking to young Hamilton. Hamilton later became Washington's military aide, then joined his first Presidential Cabinet.

Trenton. Explain why the Americans, not the Hessians, won the Battle of Trenton.

2. Imagine that a British spy had warned the Hessians about Washington's plan of crossing the Delaware. Describe what you think would have happened to Washington and his army. Do you think Americans would still be British citizens if the Hessians had been wide awake at Trenton on Christmas night, 1776?

3. On a piece of paper, trace or copy a map of New Jersey. Then use the map in Chapter 15 as a source for the following exercise: Show three places on the map where important events took place: (a) Trenton; (b) Princeton; and (c) Morristown. Also indicate Washington's route from Trenton to Morristown.

Chapter 15

The Defeat of Gentleman Johnny

"Gentleman Johnny" Burgoyne (burr-GOIN) did not have much use for American soldiers. He believed that his own British troops were better fighters on the battlefield. They fought like Europeans. American troops fought like people from the backwoods. They pretended to surrender and then fired on the enemy. They sniped at the British from behind trees. They surprised their foes and caught them in ambushes (traps). At least the British knew how to stand up and fight like gentlemen, General Sir John Burgoyne thought.

Burgoyne knew that the Americans were troublesome. They could be as annoying as a swarm of buzzing flies. But Burgoyne was very sure of himself. He had no doubt that he could defeat the Americans — no doubt at all.

His faith in himself was clear to British leaders. Early in 1777 it won him a leading role in the war. His job was to cut off New England from the rest of the colonies. New England had given the colonies many of their soldiers. It had been giving the Continental Army much of its meat. Without help from New England, the Continental Army would be greatly weakened. Then, the British believed,

the war could be brought to a speedy end.

The plan to cut off New England had been made before the Battle of Trenton. It involved British forces under three commands. Burgoyne was to lead his soldiers down from Canada and southward across Lake Champlain. Lieutenant Colonel Barry St. Leger was to move another force from Fort Oswego (ah-

If American soldiers had been the drunken cowards they are made to seem in this British cartoon, the Revolutionary War would have ended swiftly indeed.

82

SWEE-go) on Lake Ontario to the Hudson River. General Sir William Howe was to lead a third force up the Hudson from New York. All three forces would come together at Albany. They would defeat any enemy troops in the area. They could then take firm control of the Hudson. Without crossing points along the Hudson, Americans would not be able to get supplies from New England (see the map in this chapter).

British blunders. To British leaders in London, the plan looked almost ideal. But when their generals tried to follow it, they blundered all along the way. St. Leger ran into fighting in the Mohawk Valley. Finally he fell back to his starting point, Fort Oswego. Howe, meanwhile, never took part in the plan at all. He may have misunderstood his orders. Or he may have figured that Burgoyne did not need his help. Whatever the case, Howe gathered his troops in New York City. Then he sailed in the *opposite* direction from Albany — southward toward Chesapeake Bay.

At first Burgoyne did make some headway. He set out from Canada in June 1777 with more than 7,000 men. His army easily captured Fort Ticonderoga (tie-kon-deh-ROE-guh) on the southern edge of Lake Champlain. But soon Burgoyne ran into trouble. His army had to cut its way through thick forests. It had to cross swamps and streams. It had to build some 40 bridges along the way. Burgoyne's men became weak and sick.

To add to his troubles, Burgoyne made a serious mistake. He sent about 700 of his Hessian soldiers to Vermont (then still part of New York) to grab food and horses for his men. At Bennington they were attacked by untrained Ameri-

General Sir John Burgoyne

can soldiers. These soldiers called themselves the Green Mountain Boys. Almost all of the Hessians were killed or captured. Many of the soldiers sent to help them were also lost. In all, Burgoyne lost about 900 men.

On September 19, Burgoyne's army met a larger American army near Saratoga. The British marched out of a forest into an open field. Up ahead, men with fur caps and long rifles lay in wait, hidden among the trees. Suddenly there was the crack of American rifles. Their main targets were British officers. Many were killed. British gunners were picked off before they could load their cannons.

The British fled back to the woods. When the Americans charged them, the British drove them back. For three hours the two armies fought back and forth across a field. The Americans finally pulled back, but the British had lost more than 600 men.

Final retreat. Burgoyne waited for help but none came. Then, on October 7, the two armies fought it out again. This

Blocking the British, 1777

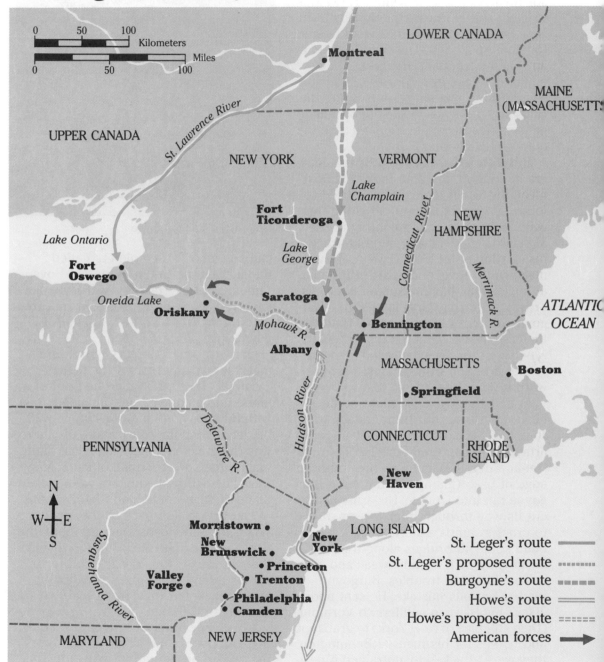

time an American general named Benedict Arnold was the hero of the day. Riding horseback, he led three charges against the British lines. On one charge, British troops under young General Simon Fraser held their own.

"Pick off that Fraser!" Arnold shouted. "Get him and the day is won!" A moment later a sharpshooter aimed his rifle and fired. Fraser fell from his horse, badly wounded. His troops fell back. Soon Arnold also fell from his horse with a bullet wound in his leg. He was carried from the field.

But the Americans won the day. Burgoyne's bleeding, starving troops retreated toward Saratoga. Soon his entire force was surrounded. He had never figured that "soldiers from the backwoods" would beat him on the battlefield. The Americans had proved him wrong. On October 17, Burgoyne surrendered his army of more than 5,000 British and Hessian troops.

The victory at Saratoga was the most important the Americans had won so far. When news reached Europe, it led to a victory of another sort. For several months, Americans had been trying to win France over to their side. Now they finally succeeded. In February 1778 the French signed a treaty of friendship with America. The treaty gave America a powerful ally in its struggle for independence.

Yet the tide of war did not turn overnight. That winter Washington camped at Valley Forge in Pennsylvania. His aim was to keep watch on the British in nearby Philadelphia. After Saratoga, the winter at Valley Forge was a low point for the American army. There was not much food. Soap was as scarce as meat. Soldiers stood in the snow in bare feet.

At Valley Forge, Washington did get some unexpected help. It came with the arrival of a tough drill master, Baron Friedrich von Steuben (FREED-rick vahn STYOO-bun). Von Steuben came from Prussia (PRUSH-uh), a powerful German kingdom. He was put in charge of training Washington's men. He taught them to use bayonets and march in perfect order. Washington's men respected him and worked hard.

In June they marched away from Valley Forge. With Von Steuben's help, the American army had been reborn. It had become a tough, well-trained body of soldiers. It was ready now for the hard fighting ahead.

A Second Look. . . .

1. *What did "Gentleman Johnny" Burgoyne expect to achieve by marching south from Canada? Why did he fail?*

2. *Many times General Sir John Burgoyne had risked his life in battle. He was very well liked by his own British troops. But he failed to measure the strength of the independence movement in America's small towns. And he had little knowledge of the American landscape. How do you suppose these weaknesses led to his defeat at Saratoga? Can you think of any similarities between these weaknesses and recent U.S. fighting in Vietnam? If so, what are they?*

3. *Imagine that John Burgoyne, Barry St. Leger, and William Howe have met in New York City in 1778. Each blames the other two for the failure of the campaign that led to Saratoga. Create a conversation among them. (Bear in mind that such a conversation never did take place.)*

Chapter 16

"I Would Have Hanged My Brother"

Six hungry men walked up to a log cabin in the woods of Georgia. They found a turkey and shot it. Then they pointed their rifles at a woman in the house. "Cook it for us," they said. The woman took the dead bird and began to pluck out its feathers.

The men found some whiskey in the house and began to drink it. They talked and laughed about the man they had killed a few hours before. He had been an officer in the Georgia militia. They had shot him in his bed.

The woman told her daughter to fetch some water. She also managed to whisper another message into her ear. "Call your father," she said. The girl left the house.

The men were careless. They did not know the woman they were dealing with. Her name was Nancy Hart. She was six feet tall, and she knew about guns. She waited for her chance to grab one of the men's guns. Finally she reached out and took it. The man leaped at her. She killed him with one shot. Another came at her. She shot him too. The others she held as prisoners.

Soon her husband entered with a group of friends. They wanted to shoot the invaders on the spot. But Nancy Hart said that would be too good for them. Hanging them would be better, she said. That is how her enemies died, hanging from a tree outside her cabin door.

Nancy Hart and her husband were farmers, not soldiers. The men they killed were not really soldiers either. These men were Americans who supported the British king. This scene that took place in the woods of Georgia was a fairly common one. For the American Revolution was much more than just a soldiers' war.

"Enemy country." The fact was that Americans were badly divided among themselves. Many of them believed as Nancy Hart did. They wanted independence even if it took a war to win it. But perhaps as many as a third of all American colonists remained loyal to the British king. The people in this second group were called *Loyalists.*

Which colonists were Loyalists? Generally those who thought they had most to gain by siding with the British. Many were merchants, large landowners, and other wealthy people who feared great change. But not all Loyalists were wealthy — not by any means. On the Southern frontier, for example, the group included many poor farmers and hunters. These people looked to Britain for protection. They opposed the Revolution because it was being led by the very people they most disliked. These leaders were the wealthy planters and merchants along the east coast.

Loyalists lived in all 13 colonies. But they were perhaps most common in five — New York, New Jersey, Pennsylvania, Maryland, and Delaware. In New York, Loyalists may have made up more than half of all the colonists. In Pennsylvania, many Quakers were suspected of being Loyalists because they refused to fight. Patriots from New England and Virginia were aware of Loyalist strength in the middle colonies. They sometimes spoke

This British cartoon is a defense of the Loyalists. "O cruel fate," the kneeling Loyalist cries. "Is this the return for our loyalty?" Patriots are shown as Indian savages, who reject European ways. "I'll tomahawk the dog," one snarls. In what ways is the cartoon unfair to American Indians?

of this area as "the enemy's country."

Most patriots hated Loyalists more bitterly than they hated the British. They blamed Loyalists for persuading the British to fight. Loyalists were treated as traitors and outlaws. They could be arrested for writing letters to British friends. They could be punished for traveling in stagecoaches without identification cards. It was even risky to drink to the health of the British king. One Loyalist who tried this was pushed into a large barrel. There he was forced to dance all night to the tune of "Yankee Doodle."

The homes of Loyalists were raided. Their property was stolen. Sometimes they were put to death. Patriot leaders such as John Adams raged against Americans who sided with the British. "I would have hanged my brother," said Adams, "if he took part with our enemy in this country." (Luckily for Adams' brother, he, like Adams, was a patriot.)

Loyalists were no friendlier to patriots — at least not in areas where they had control. One of these was New York City, held by the British for most of the war. The British used New York churches as prisons for "rebels." They often let prisoners starve to death. Bodies were then piled in carts and hauled through the streets. Loyalists laughed and hooted as they saw these carts go by. "There goes another load of rebels," they would say.

Making choices. Thousands of Americans did not care who won the war. They were neither Loyalists nor patriots. They just wanted to be left alone. James Moody, for example, was a New Jersey farmer. His neighbors tried to make him sign a paper swearing loyalty to the new American government.

He refused to do it, explaining that he just wanted to be left in peace. But his neighbors kept threatening him. One day they even shot at him while he was out farming. That made Moody so angry he decided to leave his farm and fight for the British.

The war brought suffering and fear to many. It also brought new opportunities. In Virginia the royal governor made a promise to those slaves owned by rebel planters. He promised them freedom if they ran away from their masters and served the British army. Hundreds of slaves in Virginia and other states joined the British. But few were set free. Instead they became the property of British officers. They were made to do the heavy labor of building forts and hauling cannons and supplies.

A Second Look. . . .

1. *In the American Revolution, patriots had to fight more than British soldiers. They also feared trouble from Loyalists. Who were these Loyalists? In which colonies were they strongest? How were they treated by the patriots?*

2. *Nancy Hart and her husband killed their prisoners without a trial. Would you say that they were guilty of committing a crime? Or were they simply acting in their own defense? Do you think Nancy Hart and her husband were justified in killing the prisoners? Explain.*

3. *During the Revolution, many Americans refused to take sides. Pretend that you are a patriot trying to persuade a local farmer to join your side. Draw up a list of five points you would want to make to the farmer. What reasons would you give for your views?*

When Benjamin Franklin lived in Europe, he used this engraving as his calling card. Britain, having lost her limbs (colonies), can no longer wield her once-mighty spear and shield. Slowly, she slips off the globe. Brooms fly from the masts of British ships to indicate that the ships are for sale.

Chapter 17

Surrender at Yorktown

The British drummer boy hammered at his drum as hard as he could. But the noise of the cannons drowned out his message. Gunsmoke curled around his legs. Finally the Americans and French let up on their firing for a moment, and the drum beat could be heard. The message was clear: The British were asking for a meeting.

A British officer stepped out, waving a white cloth. Soon he was blindfolded and taken to General Washington's headquarters. The British officer had a message for Washington. Lord Cornwallis, the British commander at Yorktown, wanted to surrender. It was a great victory for the Americans and the French. It would end the Revolutionary War.

How was the victory won?

When the French entered the war in

1778, they gave the British cause for great alarm. France was one of the most powerful countries of Europe. Its aid to the Americans was sure to lengthen the war. Now the British decided on a new course. British commanders turned much of their attention to the area south of the Potomac River. There they expected to find many Loyalists who might aid their cause.

Southern campaign. In December 1778 the British took Savannah, Georgia. A year-and-a-half later they seized Charleston, South Carolina. There they took 5,000 American troops prisoner. That was nearly all of the Continental Army south of the Potomac.

Yet the British found themselves in trouble in the Carolinas. They suffered stinging defeats at King's Mountain in 1780 and at Cowpens in South Carolina the next year. In 1781 they decided to leave the Carolinas and move north. They built up an army of 7,200 men in Virginia. Lord Cornwallis took charge of this army and camped it at Yorktown, on the coast. Facing it was a much smaller army made up of French and American troops. These troops were led by the Marquis de Lafayette, Count Von Steuben, and General Anthony Wayne of Pennsylvania.

General Washington had a much larger American army outside New York City at this time. And Washington had a big decision to make. Should he attack the British in New York? Or should he march south and strike against Cornwal-

lis in Virginia? Washington favored attacking New York. If it were captured, the war might be ended.

Washington had a meeting with Count Rochambeau (roe-sham-BOH), the French commander. Rochambeau had an army of 5,000 men, but he was against an attack on New York. "The British are too strong in New York," he said. "It would be much better to attack Cornwallis in Virginia."

This painting is a French view of the British surrender at Yorktown in October 1781. Notice the importance the artist gives to the French fleet, which came to Yorktown to block a British escape.

By land and by sea. Washington and Rochambeau knew that their armies alone could not defeat Cornwallis in Virginia. They would have to have sea power as well. What if the armies trapped Cornwallis at Yorktown, and then Cornwallis sailed away in British ships? Cornwallis would have to be blocked on sea as well as land.

Washington and Rochambeau sent a message to French Admiral de Grasse in the West Indies. They asked for the help of his fleet. It was the middle of August before they got their answer. De Grasse was sailing for Yorktown to block a British escape by sea. He would also land extra troops.

Washington and Rochambeau began racing south to Yorktown with their troops. By the middle of September they had joined the small French and American army that was already there. And in

the meantime, De Grasse had won a victory at sea. He had beaten a British fleet sent from New York to help Cornwallis. Now Cornwallis was hemmed in by land at Yorktown — and blocked at sea by the ships of Admiral de Grasse.

The Americans and their French allies had 16,000 men at Yorktown. Cornwallis had less than half that many. Soon the allied cannons were pounding the British defenses day and night. Then, on October 14, French and American troops attacked. They struck swiftly after dark. They captured two British outposts.

Allied cannons pushed closer to the front. Soon 100 of them were blasting the British lines. Now the British position was hopeless. Their defenses were smashed. Finally, on October 17, the British drummer boy began hammering out his message. Cornwallis was finished.

After the fighting, British fifes and drums struck up an old tune. It was called "The World Turned Upside Down." The song was a fitting end to the Revolutionary War. For the British, the world had indeed been turned upside down. They had lost a war they had once expected to win. They had lost their 13 American colonies as well. The peace treaty ending the war was not to be signed until September 1783. But Yorktown was the last major battle. Already it was becoming clear that the 13 British colonies were to be 13 "free and independent states."

The War Moves South

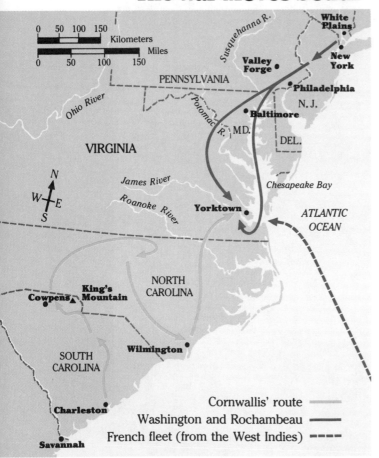

Cornwallis' route ——
Washington and Rochambeau ——
French fleet (from the West Indies) ----

A Second Look. . . .

1. *Americans won a victory at Yorktown by trapping British troops. How did they do so?*

2. *Compare Washington's leadership at the Battle of Yorktown with his leadership at the Battle of Trenton. Which battle, in your opinion, better showed Washington's greatness as a commander? Which battle was more important — or were both equally important? Why?*

3. *Turn to "Putting Events in Order" at the end of Part 3. Make a list of the three events you consider the most important in bringing an American victory in the Revolutionary War. Defend your choices briefly in writing.*

Chapter 18

A Most Loved Man

Everywhere people went in Paris, France, in 1781, the same face seemed to stare out at them. His portraits hung over the fireplaces of French homes. His picture was painted on clocks and pocket watches. He was one of the most famous people in France. He was not a French king or count but plain old Benjamin Franklin from America.

Franklin wore a simple fur hat on his head and plain spectacles on his nose. In France anyone who was at all important wore a fancy powdered wig. But not Franklin. He simply let his gray hair hang down to his shoulders.

Ben Franklin was a charming and witty man. He knew how to use his charm and wit to help the American cause. Without his work in Paris, Americans could not have won the Battle of Yorktown. After all, the Yorktown victory depended on a combined attack by French and American troops and French ships. Why were the French helping the Americans? Partly because Ben Franklin had talked them into it.

Franklin was clever. He had a way with words and an understanding of complex ideas. He was also willing to try anything new. He had been this way ever since he first ran away from home in 1723.

Ben was only 17 years old then. He had become tired of working in his older brother's Boston print shop. So he ran off to seek his fortune. He had only a dollar in his pocket when he finally reached Philadelphia. But he soon found a good job working for a German printer. After a while he was able to open his own printing shop.

Ben worked hard. Soon he was printing a newspaper. It sold more copies than any other paper in the American colonies. In 1732 Ben began to print *Poor Richard's Almanac.* It had news of the weather, holidays, and the best time to plant seeds or pick grapes. It also had many wise and funny sayings that Franklin made up. Some of them were:

"God helps them that help themselves."

"Lost time is never found again."

"Half the truth is often a great lie."

People loved Poor Richard's sayings. They bought many copies of the *Almanac,* and Ben became rich. He also became a leading citizen of Philadelphia. He did many things to make Philadelphia a good town to live in. He became its postmaster and speeded up the mail service. He started a fire department and a police department. He began the town's first library and first hospital. He also started the school that later became the University of Pennsylvania.

At the age of 42, Franklin had made enough money to retire from business. He liked science and wanted to learn more about electricity. Soon after,

Franklin invented the lightning rod. This kept houses from catching fire when struck by lightning. Franklin won many honors for his work.

As time went on, Franklin became more and more active in public affairs. He went to England to try to make the British government deal fairly with the colonies. When the Revolutionary War broke out, he helped Thomas Jefferson write the Declaration of Independence. Soon after that, in 1776, he sailed for France to try to get some help for Washington's struggling army.

Winning over France. Franklin said he represented a nation called the United States. But no government in Europe thought this nation even existed. The United States then was only an idea in the heads of a few colonial rebels. Franklin now had to persuade the French king to recognize his government as the true one for America.

France wanted to strike back at its old enemy, England. But the young French king, Louis XVI, was afraid of losing

Benjamin Franklin made a great hit at the French court. Once the French queen, Marie Antoinette, crowned Franklin with a laurel wreath.

another costly war. He would help the Americans secretly, but would not yet dare to recognize their government. Then came news of the Americans' surprising victory at Saratoga in 1777. Franklin wept with joy when he heard it.

Yet even now the French king hesitated about getting mixed up with the Americans. So Franklin came up with another scheme. He met secretly with a representative of the English government. This Englishman said George III was ready to make peace. England would now give Americans almost complete freedom to govern themselves. But they would still have to be part of the British empire.

Franklin probably did not take this meeting seriously. He just wanted to scare the French king into thinking that the Americans might make peace. Suddenly the king decided he would have to act. He signed a treaty of alliance with the United States. (An *alliance* is an agreement between nations to promote their shared interests.) The final result of this alliance was the victory at Yorktown.

Reaching terms with Britain. Later, in 1781, one more treaty had to be worked out in Paris. That was the treaty of peace with England. Franklin worked on its terms with John Adams of Massachusetts and a New York lawyer, John Jay. Again Franklin helped give Americans the best bargain they could hope for. Britain said the western border of the United States should be the Allegheny (al-uh-GAY-nee) Mountains. The U.S. Congress said it should be much farther west — along the Mississippi River.

In Paris, Franklin wrote a clever note

for the British to look at. It suggested that Britain pay the United States for all the houses and property its armies had destroyed. Perhaps, Franklin suggested, Britain should pay for this damage by giving Americans all of Canada. Franklin knew that the English would never agree to give up Canada. But he made the threat anyway. In the end, the British found a way to avoid a showdown over Canada. They agreed to make the Mississippi River the western border of the United States.

The Treaty of Paris was signed in Sep-

Benjamin Franklin printed his first Poor Richard's Almanac *in 1732 (below). He kept on playing the role of Poor Richard even in the 1780's at the French court. Above is a detail of a portrait of Franklin painted by John Trumbull.*

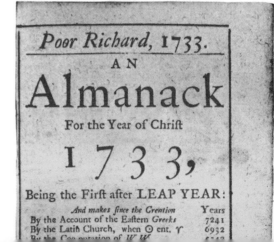

Poor Richard, 1733.

AN

Almanack

For the Year of Chrift

I 7 3 3,

Being the Firft after LEAP YEAR:

And makes fince the Creation   Years

By the Account of the Eaftern *Greeks*   7241

By the Latin Church, when ☉ ent. ♈   6932

95

Benjamin West painted American signers of Treaty of 1783, (left to right) John Jay, John Adams, Ben Franklin, Henry Laurens, and William Franklin. But painting went unfinished. British signers would not pose.

not walk. He had to be carried out of Paris on a seat strapped between two mules. People who lined the streets wept to see him go. They knew they would never see anyone quite like him again. Neither would the nation he had done so much to create.

A Second Look. . . .

1. *Benjamin Franklin never fought in the American War for Independence. How then did he help the United States to win freedom from Britain? Give at least two examples.*

2. *This chapter describes Benjamin Franklin as charming, witty, and powerful. What other words would you use to describe him? For example, was he honest or dishonest? Timid or bold? Generous or selfish? Flexible or stubborn? Lazy or energetic? What reasons can you give for your answers?*

3. *Franklin was famous for his sense of humor. Even when writing about serious subjects, he sometimes told amusing stories. Imagine that you are Ben Franklin preparing to leave Paris in 1785. Write a letter to the French king thanking him for his help. You may make the letter as humorous as you wish.*

tember 1783. In the treaty Britain recognized the independence of its former colonies. It gave the new nation all the land westward to the Mississippi from the Great Lakes to Florida. It also gave Americans the right to fish off the shores of what is now Canada. The French were amazed that the British had been so generous.

Benjamin Franklin was 70 years old when he first arrived in Paris. He was almost 80 when he left for home in 1785. He was so sick and lame that he could

Looking Back: Fight for Independence

A	B	C	D	E	
January 1775	January 1777	January 1779	January 1781	January 1783	January 1785

Putting Events in Order

Chapters 12 through 18 have shown how Americans won their War for Independence. Ten events in this war are listed here. Your job is to match each event to the correct period shown on the timeline above. On a piece of paper, number from **1** to **10**. After each number, write the letter of the period in which the event occurred.

1. "Give me liberty or give me death," Patrick Henry tells Virginia lawmakers.

2. George Washington's army suffers a hard winter at Valley Forge, Pennsylvania.

3. Treaty of peace between Britain and the United States is signed at Paris.

4. Thomas Jefferson writes the Declaration of Independence.

5. George Washington attacks the Hessians at Trenton, New Jersey.

6. George Washington retreats from the Battle of Long Island.

7. France and the United States sign a treaty of alliance.

8. A British army under General Cornwallis surrenders to George Washington at Yorktown, Virginia.

9. A British army under General John Burgoyne surrenders at Saratoga, New York.

10. Baron Friedrich Von Steuben is put in charge of training Washington's army.

Interpreting a Source

A young Loyalist, Nicholas Cresswell, kept a diary during the American Revolution. Much of his diary was written while he was living near Alexandria, Virginia. As you read his diary, look for signs of bias, or strong personal opinion, that color his account of events.

Monday, January 6, 1777. News that

Washington had taken 760 Hessian prisoners at Trenton in the Jerseys. Hope it is a lie. This afternoon hear he has likewise taken six pieces of brass cannon.

Tuesday, January 7, 1777. The news is confirmed. The minds of the people are much altered. A few days ago they had given up the cause for lost. Their late successes have turned the scale and now they are all liberty-mad again. Their recruiting parties could not get a man ... no longer since than last week, and now the men are coming in by companies. Confound the turncoat[1] scoundrels and the cowardly Hessians together. This has given them new spirits ... and will prolong the war, perhaps for two years....

Wednesday, January 8, 1777. This is a most unhappy country. Every necessary of life is at an extravagant[2] price, some of them indeed not to be had for money. Poor people are almost naked....

Tuesday, January 14, 1777. News that Washington had entirely routed[3] our army, and the few that had escaped had been obliged to take refuge on board the ships. This must certainly be a lie.

Leesburg, Loudoun County, Virginia — Friday, January 17, 1777. Left Mr. Nielson's. Got to Leesburg to my old lodgings. Dined and spent the evening at Mr. Kirk's.... Their late successes have made him believe that they will have a free and open trade to all parts of the world very soon. Such is the instability of human affairs. Six weeks ago this gentleman was lamenting the unhappy situation of the Americans, and ... supposing [George Washington's] want of skill and experience in military matters had brought them all to the brink of destruction. In short, all was gone, all was lost. But now the scale is turned and Washington's name is extolled[4] to the clouds.... Poor General Howe is ridiculed in all companies and all my countrymen abused. I am obliged to hear this daily and dare not speak a word in their favor. It is the ... Hessians that have caused this, curse the scoundrel that first thought of sending them here.

1. *Cresswell was living near Alexandria, Virginia, when he wrote much of his diary. How long did it take for news from the Battle of Trenton to reach Virginia?*

2. *What sentences in his diary most strongly show Cresswell's bias?*

3. *Suppose a friend of the American cause had also kept a diary in January 1777. How would this account probably differ from Cresswell's account?*

4. *Do you think that Mr. Kirk knows that Cresswell is a Loyalist? Why or why not?*

Sharpening Your Skills

Some years in the Revolutionary War were more violent than other years. The bar graph at the right shows how many Americans were killed and wounded in battle in each year of the war.

---

[1] A *turncoat* is a person who switches to an opposing side. In this case, Cresswell is referring to those joining the patriots' side.

[2] *Extravagant*, in this sense, means very high in price.

[3] *To rout* is to drive out by force.

[4] *To extol* is to praise highly.

1. Compare graphs for the years 1778 and 1780. What is the major difference between them?

2. To judge from this graph, what were the three most violent years of the Revolutionary War? What were the three least violent years, in terms of battle losses?

3. Why do you suppose the number of battle losses in 1777 was so much higher than the number of battle losses in 1783?

4. In addition to those killed in battle, about 18,500 other Americans died either in their own army camps or as prisoners of the British. Given this fact, would you say more deaths occurred on the battlefield — or off it?

American Battle Casualties, 1775-1783

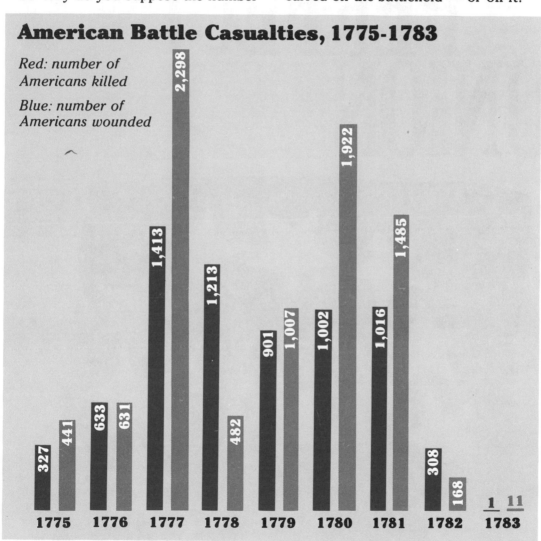

Red: number of Americans killed

Blue: number of Americans wounded

	1775	1776	1777	1778	1779	1780	1781	1782	1783
Killed	327	633	1,413	1,213	901	1,002	1,016	308	1
Wounded	441	631	2,298	482	1,007	1,922	1,485	168	11

4 A MORE PERFECT UNION

Looking Ahead: "Limping Government"

A huge crowd gathered in the streets of Philadelphia on July 4, 1788. People had come to watch a parade. Twelve years had passed since the Declaration of Independence was first read in this city. Now the people had something else to celebrate. They had a new plan of government. A document called the *United States Constitution* had recently been approved by nine states. This was enough to make it the law of the land.

The parade in Philadelphia lasted all day. People hooted and laughed as one wagon went by. It carried a ship called the *Confederacy*. This stood for the old plan of government that was being replaced. The ship was falling apart.

Another wagon carrying another fake ship rumbled down the cobblestone street. People cheered and applauded. This ship was called the *Federal Constitution*. Unlike the other ship, this one

A flag battered in the American Revolution.

was solidly built. The horses that pulled it had the names of different states written on their foreheads. The horse "Delaware" was in front. That was because Delaware was the first state to approve the Constitution.

What was the Confederacy? Why was it shown falling apart? Why did many people think the new plan of government, the federal Constitution, was stronger? Were they right?

The Confederacy was the first plan of government for the United States. It was created by the Second Continental Congress during the Revolutionary War. Like all plans of government, this one said how laws would be made. The rules for making American laws were listed in a document called the *Articles of Confederation*. For seven years, from 1781 to 1788, the United States was governed according to this plan.

The Articles gave power to make laws to a group called *Congress*. Congress

101

was made up of representatives elected by the lawmakers of each state. Congress had power to make treaties with foreign nations. It had authority to run a post office. It could raise an army and navy, and coin money. Each of the 13 states could cast only one vote in Congress. An important law could be passed only if nine of the 13 states voted for it.

These rules sounded fair enough, but they did not work well in practice. They caused trouble mainly because they left too much power to the states. Each state had its own government and made its own laws. Each state could coin its own money. Each could arm its own soldiers and build its own navy. Each could make laws that hurt neighboring states. The Articles did not keep the 13 states from acting as if they were 13 separate nations.

Because of this, Americans suffered badly during their first years as a nation. These were a few of their troubles:

Confusion about money. What could money buy in 1785? That depended on the kind of money a person had. Many different kinds of coins were used. There were British coins, French coins, and Spanish coins. Colonists had trouble determining a fair value for each.

Congress set up a national coinage in 1785. But few national coins were actually made until 1793. How did Americans deal with the problem? Some of them traded with coins minted by the states. Others used foreign coins. Still others traded with something besides coins. Some people in New York used salt pork. Some people in North Carolina used whiskey.

Even more confusing was the paper

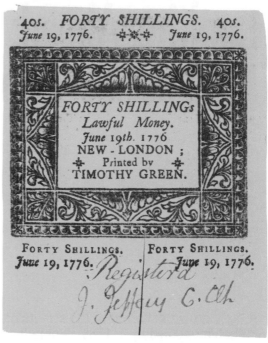

money printed by the different state governments. Farmers wanted paper money because the more valuable coins were scarce. They needed something with which to pay their debts to city merchants. But the merchants often thought this paper money was worthless.

Confusion about trade. The 13 states competed with each other for business. They hated to see their own merchants and farmers losing business to people in other states. The merchants of New York, for example, complained about people buying firewood from Connecticut merchants. To stop this trade, the New York state legislature placed a very high tax on firewood from out of state. Connecticut merchants tried to get even. They signed an agreement refusing to sell *anything* to New

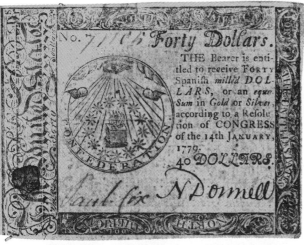

Money was confusing in the young United States. How was one to pay for a new horse? With colonial money such as the Connecticut bill (top left)? Or with state money such as the South Carolina dollar (left)? Money issued by the Continental Congress (above) was no stronger than the U.S. government itself. Was this strong enough?

York for one year. Business was hurt badly everywhere because of this fierce competition between states. And the United States Congress was helpless to do anything about it.

Confusion about foreign policy. Like any nation, the United States needed to make treaties with other countries. But in 1785 most European nations laughed at the United States government. They knew how weak Congress was. Congress was too weak to collect enough taxes. It was too weak to raise and equip a strong army. Therefore, foreign nations did not respect American power.

This left American diplomats helpless. They could not even strike bargains with countries such as Spain. Spain controlled the city of New Orleans and the lower Mississippi River. Spanish officials stopped Americans from using New Orleans for their trade. Americans complained bitterly. But the King of Spain only shrugged. He knew that the U.S. Congress was too weak to do anything about Mississippi trade — or almost anything else.

The problem was clearly with the Articles, not with Congress itself. Members of Congress proved they had great vision when given the power to use it. In 1787 Congress passed a law known as the *Northwest Ordinance.* It concerned western lands north of the Ohio River. The United States had gained these lands from Britain in the Treaty of Paris of 1783. Now Congress drew up a far-sighted plan for governing them.

Congress could have simply set up a government for the Northwest Territory. It could have made these lands dependent on the Confederacy and let it go at

103

that. Instead lawmakers went much farther. They created a plan for Western lands to become equal in the long term with the 13 original states. Their plan even allowed settlers in this area to form states of their own.

Model for statehood. The plan worked this way: The Northwest Territory would first be ruled by a governor, a secretary, and three judges named by Congress. Settlers in the area would reach self-government in two steps. The first step would be reached when the area had 5,000 free males of voting age.

Northwest Territory, 1787

At that point, the people of the territory might elect a legislature. The second step would be reached when one part of the territory had 60,000 settlers. Then that part could become a state.

Congress set limits on the number of states that could be formed in the territory. It put these limits at no fewer than three and no more than five. It promised freedom of worship in Western lands. It encouraged public support of schools and colleges in the area. It barred slavery from the Northwest Territory.

In short, Congress made the Northwest Ordinance a model for the creation of additional states. The trouble was that it took action too late to head off criticism of the central government. By 1787 many Americans had begun to doubt that the Articles of Confederation were strong enough. Some of them were saying that their central government was a failure. George Washington called it a "half-starved, limping government, always moving upon crutches and tottering at every step."

How could the government be strengthened? One way was to make changes in the Articles of Confederation. Another way was to throw out the Articles and start over again. Meeting in Philadelphia in 1787, a group of 55 men decided that the second way was best. They created a Constitution that gave a new Congress far more power than the old Congress had. They also created the office of President and a national court called the *Supreme Court*.

How did this new plan of government work? Did it work better or worse than the old plan? The chapters in this part will attempt to give the answers.

Chapter 19

The Leaders Gather

It was a sunny springtime Sunday in Philadelphia in 1787. Crowds of people lined the streets. It seemed as if the whole city had turned out to greet one man. He was George Washington, America's hero and commander-in-chief during the Revolutionary War.

Washington arrived in his old buff-and-blue uniform with three gold stars on each shoulder. He also wore a powdered wig under his three-cornered hat. Sitting straight and easy on his carriage seat, Washington didn't smile much. But his eyes looked very blue under their bushy brows.

"Speech, General! Speech!" shouted the crowds again and again. But Washington didn't stop his carriage to give a speech. He and the other men who had come to Philadelphia had far more important business to consider.

Dangers from within. These men were worried that their young nation was tearing itself apart. They remembered all too well what had happened only a few months before. In the fall of 1786, a group of Massachusetts farmers had rebelled against their state government. Their leader was a hero of the Revolutionary War, Daniel Shays.

The farmers had no money. They could not pay a tax recently passed by Massachusetts lawmakers. The state had therefore threatened to take away their land. To prevent this, Shays and other poor farmers had marched against the state courthouse. They had pointed a gun at the judge and forced him to leave the court. They had burned the barns and property of other state officials.

The state government was too weak to fight the rebel farmers. The United States Congress could not do anything either. Finally, a group of Massachusetts merchants asked people to donate money. The money went to support a large force of state troops. These troops then captured Shays. The rebellion was finally crushed.

But it was not so easily forgotten. Shays' Rebellion raised questions that frightened many people — especially wealthy ones. What if other rebels took up arms? Would the states be able to put them down? What would happen if rebels took over a state government? What if several rebellions broke out? How much bloodshed would there be? How much damage to property? The whole nation, just getting started after a hard-fought battle for freedom, could fall apart.

During the crisis of 1786, some leaders were meeting in Annapolis, Maryland. They had been called there by the U.S. Congress to discuss trade regulations between the states. But four states did not send representatives. Representatives from four other states did not arrive in time to take part in the meeting. The representatives who did appear saw no point in going on with the meeting. There were not enough leaders attending it. So they called for another meeting. They said this meeting should discuss a broader subject: how to make the central government work.

Danger of delay. Two leaders, James Madison of Virginia and Alexander Hamilton of New York, felt that it would be dangerous to wait too long. They believed that Americans simply had to face facts. The Articles of Confederation just weren't working well enough. They would have to be done over from top to bottom. Congress finally agreed. It sent out a call to all the states for the meeting, or convention, to do the job. The meeting was to be in Philadelphia, starting in May 1787.

Travel was slow in those days. It took a long time for some of the states' delegates, or representatives, to arrive. New Hampshire's men came late. Rhode Island never sent any at all. After long days of waiting, the delegates settled down to business. There were 55 of them in all.

What kind of men were these early leaders of the United States? They were mostly men of wealth and education. They were lawyers, businessmen, bankers, professors, and planters. About half of them were college graduates. This was unusual in a time when very few people went to college.

The men who met in Philadelphia were chosen by their states. Two of the most famous leaders were George Washington and Benjamin Franklin. Others were James Madison of Virginia and Alexander Hamilton of New York. But not all of America's great leaders met in Philadelphia in 1787. John Adams was in England at the time. Thomas Jefferson was in France. Patrick Henry, the Virginia patriot, refused to go to the meeting. He was sure that it would come up with a plan that would take too much power away from the states.

Many of the delegates knew from the start that the old Articles of Confederation would have to go. There was no point in trying to patch them up. The real job of the delegates was to draw up a new plan of government — a new Constitution.

The first thing the delegates did was elect George Washington to head the meeting. They all agreed on this. But for a long time afterward they agreed on little else. Writing the Constitution was not an easy thing to do. Even so, the delegates were able to finish their great task in less than four months.

A Second Look. . . .

1. *Why had many Americans decided by 1787 that the Articles of Confederation were not working well? How did Shays' Rebellion serve as evidence?*

2. *In 1787 Congress instructed delegates from the states to propose changes in the Articles. However, Congress did not instruct the delegates to create a new plan of government. And yet the dele-*

Many Americans did not like the idea of a strong national government. Some, like the person who drew this cartoon, thought of the Philadelphia meeting as a plot by the rich to hold on to their wealth and power. In the cartoon, the rich are carried to Philadelphia, but the "majority" must walk.

gates started working right away on a new plan. Does this mean that they were acting in an illegal way? Why or why not? Were the delegates right, do you think, to do away with the Articles altogether? Or would they have been better to change the Articles slightly?

3. The Constitution begins with the words: "We, the people of the United States. . . ." The first paragraph or Preamble *then states the six purposes of the government. Study the Preamble to the* Constitution, to be found at the back of this book. Select one of the purposes it states. Write it at the top of a piece of paper. Then write three examples of how our government serves this purpose today. (Here is what some of the words in the Preamble mean: Domestic tranquility *means a state of calmness at home.* Common defense *means safety from enemy attack.* Our posterity *means those Americans who will live in the future.* To ordain *is to establish by law.*)

Chapter 20

Moving Toward Middle Ground

That summer of 1787 was a hot one in Philadelphia. But the men who sat in the State House kept all the windows and doors closed. They also posted guards at the doors. Why? Because they wanted the meeting to be free from all outside pressures. And they wanted their discussions to be secret. These delegates wanted to be known for *what* they did, not *how* they did it.

Still, one delegate, James Madison of Virginia, kept some careful notes. More than 50 years after the meeting, these notes were printed. As a result, we now know quite a bit about what went on there. One of the things that went on — and on and on — was argument.

Delegates of the large states argued with the delegates of the small states immediately. One thing they argued about was how the new Congress should be set up. Under the Articles of Confederation, each state had one vote in Congress. But the delegates from the larger states now said: "We have more people and pay more taxes than the smaller states. So it is only fair that we should have more say in making laws." Delegates from the smaller states said: "We don't want to give up any of our rights

and powers in the new Congress."

For a while it looked as if the two sides would never agree. But finally they worked out a *compromise* — a way that satisfied both sides. Instead of having just one house, the new Congress would have *two* houses: the *House of Representatives* and the *Senate*. In the House of Representatives, the number of members from each state would depend on how many people it had. But in the Senate, each state, large or small, would have the same number of members — two.

States' rights. Another thing the delegates argued about was how much power the new government should have. Most leaders of the large states wanted a strong national government. They wanted it to have much more power than the state governments. Many delegates from the smaller states wanted a government that would be a fairly loose union of states. They wanted the states to keep much of the power they had under the Articles.

Again there was a compromise. The Congress was given many new powers. Now it would be able to collect taxes. It could borrow money to pay the government's bills. It could control all business done with foreign countries as well as business between states. No state would be able to print and coin its own money any more. Now Congress would do that — and for the whole country. Only Congress could declare war and order men into the armed forces.

All powers not given to the central government were left to the states. It was still up to each state to control all the local governments inside its borders. Cities, towns, and school districts would be under the control of the states. Each state still had the power to regulate any business firm that operated

This view of the meeting in Philadelphia was painted several years after it took place. George Washington delivered only one speech in the convention debates. But the artist who painted the picture let Washington have the floor. The artist seems more impressed by Washington as a speaker than some gentlemen at the table do. They look as if they have other matters on their minds.

only inside the state's borders. In fact, the state government was left in charge of almost everything that took place inside the state. The national government was in charge of affairs that went on between the states, or between the United States and foreign countries.

Counting slaves. There was still a third major area of disagreement. It concerned the counting of slaves. Delegates from the South wanted their slaves to be counted to decide the number of representatives they had in the House of Representatives. But they did not want slaves to be counted in figuring the amount of taxes to be paid by each state. Delegates from the North wanted just the opposite. They did not believe slaves should be counted toward representation. They *did* believe slaves should be counted in determining each state's taxes.

Argument on this issue led to yet another compromise. The word *slavery* was never mentioned in the Constitution. But the delegates in Philadelphia accepted slavery. If they had not done so, about half the states would not have agreed to the Constitution. The delegates decided to count each slave as three fifths of a person. They said this fraction should be used in determining the number of Representatives each state had in the House. They also said the fraction should be used in figuring the taxes to be paid. (See Article I, Section 2, Paragraph 3 of the Constitution at the back of this book.)

The men who wrote the U.S. Constitution in 1787 knew that it was not perfect. Even Ben Franklin said that he did not agree with everything in it. But Franklin said he would sign it anyway. He hoped that the other delegates would do the same. Why? Because Franklin doubted that any other meeting would be able to make a *better* Constitution.

In some ways the Constitution was not as democratic as it could have been — not by today's standards. Yet it was the best and most democratic plan of government *for that time.* The plan worked in 1789, the year the Constitution went into effect. It was tested by a bloody Civil War for four years, from 1861 to 1865. It is still working today.

A Second Look. . . .

1. *What is meant by the word* compromise? *Name at least two compromises reached in Philadelphia in 1787.*

2. *In 1790 the largest state was Virginia with a population of 821,287. The smallest was Delaware with a population of 59,096. How many Representatives should Virginia have been allowed to send to the proposed new House of Representatives? How many Representatives should Delaware have been allowed to send? Write your answers on a slip of paper. Then compare them with the Constitution itself. (See Article I, Section 2 of the Constitution at the back of this book.) Do you think it was fair that both Delaware and Virginia were represented equally in the Senate? Why or why not?*

3. *Here are some powers granted to Congress by the U.S. Constitution: (a) the power to collect taxes; (b) the power to regulate commerce or trade; (c) the power to coin money; (d) the power to establish post offices; (e) the power to declare war. Copy each of these powers on a sheet of paper. Next to each power, explain why a strong government needs to have this power to serve public needs.*

Chapter 21
Checks and Balances

The delegates in Philadelphia not only got ideas from one another. They also drew ideas from European thinkers of the past. Some of their most important ideas came from a book called *The Spirit of Laws.* It had been written some 40 years earlier by a Frenchman, Charles de Montesquieu (mon-tess-KYOO).

The Spirit of Laws talked about hundreds of subjects. It talked about the practice of killing unhealthy children in ancient times. It talked about how European princes treated prisoners. But the most famous part of Montesquieu's book

Charles de Montesquieu

talked about the English system of government.

The English, Montesquieu said, did not give all the power of government to one single group. Instead the English divided power among three separate parts, or branches, of government. One branch had the *legislative* power to make laws. Another branch, headed by the king, had the *executive* power of enforcing and carrying out laws. And a third branch had the *judicial* power of hearing evidence in court and deciding a person's guilt or innocence.

Why was it important to divide power in this way? Because, said Montesquieu, the power of government can be dangerous. It can destroy a citizen's liberty. But if power is divided, one part of government can *check and balance* the other two parts. The executive branch, for example, can stop the legislative branch from becoming too powerful. The judicial branch can check, or stop, the executive branch, and so forth.

The Spirit of Laws was not very popular in France. But it made a great hit in England. Montesquieu became very well known there. The English even started buying the wine he made on his French farm.

Montesquieu died in 1755. But his ideas lived on in Britain and America after his death. They influenced the delegates in Philadelphia in the way

111

they organized the new government. The delegates were very much aware of the need for checks and balances. So they divided the government into the same three branches Montesquieu had mentioned.

The *Legislative Branch* was to be made up of the two houses of Congress. Members of this branch were given most of the power to make laws for the nation.

The *Executive Branch* was to be made up of the President and the Vice-President. Members of this branch were given most of the power to enforce or carry out the laws.

The *Judicial Branch* was to be made up of the federal courts. Members of this branch were to sit in judgment in cases involving federal laws. The highest of these courts was the U.S. Supreme Court. It was to settle arguments about the Constitution and hear the most important law cases in the land.

Ever since 1789, checks and balances have prevented any one branch of the government from becoming too powerful. They make each branch depend in some ways on the other two.

How the President and the Supreme Court check one another. For example, the President has some control over the Supreme Court. He is the one who appoints a new member of the Court whenever a Supreme Court Justice dies or retires. The Supreme Court has some control over the President too. It can declare that the President's action or order is *unconstitutional* — not allowed by the Constitution. It can also rule that a law strongly favored by the President is unconstitutional. When the Court does so, that law is no longer valid.

How the President checks Congress. How do the President and Congress check and balance each other? For one thing, the President can tell Congress what new laws he would like it to pass. He can call special sessions, or meetings, of Congress. Calling a special session of Congress shows that the President really wants it to pass laws that he thinks are badly needed. The President can *veto,* or stop, any bill passed by Congress. If the President vetoes a bill, it does not become law in most cases.

How Congress checks the President. But Congress can check and balance the President by repassing the bill — passing it over his veto. It takes two thirds of the votes in Congress to do this, so it doesn't happen very often. Congress can refuse to give the President the money he needs to carry out his programs. The Senate can block any treaty the President makes with a foreign country. The President may ask a person to represent the U.S. in a foreign country, or to be a member of his Cabinet, or the Supreme Court. But if the Senate does not like the person the President has selected, it can block the appointment.

If Congress thinks that the President himself is unfit, it can remove him from office. The House of Representatives can *impeach* the President, or charge him with crimes or misconduct. Then the Senate can put the President on trial. Only once has Congress ever impeached a President and put him on trial. That was in 1868, and the President was Andrew Johnson. The Senate did try Johnson and came within one vote of removing him from office. Johnson finished out his term as President.

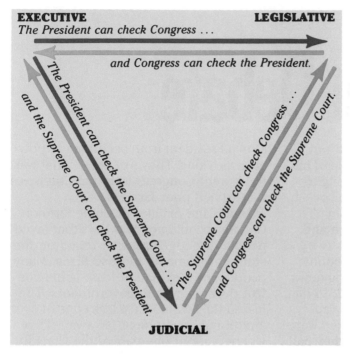

EXECUTIVE — LEGISLATIVE
The President can check Congress . . .
and Congress can check the President.
The President can check the Supreme Court . . .
and the Supreme Court can check the President.
The Supreme Court can check Congress . . .
and Congress can check the Supreme Court.
JUDICIAL

How the Supreme Court checks Congress. The Supreme Court and Congress check and balance each other in several ways. Congress can pass a bill. The President can sign the bill and make it a law. But any citizen can protest that the law goes against the Constitution. He or she can try to get the Supreme Court to listen to the case. If the Supreme Court does listen, it may decide that the law is unconstitutional. In that case, the law is no longer valid.

How Congress checks the Supreme Court. Congress can remove a Supreme Court Justice who does something Congress feels is wrong. Congress can also change the number of Justices on the Supreme Court. Today there are nine Justices. The first Court had only six. Congress can also

make changes in the lower federal courts.

So Congress, the President, and the Supreme Court check and balance and control each other. Each one holds some of the government's power. None of them holds all of the power. This is how American leaders intended it when they drew up the Constitution more than 190 years ago.

A Second Look. . . .

1. Each branch of the U.S. government is given a way to check, or hold back, the other two branches. Give one example of how the President can check Congress. Give one example of how Congress can check the President. Give one example of how the Supreme Court can check Congress. Give one example of how the President can check the Supreme Court.

2. Suppose that 230 members of Congress want to make major changes in the tax laws. The other 205 members are opposed to such a change, and so is the President. What do you think would probably happen? Would the tax laws be changed — or not? Do you think the President should have the power to check the action of members of Congress? Why or why not?

3. Turn to the Constitution in the back of this book. Study Article II, Section 2 on the President's powers. How many checks on the President's power can you find in this section? List them on a piece of paper.

113

Chapter 22

The Great Debate

A man holding a shovel climbed out of the large hole he had dug. A group of his friends came toward him, carrying a black coffin. One of them made a speech about the death of "liberty." They lowered the coffin into the grave and shoveled dirt on top of it.

These farmers from South Carolina had recently heard very upsetting news. They had learned that on May 23, 1788, their state had *ratified* (formally approved) the U.S. Constitution. They were sure this would end the liberty they had fought for in the Revolution. South Carolina was the eighth state to ratify the Constitution. If only one more state ratified it, the Constitution would be the new law of the land.

Anti-Federalist attack. To show how they felt about this, the farmers pretended to bury "liberty" in a mock funeral. They were not the only Americans who felt this way in the spring of 1788. Many feared the Constitution and worked hard to defeat it. These people were called *Anti-Federalists*. They were called this because they did not want a *federal* plan of government. They feared that the Constitution gave too much power to the national government. They wondered what was to

stop a President from becoming as powerful as a king. They wondered what was to prevent Congress from passing taxes that ruined poor farmers.

Under the Articles of Confederation, Congress could not pass laws that taxed people directly. Instead it relied on the state governments to raise taxes. Many people felt they had at least some control over their state governments. They feared they would have less control over a national government far away. They worried about one part of the Constitution more than any other. It was the phrase allowing Congress to "lay and collect taxes."

Many other Anti-Federalists were worried by something the Constitution

North Carolina, Rhode Island were last to approve the Constitution. A Federalist cartoon made these states the last columns of the federal structure.

left out. There was no listing of the rights of the people — no bill of rights. What was to stop the government from taking away people's right to worship freely? What about the right to speak freely? Most state constitutions had a bill of rights. Why then was it left out of the federal Constitution?

Federalist defense. These were serious questions. They were answered by supporters of the new Constitution — the Federalists. At first the Federalists explained that the Constitution had no bill of rights on purpose. It was thought that people's rights should be matters for the states to decide. But some Federalists now began to sense the need for a bill of rights. They admitted that there might be faults in the Constitution. But they did not believe these faults as serious as those in the Articles of Confederation.

The Federalists had the best writers on their side. They had James Madison of Virginia, and John Jay and Alexander Hamilton of New York. These three talented leaders took turns writing articles for New York City newspapers. Between October 1787 and April 1788, they wrote 85 articles. These articles were later put into a book called *The Federalist.*

In one of the articles, James Madison poked fun at the Anti-Federalists. Under the Articles of Confederation, he said, the American nation had been like a sick patient. The best doctors had been called together in Philadelphia to suggest a cure. They all agreed that the Constitution would make the United States stronger and healthier. But then some fussy critics — the Anti-Federalists — fretted over the doctors' wise advice. Each Anti-Federalist gave a different opinion about what was wrong with the Constitution. One thought it unfair to the small states. Another thought it unfair to the large states. The Anti-Federalists, said Madison, were very confused.

The Federalist articles kept stressing one idea. They said the Constitution was

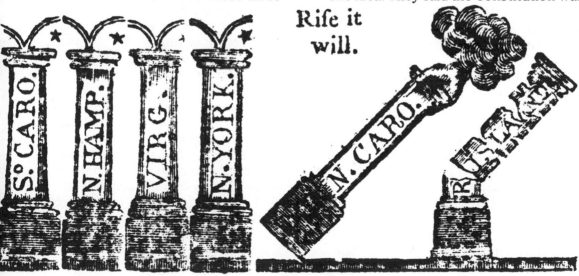

Rise it will.

The FEDERAL EDIFICE.

needed to keep the nation united. Remember, they said, that the Constitution began with these words: "We, the people of the United States, in order to form a more perfect Union...." Under the Constitution, the states would not be allowed to print their own money. They would not be allowed to tax the goods traded between states. Therefore there would be less quarreling and confusion between states under the Constitution. Businesses would be healthier. People would be happier. The country would be strong and united.

People argued for months about each rule in the Constitution. In every state, Federalists and Anti-Federalists prepared for a great debate and final vote. In each state, the question of whether to approve the Constitution was settled at a convention. Only 26 delegates took part in the smallest convention in Georgia. Massachusetts held the biggest convention with 370 delegates elected from all over the state.

Battle of words. The new plan gave small states an advantage in the Senate. So in three small states — Delaware, Georgia, and New Jersey — the Constitution won easily. The greatest struggle came in the big states — Massachusetts, Pennsylvania, Virginia, and New York. In Virginia there was a great battle of words between two great men. Patrick Henry attacked the Constitution. James Madison defended it. Henry said liberty would not be safe under the Constitution. Madison promised that it would be. Madison and the Federalists finally won by a vote of 89 to 79.

By the time of Virginia's vote, New Hampshire had become the ninth state to ratify. The Constitution had already been adopted by the needed two thirds of the states. Before the victory in Virginia, however, the Federalists were forced to make a promise. They said they would add a bill of rights to the Constitution as soon as it was ratified. Soon afterward, they set out to keep their promise.

Only one week after Virginia ratified, Americans celebrated the Fourth of July. It was a happy day for the Federalists, a sad day for the Anti-Federalists. The Constitution was now the law of the land. There were parades and bonfires in every American city. In Philadelphia a doctor, Benjamin Rush, watched the parade with high hopes for the future. At home, still rejoicing, he wrote a letter to a friend. "'Tis done," he wrote. "We have become a nation."

A Second Look. . . .

1. *Some Anti-Federalists feared that the Constitution threatened people's liberty. Why did they fear this?*

2. *James Madison argued that strong laws and a strong government were needed to protect people's liberty. What do you think he meant by this? Do you agree with him? Why or why not? If not, do you think that strong laws reduce a person's freedom? If so, how?*

3. *On a piece of paper, number from* **1** *to* **13.** *Next to these numbers, write the names of the original 13 states in the order that they ratified the Constitution. (The order of ratification is the same as the order of entry into the Union. You can find that information given in "Facts About the 50 States" at the end of this book.) Circle the name of the ninth state to ratify. Explain why ratification by this state was especially important.*

Cannons boom a 13-gun salute as George Washington arrives in New York harbor. New York was the first capital of the U.S. under the Constitution, and Washington was about to become the first President.

Chapter 23

The Bill of Rights

In little more than 10 years, Americans had put an end to two systems of government. The first was the colonial system ruled by Britain. The second was the system drawn up in the Articles of Confederation. Now, in 1789, Americans began setting up a third system. This was the federal system created by the new Constitution.

Under this plan, the President was to be chosen by a panel of electors. In some states these electors were picked by the legislature. In other states they were chosen directly by the people.

(One state, New York, did not choose electors for the first Presidential election.) The electors voted on February 4, 1789. The ballots were counted in the new Senate on April 6. George Washington turned out to be the unanimous choice as President.

Ten days later Washington set out from his home in Virginia for New York City. New York was then the temporary capital of the U.S. Washington arrived in New York on April 23. He took the oath of office on April 30, 1789.

Few people noticed the short man

James Madison

who walked directly behind Washington that day. James Madison had come to New York to sit in the first session of the House of Representatives. He came even though his frost-bitten nose still bothered him. Madison's nose had frozen one cold night while he was out campaigning for office. But a frozen nose did not cause Madison to forget an old promise.

Keeping his word. Madison had made the promise to the Anti-Federalists. He had said again and again that the first Congress would add a bill of rights to the Constitution. He waited four days after Washington took office. Then he went to work to *amend* (change) the Constitution.

The rules for amending the Constitution were written into the Constitution itself. One way of making amendments was to start with the state legislatures. Two thirds of the states could propose an amendment to the Constitution. Then

a nationwide convention would have to approve their work. A second way of amending the Constitution was to start with Congress. A two-thirds vote of each house of Congress was required to pass an amendment. Then three quarters of the state legislatures would have to ratify it. Madison chose this second method as the quicker way.

He stood up in the House of Representatives and made a long speech. He explained why a government should not interfere with people's rights. He then suggested that the House guarantee certain rights to the American people. A few of Madison's ideas for basic rights were rejected. But 17 were passed by the needed two-thirds vote.

These 17 amendments were then sent to the Senate. The Senate did not agree on all of them. In the end, a committee of Senate and House members agreed on 12 amendments. The 12 were sent to the state legislatures. Ten were finally ratified. They became part of the Constitution on December 15, 1791.

Listing people's rights. These 10 amendments are now known as the *Bill of Rights.* Some of them do not seem as important today as they once did. Take the Third Amendment, for example. The Third Amendment says that soldiers cannot be put up in a private home without the owner's consent — except in wartime. Hardly anyone pays much attention to this amendment anymore. But other amendments in the Bill of Rights seem to be just as important now as they were in 1789. Here are the ones that mean the most to us today:

The First Amendment says that Congress cannot make laws to work for or against any religion. It says that Congress cannot make laws against freedom of speech or freedom of the press. It also says that Congress cannot make laws against the people's right to hold peaceful meetings — and to ask the government to correct wrongs.

The Second Amendment says that people have the right to "keep and bear arms."

The Fourth Amendment says that a person's house and belongings cannot be searched without a legal permit — a *warrant* — from a court. Any search for evidence of a crime has to be carried out in a legal and careful way.

The Fifth Amendment says that if a person is found "not guilty" in a trial, he or she cannot be tried again for the same crime. Nor can people be forced to be a witness against themselves. That is, they cannot be made to say things that would get them in trouble with the law.

The Sixth Amendment says that a person accused of a crime must have a "speedy and public" trial by jury. The accused person must be told what he or she is accused of. Any witness who has something to say about the accused person must say it to the person's face at the trial. And if the accused person wants a lawyer for defense, he or she has a right to have one.

The Eighth Amendment says that an accused person does not have to put up "excessive bail." *Bail* is money left with the court when an accused person is released until his or her trial comes up. If a person is found guilty of a crime, the punishment must not be "cruel or unusual." If the person has to pay a fine, it must not be too high.

These were not the only rights listed in the Bill of Rights. But they were the most important protections for the individual citizen. Other rights were more general. The Tenth Amendment, for example, talked about the power of state governments. It said the states could do anything, except those few specific things which the Constitution said they could not do. (They could not coin money, for example.)

The Constitution created in 1787 told the United States government what it *could* do. The first 10 amendments — or Bill of Rights — said what the government could *not* do. At first, these amendments protected people only from unfair actions of the national government. But in recent years the Supreme Court has told state governments that they too must uphold the U.S. Bill of Rights.

Today every citizen of every state in the country has the legal right to a fair trial. Every citizen has the right to worship freely and speak and write opinions freely. The work begun by James Madison in the spring of 1789 is still an important part of every American's life.

A Second Look. . . .

1. *In your own words, describe the way that the first 10 amendments were added to the Constitution.*

2. *Review the list of rights mentioned in this chapter. Which three rights seem to you to be the most important? Why?*

3. *The right to free speech does not mean you can shout "Fire!" in a crowded theater. Why not? Can you give three other examples of speech that may be so harmful to others that you can be stopped from saying it? List them on a sheet of paper. Be prepared to defend your list in class.*

Chapter 24

The First President

Back in Virginia, George Washington had been more easygoing. In New York City, he found it hard to relax with callers. As President, he opened his home to casual visitors only one hour a week — on Tuesdays. These social hours were usually stiff and formal.

Though Washington seemed uncomfortable, he kept on with the Tuesday custom. He was, after all, the first President his country ever had. Everything he did was important. Every move that he made might set an example for future Presidents.

The Constitution described a President's duties in a general way. But it said nothing about how to receive visitors. It did not tell Washington exactly how to deal with Congress. It did not tell him how to work with a Cabinet of advisers. In fact, it did not even tell him he had to have such a Cabinet. Washington had to figure out what was best to do from day to day. He often had doubts about his own ability and wisdom. And yet, because he cared so much about the Constitution, he held the country together for eight difficult years.

How did he do it? Why do many scholars still think that America's first President was also its best? Here are three reasons for Washington's success:

Washington chose able people to help him. The President heads the Executive Branch of the United States government. It is his job to see that laws passed by Congress are properly enforced throughout the country. He cannot do this alone. Instead he must seek the help of the most able people he can find.

Washington surrounded himself with talented people. He chose Thomas Jefferson to take charge of foreign affairs as Secretary of State. He selected Alexander Hamilton to raise and spend government money as Secretary of the Treasury. He named Henry Knox to take charge of the nation's military needs as Secretary of War. And he chose Edmund Randolph to enforce federal laws as Attorney General. When these four men met together, they became known as the President's Cabinet.

Two members of the Cabinet were already well-known. Tall, red-haired Thomas Jefferson, now 47, had written the famous Declaration of Independence. Short, handsome Alexander Hamilton, now 33, had worked hard to get the Constitution ratified. These two men were certainly not close friends. Jefferson thought Hamilton cared too much about the problems of wealthy businessmen. He accused Hamilton of favoring a government ruled by kings. For his part, Hamilton thought Jefferson

As this painting from about 1800 shows, George Washington was an admired American in his day.

Anti-Federalists thought their worst fears had come true when government agents showed up to collect the new whiskey tax. Some farmers tarred and feathered the tax collectors — or worse. One Anti-Federalist considered the whiskey tax the work of the devil (above). But the new Commander-in-Chief stood firmly with the Federalists. The painting below is by Frederick Kemmelmeyer. Kemmelmeyer was there when Washington reviewed troops about to try to put down the Whiskey Rebellion.

122

much too eager to stay popular with the masses. He believed that Jefferson's ideas would ruin the national government. The two men, then, had little in common. But they did share one view. They both admired George Washington and worked hard to serve him.

Washington gave leadership to Congress. Washington did not sit back and wait for Congress to pass laws. He told Congress what laws he thought necessary. The country needed strong leadership. It owed millions of dollars to foreign countries. How was it going to pay these debts? How was it going to protect business from foreign competition? Congress was too divided to come up with the answers. Leadership could only come from one place — the President and his Cabinet.

Actually, it was Hamilton who came up with most of the ideas. He wanted the federal government to create a national bank, the Bank of the United States. He wanted the national government to pay off all the debts owed by the state governments. To raise money for this and other purposes, he recommended a *tariff* (import tax). This tax would be placed on those foreign-made goods that competed with goods made in the U.S. In addition, he thought certain goods sold at home should also be taxed — whiskey, for example. He persuaded Washington that a national bank, a tariff law, and a whiskey tax were needed.

Then Hamilton and Washington had to persuade Congress to pass the laws they recommended. They ran into fierce opposition, some of it from Jefferson and his supporters. But at last the President's program passed both houses. Partly because of these laws, business improved. The nation paid off most of its debts. The American people gained confidence in their new government.

Washington had the courage to make hard decisions. Many times, Washington acted in ways that were certain to make people angry. In 1794, for example, a group of farmers in western Pennsylvania refused to pay the new tax on whiskey. They attacked the house of one of the tax officials. They tarred and feathered officers of the law.

Washington decided that the Whiskey Rebellion, as it was called, had to be crushed. He called together 15,000 troops to march across Pennsylvania. Washington himself put on a uniform and led the army at the beginning of the march. Against the huge federal army, the small band of farmers did not stand a chance. They surrendered without a fight. Washington's actions angered some people. These people accused him of acting like a bully and a tyrant. But the President believed that he had done what was best for the country.

The next year, 1795, Washington faced an even more difficult decision. The United States was again having trouble with its old enemy, Britain. Washington wished to avoid another war. He asked John Jay, Chief Justice of the United States, to go to Britain to arrange a treaty. Jay did come back from Britain with a treaty. But it was much weaker than the one Washington wanted. The treaty was supposed to stop the common British practice of seizing sailors from U.S. ships and forcing them into the British navy. Yet Jay's Treaty said nothing about this at all. The treaty also promised that the United States would pay debts owed to British mer-

123

chants before the Revolutionary War.

Washington knew how unpopular this treaty would be. At first he locked it away in his desk drawer, afraid to show it to anyone. Finally he released it to the newspapers. Many people who read the treaty went wild with anger. Some of the angriest people were followers of Thomas Jefferson. Mobs gathered in the streets. They stuffed old clothes with straw. Then they wrote "John Jay" on the straw body, and set it on fire.

George Washington was in a fix. What should he do? Should he give in to this public fury? Or should he deliver the treaty to the Senate and urge that it be ratified for the sake of peace? Washington sent it to the Senate. Jay's Treaty was ratified on June 24, 1795.

As his second Presidential term wore on, George Washington became eager to retire to private life. He had never wanted to be President. He did not have the same confidence in himself that other people had. Now he had also grown weary of the arguments between Hamilton and Jefferson and their followers. In 1796 a third election for President was due to take place. Twice before, Washington had been elected by a unanimous vote. But now Washington announced that he would not again be a candidate for President.

Like many things that Washington did, this decision also set an example for future Presidents. It became the custom after that for Presidents to retire after two terms. The custom lasted until 1940, when President Franklin Roosevelt ran for a third term.

In his farewell address, Washington admitted that he might have made some mistakes. He asked that people forgive him for these and remember the good that he tried to do. He urged that Americans remain steadfast in support of the Union. He tried to discourage the growth of political parties. He thought such parties would divide the nation. He also warned against forming "permanent alliances" with foreign powers. He feared that such alliances would keep the nation from acting in its own best interests.

A Second Look. . . .

1. *What were two challenges that Washington faced as the first President?*

2. *Why did Washington believe that a whiskey tax was needed? What did he do when farmers refused to pay the tax? Why did Washington at first hesitate to support Jay's Treaty? Why did he finally decide to give the treaty his support?*

3. *Compare Washington's problems with the problems of the current President. Make a chart, writing the names of Washington and the current President at the top. Down the left side of the chart, write these categories: problems in foreign affairs; problems with Congress; economic problems; problems in communicating with people. Complete the chart by filling in all blank spaces.*

Alexander Hamilton

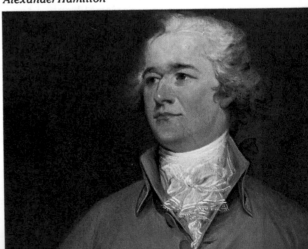

Looking Back: A More Perfect Union

	A	B	C	D	
1780	1785	1790	1795	1800

Putting Events in Order

Chapters 19 through 24 have shown how Americans created, approved, and then amended the U.S. Constitution. Ten events in this history are listed here. Your job is to match each event to the correct period shown on the timeline above. On a piece of paper, number from **1** to **10.** For each number, write the letter of the period in which the event occurred.

1. Congress passes the Northwest Ordinance.

2. George Washington is sworn in as the nation's first President.

3. The Articles of Confederation are adopted as the first government of the United States.

4. Delegates from 12 states meet in Philadelphia to write a new Constitution.

5. Daniel Shays leads a rebellion against Massachusetts laws.

6. New Hampshire becomes the ninth state to ratify the Constitution.

7. The Bill of Rights is added to the Constitution.

8. George Washington puts down the Whiskey Rebellion in Pennsylvania.

9. George Washington warns against permanent alliances in his farewell address.

10. James Madison, Alexander Hamilton, and John Jay write the articles that later become a book called *The Federalist.*

Interpreting a Source

In 1788 John Jay of New York prepared a speech to give to the people of his state. This passage is adapted from the speech he gave. In this speech he discussed the condition of the United States under the Articles of Confederation.

Almost every national object of every kind is at this day unprovided for. And other nations are putting more and more restraints on our trade. Our fur trade is gone to Canada, and British troops keep the keys of it. Our shipyards

125

John Jay

2. *What does he mean by saying that "British troops keep the keys" to the fur trade?*

3. *Does he seem to be calling for adoption of the Constitution? Or condemning it?*

4. *What does Jay mean by "interest" on debts? Can you think of any cases in which you have collected such interest? What is meant by "credit"? How can lack of credit damage a person's ability to get rich? How do you suppose it can be harmful to a nation?*

Sharpening Your Skills

What groups supported the Constitution? What groups opposed it? To find out, one historian, Jackson Turner Main, studied the delegates to the ratifying conventions of three states. (The states were Pennsylvania, Connecticut, and New Hampshire.) The table at right sums up what Main found out.

1. Does the information in the table support this statement: "Most delegates to the state ratifying conventions were farmers." Why or why not?

2. Does the information support this statement: "Lawyers generally opposed the Constitution." Why or why not?

3. Is this statement correct: "The Constitution received support from two groups. Most wealthy merchants and professionals supported it. Most small businessmen supported it." Why or why not?

4. Do you agree with this statement: "The Anti-Federalists seemed to have less wealth and property than the Federalists." Give reasons for your answer.

have almost ceased to disturb the sleep of the neighborhood by the noise of the axe and hammer. Most of our hardy seamen are plowing the ocean in foreign pay. Our agriculture and industry multiply the goods we produce. But the goods get lower in value....

How many fine cattle have returned from this city [New York] to the country for lack of buyers? What goods still lie useless in storehouses? How far below the former price is our corn and wheat and flour and lumber rapidly falling? Our debts are as great as ever, and the interest on them is growing. Our credit abroad is nearly gone, and at home it has not been improved.... Hardly any man can borrow from his neighbor....

1. *Is John Jay pleased about the events he is describing? Why or why not?*

State Convention Delegates' Vote on Ratification

	Federalists (for ratification)	Anti-Federalists (against ratification)
Wealthy Merchants and Professionals		
Merchants	29	4
Large manufacturers	3	1
Lawyers	49	7
Large landowners	13	2
Doctors	14	3
Ministers	9	5
Small Businessmen		
Innkeepers	7	3
Millers	12	10
Artisans	1	0
Shopkeepers	2	2
Surveyors	1	0
Small manufacturers	1	0
Ferry owners	1	0
Traders	3	1
Miscellaneous	4	2
Farmers	32	38
Unknowns	49	32
Totals	**230**	**110**

5 THE NATION EXPANDS

Looking Ahead: Growing Pains

The United States was a large country at the end of the Revolutionary War. In fact, the new nation controlled an area more than twice the size of the original 13 colonies. The peace treaty in 1783 gave the United States all of Britain's land from the Appalachian Mountains to the Mississippi River. This land ran from Canada to Florida.

Many of Europe's leaders were surprised by the peace treaty. They hadn't expected Britain to give up so much land. American leaders were pleased. It looked as if the young republic had all the growing room it would need for a long time to come.

But then, in 1803, the United States signed another treaty — one that has been called "the greatest real estate bargain in history." By this treaty, the United States bought from France a huge piece of land called the *Louisiana Purchase*. The purchase nearly doubled the size of the United States. The Louisiana Territory stretched from the Mississippi River to the Rocky Mountains, and from the Gulf of Mexico to Canada. This was about 828,000 square miles (2,144,000 square kilometers) of some of the world's most fertile land. At a price of 15 million dollars, the United States paid three cents an acre for it.

Few Americans knew much about this new land their government had bought. The government wasn't even sure where some of the borders were. Soon the U.S. was arguing with Britain about the border with Canada. The U.S. argued with Spain about the borders with Florida and Mexico.

What lay behind all this arguing was nothing less than the future of a continent. Americans of the time were eager to control that future as best they could.

From this point west of Baltimore, wagons caught the Frederick Road westward. Roads such as this helped push the wilderness past the Appalachians.

And that was little wonder, since the U.S. population was growing rapidly in these years. In 1790 government officials took a census (count) of the American population. They counted 3,929,000 men, women, and children. Every 10 years another census was taken. The census of 1820 showed a population of 9,638,000. In other words, in 30 years, the population had increased about 2¹/₂ times.

The United States was still uncrowded. Most of its land was still a giant, unsettled wilderness. Yet many people in the western woods kept pushing farther and farther westward. They would clear some land, farm it for a few years, and then move on. Slowly the wilderness east of the Mississippi River began to disappear.

The flag of the United States showed how America was growing. In 1790 there were only 13 stars on the flag. But as people moved west, they set up new state governments. Vermont, Kentucky, and Tennessee were the first new states to join the Union. Other states followed rapidly. Every year from 1816 to 1821 a new state was added. In 1821 the U.S. flag had 24 stars. It had almost as many new Western states as old Eastern ones.

The years between 1790 and 1829, then, were years of steady growth. There were many signs of "growing pains" all through this period. The nation divided its loyalties and its votes between two political parties. It fought a war with Britain. Finally it was changed greatly by the invention of two machines.

Louisiana Purchase, 1803

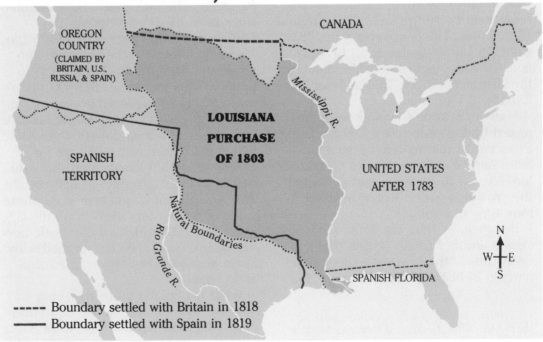

Boundary settled with Britain in 1818
Boundary settled with Spain in 1819

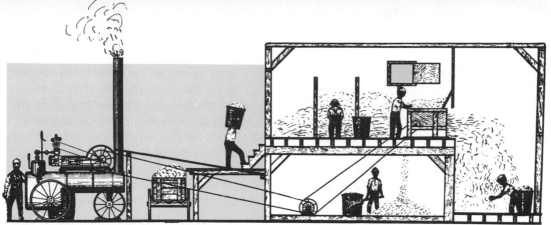

New machines such as this steam-powered cotton gin did the work of many humans. The machines didn't make life easier for the slaves who ran them. But they meant more money for planters who owned them.

Political parties. A political party is a group set up for the purpose of directing the policies of a government. There were no political parties in the United States in 1790. Americans were loosely divided between Federalists and Anti-Federalists. That is, they were split between those who favored the U.S. Constitution and those who didn't. In 1790, however, neither of these groups was a political party as we know such parties today.

Only 10 years later, however, two parties were clearly competing with each other for power. One was the Federalist party. It was the party of John Adams and Alexander Hamilton. The other was the Democratic-Republican party. It was led by Hamilton's old rival, Thomas Jefferson. The great clash between these two parties occurred in the election of 1800, as we shall see.

War. The war began not in the United States, but in Europe. It broke out there because of a revolution in France. The French people rose up against their government in 1789. They beheaded their king and queen in 1793. In the same year, the new government of France declared war against England. This war

lasted, off and on, for more than 20 years. It became especially bitter after 1799 when a soldier named Napoleon Bonaparte seized power in France. He became emperor in 1804.

Americans watched this war closely. Starting with George Washington, one President after another had to deal with it. Each tried to keep the United States from taking sides. But neither France nor Britain respected United States ships. The navies of both countries stopped U.S. ships on the high seas. They seized the ships' cargoes and captured U.S. sailors.

Finally, in 1812, the U.S. Congress declared war against Britain. The war changed America greatly. It strengthened people's pride and patriotism. Speakers on the Fourth of July told about the glory of their young country. It was the greatest country in the history of the world, they said. The war also gave Americans a new song to sing: "The Star-Spangled Banner."

Inventions. In the 1700's a great change swept over Europe. It was a change in manufacturing and industry. The driving force behind it was the invention of a steam engine. Today we call

131

this change the *Industrial Revolution.*

This revolution was soon brought to the U.S. It led, in turn, to several other new inventions. They were important because they greatly changed the course of U.S. history. One invention was only as big as a bread box. Another was as big as a river boat — in fact, it *was* a river boat.

The smaller machine was called a cotton gin. It was invented in 1793 by Eli Whitney from Connecticut. Whitney had once watched a slave take a whole day to pick seeds from one pound of cotton. Whitney built his cotton gin as a way to speed up this job. The gin was a wooden box with a metal cylinder inside. The cylinder had teeth and could be turned by a crank. As the cylinder turned, the teeth separated the seeds from the cotton. By using the cotton gin, a slave could produce 50 pounds (22½ kilograms) of seedless cotton fiber a day.

All of a sudden, farmers in the South could make a handsome profit growing cotton. All they needed was land to grow it on — and slaves to pick it and bale it. In a short time, cotton farms spread westward all the way from Georgia to Mississippi. Sadly, the invention of the cotton gin was a disaster for the slaves. Before this, many tobacco growers in the South had thought seriously about giving up slavery because it was getting too costly. But now cotton and the cotton gin made white Southerners think that they needed even more slaves.

The other invention, the river boat,

was one powered by steam. It had as great an effect on the West as the cotton gin had on the South. Before the steamboat, Western farmers shipped their products on flatboats. But flatboats could only go in one direction — downstream. Since they could not go upstream, goods had to be hauled in this direction by land. It took weeks, even months, to get them to market this way.

Steamboats could move in both directions. The first person to build one was a Kentucky farmer, John Fitch. Fitch built three of these boats in the late 1700's. But he was unable to make a commercial success of them.

By 1807, however, America was ready for steamboats. In that year Robert Fulton attached two paddle wheels to the side of a boat called the *Clermont.* He hitched the wheels to a steam engine. Then he steered the boat up the Hudson River to Albany.

In a short time, steamboats were moving up and down rivers in many parts of the country. Aboard them, farmers' goods could travel to market in a week's time. The steamboat made it possible for towns and cities to be built in the South and the Middle West. It helped America grow with greater speed — westward, ever westward.

No invention changed America more than the steamboat, perfected by Robert Fulton. Fulton drew this sketch of his own boat, the Clermont.

Chapter 25

The Wilderness Moves West

Even as he got older, Daniel Boone could still hunt furs and game. He could hunt and trap better than he could write his own name. When he wrote a letter, he did not know whether to sign it "Daniel" or "Daniell." Sometimes he spelled it one way, and sometimes the other.

Boone may have been a poor speller, but he was a good frontiersman. In the 1770's he blazed new trails with his gun and axe. He opened a trail through the mountains — the Wilderness Road. This trail was followed by many other settlers as they made their way west.

Boone was not the first white person to travel through Kentucky. But he was the first to start a permanent settlement there. In 1775 he built a fort on a site later to become Boonesborough. The same year he brought his family and several men to settle here. He lived in Kentucky off and on for the next 13 years.

But times were changing. After the Revolution, hundreds upon hundreds of white settlers pushed into Kentucky over Boone's Wilderness Road. The town of Louisville was organized in 1779. Lexington was chartered three years later. By 1792 enough people had come to Kentucky to allow it to become a state.

Boone was puzzled by all this growth. He thought he deserved to own the thousands of acres of land that he had explored. Instead he discovered sadly that ownership of land depended on understanding the law. Boone did not understand the law. He lost most of his claims to Kentucky land. He fell badly into debt.

In 1796 he hoped to make some money working on a new road that the government was planning to build. Boone therefore wrote this letter to Kentucky's first governor:

Sir — I have sum intention of undertaking this new Rode that is to be cut through the Wilderness ... and Sepose I am no Statesman I am a Woodsman and think My Self as Capable of Marking and Cutting that Rode, as any other man ... I am Dear Sir

your very omble servant
DANIEL BOONE

Boone did not get the job. Kentucky was no longer a wild enough place for an old pioneer such as he. It was a much

133

better place for farmers, ministers, storekeepers, and lawyers. It was a perfect place for an ambitious young man such as Henry Clay to win success and fame.

Kentucky lawyer. Clay was 20 years old when he first arrived in Kentucky in 1797. He was not wealthy, but he had studied the law. He could help people figure out who had a legal right to a certain piece of land. In return for his services, he often got a part of the land for himself. He was soon rich enough to own a plantation, train racehorses, and gamble for high stakes in card games.

In 1803 Clay won election to the state legislature. Three years later he went to Washington, D.C., to sit in the U.S. Senate. He served in one house of Congress or the other for most of the rest of his life. In Congress, Clay was much more than just a lawmaker. He was a symbol of the rapidly expanding West.

The West had many kinds of heroes. Daniel Boone blazed trails as a pioneer. Henry Clay dazzled people with his clever speeches. But few of the people who were moving west were pioneers or lawyers. Most were farmers looking for good, cheap land.

Western farmers. They came from the East in plain wagons over rough roads. After weeks of hard traveling, they found a location for a new community and helped each other build log

Daniel Boone knew the Appalachian Mountains as well as any American of his time. In this George Caleb Bingham painting, he is shown (center) escorting families through mountains he had explored. Pioneers were followed by lawyers such as Henry Clay (inset), a man of the new West.

135

Pioneers cleared the forest for farmland. Then they used the trees for fences. When they took short trips, they took nature's roads — rivers. Indian canoes sometimes served as river taxis.

cabins. It took only a day for a group of neighbors to chop down logs for the cabin walls and split other logs for the roof and floor. It took another day to notch the logs and lift them into place. The new homeowner was then expected to throw a housewarming party. Somebody played the fiddle while neighbors danced, drank cider, and feasted on pork and bread.

Life in the West was anything but easy. Few farm families ever got wealthy from their hard work in the fields. Many lived in cabins that were damp and cold. Settlers often got diseases such as forest fever and malaria. When they did, they usually had to get along without medicine. The West had few doctors or druggists to treat such illnesses. Many Westerners died at an early age.

Still Americans kept on moving west. More and more farms kept springing up in the Northwest Territory. Villages turned into towns. As the area grew, Westerners soon saw that they had several pressing needs in common. Perhaps the greatest was the need for a better system of roads.

Need for roads. Most early Western roads were very crude. Many of them followed paths first laid out by Indians or white fur trappers. Such roads were almost never paved in any way. They became very muddy after a hard rain — sometimes too muddy to be used. Westerners would often joke about their bad roads. One stage driver said he did not know the color of his own mules. Though he had driven them for many months, they had been buried in mud. He had seen nothing of them but their ears.

In the East, much road-building was done by private companies. These companies made a profit by charging tolls. But private companies did not have great interest in road-building in the West. They did not believe they would earn enough profit to offset their expenses.

How, then, could the Westerners' need for roads be answered? The federal government took a first step toward answering it in 1806. It set aside money for building a road from Cumberland, Maryland, to Wheeling on the Ohio River. This road, called the National Road, would stretch across the Appalachian Mountains.

Crews began building the road in 1811. First they cleared the roadway. Then they paved it with crushed stone. They completed their work as far as Wheeling in 1818. Later the road was extended farther — into Illinois.

This road brought still more Americans westward. But by this time the Northwest Territory was no longer a wild frontier. People had moved there so fast that three states had been carved out of it in only 15 years. The state of Ohio was admitted to the Union in 1803. Indiana became a state in 1816. Illinois followed only two years later. By the year 1820, much of the land east of the Mississippi River was settled.

The Western frontier had moved beyond the Mississippi to territories such as Missouri. There, in a lonely log cabin, a very old man with long, white hair had settled down. His name was Daniel Boone. Boone had left Kentucky years ago to get away from all the people and the confusing laws. Now even Missouri was getting crowded.

In 1820 Daniel Boone got a stomach-ache from eating too many sweet potatoes. He died at the age of 87. The very next year, 1821, Missouri entered the Union. It became the 24th state.

A Second Look. . . .

1. Why was young Henry Clay better able to live in Kentucky in 1798 than old Daniel Boone? Explain why Boone's efforts in the 1770's were necessary before people such as Clay could succeed in Kentucky.

2. Three kinds of Westerners are described in this chapter — the hunter, the lawyer, and the farmer. Which of these do you admire the most? Why? Which do you admire the least? Why? Which was most important to the growth and settlement of the West — or were all equally important? Give reasons for your answers.

3. At the end of this book, you will find a chart called "Facts About the 50 States." It tells when each state entered the Union. Divide each century into 25-year periods. Start with the period 1776-1800, then 1801-1825, and so on to the last period, 1976-2000. Count the number of states that were admitted in each period. In which period did the most states enter the Union? Do you think any more states will be added in your lifetime? If so, which ones?

Roads Leading Westward

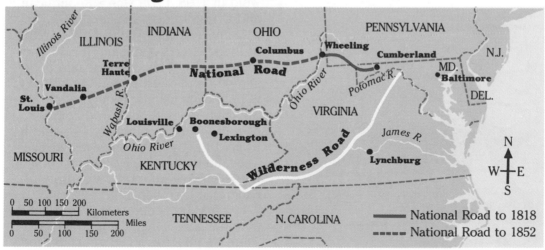

Chapter 26

Congress Picks A President

Enemies of Matthew Lyon called him the "Spitting Lyon." Lyon was a Congressman from Vermont. He had earned his nickname by spitting in the face of another Congressman, Roger Griswold. Griswold got even the next morning by knocking Lyon on the head with his walking stick. Lyon struck back with an iron poker. Business in the House of Representatives stopped briefly while Lyon and Griswold tried to club each other.

The two men belonged to different

Cartoon shows Matthew Lyon and Roger Griswold trying to club each other.

political parties. Their dispute was the kind of thing George Washington had warned against in his farewell address. Washington had not been in favor of political parties. Yet two parties had grown up during his term as President. One was the Federalist party. It was the party of John Adams and Alexander Hamilton. The other was the Democratic-Republican party. It was led by Thomas Jefferson, and its members usually called themselves Republicans. The growth of these parties brought about the feud between Lyon and Griswold in 1798. Lyon was a Republican, and Griswold was a Federalist.

Many Federalists doubted the abilities of the average American citizen. They thought only the best-educated people should be allowed to run the country. Republicans usually thought just the opposite. They thought the common people — farmers, mostly — could be trusted to govern themselves wisely. They did not think government could be trusted if it were run by wealthy Federalist merchants.

In 1798 the Federalists controlled the national government. The President, John Adams, was a Federalist. So too were most members of both houses of Congress. The Federalists worried, however, that they were fast losing ground to the Republicans. They feared the votes Republicans might get if newcomers from Europe were given the rights of citizens. So Federalists put four laws through Congress. Together these four laws were known as the Alien and Sedition (sih-DISH-un) Acts.

Alien and Sedition Acts. Three of the laws dealt with aliens. *Aliens* are people who are citizens of a foreign country. The first law had to do with their becoming citizens of the U.S. Before 1798 aliens could apply to become citizens once they had been in the U.S. five years. Now the time limit was raised to 14 years. The second law gave the President the power to order "dangerous" aliens to leave the country. The third law allowed him to jail certain aliens at his own wish during wartime. (The second and third laws were never put into force.)

The fourth law was the Sedition Act. *Sedition* meant, in this sense, spreading ideas that made people unhappy with the government. This law made it illegal for anyone to publish "false" or "scandalous" reports about officials of the government. Anyone who did so could receive a fine or a jail term. This act, then, put limits on freedom of speech and freedom of the press.

Owners of Republican newspapers were now in great trouble. They had often used vicious language to describe John Adams. One newspaper had called him a "ruffian." Another had called him "blind, bald, and toothless." Matthew Lyon, the spitting, fighting Congressman, put out a newspaper in Vermont.

Electoral Vote, 1800

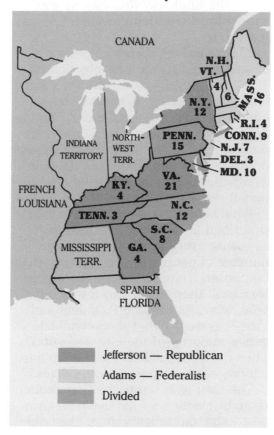

He was the first Republican to be jailed under the Sedition Act.

But this law soon backfired. It made Republicans more popular than ever. Lyon became a hero. A mob of people came to set him free. They almost tore the jail down. While he was still in jail, the voters of Vermont elected Lyon to another term in Congress.

State lawmakers in Virginia and Kentucky passed resolutions against the Alien and Sedition Acts. They said these laws violated rights set down in the Constitution. Therefore such laws did not need to be obeyed. The man who wrote the Kentucky Resolutions was none other than Vice-President Thomas Jefferson.

Electoral system. Voters now looked ahead to the next election in 1800. They could guess who the candidates for President would be. Republicans would choose their leader, Thomas Jefferson. And Federalists would once more choose John Adams. Both Adams and Jefferson had been candidates in 1796. Adams had beaten Jefferson by only three votes — three *electoral* votes.

What is an electoral vote? This vote is described in the U.S. Constitution. It says that every four years a certain number of people, called *electors,* shall be chosen from each state. These electors shall then decide, by a majority vote, who shall be the President and Vice-President. What if no candidate gets a majority of the electors' votes? Then the House of Representatives must choose between the two candidates.

The men who wrote the Constitution thought electors would use their own best judgment when voting. They did not expect the electors' choice to be made for them, long before the election, by two political parties. Yet this is what happened in 1800.

Federalists in Congress chose John Adams and Charles Pinckney as their party's two candidates for President. Republicans chose Thomas Jefferson and Aaron Burr. They chose two men, not just one, because each elector was allowed to cast *two* votes for President. The person who got the second highest total of the electors' votes would become Vice-President. As it turned out, this system led to serious trouble.

In the fall of 1800, people cast their votes for electors. They chose 73 Republicans to be electors from different states. Only 65 Federalist electors were chosen. The Republican party had won. Still, no one knew who would be President. All the Republican electors had cast both of their votes for their two party favorites. Jefferson got 73 Republican votes — but so did Aaron Burr. Jefferson and Burr were tied. The outcome now had to be decided in the House of Representatives.

Vote in the House. Here matters became even more complex. The Constitution said that each state could cast one vote for President. For example, Vermont could cast one vote for Jefferson if Vermont's two Representatives both liked him better than Burr. If they disagreed on a candidate, however, Vermont could not vote for anyone. If several states were divided, it would be hard for any candidate to win enough votes for a majority.

Federalists in Congress hoped to ruin the election for the Republicans. They voted for Burr for President to turn the vote away from Jefferson. On the streets of Washington, people hooted at the Federalists for playing such tricks. Some Republicans even talked of civil war.

Voting in the House went on and on. The crisis lasted five days. Then a Federalist from Maryland switched his vote from Burr to Jefferson. After 35 ballots, Thomas Jefferson was elected President. Burr was chosen as Vice-President.

When they heard the news, Republicans gathered in the streets to sing this party song:

Rejoice! Columbia's sons, rejoice!
To tyrants never bend the knee,
But join with heart and soul and voice
For Jefferson and Liberty.

There would be no more alien and sedition laws under President Jefferson. No Federalist printer would go to jail just because he attacked a Republican President in print.

The electoral system changed after this too. The 12th Amendment was added to the Constitution in 1804. It gave to each elector *one* vote for President and a *separate* vote for Vice-President. That helped to prevent the confusion that had taken place in 1800 from happening again.

Jefferson himself helped to end some bitter feelings left over from the election. He did so as he took office on March 4, 1801. He promised to pay U.S. debts. He said he would try not to make too many changes in the government. His address pleased most Federalists. His term of office began on a note of harmony.

A Second Look. . . .

1. Why did Federalists think the Sedition Act would help them defeat Republicans? Did it actually help them in the election of 1800? Why or why not?

2. The U.S. electoral system has changed very little since 1804. A majority of electors still chooses the President and Vice-President. The House of Representatives must still make the choice, if no candidate gets a majority of the electoral votes. Do you think this is a good system? If not, how would you change it?

3. Compare the election of 1800 with the most current election for President. How many electoral votes did the current President get? How many electoral votes did his opponent get? What were the results of the election in your state? You might want to make your own chart of the state-by-state electoral vote, consulting an almanac for your information.

Jefferson's followers celebrated his election victory in 1801 with this flag.

Chapter 27

All the Way to the Pacific

Captain Meriwether Lewis froze in his tracks. Only 20 yards (18 meters) away — coming right for him — was a huge grizzly bear. Lewis was in a tight spot. He had just killed a buffalo — and forgotten to reload his rifle. Now there was no time. When the bear broke into a run, Lewis made a dash for a stream. He waded out into deep water. Then he turned, faced the bear, and held out his bayonet. The bear looked at Lewis in the water — and then suddenly ran away. So Lewis lived to tell the tale.

Who was Meriwether Lewis — this man with the unusual first name? What did his battles with grizzly bears have to do with the growth of the United States?

Lewis was President Thomas Jefferson's private secretary. Jefferson wanted him to find out what the Western half of the United States looked like. Jefferson

When President Jefferson sent Meriwether Lewis and William Clark to explore the West, he warned them to beware of dangerous beasts. The explorers didn't get eaten, but they did have their troubles. Someone on the journey drew this picture of one mishap. The two explorers seem to have bumped into a tree.

had hundreds of questions about the lands that lay west of the Mississippi River. Were the Indians who lived there peaceful or warlike? Was the land good for farming? Did it contain valuable ores and minerals? What kinds of plants and animals lived along the Missouri River? What was the safest route over the Rocky Mountains to the Pacific Ocean?

The President instructed Lewis to explore the Western country. He expected his secretary to come back with a full description of the land. For a helper and friend to go with him, Lewis chose a fellow Army officer, Lieutenant William Clark. Clark had lived on the frontier.

There was good reason why the President knew so little about the Western half of his country. Until 1803 it belonged to foreign nations. The name of the territory, Louisiana, honored a French king who once controlled it — Louis XIV. Spain had taken over the territory in 1762 after the French and Indian War. In 1800 Spain had returned it to France. Three years later, in 1803, the French leader Napoleon had sold it to the U.S. for about 15 million dollars.

The purchase of Louisiana was one of the greatest land bargains in history. The territory was huge. It had never been completely explored, so the U.S. government did not know exactly how big it was. Its boundaries were not yet clearly drawn. The land stretched roughly from the Mississippi River in the east all the way to the Rocky Mountains in the West. It went from the great river port of New Orleans to some unknown point in Canada, about a thousand miles (1,600 kilometers) north.

William Clark kept a careful record of what he and others discovered. On March 16, 1806, he gave a page in his record to the "white salmon trout."

Choosing a route. Now Meriwether Lewis and William Clark prepared to find out what this land was really like. They carefully chose men and supplies for the trip. From St. Louis they would travel up the Missouri River in three boats. Then they would cross the Rocky Mountains on horses. Once across, they would paddle canoes down the Columbia River to the Pacific Ocean.

On May 14, 1804, the explorers and their men started out from St. Louis. The Indians they met were friendly — all except the Sioux (pronounced "soo"). They gave the white men trouble. Once a group of Sioux surrounded Clark. They drew their arrows and took aim at him. 143

Exploring the West, 1804-1807

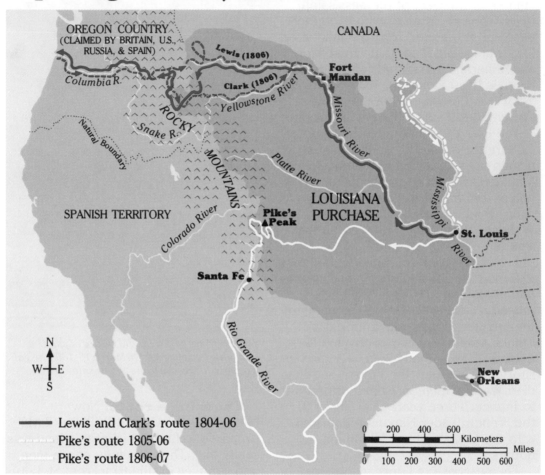

OREGON COUNTRY
(CLAIMED BY BRITAIN, U.S.,
RUSSIA, & SPAIN)

CANADA

Lewis (1806)

Fort
Mandan

Columbia R.

Clark (1806)

Yellowstone River

ROCKY

Missouri River

Snake R.

Natural Boundary

MOUNTAINS

Platte River

Mississippi River

SPANISH TERRITORY

Colorado River

Pike's
▲Peak

LOUISIANA
PURCHASE

St. Louis

Santa Fe

Rio Grande River

N
W—E
S

New
Orleans

——— Lewis and Clark's route 1804-06
········ Pike's route 1805-06
– – – Pike's route 1806-07

0   200   400   600
Kilometers
0   100   200   300   400   500   600
Miles

But Lewis and 12 of his men aimed their rifles at the Indians. Finally the Indians let Clark go.

In November the explorers reached a large Indian village in what is now North Dakota. The explorers and the Indians got along well together. Lewis and Clark decided to spend the winter there.

They hired a French-Canadian trapper to help them with Indian languages. His wife, Sacajawea (sack-ah-jah-WEE-ah; Bird Woman), was a member of the Shoshone (shuh-SHOW-nee) tribe that lived near the Rockies. Lewis and Clark would need horses from the Shoshones to cross the mountains. So they invited Sacajawea to join them.

In the spring the explorers started westward again. The trip up the Missouri River now became harder. Often the men had to tow the boats, standing in icy water up to their shoulders. After a long search, they found the Shoshones. With Sacajawea's help, they got horses for the trip across the Rockies.

Hard crossing. The men suffered terribly crossing the Rockies. The cold was bitter. Food gave out. Horses fell down the steep slopes. Finally the half-starved men reached the other side of the Rockies. There they set up camp among friendly Nez Perce (nez purse) Indians. They rested and got back their strength.

Then the men made dugout canoes for the trip down the Columbia River. Going over rough rapids was dangerous. Once the canoes were almost smashed. But in November 1805 the explorers reached the Pacific. Clark wrote in his journal: "Ocean in view! Oh! the joy!"

At this point Lewis and Clark had only completed half their journey. Now they had to turn around, cross the Rockies again, and paddle back down the Missouri River. When they finally got back to St. Louis, they had gone 8,000 hard and dangerous miles (12,800 kilometers).

Before these men ever reached the Pacific, another explorer set out from St. Louis in another direction. He too had an unusual name: Zebulon Pike. In 1805 Pike headed north seeking the source of the Mississippi River in what is now Minnesota. That winter he believed (wrongly) that he had found it. In 1806 he returned to St. Louis, then made another trip, this time heading west. In what is now Colorado he tried to climb the mountain that still bears his name — Pike's Peak.

Lewis and Clark and Pike had helped to open up the West. The first two explorers had proved that the continent could be crossed. They had made many maps and kept careful records of plants, animals, and Indian tribes. Traders and settlers would soon follow in their path.

Exploring the Louisiana Territory was a great feat. But Lewis and Clark had done even more than this. They had journeyed beyond Louisiana into Oregon. In 1803 three nations — Spain, Russia, and Great Britain — claimed that they were the rightful owners of Oregon. But the Lewis and Clark journey through Oregon gave the United States an even better claim. Many years later, in 1846, most of Oregon became U.S. territory. Sadly, neither Lewis nor Clark lived long enough to see the final result of his daring adventure.

A Second Look. . . .

1. *What did Americans learn about their country from Lewis and Clark's great journey?*

2. *Which of these statements, in your opinion, best describes Lewis and Clark's experience with Indians? (a) The explorers could not have survived without the help of Indians. (b) Surprise attacks by Indians were the worst danger that the explorers faced. (c) Except for Sacajawea, Indians did not give much help to Lewis and Clark. Explain your choice.*

3. *Discover in a small way what it is like to explore and map the territory around a river or trail. Walk with a friend for about a mile along a river or trail that runs close to your home. Try to draw a map of it as you walk. Also record in a notebook what you observe about the land and wildlife on either side of the river or trail. Post your map and your notes on your class bulletin board. How does your experience compare with that of Lewis and Clark?*

Chapter 28

Sailing into War

John Pierce, an American sailor, was killed at sea one April day in 1806. He had been standing on the deck of a U.S. ship. A British warship came into sight. Suddenly a cannonball from the British ship came crashing through the masts and rigging overhead. A heavy beam fell on John Pierce. It crushed him to death.

The British had not meant to kill this unlucky sailor. In 1806 they were at war with France, not the United States. They fired the cannon just to make the U.S. ship stop in the water. After that the British only wanted to inspect the cargo that the Americans were carrying. If it came from France, they would either seize it or destroy it. Their chief goal was to cut off all trade between Americans and their French enemy. To do this they had to stop and search U.S. ships.

John Pierce's death was an accident. His friends, however, called it murder. They sailed their damaged ship into New York harbor. They carried Pierce's body through the streets. "See what the British have done!" they shouted. Many in the crowd wondered when events like this might lead the United States to war.

The conflict in Europe was not new. Britain and France had been at war, off and on, since 1793. The two countries would use any means to win the war. One way to win was to strangle the enemy by cutting off its trade. In 1806 and 1807 France announced to the world that all ships trading with Britain would be captured. Britain issued exactly the same kind of warning about ships trading with France. Both sides then tried to *blockade* (seal off) each other's harbors.

U.S. trading ships were caught in the middle. Both sides stopped these ships at sea. Cargoes were destroyed. Ships were set on fire and sunk. Sailors were sometimes dragged off ships and thrown into prisons. And yet U.S. ships kept trying to break through both the British and French blockades. Those that made it returned home with huge profits.

President Jefferson faced a great problem. How could he protect his country's rights to trade freely without fighting a war? Finally, in 1807, he decided on a plan. He would ask Congress to place an embargo on U.S. exports. This meant that no U.S. ship would be allowed to leave for foreign parts. All U.S. trade with Europe and the rest of the world would stop. Jefferson hoped that France and Britain would both suffer from the loss of American goods. They would not have enough food and cotton to live on. After a while, they might be forced to lift their cruel blockades.

But Jefferson's embargo did not work. Americans suffered from it more than the French or British. Sailors were thrown out of work. Merchants lost millions of dollars in business. Farmers could no longer sell their flour and cotton overseas. One unhappy American said the embargo was like "cutting one's throat to cure the nosebleed." Congress ended the embargo in 1809.

A few days later, a new President, James Madison, inherited Jefferson's problems. He had no better luck dealing with them. His long struggle to keep the peace ended on June 1, 1812. On that day, he asked Congress to declare war against Britain.

Why did Britain become the enemy — and not France? There were at least four reasons why Britain became the enemy:

Impressment. When the British boarded U.S. ships, they did more than inspect the cargo. They also ordered the sailors on board to line up on the deck. They had the sailors pronounce certain words. If a sailor spoke with an Irish or British accent, he was made prisoner. He was then *impressed* (forced) into the service of the British navy. The British figured that anyone with an Irish or British accent had deserted from the British navy in the first place. But many impressed sailors were U.S. citizens. Some died from the brutal whippings and bad food that was the common lot of British sailors.

The U.S. fought the War of 1812 against Britain, but France threatened the United States nearly as much. French ships, like British ones, stopped U.S. ships at sea to inspect them. Here a U.S. merchant ship, the Planter, drives off a French attack. U.S. merchants armed their ships for self-defense.

147

Deaths at sea. Most American deaths caused by the British navy were accidents. But at least three deaths might be called murders. They took place in 1807 aboard the *Chesapeake,* a U.S. warship. A British ship, the *Leopard,* pulled alongside the *Chesapeake.* The British ordered the U.S. captain to permit a search. The captain refused. The *Leopard* fired cannonballs into the *Chesapeake* at close range. It pounded the U.S. ship for 15 minutes. U.S. sailors were given no chance to defend themselves. Three died and 18 were badly wounded. Long afterward, many Americans remembered the affair with great anger.

Desire for more land. By 1812 Westerners had almost swept beyond the forest lands. Now many of them were growing hungry for land in Lower Canada. The catch was that Canada was still ruled by Britain. Many pioneers hated the British anyway. They blamed the British in Canada for secretly helping Indians to attack U.S. settlements.

Here is one cartoonist's view of world politics in 1805. Britain (left) and France (right) empty the pockets of the United States (represented by Jefferson) to pay for their war against each other.

Indian problems. Some Indians were eager to stage such attacks. They thought of white people as a threat. White people had convinced or forced Indian tribes to give up their lands. Whites had also broken promises made to the Indian people. Now many Indians wanted to keep whites from expanding farther.

Indians did have some British help. In 1811 U.S. troops under General William Henry Harrison fought Indian warriors in the Indiana territory. The battle took place where the Tippecanoe (tip-eh-kuh-NOO) River flows into the Wabash (WAH-bash). The Indians retreated and left behind 90 British rifles. Here was one more example, Westerners thought, of British trouble-making.

War fever in Congress. Why was war declared in 1812 and not before? Because in 1812 a group of Westerners had taken control of Congress. They were called "War Hawks" because they so badly wanted to fight the British. Their leader was Henry Clay, the lawyer from Kentucky. People sometimes called him "Harry of the West." The War Hawks chose Clay to be the new Speaker of the House of Representatives. Clay's speeches for war swept people off their feet. Americans' honor had suffered too long already, said Clay. Besides, he said, look at all the new farmland U.S. settlers could conquer if they marched against British Canada.

People in the U.S. had nothing to gain from a war with France. But a war with Britain might give them Canada. In 1812 Henry Clay and other War Hawks in Congress were more powerful than the President himself. Like Madison, they wanted war — and they got it.

Some U.S. merchants tried to beat the 1807 embargo. Here the snapping turtle Ograbme (embargo spelled backward) nabs a merchant smuggling tobacco.

A Second Look. . . .

1. *How did Jefferson try to keep the United States from going to war? Why was he unsuccessful?*

2. *In 1806 a British warship killed John Pierce. In 1807 another British warship killed three Americans aboard the* Chesapeake. *Did the United States have good reason to go to war in 1807? If you had been President and had just heard about the* Chesapeake *deaths, would you have asked Congress for a declaration of war? Why or why not?*

3. *Imagine that your class is the United States Senate in June 1812. Organize two committees. One committee should present arguments in favor of going to war. The other committee should present arguments for not going to war. After this debate, all "members of the Senate" should vote on whether to declare war against Britain.*

149

Chapter 29

New Pride for the Nation

"You must save yourself, madam," cried the mayor of Washington, D.C. "Half the city has already run away. If the British win this battle, they will have no mercy on Washington."

The mayor was standing at the door of the White House. He was talking to Dolley Madison, the wife of President James Madison. But Dolley Madison was not afraid. Instead she tried to get the mayor to calm down. Then she went on helping to set the table for dinner.

It was August 24, 1814. The United States and Britain had been engaged in the War of 1812 for two years. During this time the British had not done much fighting with the Americans. Some U.S. troops had tried to invade Canada. Against orders, they had set fire to government buildings at York (now Toronto). But Canadians had defended their homeland. The U.S. troops had been driven back.

Then, in 1814, the French empire collapsed. This left Britain free to send more of its forces against the U.S. And now, in August 1814, the British meant business. They had landed an army in Maryland. Both Baltimore and Washington were in danger.

While Dolley Madison was getting ready for dinner in the White House, her husband was only a few miles away in Bladensburg (BLAY-dinz-burg), Maryland. About 7,000 U.S. troops were there too. They were getting ready to fight a British army of about 4,000 men. This British army was made up of tough veterans of the wars against France. The U.S. troops, on the other hand, were mostly untrained militia.

Battle of Bladensburg. The British brought rockets to the Battle of Bladensburg. These noisy, smoky weapons did little damage, but they scared the militia badly. Some of the Americans began running away from the battle. Soon the entire Army was fleeing toward Washington.

There was only one bright spot for the Americans at Bladensburg. Joshua Barney, an old seaman who had fought in the Revolutionary War, was in command of some 500 sailors. There wasn't much need for sailors at Bladensburg, so Barney's brave seamen fought as soldiers instead. Most of them were free blacks.

Before the battle started, President Madison asked Barney if his sailors would run from the British. "They don't know how to run," Barney answered. "They will die by their guns first."

Barney and his men held out against the British for two hours. Finally Barney had to order his men to escape. He himself was taken prisoner with a bullet in his hip. The British liked Barney and treated him kindly.

While the Americans were fleeing Bladensburg, Dolley Madison was pack-

British troops burned the White House and most of Washington, D.C., during the War of 1812 in return for the burning of York, Canada. Adding insult to injury, the British ate President Madison's dinner.

ing her husband's papers. Then a messenger brought her a note from Madison. It told her to leave Washington at once. Only then did she make her escape.

Soon the British entered the city. They sought to pay back the Americans for the burning of York. Some of their officers went into the White House. While they were there, they ate President Madison's dinner. Then they ordered their soldiers to make a pile of the White House furniture, and set it on fire. Within a few minutes, the flames roared up the staircase and through the roof. The British also set fire to the Capitol and other government buildings. Smoke and flames rose high above the city. The fires could be seen for miles.

Defense of Baltimore. After burning Washington, the British decided to attack Baltimore. On September 12, they landed their army about 15 miles from the city. While the army marched overland, the fleet sailed toward the city's harbor. Its aim was to knock out Fort McHenry, which guarded the city.

The next day the British were surprised to find a large U.S. Army waiting for them outside Baltimore. This Army was well armed and well trained. The British decided not to attack such a strong force until they had help from their fleet.

The British fleet was pounding away at Fort McHenry. It fired rockets and shells at the fort all day. On one of the

The U.S. ship Hornet *defeated the British ship* Peacock *in an important battle in the War of 1812. "Free Trade and Sailors' Rights, you old Rascal," hornet buzzes in the cartoon above. Peacock has the head of a bull because the symbol of Britain is John Bull. Painting below shows the firing on Fort McHenry in Maryland, which led Francis Scott Key to write of the "rockets' red glare."*

152

British ships there was an American lawyer named Francis Scott Key. He had gone on board to ask the British to free an American prisoner. Key watched closely while the British tried to knock out the fort. Hour after hour went by, and darkness fell, but still the fort held out. At night, by the glare of the rockets, Key could see that the American flag was still flying. Key felt so proud about the way the fort held out that he wrote a poem about it. Later this poem became the national anthem of the United States: "The Star-Spangled Banner."

After firing on Fort McHenry for a day and a night, the British decided they could not take Baltimore. The next morning they left. The attacks on Washington and Fort McHenry gained nothing for the British. But the burning of the capital made many Americans very angry.

Battle of New Orleans. The greatest U.S. victory occurred, strangely enough, after the war was over. It was won by General Andrew Jackson in the Battle of New Orleans. The battle was fought on January 8, 1815. Jackson had command of 4,500 U.S. troops. More than 400 of them were free blacks. In a fight that lasted only half an hour, Jackson's army killed and wounded about 800 of the enemy. Only eight U.S. soldiers were killed.

Americans all over the country cheered Jackson's great victory at the Battle of New Orleans. They did not realize that the war was already at an end. Peace had come on December 24, 1814, in the city of Ghent in Belgium. There five Americans had met with the British and signed the Treaty of Ghent. But news of the peace traveled very slowly across the Atlantic Ocean. Word

153

of the settlement had not arrived when the Battle of New Orleans was fought.

The treaty did not change much. The United States did not win any land from Britain as a result of the war. Britain did not win any land from the United States either. But both sides were glad to sign the treaty. They were tired of fighting.

The United States may not have "won" anything in the War of 1812. But it did gain a new spirit of nationalism — a feeling of pride as a nation. The American people had fought a Second War for Independence. They had won their right to remain free.

A Second Look. . . .

1. *Americans thought both Dolley Madison and Andrew Jackson were heroes of the War of 1812. Can you explain why?*

2. *Was there a victor in the War of 1812? If so, which side won and why? If not, why not?*

3. *There were other heroes of the War of 1812 besides those mentioned in this chapter. Look up the following three people in the reference room of your local library: William Henry Harrison, Thomas McDonough, and Oliver Hazard Perry. One good source you should know about is the* Dictionary of American Biography. *Using this source or an encyclopedia, write a one-paragraph description of what each of the above men did in the War of 1812.*

Andrew Jackson's blue-clad troops drubbed the British at the Battle of New Orleans — the greatest American victory of the War of 1812. But Americans and British had already settled their differences.

Chapter 30

The Greatest Judge

He was tall and a bit clumsy. He was so forgetful that he often lost his hat or coat. He had a lot of hair which he seldom combed. He wore dirty boots and old clothes. Yet he was the most important judge in United States history. His name was John Marshall.

Marshall had much in common with another powerful person in government — Thomas Jefferson. Like Jefferson, he was more than six feet tall. Like Jefferson, he came from Virginia. Like Jefferson, he wore plain clothes that never quite fit him properly. Jefferson and Marshall even belonged to the same family; they were cousins. Yet they were certainly not close friends.

In fact, they despised each other. Marshall was a Federalist. Jefferson was a Republican. Marshall believed that the national government should be much stronger than the states. Jefferson thought that states' rights should be carefully preserved.

The two cousins did not trust each other for another reason. They belonged to different branches of the U.S. government. As President, Jefferson led the Executive Branch. As Chief Justice of the Supreme Court, Marshall led the Judicial Branch. He had been named Chief Justice by the last Federalist President, John Adams, in 1801. President Adams had also appointed many other federal judicial officers. Among them

were several justices of the peace for the District of Columbia. Soon after that, Jefferson became President. Because of the system of checks and balances, Jefferson and Marshall could try to block each other's policies.

They could — and they did. The result was the first great tug of war between a President and a Supreme Court Justice. President Jefferson hated to see Federalists such as Marshall in the Judicial Branch of government. Jefferson and his Secretary of State, James Madison, did what they could to prevent this. Among other things, they tried to stop a Federalist, William Marbury, from becoming justice of the peace in the District of Columbia.

Requesting a writ. President Adams had appointed Marbury just before leaving office. He had signed a legal paper called a *commission* giving Marbury the right to hold the office. But Marbury had not yet received the commission when Jefferson became President. Jefferson ordered Madison *not* to deliver the commission to Marbury. After waiting two years for the commission, Marbury became annoyed. He asked Marshall's Court to force the President to give him his commission. He tried to persuade the Court to issue an order known as a *writ of mandamus* (man-DAY-mus). This writ orders a public official or a lower court

155

to do something they should legally do.

Marshall would have liked to help Marbury. But in 1803 the Supreme Court was weak. If Marshall had ordered Jefferson to deliver the commission to Marbury, Jefferson would have laughed at him. Marshall and the Court would have looked silly. What could Marshall do?

Marshall came up with a very clever solution. He announced it in his decision in the case of *Marbury v. Madison.* He first said that Marbury had a right to be a justice of the peace and that Jefferson was wrong in not giving him his commission. But then Marshall said that there was nothing the Supreme Court could do about it. The right to issue a writ of mandamus had been granted by Congress in 1789, *not* by the Constitution. Because that right went beyond the Constitution, Marshall declared it was unconstitutional. The Supreme Court therefore did not have the right to issue a writ of mandamus at all.

It was a brilliant decision for several reasons. First, it gave Marshall a chance to scold the President and tell Jefferson he was wrong. Second, it seemed to limit the power of the Supreme Court by saying that the Court could do nothing about Marbury's appointment. But at the same time the decision showed how powerful the Court could be. Marshall was saying that the Court had the power to declare a law of Congress unconstitutional.

Poor Marbury never did get his job as justice of the peace. Jefferson had his way on that. Even so, the real victors in this case were Marshall and his Supreme Court. Ever since this decision, the Supreme Court has had the final say on laws of Congress. Its power to overrule acts of Congress because they are unconstitutional is called *judicial review.*

John Marshall continued to make decisions that surprised people. One of his greatest involved the Bank of the United States. Another involved steamboats. Both decisions had the same effect. They gave more power to the national government and took power away from the states.

Taxing a bank. Marshall's decision on the bank came in 1819 in the case of *McCulloch v. Maryland.* The case arose from an attempt by the state of Maryland to tax the bank heavily and therefore destroy it. For 25 years, people had wondered whether the Bank of the United States was legal. As we have seen, the bank had been the pet idea of Alexander Hamilton. Hamilton wanted Congress to create a bank that would serve the goals of the United States government. He said a national bank would help the economy to run smoothly. But did the Constitution give Congress the power to create such a bank? No, said many Republicans. Yes, said most Federalists.

Who was right? John Marshall agreed with Hamilton. Congress, he said, *did* have the power to charter a bank. True, in the list of powers granted to Congress, the Constitution said nothing about banks. But it did say this: "The Congress shall have power ... to make all laws which shall be necessary and proper" for carrying out its other powers.

Two of these specific powers listed in the Constitution are Congress' power to collect taxes and Congress' power to pay off debts. Could a bank help the government to collect taxes and pay off

John Marshall

debts? ~~Yes, said Marshall,~~ speaking for the Court. Therefore, the bank law was "necessary and proper." The Bank of the United States was constitutional. The state of Maryland did not have the right to tax it because this would give the state a right to destroy it.

Controlling commerce. Steamboats gave Marshall another chance to increase the power of the national government. A New York law said that only one company could operate steamboats on New York's Hudson River. But what if a steamboat company in the neighboring state of New Jersey wanted to carry passengers across the river to New York? The judges of New York state said this was against the law. Not so, said

John Marshall in 1824. In a case called *Gibbons v. Ogden,* he said Congress alone could control commerce between the states. The New York law was judged unconstitutional. New Jersey's steamboat company could do business in New York.

John Marshall spent 34 years — half his life — on the Supreme Court. He served as Chief Justice during the Administrations of five Presidents. He did as much as any President to strengthen the United States government. When he died, in 1835, Americans honored him by ringing the Liberty Bell in Philadelphia. It had not rung for many years. While tolling in memory of the greatest judge, the Liberty Bell cracked. It would never ring again.

A Second Look. . . .

1. *What is meant by* judicial review? *In what famous case was this doctrine first established? How does this doctrine add to the system of checks and balances set up in the Constitution?*

2. *This chapter describes three of Marshall's decisions in the Supreme Court:* Marbury v. Madison, McCulloch v. Maryland, *and* Gibbons v. Ogden. *In your opinion, which of these decisions did the most to strengthen the national government? Why?*

3. *Imagine that three friends have met in Washington on February 24, 1803. One is a Federalist, the second is a Republican, and the third is a visitor from Spain. John Marshall has just announced the Supreme Court decision in* Marbury v. Madison. *The Federalist is delighted, the Republican is furious, and the Spaniard is a bit puzzled by it all. Create a conversation among them.*

Chapter 31

America for Americans

"The Eagle of the United States — may she extend her wings from the Atlantic to the Pacific."

That was how people in Waterville, Maine, toasted the new nation on July 4, 1815. The toast promised great things for the U.S. Only a few years earlier, large numbers of Americans had thought of their state first and their country second. Now more and more of them were thinking in national terms first.

The nation had come through the War of 1812 with some success. There was a new spirit of *nationalism* — national pride — in the air. It could be seen most clearly in the nation's capital. Government buildings in Washington, D.C., had been burned by the British in 1814. After the war, new buildings had begun rising from the ashes of the old. The White House was being enlarged, repaired, and repainted. In September of 1817 it was ready to be occupied. A new President, James Monroe of Virginia, and his wife moved in.

Monroe was an old Republican friend of Thomas Jefferson. Monroe's election in 1816 had been just another sign that the Federalist party was dying out. Almost all national leaders now called themselves Republicans. During Monroe's first term as President, the U.S. seemed more united than ever before. A Boston newspaper called this period an "Era of Good Feelings." The term stuck.

During these years, the spirit of nationalism grew. Some Americans took special pride in comparing their government to European ones. In Spain and France, Russia and Austria, kings and emperors still ruled. Citizens there had few rights.

The U.S. still had to pay attention to Europe. For the young nation was surrounded by European colonies. Britain remained in control of Canada. It also claimed to own parts of Oregon and other areas in the Northwest. Russia claimed a huge piece of land that went from Alaska to Oregon. Spain held Florida, Texas, Cuba, Mexico, and most of South America.

But Spain was growing weaker. Its huge American empire was fast falling apart. Starting in 1810, a series of revolts had broken out from Mexico in the north to Argentina in the south. One after another, new nations were becoming independent.

Unrest in Florida. In Florida, Spain also had problems. The border between Georgia and Florida was an area of unrest. In 1817 the U.S. tried to drive Seminole (SEM-uh-nole) Indians from a settlement in Georgia. Seminoles in Florida became very angry at this. They staged raids over the border into Georgia. Their raids led to a wider war with the U.S.

In 1818 the U.S. sent a small Army to the area. It was led by the hero of the Battle of New Orleans, General Andrew Jackson. Jackson was expected to chase Indian raiders back into Florida and punish them. But it was not clear how much farther he should go.

Jackson swept into Florida and then across it. He put two Indian chiefs to death without trial. He took two forts from the Spanish, though he had no orders to do so. Then he left the area, believing that he had conquered it.

President Monroe was shocked when he heard what Jackson had done. He did not want to go to war with Spain. He ordered Jackson to withdraw his troops from Spanish forts. But he stopped short of telling Spain he was sorry about the invasion. His Secretary of State persuaded him against this.

The Secretary of State was John Quincy Adams, the son of Abigail and John Adams. Adams' parents had been stern patriots. Now he was proving to be as stern a nationalist. He not only approved of what Jackson had done in Florida. He also held out against other

James Monroe

Florida, 1810–1819

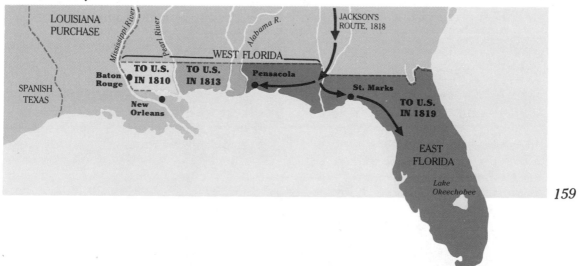

159

members of Monroe's Cabinet, who opposed it. In the end, he acted almost as boldly as Jackson. If Spain could not keep peace in Florida, Adams warned, it should turn the area over to a nation which could.

After this, Spain saw that it could not hold onto East Florida much longer. In 1819 it signed a treaty giving the area to the United States. In return, Americans gave up claims to the five million dollars that Spain owed them. And they gave up all claims to Texas (which the Spanish also claimed).

The treaty gave a further boost to American pride. Monroe was re-elected President by all but one electoral vote the next year. Yet his re-election did not end worries about the nations of Europe. If anything, these worries became greater in his second term.

As Spain withdrew from South America, it left behind a continent divided among weak nations. At the same time, some European nations were hungry for new colonies overseas. Was it possible that France, Russia, Prussia, and Austria might join forces in South America? Might they try to grab off former Spanish colonies for themselves? There were no clear signs of this. But there were many rumors.

Threats in the Pacific. There was also a sharper threat from Russia. In 1821 Russia told other nations to keep their ships out of the North Pacific. This angered Monroe and Adams. It also

John Quincy Adams had himself painted by the portrait-maker Thomas Sully.

angered the British. Like Russia, both the U.S. and Britain had claims to parts of Oregon. They were not going to let the Russians seal off the Pacific Coast.

Still, what was to prevent trouble on the high seas? And what was to prevent it in the newly independent nations to the south? British leaders thought they saw a way. In August 1823 they suggested that the U.S. join them in a warning. They would tell European leaders not to interfere in the Americas.

Monroe liked the idea. So did some other U.S. leaders. But John Quincy Adams had misgivings. He held high hopes of being elected President in 1824. Any pact with Britain could hurt his chances. Besides, he doubted the rumors about Europe's plans for South America. And he thought it more dignified for the U.S. to make the warning by itself.

Adams was a stubborn man. He held his views even when others disagreed. Slowly he persuaded Monroe to "go-it-alone" in his warning to Europe. In the end, he won his point.

Monroe issued the warning in his regular message to Congress on December 2, 1823. In the message, Monroe made two points about Europe and the Americas. First, he said that no European nation could start a new colony anywhere in the Americas. Second, he said that the U.S. and Europe should stay out of each other's territory. European armies should stay out of the Americas. In return, American armies would stay out of Europe.

This policy has come to be called the *Monroe Doctrine*. The ideas it stated were not completely new ones. In 1796 George Washington had warned against permanent alliances with Europe. Now Monroe was carrying Washington's warning one step further. He was saying that all independent nations of America should stay separate from Europe.

His doctrine was a bold one for its time. It was bolder still because it had been set forth by the U.S. alone. In 1823 Britain held control of shipping in the Atlantic Ocean. Only Britain could enforce the Monroe Doctrine. Yet the U.S. had chosen not to join Britain in the warning. By "going-it-alone," the U.S. had made the separation between Europe and the Americas all the more clear.

The Monroe Doctrine became a key part of American policy. Other Presidents followed the doctrine for more than 100 years. The doctrine clearly said to all the world: Keep out of the Americas. Since Monroe's time, other governments have usually heeded the warning.

A Second Look. . . .

1. *What two points did James Monroe make in his message to Congress on December 2, 1823? Why are these points considered an important part of American history?*

2. *What is your opinion of Andrew Jackson's invasion of Florida? If you had been a newspaper editor in 1818, would you have praised Jackson or criticized him? Why?*

3. *On a piece of paper, trace a map of North and South America. Entitle it: "The Americas in 1825." Shade in countries which, by 1825, had won independence from Europe. Use a historical atlas or an almanac as your source of information.*

Looking Back: The Nation Expands

	A	B	C	D	
1790	1800	1810	1820	1830

Putting Events in Order

Chapters 25 through 31 have shown how the United States grew and changed between the years 1790 and 1830. Fifteen events in this history are listed here. Your job is to match each event to the correct period shown on the timeline above.

On a piece of paper, number from **1** to **15.** After each number, write the letter of the period in which the event occurred.

1. The Embargo Act stops U.S. trade with foreign nations.

2. British troops burn Washington, D.C.

3. Meriwether Lewis and William Clark explore the Louisiana Territory and Oregon Country.

4. John Marshall's Supreme Court reaches a decision in the case of *McCulloch v. Maryland.*

5. President James Monroe issues a warning to Europe not to start new colonies in the Americas.

6. The United States purchases the Louisiana Territory for about 15 million dollars.

7. A British warship, the *Leopard,* fires at the *Chesapeake,* killing three Americans.

8. Congress passes the Alien and Sedition Acts.

9. Andrew Jackson leads Americans to victory at the Battle of New Orleans.

10. Andrew Jackson leads an invasion of Spanish Florida.

11. Thomas Jefferson serves two terms as President.

12. General William Henry Harrison wins the Battle of Tippecanoe.

13. Missouri becomes the 24th state.

14. Kentucky becomes the 15th state.

15. Congress declares war against Britain.

Interpreting a Source

The song below was first sung at about the time of the War of 1812. From it, we can learn about the hopes, dreams, and prejudices of American pioneers.

Banks of Ohio

Come all young men who have a mind for to range,
Into the Western country your station for to change,
For seeking some new pleasures we'll altogether go,
And we'll settle on the banks of the pleasant Ohio.

The land it is good, my boys, you need not to fear
'Tis a garden of Eden in North America:
Come along, my lads, and we'll altogether go
And we'll settle on the banks of the pleasant Ohio.

There's all kind of fish in that river for our use,
Besides the lofty sugar tree that yields us their juice,
There's all kinds of game besides the buck and doe,
And we'll range through the wild woods and hunt the buffalo.

This river as it murmurs it runs from the main,
It brings us good tidings quite down from New Spain:
There's all kinds of grain there and plenty it doth grow,
And we'll draw the Spanish gold right from Mexico!

Those blood-thirsty Indians you need not fear,
We will all united be and we will be free from care,
We'll march into their towns and give them their deadly blow,
And we'll fold you in our arms in the pleasant Ohio.

Come all you fair maidens, wherever you may be,
Come all join in with us and rewarded you shall be.
Girls, if you'll card,* knit, and spin, we'll plow, reap, and sow,
And we'll settle on the banks of the pleasant Ohio;
Girls, if you'll card, knit, and spin, we'll plow, reap, and sow,
And we'll fold you in our arms while the stormy wind doth blow.

To card was to clean and arrange fibers before spinning.

1. *What reason does this song give for moving west and settling on the Ohio River?*

2. *Do you think the songwriter was a man or a woman? Why?*

3. *Judging from this song, how do you think Western settlers felt about Indians? How do you think Indians felt about white settlers?*

4. *Do you think this song presents a fairly accurate picture of life on the Western frontier? Does it suggest that there could be any chance of failure? Was there, in fact, a chance of failure?*

Paintings such as this one by George Caleb Bingham helped create the stories we still hear about the good old days of the West.

Sharpening Your Skills

Did Americans in every part of the country support the War of 1812? The answer may be found in the table at right. It shows how U.S. Representatives from different states voted on going to war.

1. What section(s) of the country seemed to want war the most?

2. What section(s) of the country seemed to want war the least?

3. Of the following people, which was probably most enthusiastic about the War of 1812: (a) a New York banker; (b) a Kentucky farmer; (c) a Vermont farmer; or (d) a New Hampshire ship captain? Why?

Vote in the U.S. House of Representatives on the War of 1812

	Representatives for War	Representatives Against War
Frontier New England		
New Hampshire	3	2
Vermont	3	1
Commercial New England		
Massachusetts	6	8
Rhode Island	0	2
Connecticut	0	7
Commercial Middle States		
New York	3	11
New Jersey	2	4
Delaware	0	1
Jeffersonian Middle States		
Pennsylvania	16	2
Maryland	6	3
Jeffersonian Southern States		
Virginia	14	5
North Carolina	6	3
South Carolina	8	0
Georgia	3	0
Frontier West (home of the War Hawks)		
Ohio	1	0
Kentucky	5	0
Tennessee	3	0
Totals	**79**	**49**

6 ANDY JACKSON'S AMERICA

Looking Ahead: The People's President

No one had ever seen anything like this before. Woodsmen — rough men who lived in log cabins out West — were pouring into Washington, D.C. Many wore coonskin caps and muddy boots. Their mouths were full of chewing tobacco. These were real pioneers — farmers, hunters, and Indian fighters.

What were they doing in Washington? They had come to see their hero, Andy Jackson, sworn in as President. Wasn't Andy "one of the boys"? Wasn't he born in a log cabin, just as they had been? You bet he was!

And now it was March 4, 1829, the day Andy was sworn in. Andy took the solemn oath and then rode on horseback to the White House. His friends followed him to the White House and pushed

Ralph Earl painted this portrait of Andrew Jackson about 1820. The artist lived in the Hermitage, Jackson's mansion near Nashville, Tennessee. Later Earl married Jackson's niece.

their way in. Inside, some of them stood on fancy, velvet chairs to see their hero. Others pushed toward the tables to eat. Plates were broken, and food and drink were spilled on the beautiful carpets. The President was shoved against a wall. Finally a few friends helped him to escape. Andrew Jackson spent his first night as President in a hotel.

This wild day in the White House started a new period in American history. Scholars call it the period of Jacksonian Democracy. In the early years of the republic, the government of the United States had been partly democratic. But in some states, citizens could not vote unless they owned a certain amount of property. In these areas, the poorer citizens were therefore left out of government.

Vermont was the first state to change this. When it entered the Union in 1791, it gave *all* adult white males the vote. Other states — Alabama, Tennessee,

Missouri — soon did the same. In the 1820's, the older states began following the example of the newer states. They changed their laws about *suffrage* (the right to vote). Now any citizen who was white and adult and male could vote. The poorer citizen's vote counted just as much as the richer citizen's vote.

Most of the poorer citizens voted in 1828 for their hero, Andrew Jackson. They believed in him because Jackson believed in them. Jackson was not a poor man himself. Certainly he was no wild-eyed radical. But in his speeches, Jackson said again and again how much he admired the people — the "common people." At the same time, he was much cooler toward people who used money to gain power. He distrusted Eastern bankers because he thought they could cheat people out of their money. He dis-

168

While running for President, Andrew Jackson called himself the "common man's" candidate. After his swearing in as President, he invited a crowd to the White House — and they nearly destroyed it (above). Cartoon below shows Jackson stringing up a wealthy man, possibly a banker.

trusted college graduates who acted as if they were smarter than other people.

The people Jackson respected were those who sweated for a living on the farms and in the factories of America. Because of them, Jackson won the electoral votes of every Western and Southern state. His opponent, President John Quincy Adams, won only the votes of his own region, New England, plus New Jersey and Delaware (see map at right).

Jackson was the candidate of farmers, factory workers, and poor people. He was also the candidate of the Democratic-Republican party. When Monroe was President, the Democratic-Republican party had been the only one strong enough to have broad support. But now the party had broken apart. Andrew Jackson and his followers still called themselves Democratic-Republicans. The followers of John Quincy Adams and Henry Clay called themselves National Republicans. In a short time, the Democratic-Republicans would shorten their name. Followers of Jackson would call themselves Democrats. Jackson's opponents would call themselves Whigs. The Democrats and Whigs would remain the two major parties for the next 20 years.

Andrew Jackson, the people's President, served two terms (1829-1837). In that time, a lot happened to change America. Some Northerners became wealthy from their new factories and machines. Many Southerners became fearful of the growing power of the North. And in many areas dedicated people were fighting against injustices they saw around them. The names for these three great movements were: *industrialism, sectionalism,* and *reform.*

Electoral Vote, 1828

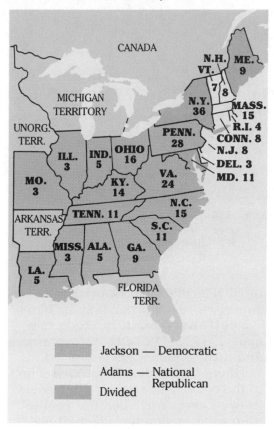

Jackson — Democratic

Adams — National Republican

Divided

Industrialism. Early every morning, men, women, and children took their places behind noisy machines. The machines might turn out cotton cloth or farm tools or rifle barrels. The development of this method of making things was called *industrialism.* The system was fairly new in the 1830's — but it was growing fast. More and more factories were being built in northeastern states such as Massachusetts and Connecticut. More and more people were leaving their farms to work in the factories. The economy of the North was changing

169

American pioneers are said to have conquered
the West. But, as the 1839 cartoon shows,
the West "conquered" some of the pioneers.

rapidly. Its mills and factories were now
almost more important than its farms.

Sectionalism. In Jackson's day,
many Easterners distrusted Westerners.
And many Southerners distrusted
Northerners. Leaders from one section
of the country quarreled with leaders
from another. Why? Because people
from each section had different needs.

Factory owners in the North needed
to sell factory goods. To protect themselves from cheap foreign imports, they
wanted Congress to put a high tariff on
foreign-made goods. Southern cotton
farmers, however, needed to buy cheap
factory goods — farm tools and clothes.
A high tariff made them pay higher
prices. They also thought it hurt their
chances of selling Southern goods —
mainly cotton — to European nations.

Congress could not be fair to all sections of the country at the same time.
Laws that helped the North hurt the
170   South. Laws that helped the South hurt

the North. Southerners were especially
worried because the North was growing
so fast in population. It was gaining
more and more power in Congress.
Northerners therefore had a better
chance to hurt the South than the other
way around.

Reform. After 1828 the nation
thought of itself more and more as a
democracy. This new way of thinking
brought with it new hope. In many parts
of the country people tried to find ways
to right the wrongs of the past. They
wanted to make life better for others.
These people were called *reformers.*

Reformers tried to help people who
needed special care. A doctor in Boston,
Samuel Gridley Howe, set up the first
center for the teaching of blind children.
Dorothea Dix, a New England schoolteacher, tried to improve life for the
mentally ill. A young lawyer named
Horace Mann fought for the right of
every child to attend a public school.

The United States in Andrew
Jackson's day was more democratic
than ever before. But there were still
large groups of people who did not

American know-how has created unusual things.
An inventor of the 1830's proposed this top hat.
It holds a man's glasses, snuff box, and cigar.

After 1828 some artists began paying more attention to the "common man." William Sydney Mount admired the life of Long Island (New York) farmers. In the painting at left, he shows them taking a break from work at noon. David Blythe, on the other hand, made fun of the "common man." In the painting above, he mocks a country lawyer and sleepy jury members.

171

Vol. 2.]   "GO AHEAD!!"   [No. 3.

THE CROCKETT ALMANAC 1841.

Tussel with a Bear. See page 9.

**Containing Adventures, Exploits, Sprees
& Scrapes in the West, &
Life and Manners in the Backwoods.**

Nashville, Tennessee. Published by Ben Harding.

*Western leaders such as Davy Crockett gained
fame during the Jackson Era. By 1841 Crockett
was a legend, and an almanac was named for him.*

share in this democracy. A young French writer, Alexis de Tocqueville (ah-LECK-sis duh TOKE-vill) noticed this fact while traveling in America in 1831. He noticed that there were three main groups in America — whites, Indians, and blacks. Only white people were treated with respect.

Indians were fast losing their lands and their way of life. As white settlers moved into their homelands, many Indians were forced to keep moving farther and farther west. Those who could not adjust to the change perished. Many died of starvation. De Tocqueville once told a white innkeeper that an Indian was dying outside his hotel. The man just shrugged his shoulders. White Americans did not seem to care about the suffering and dying of Indians.

The Frenchman also observed how blacks were treated in both the North and the South. In the North, slavery was against the law in most states. But whites would not mix with blacks or treat them fairly or as equals. Blacks were kept out of white churches, white schools, white jobs, and white hotels.

In the South, two million blacks lived as slaves. In many areas, black slaves greatly outnumbered white farmers and planters. Would the slaves someday rise up and revolt against their masters? White Southerners often worried about this. They were afraid of what blacks might do if they ever became free.

Returning to France, De Tocqueville wrote a book about his travels. He called it *Democracy in America*. Even today this book gives a fine account of Jacksonian Democracy. It shows how American democracy was strong and growing — but not yet complete.

Chapter 32

A Time of Conflict

Two tall men sat at either end of a long table. The white-haired man was President Andrew Jackson. The younger man with jet black hair and piercing eyes was his Vice-President, John C. Calhoun. They were eating dinner in a Washington hotel with other members of the Democratic party. The date was April 13, 1830.

Waiters brought in trays loaded with turkey, duck, and pickled oysters. But neither Jackson nor Calhoun ate much. Something was the matter. The other Democrats in the room guessed what it might be.

Calhoun had recently challenged the power of the United States government. He had written an essay saying that a state government could refuse to obey a law of the national government. It could, in other words, *nullify* an act of Congress. The law that Calhoun especially hated was a high tariff passed by Congress in 1828.

Southerners called it the *Tariff of Abominations,* meaning "the hated tariff." Why did they hate it so? They believed it made them pay more for items such as shoes, made in the North. They also thought it hurt the sales of Southern goods — chiefly cotton — to nations overseas.

Calhoun came from South Carolina. He was a Southerner. Jackson had been raised in the Carolinas and had settled in Tennessee. Nobody knew the President's opinion about Calhoun's idea of nullifying a national law. Many Democrats, however, thought he probably approved of it. After all, as a Southerner Jackson disliked the tariff of 1828 as much as Calhoun.

The dinner was finally coming to an end. Waiters filled the wine glasses. One of the men at the table rose to offer a toast. He suggested that people drink to the idea of states' rights. One by one, 23 other men stood up. Most of them made similar toasts. So far everyone seemed to be supporting the ideas of Calhoun.

Then Andrew Jackson stood up. He looked directly at Calhoun. "Our Union," he said. "It must be preserved." People gasped. They understood very well what Jackson meant. He was saying that he

John C. Calhoun

173

thought the nation's laws were more important than the rights of the states. It was almost as if the President had slapped the Vice-President across the face.

Calhoun's hand trembled as he raised his glass. Staring angrily at Jackson, he said: "The Union: Next to our liberties, most dear."

Nullification issue. The dinner was over. But the quarrel between Jackson and Calhoun had just begun. A new tariff law passed Congress in 1832. Again Calhoun and the South reacted angrily. Calhoun wrote a letter to the governor of South Carolina. It explained why unfair federal laws should be resisted, not obeyed.

The governor called a state convention. He asked the delegates: Should South Carolina obey the tariff laws of 1828 and 1832? No, said a majority of delegates. They passed a law called the *Ordinance of Nullification*. It declared that U.S. officials would not be allowed to collect a tariff in South Carolina. What if the United States government used force to collect the tariff duties? Then, said the ordinance, South Carolina might *secede from* (leave) the Union.

Americans panicked when they heard this news. Their President was famous for his angry temper. They feared he might send troops into South Carolina and start a civil war. But Jackson acted with words, not guns. He sent a message to South Carolina explaining that he did not wish to use force. He also explained, however, that he had a duty to enforce the laws of the nation. This duty was part of the oath he had taken under the U.S. Constitution.

174   Then Jackson gave South Carolina a

good reason for changing its nullification law. He sent a message to Congress asking for a lower tariff — a tariff that would be fairer to the South. He also asked for a second law that would allow him to use force in South Carolina, if he needed it. Both the new tariff and the Force Act were passed in 1833.

Another convention was called in South Carolina. This time the delegates voted to take back the Ordinance of Nullification. They would pay the lower tariff duties, they said. The threat of a civil war was over — at least for the time being. Neither side had won a clear victory.

Most scholars agree that Andrew Jackson was one of the strongest Presidents in American history. Many of them admire the way he overcame the threat

Henry Clay led Senators who wanted to silence Andrew Jackson on the national bank. One cartoonist thought Clay won.

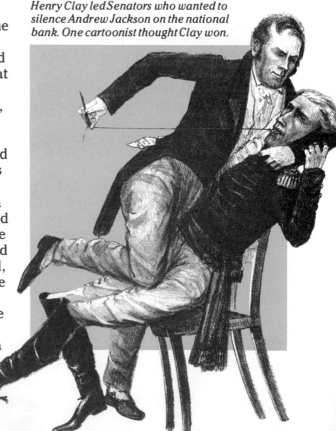

Aided by Vice-President Martin Van Buren, Jackson slays the "many-headed monster" — the Bank of the United States. Jackson actually killed the national bank by putting government money in state banks.

of disunion and civil war in 1833. Some of them also admire the courage he showed in a second and even greater struggle. This was a struggle between the President of the United States and the Bank of the United States.

Struggle over the bank. In 1832 Jackson called the national bank a "monster." He believed that the bank served Eastern businesses and cheated Western and Southern farmers. He believed that too many people were at the mercy of this powerful bank. He also suspected that the bank was secretly trying to defeat him in the 1832 election. The President told his friend, Martin Van Buren: "The bank, Mr. Van Buren, is trying to kill me, *but I will kill it!*"

How could a President "kill" a bank? He could simply refuse to allow it to go on living. The bank depended for its existence on a charter from Congress. In 1832 the bank's president, Nicholas Biddle, asked Congress to renew the bank's charter. Congress passed the law that

Biddle wanted. But then the President vetoed it. That is, he refused to sign his name to the bank act.

Back in 1819, in *McCulloch v. Maryland,* the U.S. Supreme Court had ruled the bank was constitutional. Now Jackson disagreed. He wrote an angry message to Congress, explaining his veto. The national bank, Jackson said, went *against* the Constitution. It placed too much power in the hands of a few wealthy bankers. It was an enemy of the common people.

Many people thought the President was being unfair. Nicholas Biddle thought he was being high-handed. Didn't Jackson know that an election was coming soon? Didn't he know that he would probably lose the election if he tried to smash the powerful Bank of the United States? Didn't he know that the whole economy might be badly hurt if there were no bank? Yes, Jackson knew the risks. But he took them anyway.

In November 1832, the voters decided the winner of the so-called "bank war." Henry Clay, the candidate of the Whig party, was a good friend of Nicholas Biddle's bank. If he won the election, the bank would be sure to be revived. But Clay won only 40 electoral votes. Andrew Jackson won 219 electoral votes. Jackson had won the greatest political fight of his life. He had killed the "monster"; the "monster" had not killed him.

A Second Look. . . .

1. *Andrew Jackson was opposed by two powerful men — John C. Calhoun and Nicholas Biddle. What was Calhoun's reason for opposing Jackson? What was Biddle's?*

176 **2.** *As it turned out, Biddle was partly right about the bank. After Jackson killed it with his veto, business suffered. Thousands of people were thrown out of work in 1837. Was Jackson wrong then to kill the "monster"? Do you think you would have voted for him in the election of 1832? Why or why not?*

3. *Compare Andrew Jackson with the current President. Write one paragraph comparing the personalities of these two Presidents. Write another paragraph comparing their ability as leaders. For more information, consult a biography of Andrew Jackson in your local library. You may also want to look at magazine articles on the current President.*

Andrew Jackson's many vetoes stirred one cartoonist to show how he felt about the people's President.

BORN TO COMMAND.

OF VETO MEMORY.

HAD I BEEN CONSULTED.

KING ANDREW THE FIRST.

Chapter 33

Lowell's Mills

The young woman in the plain cotton dress felt lonely and lost. What was she doing here in Lowell, Massachusetts? Oh, Lowell was a model factory town all right. There were some quiet canals and plenty of trees, and the streets were very clean. Still it didn't look quite like her family's farm back home. Plumy Clay was a little scared.

She stepped down from the black wagon that had brought her here. An older woman came toward her. The woman said she was in charge of one of the boarding houses where the working girls lived. Plumy Clay followed the woman into a three-story boarding house. They entered a small room with four beds in it — something like the bedrooms on nearby farms. The woman pointed out which bed was Plumy Clay's. She also explained the rules of the house. No dancing. No drinking. Into bed by 10 o'clock at night. Be sure to attend church on Sunday.

The young woman sat on the edge of the bed and waited for her roommates to return from the cotton mill. Perhaps they would be able to tell her about life as a factory worker. What happened to Plumy Clay after this is not known. We know about her arrival in Lowell only because another woman, Harriet Robinson, wrote about it.

Probably Plumy Clay soon learned the routine. The machines in the cotton mills of Lowell would begin buzzing and hissing at five in the morning. The women would have to tend them for two hours before sitting down to breakfast for half an hour. They could look forward to another half-hour break for dinner at 12:30. After that, they had to work straight through the afternoon until 7:30.

They worked 13 hours a day, six days a week. For many of them, pay amounted to about $2.25 for a week's work. (Lowell's wages in 1830 averaged $3.50 a week, less $1.25 taken out for room and board.) This may seem like very poor pay. But it was fairly high by the standards of the day. The girls at Lowell were glad to get it. It meant that they had money of their own to spend or save.

Chance for independence. Until the 1830's, it had been usual for most women to depend on men — husbands, fathers, or brothers — for their support. But the mills in Lowell, Massachusetts, gave young women a greater chance to be independent. Plumy Clay's friend, Harriet Robinson, explained what this meant to women: "After the first payday came, and they felt the jingle of silver in their pockets, their bowed heads were lifted. They looked you in the face."

The women who came to Lowell from the farms of New England were like pioneers. They were beginning something new and important in American life. They were part of an experiment in large-scale manufacturing. They were producing cotton cloth in a way that had never been tried before in the United States.

Factory system. Their system for making cloth worked like this: At one end of the factory, they received shipments of raw cotton from the South. Then, with the help of giant machines, they twisted it, spun it, and wound it into cotton thread. They placed the thread on huge power looms and wove it into yards of cotton cloth. The cloth was then ready to be shipped and sold all over the country.

What was so new and different about this? People had been making cotton cloth for hundreds of years. The difference was that, before this, cloth was spun and woven at home for family use. Families still had spinning wheels and hand looms in their homes in the 1830's. But Lowell's mills made cloth much faster and more cheaply than the old way.

This new system meant doing everything on a large scale. Large machines had to be built. Large sums of money or capital had to be spent on them. Large numbers of workers had to be brought together to work with large amounts of raw material. Finally large quantities of the finished product could be sold to a large market for a large profit.

One of the first Americans to try manufacturing on a large scale was a Boston merchant, Francis Cabot Lowell. He built a cotton mill in Waltham, near Boston, in 1813. It made so much money that

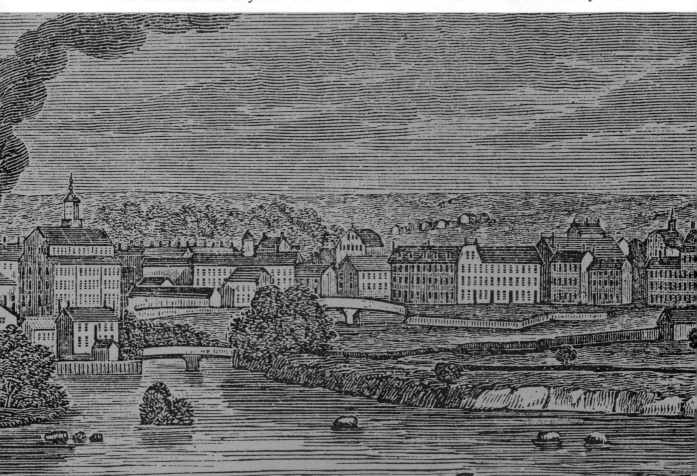

Lowell and his partners looked for a place to build a larger mill. Lowell found a village of 200 people on the Merrimack River. But before he could build there, Lowell died at an early age. His partners went on to start the mill in the village he had chosen. They renamed the village after Lowell. They mostly hired young women because they could pay them less than men.

In its early years the village was a worker's dream-come-true. It had gentle canals, orderly mills, and good living conditions. Soon Lowell grew into a town. Then the town became a city. In 1836 there were 17,633 people (most of

Many early factory workers were farm girls who came to towns such as Lowell, Massachusetts (below), to escape farm life. By the 1840's, such women were being replaced by Irish.

them young women) living in Lowell.

Labor troubles. But as the mill town grew, the workers' lives became harder. The mill owners cared less and less about the workers' welfare and more and more about making money. One manager explained his attitude: "I regard my work people just as I regard my machinery. So long as they can do the work for what I choose to pay them, I keep them, getting out of them all I can."

In 1836 the girls in the Lowell mills received shocking news. The owners announced that each worker's weekly wages would be cut by one dollar. That meant that many workers would be getting only pennies a week. Hundreds of workers walked off the job and paraded up and down the streets of Lowell. Theirs was one of the first strikes in their industry in American history. As they marched, they waved handkerchiefs in the air and sang:

Oh! Isn't it a pity, such a pretty girl as I —
Should be sent to the factory to pine
away and die?

The owners did not listen. They cut wages anyway. Their job was to make cotton cloth faster and cheaper than it had ever been made before. But Lowell's women workers did not forget the need to stand united. Nine years later a Lowell worker, Sarah Bagley, organized the Female Labor Reform Association. This group was formed to campaign for a 10-hour workday.

What was happening in Lowell was only an early chapter of a much larger story. By the 1840's, other industries were also growing in most large states of the North. Men, women, and children were going to work in factories, for bet-

180

ter or for worse. Often they were made to work long hours in dingy rooms for very little pay.

Industrialism, then, was a mixed blessing. Factory life was hard on many people engaged in it. It was especially hard on children, who made up a very large part of the work force at this time. On the other hand, industrialism added to the wealth and power of the Northeast. It gave jobs to the jobless, many of them from overseas. And in the long run it would help Americans build a better way of life.

A Second Look. . . .

1. *Payday in Lowell had a special importance. What was it? Why did many of the workers there believe at first that they were doing something new and different?*

2. *The coming of the factory system changed U.S. life. In what ways was the change for the better? In what ways was the change for the worse?*

3. *Before the rise of manufacturing, items such as cotton shirts or blouses were made by one person and by hand. People who did this sort of work for a living were* artisans — *those skilled in a special trade. Artisans still exist in many U.S. communities. Here are some examples: basket-weavers, potters, tailors, cabinet-makers. You might want to invite one or more local artisans to speak to your class. These are some questions to keep in mind to ask them: Do you enjoy making use of your special talent? If so, why? Do you believe that your enthusiasm shows in the finished product? In what ways? Would you recommend your products over manufactured items of the same kind? Why?*

Chapter 34
She Cared

She cared about the poor, the sick, and the insane (mentally ill). Especially the insane. In her day, these people were treated as though they had fallen to the level of wild animals. They were not put in hospitals but in jails or poorhouses. They were often locked up in dark cages, closets, or cellars. Many were chained. They were sometimes whipped by cruel or ignorant keepers. They had little or nothing to wear and got very little to eat. Some of them looked like skeletons.

But this woman, almost alone, changed these conditions. Her name was Dorothea Dix. Because of her, new hospitals were built, and the mentally ill began to get better treatment. Kindness began to take the place of chains and the whip. As a result, many mentally ill people got better.

Dorothea Dix had been born in Maine in 1802. In those days, Maine was mostly woods with few people and few roads. Dorothea lived in a lonely log cabin. Her father was a traveling preacher. Usually he was paid with food. Sometimes he wasn't paid at all. Then Dorothea and her two brothers would go hungry.

Dorothea hated the lonely, dreary life she led. At 12, she ran away. She lived for a while with her grandparents in Boston. Later she went to live with some cousins nearby.

Dorothea Dix

Running schools. At 14, Dorothea became a schoolteacher. Before long, she was running *two* schools. One was for children who could pay. The other was for poor children. Dorothea worked very hard. Her day was very long, and she hardly had time to sleep. She got up at four o'clock in the morning to study and read her Bible. Sometimes she didn't go to sleep until midnight.

The strain was too much for her. Her health finally broke down. She spent years trying to get well. All the while, she wanted to help other people. But what could she, a woman, do? Women had few rights in those days. They couldn't even vote. Then one day in 1841 Dix was asked to visit a jail near Boston. Would she read the Bible to the women prisoners there? She went to the jail and was shocked by what she saw. It was winter, but there was no heat to keep the women warm. Some of the prisoners were insane. Dix told the jail keeper that he should put in a stove to heat the drafty rooms. The jail keeper told her "crazy people" didn't need stoves.

Helping the insane. Dorothea Dix became very angry. She felt she had to do something to help these people. For the next two years, she traveled all over Massachusetts. She went to every jail, poorhouse, and home where insane people were kept. She made notes about the horrible things she saw. She saw men and women chained in dark, filthy rooms behind iron doors. One man was even kept in a hole in the ground. Many of the insane were very thin from lack of food. Dix rubbed the hands of one man, trying to warm them. She spoke to him kindly and told him that someday he could go home. The man said nothing, but a tear ran down his cheek.

Dix then gave all her notes to an important man in Massachusetts. He read them to the state's lawmakers. Many people did not like what Dix had done. They felt that the insane were no better than wild animals. Others believed that the insane were being punished for their "sins." But finally the lawmakers voted money for a decent hospital for the mentally ill.

Dix then traveled all over the United

Before the 19th century, most Americans considered insane people sinful, not sick. But some doctors of the 1800's believed they could cure insanity. One of the devices they used was this "crib."

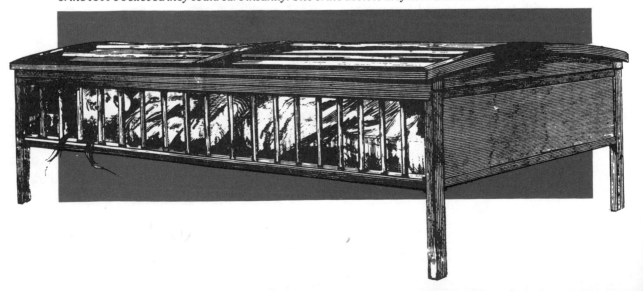

States visiting the insane. At a time when long trips still meant hardships, she traveled more than 60,000 miles (96,000 kilometers). Nothing stopped Dorothea Dix, not even her bad health.

Everywhere she talked to lawmakers about "God's poor and outcast." She would not take "no" for an answer. In almost every state she visited, money was voted for new hospitals for the insane. Dorothea, who never married, called these hospitals her children.

Later she went to Europe to help the insane. In the Civil War, she became head nurse for the Union army. After the war, she trained nurses to care for the mentally ill. She did not retire until she was 80.

Dorothea Dix died at the age of 85 in 1887. At the time of her death, an English doctor called her "the most useful and distinguished woman that America has ever produced."

A Second Look....

1. *Give three reasons for thinking that Dorothea Dix was one of the "most useful and distinguished" women in American history.*

2. *How were the mentally ill treated in Dorothea Dix's day? How are they generally treated today? What was Dix's opinion of the way these people were treated in her own time? What did she do to try to change conditions for the mentally ill? Did she succeed in her efforts on their behalf? Explain your answer.*

3. *Imagine that you are a state lawmaker in the 1850's. Dorothea Dix has*

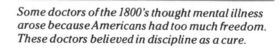

Some doctors of the 1800's thought mental illness arose because Americans had too much freedom. These doctors believed in discipline as a cure.

visited several jails and poorhouses in your state and criticized the treatment of the mentally ill. Now you must make a tour of the state to see conditions for yourself. Make a list of 10 questions you will want to ask as you go from place to place.

183

Chapter 35

Father of Free Schools

Picture a one-room school with a dirt floor. The windows are broken, and the doors don't shut well enough to keep out the cold. The roof leaks when it rains. There are no blackboards, charts, or maps on the walls. But there is a whip in the room. And every once in a while the teacher uses it — on students who cannot recite their lessons.

This is what many schools were like in the early 1800's. About one school out of three was very rundown. Yet the young people who were students in them were *lucky*. In those days, most children did not get much schooling. Many of them lived on farms that were too far away from schools. Thousands of city children had to work in factories 10 to 12 hours a day.

A reformer named Horace Mann wanted to do something about this. His urge to improve education sprang partly from his own early schooling, which was poor. When he grew up, he could have made a lot of money as a lawyer. But he took a school job at low pay instead.

Horace Mann was born in a small Massachusetts town in 1796. As a child he worked from morning to night on his father's farm. It was a hard life. He had little time to play, and he never went to school more than 10 weeks a year. But Horace liked books. He read every history book in the town library.

Horace thought he wanted to be a lawyer. Every chance he got he studied the subjects he needed to get into college. At the age of 20, he entered Brown University. There he proved himself a brilliant student, the best in his class.

Horace Mann became an able lawyer. He was tall and thin, and his eyes seemed to shine when he talked. In 1827 he was elected to the Massachusetts legislature. He worked hard to help the sick and the poor. But most of all he wanted to do something about the schools.

School reforms. Massachusetts had had public schools since 1647. But these schools were controlled by local school districts which kept very strict limits on their spending. As a result, public schools had grown weaker. In the 1830's, reformers wanted to improve them. In 1837 they won a victory. A state Board of Education was set up.

Horace Mann was asked to become the head of this board. The pay was very low. Many of Mann's friends told him not to take the job. "Stick to the law," they said. "Someday you'll be governor of the state." But Horace Mann took the school job anyway. It meant that on most days he would have to skip lunch to save money.

Why did Mann give up being a lawyer to go into education? Because he believed that in the United States *everyone* should be educated. In

Europe only the ruling classes and the very rich got an education. The rest of the people didn't matter. But in the United States, Mann said, the *people* are the rulers. Democracy cannot work unless everyone goes to school.

Mann repeated these ideas again and again. He stressed other points as well. He did not believe in "thwacking" a student over the head as a punishment for failure. He thought this was as wise "as it would be to rap a watch with a hammer because it does not keep good time."

Teacher training. Mann traveled to almost every town and village in Massachusetts. Everywhere he went he told the people why they needed good schools. He got them to vote money for grade schools that were clean and well run. He got them to vote money for building high schools and for setting up

libraries in the schools. Mann also set up three state colleges, called *normal schools*, to train better teachers. These were the first state-run normal schools in the United States.

Many people did not like the work Mann was doing. They said that schools for poor children were a waste of money. Why should they pay school taxes for children who didn't need an education? People who felt this way tried hard to stop Mann's work. But Horace Mann could not be stopped. In fact, many other states began to copy the work Mann was doing in Massachusetts. Countries in Europe began to copy it too. Horace Mann became known as the "father" of free public schools for all children.

A Second Look. . . .

1. *Why did Horace Mann think that free public schools were so important? Why did he think democracy could not work without them?*

2. *In both Europe and Asia, teaching has been thought of as a noble calling for centuries. Why should this be true? What is so important about education? What do you like most about school? What do you like least? Explain your answers.*

3. *Two months before his death in 1859, Horace Mann gave an address to students at Antioch College in Ohio. "Be ashamed to die," he told them, "until you have won some victory for humanity." Write at least one paragraph explaining what you think Mann meant by that statement. Be sure to point out at least one of the "victories" he won in his lifetime. Also indicate what "victory" you would like to win.*

A great many Americans of the 1800's got their educations in one-room schoolhouses such as this.

Nat Turner's Rebellion

"All men are created equal," the Declaration of Independence had proclaimed back in 1776. By the 1830's this idea had been accepted by most Americans as a basic part of their political beliefs. Yet not all Americans were equal. Those most forcefully denied equality were America's two million black slaves.

From 1700 to 1800, about seven million Africans had been taken by force to various parts of the New World. About half a million of them had been brought to America, mostly to the South. Slaves were not much needed on the smaller farms of the North. Shortly before 1800, in fact, most Northern states enacted laws to do away with slavery completely.

In 1808 the U.S. Congress had passed a law against bringing any more slaves

A slave who ran away had little chance of escaping. Owners organized "Negro hunts," chasing down the runaway with dogs, horses, guns. Despite the odds, thousands of slaves tried to escape. Some made it.

into the country. But many slaves were still brought in against the law. By this time many Southern farmers were relying on cotton as their main crop. Cotton-growing required a large supply of laborers, and slavery could provide it. And so by the 1830's many white Southerners had come to believe that their way of life depended on slaves.

The laws for white people were very different from the laws for blacks. A white person could go to jail for beating up another white person. But white masters were almost never punished for whipping or even killing their black slaves. Laws in the Southern states said that black slaves *belonged* to their masters — like property. Black people's children belonged to the masters too. And all black slaves could be bought and sold as their masters saw fit.

White Americans disagreed about what should be done about slavery. Some thought it was a terrible evil and should be quickly ended. Others thought slaves should be freed slowly, a few at a time. A third group thought slaves should be sent to Africa to start new colonies.

A fourth group thought nothing should be done. These people did not believe there was anything wrong with slavery. John C. Calhoun, for example, argued that slavery was "good — a positive good." After all, he said, blacks were taken care of by their white masters. Throughout their lives, they were given food, housing, and medical care.

Calhoun failed to mention that the slaves' food was usually poor and fatty. Their clothing was usually rough and ragged. Few of them wore shoes, except in the winter months. Most

Many escaping slaves went off to look for their families, from whom they had been separated.

died much younger than their masters.

White people at least had a choice about whether they liked or disliked the idea of slavery. Slaves themselves had no say in the matter at all. Some of them showed their feelings by destroying crops or burning forests. Others simply tried to run away. If they were caught, however, they would be whipped. Some runaways were even burned on their faces with a red-hot iron.

Slaves' despair. Slavery led to despair, and despair sometimes led black people to take their own lives. Or in some cases it led them to revolt against white slaveholders. One of the most famous slave revolts was led by a young black named Nat Turner.

Nat Turner was a slave on a plantation in Southampton, Virginia. The known facts about his early life are few. His parents and grandparents had been slaves. His parents had taught him to read and write. His grandparents had given him his religious faith.

187

At slave auctions (right), black men and women were bought and sold. Families and friends were often torn apart. Even so, family ties remained very strong. Slaves held on to their loved ones and their customs. In the South Carolina scene shown above, slaves are using a drum and stringed instrument of African origin. The dance they are doing is thought to have come from the Yorubas of West Africa.

Turner was a religious man and prayed very often. He believed that he heard voices that were messages from God. They told him that he would do some great work. But Turner did not know what this would be.

Then one day Turner felt that he was seeing a vision. He believed that he saw black spirits fighting white spirits in the sky. He saw blood dripping from the heavens. Now Turner felt that he understood what he was to do. He was to lead the slaves in a battle for freedom.

Turner waited for a sign to begin his work. He waited nearly three years. On February 12, 1831, there was an eclipse of the sun. Turner took this to be his sign. He then told his plan to a few slaves he felt he could trust. Together they set July 4 as the date for the revolt. But Turner let that day pass without doing anything.

Then, in August, Turner was sure he saw another sign. For three days the sun seemed to turn a greenish blue. For three nights there was "blood on the moon." Turner called a meeting of his trusted followers. It was held in a forest on August 21.

Plan for revolt. Turner's plan was to march from one plantation to another, killing the slave-owners. He would also call on the slaves to join him in an attack on Jerusalem, the county capital. If they could capture the town, their revolt would become famous. Then maybe all the other slaves would revolt for miles around. If the attack on Jerusalem failed, they would retreat to a swamp. From there they would fight on. They would gather more followers, and one day they would take over the whole state of Virginia.

Turner and his followers decided to start the revolt that night at the house of Joseph Travis. Travis was Turner's master. He had not been a hard master. But he was not going to escape.

After dark, the six men moved quietly toward the Travis house. Once inside, they killed the whole family. They took all the guns they could find. Then they went to other houses, murdering people in their beds. Only a few slaves joined the revolt. Most of the slaves were either too frightened or felt loyal to their masters. They would not take part.

That night Turner's band killed 55 men, women, and children. The next morning it headed for Jerusalem. But soon the slaves ran into armed white men. After some fighting, the slave band broke up. Turner went into hiding only two miles from the Travis home. Then the Virginia state militia took a terrible revenge. More than 100 innocent blacks were shot down in cold blood. Dozens of others were tortured to make them "talk."

Finally 53 slaves were put on trial. Some were hanged, and a few were let go. Turner was caught in October and tried for murder. He pleaded "not guilty." His lawyer asked him if he had any regrets about what he had done. Turner said "no." He went to his death calmly on November 11, 1831.

Nat Turner's uprising shook the whole South. Whites everywhere were very frightened. Hard laws were passed against all blacks, free or slave. These laws did not solve the problem of slavery. In fact, they made the problem even worse than before.

In the years to come, arguments about slavery would divide Americans very

189

deeply. In the end, slavery would lead the nation into the worst war in its history — the Civil War.

A Second Look. . . .

1. *How did Nat Turner plan to take over the state of Virginia? Why did his plan fail?*

2. *Suppose you were a slave in Southampton County in the 1830's. Do you think you would have joined Nat Turner's rebellion? If not, what would you have done? Give reasons for your answers.*

3. *In 1830 slavery was allowed by law in 12 states: Alabama, Delaware, Georgia, Kentucky, Louisiana, Maryland, Mississippi, Missouri, North Carolina, South Carolina, Tennessee, and Virginia (which then included what is now West Virginia). After 1810 the greatest growth in numbers of slaves took place in three of these states — Alabama, Louisiana, Mississippi. Make your own map showing the spread of slavery by coloring in an outline map of the U.S. First label all of the states which existed in 1830. (Consult the chart of the states at the back of this book for dates of admission to the Union.) Then color in the three states with the greatest growth in numbers of slaves. Apply a different color to the other slave states and a third color to states outlawing slavery. Why did slavery grow more in some states than it grew in others?*

Many slave-owners must have had nightmares about what would happen if their slaves turned on them. In Virginia in 1831, the nightmare came to life. Nat Turner's revolt spread terror through the white South.

HORRID MASSACRE IN VIRGINIA

Looking Back: Andy Jackson's America

	A	B	C	D	
1825	1830	1835	1840	1845

Putting Events in Order

Chapters 32 through 36 have shown some of the changes that took place in "Andy Jackson's America." Ten events of this period are listed here. Your job is to match each event to the correct period shown on the timeline above. On a piece of paper, number from **1** to **10**. After each number, write the letter of the period in which the event occurred.

1. Nat Turner leads a slave revolt in Virginia.

2. Congress passes the Tariff of Abominations.

3. Western pioneers tramp through the White House to celebrate Andrew Jackson's swearing in as President.

4. Massachusetts reformers set up a state Board of Education.

5. South Carolina votes to nullify a U.S. tariff law.

6. Dorothea Dix begins her crusade for better treatment of the insane.

7. Andrew Jackson vetoes a bill of Congress concerning the Bank of the United States.

8. Factory workers in Lowell, Massachusetts, protest a cut in their wages.

9. Andrew Jackson wins election to a second term as President.

10. Congress passes a new tariff law that is fairer to the South.

Interpreting a Source

In 1826 a hunter and pioneer from Tennessee named Davy Crockett won election to Congress. Crockett admitted that he knew nothing about government. But his jokes and Western style of speaking made him a popular figure in the early 1830's. Here is Crockett's account of his first campaign for office.

[I had never seen a public document], nor did I know there were such things. How to begin I couldn't tell. I made many

191

apologies, and tried to get off, for I know'd I had a man to run against who could speak prime. And I know'd too that I wa'n't able to shuffle and cut with him. He was there, and knowing my ignorance as well as I did myself, he also urged me to make a speech. The truth is, he thought my being a candidate was a mere matter of sport; and didn't think, for a moment, that he was in any danger from an ignorant backwoods bear hunter. But I found I couldn't get off, and so I determined just to go ahead, and leave it to chance what I should say.

I got up and told the people, I reckoned they know'd what I come for. But if not, I could tell them, I had come for their votes, and if they didn't watch mighty close, I'd get them too. But the worst of all was that I couldn't tell them anything about government. I tried to speak about something, and I cared very little what, until I choked up as bad as if my mouth had been jam'd and cram'd chock full of dry mush. . . .

At last I told them I was like a fellow I had heard of not long before. He was beating on the head of an empty barrel near the roadside, when a traveler . . . asked him what he was doing that for. The fellow replied that there was some cider in that barrel a few days before, and he was trying to see if there was any then, but if there was he couldn't get at it. I told him that there had been a little bit of speech in me a while ago, but I believed I couldn't get it out. They all roared out in a mighty laugh, and I told some other anecdotes [stories] . . . and believing I had them in a first-rate way, I quit and got down, thanking the people for their attention. But I took care to remark that I was as dry as a powder horn,

192

and that I thought it was time for us all to wet our whistles a little; and so I put off to the liquor stand, and was followed by the greater part of the crowd.

I felt certain this was necessary, for I knowed my competitor could open government matters to them as easy as he pleased. . . .

But to cut this matter short, I was elected, doubling my competitor, and nine votes over.

1. *Is Crockett's election a good example of Jacksonian Democracy? In what way?*

Labor Force and Employment by Industry: 1820 to 1840

(In thousands of persons 10 years old and over)

LABOR FORCE

Year	Free	Slave	Total
1820	2,185	950	3,135
1830	3,020	1,180	4,200
1840	4,180	1,480	5,660

2. *Is politics today anything like politics in Davy Crockett's day? Can a candidate who knows very little about government win an election because of his or her pleasing personality? Explain.*

Sharpening Your Skills

This table shows how people earned their living in the years 1820 to 1840. Study it carefully. Then answer the questions.

1. Were there more farmers or factory workers in 1820? Were there more farmers or factory workers in 1840?

2. Between 1820 and 1840, which type of labor showed the greater increase — free labor or slave labor?

3. What job existed in 1840 that did not exist in 1820?

4. You can see from this table that the number of teachers doubled between 1820 and 1840. In the same period, the number of jobs in one industry increased *six times*. Which industry was that?

5. Can you tell from this table how many slaves worked in agriculture? (Explain your answer.)

EMPLOYMENT

Year	Agri-culture	Fishing	Mining	Cotton Textile Wage Earners	Primary Iron and Steel Wage Earners
1820	2,470	14	13	12	5
1830	2,965	15	22	55	20
1840	3,570	24	32	72	24

Year	Workers on Ocean Vessels	Railway Workers	Teachers	Domestics
1820	50	0	20	110
1830	70	0	30	160
1840	95	7	45	240

Book Two

Old Hate–
New Hope

2

1 FROM SEA TO SHINING SEA

Looking Ahead: New Land–New Troubles

Francis Parkman noticed a wooden board sticking out of the ground. There was nothing else in sight except miles and miles of grass and a bright blue sky. Parkman rode his horse up to the board. On it were written these words:

MARY ELLIS
DIED MAY 7TH, 1845
AGED TWO MONTHS

Parkman was not too surprised. The Bostonian had seen other graves along his route. A few years later, he was to write about them in a famous book describing his journey, *The Oregon Trail.* The graves were simple proof that a journey down the Oregon Trail could be a hard and dangerous trip.

This dirt trail went from Missouri all

"Go west, young man," editor Horace Greeley told Easterners in the 1850's. They learned what to expect in the West from paintings such as the one at left. William T. Ranney sketched it in Texas, painted it after returning home.

the way to Oregon Country and the Pacific Ocean. The first 700 miles (1,100 kilometers) led through land as flat as a football field and as broad as an ocean. Then the trail climbed slowly upward through the Rocky Mountains and down into Oregon.

In the 1840's, hundreds of families followed this trail in covered wagons. Oxen pulled them along through mud, over rivers, across mountains. The fastest the travelers could go was two miles (fewer than 3½ kilometers) an hour. They suffered from disease, hunger, and cold. Some died along the way. But this did not stop other families from heading west. Every year more wagons rumbled — mile after weary mile — over the Oregon Trail. Those who finally made it started farming in the good Oregon Country soil.

But did the soil of Oregon really belong to Americans? Or did it belong to the British? And what about other Western territories such as California and Texas? As late as 1835, none of these lands clearly belonged to the United States.

In 1835 the western border of the United States was the Rocky Mountains. On the Pacific Coast, the beaches and palm trees of California belonged to Mexico. The wide-open spaces of Texas also belonged to Mexico. And yet some U.S. pioneers believed this land should really belong to them. They thought they had a natural right to it. A newspaper article in 1845 put their thoughts into words. It said God had set aside America from the Atlantic to the Pacific for the United States. It said God's design was *manifest* (obvious). In fact, the article said the U.S. had a *Manifest Destiny* to expand to the Pacific Coast.

Within three years after this article appeared, the United States had done just that. Between 1845 and 1848, the U.S. gained almost a million square miles (almost 2.6 million square kilometers) of Western lands. The U.S. gained Texas in 1845. It gained Oregon a year later and California in 1848. How did this come about?

How Oregon became U.S. territory. Thousands of beavers once lived on the banks of Oregon's rivers. With the help of Indians, a British trading company set traps for the beavers. The British made a good profit killing the animals, skinning them, and selling the skins to British hat-makers. In the early 1800's, a New York fur merchant, John Jacob Astor, set up companies to

German-born Albert Bierstadt imagined the American West as a rugged Garden of Eden, a wilderness meant by God to be part of the U.S.

198

"What! You young Yankee-Noodle, strike your own father?" cries Britain to its offspring, America, in this cartoon. British cartoonist was making fun of U.S. claims in the West.

develop this trade. Before the 1830's, however, there were few Americans in Oregon. Then, beginning in 1836, U.S. farm families started arriving over the Oregon Trail. Soon there were more U.S. settlers than British trappers.

Both Britain and the U.S. had strong claims to Oregon. In the 1840's, some U.S. leaders demanded that the British give up their claim. The British refused. It looked as if Britain and the United States might fight another war. But in 1846 governments of the two nations signed a treaty. They divided the Oregon lands between them. The British took the northern half of the territory. The U.S. took the southern half. (The northern part of Oregon is now the Canadian province of British Columbia).

How Texas became U.S. territory. Before 1836 Texas was the northern part of Mexico. But since 1821 farmers from the U.S. had been

Three Ways West, 1840

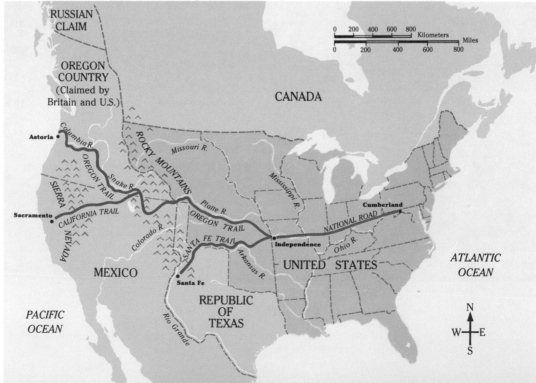

planting cotton and raising cattle in this foreign country. Soon there were more U.S. citizens than Mexicans living in Texas. The Mexican government passed laws against these settlers from the U.S. In 1836 the settlers revolted. They set up their own government.

For almost 10 years, they had a *republic* (democratic nation) of their own. Meanwhile, in the United States, people wondered what they should do about Texas. Should they make it part of the United States? Or should they let Texas remain an independent nation? After several years of bitter argument, the question was finally settled in 1845. Texas was *annexed* (added to the U.S.) by an act of Congress.

How California became U.S. territory. In California in 1845, few people spoke English. Mexican ranchers and priests controlled the country. The priests converted many Indian people to Christianity. They also made Indians do most of the work on huge, church-run farms. Most Mexicans thought the rocky, snow-capped Sierra Nevada Mountains would keep U.S. settlers out of their country. But in the 1830's, daring trappers from the U.S. crossed the mountains and settled in California. The Mexican government was far away. It had a hard time enforcing its laws.

In 1846 Mexico and the United States quarreled over the southern boundary of Texas. The quarrel led to war. News of the war touched off a revolt of U.S. settlers in California. These settlers declared their independence from the Mexican government. They made their own flag. In the center of the flag was a cutout of a brown grizzly bear.

Meanwhile, a U.S. army marched through Texas and invaded Mexico. Another U.S. army landed at Veracruz (ver-uh-KROOS) on the Gulf of Mexico. It fought its way to Mexico City, the Mexican capital. After two years of battles, the Mexican government surrendered in 1848. In the treaty of peace, all of California and much of the present Southwest were given to the United States for 15 million dollars.

By war and by treaty, the United States had gained Oregon and California on the Pacific Coast. By war and by treaty, it had gained Texas, Utah, Nevada, and much of the Southwest. It had pushed westward as far as the Pacific. In 1848 the nation stretched from ocean to ocean — "from sea to shining sea."

Texas entered the Union as a state. But Texas was an exception. In the other lands, settlers first organized *territories*. Then the territories applied for admission to the Union as *states*.

When California tried to become a state, a great question arose. Should slavery be allowed there? Southerners said that it should be allowed. Northerners said that it should not be allowed. The problem threatened to tear the nation apart.

Then a powerful old Senator, Henry Clay, came up with some ideas to settle the quarrel. After long and fierce debates, his ideas were passed into law. They are known as the *Compromise of 1850*. One law made California a new state — a *free* state where slavery was outlawed. Another law, the *Fugitive Slave Act,* was supposed to help slaveowners in the South. Would Henry Clay's compromise really work? Would it settle the question of slavery and hold the country together? Only time would tell. *201*

Chapter 1

A Soldier and a Priest

Father Serra wiped the sweat from his brow. The waters of San Diego harbor sparkled behind him. At the priest's side stood a tired and unhappy soldier, Gaspar de Portolá (por-toh-LAH). Sadly the two Spaniards inspected the weary men who had survived the long journey from Mexico.

Two months earlier they had left the Mexican town of La Paz. With 219 men they had sailed to what is present-day California. What a terrible journey it had been! One of their three ships had been lost at sea. Almost the entire crew of

Father Serra

another ship had fallen ill and died. Now, in San Diego harbor, Junípero Serra (hoo-NEE-pay-roh SAY-rah) and Portolá were left with little more than a hundred men. Most of the survivors were sick and weak from the journey.

Should they turn back? Should they return to the thriving Spanish colonies of Mexico? No, the priest and the soldier were determined to stay. They had traveled to the shores of San Diego in this year of 1769 with a goal. They wanted to establish Spanish settlements throughout California. They wanted to strengthen Spain's holdings in the New World. And strengthen them they would.

To do this, they would attempt to build in California three kinds of Spanish settlements: *missions, presidios* (pray-SEED-yohs), and *pueblos.*

Missions housed Roman Catholic priests such as Father Serra. Priests used the missions to try to convert Indians to Christianity.

Presidios were military forts. They protected the Spanish from attacks by Indians and Spain's European rivals.

Pueblos were farming villages where crops and livestock were raised.

The priest and the soldier dreamed about how they could change California. Father Serra dreamed about a string of missions stretching from San Diego northward through California. Portolá had heard the Bay of Monterey described by an earlier explorer. Now he hoped to find it.

The dreams of these two men were much like the dreams of other Spaniards before them. For more than 250 years, Spanish explorers, missionaries, and farmers had been spreading out all over South and Central America. The Spanish colonies in the New World were now 20 times larger than Spain itself.

North of these colonies lay lands that later became the Southwestern U.S. The Spanish had first explored these lands in 1540. The man who had led this exploration was Francisco Vasquez de Coronado (fran-SEES-koh VAHS-kays day koh-roh-NAH-doh). Coronado had hoped to find seven cities built of gold. Instead he had found only small Indian villages and vast stretches of desert. Coronado had been bitterly disappointed.

Now, more than 200 years later, the priest and the soldier were also disappointed. The land they found in San

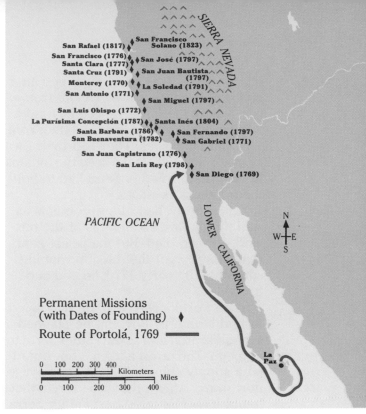

A French traveler, possibly a fur-trapper, painted this California Indian about 1787, as Spanish began to settle the West.

California Missions

Diego gave no promise of wealth or splendor. The Indians were suspicious of them. But nothing could stop the two men from pursuing their dreams. Father Serra was lame in one leg. This did not stop him either.

First settlement. The two men hardly paused to catch their breath. Portolá constructed a *presidio* in San Diego within two weeks. Then he began his journey northward in search of Monterey Bay. Those men who stayed behind with Father Serra put up a crude, brushwood shelter. This small shelter, built in a few days, became the first Roman Catholic mission in California.

In this church, Father Serra tried to convert the Indians to Christianity. But the Indians resented his attempts to   203 change their lives. After all, they had a civilization of their own. (A *civilization* is a way of life far advanced beyond a savage level.) The Indians had their own arts and languages. They had their own customs and beliefs. To keep the Indians in his mission, Father Serra had to hold them almost as slaves.

Father Serra had other problems as well. In his first six months at the mission, 19 men died. But the priest kept struggling to get the mission running smoothly. By early 1770, he had succeeded.

Then Portolá returned. He had failed to find Monterey Bay. But he planned a second search and asked Father Serra to join him. The priest agreed. They boarded a supply ship and began the voyage northward. After a month's search, they found it — Monterey Bay! Father Serra, Portolá, and their followers held a joyous celebration. They raised the Spanish flag over the site of another settlement. Soon a mission and a *presidio* were constructed from timbers gathered near the harbor.

Later settlements. Portolá had accomplished his goal. He bade farewell to Father Serra and returned to Mexico. The priest's work, however, was far from finished. There were other missions to be built along the California coast. In 14 years, he guided the building of seven of them. Each mission was only about one day's travel from the next.

Within the missions, priests did more than teach Christianity. They also taught Indians how to grow new crops and raise livestock. Many crops were introduced to the American Southwest — rice, wheat, citrus fruits, and grapes. The Spanish also imported the first livestock

in this region. Cattle ranches began to appear, stocked with cattle from Mexico. The first American cowboys were Spaniards. Spanish words became part of American speech.

In 1784 Father Serra died at his mission in Monterey. Indians came to his funeral to mourn his death. They now thought of him as their friend. California had changed because of this Spanish priest. Some parts of the California wilderness had been transformed. Livestock in the missions numbered more than 30,000.

Driving through California today, the traveler is often reminded of the state's Spanish heritage. Many of the houses have sloping red tile roofs and stucco walls like early Spanish houses. Many California cities have Spanish names. These signs of Spanish heritage show the power of a dream held long ago by a soldier and a priest.

A Second Look. . . .

1. *What were some of the things Father Serra tried to achieve in California? Why?*

2. *Do you think that the Spanish helped to enrich the lives of the Indian people of California? Why or why not? Did the Spanish give the Indians any reason to resent them? If so, how?*

3. *Using an encyclopedia, look up the history of one of three major California cities. They are San Diego, Los Angeles, and San Francisco. Write a research report on when and how the city was founded. Indicate the city's location and explain how this location has affected its growth. Also list the city's largest ethnic minorities. Explain how at least one of these groups happened to settle there.*

Chapter 2

Vaqueros

The long, flat plains of New Mexico lie silent in the sunset. Somewhere far away a lone coyote wails into the evening shadows. For a long moment, all seems empty and calm. Then, as the sun sinks down into the distance, the earth begins to tremble.

A low rumbling sound comes out of the west. Slowly it grows louder. A cloud of dust rises to the graying sky. The rumble becomes a roar. The earth seems to shake with excitement. Hoofbeats! The plains rock with the pounding of hundreds of hooves.

A herd of wild cattle thunders across the land. Their long horns are tossing. Their feet trample every living thing on the ground. Then, as they pass, the roar returns to a rumble. Very soon the

plains are silent once more, and dark.

These dry plains rumbled often to the hoofbeats of great cattle herds. This was in the 1700's, when the first cowboys rode. The cattle herds they tended had first been brought to North America by

This proud vaquero rode the ranges of California before 1860. He was drawn by James Walker, who served with the U.S. Army in the 1840's.

A favorite vaquero sport was catching bears and watching them fight bulls. Painting is by James Walker.

the Spanish. The cowboys roped and branded the cattle while the animals were still wild. These cowboys rode the ranges of Texas and New Mexico long before any settlers from the U.S. moved into these lands.

Who were these first cowboys? They were Mexican Indians. They were the men who worked the ranches of Spanish missions. Many of the missions were both churches and forts. These men looked upon their cattle as a way of supporting themselves.

The Indians did not become cowboys by choice. In Mexico, their native land, they had been conquered by the Spanish. Then they were brought by force to what is now the Southwestern

U.S. Here, at the missions, they were taught how to ride and to rope. Many of the Indians had been branded on the cheek with the letter "G" — for *guerra* (GARE-uh), the Spanish word for war. It is a fact that many of these cowboys wore brands before their cattle did.

Proud herdsmen. But these Mexicans became excellent cowboys. They took great pride in their work. And they took pride in the special outfits they wore. Around their heads they wrapped bright kerchiefs. They wore wide-brimmed hats to protect themselves against sun and rain. Their knee-length pants buttoned on the sides and folded into buckskin shoes. Each man had a long knife fastened to his right leg. He also wore great slabs of cowhide, called *chaparreras*. These covered his legs when he rode through heavy brush.

He called himself *vaquero* (vah-CAY-roh) — the cowboy, or mounted herdsman. He carried no gun. His main weapon and tool was the *lariat* (LAR-ee-ut), a strong rawhide rope. Sometimes it was 110 feet (33 meters) long. With it he could bring a wild bull to the ground — or a man, if necessary.

In the time of the vaquero, cattle were not herded to market. When it came time to take hides, the vaqueros held large-scale killings, called *matanzas* (mah-TAHN-sahs). They drove the cattle to the *matanza* grounds, roped them down with their lariats, and killed them with lances.

Their work was hard. So was their fun. A favorite sport was *corrida de toro* (koh-REE-dah day TOE-roh). Inside a fenced area, they let loose a live bull. On horseback, the vaqueros waved capes at him. The bull charged. On foot, the vaqueros chased him. The aim? To grab hold of his tail, twist it, and dump the big bull to the ground.

Vanishing breed. The vaquero way of life came to an end in the 1800's. In 1821 Mexico threw off Spanish rule and became independent. The same year, the Mexican government opened the vast mission lands to settlers. Then the vaqueros were let go from the missions' control. They were free men.

But the vaqueros didn't have much time to know freedom. More and more settlers from the U.S. began moving into the cattle lands. These settlers divided the land into ranches of their own. Soon the vaquero had less room to ride. The land was no longer his.

Today great highways wind where cattle trails used to be. Large cities stand where many of the missions once ruled. The plains still roll out toward the horizon, flat and silent. But wild herds of cattle thunder across these lands no more. And the men who spent their days following the herds under the hot western sun have vanished. They live now in our legends of the West — legends that endure in the movies and on television.

Some five to seven million Spanish-speaking Americans live in the Southwest today. Many of them can trace their families back to the times when Mexico ruled this land. Some have proud vaquero blood. Most have come from Mexico more recently. All of these Americans look back with pride on the days when the vaqueros rode.

A Second Look. . . .

1. *Where did the vaqueros ride in the year 1800? For whom did they work? How did settlers from the U.S. change the vaqueros' way of life?*

2. *Nowadays TV and the movies usually show cowboys as adventurous people. Do the vaqueros seem adventurous to you? How did their way of life differ from the lives most Americans live today? If you had lived in 1800, would you have wanted to be a vaquero? Why or why not?*

3. *The chapter describes the clothing and equipment worn by the vaqueros. How did this clothing and equipment fit the vaqueros' surroundings? Review the chapter to answer this question. Then select one present-day type of work. Write a paragraph describing how people in such jobs dress for the kind of work they do.*

207

Mexican soldiers open fire on the Alamo. Woodcut of the scene is from Davy Crockett's Almanac, *1837.*

Chapter 3

The Alamo

"Within a very few days, we will all be dead. We must sell our lives as dearly as possible. For myself, I will fight as long as there is breath in my body."

These words were spoken by Colonel William B. Travis. Listening to him were 187 Texans. They were defending the Alamo, a long-unused Spanish mission in San Antonio, Texas. Outside the walls of the Alamo, completely surrounding them, was a Mexican army of 3,000 men.

The leader of this army was the Mexican dictator, General Antonio López de Santa Anna. Not far away, from the top of the main church in San Antonio, a red flag was flying. The red flag meant "no quarter" — Santa Anna would take no prisoners. The date was March 5, 1836.

What had brought Santa Anna to the Alamo? He had come to put down a revolt. U.S. settlers in Texas had made trouble for the Mexican government for years. But now they had gone too far. On March 2, they had declared Texas independent of Mexico.

This was an outrage to the Mexicans. They had invited many of these people from the U.S. to settle in their country. They thought U.S. settlers would be thankful for the lands Mexico had given them. They thought the settlers would build up the almost empty country and become loyal Mexican citizens.

Mexico had asked for Roman Catholic settlers. But most of those who came from the U.S. were Protestants. Mexico did not allow slavery. Many of the U.S. settlers owned slaves. Some of the U.S. settlers were outlaws.

Cracking down. Before long, Mexico began passing laws against the settlers. One law said that no more slaves could come in. Another said that no more settlers could enter from the U.S. Other laws began to take back some of the lands the settlers had been given. Then Santa Anna came to power in 1834. He did not trust anyone from the U.S. And U.S. settlers did not trust him. Santa Anna sent troops into Texas to keep control of things. Soon after, fighting broke out.

Santa Anna decided to teach the settlers a lesson. He marched into Texas with a large army. He and his troops reached San Antonio in February 1836. Most of the rebels fled. But one small band withdrew to the Alamo. With these men were several friendly Mexicans. Some were women and children.

The Alamo was a strong fort, as well as a mission. Though it was a roofless ruin, its walls were 10 feet (three meters) high and three feet (one meter) thick. It had about 20 cannons. Besides Colonel Travis, the Texans were led by Jim Bowie (BOO-ee), inventor of the bowie knife used for hunting. Another leader was Davy Crockett, the former U.S. Congressman from Tennessee.

Holding out. For several days, Mexican cannons ripped the walls of the Alamo. Then, at five o'clock on the morning of March 6, a bugle call rang out. Thousands of Mexican soldiers began charging toward the Alamo's walls. The Texans grabbed their guns.

"Come on, let's give it to them!" Travis shouted. Then the cannons of the Alamo blazed. One Mexican soldier saw 40 of his comrades fall dead or wounded around him. Others tumbled off ladders as they tried to climb the walls. Finally, the Mexicans fell back. A second attack was also driven back by deadly fire.

Antonio López de Santa Anna in 1833.

209

Texas Goes to War, 1836

On the map:

UNITED STATES

MEXICO

OREGON COUNTRY

AREA DISPUTED BY TEXAS AND MEXICO (1836-1845)

REPUBLIC OF TEXAS (1836-1845)

THE ALAMO

San Antonio

Laredo   Corpus Christi

San Jacinto

Galveston

GULF OF MEXICO

GULF OF CALIFORNIA

Rio Grande

Nueces R.

Red River

Arkansas R.

Sabine R.

N W E S

— — — Santa Anna's Army (1836)

——— Texas Army (1836)

0 100 200 300 Kilometers
0 100 200 300 Miles

Santa Anna's losses had been terrible. But he ordered a third charge. This time some Mexicans were able to get over the north wall. Then Colonel Travis slumped over a cannon, a bullet through his forehead. Other Mexicans climbed over the south wall and opened the gate. Mexicans poured into the Alamo.

Davy Crockett fought as long as he could stand. Finally he fell, riddled by bullets. The defenders who were left ran inside a building. There they made a last stand. All were finally killed.

In the Alamo's chapel, Jim Bowie lay sick on a cot. Women and children huddled around him. When the Mexicans rushed in, Bowie was waiting. He fired two pistols until he too was killed by bullets and bayonets. Before long, all the defenders in the chapel were slain. Only a few women and children survived.

Santa Anna's victory had cost him 1,500 dead and wounded. But for Texans the Battle of the Alamo stood as the highest example of bravery and heroism.

Fighting back. A month later, at the Battle of San Jacinto (san hah-SEEN-toh), another Texas army met Santa Anna. With shouts of "Remember the Alamo!" this army smashed the Mexican forces and captured Santa Anna himself. Then the prisoner signed a treaty giving Texas its freedom.

Texas was now an independent republic. Yet Santa Anna and the Mexican government could not accept this fact. Mexican maps still showed Texas as a part of Mexico.

The Texas leaders wanted the United States to let Texas into the Union as a state. But Texas was kept waiting for a long time, as we shall see.

A Second Look. . . .

1. *Why were Mexicans outraged by U.S. settlers in Texas? Why did the settlers revolt against the Mexican government?*

2. *Why did Texans regard those killed at the Alamo as heroes? Do you suppose Mexicans thought of them in the same way? Does the defense of the Alamo seem courageous to you? Why or why not? How do you suppose deaths in this battle affected the Texans' will to fight?*

3. *Pretend that you are Colonel Travis at the Alamo. You and your small band are surrounded by Santa Anna's army. There is no hope of escape. Now you must stir your comrades to fight to the death to defend the mission. Deliver a three-minute speech giving them courage to go on.*

Chapter 4

War with Mexico

A Mexican army of 15,000 men was marching north. Its aim: to destroy a much smaller U.S. army at a mountain pass in Mexico. Its leader: Santa Anna, the man who had captured the Alamo.

It was February 1847, more than a year after Texas had become a state. The United States and Mexico were at war. How did it come about?

Texans had gained independence from Mexico in 1836. They had set up their own nation, nicknamed the "Lone Star Republic," the same year. But the future of the republic had never looked very certain. For one thing, Mexico had refused to accept the loss of Texas. For another, many Texans had hoped that their republic would soon become one of the United States.

Their hope had been shared by their president, Sam Houston. But Congress had kept Houston waiting for nine long years. Why? Part of the trouble was slavery. Many Texans, including Houston, owned slaves. If Texas were added to the U.S., slavery would spread to the Southwest. Many white Southerners hoped that this would happen. But Northerners did not want another slave state. Leaders of Congress were afraid of making Northern voters angry. They were also afraid of starting war with Mexico. So they left Texas to struggle on its own.

In 1844 a U.S. Presidential election took place. Democrats demanded that Texas be admitted to the Union as a state. The Democratic candidate, James K. Polk, won the election. His victory set events in motion. The outgoing Whig President, John Tyler, now persuaded Congress to allow Texas to join the Union.

Polk's demands. Once Polk took office, he made it clear he wanted more than Texas. He hoped Mexico would turn over the entire area from Texas to the Pacific Ocean. This area included what are now the states of New Mexico, Arizona, Nevada, Utah, and California. In November 1845 Polk sent a representative to discuss this with Mexican lead-

Sam Houston, shown as governor of Texas, 1861.

212

ers. The following month, Texas became the Union's 28th state. At this point, Mexico broke off all ties with the U.S. Any hope of obtaining more land from Mexico now seemed at an end.

Polk became impatient. General Zachary Taylor had already assembled an army at Corpus Christi. In January 1846 Polk ordered this army to march to the banks of the Rio Grande. The Rio Grande, Texans said, was their border with Mexico. But the Mexicans claimed the Rio Grande was well inside the Mexican border. Soon Mexican and U.S. troops were fighting. On May 13, 1846, the United States declared war.

Taylor's march. The U.S. carried the war to the heart of Mexico. Taylor and his men captured Monterrey, Mexico, in September 1846. The next February, Santa Anna sent Mexican forces to check Taylor at Buena Vista (BWAY-nuh VEES-tuh; beautiful view). Taylor had an army of fewer than 5,000 men. Most of them were untrained volunteers. Santa Anna decided to attack. Taylor, called "Old Rough and Ready" by his men, welcomed another fight. He placed his men in position at a mountain pass. There they would have an edge over Santa Anna's forces.

On February 22 — George Washington's birthday — Santa Anna attacked at Buena Vista. All that day, U.S. riflemen and cannons beat back the Mexicans. As they fired, bands played "Hail, Columbia," and men shouted,

With only 5,000 troops, General Zachary Taylor defeated a Mexican army of 20,000 at Buena Vista in 1847. At left, Taylor rides his horse, Old Whitey, into battle. The next year, he ran for President as a Whig and won the election.

"Honor to Washington!" When darkness came, the fighting stopped. Both armies shivered through a night of rain.

The next day, Santa Anna lined up his troops for an all-out attack. Mexican bands played sacred music. The Mexican soldiers and horsemen wore uniforms with bright colors — red, green, yellow, crimson, and blue. Some carried silk banners and long, handsome feathers. As a battle cry, they shouted, "Viva!" (long life!) to their leaders. They made a wonderful sight as they marched proudly to their positions. Some of the U.S. soldiers were a little scared of them.

Soon the battle was on. The Mexicans hit hard and fought bravely, but U.S. troops drove them back. Late in the afternoon, another Mexican force opened a powerful attack. Bullets could not stop it. Many Mexicans fell. But others swept forward, shouting, "Viva! Viva!"

General Taylor calmly watched the fighting from the saddle of his horse. One bullet ripped through the front of his coat. Another tore his left sleeve. Near him cannons were firing. "Double your shot!" Taylor shouted to his men.

The cannons blasted the Mexicans at short range. Soon Santa Anna's men could stand the pounding no longer. They fell back into the mountains, and the firing stopped. It was a close battle, but the Mexicans had lost twice as many men as the U.S.

Scott's truce. On September 14, 1847, U.S. troops under General Winfield Scott entered Mexico City. Scott arranged a truce with Santa Anna. Four months later, Mexican and U.S. agents met in the village of Guadalupe Hidalgo (gwah-duh-LOO-pay ee-DAL-goh) near Mexico City. The Mexican agents signed a peace treaty with the United States government.

By the Treaty of Guadalupe Hidalgo, Mexico signed over to the U.S. a huge block of land. It came to be known as the *Mexican Cession*. It included all of what are today the states of California, Nevada, and Utah. It also included parts of Arizona, New Mexico, Colorado, and Wyoming. Mexico agreed that the Rio Grande would be the boundary of Texas. In return for all this land, the United States paid Mexico 15 million dollars. The U.S. also agreed to pay all the money that Texas citizens said Mexicans owed them.

Five years later the United States paid Mexico 10 million dollars for another piece of land. This was the *Gadsden Purchase*, named after the U. S. agent who arranged the sale. The Gadsden Purchase was much smaller than the Mexican Cession. But it finally settled the boundary between the two coun-

tries. Today the land obtained in the Gadsden Purchase makes up the southern parts of Arizona and New Mexico.

A Second Look. . . .

1. *What caused the United States to go to war with Mexico in 1846? What did Mexico gain from the war? What did the U.S. gain?*

2. *What were Mexicans defending in their war with the U.S.? Did they have good reason to fight? Why or why not? Did President Polk have good reason to send U.S. troops across the Rio Grande? If so, what was it?*

3. *The U.S. obtained land in the Southwest in four separate parcels. Three are mentioned in this chapter. Consult the map which accompanies the chapter. Use it to trace an outline of the area. Then shade in the four different parcels of land and identify them. Under each label, identify the year the land became a U.S. state or territory.*

U.S. Territorial Gains, 1848-1853

214

Clipper-ship owners advertised trips to California on cards such as this. But this card is not really serious. It is making fun of the Gold Rush. What won't money-crazed people do to get at the gold? The cartoonist says some will do almost anything — even fly a rocket or take a ride in a balloon.

Chapter 5

Gold! Gold!

James Marshall was shaking all over with excitement. He was dripping wet. He had just ridden through the rain to John Sutter's house in California. Sutter had sent Marshall to build a sawmill on his large property. Now Marshall wanted to see Sutter — alone. He made Sutter lock the door of his room.

Inside, Marshall pulled a bit of cloth out of his pocket. In it were small bits of yellow metal. Marshall had found them in the sawmill stream on January 24, 1848. "It looks like gold," Sutter said. "Let's test it." The tests proved the yellow metal was really gold. And, Marshall said, there was a great deal more where it came from.

At first Sutter tried to keep the news a secret. He did not want groups of prospectors (people who looked for gold) on his property. But a storekeeper found out about the gold. He saw a chance to make money selling supplies to gold miners. In May, he went to San Francisco with a bottle of gold dust. He went around shouting, "Gold! Gold! Gold from Sutter's Mill!"

Soon San Francisco was burning with gold fever. Men dropped everything they were doing and rushed to Sutter's Mill, about 100 miles (160 kilometers) northeast of San Francisco. Women and children joined them. In a few days, San Francisco became a ghost town. The fever spread to other California towns and to Mexico. The Gold Rush had begun.

By September the news reached the Midwest and the East Coast. By the end of the year, it reached across to Europe. Tens of thousands of people from many distant places set out for California to strike it rich.

Routes to the West. In 1849 there were three ways to get to California from the eastern U.S. All of them were dangerous.

One way was to sail from the Atlantic Coast, around South America, and north to San Francisco. This trip took six to eight months. Usually the ships were crowded and the food was bad. Many ships were rotten and leaky. Some of them sank during storms.

Another way was the "short cut" across Panama. The traveler went by ship to the Atlantic Coast of Panama. Then he or she crossed by mule over 75 miles (120 kilometers) of steaming jungle to the Pacific Coast. Some travelers were left stranded by mule drivers. Others were victims of poor food, bad water, or disease. Once travelers reached the Pacific, they had to wait for weeks or months for a ship to California.

The third way was by wagon train on overland trails. This way, across snowy mountains and sizzling deserts, was not much easier. Some travelers died of disease and were buried along the way. Wagons broke down, and animals died of hunger and thirst in the desert. Along the trails lay the bodies of mules, horses, and oxen.

What happened when the miners reached California? They had to work harder than ever before. Gold-mining was backbreaking work. The miner had

Gold-seekers used troughs called Long Toms *(below). Dirt was placed in the trough, and water was run through it. Loose dirt floated off with the water. Gold settled to the bottom of the trough.*

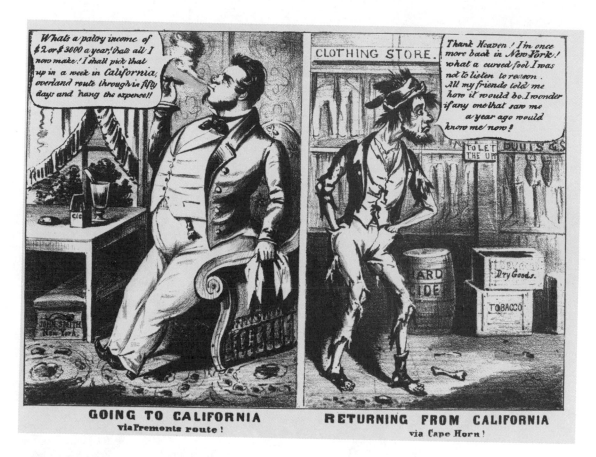

GOING TO CALIFORNIA
via Fremonts route!

RETURNING FROM CALIFORNIA
via Cape Horn!

to shovel dirt from streams all day and then wash it out in tin pans. Sometimes he got only an ounce or two of gold. A few men did strike it rich. Some men dug as much as $1,500 worth of gold in a single day. But most just broke even, or lost money.

Forty-niners. In 1849 more than 50,000 people (called *forty-niners*) rushed to California. People kept coming in 1850 too. Most were citizens of the United States. But several thousand were Mexicans, and a few thousand more came from South America. In time, news of the Gold Rush even reached China. The number of Chinese coming to

Easterners headed for California with shiny shovels and pans (below). Many who expected to make a fortune were as disappointed as the ragged figure in the cartoon above.

217

America took a sudden jump. Before 1850 fewer than 1,000 Chinese had arrived in America. Then, in 1852 alone, more than 18,000 Chinese entered California.

Not all the forty-niners came to mine for gold. Some of the most successful came with other ideas in mind. One, for example, was a German Jewish merchant named Levi Strauss. Strauss arrived in San Francisco with large rolls of canvas. He hoped to sell the canvas to miners for use in making tents. But he quickly learned that many miners needed work pants most of all. So he began making pants out of the canvas. The pants were warm, rugged, and perfect for hard work. Strauss called them "Levi's." Soon he was selling as many of them as he could produce.

Rattlesnake Diggings. By this time, northern California was swarming with miners. They gave strange names to their camps. They called one place Hangtown. A second was named Rattlesnake Diggings. The forty-niners wore broad-brimmed hats, red shirts, and boots up to their knees. Many of them slept with weapons at their sides. They did not have police to protect them from robbers or murderers. Outside of San Francisco, there was not yet much local government of any kind.

The fact was that California's future was still hanging in the balance. During the war with Mexico, a U.S. soldier, John C. Frémont, had led a revolt of American settlers in California. They had fought Mexican troops — and won. After the Treaty of Guadalupe Hidalgo, California stayed in the hands of the U.S. But the nation's lawmakers could not decide what to do with the territory. Their problem was a hard one to solve.

The root of the problem was slavery. The question was whether or not slave-owners from the South should be allowed to bring their slaves to California. Most Northerners believed that making more slave states would be wrong. Most Southern leaders thought that owning slaves was a person's natural right. The two groups argued bitterly. They called each other names. Some Southerners threatened to leave the Union if the issue was not decided in their favor.

California could not be a state until this quarrel was settled. But some Americans said that the problem could not be settled without violence and war. Then Henry Clay, a U.S. Senator from Kentucky, stepped forward with proposals to end the argument. Clay's plan set the stage for one of the most dramatic debates ever to take place in the U.S. Congress.

A Second Look. . . .

1. *Suppose a young person from Philadelphia wanted to go to California in 1849. What three routes could he or she have taken to get there? What were the risks involved?*

2. *Many forty-niners suffered hardships while trying to get rich. Do people today still do so? If so, how? Is wealth worth such hardships? Why or why not?*

3. *Imagine that a friend of yours found gold 50 miles (80 kilometers) from your home. Write a short essay describing what you think might happen.*

Artist Albertus Browere, himself a prospector, painted this bearded forty-niner, decked out in a red shirt, the "uniform" of his trade.

219

Chapter 6

A Plan To Save the Union

Henry Clay popped a peppermint candy into his mouth. He was sitting at his desk in the United States Senate. Clay looked around the room. He noticed an old friend with bushy gray hair. This man was so weak he could hardly walk. Clay knew that his friend was dying. Yet the man still had great political power. He was Senator John C. Calhoun from South Carolina.

Clay noticed another Senator walk into the room. It was his old friend from Massachusetts, Daniel Webster. What a face Webster had! His brows were shaggy and black. His eyes were set deep in their sockets. His balding forehead seemed to be twice the size of a normal person's. Webster was the greatest speech-maker in American history — even greater than Clay himself. Friends of the Massachusetts Senator called him the "godlike Daniel."

Clay had known Calhoun and Webster for many years. All three remembered the days, back in 1814, when the British had set fire to the Capitol. They had been young men then with high ambitions. Each had hoped to be President. Each had been disappointed. Now all three had grown old.

Debate over slavery involved three famed U.S. Senators: (left to right) Kentucky's Henry Clay, Massachusetts' Daniel Webster, and South Carolina's John C. Calhoun.

But Henry Clay still had one ambition. He wanted to save the Union from breaking up over slavery. Clay had helped to save the Union once before. That was 30 years ago, in 1820. The question then was what should happen to Missouri. Should slaves be allowed there or not?

Missouri Compromise. Northerners and Southerners had argued fiercely about it. Clay and some other U.S. Senators had finally worked out a compromise plan. They had suggested that slaves be allowed in the new state of Missouri. At the same time, the Senators had said, Maine should enter the Union as a free state. Then the number of slave states and the number of free states would still be exactly the

same. The North and the South would still have about equal power. And what about new Western states that might be added after 1820? The Senators had pointed to a line on the map running through the territory of the Louisiana Purchase.

This line ran along the parallel 36° 30′, or 36 degrees, 30 minutes. (A *parallel* is an imaginary line, a circle on the world globe, which runs in the same direction as the Equator.) The Senators had chosen the 36° 30′ line because it marked the southern border of Missouri. They had proposed that slavery be made illegal north of this line, except in Missouri, where it would be permitted. Their proposal would allow slavery south of this line. The idea passed the House and the Senate. It was known as the *Missouri Compromise.* For a while, it ended the angry talk about slavery.

California's constitution. But now the year was 1850. California was asking to come into the Union as a new state. Its constitution outlawed slavery.

California would not allow slavery anywhere in its borders — not even south of the 36° 30′ parallel. This angered white Southerners. They said the North was trying to cheat them. The North was claiming for itself all the lands won in the Mexican War. Didn't Southerners have as much right to this land as Northerners? The South needed to grow westward, many Southerners believed. Otherwise it would die.

At least this is the way Southern leaders talked. They said they would fight for their rights. And what if they lost the fight over California? Then, they warned, they might secede from (leave) the United States. The South might become a separate country.

Henry Clay wanted to prevent this. Part of his plan, he hoped, would satisfy the North. The other part, he hoped, would satisfy the South. On February 5, 1850, the old Senator from Kentucky climbed the steps of the Capitol building. He had come to make the most important speech of his life.

Missouri Compromise of 1820

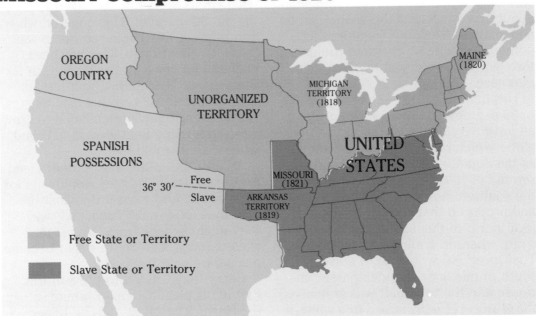

OREGON COUNTRY

SPANISH POSSESSIONS

UNORGANIZED TERRITORY

MICHIGAN TERRITORY (1818)

MAINE (1820)

UNITED STATES

MISSOURI (1821)

36° 30' — Free / Slave

ARKANSAS TERRITORY (1819)

Free State or Territory

Slave State or Territory

Clay's compromise plan. Clay spoke for hours about his ideas. First, he said, California should be admitted to the Union as a free state. Second, Utah, Nevada, and the other territories obtained in the Mexican Cession could be either slave or free. The question there, he said, should be decided by a vote of the settlers themselves. Third, Northerners should help the South to "crack down" on the problem of runaway slaves. A federal law should punish more strictly any Northerner who helped a slave gain freedom. Fourth, the slave *trade* in Washington, D.C., should be stopped. (Slave *ownership* in the district would not be affected.)

This was Clay's plan. In his speech, he defended the plan with all his strength.

Some Senators applauded the plan. But the dying Senator, John C. Calhoun, attacked it. He thought it was unfair to the South. Calhoun was too weak even to read his own speech about Clay's plan. Another Southern Senator had to read it for him. It explained why the South could not compromise. It said: "The South asks for justice, simple justice, and less it should not take." The sick man's eyes blazed as his speech ended.

A few days later, people again crowded into the Senate balcony. They had come to hear the "godlike Daniel." They were thrilled by Webster's booming voice. Like Clay, Webster wanted to save the Union with his speech. He told his audience he wished to speak "not as a Northern man, but as an American." For three hours, he gave reasons why the Senate should vote for Clay's plan.

While Webster spoke, a feeble old man came into the room and slumped into an armchair. Webster did not notice him. Twice the speaker mentioned Calhoun. He wished, he said, that the great Southern Senator were well enough to be present. Slowly, painfully, the old man rose from his chair. He called to Webster in a hollow voice: "The Senator from South Carolina is in his seat." Webster turned. His eyes filled with tears. He stretched out his arms and bowed to Calhoun.

The old Southerner lived only three weeks longer. Clay and Webster attended his funeral. They helped to carry Calhoun's coffin to the grave.

Heated debate. What happened to Clay's compromise plan? People quarreled over it for months. Northerners accused Webster of being a traitor. They hated the part of Clay's plan punishing Northerners for helping runaway slaves. How could Webster defend such a plan? they asked. Many people in both the North and the South attacked Clay's plan. But finally, in September 1850, Congress voted the plan into law. The law concerning runaway slaves was called the *Fugitive Slave Act*. The entire plan became known as the *Compromise of 1850*.

For the moment, Henry Clay had saved the Union from breaking up. California now joined the Union as the 31st state. But strong feelings about slavery in the territories lingered. They were part of a larger question about slavery itself.

Slavery and what do to about it worried Americans throughout the 1850's. In the end, the problem led to the worst

Compromise of 1850

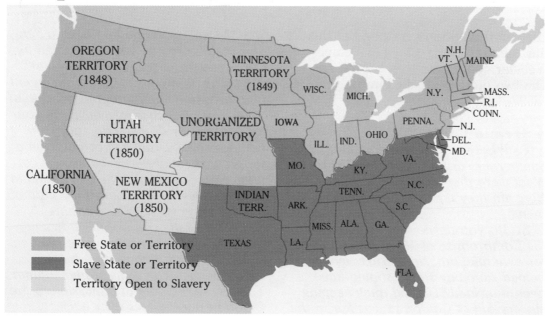

Free State or Territory

Slave State or Territory

Territory Open to Slavery

San Franciscans celebrated on October 29, 1850, when California joined the Union. But the entry had rekindled a bitter debate over slavery. A few years later, the debate would tear the Union apart.

crisis in the nation's history. But this time neither Henry Clay nor Daniel Webster could help to solve the crisis. The two old friends died in the year 1852.

A Second Look. . . .

1. *What were Northerners and Southerners arguing about in 1820? What were they arguing about in 1850? How did they try to settle each argument?*

2. *Do you agree with every part of the Compromise of 1850? Do you think, for example, that Northerners who helped runaway slaves should have been punished? Do you think keeping slavery out of California was fair to the South? Explain. If you had been a Senator in 1850, would you have voted for Clay's compromise? Why or why not?*

3. *The admission of California meant that the Union had more free states than slave states. Which were which? Find out for yourself by drawing up your own balance sheet. Draw two columns on a separate sheet of paper. Label one column "Free States" and the other column "Slave States." Then consult the map of the Compromise of 1850 with this chapter and the chart of the states at the back of this book. List all of the states admitted to the Union before 1850. Put each state in its proper column. Then write the date of admission to the Union in parentheses after each.*

Looking Back: From Sea to Shining Sea

A	B	C	D	E	
January 1, 1830	January 1, 1835	January 1, 1840	January 1, 1845	January 1, 1850	January 1, 1855

Putting Events in Order

Chapters One through Six have described how Texas, Oregon, California, and other areas became part of the United States. Ten events of this period are listed here. Your job is to match each event to the correct period shown on the timeline above. On a piece of paper, number from **1** to **10**. After each number, write the letter of the period within which the event occurred.

1. Discovery of gold touches off a rush to California.

2. The U.S. takes over sole possession of Oregon.

3. Texas becomes the "Lone Star Republic."

4. Mexico still controls and governs the territory of Texas.

5. Henry Clay and Daniel Webster die.

6. U.S. troops win the Battle of Buena Vista.

7. Questions linger after leaders of Congress reach a famous compromise.

8. Large numbers of families begin to follow the Oregon Trail.

9. Texas joins the Union.

10. A red flag flies from the top of the main church in San Antonio, Texas, as a famous battle begins.

Interpreting a Source

In the 1840's and 1850's, many Americans thought it was their destiny to control Western lands. Some parts of the West were still wild and unsettled. But other parts in the Great Lakes area were growing fast partly because of the railroad. How important the railroad was to Western life is shown in the letter below. It was written by an immigrant, Frithjoff Meidell (FRITCH-off MY-dell), to his mother in Norway. He wrote it from Springfield, Illinois, on August 7, 1855.

Dear Mother:

...Here in America it is the railroads that build up the whole country. Be-

225

cause of them the farmers get wider markets and higher prices for their products. They seem to put new life into everything. Even the old apple woman sets off at a dogtrot, when she hears that whistle, to sell her apples to passengers. Every 10 miles [about 15 kilometers] along the railways there are stations, which soon grow up into towns....

Since I have nothing else to write about this time, I shall attempt to describe how these towns spring up.... First, I say, the railroad company builds a depot. Next, a speculator[1] buys the surrounding 100 acres [40 hectares] and lays it out in lots, streets, and a marketplace....

A young wagonmaker who has just completed his apprenticeship[2] hears about the station, that it is beautifully located in a rich farming country ... and, most important of all, that it has no wagonmaker. Making a hasty decision, he buys the barest necessities[3] for setting up in his profession, hurries off to the place, rents one of the old log houses, and is soon at work. One absolute necessity he still lacks, however: a sign, of course, which is the most important part of a man's equipment here in America. The next day he hears that there is a ... painter aboard the train; he gets him off, puts him to work, and the very next day the farmers are surprised to see a monstrous sign straddling the roof of the old log house.

The sign is an immediate success, for the farmers rush to the shop and order wagons, wheels, and the like....

The train stops again, and off steps a blacksmith who went broke in one of the larger towns. He saunters[4] over to the wagonmaker's shop as unconcerned as if he only wished to light his cigar. In a casual way he inquires about the neighborhood and wonders what its prospects are, without indicating that he intends to settle there — by no means! But the wagoner, with his keen Yankee nose, soon smells a rat and starts boosting the place with all his might. This inspires the smith with ecstasy[5]; he starts jumping around and making sledge-hammer motions with his arms. Off he goes and rents the other log house and nails a horseshoe over the door as a sign....

Within a short week, a carpenter, a tailor, and a shoemaker also arrive in town. The wagoner orders a house from the carpenter and rents the second story to the tailor and the shoemaker. Soon the blacksmith also builds a house, and things progress with giant strides toward the bigger and better.

1. *The writer says that "it is the railroads that build up the whole country." What does he mean by this? How did the railroads help to settle the West?*

2. *The writer mentions a number of trades and occupations. List these trades on a piece of paper. How many of them*

---

[1]A *speculator,* in this sense, is one who buys or sells something risky with the hope of profiting from a change in prices.

[2]An *apprenticeship* is a time during which one person works for another in order to learn a trade.

[3]*Necessities* are those things a person needs for getting along.

[4]*To saunter* is to stroll idly.

[5]*Ecstasy* is extreme joy.

are still important ways of earning a living today?

3. *The writer says that a sign "is the most important part of a man's equipment here in America." Is this more true or less true today than it was in the 1850's?*

4. *The letter fails to say how the town grows after the first five men arrive. Who would you guess would be the next five citizens of the town?*

Sharpening Your Skills

By 1850 the borders of the United States stretched from the Atlantic Ocean to the Pacific. But it took many years for this huge territory to be settled. The map on this page shows how settlement moved westward between 1790 and 1890. Study the map carefully. Then answer the questions below.

1. Between 1820 and 1850, what territory became settled for the first time? (Name six states whose lands were being settled in these years.)

2. What states were mainly wild, unsettled country before the year 1850? (Name at least 10 of them.)

3. What state was settled first — Texas or California? What parts of California were mostly settled after 1870? What parts of Texas were mostly settled after 1870?

4. True or false? "Every state on the Atlantic Coast from Maine to Florida was fully settled by 1890." Explain.

Americans Move West, 1790-1890

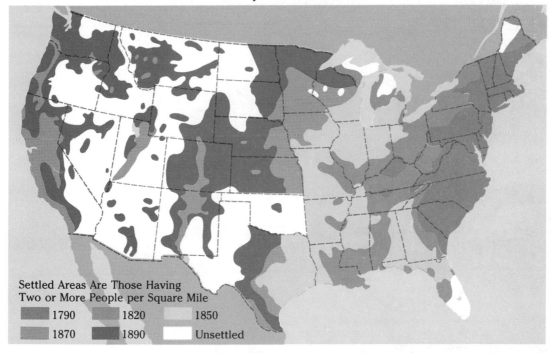

Settled Areas Are Those Having
Two or More People per Square Mile

▪ 1790	▪ 1820	▪ 1850
▪ 1870	▪ 1890	▫ Unsettled

2 ROAD TO WAR

Looking Ahead: Anger, Violence, and War

An old slave named Tom refused to obey his boss, Simon Legree. Legree struck Tom with his whip and said:

"What! ye blasted black beast! tell *me* ye don't think it *right* to do what I tell ye! What have any of you cussed cattle to do with thinking what's right? I'll put a stop to it!"

Tom received an awful beating. But Legree did not break down his spirit. Tom disobeyed Legree a second time. This time Legree killed him.

Shortly after Tom's murder, the story of *Uncle Tom's Cabin* ended. It was not a true story. It was only a novel written in 1851 by a Northern woman, Harriet Beecher Stowe. Still, the story seemed very real to people in the North who read it. It seemed to them to give a true picture of slavery in the South.

In one way or another, *Uncle Tom's Cabin* angered almost all its readers. It made Northerners angry by showing Southern slavery to be evil and cruel. Southern readers were angry because the book seemed, to them, to give a wrong idea of slavery. It seemed to attack the South in an unfair way. *Uncle Tom's Cabin* was one of the things that stirred up the old quarrel between the North and the South. In the 1850's, more and more people began to wonder whether the Union could hold together.

Slavery was the main reason for arguments between the North and the South. But there were other reasons too. The people of the two sections had different ideas about democracy and how to run the national government. In fact, these two groups of people were different in so many ways that the U.S. seemed almost like two nations. One was the North. The other was the South.

According to legend, the South of the early 1800's was a region of rich, slave-supporting plantations such as the one at left. In fact, however, it was mainly a region of small farms.

229

135,000 SETS, 270,000 VOLUMES SOLD.

UNCLE TOM'S CABIN

FOR SALE HERE.

AN EDITION FOR THE MILLION, COMPLETE IN 1 Vol., PRICE 37 1-2 CENTS.
" " IN GERMAN, IN 1 Vol., PRICE 50 CENTS.
" " IN 2 Vols., CLOTH, 6 PLATES, PRICE $1.50.
SUPERB ILLUSTRATED EDITION, IN 1 Vol., WITH 153 ENGRAVINGS,
PRICES FROM $2.50 TO $5.00.

The Greatest Book of the Age.

Poster above was used to build sales for Harriet Beecher Stowe's much-debated novel.

Economic differences. There were great differences in the way the people of the two sections made their living. Most of the South's wealth had always come from farming. Cotton was the most important crop of all. The South's cotton was sold to cloth factories in the North, in Britain, and in France. Besides cotton, the South raised large amounts of tobacco, rice, and sugar. These crops were also sold to the North and to Europe. Even so, cotton was the big money-maker. "Cotton is king," Southerners said.

230   Cotton, tobacco, and other crops were often raised on large farms called *plantations*. Plantation owners thought that they needed slave labor in order to make a profit on their crops. Black slaves and "King Cotton" kept the South going. They were part of the Southern way of life. Most white people in the South thought it was the right way.

Most of them did not own slaves. Only about one white Southerner in four was a slave-owner. Almost three fourths of the slave-owners had fewer than 10 slaves each. In the whole South, fewer than 3,000 people owned more than 100 slaves. Yet these owners of large plantations were very powerful. They controlled politics in the South and ran things their own way.

They did not speak for all the white people in the South. Many whites refused to defend slavery. Like Thomas Jefferson in an earlier day, these people frowned upon the whole idea of slave ownership. Some even freed their own slaves. Many other white people in the South neither defended slavery nor attacked it. They simply had no opinion about slavery at all.

Even so, plantation-owners controlled Southern politics. Why? Partly because most white Southerners believed in slavery — even if they didn't own any slaves themselves. They thought slavery was good for the South and good for the slaves too.

Of course there were farms in the North too. Most of them were small. They were worked by the farmer with the help of his family and sometimes a hired man. In fact, most of the people in the U.S. at this time were country people, North and South.

Yet there was a big change taking

place in the North. More and more of its wealth was coming from manufacturing. It already had far more mills, factories, and railroads than the South. More were being built all the time. Northern mills and factories turned out 10 times as many goods as Southern factories. Manufacturing and business were becoming the Northern way of life. It was a way of life that did not need slaves.

Abolitionism. In the 1830's, some Northerners became more and more upset by the idea of slavery. They thought it was immoral (wicked and wrong). They wanted to abolish it (do away with it) everywhere in the nation. These people were called *abolitionists.* One of them, William Lloyd Garrison, attacked slavery in his Boston newspaper. Another, a black man named Frederick Douglass, delivered speeches against slavery in many parts of the North. A third, a black woman named Harriet Tubman, took more direct action. She helped hundreds of black slaves escape from the South. Both Douglass and Tubman were former slaves themselves.

Free-soil dispute. The more slavery was attacked, the more Southerners defended it. Some of them wanted to see slavery spread into new territories of the West. The Compromise of 1850 had closed the door to slavery in California (see Chapter Six). But it had left the question unsettled in other areas of the West.

In 1854 Congress opened the question of slavery in Western lands to further dispute. It did so by passing a law called the *Kansas-Nebraska Act.* This act allowed settlers in Kansas and Nebraska Territories to choose for themselves whether to allow slavery or not. Fighting soon broke out in Kansas between those who favored slavery and those who opposed it. Before long the trouble in Kansas had become a national issue.

Many Northern factory-owners used women to keep the wheels of industry spinning. In factories, there was no need for slaves.

The possible spread of slavery to Kansas outraged abolitionists. It also angered a group of Northerners called *free-soilers*. Like abolitionists, free-soilers opposed slavery. But before the struggle in Kansas they had not demanded that slavery be abolished in the South. They only wanted to keep it from spreading into Western lands.

Now the struggle in Kansas united the free-soilers and abolitionists against the South. A new political party was formed in the mid-1850's. It called itself the *Republican party*. The party grew very rapidly. Its major purpose was to keep slavery from spreading.

Growing anger. By this time the anger between Northerners and Southerners seemed to get worse every year. In 1856 Senator Charles Sumner of Massachusetts delivered a speech in the Senate. In the speech, he used heated words to describe the South. Preston Brooks, a Southern Congressman, became so angry that he attacked Sumner on the Senate floor. He broke a wooden cane over the Senator's head. Southerners treated Brooks as a hero. They

South Carolina's Preston Brooks attacks Massachusetts' Charles Sumner with his cane.

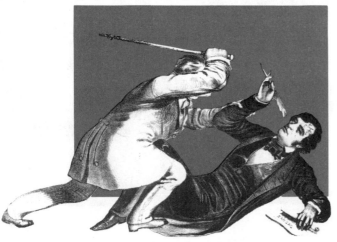

sent him other canes to replace the one he had broken. They urged Brooks to use them to hit more Northerners.

Slavery remained the root of the trouble. In 1857 the U.S. Supreme Court tried to put one legal question over slavery to rest. Among other things, it ruled that Congress could not keep slavery out of the territories. This ruling made Northerners even angrier than before.

Anger, both in the North and the South, became almost unbearable in 1859. In that year a Northerner named John Brown tried to lead a slave revolt at Harpers Ferry in what was then Virginia. Brown's attempt failed. The government of Virginia put him to death. Yet the damage had been done. Northerners hailed Brown as a hero and a saint. Southerners were terrified by such praise for Brown. They feared that most of the North was now against them.

In 1860 the Republican candidate for President was a lawyer from Illinois, Abraham Lincoln. Lincoln was a free-soiler, not an abolitionist. But Southerners thought all Republicans threatened their way of life. Lincoln did not win a single electoral vote in the South. (*Electoral votes* are those cast by people specially chosen to elect the President and the Vice-President of the U.S.) And yet Northern votes elected Lincoln President.

Angry Southerners decided that they had had enough. On December 24, 1860, a few weeks after the election, South Carolina declared its independence from the Union. Other Southern states also pulled out. Then, on April 12, 1861, Southerners fired cannons at a United States fort. They were the first shots of a long and terrible civil war.

Chapter 7

"I Will Be Heard!"

An angry mob dragged William Lloyd Garrison through the streets of Boston. They put a rope around his neck. They wanted to hang him. But the mayor of Boston was able to stop the mob just in time. He put Garrison in jail for a while to protect him. The date was October 21, 1835.

Why did the mob want to hang this man? Because he ran a newspaper that was very strongly against slavery. It was called *The Liberator*.

Slavery had never taken hold in the North the way it had in the South. And by this time all the Northern states had passed laws against slavery. But many white Northerners discriminated against black Americans. That is, they looked down upon black people and mistreated them in certain ways. Still, few Northerners defended slavery. Many hoped that slavery would die away in the South by itself. Or they thought that the government might be able to get rid of it slowly, step by step.

William Lloyd Garrison was not willing to wait. He wanted slavery in the South ended *right away*. He fought against slavery day and night.

There were many people in the North

By the early 1800's, some Northern towns and cities were setting up separate schools for blacks. But many whites opposed this idea. In the 1830's, from Connecticut to Ohio, mobs attacked such schools.

who did not like Garrison. They said he was a troublemaker. If people in the South wanted slavery, they said, that was the Southerners' business. Many workers in the North were afraid they would lose their jobs if the slaves were freed. The blacks, they said, would work for less money. And there were factory-owners and other business leaders in the North who made their money from cotton. They did not want to see an end to slavery, either.

Target of mob action. So Northern mobs often attacked people who were in the movement against slavery. The people who wanted to end slavery right away were called *abolitionists*. They were a favorite target of the mobs. Their lives were not safe. But Garrison — and other abolition-ists — would not quit. Garrison was not afraid of anyone. Nothing could make him stop writing and talking against slavery. When he started his newspaper, Garrison said:

"I am in earnest.... I will not excuse [anyone]. I will not retreat a single inch. *And I will be heard!*"

Garrison made many enemies by taking

William Lloyd Garrison led the fight against slavery. He was jailed and widely resented.

234

a stand like this. He also won many friends. And he lived to see the day when slavery was ended in the United States.

William Lloyd Garrison was born in a small town near Boston in 1805. His father drank very heavily and left the family when William was three years old. Many times as a boy William had to beg for scraps of food. Many times he went hungry.

When he was nine, William had to leave school and go to work. After a while, he became a printer's helper on a newspaper. William liked good writers. He read their books at night. When he was only 17, he began to write articles for the newspaper.

Later Garrison became the editor of a Baltimore newspaper that was against slavery. He could not understand the American people of his time. They were very proud of the Declaration of Independence which said, "All men are created equal." Yet they did not seem to care that millions of blacks were slaves. "I am ashamed of my country," Garrison said.

"No neutrals." In 1831 Garrison started his own paper, *The Liberator,* in Boston. He didn't pull any punches when he wrote against slavery. He called slavery "sinful." He thought the South wicked for supporting it. Many people — even some who were against slavery — did not like Garrison's strong language. One minister said that Garrison did not write "like a Christian gentleman." Garrison did not care. "Men shall either like me or dislike me. There shall be no neutrals," he said.

In 1833 Garrison also started one of the first groups to fight against slavery. It was called the *American Anti-Slavery Society*. Many people laughed at it at first. But by 1840 it had about 200,000 members.

Garrison kept up his attack on slavery with full force. While in jail in Boston in October 1835, he wrote these lines on the wall of his cell: "Keep me as a prisoner, but bind me not as a slave. Punish me as a criminal, but hold me not as a chattel [slave]. Torture me as a man, but drive me not like a beast."

At home, Garrison was a kind husband and father. Some people were amazed when they met him for the first time. They thought he would be as outspoken as his newspaper articles.

Garrison did not think that force was the way to end slavery. He was against war. He thought slavery should be ended by peaceful means. But when the Civil War broke out, Garrison gave his support to President Lincoln and the North.

In 1865 slavery was ended everywhere in the United States by the 13th Amendment. Garrison then stopped printing *The Liberator.* The battle he had fought for more than 30 years was won.

A Second Look. . . .

1. *What were William Lloyd Garrison's views on slavery? Why did they annoy many Southerners? Why did they frighten some white Northerners?*

2. *Who are some people today who remind you of William Lloyd Garrison? What is it about them that seems similar to Garrison?*

3. *Pretend that you are a slaveowner in Georgia in the 1830's. Write a letter to the editor of* The Liberator *telling him what you think of his newspaper. Then pretend that you are Garrison. How will you respond?*

Chapter 8
She Ran a Railroad

A poster in a Southern railroad station read:

"WANTED — dead or alive — Harriet Tubman. A reward of $40,000 is offered for capture."

Why was such a large reward offered for the capture of a black woman? The answer is in the story of her life.

Harriet Tubman was born a slave on a Maryland plantation in 1821. She was whipped constantly while she was a child. Harriet had scars on her neck from these beatings. Once, when she was 14, she tried to save a slave from a whipping. She stood in the way of the "boss" with the whip. The slave started to run. Then the boss picked up a heavy iron weight. He threw it at the slave, but it struck Harriet's head instead. Harriet fell to the ground. For days she lay near death. Finally Harriet grew stronger. But she never got completely well. She had a deep scar where the iron weight had hit her. For the rest of her life, she had strange spells of suddenly falling asleep.

Dash to freedom. Tubman hated being a slave. She wanted to escape to the North where there was no slavery. One night in about 1849 she and two of her brothers made a break for freedom and headed north. But the brothers

Harriet Tubman was a woman of great courage. Had she been caught on one of her journeys, she would have been enslaved again — or worse.

soon became frightened and turned back.

Tubman went on alone. She hid by day and moved north by night. She guided herself by the North Star. She was also helped by the *Underground Railroad.* This "railroad" was not really a railroad at all. It was a secret escape route to the North. But the "railroad" did have many "stations." These were the homes of people who hid slaves by day and sent them on to other homes after dark. This secret network stretched from the South to the North and to Canada. With its help, Tubman finally reached Philadelphia.

Slavery had long been outlawed in Pennsylvania. Tubman was free at last. But she was not content. She wanted to help her family and other slaves to escape. Soon she became a "conductor" on the Underground Railroad. She made trip after trip to the South to lead groups of slaves to freedom. In all, she helped free more than 300 slaves. Among them were her aged parents and the rest of her family. Southern slave-owners tried again and again to capture her. Finally they offered the $40,000 reward.

Rescue work. Here is the story of one of her adventures:

Led by Harriet Tubman, 11 slaves walked through the woods. They were cold and hungry. It was so dark they couldn't see each other. Yet Harriet Tubman led them as if the sun were shining. The slaves spoke in whispers. They were frightened — they could hear the barking of dogs. They knew that slave-catchers (men who made money catching escaped slaves) were after them.

Tubman knew of a stream nearby. It

This 1844 drawing advertised the "Liberty Line," part of the Underground Railroad. The ad told of "splendid locomotives" and free seats.

was icy cold, but Tubman told the slaves to go into the water. She knew the dogs could not smell them in the water and track them down. The slaves stayed in the water until they no longer heard the dogs barking.

They walked for days and weeks — and still they were far from freedom. Their goal on this trip was Canada. Why Canada instead of one of the Northern states? As we have seen, Congress passed the Fugitive Slave Act in 1850. This law was part of Henry Clay's compromise of that year. It said that any runaway slaves caught in the North would have to be sent back South. So after 1850 the Underground Railroad ended in Canada.

The group went on together, hiding in swamps when danger was near. One day while they were hiding, Tubman began to wonder where the man from the next "station" was. He was very late. She prayed that the Underground Railroad had not let her down. Finally a man did come. He told Tubman he had a horse and wagon and food in his barn. That

Charles T. Webber led slaves to the North and Canada on the Underground Railroad. Later he painted some of the journey's hardships (above). The "railroad" operated mostly at night. Passengers had to carry their own luggage. But for most slaves, the Underground Railroad was the only hope for freedom.

night Tubman went to the barn. There was everything the man had promised. "Praise God," the slaves said. They were another step closer to freedom.

Harriet Tubman's journeys were almost always dangerous. They took careful planning and great skill. There was usually a danger of being arrested. To reduce this danger, Tubman had one important rule. No slave should think of trying to surrender or of returning South. Any slave who did was threatened with death.

In time Tubman became well known for her rescue work. Now and then she spoke to Northern anti-slavery groups of the hazards she had faced. Among her own people, she was considered a true heroine. She knew the hardships of slavery and had the courage to help others overcome them.

A Second Look. . . .

1. What was the Underground Railroad? Why was it important?

2. Harriet Tubman escaped from slavery, breaking the laws of Southern states. Later she helped other slaves escape, violating the Fugitive Slave Act passed by Congress. Is it right, therefore, to call Harriet Tubman a criminal? Should she have been punished for breaking the law? Why or why not?

3. Pretend you are a slave living on a plantation in northern Virginia in the 1850's. You have been offered the chance to escape to Canada. You have given a lot of thought to whether you want to escape or not. You have had to consider all the benefits and drawbacks of leaving home. Now you must give a one-minute explanation for the choice you have made. What will you say?

Chapter 9

Freedom Fighter

"I will run away. I will not stand it. I would rather be killed running than die as a slave."

It was Frederick Douglass talking about his early life. He was making a speech in Nantucket, Massachusetts, in August 1841. The audience was shocked. This tall, handsome young man had once been a slave!

Yes, it was true. This man, who became one of the greatest leaders of the fight against slavery, was born a slave. The year was 1817. The place was a plantation in Maryland. While still a boy, Frederick was sent to live with his master's relatives in Baltimore. The wife of his new master taught him to read and write. For Frederick, nothing was more exciting. But then Frederick's master stopped his lessons. He did not think it was good for a slave to know how to read and write. In fact, it was against the law to teach a slave such things. White Southerners did not want slaves to get any "dangerous ideas."

When his lessons stopped, Frederick knew for the first time how evil slavery really was. He dreamed of freedom from that day on.

Resisting a "slavebreaker."

When he was 16, Douglass had his darkest hours as a slave. His master hired him out to a very cruel man named Edward Covey. Covey was known as a "slave-breaker," because he knew how to break the spirit of any slave who did not obey. Covey whipped Douglass without mercy many times. At last Douglass could take it no more. When Covey tried to whip him again, Douglass put up his fists. He and Covey fought for nearly two hours. Finally Covey quit. He never tried to give Douglass a whipping again. Douglass was lucky. Some slaves who fought back were severely punished — or even killed.

Frederick Douglass was 21 when he decided to escape to New York. At the time, he was working as a slave in a Baltimore shipyard. He borrowed the papers of a free black sailor and dressed himself in a seaman's outfit. Then he got on a train headed north. It was a dangerous trip. Slave-catchers were always on the lookout for runaway blacks. But Douglass made it safely to New York. There he got in touch with people who belonged to the Underground Railroad. They sent him to New Bedford, Massachusetts.

Douglass wanted to live quietly. He did not want to do anything that would let slave-catchers know where he was. Then one day he was asked to speak at an anti-slavery meeting in Nantucket. Despite the danger, he accepted. Soon other anti-slavery meetings wanted to hear him speak.

Douglass was a fine speaker. Large crowds came to hear him wherever he went. Sometimes they were not very friendly. In a few towns, Douglass was beaten by angry mobs. But he did not give up speaking to groups.

Douglass spoke so well that he ran into trouble. Some people doubted he had ever been a slave. He sounded too well educated. Actually, Douglass had never gone to school. He was well educated because he had read a great number of books on his own. But the leader of one anti-slavery group told Douglass to prove he was a runaway slave.

Escaping from slave-catchers. As a result, Douglass wrote a book about himself called *The Narrative of the Life of Frederick Douglass.* In it he told all about his life as a slave. He named his masters and gave his own real name — Frederick Augustus Bailey. Soon slave-catchers were sent to arrest him. Douglass went to England to escape them.

Douglass liked England, and many English people liked him. They got together and bought his freedom from his former master. In 1847 Douglass returned to the United States. He moved to Rochester, New York, and started an anti-slavery newspaper. He called it *The North Star* after the star that guided runaway slaves at night.

The newspaper did not bring in much money. Yet Douglass managed to keep it going for the next 15 years. It gave a voice to other black writers. It was read by many abolitionists, both blacks and whites.

During these years, Douglass kept up his attack on slavery. His editorials tried to show why slavery was wrong. Douglass aided many runaway slaves, giving them money he had earned making

speeches. He also helped a great many blacks to escape over the border into Canada.

Douglass called for equal treatment of the free black people of the North. He protested "White Only" signs in public places. He quarreled with black barbers who would cut only white men's hair. Moreover, Douglass called for equal treatment of women. He was one of the first American men to join the women's rights movement of the time.

But it was Douglass' brave fight against slavery that people remembered best. In this battle, there was no greater hero than he.

A Second Look. . . .

1. *How did Frederick Douglass, who grew up as a Southern slave, become famous in the North and then in England?*

2. *Frederick Douglass learned to read and write from his master's wife. He did not attend school as a child. Yet he ended up putting out his own newspaper. Why is this considered remarkable? Do you think you could learn to read and write without going to school? Why or why not?*

3. *Suppose you had the job of carving a few words of praise on Frederick Douglass' tombstone. The top of the stone reads: FREDERICK DOUGLASS (1817-1895). You can fit 25 additional words on the stone. What would you say?*

As a young slave, Frederick Douglass was kept from his lessons by his owner. The owner feared school would make Douglass "unmanageable" and "unhappy." When the schoolwork stopped, Douglass began to dream of escaping to freedom.

In the mid-1850's, the debate over slavery came to a boil in the prairie towns of Kansas Territory. Free-soilers and supporters of slavery locked horns in settlements such as Hickory Point (above).

Chapter 10

Bleeding Kansas

Two women were driving a wagon on the road to Lawrence, Kansas. They were stopped by men with rifles in their hands. The women had recently moved to Kansas from the North. The men with the guns had come from the South.

The women were nervous. They were trying to smuggle gunpowder and bullets to their Northern friends in Lawrence. They had hidden these supplies of war inside their skirts and petticoats. The men searched the wagon and found nothing. So they let the women drive on into Lawrence. Inside the town, the women proudly passed out bullets to their friends. The people of Lawrence were now ready to fight.

In the winter of 1855, Kansas had become a battleground. What was the trouble all about? The people of Kansas were trying to decide on their future. Would Kansas come into the Union as a free state or a slave state? This question had already divided the people of the territory and brought them close to war.

The issue had first been raised the year before. It had grown out of some proposals put forth by a U.S. Senator from Illinois, Stephen Douglas. Douglas was a short man with a powerful voice.

People called him the "Little Giant."

Douglas had not meant to cause trouble. He was mainly interested in opening up the West so that railroads could come through. And the parts of the West that interested Douglas most were the flat, grassy plains to the west and northwest of Missouri. This land was known as Kansas Territory and Nebraska Territory. Who would settle on this land if it were open to everybody? Northern farmers would probably move west from Ohio. Southern farmers would probably move west from Missouri.

Douglas' proposals. But should Southern farmers be allowed to bring their slaves with them? Douglas thought so. Later the settlers could elect their own government and decide about slavery. All would depend on what Douglas called *popular sovereignty*. This meant that the settlers themselves would vote whether to permit or to outlaw slavery. The U.S. Congress would not decide the question for them.

Most white Southerners liked Douglas' idea. Kansas and Nebraska lay north of the famous 36°30′ parallel. This parallel had been set as the dividing line between slave states and free ones ever since the Missouri Compromise of 1820. Now Douglas was proposing to repeal the 1820 law that had set up the 36°30′ line. If Douglas had his way, the South would have a chance to push slavery into Western and Northern lands.

Of course many Northerners were against Douglas' idea. It made abolitionists angry. It made free-soilers angry. A whole new party was formed to fight Douglas' plan. At a convention in 1854, members of this party decided to call themselves *Republicans*. They had taken the name once used for Thomas Jefferson's party. Before long the Republican party was almost as strong as the old Democratic party.

Kansas-Nebraska Act. But in 1854 Republican leaders were not yet strong enough to stop the Little Giant. Douglas managed to get his new law through Congress. It was called the *Kansas-Nebraska Act*. It laid down rules for settling in Kansas and Nebraska. Northerners and Southerners could settle there. Whichever group was largest could finally decide the question of slavery. It was like setting up a race between the North and the South. Douglas assumed the race would be decided peacefully.

There was no race between North and South in Nebraska. Few Southerners went there. Slavery was not an issue. But the race to control Kansas turned out to be anything but peaceful. The North *must* win the race, said abolitionists in Massachusetts. They formed the New England Emigrant Aid Society. (*Emigrants* are people who leave their states or countries to settle in another.) This group persuaded hundreds of New England farmers to move to Kansas. It sent them guns to use to fight their Southern neighbors.

Southerners too rushed into Kansas. Most of these Southerners came from the slave state of Missouri. Few of them planned to settle in Kansas. They just wanted to vote in the election of the Kansas legislature and then go home.

Their illegal votes were probably not needed. The people favoring slavery in Kansas were far greater in number than those opposing it. When the election took place in March 1855, pro-slavery forces won a thumping victory. Law-

makers quickly met to make laws for the new territory.

Two governments. The laws they enacted were very hard on those who opposed slavery. One law made slavery legal. Another said that any citizen who spoke against slavery could be put in jail. Some lawmakers opposed to slavery were driven out of this legislature. This made Northerners in Kansas angrier.

They, in turn, fought back. They said the election of 1855 was a fraud. They held another election. The pro-slavery group refused to take part in it. This time anti-slavery lawmakers were chosen. Now there were two separate governments in Kansas. The pro-slavery one met in Leavenworth. The anti-slavery one met in Topeka. Each claimed to be Kansas Territory's legal government.

Now it was December 1855. Two women had smuggled bullets into Lawrence, a stronghold of anti-slavery forc-

In March 1855, voters went to the polls in Kickapoo (above) and other Kansas towns. They were to decide whether their territory would be a slave state or a free state. The pro-slavery voters won the election. But anger over the issue did not fade. In the spring of 1856, violence flared in Lawrence, an anti-slavery stronghold. The town's Free State Hotel was burned to the ground (right), setting off the Pottawatomie Massacre.

244

es. Everybody waited for the Southern sheriff to command his men to attack the town. But it did not happen. A cold winter storm swept across the Kansas plains. The sheriff and his men retreated to the shelter of their homes.

They returned to Lawrence in the spring of 1856. Nobody tried to stop them this time. They set fire to the town's hotel. They looted stores and did a great deal of damage.

Pottawatomie Massacre. Revenge came swiftly. It was taken by a Northern radical named John Brown. Brown had followed five of his sons to Kansas in 1855. Now, with four of his sons and three other men, he staged a bloody attack. The group marched to a Southerner's cabin in the middle of the night. There they killed three men. They marched to two other cabins that night and killed two more Southerners. None of their victims was a slave-owner. But all were supporters of the slave system.

The next morning, people heard about the terrible murders near Pottawatomie (pot-ah-WAHT-oh-me) Creek. Angry farmers from Missouri crossed the Kansas border to form a Southern militia. Northern settlers in Kansas formed a Northern militia. For months the two

forces threatened to attack each other.

No real battles took place. Only a few lives were lost. But throughout the U.S., Americans talked about the "war" in Kansas. They had a nickname for the place. "Bleeding Kansas," they called it. For years the nation's leaders had compromised on the issue of slavery. Now, in two short years, all their compromises had come apart.

A Second Look. . . .

1. *What was the Kansas-Nebraska Act? Why did most white Southerners favor it? Why did many Northerners oppose it?*

2. *Does Stephen Douglas' plan for solving the slavery issue in Kansas seem sensible to you? If not, why not? If so, why didn't it work?*

3. *In the 1850's, the nation's leaders seemed unable to reach a fair settlement of the Kansas problem. Can you and your classmates do any better? One group could pretend to be Southerners in Kansas, and a second group to be Northerners in Kansas. A third group could suggest three ideas for bringing peace to the territory. After discussing the proposals, Northern and Southern groups can decide whether to accept any of them.*

Kansas-Nebraska Act, 1854

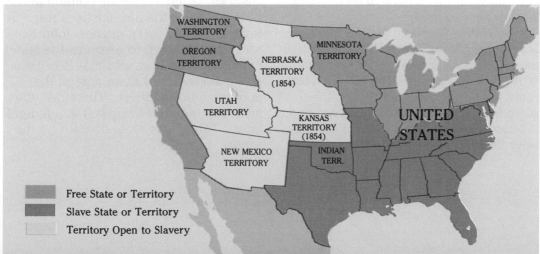

WASHINGTON TERRITORY

OREGON TERRITORY

NEBRASKA TERRITORY (1854)

MINNESOTA TERRITORY

UTAH TERRITORY

KANSAS TERRITORY (1854)

UNITED STATES

NEW MEXICO TERRITORY

INDIAN TERR.

Free State or Territory

Slave State or Territory

Territory Open to Slavery

Chapter 11

The Slave Who Took His Case to Court

Were slaves human beings with rights — or were they just pieces of property? If they were taken into a state or territory that did not allow slavery, did they become free — or remain slaves? Could a slave become a citizen?

Questions like these divided the nation very deeply in the 1850's. By this time, large numbers of people in the North had been won over to the movement against slavery. Many abolitionists wanted to do away with slavery — *abolish* it — everywhere in the country.

In the South, most whites believed that they had a right to own slaves. Not only that — they also believed that they had a right to take their slaves with them into any part of the country, even free states and territories. People who felt this way believed that the abolitionists were nothing but troublemakers. Many Northerners agreed.

In 1857 it looked as if the U.S. Supreme Court would finally settle the question of slavery in the territories. This was because of a black man named Dred Scott. Years earlier Scott, a slave, had been taken by his master from the slave state of Missouri to the free state of Illinois. Later he had been taken to free territory in what is now Minnesota. Then he had been brought back to Missouri.

In Missouri a group of abolitionists decided to help Dred Scott win his freedom. They argued that, because Scott had been taken to a free state and to a free territory, he must have become a free man. He was no longer a slave when he returned to Missouri. This argument was first heard in the courts of Missouri in the late 1840's. Finally it was taken to the U.S. Supreme Court.

On March 6, 1857, the Supreme Court announced its decision in the Dred Scott case. Excitement was high. A hush fell over the crowd as Chief Justice Roger Taney led the other eight Justices into the courtroom. Five of the Justices, including Taney, were Southerners.

Separate opinions. Each of the Justices issued a separate opinion in the case. Seven of the nine Justices ruled in favor of Dred Scott's master, John Sanford. They refused to overturn the state court decision that said that Scott was still a slave. Six of them agreed that Scott was not a citizen. Therefore, they said, he could not bring suit in a federal court. Taney was most definite on the point.

Long before the U.S. Constitution became law, Taney argued, black people had been thought of as "beings of an inferior order." That is, they were not thought to be as good as whites. They had "no rights which the white man was bound to respect." After 1787 free blacks did not become citizens just because they gained the right to vote in some states, Taney claimed. In fact, they could not be U.S. citizens at all.

This was a very weak argument. Free blacks had clearly been citizens of several states for many years. Only two Justices said they agreed with Taney on this point. But Taney had made the point quite forcefully. It aroused great anger among everyone opposed to slavery.

Taney and five other Justices went further. They agreed that Congress could not keep slavery out of the territories. The Missouri Compromise of 1820 had said that there could be no slavery north of Missouri. Now, the Court was ruling, the Missouri Compromise had been illegal all along.

On this point, Taney called attention to the Fifth Amendment to the U.S. Con-stitution. It said that no person could have his or her property taken away without *due process* of law. (Due process is an orderly set of rules for bringing a lawsuit or a person accused of a crime to trial.) Slaves were property, just as the clothes one wore or the horses one owned, Taney argued. Congress could not take away a Northerner's right to own horses, the Chief Justice seemed to be saying. It stood to reason, then, that Congress could not take away a Southerner's right to own slaves.

Judicial review. In the Dred Scott case, the Supreme Court was making use of a power it had used only once before — in *Marbury v. Madison.* This was *judicial review,* the power to decide whether the acts of Congress and the President are allowed by the U.S. Constitution. As in *Marbury v. Madison,* the Court was declaring an act of Congress unconstitutional. For the first time, in fact, it was throwing out a *major* act of Congress.

Many Southerners were joyful about the Court's decision. Slave-owners felt that they had won a great victory. But in

Dred Scott

247

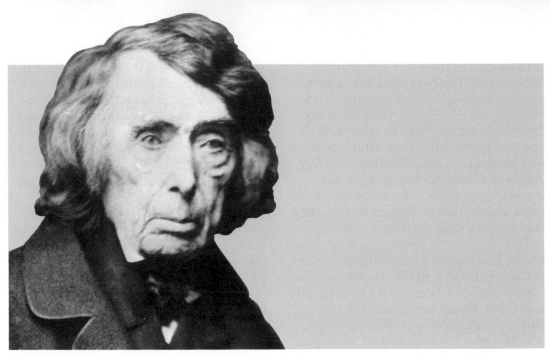

Despite the Dred Scott ruling, Roger Taney (above) disliked slavery, had once freed his own slaves.

the North and the West, mass meetings of protest were held. More and more people felt drawn to the abolitionist movement. And more and more people were attracted to the Republican party — the party that was against the spread of slavery into the territories.

Some abolitionists were very discouraged by the Supreme Court's decision. Black people were especially upset. But Frederick Douglass, one of the leading fighters against slavery, said: "My hopes were never brighter than now. . . . The Supreme Court is not the only power in this world. . . . Judge Taney cannot pluck the silvery star of liberty from our northern sky."

Nor, in the end, did the Court settle the matter of Dred Scott's liberty. A few months after the decision, Scott and his family were turned over to a new slave-owner in St. Louis. This owner gave the Scotts their freedom. Dred Scott died in

1858, the free man he had wanted to be.

His case did not end the dispute over slavery. Four years after the Dred Scott decision, Americans would be fighting each other in the Civil War. The long conflict between the North and the South over the slavery question would be one of the main causes of this war.

A Second Look. . . .

1. *Why did the Supreme Court's decision in the Dred Scott case please many Southern whites? Why did it anger blacks and others opposed to slavery?*

2. *Review each of the points made in Roger Taney's opinion. Do you agree with Taney or not? Why?*

3. *The Supreme Court can no longer rule the same way that it ruled in 1857. To find out one reason why, look up the 13th Amendment to the U.S. Constitution. Write a paragraph explaining what this amendment says about slavery.*

Chapter 12

Raid on Harpers Ferry

The Dred Scott decision had divided the nation as never before. The more Northerners thought about it, the angrier they became. Then, in 1859, some Americans began wondering if their Union was really a Union at all. What touched off this question? The work of a daring, if bumbling, Northerner named John Brown.

"Old Brown," as he was often called, was a restless man. For most of his life, he had floated from place to place and job to job. In the 1840's, he somehow got interested in helping black slaves. In the next few years, he became caught up in this cause.

In 1855 he followed five of his sons to Kansas Territory. As we have seen, he and his sons killed five men. Brown had no feelings of guilt about this deed. He thought God intended his victims to die. Brown was sure that God was against slavery. He was also sure that bloodshed was the only way to end the system.

After the raid in Kansas, John Brown set out on the great plan of his life. He hoped to raise a small army in the North and move South. He would set up a stronghold in the mountains of Virginia. From there he would help to free Virginia's slaves. After this, he hoped that slaves all over the South would rise up and kill their masters. And this, Brown thought, would end slavery in the United States once and for all.

The plan was so daring that some people later called it insane. Yet Brown kept looking for ways to put his ideas into action. He raised money among abolitionists — first in upstate New York, then in Boston. He told his friends that he could not fail. "If God be for us," he asked, "who can be against us?"

Time of testing. In July 1859, Brown rented a farm near the Virginia-Maryland border. The farm was about five miles (eight kilometers) from Harpers Ferry where federal arms were stored. Brown's men — 16 whites and five blacks — had enough guns for themselves. They must have wanted guns to give to slaves who joined them. Whatever their reasons, Brown and his men attacked Harpers Ferry on October 16. They captured the federal warehouse where guns were stored. Some of Brown's men rounded up slave-owners and took them prisoner.

Brown's plans now called for a march to the Virginia mountains. From there he and his men would start a war against slavery in the South. But Brown stalled, waiting for local slaves to join him. The slaves didn't, probably because they feared federal troops nearby. Instead of fleeing, Brown took refuge with his men in the fire-engine house. And he let a train go through that carried news of his raid.

249

U.S. troops put an end to John Brown's raid.

The next day, 1,500 U.S. soldiers and marines surrounded the engine house. They were commanded by Colonel Robert E. Lee, the future military leader of the South. Brown and his men refused to surrender. But their fight was hopeless. One by one they were shot down.

The next morning, Brown was again asked to surrender. One of his sons was dead, and another dying. Brown himself was wounded. Yet he still refused to give up. Then marines rushed the building and battered down the door. An officer entered in and knocked Brown out with the flat of his sword. Only two other men were still alive.

Trial for treason. A week after being captured, Brown was put on trial for treason (disloyalty toward the government). His lawyers told him to make a plea of insanity. But Brown refused to do so. He said he knew what he was doing. He had come to free the slaves. What he had done, he said, "was not wrong, but right." He said that freeing slaves was "the greatest service man can render [give] to God."

During the trial and after it, Brown handled himself with great dignity. Vir-

ginia's Governor Wise was moved to call him "a man of clear head" and "courage." Even so, a jury found Brown guilty of treason. On December 2, 1859, he was hanged at Charles Town, Virginia (now in West Virginia).

Northern newspapers outdid themselves in praising Brown. Abolitionists spoke of him as if he were a saint. One famous writer, Ralph Waldo Emerson, compared Brown's death to the way Jesus had died on the cross. Another writer, Louisa May Alcott, said the gallows were "a stepping stone to heaven" for Brown.

Some went even further. They used Brown's death to make a ringing protest against the South and all its slave-owners. One abolitionist, Wendell Phillips, was especially outraged. "John Brown has twice as much right to hang Governor Wise," Phillips said, "as Governor Wise has to hang him." Phillips and others went on to call for slave uprisings. These abolitionists said they supported such uprisings even if they meant more bloodshed.

Southerners did not take Northern protests lightly. Some of them may have admired Brown's courage. But they did not admire his goals. These Southerners were even more disturbed to learn that Brown had drawn support from some famous people in the North. It looked to some people as though Northerners were about to promote terror all over the South.

Was the Union really a Union at all? some Southerners began asking. By early 1860, this question had become a very vital one. Within a few months, Americans would elect a new President. And it was becoming plain that the future of the Union would depend heavily on the President they chose.

A Second Look. . . .

1. *How did the life and death of John Brown help to cause unrest among many white Southerners? What did abolitionists think of him? Why?*

2. *Not all Northerners agreed with Brown's methods of ending slavery. Abraham Lincoln did not approve of Brown's use of "violence, bloodshed, and treason." What is your view? Is violence ever a proper way to right a wrong? If so, under what circumstances? If not, why not?*

3. *After the start of the Civil War, Northern soldiers marched to battle to a song called "John Brown's Body." The song was meant to build support for the Northern side in the war. Pretend you are a songwriter in 1861. Your job is to write a song favoring John Brown or attacking what he did. Try to write your song to a well-known piece of music.*

John Brown created his own legend. He grew a beard as a disguise (above), then planned a slave revolt. The revolt never took place, but Brown became a hero to many. In 1942 black artist Horace Pippin painted Brown going to his hanging under a wintry Virginia sky (below).

251

Chapter 13

The Union Breaks Up

Abe Lincoln stood on the rear platform of the train in Springfield, Illinois. He was leaving for Washington, D.C. — to be sworn in as President of the United States. The date was February 11, 1861.

A large crowd had come to see Lincoln off. The tall, thin Lincoln looked pale. He was worried, and he was sad. He knew that war might come. He looked out at the crowd and told the people that he faced a problem greater than George Washington's. But he said he would trust in God. Then he said farewell, and the train pulled out.

Lincoln had not believed that he would be elected President. He thought that he wasn't well enough known. But some things he had said in debates about slavery had made him famous.

These debates had been held in 1858 with Senator Stephen A. Douglas. Douglas had been running for re-election to his Senate seat from Illinois. Lincoln had been running against him. The two men held the debates so they could get their ideas out to the people.

Settling the future. Douglas was a Democrat. He stood for the idea of *popular sovereignty*. He believed, that is, that the people of the territories should vote whether to permit or outlaw slav-ery. The U.S. Congress should not decide the question for them.

Lincoln was a Republican and did not want any more slave states. He did not believe that the United States could remain "half slave and half free." Sooner or later, Lincoln said, the country would become "*all* one thing, or *all* the other."

In 1861 the South began building a sense of national pride. Musicians pounded out new tunes which were printed as sheet music (below).

Abraham Lincoln posed for some of the first portrait photographs. This one was taken in 1860, a few months before he became President.

Lincoln was against the idea that the people of each new state should decide for themselves whether or not to have slavery. If slavery is wrong, Lincoln said, then people do not have a right to choose it. Lincoln did not believe that any people have the right to choose to do wrong.

Lincoln lost the election for the Senate seat. Still, the Lincoln-Douglas debates made Lincoln famous. Soon he was invited to speak in other states of the North. His speeches against slavery received loud cheers. People in the North began to think of Lincoln as a leader. In 1860 the Republican party chose Lincoln to run for President. It also came out strongly against the spread of slavery.

The Democratic party split between North and South. Northern Democrats chose Stephen A. Douglas to run for President. Southern Democrats picked John C. Breckinridge, a strong supporter of slavery. Breckinridge believed that if the U.S. government made any more laws against slavery, the South should secede (withdraw) from the Union.

Choosing a President. The election was held on November 6, 1860. Lincoln won. He beat Douglas by nearly 500,000 votes.

The South was in an uproar. "What! Lincoln for President? Impossible!" Some Southern states had already said they would secede if Lincoln won. On December 20, South Carolina said that it was no longer part of the Union. By February 1, six other states had also dropped out. When Lincoln's train left

Senator Stephen A. Douglas of Illinois

for Washington on February 11, the Union was already breaking up.

Lincoln was to be sworn in on March 4. The train trip from Springfield to Washington was stretched out to 12 days. This was to allow as many people as possible to see and hear the new President as he traveled to the capital. Worried crowds gathered at every town and city along the way. They hoped that Lincoln would promise them peace. But the President made no promises.

At six o'clock in the morning on February 23, Lincoln's train slipped quietly into Washington. This was not the same train he had taken from Springfield. It was a private train. Lincoln had switched to a private train because of

To get to Washington, the new President Lincoln had to pass through the slave state of Maryland. A Southern cartoonist imagined a frightened Lincoln sneaking through Baltimore in a boxcar.

reports that someone might try to assassinate him. In Washington, Lincoln was met by an old friend and taken by guards to a hotel.

Offering friendship. On March 4, 1861, Lincoln rode to the Capitol to be sworn in. Soldiers guarded him all along the way. In his speech, Lincoln said that no state had the right to secede from the Union. At the same time, he offered the South peace. "We are not enemies, but friends," he said.

It was too late. The South had made up its mind. Seven Southern states — South Carolina, Mississippi, Florida, Alabama, Georgia, Louisiana, and Texas — had seceded from the Union. They had formed the Confederate States of America. They said it was a new nation independent of the United States. In a few weeks, America would be torn by a bloody and tragic Civil War.

A Second Look. . . .

1. *Why did some Southern states secede from the Union after Lincoln was elected President?*

2. *Suppose that Stephen Douglas had been elected President instead of Lincoln. Many white Southerners trusted Douglas more than Lincoln. Do you think Douglas might have been able to hold the Union together better than Lincoln? Might Douglas have been able to stop the Civil War? Give reasons for your answers.*

3. *Imagine that you are a U.S. Senator from South Carolina in December 1860. Abraham Lincoln has been elected President, and many Southerners have talked of seceding from the Union. Now you must give a short speech in favor of secession. What will you say?*

255

Sounds of cannon fire echoed across the marshes of Charleston harbor, South Carolina, in April 1861. Southerners had opened fire on Union-held Fort Sumter (on island at left). The Civil War had begun.

Chapter 14

Fort Sumter

The fort was neither large nor handsome. It was an old brick building on an island in the Charleston, South Carolina, harbor. Yet in the spring of 1861, Fort Sumter became the center of the dispute between North and South. The future of the fort, like the future of the Union, fell into doubt.

Seven Southern states had already left the Union. They were calling themselves the Confederate States of America — the Confederacy, for short. They had claimed they were a new nation, sepa-rate from the United States. They had even formed their own army. They wanted to be prepared in case President Lincoln tried to force them back into the Union.

One by one, the Confederate army had taken over Union forts in the South. Some of the soldiers in the forts were Southerners. Many of them joined the Confederate army. Others said they were loyal to the United States. They were sent North.

But not all Union forts passed into

Confederate hands. Fort Sumter remained in the control of the U.S. government. It was an important fort partly because of its location. It stood at the mouth of Charleston harbor. Ships sailing into and out of the harbor had to pass it at close range.

The fort was commanded by Major Robert Anderson. He held it with eight other officers and 68 men. Though Anderson was a Southerner, he was loyal to the Union. At the same time, he was in no hurry to start a civil war. In fact, he tried to avoid doing anything to bring on a Confederate attack.

Anderson's worry. By the end of 1860, food and supplies at Fort Sumter had begun to run low. The U.S. War Department had sent a steamer loaded with men and supplies to help the fort. As the ship drew near Charleston, Southern troops had opened fire on it. The ship was not badly damaged. But it never completed its mission. Instead, it made a fast retreat to New York.

As winter wore on, supplies at the fort ran even lower. Late in February, Major Anderson wrote to the War Department. He said that there was no way to stock the fort with new supplies. He claimed that he and his men could last there no more than six weeks. His note reached Washington, D.C., as Abraham Lincoln was about to become President. Its message was clear to Lincoln. Time was running out.

What was Lincoln to do? If he sent supplies, the South would take this as an act of war. If he didn't, the fort would fall to the Confederacy. In this case, Lincoln would appear to have *allowed* the South to secede. Lincoln could not put himself in such a position. Toward the end of March, he made plans to send supply ships south to help the fort.

Beauregard's orders. When Southern leaders learned of this, they decided to act. General Pierre Beauregard (BOH-ruh-gard) was the commander of the Confederate army in Charleston. The Confederate government gave him new orders. If the fort did not surrender, the orders said, he was to take it by force. On April 11, Beauregard sent a message to Major Anderson. It ordered him to give up the fort. Anderson refused. But he also said, "If you do not batter the fort to pieces, we shall be starved out in a few days." There was no real need for the Confederates to fire on Fort Sumter. All they had to do was keep away any supply ships that came along. But the South wanted to show that it was ready to fight for its independence.

At 4:30 in the morning of April 12, 1861, U.S. officers stood guard along Fort Sumter's outer rim. They stared out into blackness and waited for dawn. Then, suddenly, a cannon roared from a nearby marshland. A shell sailed across Charleston harbor and burst on the fort. There was a pause. Then other guns began firing. In an instant, the Civil War had begun.

Anderson's delay. Soon the sky was lit up by bursting shells. Fort Sumter's bricks began to crumble under the pounding. Fires broke out in the soldiers' bunk rooms. Major Anderson was short of ammunition. He couldn't waste any. So he waited till daylight before he ordered his men to return the Confederate fire.

For 34 hours, Confederate guns pounded the fort. In Charleston, men and women watched the shelling from

257

the roofs of houses. Finally, on the afternoon of April 13, Major Anderson knew he had to surrender. Fort Sumter was in ruins. His men were tired and starving. He and his men gave themselves up the next day and were allowed to leave safely on a Union ship.

In the South, news of the surrender brought many cheers. In the North, one man said, "Sumter is lost, but freedom is saved."

Now that the actual fighting had broken out, eight other slave states had to choose sides. Four of them — Maryland, Delaware, Kentucky, and Missouri — stayed in the Union. Four others — Virginia, North Carolina, Tennessee, and Arkansas — joined the Confederacy. In all, the Confederacy had 11 states to carry on the war. The Union had more than twice as many — 23 in all.

A Second Look. . . .

1. *What army held Fort Sumter in March 1861? Why was this army forced to surrender the fort?*

2. *What choices did Abraham Lincoln have in the crisis? Why did he make the decision he did? Was the Civil War "inevitable," as some people have said? Give reasons for your answer.*

3. *After Fort Sumter, both the Union and the Confederacy set out to expand their armies. Pretend that you have the job of urging citizens to join one army or the other. Create a poster that does so. The best posters might be displayed on the class bulletin board.*

The South Secedes, 1860-1861

States Seceding Before Attack on Fort Sumter

States Seceding After Attack on Fort Sumter

States Remaining in Union

U.S. Capital ⊚

Confederate Capital ●

Looking Back: Road to War

A	B	C	D
January 1830	January 1840	January 1850	January 1860	January 1870

Putting Events in Order

Chapters Seven through 14 have described the causes of the Civil War. Ten events of this period are listed here. Your job is to match each event to the correct period shown on the timeline above. On a piece of paper, number from **1** to **10.** After each number, write the letter of the 10-year period within which the event occurred.

1. The U.S. Supreme Court rules that Dred Scott is not entitled to his freedom.

2. Harriet Beecher Stowe writes *Uncle Tom's Cabin.*

3. South Carolina secedes from the Union.

4. Frederick Douglass escapes from slavery.

5. U.S. officials start to enforce the Fugitive Slave Act.

6. *The Liberator* begins its attack on slavery.

7. Abraham Lincoln is elected President.

8. Confederate troops fire on Fort Sumter.

9. The Kansas-Nebraska Act replaces the Missouri Compromise and makes it possible for slavery to spread.

10. John Brown is hanged for his raid at Harpers Ferry, Virginia.

Interpreting a Source

The two letters below show how much the attitudes of master and slave differed by 1860. The first letter was written to o former slave by Mrs. Sarah Logue of Tennessee on February 20, 1860. The former slave, the Reverend J.W. Logan of Syracuse, New York, answered her letter on March 28, 1860. Logan had been Mrs. Logue's slave "Jarm" before he escaped to the North.

To Jarm: I take my pen to write you a few lines, to let you know how we all are. I am a cripple, but I am still able to get about. The rest of the family are all well.

I write you these lines to let you know the situation we are in — partly [as a result] of your running away and stealing Old Rock, our fine mare. . . . As I now stand in need of some funds, I have determined to sell you. . . . If you will send me $1,000, and pay for the old mare, I will give up all claim I have to you. Write to me as soon as you get these lines, and let me know if you will accept my proposition.[1] In consequence[2] of your running away, we had to sell Abe and Ann [Logan's brother and sister] and 12 acres [almost five hectares] of land; and I want you to send me the money, that I may be able to redeem[3] the land that you was the cause of our selling, and on receipt [delivery] of the above-named sum of money, I will send you your bill of sale. . . . You had better comply[4] with my request.

Mrs. Sarah Logue: Yours of the 20th of February is duly received, and I thank you for it. . . .

You are a woman; but, had you a woman's heart, you never could have insulted a brother by telling him you sold his only remaining brother and sister, because he put himself beyond your power to convert[5] him into money.

You sold my brother and sister, Abe and Ann, and 12 acres of land, you say, because I ran away. Now you have the . . . meanness to ask me to return and be your miserable chattel,[6] or in lieu[7] thereof, send you $1,000 to enable you to redeem the *land*, but not to redeem my poor brother and sister! If I were to send you money, it would be to get my brother and sister, and not that you should get land. You say you are a *cripple*, and doubtless you say it to stir my pity . . . I do pity you from the bottom of my heart. Nevertheless I am indignant[8] . . . that you should be so sunken and cruel as to tear the hearts I love so much all in pieces; that you should be willing to impale[9] and crucify us all, out of compassion[10] for your poor *foot* or *leg*. Wretched woman! Be it known to you that I value my freedom, to say nothing of my mother, brothers, and sisters, more than your whole body; more, indeed, than my own life; more than all the lives of all the slave-holders and tyrants under heaven.

1. *The Reverend Logan calls Mrs. Logue "sunken and cruel." Why? Do you agree with him? Does she intend to be "cruel"?*

2. *What are Mrs. Logue's attitudes about how a slave should behave? Do you think her neighbors in Tennessee probably shared these attitudes? Might some neighbors have different attitudes? Why or why not?*

---

[1]A *proposition* is a plan or proposal.

[2]A *consequence* is a result or outcome.

[3]*To redeem* is to buy back or regain possession of something by payment in money or action.

[4]*To comply* is to act as requested or ordered.

[5]*To convert* means, in this sense, to change from one form to another.

[6]A *chattel* is, in this sense, a slave.

[7]*In lieu* means instead.

[8]To be *indignant* is to be angry at something considered unfair, mean, or cruel.

[9]*To impale* is to torture or kill by fixing on a sharp stake.

[10]*Compassion* is a feeling of sorrow or sympathy for others.

Electoral Vote, 1860

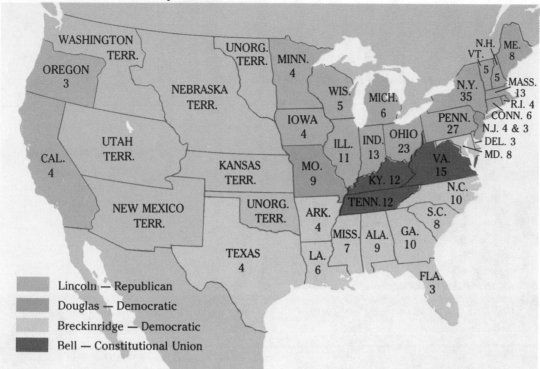

WASHINGTON TERR.

OREGON 3

UNORG. TERR.

MINN. 4

N.H.
VT. 5
ME. 8
5
MASS. 13

NEBRASKA TERR.

WIS. 5

MICH. 6

N.Y. 35

R.I. 4

CAL. 4

UTAH TERR.

IOWA 4

ILL. 11
IND. 13
OHIO 23

PENN. 27
CONN. 6
N.J. 4 & 3
DEL. 3
MD. 8

KANSAS TERR.

MO. 9

KY. 12
VA. 15

NEW MEXICO TERR.

UNORG. TERR.

ARK. 4

TENN. 12
N.C. 10

S.C. 8

TEXAS 4

LA. 6

MISS. 7
ALA. 9
GA. 10

FLA. 3

■ Lincoln — Republican
■ Douglas — Democratic
■ Breckinridge — Democratic
■ Bell — Constitutional Union

3. *For which of the two letter-writers do you have more sympathy? Is it possible to have sympathy for both? Explain.*

Sharpening Your Skills

How did Abraham Lincoln win the election of 1860? How did this election show the divisions in the country, North and South? Find out by studying the map on this page and answering the following questions.

1. How many electoral votes did each candidate receive? (To answer, list the votes received by each candidate in the different states and add the total.)

2. The popular vote received by each candidate was as follows: Lincoln, 1,866,352; Douglas, 1,375,157; Breckinridge, 847,953; Bell, 589,581. Notice that Douglas came in second in popular votes but last in electoral votes. Can you explain how this happened?

3. The statement that follows is true: "The United States in 1860 was deeply divided between North and South." How does the map show that this statement is true?

4. The statement that follows is false: "In 1860 the South had a larger population than the North." The map does not give population figures. Yet it can be used to show that the above statement is indeed false. How?

3 A NATION TORN AND BLEEDING

Looking Ahead: Brother Against Brother

The Civil War lasted four years, from 1861 to 1865. It was the most terrible war in U.S. history. More Americans died in the Civil War than in the Revolutionary War, the War of 1812, the Mexican War, the Spanish-American War, World War I, World War II, and the Korean War all put together.

About 620,000 Americans gave their lives in the Civil War. This figure included some 38,000 black Americans. This means that the Civil War cost an average of more than 420 lives a day, every day, for four years.

The Civil War tore the nation apart. In some families, one brother fought for the North, and another for the South. The Civil War caused very heavy damage, as well as many deaths. Most of the

Civil War soldiers found their truths in "the watch-fires of a hundred circling camps." This 1862 Winslow Homer painting shows Union troops numbed by homesickness, boredom, and cold.

fighting took place in the South. It left many Southern towns and cities in ruins.

When the war began, each side was confident that it could win. And each did indeed have certain advantages. The North was better equipped than the South to fight a long war. Northern factories could produce rifles, bullets, boots, uniforms — as much as its army needed. But in the South, factories were few. Southern soldiers soon were marching barefoot. They lacked decent guns, decent uniforms, and decent food.

But the South also had advantages. For one thing, it had a greater number of trained military leaders than the North. For another, Southerners most often fought on their own soil against Northern invaders. The feeling that they were defending their homes and families helped Southerners to keep up a strong fighting spirit. People of the North were much less united. Many of them did not know at first what they were fighting for.

263

Lee's greatness. The coming of war posed an especially sad problem for one old soldier. He was Lieutenant Colonel Robert E. Lee of Virginia. Lee did not want to leave the United States Army. He had served it all his adult life. Yet to stay in the Army meant that he would have to fight against his own people — Virginians. He could not bring himself to do this either.

Lee explained his problem to a Northern girl who asked him for his photograph. He wrote to her: "I cannot raise my hand against my birthplace, my home, my children." Lee understood what war would mean. He understood that it would bring terrible suffering to both the North and the South. Lee finished the letter to his Northern friend with these words: "May God direct all for our good, and shield and preserve you and yours!"

Lee then put on a new uniform — the uniform of the Confederacy. He became the South's greatest military leader. For four years, he led Southern troops in one grim and bloody battle after another. He suffered two great setbacks. In 1862 he invaded the North and fought the costly Battle of Antietam (an-TEET-um) in Maryland. In 1863 he lost even more men at the Battle of Gettysburg in Pennsylvania. Robert E. Lee knew what war was — a tragedy.

Lincoln's leadership. The North's great leader, Abraham Lincoln, was also saddened by the war. As President, Lincoln had many enemies in both North and South. Members of his own Cabinet sneered at him behind his back. Because he was so tall and awkward, one Cabinet member called him a "gorilla." Children in the South mocked him with a song. It compared Lincoln with the President of the Confederacy, Jefferson Davis. The song went like this:

Jeff Davis rides a snow-white horse;
Abe Lincoln rides a mule;
Jeff Davis is a gentleman;
Abe Lincoln is a fool.

Since then, people have changed their minds about Lincoln. They understand now that he was a great leader — and a great human being. What made him so great?

For one thing, he was shrewd at politics. He first ran for political office when he was only 25. Ever since, he had watched political leaders work. He had seen how they bargained with one another for power. This knowledge was useful to him as President. It helped him to deal with the quarreling members of Congress. It helped him to get through the first year of war when the North suffered many defeats on the battlefield.

Lincoln also had a gift for political timing. Many Northerners wanted him to declare an end to slavery when the war began in 1861. Yet Lincoln waited until just the right time to do this. He proclaimed slaves in the Confederacy to be free only when he knew this would help to win the war.

Lincoln's greatness. But Lincoln's claim to greatness went much deeper. He was gentle as well as strong. As an eight-year-old boy, he had gone out hunting with his father in the woods of Indiana. He had shot and killed a turkey. The death of this wild creature had so upset him that he had never again shot

Even very young soldiers gave their lives in battle. This Georgia private gave his in 1862.

264

an animal. He had the same tender feelings about people. He never punished his four children. When they misbehaved, he just asked them kindly why they did it.

As President, Lincoln did not think of Southerners as enemies. He saw Confederate soldiers as human beings who were suffering as deeply as Union soldiers. He hated the bloodshed and death that the war caused. But it pained him even more to see fellow human beings treated as slaves. "If slavery isn't wrong," he once said, "then nothing is wrong."

In March 1865, it seemed that the war was almost over. Lincoln made his last great speech to the American people. He asked that, after the war, people treat each other "with malice toward none, with charity for all." Only a few weeks later, an assassin shot and killed him. It was a bitterly sad ending to a bitterly sad war.

Even before the Civil War, Northern industries turned out iron, steel, and guns. During the war, industry grew stronger. John Ferguson Weir painted the steel mill below soon after the war's end.

Chapter 15

"Forward to Richmond!"

It started out as a picnic. In the city of Washington, people packed picnic lunches. Then they followed the Union army up the road to Virginia. They wanted to watch the first battle of the Civil War. The Union soldiers looked very fine indeed marching off to battle. Some wore bright red pants and blue jackets. Others wore yellow sashes around their waists. Each regiment showed off its own splendid silk flag. Yes, July 21, 1861, promised to be an exciting day.

People spread out their lunches a few miles from a stream called Bull Run. That was where the battle was expected to take place. The spectators could not see much of the fight. But they could hear the booming of the cannons. They could see puffs of gunsmoke drift up into the summer sky.

Then, all of a sudden, the fun stopped. A few wounded soldiers stumbled down the road past the picnickers. The soldiers were heading back to Washington. The picnickers became a little worried. They decided to hitch up their buggies and start the long ride home. Hundreds of buggies tried to get on the road at the same time. There was a traffic jam.

Panicky retreat. Great numbers of Union soldiers came toward the picnickers from the battlefield. They looked beaten, tired, and afraid. They had lost the Battle of Bull Run, and they were trying to retreat. But the road was blocked by all the civilian buggies. Was the Confederate army pursuing the defeated Northerners? People feared that it was. They began to panic. Some soldiers started to run. There was a lot of shoving, shouting, and screaming.

In fact, the Confederate army did not pursue its foe. Southern generals thought their troops too weary and disorganized for that. After hours of agony and fear, Northern soldiers and civilians made it back to Washington. Hundreds of soldiers, however, did not return. Their dead bodies were buried where they fell — on both sides of Bull Run.

People now understood what the Civil War would be like. It would not be a picnic. Instead, it would be a grim, life-and-death struggle. How long would it last? Nobody knew. Who would win? Nobody could be sure of the answer to this question either.

One way the North believed it could win was to attack and capture the South's capital city — Richmond, Virginia. That was where the Union army was heading before it was stopped at Bull Run. Northern newspapers, eager for victory, urged another attack. "Forward to Richmond! Forward to Richmond!" cried the New York *Tribune.* But the commander of the Union armies was not so eager to fight. He was the brilliant-but-cautious General George B. McClellan. The soldiers under his command loved him. For months they practiced marching back and forth in the giant tent camps outside Washington. At last, in the spring of 1862, McClellan was ready to march against Richmond.

Seven days' campaign. In Virginia two Southern generals were ready for McClellan's invading army. One of them was General Robert E. Lee. The other was General Thomas "Stonewall" Jackson. They allowed McClellan's army to get within a few miles of Richmond. Then Lee and Jackson threw all their strength against the Union lines. There were seven days of fierce fighting. The Union army did not take Richmond. McClellan was forced to retreat.

General George B. McClellan took eight months to organize an invasion of Virginia. But when Confederate armies struck, McClellan retreated so fast that he had to leave injured men behind (right). Later an angry Abraham Lincoln met McClellan face to face at the general's camp (below). Finally Lincoln dismissed McClellan.

The tough Southern army could fight off the Northern invaders. But the South could be beaten in another way. The Southern economy could be strangled by the Northern navy. Soon after the war began, President Lincoln set up a blockade. That is, he ordered Northern warships to block traffic in and out of every major Southern port. The South needed to trade its cotton for guns, bullets, and clothing from Europe. But the Northern blockade cut off most of these supplies. It cut the South's life line.

The longer the war lasted, the harder it would be for the South to survive. The Confederate general, Robert E. Lee, un-derstood this very well. The South, he decided, needed one more great victory. It needed to scare the North with its fighting power. Even more important, it needed to impress the government of Britain. Before the war, the British had bought a great deal of Southern cotton. Now British aid could help the South win the war.

In September 1862, Lee led his army into Maryland — Northern territory. Part of his aim was to draw Maryland into the Confederacy. With a little luck, his daring plan might have worked. But Lee was not lucky. By accident, a copy of his battle plans fell into the hands of the

269

War Without Victory, 1861-1862

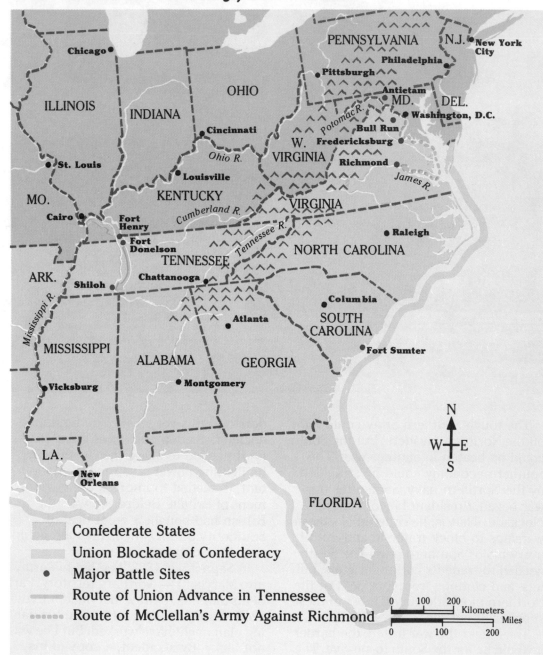

Confederate States

Union Blockade of Confederacy

• Major Battle Sites

Route of Union Advance in Tennessee

Route of McClellan's Army Against Richmond

Union army. The Northern general, McClellan, knew exactly what Lee was planning.

Battle of Antietam. Two huge armies clashed near the little farming village of Sharpsburg, Maryland. Attacking soldiers were ripped apart trying to cross an open cornfield. Other soldiers fought and died on a stone bridge that crossed Antietam Creek. Still others died fighting behind a small village church. The fighting lasted all day. Bodies of the dead lay everywhere. In one day, the Union army lost 12,000 men killed and wounded. Lee's army lost at least as many. It was one of the bloodiest days in the whole war.

Neither side could claim a true victory at Antietam Creek. But Lee's army was forced to retreat to Virginia. Its invasion of the North had failed. Hearing of the battle, the British government backed away from its plan of aiding the South.

The North and the South had now both survived one full year of war. It had been a terrible year. Three more years of pain and death lay ahead. The war had only begun.

A Second Look. . . .

1. *What were the results of the Battles of Bull Run and Antietam? Who won, who lost, and why?*

2. *General George B. McClellan had great support from his soldiers. Yet he was unable to bring forth any major victories in the first year of the war. Which quality seems more important in a general — an ability to make decisions or an ability to build fighting spirit? Why?*

3. *Pretend that you are either Jefferson Davis, President of the Confederacy, or Abraham Lincoln, President of the United States. Imagine that you have a total of 100 million dollars to spend on the war effort. You must make three decisions about fighting the war in the year 1863. (a) How much money should you spend on your army? How much should you spend on your navy? (b) Should you plan to invade enemy territory? Or should you keep troops in your own home territory for defense? (c) How much help do you need from foreign governments? How will you go about getting it? For each question, write your decision and your reason for it.*

In September 1862, Robert E. Lee's Confederate army met George McClellan's Union troops in the Battle of Antietam. When the fighting was over, thousands lay dead in the Maryland fields.

271

Chapter 16

Emancipation

President Lincoln was troubled. It was the summer of 1862, and the Civil War had been going on for more than a year. Victory was still nowhere in sight. In fact, the South had won every major battle fought so far. Lincoln was beginning to wonder if he could ever defeat the Confederate armies and bring the South back into the Union.

Besides these problems, the President was having trouble with his Cabinet and with Congress. Some members of the Cabinet and Congress were saying that Lincoln should give an order to *emancipate* (free) all the slaves. Lincoln himself had been thinking about this idea for a long time. But he hadn't made up his mind about it yet.

Lincoln had not hesitated for any personal reasons. He had deeply opposed slavery for many years. His record was well known. Yet he realized that slavery was a political problem. Freeing slaves too quickly could cause more problems than it solved.

When Lincoln was elected, he saw

Before emancipation, a great many slaves were field workers, made to till the soil of Southern farms.

that he had two main jobs to do. One was to save the Union. The other was to stop the spread of slavery. In his speech upon taking office, Lincoln said that he had no plans to free the slaves, only to save the Union. Many people agreed with this stand. But as the war went on, more and more Northerners began saying that the real purpose of the war was to free the slaves.

Republicans argue. The Republicans in Congress and the men in the Cabinet were split on the question. Some of them — called *Radical Republicans* — were for freeing the slaves right away. They said that slavery had really started the war. They also said that the South was able to fight only because it had slaves to do most of its work. Slave labor supplied the South with cotton to trade for guns and war supplies. Slave labor raised the food that fed Southern armies. The Radicals said that freeing the slaves would help to win the war and save the Union. It would encourage slaves to disobey their masters — or better yet, to run away. Some Radicals argued that Lincoln should ask the slaves to join the Union army.

Other leaders said that Lincoln should forget about the slaves and stick to his main job — winning the war. They said that the war wasn't being fought over the question of slavery. It was being fought to preserve the Union, nothing more and nothing less.

Lincoln takes a stand. The President listened to both sides. He saw that both sides had good arguments. But in the summer of 1862, Lincoln leaned toward the Radicals' viewpoint. Why? For one thing, he saw that Northerners were growing impatient on the issue. Many of them wanted action to rid the nation of slavery — fast. For another, Lincoln thought such an action would be popular in Europe. It would greatly lessen the chance that European nations might enter the war on the side of the South. Perhaps the most important reason was what such an action would do for the spirit of the Union army. It would give the war a purpose which it now seemed to lack.

Finally, one hot summer day, the President came to a decision. He did so while waiting in the White House telegraph office for news of the fighting. He borrowed some paper. He sat down at an old desk and began to write. He crossed out words, chewed his pen, and listened to the telegraph. After a long time, he finished. He put his notes in his pocket and went back to the White House.

What had he written? It was one of the most important papers in American history. It was the *Emancipation Proclamation.*

The Emancipation Proclamation was an order that would declare free *most* of the slaves in the Confederate states. It would not free the slaves in four slave states that had stayed loyal to the Union. These were border states. Lincoln did not want them to secede. But his order would declare free all the slaves in any parts of the South that were still in rebellion against the Union.

Lincoln did not sign the Emancipation Proclamation right away. His Secretary of State, William Seward, warned him against it. Seward said that Lincoln must wait for a Union victory before signing it. Otherwise it might seem that a weak Union was *begging* the slaves for help.

Lincoln agreed. He kept the Emancipation Proclamation locked in his desk for weeks. Then came the news of Lee's retreat at Antietam on September 17. Lincoln felt he was now ready to act. Five days later, he gave the Confederate states a warning. He said they must come back to the Union by January 1, 1863. Otherwise all their slaves would be "forever free."

Lincoln signs an order. The nation waited. The year was coming to an end. The Confederate states had not come back to the Union. Would Lincoln sign the Proclamation? Or would he hold back?

On January 1, 1863, thousands of people flocked to the White House. Lincoln greeted them all. Then he took an old steel pen in his hand. He signed the Emancipation Proclamation. The slaves in the Confederacy were declared free.

"If my name ever goes down in history," Lincoln said, "it will be for this act. My whole soul is in it."

In many parts of the North, guns were fired to greet the signing. Many people wept with joy. Yet a few Northerners claimed that the Proclamation was meaningless. They pointed out that the President had freed only slaves in the Confederacy, not in states loyal to the Union. One member of Lincoln's Cabinet criticized the President. He said that the order had freed slaves where it could not touch them. And it had left them slaves where it could have set them free.

Such criticism missed the broader point of Lincoln's order. The point was that slavery would be ended if the Union won the Civil War. The first nation to promise liberty for all had begun to keep its promise. Later the 13th Amendment to the Constitution would outlaw slavery everywhere in the United States.

A Second Look. . . .

1. *Why did Lincoln wait so long before issuing the Emancipation Proclamation?*

2. *Do you think Lincoln waited too long to do so? Should he have issued the Proclamation as soon as the war began? Why or why not? How much truth was there in the criticism of the Proclamation? Do you agree with the criticism? Why or why not?*

3. *On January 1, 1863, the day the Proclamation took effect, a group met in Boston to celebrate it. Members of the group included William Lloyd Garrison, Frederick Douglass, and Harriet Beecher Stowe. Create a conversation among these three people. Each should tell what he or she thinks emancipation will mean for the future of the U.S.*

Southern cartoonist Adalbert Volck showed Lincoln drafting the Emancipation Proclamation while treading on the U.S. Constitution.

Confederate and Union troops met at Gettysburg amid a rolling cloud of smoke (above). When the smoke cleared, Gettysburg was seen as a turning point, the beginning of the end for the Confederacy.

Chapter 17

Gettysburg

The people of Cashtown, Pennsylvania, could hardly believe their eyes. It was early summer, 1863. The fields were green, and the trees cast cool shadows on the grass. But in this quiet little Pennsylvania town, Confederate troops jammed the dusty streets. Most of them were barefoot and hungry. They broke shop windows to get shoes. They grabbed pigs and chickens for food.

Angry crowds of citizens met at a church. One man said, "Them Southerners got no right coming North to fight. Let 'em stay where they belong, in Georgia or Tennessee."

"Well, what I heard," said another,

275

"was that General Lee aims to give us Yanks a taste of what war is like. In our own backyard."

It was true. Confederate General Robert E. Lee had made up his mind to invade Pennsylvania. A victory there would be a big boost for the fighting spirit of the South. Lee had 75,000 men. Union General George Meade was marching to meet him with 90,000 men.

Collision course. On July 1, a large group of Confederate soldiers headed toward the town of Gettysburg. The soldiers — that day, at least — were looking only for shoes and provisions (food supplies). Instead, they ran into Union soldiers — and one of the greatest battles of the war began.

Back and forth the armies fought for three days. Soldiers on both sides attacked with bayonets or fired up close. One wheat field was won, and lost, six times. Cannonballs cut down the ranks of soldiers. Union gunners, their faces black with smoke, screamed, "Feed it to 'em!" Moans came from the wounded who lay helpless in the hot sun.

Cemetery Ridge. On July 3, Lee decided to attack the center of the Union line on Cemetery Ridge. First, Confederate cannons opened up with the heaviest fire of the war. One man on Cemetery Ridge wrote: "We see the poor fellows [Union soldiers] lying on the ground with the stump of an arm or leg, dripping their life blood away; or with a cheek torn open."

Then 15,000 Confederates led by General George Pickett moved through a peach orchard and charged the Union soldiers on Cemetery Ridge. As the Confederate soldiers marched up the slope, Union cannons blasted big holes in their

ranks. Then rifle fire came down on them. Only a few of the Confederate troops reached the top of the ridge. There they held on for 20 minutes. Finally they were driven back. One Confederate soldier shouted: "It ain't so hard to get to that ridge. The hard part is staying there."

The next morning Lee's broken army pulled back toward Virginia. Gettysburg was the South's "high water mark" — the farthest point the Confederates ever reached in the North. Lee's retreat was also a turning point in the war. Lee had lost more than 23,000 men dead and wounded. He would never again be able to stage a major attack against the North. After Gettysburg, the Civil War would be fought — and finished — in the South.

A Second Look. . . .

1. The Battle of Gettysburg was a turning point in the Civil War. Why?

2. Why did General Lee try to invade Pennsylvania? Why do you suppose a victory in the North would have helped the South's fighting spirit? Would you have risked an invasion of Pennsylvania had you been in Lee's place? Why or why not?

3. After the Battle of Gettysburg, the governors of several Northern states planned a cemetery for the men who had fought there. The cemetery was dedicated in November 1863 by Abraham Lincoln. The speech he delivered that day can be found in most almanacs. One student might read this speech aloud. Then discuss why the speech is thought to be one of the greatest ever made. Does it contain an important message for Americans today? Why?

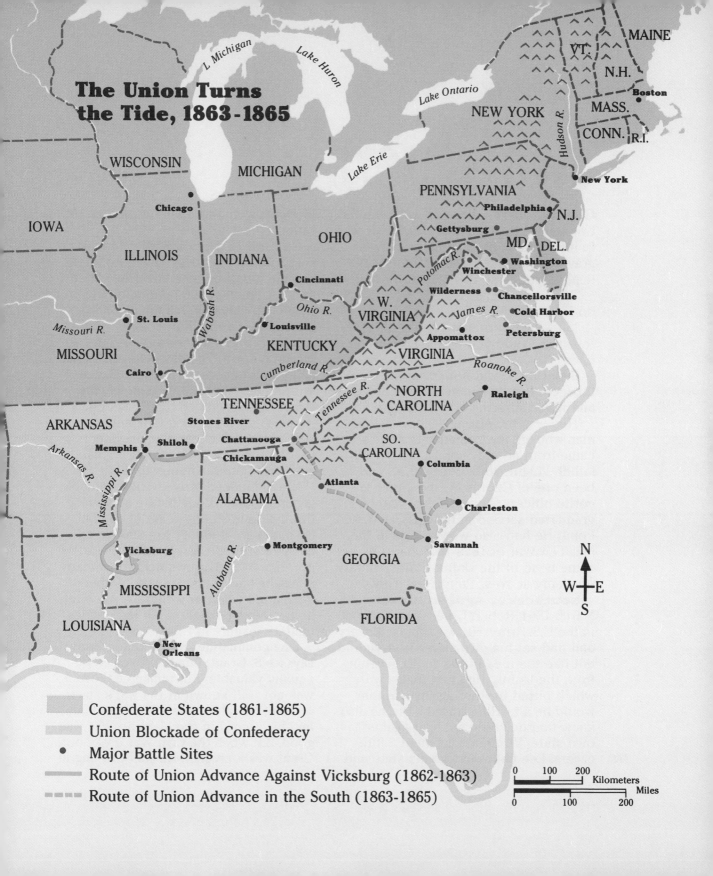

The Union Turns the Tide, 1863-1865

L. Michigan

Lake Huron

Lake Ontario

Lake Erie

MAINE

VT.

N.H.

MASS.

Boston

CONN.

R.I.

NEW YORK

Hudson R.

New York

WISCONSIN

MICHIGAN

IOWA

ILLINOIS

INDIANA

OHIO

Chicago

PENNSYLVANIA

Philadelphia

N.J.

Gettysburg

MD.

DEL.

Cincinnati

Potomac R.

Winchester

Washington

Ohio R.

W. VIRGINIA

Wilderness

Chancellorsville

St. Louis

Louisville

KENTUCKY

James R.

Cold Harbor

Missouri R.

VIRGINIA

Appomattox

Petersburg

MISSOURI

Cairo

Cumberland R.

Roanoke R.

Wabash R.

NORTH CAROLINA

Raleigh

ARKANSAS

TENNESSEE

Tennessee R.

Stones River

SO. CAROLINA

Memphis

Shiloh

Chattanooga

Columbia

Arkansas R.

Chickamauga

Atlanta

Charleston

Mississippi R.

ALABAMA

Savannah

Vicksburg

Alabama R.

Montgomery

GEORGIA

MISSISSIPPI

FLORIDA

LOUISIANA

New Orleans

N
W + E
S

Confederate States (1861-1865)

Union Blockade of Confederacy

● Major Battle Sites

Route of Union Advance Against Vicksburg (1862-1863)

Route of Union Advance in the South (1863-1865)

0   100   200   Kilometers

0   100   200   Miles

Chapter 18

Two Generals

General Robert E. Lee was watching the Union lines through field glasses. He was in his middle 50's, and his beard was gray. He stood tall and straight. Suddenly a young soldier was at his side.

"Yes, my son," Lee said, "what can I do for you?"

"Sir," the boy answered, "I'm all out of tobacco. Could you let me have a chew?"

General Lee did not smoke or chew tobacco. But he called over an officer and made sure the boy got some.

This was the strong, kind, religious man who led the Confederate armies. He came from an old Virginia family. His father, "Light Horse Harry" Lee, had been one of George Washington's favorite officers. Robert E. Lee had been graduated second in his class at West Point. He had also won honors in the Mexican War of 1846-1848. Later he became head of the United States Military Academy at West Point, New York.

Southerner against slavery. In March 1861, Robert E. Lee was a colonel in the U.S. Army. He was against slavery and had set his own slaves free. He did not like the idea of the South seceding from the Union. He knew that a war which pitted brother against brother would be a terrible tragedy. But he also knew that he could not fight against his own state, Virginia. Like most Southerners, Lee believed that his state and

its rights were more important than the Union.

On April 18, five days after the fall of Fort Sumter, President Lincoln offered Lee the job of commanding the Union army. A Union general had told Lincoln, "Lee is so valuable, his life should be insured for five million dollars." Lincoln's offer was a great honor, but Lee turned it down. The day before, Virginia had voted to secede from the Union. With a heavy heart, Lee then left the U.S. Army and joined the Confederacy.

Lee said: "If I owned four million slaves, I would cheerfully give them up to save the Union. But to lift my hand against Virginia is impossible."

Lee did indeed prove to be a valuable general. He led Confederate soldiers through four bloody years of combat. He had a great ability to measure an enemy's strength and location. He knew how to move an army quickly over many miles. He had a superb sense of when to attack and when to withdraw. All in all, he has been judged one of the greatest military leaders in U.S. history.

One commander of the Union army, Ulysses S. Grant, finally proved to be equally valuable. But unlike Lee, Grant was not well known at the war's start.

Grant was also a West Point graduate, and his record in the Mexican War was good. But when the Civil War broke out, Grant was a civilian. He was working in

his brother's leather-goods store in Illinois. He thought of himself as a failure, "stuck in the mud," washed up at 40. When he tried to rejoin the army in 1861, he had to beg for a job. Finally he was made a colonel.

Northerner against retreat. As a soldier, Grant believed, "When in doubt, fight." And he did fight. He won fame for demanding unconditional (complete) surrender from the Southern commanders he was fighting. In fact, people in the North began saying that Grant's initials, "U.S.," stood for "Unconditional Surrender."

In battle, Grant was tough and hard. He was not "a retreating man." As cannons roared, he sometimes carved wood or smoked big cigars. Sometimes he took a drink.

Soon Grant was made a general. He became a leading figure of the war in the West. In 1863 he captured the city of Vicksburg, Mississippi. He starved the city into surrender. Grant's victory at Vicksburg came the same day as Lee's retreat from Gettysburg. With Vicksburg in Union hands, the North had control of shipping on the Mississippi River.

Lincoln had searched for a winning commander for two years. Six top generals had come and gone. None of them had made great headway against the South. But now there was Ulysses S. Grant. "Grant is my man," Lincoln said. "He pounded Vicksburg — and won. He *fights!*"

Early in March 1864, Grant was called to the White House. There he met Lincoln for the first time. Grant didn't look much like a general. He didn't even look

General Robert E. Lee

like a soldier. He was sloppy in his dress uniform. He didn't stand straight, the way a general should. And he had a rough, untidy beard. But his blue eyes were bright and cold.

A few days later, Lincoln promoted Grant to the highest rank in the army. Other officers grumbled. Some said that Grant drank too much. But Lincoln didn't care. He said that Grant was the man he needed. Grant was afraid of no one, not even Robert E. Lee.

When Grant became commander of the Union armies, he attacked without letup. He lost 50,000 men, all told. Some people called him a "butcher." This hurt him, but he knew only one way to win — attack. Such was the man who finally pounded the South into surrender.

A Second Look. . . .

1. In 1863 both Robert E. Lee and Ulysses S. Grant fought famous battles. Where did they take place? How did the two battles lead to a Union victory in the war?

2. Suppose you had been of fighting age in 1861. Which general would you have preferred to serve under — Ulysses S. Grant or Robert E. Lee? Why?

3. There were other heroes of the Civil War besides those mentioned in this chapter. Look up the following four people in the reference room of your local library: Thomas "Stonewall" Jackson, George B. McClellan, William T. Sherman, James E. "Jeb" Stuart. Using the Dictionary of American Biography *or an encyclopedia, write a one-paragraph description of what each of the above men did in the Civil War.*

General Ulysses S. Grant

Chapter 19

The South Surrenders

It is a quiet Sunday, April 9, 1865, in the tiny village of Appomattox (ap-uh-MAT-ucks) Court House, Virginia. Even the trees are still. There is only the sound of horses' hooves.

In a farmhouse parlor sits a tired man with a gray beard. He is alone with his thoughts. He wears a spotless uniform with a bright red sash. His boots are like mirrors, his buttons shine. A fine sword hangs from his side.

He is General Robert E. Lee, only recently named Commanding General of the Confederate army. His army — what is left of it — is starved and beaten. A few days before, it had given up Richmond, the Confederate capital. Then, near Appomattox Court House, Lee's army was cut off from retreat. There was not much left to do except surrender to General Grant. "And I would rather die a thousand deaths," Lee said.

Yet Lee knows when he is beaten. He also knows the folly of continuing to fight. Hours earlier one of his officers advised him to break up his army and let it go on fighting in the hills. Lee rejected the advice. To let the fighting go on, he believed, would let old hatreds go on simmering. This would mean that the South would not recover from the war for many years.

Now Lee is waiting for General Ulysses S. Grant to arrive. He remembers what he has just told an officer. "You ask why I am dressed like this? I may become General Grant's prisoner. I must look my best."

Outside, footsteps are heard. General Grant enters with half a dozen officers in blue. Grant wears a wrinkled private's coat. His boots and trousers are spotted with mud. He wears no sword. Only the gold stars on his shoulders show his rank.

Meeting at a crossroads. The two generals bow and shake hands. Then they chat for a few moments about the old days when they both fought for the U.S. in the Mexican War. Finally Lee reminds Grant of why he has come, and the two get down to business.

Grant knows what surrender must mean to Lee. Following Lincoln's instructions, Grant is kind to his enemy. He will take no prisoners. Lee's men will be allowed to go home. Southern officers may keep their swords. Soldiers owning horses or mules may keep them. "Let all the men who claim to own a horse or mule take the animals home with them," says Grant, "to work their little farms."

One thing more. "General Sheridan," Grant asks a nearby officer, "how much food do we have?" When Sheridan replies, Grant orders: "Give General Lee food for 25,000 men."

Lee shakes hands with Grant and

281

bows to the other Union officers. Then he walks out to the farmhouse porch. His horse, Traveler, is brought up. Lee mounts. Grant has his officers raise their hats in respect. Lee raises his and, without another word, rides off to his army.

His men crowd around him, shaking his hand. Some of them are crying. "God help you, General," they say. Lee is barely able to speak. "Men," he says at last, "we have fought through this war together. I have done the best I could for you. My heart is too full to say more."

Marching salute. Three days later, on April 12, Lee's men gathered for the surrender of arms. They formed into columns for the last time. Then, their flags waving in the breeze, they marched toward the troops in blue lined up on either side. As they approached the lines, a Union bugle sounded. The commander of the Union troops ordered his men to give the marching salute. This is the highest honor that fighting men can give to other fighting men.

General John B. Gordon rode at the head of the Confederate marchers. He was a proud man who had fought under Thomas "Stonewall" Jackson during the war. Now he dropped the point of his sword and shouted, "Carry *arms!*" Then his men returned the Union salute. It was a moment of quiet splendor.

At the end of the salute, the men in gray laid down their arms and flags.

The fighting was over at last.

A Second Look. . . .

1. *What were the terms of surrender Grant presented to Lee at Appomattox?*

2. *Many civil wars go on for generations. The American Civil War lasted only four years. It was ended by the peace at Appomattox. One reason the peace was successful, U.S. historian Bruce Catton has argued, was that it was generous on both sides. Using examples from the chapter, defend Catton's argument or try to show that it is wrong.*

3. *Imagine that you are a soldier in Lee's army. Earlier today you joined with your fellow soldiers for the surrender of arms. Now it is nightfall, and you are writing a letter to your family back home. Describe your feelings about the war, the surrender, and the leadership of Robert E. Lee.*

Their ordeal ended, Confederate prisoners leave for home. This 1866 painting is by Winslow Homer.

Chapter 20

The Death of Lincoln

The surrender at Appomattox marked both an end and a beginning. The Civil War was over. Now the nation could begin to think of the years ahead. For Abraham Lincoln it was a time to bind up the nation's wounds. He had called upon Americans to do so "with malice toward none."

Five days after the surrender, the President and his wife, Mary, went to see an English play. The play was being presented at Ford's Theater, not far from the White House. The Lincolns took their seats in Box Seven above stage left. They were joined by an engaged couple, Clara Harris and Major Henry R. Rathbone. The date was Good Friday, April 14, 1865.

A little after 10 P.M., a man in a black suit slipped quietly into the Lincolns' darkened box. In his right hand he held a small, single-shot pistol. In his left hand, he held a dagger. Carefully he raised the pistol behind the President's left ear. A shot rang out. The President's head fell onto his chest. He would never speak again.

How did it happen? Who was the man in the black suit who had done such a terrible thing?

John Wilkes Booth, the man who killed Lincoln, was a well-known actor. He was not insane, but he had a strong wish to win lasting fame. Booth wanted the South to win the Civil War. He hated Lincoln for trying to hold the Union together. In 1864 Booth decided he must do something to help the South win the war. Booth's idea was to kidnap President Lincoln and take him to Richmond, Virginia, the Confederate capital. This would make Booth's name famous and would also hurt the man he hated.

Kidnap plot. Booth found five Confederate supporters to help. They first planned to kidnap Lincoln from Ford's Theater on January 18, 1865. But the plan did not work. President Lincoln did not go to the theater that night as expected. On March 20, the six men again tried to kidnap Lincoln. They learned that on this day Lincoln would visit the Soldiers' Home outside Washington. On a lonely road, they waited on horseback for his carriage to pass by. But Lincoln decided not to go to the Soldiers' Home that day. So this plan also failed.

Then, on April 13, Booth heard that President Lincoln would be at Ford's Theater the next night. By this time, he had given up his kidnaping plan. Instead, Booth decided to kill the President for revenge.

The next morning Booth went to Ford's Theater and made his plans. He decided he could easily make the jump from the President's box to the stage. Outside the rear door, a horse would be waiting for him. Booth decided that 10:15 P.M. would be the right time to make his move. Then there would be only one actor on the stage.

Shortly after 10 o'clock that evening, Booth arrived at the theater. He went up to the President's box. No one was guarding the door. The man who was supposed to guard it was not at his post. Booth opened the door. In a moment, the pistol was behind Lincoln's head, and Booth fired.

Booth shouted, *"Sic semper tyrannis!"* ("Thus always to tyrants!") Then he jumped to the stage, breaking his left leg in the fall. But before anyone could stop him, he was out the back door. He got away on a horse.

Last journey home. Four soldiers carried Lincoln through the crowd to a house across the street. The doctors knew he would die. They sent for Lincoln's son, Robert, and members of the government. The end came at 7:22 the next morning. Secretary of War Edwin Stanton said at Lincoln's bedside, "Now he belongs to the ages."

Peace celebrations ended, and a period of mourning began. On April 21, the

John Wilkes Booth

President's coffin was put aboard a special funeral train. This train would take Lincoln home to Springfield, Illinois. Four years before, Lincoln had traveled by train from Springfield to Washington to become President. Now the train traveled slowly back over almost the same route.

Millions of people came out to watch the funeral train as it passed by. Day and night, in town after town, mourning people waited, stared, and threw flow-

ers. Flags were flying at half staff, bands played funeral marches, guns were fired. Church bells rang sadly.

So Abraham Lincoln made his final journey home. He was buried on May 4, 1865. About 75,000 people crowded into the cemetery to watch the burial.

What happened to John Wilkes Booth? On April 26, 12 days after he shot Lincoln, he was cornered in a burning barn in Virginia. A soldier, disobeying orders to capture him, shot him to death.

A Second Look. . . .

1. *What was John Wilkes Booth's reason for killing Abraham Lincoln? How did he go about it?*

2. *Many historians rate Abraham Lincoln as one of the two greatest Presidents in U.S. history. (George Washington is usually mentioned as the other.) Why, in your opinion, was Lincoln such a great leader? How would you compare his leadership qualities to those of other Presidents you have read about in this program? How would you rate Lincoln as a leader?*

3. *Do research on one of these questions: (a) How many U.S. Presidents have been assassinated? Who were they? How were they killed? (b) What is being done to prevent assassinations of this kind today? Report your findings to the class.*

Lincoln showed the strain of war in his last photo four days before his death (left). His murder shocked the nation deeply. "O Captain! my Captain! our fearful trip is done," wrote poet Walt Whitman. Others said farewell by lining the route of the funeral train (below).

Looking Back: A Nation Torn and Bleeding

A	**B**	**C**	**D**	**E**	
April 1, 1861	April 1, 1862	April 1, 1863	April 1, 1864	April 1, 1865	April 1, 1866

Putting Events in Order

Chapters 15 through 20 have described the major events of the Civil War. Ten events of this period are listed here. Your job is to match each event to the correct period shown on the timeline above. On a piece of paper, number from **1** to **10.** After each number, write the letter of the one-year period within which the event occurred.

1. Ulysses S. Grant wins a major victory as the city of Vicksburg, Mississippi, falls to the Union.

2. Robert E. Lee's armies retreat from Maryland after the bloody Battle of Antietam.

3. John Wilkes Booth plans the assassination of Abraham Lincoln.

4. The Union army is badly defeated in the first Battle of Bull Run.

5. Abraham Lincoln drafts the Emancipation Proclamation.

6. Ulysses S. Grant is made commander of the Union army.

7. Abraham Lincoln asks the nation to go forth "with malice toward none."

8. Robert E. Lee's armies retreat from Pennsylvania after the Battle of Gettysburg.

9. Robert E. Lee surrenders at Appomattox Court House.

10. Abraham Lincoln signs the Emancipation Proclamation.

Interpreting a Source

For Southerners, the Civil War often had a more personal meaning than it did for Northerners. Because the war took place on their soil, Southern families were often raided by Yankee troops. One such raid occurred on Newstead Plantation near Jackson, Mississippi, in 1863. General Grant himself occupied the plantation house in 1863. One of the children on the plantation, Cornelia Barrett Ligon, remembered the Northern raid all her life. As an older woman, she wrote the account of it which begins on the following page.

Our Negroes huddled close to us ... and joined us in amazement at seeing the Yankee boys cook and wash dishes. For two weeks General Grant and his army ruled supreme over Newstead, living on the fat of the land. His men drilled every day. It looked as if the whole face of the earth was covered with blue soldiers. The ground was mashed to a pulp — not a blade of grass was visible. When they [Grant's army] left, they gave my mother rations[1] enough to last three days....

[1]*Rations* are food and supplies issued in a fixed amount. Food is often a ration during times of war when shortages exist.

After General Grant had moved on toward Vicksburg, my mother received a message from our neighbor, Colonel H.O. Dixon, a veteran of the Mexican War, too old to join the Confederates. The message stated that he and his wife, also quite old, were under arrest at the headquarters.... He asked that my mother lend them what assistance she could.

Our plantation had been swept clean of horses, mules, and vehicles, but my mother set out afoot to go to the rescue of her friends. She had won the respect of General Grant during his stay at Newstead and hoped that she might

In the closing months of the Civil War, Union general William T. Sherman tried to batter the South into surrender. He led 60,000 troops on a march from Atlanta, Georgia, to Savannah by the sea. Along the way, the troops burned homes and farms, tore up railroad tracks (below), and killed thousands.

have some influence in behalf of the Dixons.

It was a walk of several miles to the new headquarters, but my mother was rewarded with an immediate interview with the old couple. They said that when the Yankees entered their home to plunder,[2] Mrs. Dixon rushed to the piano and began to play "Dixie." The colonel took down his flag of the South and marched up and down the room, waving it. This was too much for the men in blue. They set fire to the house, threw the piano outdoors, and split it into kindling wood. They arrested the old couple, threatening to send them north to prison.

Upon request, my mother was granted an audience[3] with General Grant. She told him of the valiant[4] service Colonel Dixon had rendered the country during the war with Mexico and pointed out their age and infirmities.[5] The general shook his head and started to walk off as a signal of dismissal of the subject, but my mother grabbed his coat tail and refused to let go until her request had been granted.

General Grant had a sense of humor. With a chuckle he said, "Take the old couple. I'll hold you responsible for them." Then he called a mounted guard to escort the three back to Newstead. We cared for Colonel and Mrs. Dixon until arrangements could be made for them to return to what was left of their own plantation.

---

[2]*To plunder* is to loot or rob.
[3]*To be granted an audience* means to be allowed to see.
[4]*Valiant* means showing great bravery.
[5]*Infirmities* are weaknesses.

1. *Why do you suppose people at Newstead were amazed to see "Yankee boys cook and wash dishes"?*

2. *Do you think Colonel and Mrs. Dixon deserved the treatment they received at the hands of Yankee troops? Why or why not?*

3. *From the above story, what can you say about General Grant's personality? What can you say about the personality of Cornelia Ligon's mother? Of Colonel and Mrs. Dixon?*

4. *What were some of the troubles Southern families suffered as a result of Yankee raids?*

Sharpening Your Skills

The chart on the next page presents information about the major battles of the Civil War. Study the chart. Then answer the questions below.

1. How many months went by between the first and second Battles of Bull Run?

2. What was the total number of losses suffered by North and South in the Vicksburg campaign of 1863?

3. To judge from the information in the chart, what were three major Northern victories?

4. To judge from the chart, what were three major Southern victories?

5. Did the efforts of attacking armies *usually* succeed or fail?

6. To judge from the information in the chart, which state saw the greatest amount of fighting?

7. What was the "worst" battle of the Civil War? First, you should define what you mean by "worst." Then find the battle that meets your definition.

288

Major Battles of the Civil War

	When Battle Occurred	Where Battle Occurred	Southern Losses[1]	Northern Losses[1]	Result of Battle
Antietam	Sept. 17, 1862	Maryland	12,000	12,000	Draw, ending in Southern retreat
Atlanta (campaign)	May 7-Sept. 2, 1864	Georgia	25,000	27,000	Northern advance successful
Bull Run (First)	July 21, 1861	Virginia	2,000	1,000	Northern attack defeated
Bull Run (Second)	Aug. 29-30, 1862	Virginia	9,000	10,000	Northern attack defeated
Chancellorsville	May 1-4, 1863	Virginia	11,000	11,000	Northern attack defeated
Chattanooga (battles around)	Nov. 23-25, 1863	Tennessee	3,000	5,000	Northern attack successful
Chickamauga	Sept. 19-20, 1863	Georgia	17,000	12,000	Southern attack successful
Cold Harbor	June 3, 1864	Virginia	2,000	6,000	Northern attack defeated
Fredericksburg	Dec. 13, 1862	Virginia	5,000	12,000	Northern attack defeated
Gettysburg	July 1-3, 1863	Pennsylvania	23,000	18,000	Southern attack defeated
Petersburg (campaign)	June 14, 1864-April 2, 1865	Virginia	13,000	17,000	Northern attack finally successful after long siege
Seven Days' Battles	June 26-July 1, 1862	Virginia	20,000	16,000	Southern counter-attack successful
Shiloh	April 6-7, 1862	Tennessee	11,000	13,000	Southern attack defeated
Spotsylvania	May 10-12, 1864	Virginia	9,000	11,000	Northern attack partly successful
Stones River	Dec. 31, 1862-Jan. 2, 1863	Tennessee	9,000	9,000	Southern attack partly successful
Vicksburg (siege of)	May 22-July 4, 1863	Mississippi	10,000	9,000	Northern attack successful
Wilderness	May 5-6, 1864	Virginia	10,000	18,000	Draw but Northern attack defeated
Winchester	Sept. 19, 1864	Virginia	4,000	5,000	Northern attack successful

[1]Killed and wounded to the nearest 1,000. Most figures are unofficial estimates.

4 TRYING TO BUILD AGAIN

Looking Ahead: Reconstruction

What was the South like at the end of the Civil War? Much of it was a land of ruins. Thousands of houses and farms were nothing but chimneys and broken walls and empty fields. Many towns and cities had been burned to the ground. Crops and cattle had been destroyed. Railroads and bridges had been blown up. And there was hardly a family in the South that had not lost a father or a son or a brother in the war.

People all over the South felt very confused after the war. They knew that the Old South of slaves and King Cotton was gone. Somehow the South would have to be built up again. But how? And what about the four million black people in the South who were now free? Many of them had no way of making a living. Few of them could read or write. What

was to become of them? There was another big question too: How would the Southern states get back into the Union?

These were the problems to be solved. Right from the start there were big arguments about ways of solving them. Between 1865 and 1877, various ways were tried. Many of these ways were aimed at rebuilding the South. That is why the 12 years from 1865 to 1877 are called the *Reconstruction Period,* or just Reconstruction for short.

In Congress, a strong Republican group had a ready answer for one Reconstruction problem. What was to become of the freed slaves? The Republicans said, "Let Negroes vote, go to school, own land, and hold office. Let them live as equals with the whites."

These ideas were not popular ones in most of the South. Many white people in the South hated the Republicans in Congress. They wanted the South to be left alone to solve its own problems.

After Appomattox, guns fell silent in a South smashed by war. Then cities such as Charleston, S.C., (left) slowly began to bind up their wounds.

They especially hated those Northerners who had come south to help black people or to go into business. Some people thought these Northerners were just trying to make money out of the South's problems. They called these newcomers *carpetbaggers* because their suitcases were often made of carpet material.

Black Codes. Soon Southern states began passing *Black Codes.* These codes tried to take away many of the black people's rights. Jobless blacks could be arrested and forced to work for a white boss. Black people could not serve on juries or go to school with whites. They could be arrested if they walked in the streets after dark.

Black people in the South felt angry and frustrated by laws such as these. The 13th Amendment had just been added to the Constitution. This amendment had done away with slavery once and for all. Now it looked as if the Black Codes were setting up a new kind of slavery. The codes also angered many white Northerners. Among them were powerful Republicans in Congress.

Some Republicans said the Black Codes showed that the South had not learned any lessons from the war. They said that the South wasn't really going to change at all if it could help it. The angry Republicans who felt this way were called *Radicals.* The Radicals said that it was up to the U.S. government to *force* the South to change. They said that no Southern states should be let back into the Union until many conditions had been met.

The Radicals came out with a tough Reconstruction plan. This plan would divide the South into U.S. Army dis-

tricts. Each district would be governed by an Army general with U.S. troops to back up his orders. Then the Southern states would have to write new state constitutions. They would have to set up new state governments. They would also have to accept the 14th Amendment. This amendment made all black Americans citizens of the U.S. and the states they lived in. It also required all states to respect the rights of blacks and other citizens to live in peace. Black people would have to be given the right to vote too.

When all these conditions had been met, then the Southern states would be let back into the Union. But the U.S. troops might stay on in the South even then. For how long? They would stay in any state until Congress was sure that the state had been fully "reconstructed."

Johnson's plan. President Andrew Johnson did not agree with the Radical plan for Reconstruction. Johnson had been Vice-President under Lincoln. After Lincoln's death, he decided to follow a plan like the one Lincoln had wanted. This plan said that the Southern states had to do only three things to get back into the Union: (1) They had to repeal (take back) the laws that said they were no longer in the Union. (2) They had to promise never to pay off any of the Confederacy's war debts. The U.S. did not want its enemies to get back any money they had lent to the Confederacy. (3) They had to ratify (approve) the 13th Amendment. This was the amendment that ended slavery.

The elections for Congress in 1866 became a bitter fight between President Johnson and the Radical Republicans. Voters had to decide whose program for Reconstruction should be followed. Should it be Johnson's "soft" plan, or the Radicals' "hard" plan? Johnson fought stubbornly for his plan. He even went on a speaking tour of the North. But the Radicals won the election — and Congress controlled Reconstruction from that time on.

Now the Radicals put their plan for Reconstruction into operation. The rights of blacks in the South were backed up by a strong Congress. They were also backed up by new laws and U.S. troops. Blacks began to vote. Running as Republicans, black leaders were elected to Congress for the first time. Two from Mississippi served in the U.S. Senate.

On the state and local levels, black and white Republicans in the South passed many laws to help *all* people in the South. These laws set up public schools for blacks and whites. They allowed streets, roads, and bridges to be rebuilt. They gave relief to the poor. They made taxes fairer.

Republican lawmakers made some mistakes too. Some of these men, both blacks and whites, were dishonest. But there were crooked men in politics in the North as well. And there were crooked men in both parties, Democratic and Republican. Dishonesty in government and business was common in the time right after the Civil War.

Many white Southerners hated Republicans in the state and local governments just as much as they hated the Republicans in Congress. "The only way to get rid of these Republicans," they said, "is to keep black people from voting." There were many ways of doing this. Sometimes just a word of warning would stop a man from voting. Then there were secret terror groups such as the *Ku Klux Klan.* Sometimes they rode around at night, beating black people in their homes. Sometimes blacks were murdered in cold blood.

Meanwhile, the Radicals were losing their hold on Congress. Some of their leaders had died. General U.S. Grant had become President in 1869. As time went on, Grant felt he could not keep U.S. troops in every Southern state where black people and Republicans needed support. He began to pull troops out. As the troops left, white Democrats took over the governments in state after state. By 1877 the last troops had left. Republican rule in the South was finished. So was Reconstruction.

During Reconstruction, black Southerners served in Congress for the first time. Man at far left below is U.S. Senator Hiram Revels of Mississippi. Others are Representatives from four Southern states.

Chapter 21
"When Freedom Came...."

Now that the war was over, the slaves were free. Thousands upon thousands of black people were overjoyed. There were many celebrations. But after the celebrations were over, black people began to have second thoughts.

Now that they were free, how would they get work? Where would they find homes? How would they get food? They were free, but very few of them had money. Very few had land to settle on. All that most of them had were the clothes on their backs. How were they going to stay alive?

Some blacks stayed on the plantations and were helped by their old masters. But most white Southerners had little help to give. They themselves had been ruined in the war. More than a few white people survived these years because of the help given them by their former slaves.

Some Southerners felt kindly toward the freed slaves. Others did not. Those who didn't sometimes shrugged: "The Yankees freed you. Now let the Yankees feed you."

Many of the freed slaves and their families took to the road. They drifted all over the South, some on foot, some in wagons and carts. Many of them crowded into towns and cities. They lived in the ruins of buildings smashed in the war. Many died of hunger and sickness. Sometimes they were given food and medicine by Northern church groups such as the Quakers. Sometimes they got help from the *Freedmen's Bureau,* which was run by the Army. Sometimes they were befriended by white Southerners, who gave them all the help they could.

The Freedmen's Bureau had been set up at the end of the war by an act of Congress. The bureau gave out food and medicine to poor black people and also to poor whites. It found jobs for blacks and acted as their friend in court. It built more than 1,000 schools for almost 250,000 black students. This was the first free public school system in the South.

Even with help from the Freedmen's Bureau, many Southern blacks faced hard times in the years after the war. Here is how three different black Americans described these years:

First black American. "When freedom came, folks went out in the streets, crying, praying, singing, shouting, yelling, and knocking down everything. Some shot off big guns. Then came the calm. It was sad then. So many folks were dead, and things all torn up. There was nowhere to go and nothing to eat, nothing to do. Folks got sick, they were so hungry. Some folks starved nearly to death...."

Second black American. "When freedom came, my mama said Old Mas-

Work changed little for most black Southerners after the Civil War. Many remained farm workers, doing tasks they had once performed as slaves.

ter called all the slaves to his house. And he said, 'You're all free, we ain't got nothing to do with you anymore. Go on away. We won't whip you anymore. Go on your way.'

"My mama said they went off, then came back and stood around just looking at Old Master and Old Mistress. They gave them something to eat and he said: 'Go on away. You don't belong to us anymore. You've been freed.'

"They went away and they kept coming back. They didn't have any place to go and nothing to eat. From what mama said, they had a terrible time. Some took sick and had no attention and died. It seemed it was four or five years before they got to places where they could live. They all got scattered."

Third black American. "People died in piles. I don't know even yet what was the matter. They said it was the change of living. I saw five or six wooden, painted coffins piled up on wagons pass by our house. Loads passed every day like you see cotton pass here. Some said it was cholera and some had TB. Lots of the colored people nearly starved. There wasn't much work to do and not much houseroom. Several families had to live in one house. Lots of the colored folks went up north and froze to death. They couldn't stand the cold. They wrote back about them dying. No, they never sent the bodies back. I heard that some sent for money to come home again. I heard plenty about the Ku Klux Klan. They scared the folks to death. People left Augusta [Georgia] in droves. About a thousand would all meet and walk, going to hunt work and new homes. Some of them died. I had a sister and brother lost that way. I had

296

another sister who went to Louisiana that way. She wrote back.

"I don't think the colored folks expected a share of land. They never got anything because the white folks didn't have anything but barren hills left. All the mules were worn out hauling provisions in the army. Some folks say the whites ought to have done more for the colored folks when they left, but they say the whites were broke. Freeing all the slaves left them broke."

Other changes began taking place. Once-wealthy planters now had little cash. Many of them sold off parts of their plantations to smaller farmers. The size of the average Southern farm decreased. The number of small farms increased greatly.

Slowly the South began to rebuild. Local government was reorganized. The court system was improved. Taxes were spread more evenly between the rich and the not-so-rich. Much of the rebuilding was carried out by Southerners themselves. During these years, blacks and whites worked together to create a stronger South.

A Second Look. . . .

1. *What were three problems faced by Southern blacks in 1865? How did the Freedmen's Bureau try to solve these problems? How did black people try to solve them?*

2. *Who, in your opinion, seems most responsible for the suffering of blacks after the war? Explain your answer.*

3. *Imagine you are a freed black person in 1866. Write a diary for one week of your life (Sunday to Saturday) telling about your daily struggle to earn a living.*

Chapter 22

A Radical Republican

He walked with a limp and had a look as hard as steel. He came from the North and had little understanding for the South. He thought of Southern plantation owners as traitors. He believed the South should be punished for its role in the Civil War. Many Southerners feared and hated him. They called him a "fanatic" — a man who pushed too hard for his beliefs.

Thaddeus Stevens had an answer to this charge. "There can be no fanatics in the cause of liberty for all men," he said. Stevens was a leader of the Republicans in Congress. He believed in trying to

Thaddeus Stevens

help the poor and downtrodden. He said that "every man, no matter what his race or color, has an equal right to justice, honesty, and fair play with every other man."

Stevens was a fighter. He fought for free public schools for the poor. He defended runaway slaves in the courts. He defended free speech for those who had unpopular beliefs. He spoke up for Indians, Jews, and black people. Yet he also offended many people. And he did little to ease bitter feelings between the North and the South after the Civil War.

Stevens had been born in Vermont in 1792. His mother ran the family farm and raised her four sons alone. Born with a twisted foot, Thaddeus was lame all his life. Young people used to tease him about it, so Stevens became shy and a "bookworm." But he was good at sports such as swimming and riding. In these, his foot didn't hold him back. He was a good student too. He went to college and became a lawyer.

"Forty acres and a mule." Then he moved to Gettysburg, Pennsylvania. There he became famous as the "runaway slaves' lawyer." In those days, before the Civil War, the law was on the side of the slaves' masters. But Stevens kept on trying to help the slaves. He did not always win in court. When he lost a case, he usually bought the slave's freedom himself.

297

Stevens was first elected to Congress in 1848. He blasted slavery in his very first speech. He said, "I look upon any man who would permit slavery to spread over one road of God's green earth as a traitor to liberty and disloyal to God."

During the Civil War, and for three years after it was over, Stevens was the leader of the House of Representatives. He wasn't just a Republican. He was a Radical Republican. He was the leader of the group in Congress — the Radicals — who wanted nothing less than *full* equality for black Americans. It was not enough, the Radicals said, to give black men their freedom. They also needed the right to vote and go to free schools. Stevens went one step further. He wanted to give every freedman a small farm — "40 acres [16 hectares] and a mule." He would do this by breaking up the big plantations of the South. The "40 acres and a mule" plan, he said, was the only way to make blacks *really* free and independent. It would also break the power of the old planter class.

"Equal protection." The "40 acres and a mule" plan raised the hopes of many black people in the South. They were disappointed when the plan failed to pass Congress. But Stevens and the other Radical Republicans did push through most of their other Reconstruction plans. Radical Republicans led and won the fight for the 13th, 14th, and 15th Amendments to the Constitution. The 13th Amendment did away with slavery everywhere in the United States. The 14th said that *all* persons born in the U.S. are citizens of the U.S. and the states they live in. The 14th Amendment also said that no person could be denied "the equal protection of the laws." The 15th Amendment said that no citizen's vote could be taken away because of his race or color, or because he was once a slave.

Stevens believed in these amendments very deeply. He especially supported the idea of giving black people the vote. Stevens was a sincere democrat. But that was not his only reason for supporting the amendments. He was also bitter in his feelings toward white Southerners. He wanted to teach them a lesson they would never forget.

Stevens died on August 11, 1868. The 13th and 14th Amendments had already been adopted by then. The 15th Amendment became law in 1870 — just over a year and a half later.

By his own wish, Stevens was buried in a black cemetery. He hoped that this would show how much he believed in the ideas he had stood for during his long life.

A Second Look. . . .

1. *Which amendments were added to the Constitution during Reconstruction? How did each amendment protect the rights of black Americans?*

2. *Some people complained that Thaddeus Stevens was a fanatic. They thought his ideas were too radical, too extreme. Do you agree or disagree with this view of Stevens? Why?*

3. *Here are three problems that disturb Americans today: (a) How to control nuclear weapons. (b) How to insure fair treatment for all Americans. (c) How to control pollution. Propose a radical solution for each of these problems. Do the other students in class think your solutions are practical or possible?*

Chapter 23

President on Trial

Every seat in the U.S. Senate gallery was filled on March 13, 1868. The 54 Senators sat as a jury. U.S. Chief Justice Salmon P. Chase acted as the judge. Never before had such a trial involved a President of the United States. Nor has it ever done so again.

The President, Andrew Johnson, had been *impeached* by the House of Representatives. That is, he had been accused of "high crimes" against Congress and the Constitution. Now he was being tried for these crimes in the Senate. If found guilty, he would be removed from office.

How had this trial come about? Why had so many people shouted, "Walk the plank, Andy Johnson"?

Andrew Johnson was born of poor parents in Raleigh, North Carolina. His father died when Andrew was three. As a boy, Andrew was hired out to a tailor to earn his food and clothing. He never went to school. After two years, Andrew

Washington's "hottest" ticket in 1868.

ran away. Later he settled down in eastern Tennessee as a tailor. At 18, he got married. His wife taught him to read and write.

Johnson was smart. He learned fast and became a good talker. He went into politics. He became governor of Tennessee and later a U.S. Senator from that state.

Johnson hated the rich slave-owners, but he was not against slavery itself. He was very much against the South quitting the Union. He was the only Southern Senator who was loyal to the Union when the Civil War began. As a result, President Lincoln made him military governor of Tennessee in 1862. His main job, at first, was to help bring Tennessee back into the Union. Three years later, Johnson became Vice-President under Lincoln.

Against the tide. When Lincoln was killed by John Wilkes Booth, Johnson became President. He faced the hard job of trying to fill Lincoln's shoes. He soon ran into trouble. Radical Republicans in Congress wanted the government to force a tough Reconstruction plan on the South. They wanted to place the South under military rule. Johnson, like Lincoln, did not want to be too hard on the South. Congress passed the Reconstruction acts. Johnson vetoed (rejected) them. Congress then passed the acts by the two-thirds majority

needed to override (defeat) the veto. Soon Johnson and Congress were fighting constantly.

Johnson also fought with Edwin Stanton, the Secretary of War. Stanton was a Radical, and he had many friends in Congress. The Radicals in Congress wanted to protect Stanton. So they passed a law called the *Tenure of Office Act.* (*Tenure,* in this sense, means length of service.) This act said Johnson could not fire Stanton or any other member of the Cabinet. Johnson was furious at this. He quickly fired Stanton. Then Congress was furious. The House of Representatives impeached Johnson for "high crimes." Some Radicals even spread false rumors that Johnson had had a hand in Lincoln's death.

Into deep trouble. Johnson was a stubborn man. He also had a hot temper. He was partly to blame for his troubles with Congress. But he could not have imagined the troubles would lead to this. He was about to become the first U.S. President to stand trial in the Senate.

Johnson was not present at his trial. He let his lawyers talk for him. On May 16th it was time to take the vote. If two thirds of the Senators found him guilty, Johnson would no longer be President. Telegraph lines were kept open to flash "guilty" or "not guilty" across the land. Bets were made about the outcome.

Finally each Senator cast his vote. Thirty-five voted "guilty." Nineteen voted "not guilty." Johnson was saved from being removed from office by *one* vote.

What would Andy Johnson do if given a chance? Make himself king, said cartoonist Thomas Nast.

Andrew Johnson

The trial weakened Johnson's ability to serve as President. After the trial, Congress took over the job of ruling the South. It took a "hard line" toward the old Confederate states. The hard line was not finally ended until 1877, when Rutherford B. Hayes became President.

A Second Look. . . .

1. *What group of people impeached Andrew Johnson? What group almost convicted him of "high crimes"? What would have happened to Johnson if in fact he had been convicted?*

2. *Has any recent President been in danger of impeachment? If so, can you name this person and state the reasons for the danger?*

3. *In class, hold a mock trial of Andrew Johnson. One group of students should argue that Johnson is guilty of high crimes. Another group should argue that Johnson is innocent. Students on both sides may want to do some library research to prepare for the debate. After the debate, poll the class on this question: "Is President Johnson guilty of high crimes as charged?"*

301

Chapter 24

The Election That Ended Reconstruction

In 1876 Democrats in the South were boiling with anger. Some of them even suggested that there might be another civil war. They thought the Democratic candidate for President, Samuel Tilden, had been elected. They hoped Tilden as President would get rid of Reconstruction in the South. But now it looked as if the Republicans meant to "steal" the election from Tilden. Southern Democrats were so angry they began shouting, "Tilden or blood!"

In 1876 only three states in the South were controlled by Republicans. They were South Carolina, Louisiana, and Florida. Everywhere else in the South, U.S. troops had been withdrawn. When U.S. troops left a state, white Democrats in that state replaced Republicans — both whites and blacks — in office. Reconstruction would probably end everywhere if Tilden beat the Republican candidate, Rutherford B. Hayes. And the Democrats — *white* Democrats — would then be in control throughout the South.

One vote short. At first it seemed that Tilden, the Democrat, had won the election. He had won many more *popular* votes than Hayes. Still, he had not yet won a majority of *electoral* votes. He was just one electoral vote short of winning. He had 184 votes; he needed 185. Hayes had won only 165 electoral votes. But in three states — South Carolina, Louisiana, and Florida — the results of the voting were in doubt. Of course, these were the only three Southern states where Republicans were still in power. If Hayes got the electoral votes from these states, he would win the election.

It was impossible to know who had really won the election in these states. Voting officials there were mainly Republicans. They tried to rig the election in favor of Hayes. The votes of whole counties were thrown out. Why? Because, Republicans said, Democrats had used force to keep black citizens from voting. And so Louisiana, South Carolina, and Florida chose electors

"Another such victory, and I am undone," says the elephant in this Thomas Nast cartoon. Nast was the nation's best-known cartoonist of his time. He first used the elephant to stand for the Republican party, then the nation's largest party. The "victory" Nast refers to is that of Rutherford B. Hayes in 1877.

HERE
LIES
THE
DEMOCRATIC
TIGER
GREATLY MOURNED
BY THE BEREAVED
FILIBUSTERS.

who would vote for Hayes. At the same time, angry Democrats in these states sent to Congress a second set of electoral ballots — all for Tilden. For a while, nobody knew what to do. There seemed to be no fair way to decide who had won the election.

One-vote difference. Finally Congress set up a committee of 15 men to look into the matter. Seven of the committee members were known to be Republicans. Seven others were known to be Democrats. The 15th member, a judge, was supposed to be neutral. Yet at the last moment the "neutral" judge resigned. A Republican judge took his place. In March 1877, the committee said that the Republicans — and Hayes — had won in all three states. In each case, the committee vote was eight in favor of the Republicans, and seven in favor of the Democrats. This meant that Hayes would be President.

It was this news that made Democrats in the South so angry. This was why they shouted, "Tilden or blood!"

Many people in the North then panicked. Northern newspapers called for "peace at any price." Finally Republican and Democratic leaders held meetings to work out the problem. The Democrats and Republicans made a secret deal. Democrats agreed to accept the election of Hayes as President. In return, the Republicans promised:

First, to allow *home rule* in the South. This meant that white Democrats would hold power there and that the 15th Amendment would *not* be enforced by the U.S. government. (The 15th Amendment was supposed to protect black citizens' right to vote.)

304   *Second,* to pull out the last U.S. soldiers from Louisiana and South Carolina.

Third, to grant the South money to rebuild itself.

So on March 2, 1877, Hayes was awarded 185 electoral votes and the Presidency. The following night he dined with the outgoing Republican President, Ulysses Grant. During the evening, Grant sent his son to get a Bible. Hayes was sworn in as President then and there. But he took his formal oath of office in public two days later, March 5.

By this time, U.S. troops had already been pulled out of Florida. Soon after, they were pulled out of South Carolina and Louisiana as well. This ended the Republican Reconstruction governments in the South. All of the South was now in the control of white Democrats. Republicans and blacks would have little or no power in the South for the next 90 years. The reforms were over, and Reconstruction was dead.

A Second Look. . . .

1. *Why did Democrats think Republicans had "stolen" the election of 1876?*

2. *What is your opinion of the bargain that Hayes and the Republicans made with the Democrats? Was it fair? Was any part of it morally wrong? Explain your answers.*

3. *Choose any state in the South. Find out how this state voted in Presidential elections from 1876 until 1956. For each election year, write down the Republican vote and the Democratic vote. Then draw a line graph that shows the pattern of voting in the state you've chosen. Use a dotted line to show the Republican vote, and a solid line to show the Democratic vote.*

Looking Back: Trying To Build Again

A	B	C	D
1860	1865	1870	1875	1880

Putting Events in Order

Chapters 21 through 24 have described some events of the era we now call Reconstruction. Ten events of this period are listed here. Your job is to match each event to the correct period shown on the timeline above. On a piece of paper, number from **1** to **10.** After each number, write the letter of the five-year period within which the event occurred.

1. President Andrew Johnson is almost removed from office.

2. The Confederate States of America fight for their independence.

3. The 14th Amendment guaranteeing "equal protection of the laws" is added to the U.S. Constitution.

4. Slavery still exists in the South.

5. Radicals win an election, gain control of Congress, and put their own plans for Reconstruction into effect.

6. Republican leaders make a deal with Southern Democrats, ending Reconstruction.

7. President Andrew Johnson goes on a speaking tour of the North.

8. U.S. troops are pulled out of Florida, South Carolina, and Louisiana.

9. Ulysses S. Grant becomes the nation's 18th President.

10. Thaddeus Stevens, leader of the Radical Republicans, is buried in a black cemetery.

Interpreting a Source

Before the Civil War, the city of Boston was the leading center for the abolitionist movement. After the war, the city became a center of Radical Republican thought. How, then, did Boston treat its own black people? A writer named Ray Stannard Baker looked into this question in his book, Following the Color Line. *The book was first published in 1904. Here are some passages from it.*

In Boston ... I was surprised at the general attitude which I encountered. ... Summed up, I think the feeling of the

305

better class of people in Boston (and elsewhere in Northern cities) might be thus stated:

We have helped the Negro to liberty; we have helped to educate him; we have encouraged him to stand on his own feet. Now let's see what he can do for himself. After all, he must survive or perish by his own efforts. . . .

Though they [white Northerners] still preserve the form of encouraging the Negro, their spirit seems to have fled. Not long ago, the Negroes of Boston organized a concert at which Theodore Drury, a colored musician of really notable accomplishments, was to appear. Aristocratic[1] white people . . . bought a considerable number of tickets; but on the evening of the concert, the large block of seats purchased by white people was conspicuously[2] vacant. Northern white people would seem to be more interested in the distant Southern Negro than in the Negro at their doors. . . .

Even at Harvard [University] where the Negro has always enjoyed exceptional[3] opportunities, conditions are undergoing a marked change. A few years ago a large class of white students voluntarily chose a brilliant Negro student as valedictorian.[4] But last year the presence of a Negro on the baseball team was the cause of so much discussion and embarrassment . . . that there will probably never be another colored boy on the athletic teams. The line has already been drawn, indeed, in the medical department. Although a colored doctor only a few years ago was house physician[5] at the Boston Lying-In Hospital, colored students are no longer admitted to that institution. . . .

The more I see of conditions North and South, the more I see that human nature north of Mason and Dixon's line[6] is not different from human nature south of the line.

1. *How does Baker show that black Americans once suffered setbacks in Boston?*

2. *What does he mean by "the form of encouraging the Negro"?*

3. *How does he sum up the attitudes of white Northerners toward black Americans around the turn of the present century?*

4. *How would you compare these attitudes to the attitudes held by white people today?*

Sharpening Your Skills

The map on the next page shows the course of Reconstruction in the South. Pictured are the 11 former Confederate states affected by special Reconstruction laws. The dates not in parentheses show when each state was readmitted

---

[1]*Aristocratic* means upperclass.

[2]To do something *conspicuously* is to do it openly or in a way to attract attention.

[3]*Exceptional,* in this sense, means very rare.

[4]A *valedictorian* is a student who usually has the highest grades in a graduating class. The valedictorian often delivers an address at the time of graduation.

[5]A *house physician* is a medical doctor who is employed by and lives in a hospital.

[6]*Mason and Dixon's line* was one drawn in 1784 to mark the southern boundary of Pennsylvania. In the years before the Civil War, the line was known as the one which separated slave states of the South from free-soil states of the North.

The Course of Reconstruction, 1865-1877

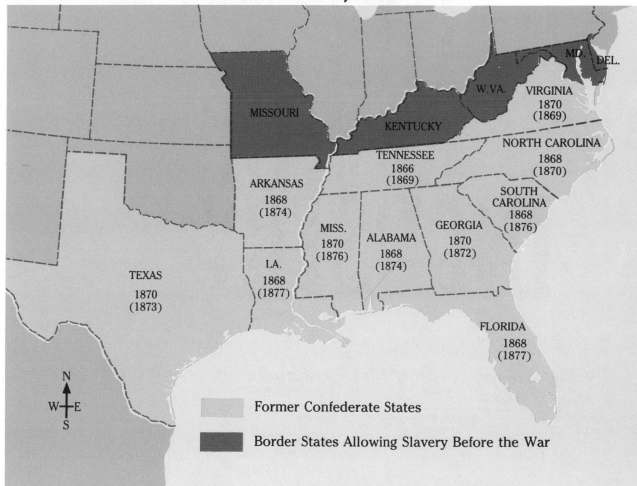

to the Union. The dates in parentheses show when state governments were taken over by white Southerners. At this point Republicans — black and white — were driven from power. Study the map, and answer the questions below.

1. Which of the 11 states was first to be readmitted to the Union? Which were last to be readmitted?

2. Which three states were the first to be allowed to set up all-white governments? Which two states were the last to be governed by Reconstruction laws?

3. Freed slaves in Kentucky were never protected by Reconstruction laws. Why was this?

4. Which of the other states shown on the map were not affected by Reconstruction laws? Why?

5 THE RISE OF INDUSTRY

Nº 323   DEC. 8th 1911   5 Cents.

FAME AND FORTUNE

STORIES ·OF· BOYS   WEEKLY.   WHO MAKE MONEY.

FRESH FROM THE WEST
OR THE LAD WHO MADE GOOD IN NEW YORK

AND OTHER STORIES   By A Self-Made Man

The two confidence men suddenly discovered they had a tartar to deal with. Jerry seized each by the ear and forced them down on their knees. The unusual spectacle immediately attracted attention, and a policeman came running to the spot.

Looking Ahead: Striking It Rich

In 1876 Americans celebrated a birthday. Their country was exactly 100 years old. Firecrackers popped and bands performed on the Fourth of July. Political leaders made speeches about the greatness of America's past — and the greatness of its future.

In Philadelphia, thousands paid 50 cents each to see one of the greatest fairs ever held. It was called the *Centennial Exhibition.* Inside its huge buildings, people were amazed by the exhibits they saw. There was a popcorn machine, a new kind of fire engine, and a new device called a typewriter. At one table, a man named Charles Hires showed how he made a drink out of roots and spices. He called it root beer. At another table, a

Nickel novels became very popular in the late 1800's and early 1900's. The success stories they told showed awareness of the vast fortunes made by a few. With a little "luck and pluck," any lad could "make good," or so the story went.

young inventor, Alexander Graham Bell, explained the use of something he called a telephone. The emperor of Brazil happened to stop at this inventor's table. He held the receiver of the telephone to his ear. "It talks!" he exclaimed.

As visitors stared at these marvels, they had reason to be amazed. How much the United States had changed in 100 years! The United States was growing fast in 1876; it was growing rich too. It seemed that, with a little luck, almost any American could make a lot of money. The president of one university certainly thought so. "I say that you ought to get rich," he urged his students. "It is your duty to get rich."

There were different ways of striking it rich in 1876. One way was to drill for oil in the fields of Pennsylvania. Another was to invest money in certain large companies by buying shares of stock in them. A few clever people made millions by buying stocks for a low price and

309

then selling them for a high price. A third road to riches was to start a business in a new or growing industry and then plow profits back into the company. A Scottish immigrant, Andrew Carnegie, did this in the steel business. A peddler's son, John D. Rockefeller, did it in the oil business.

What did millionaires in the 1870's and 1880's do with all their money? Some of them enjoyed showing it off. They built costly mansions with many more rooms than they could use. They filled these rooms with marble statues and rare paintings — things that were very expensive. One millionaire wrapped his cigars with 100-dollar bills — and smoked them. But not many showed off their wealth so openly.

It was a serious matter, striking it rich. Only a few people succeeded at it. Other Americans looked upon them with envy. They worried about the power that business leaders had. What was this power? Let's take a closer look at big business' dealings with government, labor, and farmers.

Big business and the government. Business leaders in the 1870's needed several kinds of help from the federal government. Railroad companies needed permission to build tracks through public lands. Makers of cloth and steel thought they needed tariffs to protect themselves from cheap foreign imports. (A *tariff* is a tax on goods sent from another country.) How could government officials be persuaded to give business the help it needed? A few business leaders tried to influence such officials with gifts. The gifts were usually made in money or shares of company stock.

Of course, this was illegal — but it was done from time to time in the 1870's and 1880's. In 1876, for example, Americans were shocked by scandals in the federal government. Ulysses S. Grant, the Union commander in the Civil War, was then serving his eighth and last year

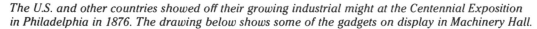

The U.S. and other countries showed off their growing industrial might at the Centennial Exposition in Philadelphia in 1876. The drawing below shows some of the gadgets on display in Machinery Hall.

310

as President. He himself did not accept gifts from business leaders. But members of his family did. And so did many government officials who worked under Grant.

At the same time, business leaders put pressure on federal, state, and local governments to do favors for them. In California, for example, the owners of the Southern Pacific Railroad controlled the politics of the state. Owners of the railroad used their money to elect candidates to office. In the 1880's, political leaders who fought the railroad almost always lost elections.

Big business and labor. Most business leaders aimed above all to turn a profit. They tried not to pay any more for a laborer's toil than they had to pay. In 1870 women working in a Massachusetts textile mill earned only five cents an hour. They worked 12 hours a

Liberty was celebrated at the 1876 fair with the exhibit of F.A. Bartholdi's torch (below). It would later become part of the Statue of Liberty. But as the U.S. entered its second century, some Americans worried about their liberties. One cartoonist feared that big businesses were running Congress (above).

311

day. Some U.S. wage-earners barely earned enough to live. If a worker dared to complain, he or she would almost surely be replaced by someone else.

What could unhappy workers do? They could pack up and head west in search of cheap land. Or they could look for better jobs. Or, like many workers after the Civil War, they could join labor unions — and go on strike, if necessary. In these years, unions were just beginning to form. But business leaders opposed them. So did many other Americans, including some workers themselves. Government officials usually took the side of business against labor.

When a union called a strike, there was often fighting and bloodshed. Strikers would set up picket lines and try to keep anyone from entering the factory or place of business. Factory owners would try to persuade courts to forbid strikes or picketing. Sometimes the owners hired armed detectives to drive the strikers off company property. The owners thought they had a right to do this. After all, they said, the factory belonged to them. They believed they could do anything they wanted with it.

Big business and the farmers. Many farmers also complained bitterly about big business. They thought they were being cheated out of their fair share of America's wealth. After all, they said, farmers supplied the cotton for Eastern textile mills. They supplied the wheat for Midwestern flour mills and hogs for the Chicago slaughterhouses. Every day, American farmers fed a nation of 50 million people. And yet, no farmer was as rich as a Chicago meat-packer or a New York banker.

In the 1870's and 1880's, in fact, many farmers seemed to be in debt most of the time. Year after year, the prices they got for their crops went down. Year after year, the prices they had to pay for bank loans, farm tools, and fertilizers went up.

Slowly many farmers decided they would have to fight for their survival. In the Middle West, they joined local chapters of an organization commonly known as the *Grange*. "Grangers" called for state laws to stop railroads from charging unfair shipping rates.

In 1892 farmers joined with factory workers to form a new political party. They called it the *People's party*. They called themselves *Populists*. Mary Elizabeth Lease, a Kansas farmer, became famous for her Populist speeches. "Raise less corn," she said, "and more hell."

In 1892 the Populist candidate for President won more than a million votes. Business leaders became worried. Would there be an uprising in the country? Would angry farmers and workers join together against big business?

The answer to both questions, finally, was no. The Populist movement faded out, and big business was not destroyed. If anything, it kept on growing bigger and wealthier — along with the nation itself. The years from 1870 to 1900 were a time of enormous growth. Americans were getting ahead in countless ways. Some workers still knew hardships. Some injustices remained. But the rise of industry put more money in more Americans' pockets than ever before.

Granger poster at right gives a romantic view of farm life. Farmers' idea of their role in the world is found in the slogan "I pay for all."

On May 10, 1869, a coal-burning Union Pacific engine met a wood-burning Central Pacific engine in the Utah desert (above). The event marked the completion of the first railroad linking East to West.

Chapter 25

The Golden Spike

Puffing steam, two railroad engines faced each other in the tiny town of Promontory, Utah. Between the locomotives stood a large group of railroad workers. They were watching a man with a sledgehammer. The man took a swing with the hammer and whammed it down on a spike of gold.

The news was flashed across the country by telegraph. In big cities, guns boomed and bells rang. The date was May 10, 1869.

What had happened with the swing of that hammer? The last piece of railroad track joining the East and the West was nailed into place. Now it was possible to

travel from coast to coast by railroad. The trip would take only six days. It had taken months by covered wagon or by ship. In those days ships had to go all the way around the tip of South America to get from New York to San Francisco.

Talk of tying East to West with a ribbon of rails had started as early as the late 1840's. But when members of Congress began discussing possible routes, they couldn't agree. Southerners wanted a southern route — from New Orleans across Texas to San Diego. Northerners wanted a northern route — from St. Paul to the Columbia River by way of the Oregon Trail. Still others favored a middle route from St. Louis to the Great Salt Lake. From there it would run up the California Trail through the Sierra Nevada Mountains to San Francisco.

The southern route seemed easiest to build. But many Northerners in Congress held out against it because of slavery. Such a route would make it easier for Southerners to move west. Northerners feared that slavery would go with them.

Middle route. The outbreak of the Civil War in 1861 ended this dispute. After the Confederate states withdrew from the Union, Congress chose the middle route. One day, members of Congress hoped, the North and the South would be reunited. A route through the center of the nation would be fair to both.

Despite the war, Congress gave the go-ahead to two railroad companies in 1862. One, the Central Pacific, was to start in California and build eastward. The other, the Union Pacific, was to start near Omaha, Nebraska, and build westward until the two lines met. The two companies faced a huge task. Together they had to lay 1,700 miles (about 2,700 kilometers) of track. They had to burrow through mountains. They had to run bridges across gorges. They had to span hundreds of miles of prairie.

For each mile of track laid, the federal government offered loans to the builders. The government also gave the two companies land along the tracks amounting to hundreds of thousands of acres. Some states offered rewards to get builders to move faster. The result:

A Railroad Spans the Nation, 1869

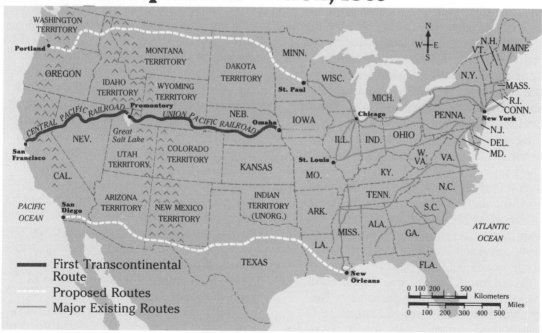

— First Transcontinental Route
--- Proposed Routes
— Major Existing Routes

The Central Pacific and the Union Pacific were soon in a race, each trying to cover more ground than the other.

As the race began, both companies ran into another problem. Thousands of laborers had to be hired to do hard and dangerous work. These men had to be ready to move far from home. They had to be willing to work a 12-hour day. They had to be able to live in constant danger.

Irish workers. The Union Pacific turned to Irish immigrants. Between 1830 and 1850, these people had arrived in America in a flood. They had fled from famine and poverty in Ireland. More than a million of them had made the trip in these years. Many men had arrived in America with little but the clothes they were wearing. Such men were game for any hard job.

The boss of the Union Pacific, General Grenville Dodge, put the Irish to work. Soon rails began to move west at the rate of about a mile a day. A tent town sprang up at the farthest point of the railroad track. Whiskey merchants, dance-hall girls, and gamblers followed the railroad crews. There was a lot of shooting and robbing. One day General Dodge heard that gamblers were "running wild" in a railroad camp. He told his assistant, Jack Casement, to "clean up" the mess.

A few days later, General Dodge came to the railroad camp. He asked Casement what he had done with the gamblers. Casement pointed to a row of new graves. "The bad men died with their boots on," he said.

The Union Pacific could make good time through the flat prairies of Nebraska Territory. But to reach the flatlands the Central Pacific had to blast its way through California's Sierra Nevada Mountains. Not many Californians wanted to struggle through snow in the Sierras. Still fewer wanted to risk their lives along the sides of the slippery peaks.

This was a problem for Charles Crocker, one of the Central Pacific's owners. In 1865 he needed at least 5,000 workers. Yet he could find only about 1,000 of them in the U.S. So he sent agents to the city of Canton in China. These agents hired Chinese laborers to come to the U.S. as railroad builders.

Chinese workers. At first American workers doubted that the small Chinese would prove strong enough for the job. To their surprise, the Chinese turned out to be very hard workers indeed. Crocker gave them the highest praise. "If we found we were in a hurry for a job," he said, "... it was better to put the Chinese on at once."

By the middle of 1868, the Central Pacific had battered its way through the mountains. Now it was lengthening eastward across the Nevada flats. The Chinese workers and the Irish workers raced to see who could put down tracks faster. The bosses of the crews encouraged the race.

One day Charles Crocker heard that the Union Pacific had laid eight miles (nearly 13 kilometers) of track in a single day. Crocker bet the Union Pacific man 10,000 dollars that his Chinese crews could do better than that. On April 28, 1869, the Chinese swung into action. Working with amazing speed, they laid 10 miles (16 kilometers) of track. Crocker won his bet.

Finally the two lines met at Promontory, Utah. Governor Leland Stanford of

The Central Pacific brought laborers from China to help lay track. In this Joseph Becker painting, Chinese workers wave at a train passing between snowsheds in California's Sierra Nevada Mountains.

California was supposed to drive in the last spike. Stanford swung and missed. He swung and missed again. Finally Jack Casement took over. He drove the golden spike home with one swing.

Now that the railroads were linked, they began spreading other lines throughout the West. These railroads made money too. They sold the lands that the government had given them. Ranchers and farmers bought the lands. Then the railroads hauled to market the crops and cattle these settlers raised.

The railroads worked hard to attract more and more settlers to the West. They put ads in newspapers read by farmers in the East. They sent agents to Europe to tell people about the great advantages of moving to America. These efforts paid off. Soon thousands and thousands of new settlers moved into the areas that had rail service. For these people, the railroad had "opened up" the West.

A Second Look. . . .

1. *Which two companies built the first railroad linking East to West? How did they happen to build it along the general route it took? Which two groups of immigrants played large roles in this work? Why was the building of this railroad line thought to be a great achievement?*

2. *Promontory, Utah, is not halfway between Omaha, Nebraska, and San Francisco. In building the railroad, one company covered more miles than the other. Take a close look at the map in this chapter. Which section of track covered more miles? Which company laid this section? Why should one company have been able to cover a greater distance than the other?*

3. *Imagine that you and other class members are serving in Congress in 1850. A committee meeting is being held to consider routes for a railroad that will run from coast to coast. Each of you should choose a route and argue for it.* 317

Chapter 26

Two Titans of Industry

The 14-year-old did not smile as he walked home from school in Cleveland, Ohio. Smiling, laughing, and enjoying himself were not important to young John D. Rockefeller. Even as a youth, all that seemed important to him was the idea of becoming rich. He once told one of his school friends: "When I grow up, I want to be worth $100,000 and I'm going to be too." He was not joking. Rockefeller rarely joked.

At an early age, Rockefeller learned an important lesson about making money. One summer, a farmer gave him the job of digging potatoes for 37 cents a day. Rockefeller saved all the pennies he earned in a blue bowl that he kept in his room. He saved 50 dollars this way. The farmer who employed him asked to be loaned the 50 dollars. The boy agreed, charging the farmer seven percent interest. As an old man, Rockefeller explained what this loan taught him. "I soon learned," he said, "that I could get as much interest for 50 dollars at seven percent ... as I could earn by digging potatoes for 10 days."

Rockefeller learned his lesson well. He developed a talent for managing his money and making it grow — and grow. As a young man, he opened up a business buying and selling grain. The business made large profits in the first year. As usual, however, Rockefeller did not spend the money on his own amuse-

Before 1859, people obtained oil by skimming it from streams. Many thought Edwin L. Drake (in stovepipe hat) was silly to drill for it. But he did so anyway, using this engine house.

ment. Instead, he used it to buy an even larger business.

Hitting a gusher. The business he bought into was an up-and-coming one — oil. Before the 1850's, oil had been mainly used in back-rub medicines and certain drugs. Then in 1859 a railroad conductor, Edwin L. Drake, dug for oil near Titusville (TITE-us-vill), Pennsylvania. He hit a gusher, and his well was soon producing 20 barrels of crude oil a day. The oil could be refined (converted) into kerosene, for use in kerosene lamps. These lamps soon became the major means of lighting U.S. homes and offices. Other fortune-seekers rushed to put down wells near Drake's. In no time at all, the pumping of Pennsylvania oil became a thriving business.

So did oil refining. It was in refineries that crude oil was turned into kerosene. Clevelanders such as Rockefeller quickly saw that their hometown was a fitting place to start refineries. Cleveland was not too far from the Pennsylvania wells. And it was close to growing Western markets.

In 1863 Rockefeller and four other men built a refinery in Cleveland. In 1865, just as the Civil War was ending, Rockefeller bought out three of his four partners. Rockefeller's refinery could turn out more barrels of oil a day than any other in Cleveland. The business made Rockefeller very wealthy — and he wasn't yet 30 years old.

Lowering prices. But the oil business was a risky one. Oil fortunes could be made and lost in a day. To stay on top of the business, Rockefeller had to sell more and more oil. He wanted his company to be more than just the biggest oil company in the country. He wanted it to

John D. Rockefeller

be the *only* oil company. He wanted to drive all his competitors out of business.

To do this, Rockefeller made deals with the railroad companies. The railroads saw future profits in shipping Rockefeller's oil. They therefore agreed to return to Rockefeller part of the money that he paid for such shipments. This returned money was called a *rebate.* Because of the rebates, Rockefeller could sell refined oil at cheaper prices than his rivals. One by one, smaller oil companies were driven out of business. They were forced to sell their businesses to Rockefeller at almost any price he offered.

By this time, Rockefeller's business was called the Standard Oil Company of Ohio. Throughout the 1870's, Rockefeller went right on buying up other com-

319

At the turn of this century, many people feared that giant companies such as Rockefeller's would swallow up small businesses. This cartoon of the period was titled "The Cave of Despair."

panies one by one. By the end of the decade, he controlled most of the piping, refining, and selling of oil in the U.S. In 1882 the Standard Oil Company was turned into the Standard Oil Trust. A *trust* was a business made up of several companies. It was run by one group of managers known as *trustees*.

But powerful as he was, John D. Rockefeller controlled only one industry — oil. Other men, using similar

methods, rose to the top of other industries. In 1880 the biggest name in the iron and steel business was Andrew Carnegie.

Carnegie was the son of a poor Scottish immigrant. At the age of 16, he earned only $2.50 a week as a messenger boy. But then he met the manager of the Pennsylvania Railroad. This businessman gave Carnegie a job with the railroad. He also gave the young Scotsman a tip about investing money. Carnegie began buying stock in other companies, usually with borrowed money. These companies grew rich, and so did Carnegie. At 33, Carnegie was making $50,000 a year.

Improving profits. In 1873 Carnegie turned his attention to the making of steel. Two years later, he decided that his mills in Pittsburgh should be using a new method of turning iron into steel. He had learned the method while visiting steel factories in England. The method was called the *Bessemer process.*

In the Bessemer process, iron was heated until it was molten (turned into a fluid). Then impurities were burned out of the molten iron with a blast of air. Before this process was discovered, steel could be made only in quantities of 25 to 50 pounds (about 12 to 25 kilograms). It took weeks to produce this much steel. Now, with the Bessemer process, steel could be turned out by the ton. And it could be made in only minutes.

Returning from England, Carnegie built the world's biggest steel mill near Pittsburgh. This mill made use of the Bessemer process. Much of Carnegie's business was in producing steel rails for railroads. His profits shot steadily up.

By 1900 the Carnegie Steel Company's profit was 40 million dollars a year. The next year, 1901, Carnegie decided that he had worked hard enough managing his business. He therefore sold his company to a group of business leaders headed by a New York banker, J. P. Morgan. Morgan paid Carnegie 492 million dollars for it. This made Carnegie the richest man in the world.

People did not know what to think about business leaders such as Carnegie and Rockefeller. It was hard to decide whether they were good men or evil men, heroes or villains. They showed no mercy toward business rivals. And they wielded enormous power. Some critics said that democracy was in danger when a few business leaders had so much power.

On the other hand, people admired all that these business leaders had built and achieved. Rockefeller had brought order to a once-risky business. Carnegie had helped to improve the manufacture of steel. And neither man used his fortune only for his own pleasure. Both gave away millions of dollars to help meet public needs. Carnegie donated nearly 60 million dollars to build 3,000 public libraries. Rockefeller gave millions of dollars to help support universities and medical research.

Was it better, then, to think of these men as "captains of industry" and praise them for making the U.S. into a strong industrial nation? Or was it better to think of them as "robber barons" who enriched themselves while hurting others? Some Americans in 1900 answered the question one way — and some the other.

A Second Look. . . .

1. *In what industry did John D. Rockefeller make his fortune? In what industry did Andrew Carnegie make his fortune?*

2. *What is your opinion of the way Rockefeller treated his business rivals? Would you call his methods wrong or immoral? Why or why not? Can you think of better ways to treat business rivals? If so, what are they?*

3. *The U.S. oil industry kept on growing long after John D. Rockefeller retired from it. Today the U.S. depends on oil as a major source of energy. List five ways in which you and your family make use of oil. Next to each item on the list, note what you think you would use as a substitute if the U.S. oil supply ran out. If no substitute seems available, explain how the lack of oil would change your life-style.*

Andrew Carnegie

Thomas Edison liked to talk about how hard he worked. Here is the "wizard" after five days' work on his phonograph.

Chapter 27

Edison "Bottles" Light

It was nearly midnight on October 19, 1879. In a workshop in Menlo Park, New Jersey, two men were working late. Thomas Alva Edison and an assistant sat staring at a glass bulb. The bulb had a thin, lighted wire inside. The bulb had glowed for about four hours without burning out. After two years of work on his light bulb, Edison seemed to be succeeding.

Of course, the invention was not Edison's alone. Scientists had been trying to perfect light bulbs for more than 40 years. Edison had taken many of his ideas from this earlier work. He was trying to develop an *incandescent* bulb — one that glowed with heat. He wanted it to give off a soft, steady light. He also wanted it to be inexpensive for use in people's homes. He had tested such a bulb again and again. But up to now his light had never lasted more than a few minutes.

This time Edison's bulb glowed on

and on. It gave off light for 40 hours before it finally burned out. Then the news traveled around the world. A practical method of electric lighting had been found. Edison became known as the "Wizard of Menlo Park."

Who was this "wizard" who became one of history's greatest inventors? Born in 1847, he was a problem child. He asked so many questions in school that his teacher said he was a trouble-maker. So his mother, who had been a teacher, took him out of school. She taught him herself. After lessons, Tom was always busy making experiments with chemicals.

Young printer. At 12, Tom became a newsboy on a railroad train. After a time, he set up a small press in the baggage car and began printing his *own* newspapers. Next to the printing press, Tom kept his bottles and jars of chemicals. One day one of Tom's chemicals started a fire that burned the baggage car. The angry train conductor threw Tom off the train, smacking him hard on the ears.

Later on, Tom began to go deaf. Some people believed it was the result of the beating he took on his ears. Whatever the reason, Edison didn't feel sorry for himself. He believed that being deaf helped him to think better. It shut out the noise.

Tom became a telegraph operator when he was 16. Later he went to New York and took a job with a company that sent the prices of gold and stocks to offices by a ticker machine. This machine worked like a telegraph, and soon Tom was making improvements on it. When he got through, the company's president asked him how much money he wanted for his improvements. Edison thought he'd settle for $3,000. But first he said, "Well, sir, suppose you make me an offer." The president said, "How would $40,000 strike you?" Edison could hardly believe it. All he said was, "Yes, I think that would be fair."

With this money, Edison started his first workshop. He was 23. In 1876 a Bostonian, Alexander Graham Bell, invented the telephone. Edison soon developed a transmitter (sender) for use in phones. In 1877 he invented the phonograph. This was his favorite invention — and his most original one. Then Edison decided to find something better than gas or kerosene for lighting homes and offices.

Drawing at left is an early demonstration of the Edison electric lamp. Electricity ran through a carbon filament made by burning thread.

323

Scientific "wizard." Like other inventors, Edison knew that an electric current could heat a wire filament white-hot. But within seconds, the wire would burn out. "If I can put that wire inside a glass bulb and keep it from burning up," Edison said, "I'd have 'bottled light.' But where to find the right filament?"

For two years Edison worked on his electric lamp. Often he worked 18 hours a day. Many times he forgot to eat. He sent current through platinum and other metal wires. He tried sending current through twine, cork, and fishing line. He even tried hairs from the beard of an old friend. He used thousands of different materials. All burned up too fast. He knew that a filament made of carbon would do the job. But keeping it burning was the problem.

Then one day he took some cotton thread and shaped it into a loop. He baked it for five hours in a special furnace. This turned the thread to carbon. When it cooled, he took it out. At first, the carbon thread broke too easily. But three days later he had a filament that held together. It was carefully set into a glass bulb, and the air was pumped out. On went the current. The lamp glowed — the "most beautiful light ever seen."

In 1882 Edison built the first electric power station to carry electricity into homes in New York City. He lived to see millions of homes and offices served by electricity. As time went on, Edison based more and more of his inventions on the work of others. In 1889, for example, he and his assistants made a movie camera. Their camera drew heavily on earlier inventions by such pioneers as George Eastman. Even so, Edison played

a part in giving movies their start.

Friends of Edison remember hearing him say that genius — being very smart — came mostly from "hard work and sweat." This summed up Edison's thinking about his work. He was a "trial-and-error" inventor. He kept on trying many different ideas until one of them succeeded.

As an inventor, Edison followed in the tradition of Benjamin Franklin. Both were self-made scientists. Both were very practical men. Franklin's most lasting discoveries were in the field of electricity. Edison was also an inventor of electrical devices. The work of this "wizard" gave rise to new industries and created new wealth.

A Second Look. . . .

1. *Several of Thomas Edison's inventions are mentioned in this chapter. Name three of them and tell the importance of each.*

2. *Here is a list of objects invented between 1876 and 1900: (a) Telephone (1876). (b) Electric light bulb (1879). (c) Electric flatiron (1882). (d) Fountain pen (1884). (e) Kodak hand camera (1888). (f) Electric sewing machine (1889). (g) Safety razor (1895). (h) Motor-driven vacuum cleaner (1899). Which of these objects do you think improved people's lives the most? Why?*

3. *Most inventions begin with the inventor's belief that there must be a better way of doing something. Try to think of an object that could be improved — a dishwasher, a pencil, a skateboard, anything at all. Think of a new kind of object that might be useful to people. Describe your idea on a piece of paper. Also draw a sketch of it.*

Chapter 28

A Voice for the Workers

One newspaper called it "the greatest battle between labor and capital [ownership] ever in the U.S."

Another newspaper said, "This rebellion must be put down!"

A third newspaper screamed, "Chicago is at the mercy of the burner's torch!"

What was all the shouting about? The workers of the Pullman Company were on strike in 1894. The Pullman Company made and ran railroad sleeping cars. George Pullman, the head of the company, thought he was good to his workers. He set up a "model" town for them, called Pullman, near Chicago. The workers lived in neat brick houses with lawns, flowers, and trees.

Yet Pullman was a *company town*. The workers *had* to live in it. They had to pay much higher rents than other people paid elsewhere. They had to buy from the company store — at higher prices.

Between 1893 and 1897, there was a serious depression in the U.S. The Pullman Company laid off many of its workers. It sharply cut the pay of those workers it kept on. As a result, most workers got less than six dollars a week. But the Pullman Company did *not* lower rents or prices in its "model" town. One worker found that his paycheck came to *two cents* after the rent money was taken out!

The Pullman Company would not raise pay or lower rents — even when business got better. Three workers who complained about conditions were fired. Then the Pullman workers called a strike.

Helping the poor. Many of the Pullman workers were members of a new union, the American Railway Union. It was led by a man who believed

Eugene V. Debs

strongly in helping the lower class. (A class is a division of the social order, usually based on wealth and social standing.) The man's name was Eugene V. Debs. Once Debs said: "While there is a lower class, I am in it.... While there is a soul in prison, I am not free."

The American Railway Union decided to help the Pullman workers. Its members would not handle any Pullman cars on trains. Railroad companies struck back. They fired any man who would "cut out" a Pullman car from a train. When this happened, all the train workers walked off. Soon almost every railroad in the Middle West was tied up by the strike.

The strike made many people angry. To begin with, large numbers of Americans simply opposed labor unions. They had lived in an older America where most business companies had been fairly small. Workers in small companies often had more control over their own lives than workers in large companies did. Many people were especially opposed to union demands for closed shops. Under *closed shop agreements,* business owners could hire only labor union members. This practice seemed unfair to many Americans, including some workers themselves. They believed that owners should be allowed to hire and fire anyone they pleased.

Even people who had nothing against unions opposed some strikes. Certain kinds of strikes could cripple businesses of many sorts. When businesses were crippled, other workers lost their jobs. Many Americans saw special dangers in railroad strikes. When railroads stopped running, goods could not reach their markets.

Eugene Debs told railway workers to be peaceful and not to damage railroad property. At first the men obeyed. But then the railroads brought in strikebreakers and armed "deputies" to run the trains. Fights and riots broke out. Railroad cars were burned.

The railroad companies turned to President Grover Cleveland. They asked him to send in troops to restore order and keep mail trains moving. President Cleveland agreed. Still the strike was not broken. It even spread. So did the disorders. When trains moved, guarded by troops, angry mobs tried to stop them. There was burning and looting.

Going to jail. Then the railroad companies played their ace. They got a federal court order that made support of the strike unlawful. Debs would not obey the order. He and three of his helpers were put in jail. So were hundreds of the striking workers. Without leaders, the workers gave up and went back to work. The Pullman strike was crushed.

Debs was let out of jail after six months. A crowd of 100,000 people met and cheered him in Chicago. Most of them were low-paid, working-class people. Many of them were immigrants who had come to the U.S. for better jobs and a new start in life. They, like Debs, didn't see why there should be such a wide gap between the income of big business owners and the pay of workers. They thought it was wrong for a few people to have millions of dollars while countless others were paid hardly enough to live on. To them, Debs stood for a fair share for the workers.

While in jail, Debs had become a *Socialist.* (Under socialism, factories, mines, and railroads are owned by the

When Pullman Company workers walked off their jobs in 1894, they threatened to snarl traffic on the nation's railroads. To keep the roads running, President Grover Cleveland sent U.S. troops to the strike area near Chicago in patrol trains (below). Groups often gathered, and troops sometimes turned on them, using force to keep the peace. The anti-union artist Frederic Remington went to the area to see it at firsthand. He painted troops giving their rifle butts to workers (above).

government.) Debs believed that workers would never have good wages and a better life under *capitalism*. (Under capitalism, factories, mines, railroads, for instance, are privately owned.)

Running for President. Debs ran for President of the U.S. five times as a Socialist. He believed that socialism could come about slowly and peacefully in the United States. He never won an election. But in 1912 he won about one million votes.

Capitalism in the U.S. has changed a great deal since Debs' time. Over the years, American workers have made gains that Debs did not think would be possible under capitalism. They have won better pay, better working conditions, and a better life. Many of these gains have been brought about by strong labor unions, the use of strikes, and changes in the law. As a result of these gains, most Americans have turned away from socialism.

A Second Look....

1. *What were two of the railroad workers' complaints against the Pullman Company in 1894? What was the outcome of these complaints?*

2. *Why did some Americans object to strikes in the 1890's? Do you think the same objections still exist today? What is your opinion of strikes? Do you believe they generally serve a useful purpose or not? Give reasons for your answers.*

3. *Copy the dictionary definitions for these three words:* capitalism, socialism, *and* communism. *Give examples, in your own words, of the differences between* capitalism *and* socialism. *Then give examples of the differences between* socialism *and* communism.

The press helped turn the American public against the strikers by making fun of Debs and his union.

328

Chapter 29

Organizing the Workers

Sam Gompers was worried. His wife Sophie was giving birth to a child. But she was having a hard time. In fact, she seemed near death. Gompers rushed out into the streets of New York to look for a doctor. But the doctor he found at first refused to help. Why? Because the doctor knew that Gompers had no money. At the time, Sam Gompers was out of work — and completely broke.

Gompers lost his temper. He seized the doctor's arm and told him: "You will come with me without another minute's hesitation or I will not be responsible for what I do to you." The doctor obeyed. Sophie Gompers and her child lived. The next day, her husband paid the doctor two dollars that he had borrowed from a friend.

Why did Sam Gompers have no money? Why was he out of work? It was because employers thought he was a troublemaker. They knew that he was a leader of a cigar-makers' union in New York. This union, like most unions, challenged the power of business owners. If owners mistreated workers or failed to pay them what they wanted, unions threatened to call a strike. In fact, Gompers' union did call a strike. It lasted through the winter of 1876-1877. The strike did not succeed. Police arrested striking cigar-makers and threw them in jail. The cigar-makers soon found that their strike was in vain. To stay alive, they had to return to work — on the employer's terms.

Blacklisted worker. But there was no work for Sam Gompers. Owners of cigar factories kept a list of union leaders. The owners agreed not to employ anyone on this so-called *blacklist.* Gompers' name was on the list. For several months in 1877, Sam Gompers' family lived on a soup made of water, salt, pepper, and flour.

Being poor was nothing new to Samuel Gompers. He had been poor all his life. He had grown up in a Jewish family in a poor section of London, England. He had attended school for only four years. Then, to help support his family, he left school to learn a trade. His father taught him how to roll tobacco with his hands and make it into cigars.

In 1863, when Sam was 13, his family left England. They came to America in search of new opportunities. Their lives did not change much. They still lived in a poor, crowded apartment. Father and son still worked more than 10 hours a day rolling tobacco into cigars. But Sam enjoyed his life, poor as it was. He made friends with another Jewish cigar-maker from England, Sophie Julian. He was 17 when they got married; Sophie was 16. They did not have much money then. In fact, they never had much money — not even after Sam Gompers became more powerful.

Gompers became more powerful because of what he did for the labor movement. He believed deeply in his cigar-makers' union. More than this, he believed that all trade unions could make life better for people. Carpenters' unions, he thought, could make life better for carpenters. Shoemakers' unions could make life better for shoemakers. But for unions to work, Gompers believed, they had to be better organized.

Knights of Labor. The leading labor union of Gompers' day was the Knights of Labor. It had been organized in Philadelphia in 1869. The Knights thought all workers — farmers and factory workers, barbers and cigar-makers — should belong to the same union. The Knights signed up *skilled workers* (those who needed training to do their jobs) as members. It also signed up *unskilled workers* (those who needed little training). By the mid-1880's, the Knights of Labor had a membership of more than 500,000 workers.

Then, in 1886, the Knights lost a railroad strike. Soon after this, membership in the union tumbled rapidly. Members of the Knights did not believe they had enough in common with one another. Skilled workers and unskilled workers did not see eye to eye.

Meanwhile, Gompers started carrying out his great plan for strengthening labor unions. In 1886 he and several other labor leaders put together a new organization. They called it the *American Federation of Labor* — or AFL, for short. They chose Gompers to be president of the organization, a full-time job. His salary was to be $1,000 a year — less than what he could make as a cigar-maker.

Samuel Gompers

New federation. The AFL was organized quite differently from the Knights. Gompers' union was a federation of separate unions. These separate unions kept their freedom to act as they wished. Most of them were *craft* unions. That is, they represented welders, carpenters, and other groups of skilled workers in a trade.

What was the purpose of the federation? Union leaders thought that different unions should help one another in their struggles with employers. Carpenters' unions should help cigar-makers' unions. Cigar-makers' unions should help bakers' unions. If unions helped each other, these AFL leaders thought, working people might become more powerful. More of their strikes might succeed. Business owners might be forced to pay higher wages. They might even give workers a shorter working day — eight hours instead of 10 or 12.

Labor leader. Gompers threw himself into his work as president of the federation. He traveled on trains from one end of the country to the other. He talked, joked, and smoked cigars with workers in different trades. He tried to persuade them to join the AFL. He told them they could belong to their own unions and the AFL at the same time. The purpose of the AFL, said Gompers, was to help the separate unions that belonged to it. For example, if a carpenters' union went on strike, it would no longer fight alone. It would have the larger AFL behind it.

Gompers had to argue for more than just his federation. He also had to defend labor's right to organize at all. Millions of Americans were still against unions. These people opposed the idea of the closed shop. They thought business owners should be allowed to run their businesses as they saw fit. Some critics were also opposed to the use of strikes in labor disputes. Strikes were bad for business, these critics said. And what was bad for business was bad for the nation.

Yet Gompers succeeded in bringing new members into his federation. As membership in the Knights of Labor slipped, membership in the AFL rose. By 1900 about 500,000 workers belonged to the federation. Sam Gompers had become a leader of organized labor, just as John D. Rockefeller had become a leader of big business. Gompers' union had become the most important labor organization in the U.S.

Unlike Eugene V. Debs, Gompers accepted capitalism. He worked within this system to get workers a better deal. He spoke for labor in the halls of Congress. He tried to get new laws that would protect workers against unfair treatment.

One day, as a guest at the White House, he got into an argument with President Theodore Roosevelt. Slamming his fist against his desk, Roosevelt said: "Mr. Gompers, I want you to understand, sir, that I am the President of the United States." Gompers did not apologize. He too banged his fist and said: "Mr. President, I want you to understand that I am the president of the American Federation of Labor."

Sam Gompers had come a long way since the days when he was out of work because of an employers' blacklist. Because of his efforts, labor unions had also come a long way. They were much stronger and better respected. They were also bigger and better organized. And they had taken their place within the American capitalist system.

A Second Look. . . .

1. *What was Sam Gompers' main goal as the leader of the AFL? What methods did he use to achieve his goal?*

2. *When (if ever) is it right for workers to go on strike? Why? When (if ever) is it right for employers to use a blacklist against labor leaders? Why?*

3. *Suppose that Sam Gompers and Eugene V. Debs have met on a railroad train in the late 1890's. Debs believes that the great hope of American workers is socialism. Gompers believes in the capitalist system. But he thinks workers need strong unions for protection. Create a conversation between them.*

Chapter 30

A Voice for the Farmers

He believed that the voice of the people was the voice of God. The people were always "right" and "good." And so he fought the battles of "the people" most of his life. He ran for President of the United States three times. He lost each time. But most of the things that he wanted for the good of the people did happen — mostly because he fought for his ideas.

His name was William Jennings Bryan. He was called the "Great Commoner," because he was the friend of the common people. He thought himself to be one of them. He was born in Salem, Illinois, in 1860. He studied law, and in 1887 moved west to Lincoln, Nebraska.

In the 1880's and 1890's, great changes were taking place in the United States. Until then the United States had mainly been a country of farmers. And the farmers were proud people. Farmers, Thomas Jefferson had said, "are the chosen people of God." But in Bryan's time the U.S. was becoming an industrial power. This was especially true in the Northeast. The U.S. was becoming a nation of factories, cities, and "big business." Farmers were no longer "the chosen people." Some city people called them "hicks" and "hayseeds."

Even worse, farmers were becoming poor. During the Civil War, they got $2.50 for a bushel of wheat. By 1890 they were getting only 50 cents for a bushel of wheat. Many farmers were in a bad way. They owed a lot of money to the banks.

Farmers blamed the factory owners, the banks, and the railroads for much of their trouble. These were "the interests," located mainly in the East. The farmers worked and sweated all day, they thought, and "the interests" in the East got all the money.

People's party. The unhappy farmers fought back. They formed a new party, the People's party. They called themselves Populists. The Populists wanted the government to control big business companies. They backed the idea that government should own the railroads. They wanted an income tax that would be heaviest on people with the most money. (In those days, there was no income tax at all.) They also supported an eight-hour day for factory workers.

Above all, Populists wanted more money to help pay their debts. They thought they could get it if the government would make silver coins. Since 1873 the government had made mostly gold coins. Populists believed that a lot of silver coins, added to the gold coins, would cause prices to rise. Then they

Democrat William Jennings Bryan made three tries for the Presidency. In this 1900 poster, he stood for some already familiar reforms.

The Issue — 1900
·LIBERTY·
·JUSTICE·
·HUMANITY·
1776
1900
NO
IMPERIALISM
W. J. BRYAN
NO CROWN OF THORNS
NO CROSS OF GOLD
E PLURIBUS UNUM
DECLARATION OF INDEPENDENCE
TRUSTS
DOLLAR OF THE DADDIES
16
TO
"GIVE US LIBERTY OR GIVE US DEATH"
EQUAL RIGHTS TO ALL
SPECIAL PRIVILEGES TO NONE.
COPYRIGHT 1900
BY
NEVILLE WILLIAMS
COLUMBUS, OHIO.

would get more dollars for their wheat and other farm products. But most bankers and business owners were against silver. They wanted only gold.

William Jennings Bryan was not a Populist. He was a Democrat. But he believed in the farmers and wanted to help them. He took over many of the ideas of the Populists. Bryan became the champion of silver and the farmers. He became the champion of reform — changing things to make them better.

At the age of 30, Bryan was elected to Congress. In 1894, when he was only 34, he ran for the U.S. Senate. He lost, but this didn't stop Bryan. He made up his mind he would run for President in 1896!

"Cross of gold." No one thought the Democrats would choose Bryan to run. But Bryan was lucky. He was asked to make a speech at the Democrats' national convention. Bryan made the most of his chance. He was young and handsome and sure of himself. Above all, he was a great speaker. Bryan talked for silver and against gold. He talked for the Western farmers against the Eastern bankers. He talked for the countryside against the cities. At the end of his speech, he shouted to "the interests" that they would not put "mankind upon a cross of gold."

The people at the convention cheered Bryan wildly. They chose him to run for President.

The Republicans went all-out to defeat Bryan. Their man was William McKinley, former Congressman from Ohio. Republicans received a lot of money from business. They promised good times for all. The Republican slogan was "McKinley and the Full Dinner Pail." Party workers flooded the country with campaign material for McKinley. There was "dirty" politics too. Some people said Bryan was "crazy." Some factory owners told their workers to vote for McKinley — or else.

Bryan didn't have much money. But he went all over the country by train talking to people. And talking was what he did best. He traveled thousands of miles and made hundreds of speeches to people everywhere. McKinley did his campaigning from his Ohio home.

The vote was close, but Bryan lost. He ran for President two more times, and also lost. But Bryan made his mark on U.S. politics. Almost all the reforms he wanted finally came to pass.

A Second Look. . . .

1. *Who were Populists? What changes did they seek? Which national leader backed many Populist ideas? What group or groups did this leader oppose?*

2. *If you had lived in 1896, would you have voted for Bryan or McKinley? Why?*

3. *The American poet Vachel Lindsay once wrote a famous poem entitled "Bryan, Bryan, Bryan, Bryan." The poem is to be found in* The Oxford Book of American Verse *and other collections of poetry. Have one of your classmates with a strong voice read the poem in class. Other classmates may want to do library research to identify three people mentioned in the poem: John Altgeld, Mark Hanna, and "Pitchfork Ben" Tillman. Some questions you may want to consider: How does Lindsay portray Bryan — as a hero or a villain? Why? How does the poet see the significance of the 1896 election? Explain your answers.*

Looking Back:
The Rise of Industry

	A	B	C	D	
1860	1870	1880	1890	1900

Putting Events in Order

Chapters 25 through 30 have described some key events in the history of U.S. industry, labor, and economics from 1860 to 1900. Ten events of this period are listed here. Your job is to match each event to the correct period shown on the timeline above. On a piece of paper, number from **1** to **10**. After each event, write the letter of the 10-year period within which the event occurred.

1. John D. Rockefeller and four partners build an oil refinery in Cleveland.

2. Thomas A. Edison develops an incandescent light bulb that glows for many hours.

3. A giant fair in Philadelphia shows off new inventions, including the telephone.

4. Thomas Edison builds the first electric power station to carry electricity into homes.

5. Federal troops battle railroad workers in the Pullman strike.

6. Samuel Gompers becomes president of the American Federation of Labor (AFL).

7. The Knights of Labor builds a membership of more than 500,000.

8. Democrats cheer William Jennings Bryan for his "Cross of Gold" speech.

9. Eugene V. Debs becomes a Socialist.

10. Andrew Carnegie, having grown rich from his investments, turns his attention to the making of steel.

Interpreting a Source

The song "John Henry" has been called "America's greatest ballad." There are at least 50 different versions of it. It is based on the story of a black man who worked himself to death building a railroad tunnel in West Virginia. His job was to drive steel drills through solid rock using a 12-pound (six-kilogram) hammer. Dynamite was placed in the holes he made to blast the rock away. In the 1870's, steam drills were introduced to hurry the work along.

John Henry

When John Henry was a little baby
Sitting on his pappy's knee,
He grabbed a hammer and a little piece of steel,
Said, "This hammer'll be the death of me, Lord, Lord,
This hammer'll be the death of me."

Now the captain said to John Henry,
"I'm gonna bring that steam drill around,
I'm gonna take that steam drill out on the job,
I'm gonna whop that steel on down, Lord, Lord,
I'm gonna whop that steel on down."

John Henry told his captain,
"A man ain't nothing but a man,
But before I'll let that steam drill beat me down
I'll die with my hammer in my hand, Lord, Lord,
I'll die with my hammer in my hand."

John Henry said to his shaker,
"Now shaker, why don't you sing?
'Cause I'm throwing 12 pounds from my hips on down,
Just listen to that cold steel ring, Lord, Lord,
Just listen to that cold steel ring."

The man that invented the steam drill,
He thought he was mighty fine,
But John Henry he made 14 feet
While the steam drill only made nine, Lord, Lord,
The steam drill only made nine.

John Henry hammered on the mountain
Till his hammer was striking fire.
He drove so hard he broke his poor heart,
Then he laid down his hammer and he died, Lord, Lord,
He laid down his hammer and he died.

They took John Henry to the graveyard,
And they buried him in the sand,
And every locomotive comes rolling by
Says, "There lies a steel-driving man, Lord, Lord,
There lies a steel-driving man."

Now some say he was born in Texas,
And some say he was born in Maine,
But I don't give a damn where that poor boy was born.
He was a steel-driving man, Lord, Lord,
He was a steel-driving man.

1. *Who was John Henry? What happened to him? Why does his story seem important enough to put into a song?*

2. *What does the song say about the changes that were taking place after the Civil War? Was it hard for people such as John Henry to adapt to these changes? Why or why not?*

3. *Do you think the story of John Henry actually happened as told in the song? Or do you think the song exaggerates? Why?*

4. *Who, in your opinion, deserves greater credit for building U.S. railroads — business leaders such as Charles Crocker, or workers such as John Henry? Or is it possible that both deserve equal credit? Why?*

Sharpening Your Skills

The line graph on this page shows how the U.S. economy was changing in the 50 years between 1850 and 1900. Study the graph. Then answer the questions below.

1. How many people worked on farms in 1850? in 1900?

2. How many nonfarm workers did the U.S. have in those two years?

3. In what year did the number of nonfarm workers equal the number of farm workers?

4. For which of the following statements does the graph provide evidence? (a) Both U.S. farming and U.S. industry increased at about the same rate between 1850 and 1900. (b) The number of farm workers and nonfarm workers increased at about the same rate in the U.S. between 1850 and 1900. (c) The growth of U.S. industry was greater than the growth of U.S. farming between 1850 and 1900. (d) The employment of nonfarm workers increased faster in the U.S. than the employment of farm workers between 1850 and 1900. Explain your answers.

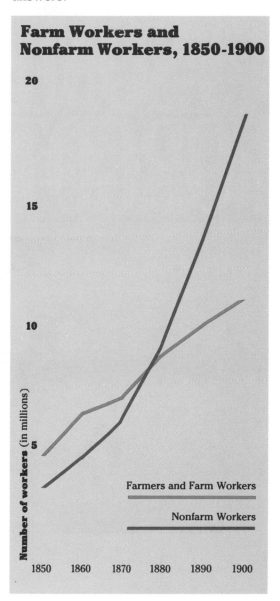

Farm Workers and Nonfarm Workers, 1850-1900

Number of workers (in millions)

Farmers and Farm Workers

Nonfarm Workers

1850 1860 1870 1880 1890 1900

6 THOSE SOMETIMES FORGOTTEN

שפייז וועט געווינען דיא קריעג!

אידר קומט אהער צו געפינען פרייהייט.

יעצט מוזט איהר העלפען זיא צו באשיצען.

מיר מוזען דיא עלליעס פערזארגען מיט ווייץ.

לאזט קיין זאך ניט גיין אין ניוועץ

יוניטעד סטייטס שפייז פערוואלטונג.

Looking Ahead: Promises Broken, Promises Fulfilled

"So at last I was going to America! Really, really going, at last! The boundaries burst. The arch of heaven soared. A million suns shone out for every star. The winds rushed in from outer space, roaring in my ears, 'America! America!' "

These words are Mary Antin's. They are taken from her book, *The Promised Land*. She is describing how she felt when she first learned she was moving to America. The year was 1894, and Mary Antin was 13. She was leaving her home in Poland to join her father in Boston.

Mary Antin was one of millions to come to America in the 19th century. Her excitement was shared by nearly everyone who came. To the tired and poor of Europe and Asia, America was a place of hope. In America there was

America offered a beacon of hope to people from lands grown old and crowded and confused. This U.S. government poster tells of America in Yiddish, the language of some European Jews.

freedom to say what one pleased. There was freedom to worship as one wished. There was cheap land and the promise of a better life. The German poet Goethe (GUR-tuh) summed it up in five words: "America, you have it better."

And so immigrants kept arriving. They crowded into ships in Europe and Asia. They endured difficult ocean crossings to get to their new land. They arrived by the hundreds in San Francisco and New Orleans, by the thousands in New York. More and more of them came with every passing year. Some wept with joy when they saw the land of their dreams.

A few were successful almost as soon as they stepped onto U.S. soil. But most had to work hard to gain a foothold in the United States. They usually had to adjust to life in the cities. They often had to learn a new language — English. They sometimes had to learn new skills in order to get jobs. The hardest thing they faced was prejudice — strong feelings of *339*

dislike formed without much reason. Other Americans often greeted them with insults because they were foreign-born.

Life in America was a struggle. But then, it had been a struggle from the very start. The first group to face hardships had been the people we now call American Indians. Later groups had also endured difficulties — especially those black Americans who had once been slaves. In the next few chapters, we'll take a closer look at the struggles of four different groups between 1860 and 1900.

From 1829 to 1838, Pennsylvania-born George Catlin painted more than 600 American Indians. He described Chief Mah-to-toh-pa of the Mandan tribe in North Dakota (left) as a person of towering "grace and manly dignity." Catlin and others feared Indian ways were disappearing. Later in the century, even lands set aside for Indians were swallowed up by whites. In 1889 Congress bought three million acres (1.2 million hectares) from Indians. On April 22, white settlers called boomers *raced into this area, part of Oklahoma, seeking free land (below).*

Struggles of American Indians.

When the first white people came to America, most of the Indians they met were friendly. Sometimes the Indians gave food to the newcomers. The Indians also showed them how to plant corn, tomatoes, and tobacco. But as the settlers took more and more land, the Indians turned against them. They did not want to lose their hunting grounds to white settlers.

When the Civil War broke out, most U.S. soldiers were called out of the West by the government. Many Indians saw their chance to strike back at the white settlers — and did so. The settlers often attacked the Indians too.

After the war, a new wave of white people rolled through the West. Some of them were miners looking for gold or silver. In some places, mining towns sprang up overnight. Behind the miners came ranchers. Close on their heels came railroad-builders and farmers. All of these white settlers wanted land and more land.

341

These newcomers quickly ran into trouble with the Indians. Many Indian tribes had treaties with the U.S. government. These treaties left the Indians large pieces of land as their hunting grounds. The treaties said that no white settlers would be allowed to settle on lands that had been left to the Indians.

These treaties were broken again and again — by whites. Finally the government decided to put all Indians on *reservations,* tracts of land set aside as living space for each tribe. It didn't matter whether or not the Indians wanted to move to reservations. They were ordered to go. Some tribes fought hard against being moved. The Sioux, the Apaches, and others made war on the U.S. Army.

As a group, however, Indians were not large enough or strong enough to score any lasting victories. They did not turn back the westward movement of white Americans. In 1890 the last of the major Indian revolts was put down in South Dakota. By 1900 almost all of the West, from the prairies to the Pacific, had been settled by cattle ranchers, farmers, and townspeople. The "Wild West" was gone. The frontier had vanished.

Struggles of new immigrants. Few newcomers to the United States had ever been greeted with open arms. Prejudice against "foreigners" had often been quite strong. Back in the 1840's and 1850's, for example, Irish Catholics had faced prejudice from Protestants. Now, in the 1880's and 1890's, immigrants faced similar problems.

"Old immigrants" had come mostly from northern and western Europe. "New immigrants" were now coming mostly from southern and eastern Europe — Russia, Poland, Italy, and Greece. A great many of these people were Roman Catholic or Jewish. They were considered "different" from other Americans. The prejudice they faced was stronger than that faced by most earlier groups.

Some of the newcomers had trouble finding jobs. Some found they could not afford to live anywhere except in city slums. The newcomers were looked down upon by many other Americans. They had to work all the harder to make a better life.

Struggles of black Americans. Even before the Civil War, some Northern towns and cities had kept black Americans separate from whites. Blacks could not stay at the same hotels. They could not occupy the same sections in theaters. These practices were known as *segregation.* After Reconstruction, segregation spread to the South.

At this time, many white Southerners were suffering from bad harvests and bad debts. They needed someone to blame for their troubles. Black people were an easy target. Some Southern leaders drummed up old hatreds against blacks. This time Northerners did not rush to the rescue. They had forgotten their old concern for equal rights.

Southern states began passing laws to separate the races. These laws were known by the name white people once used to belittle blacks — *Jim Crow.* Jim Crow laws brought many changes to the South. Blacks could no longer ride in "whites only" railroad cars on trains. They could not sit in "white" waiting rooms or take beds in "white" hospitals. They were kept separate in schools, parks, orphan homes, and prisons.

Writer Jacob Riis photographed this Italian mother and her baby on New York's Lower East Side.

Laws such as these were meant to keep black people "in their place."

Beginning with Mississippi in 1890, several Southern states adopted new constitutions. Some of these constitutions set up *poll taxes* and *literacy tests*. Poll taxes were fixed taxes required for voting. Literacy tests were exams to determine whether voters could read and write. Many Southern blacks were too poor to pay the poll taxes. Many had little education. They could not pass the literacy tests. These measures took the vote away from blacks. Now these people had little voice in the government. They had almost no way to fight for their rights.

Struggles of women. These struggles were very different from the struggles of the other three groups. Unlike American Indians, most American women had not been driven from their land. Unlike immigrants of the 1880's and 1890's, most had not been forced to live in slums. Unlike black Americans, women as a group had often shared in the power and wealth of the nation. Even so, women had faced prejudice. And their struggles against it gained much greater force after the Civil War.

In the 19th century, most men saw women as the "weaker sex." They often made jokes about women and treated them as if they were children. Husbands argued that they were the natural protectors of their wives. Men therefore could be trusted to look out for women's best interests. Women, they said, did not need to vote or hold political office.

By the 1890's, many women had rejected such ideas. They said that they had a right to vote. Not only this; they had a right to equal schooling and equal chances for jobs. A woman named Susan B. Anthony spent most of her life saying these things. Her own life story showed why women deserved to be treated as men's equals.

What do the warm, inviting lights in the distance mean to the Indian scout? Frederic Remington's painting doesn't say. But lights were signs of white settlers on lands that had once belonged to Indians.

Chapter 31

"I Will Fight No More, Forever"

Old Joseph lay dying. His people, the Nez Perce (nez purse) Indians, were peaceful. They had never killed a white person. They lived in the Wallowa Valley of Oregon. But now, in 1871, white settlers were moving in. And the government wanted the Nez Perces to move to a reservation in Idaho.

Other Indian groups had faced such problems for decades. In Florida, for example, the Seminoles had been fighting U.S. soldiers for more than 50 years. In the Northwest, the Yakimas and other tribes had been defeated in the 1850's. They had been sent to reservations. Old Joseph must have known the dangers of resisting white settlers. Yet he did not want his people to give up their land.

The old chief called his son to his bedside. This son would soon be known as Chief Joseph. The dying chief told his son never to give up the Wallowa Valley. "My son," he said, "never sell the bones of your father and mother!"

No wish for war. Late in 1876, the government ordered the Nez Perces to pack up and leave for the reservation. Chief Joseph, now 36, was a wise and gentle man. He did not want to leave the Wallowa Valley, which he loved. But neither did he want war. He said: "I will give up my country rather than have war. I will give up my father's grave. I will not have the blood of white men on my people's hands."

But many of Chief Joseph's braves wanted to fight. One night, while the chief was away, they rode out and killed at least 18 white settlers. Chief Joseph was angry. He knew it meant war.

He decided to lead his tribe of about 500 men, women, and children to safety in Canada. U.S. troops tried to cut off their escape. The Nez Perces had only about 100 warriors. The Army had many more. It also had cannons and early machine guns called *Gatling guns.* Joseph had to fight his way over high mountains. He was slowed down by the children and the old people. Yet in 12 battles, the Army was beaten back with heavy losses. Chief Joseph, a man of peace, proved to be a great and honorable warrior. He and his braves did not hurt peaceful white settlers. The Indians paid for their supplies and used guns they had captured from the Army.

Chief Joseph led his tribe over hundreds of miles of rugged territory. They

Chief Joseph as a young man.

345

crossed many mountains and rivers. Then, only 30 miles (48 kilometers) from Canada, the tribe was cut off by the troops of General Nelson Miles. The chief and his warriors could have escaped — if they had left behind the women, children, and wounded. Chief Joseph refused to do this. "I cannot bear to see my wounded men and women suffer any longer," he said.

No food for the hungry. A few days later, he gave up to General Miles and General O.O. Howard. It was October 5, 1877. Chief Joseph told them: "I am tired of fighting. . . . My people ask me for food, and I have none to give. It is cold, and we have no blankets, no wood. My people are starving. Where is my little daughter? I do not know. Perhaps even now she is freezing to death. Hear me, my chiefs. My heart is sick and sad. I have fought. But from where the sun now stands, I will fight no more, forever!"

Now Chief Joseph asked that his tribe be allowed to settle on the reservation in Idaho. This General Miles promised him. But the government broke the promise. The government was mainly interested in helping white settlers. It paid little attention to the Indians' rights or claims. Many Nez Perces were sent to a reservation in Oklahoma. Conditions there were very bad. The chief's six children and many others died of sickness.

Years later, the Nez Perces were sent to live on a reservation in Washington. Chief Joseph died in 1904, still longing for his home in the Wallowa Valley.

A Second Look. . . .

1. *Where did the Nez Perce Indians make their home? Why did they decide to leave? What was the final outcome of their attempt to go to Canada?*

2. *What is your opinion of Chief Joseph? Was he a wise leader? Do you suppose he was loved or feared by his people? Explain your answers.*

3. *Suppose you are either (a) a member of Chief Joseph's tribe, or (b) a white settler in the Wallowa Valley. It is the year 1871. The U.S. government wants to move the Nez Perce Indians off their land. Do you believe the government is right or wrong? Write a two-paragraph essay stating your beliefs and your reasons for them.*

Route of the Nez Perces, 1877

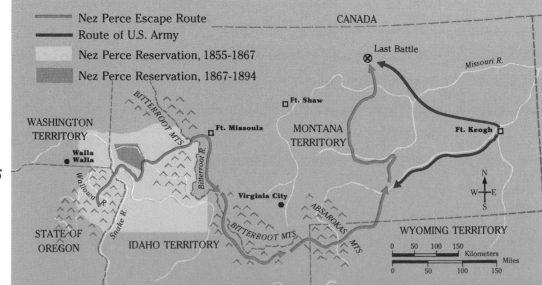

Chapter 32

Strangers in a New Land

Two young brothers from Italy looked eagerly over the rail of a steamship. Their names were Edward and Giuseppe (joo-SEP-pay) Corsi. They had lived on the crowded decks of a ship for two weeks. Now at last they were very close to what their parents called "the promised land." There, through the early morning mist, they could see it — America!

Edward shouted to his brother, "Mountains! Look at them!" Giuseppe thought it was strange that there was no snow on these mountains. Then the two boys discovered their mistake. The mountains were actually the buildings of New York City's skyline.

The Corsi brothers had never seen a city like this. There were many other surprises in store for them and their family. Some surprises were amusing. Others were unpleasant.

The first great shock for the Corsi family was their new home. It was a small, dirty, four-room apartment in a New York slum — all the Corsis could afford. Mrs. Corsi could not adjust to living in this place. It was much worse, she thought, than the Italian village they had left behind. Over there, in Italy, people lived in poverty but they lived among trees and flowers. Here, in an American city, there was also plenty of poverty — but few trees, few flowers. Even worse, the people of the neighborhood were strangers to one another. Strangers in a new land.

The Corsis were not the only immigrants to feel like strangers in America. Thousands of immigrant families had similar troubles when they first came to the United States. Throughout American history, in fact, newcomers had faced such hardships. But this did not stop more people from coming.

Growing in numbers. During the 1800's, they poured off ships in ever-greater numbers. In 1820 about 8,000 immigrants arrived from different countries. In 1840, only 20 years later, the number of new arrivals had increased to about 84,000 each year. By 1880 about half a million people were coming to the United States every year. By 1910 the number had climbed to more than a million.

These immigrants came for many different reasons. In the farming villages of Ireland, for example, most people lived on a meager diet of potatoes and milk. In the 1840's, there was a terrible drought. Potatoes would not grow. Thousands of Irish people starved to death. For thousands of others, sailing to America seemed the only way to survive. Between 1840 and 1860, more than 1.7 million Irish men and women made the trip.

Poor harvests also drove many Norwegians into ships bound for America. In Germany, meanwhile, people suffered not only from hunger but also from harsh rulers. Two revolutions broke out in Germany — first in 1830, then again in 1848. Both of them failed. Many Germans who had taken part in them fled to the United States to escape being punished.

In the 1880's and 1890's, there was even worse suffering in the countries of southern and eastern Europe. In Russia, Jews suffered from cruel laws that made it very hard for them to live. In Italy and Sicily, famine and disease wiped out whole families. There was economic misery in Poland and political trouble in Greece and Turkey. For many people in these countries, America seemed the only hope — the only possible escape from misery or death.

Growing apart. Many of those who left their old villages hoped some day to return. But only a few ever made it back. They wrote letters home about their strange new lives in America. They sometimes saved enough money to send back to relatives. But as time passed, they lost touch with people in the old villages. Slowly they were becoming Americans — even though they did not yet understand American ways.

At first, most immigrants, like the Corsi family, felt lost and homeless. Everything in America seemed strange to them. The English language seemed strange. The habit of working in a factory or a mine seemed strange. Most immigrants were farmers. They were used to living off the land, not working for wages. The constant need to buy things in a store — instead of growing or making them — seemed strange. To older immigrants, even the ways of their own children seemed strange.

The children of immigrants learned American ways more easily than their parents. They learned to speak English in American schools. They wanted to be accepted by their American friends. They often felt embarrassed by their parents' Old World language and customs. It did not seem right to them to cling to the old ways. Some immigrants therefore felt rejected by their own children. This added to their loneliness and confusion.

Newcomers suffered in yet another way. Native-born Americans took advantage of them. They were often swindled out of their money by dishonest merchants. Their bosses in mines and factories sometimes paid them barely enough to live.

To make matters still worse, immigrants were blamed for living the way they did. If they were poor, some Americans said, it was the immigrants' own fault. If they were out of work, it was *their* fault — not the fault of business. Labor unions started to blame the immigrants for accepting low wages and keeping wage rates down. Newspaper editors blamed them for bringing poverty and crime to the nation's cities.

In the 1840's and 1850's, some Americans had looked at immigration as a problem. Now, in the 1880's, it began to seem a problem again. Some native-born Americans, called *nativists,* urged laws to shut the door to foreigners. Congress listened to the call.

In 1882 Congress passed a law banning most immigration from China. This was only the first of many steps later taken against immigration from other lands. Nativists kept up the call for such laws. They forgot that they were the

IMPORTED, DUTY FREE,
by
TRUST, MONOPOLY & CO.
TO COMPETE WITH
AMERICAN LABOR.

Two 19th-century views of immigration are set forth on this page. The cartoon above comes from the humor magazine Puck. It shows Uncle Sam welcoming people from many lands with a Christmas toast. All the figures in the cartoon are clearly overdrawn. Do you think a cartoonist would draw such figures differently today? Why or why not? The cartoon at left presents the views of some labor unions toward immigrants. In the late 1800's, newcomers were often hired as strikebreakers. When they were, they ran into conflicts with labor unions. Union members were seeking higher wages. They resented anyone who would work for lower pay. As a result, many immigrants were caught between the demands of their bosses and the ill will of fellow workers. Some early unions turned their anger against all immigration.

349

children or grandchildren of immigrants themselves.

They also forgot what immigrants had done to make the nation stronger. Immigrants had played a key role in building the nation's railroads. They had dug its mines and plowed its fields. Some immigrants still thought of America as a "promised land." Yet it was they who had brought much of its promise to life.

A Second Look. . . .

1. From what countries did immigrants come to the U.S. in the 1840's and 1850's? From what countries did they come in the 1880's and 1890's? What problems did they face?

2. In your opinion, who was to blame for the poverty of most immigrant families? Was it right to blame the immigrants themselves for poverty? Why or why not?

3. You yourself may be an immigrant. If not, you are probably related to immigrant ancestors. If you are American-born, find out where your immigrant ancestors came from. (If you prefer not to use your own ancestors, substitute the ancestors of a friend or neighbor.) Then take a survey of the countries represented by the members of your class. With a tag or colored thumbtack, each student should indicate on a large map of the world the country or countries from which his/her ancestors or substitutes came.

As this man watched a baby, was he dreaming of an opera performance in his native Italy?

Chapter 33
Ghettoes

The streets were so crowded there was hardly room to walk. People had to dodge around crates, barrels, and piles of garbage. And right in the middle of all this were the peddlers with their pushcarts at the curbs. There were so many peddlers and carts that the streets were like a large department store. You could buy anything you needed — new or secondhand.

The houses had no heat or hot water. In the winter, people huddled around the kitchen stove to keep warm. In the summer, the houses were like ovens. People slept on the roofs and fire escapes to get a breath of air. One toilet in the hall served all the families on a floor.

This was the Lower East Side, a section of New York City, in the late 1890's. At that time, the neighborhood was mainly made up of Jewish people. Most of them came from Russia, Poland, and other countries of Eastern Europe. In these lands, the Jews had been treated very badly. Often they were beaten or killed by mobs, who were helped by police and soldiers.

Starting around 1880, more than a million Jews came to the United States. Earlier Jews in the U.S. had mainly come from Germany. Now most newcomers were from Russia. And most settled in the slums of the Lower East Side. This section quickly became a ghetto. In Europe the term *ghetto* had meant the section of a city to which Jews were limited. In America, the term had a more general meaning. It was applied to any section of a city in which one religious or ethnic group was dominant.

Slum conditions. The people in the Lower East Side ghetto were terribly poor. A great many had arrived in America with no money at all. They had spent all their savings to get here. Because they were poor, they had to take any kind of job they could get. Often the jobs were in small, dark, dirty factories called *sweatshops.* There they worked 12 to 15 hours a day for about seven dollars a week. Women and young girls worked in these sweatshops too. Many people became sick from the dirt, crowding, and long hours without air.

Sometimes whole families worked at home sewing clothes. A family of five or six might earn 25 dollars a week. Unskilled workers usually became pushcart peddlers. At the end of a long day, a peddler might make $2.70. That was a *good* day. Of course, everything was cheaper then. But $2.70 a day barely kept a family alive.

Many parents had problems with their children. The children wanted to become "American" as fast as they could. They didn't like using Yiddish, the language of East European Jews. They didn't understand the old customs of their parents. They made fun of their

351

parents, calling them "greenhorns."

In Yiddish, a mother would ask: "Why don't you say your evening prayer, son?" And the boy would answer in English, "Aw, what kind of junk is that?" Then he would run out into the streets to play. And he might skip Hebrew school or not go to religious services at the temple.

Small pleasures. Life on the Lower East Side was not all sad. The people had hard times, but they had many small pleasures too. They loved to go to the Yiddish theater and cheer their favorite actors on the stage. They had their favorite coffee shops where they argued for hours about politics, books, and plays. Like many immigrants, the Jews had their favorite foods and their own newspapers. Later they helped to start unions to fight against the conditions in the sweatshops.

Jewish newspapers printed letters from their readers. Some of these letters sound just as if they were written today. Here is one of them:

"My little girl wants to pierce her ears for earrings. She says all the girls here have pierced ears. But my husband says no, that in America you do not pierce ears any more. My little girl is crying. Please tell my husband what is the best thing to do."

Immigrant families often had a hard time deciding on "the best thing to do." Some customs of their new country were in conflict with the customs of the old one. Such problems arose in cities far from New York. They arose among German families in Milwaukee and St. Louis. They arose among Irish newcomers in Boston and Italian newcomers in Chicago. They arose among Chinese families in California.

In San Francisco, the Chinese were building their largest settlement in America. In 1875 this settlement had 47,000 people. It was known then as "Little China." Today it is called *Chinatown*.

New home. From San Francisco, many Chinese went out to work in the mines and on the railroads. But San Francisco was usually the place they came back to when their work was done. Here settlers could speak the Chinese language. Here they could easily obtain Chinese foods. Here they could celebrate Chinese holidays. The greatest of these took place at the start of the new year by the Chinese calendar.

At first, most Chinese had come to America as temporary workers. They had planned to build a "nest egg" for themselves, and return to China to settle down. As time went on, however, many of them decided to settle in the United States. They married or sent for their wives, then started families of their own.

In Chinatown, parents could send their children to special schools to learn the Chinese language. Mothers and fathers could raise children in the "old" Chinese ways. Above all, parents could teach young people to obey their elders and respect their teachers. They could show children the importance of getting the best education they could.

Often enough, however, young people learned different ideas in school from the ones they learned at home. When this happened, painful problems sometimes resulted. Some Chinese-American young people didn't want to live by the

Around 1900, Orchard Street in New York City's Jewish ghetto bore reminders of Central Europe. Notice the store signs in Yiddish. In the inset is Orchard Street as it appeared in the 1970's.

352

Chinese who came to California called it Gum San — *the land of the Golden Mountains. They tried to keep old customs in their new home. Above, a New Year's celebration in Los Angeles about 1900.*

customs of their parents. Like Jewish teenagers in New York City, these young people tried to become as "American" as possible.

Today the Chinatowns of most U.S. cities are changing. Many Chinese families still live there, and so do recent newcomers from Asia. But many younger, American-born people have moved away. The same is true of Jewish neighborhoods in New York City.

Parents in these ghettoes urged their children to go to school and study hard. Many children took their parents' advice. They became doctors, lawyers, teachers, or business people. Or they became skilled workers — carpenters, plumbers, taxi drivers. Some got rich, and some stayed poor. But a great many wanted to move out of the ghetto. And whenever possible, they did.

A Second Look. . . .

1. *What was a ghetto? What was a* sweatshop? *What were some of the problems of working in a sweatshop and living in a ghetto?*

2. *Imagine three members of a Jewish family living in a New York ghetto in the 1890's — a 60-year-old grandmother, a 35-year-old father, and a 13-year-old child. What special problems would each have had adjusting to American life? Which member of the family would most likely have had the most trouble adjusting? Why?*

3. *Suppose that your family were suddenly moved to a city in Africa, Asia, or Europe. What kind of neighborhood would you choose to settle in? Would you choose to live in an American colony in your new country? Or would you choose a neighborhood settled mostly by the people of the country to which you've moved? Write a 50-word essay explaining your choice. Be sure to state the drawbacks to the choice as well as the benefits.*

Chapter 34

Segregation Rides a Railroad

On June 7, 1892, Homer Adolph Plessy bought a railroad ticket in New Orleans, Louisiana. Plessy was a black man. On the train, he took a seat in a "whites only" car. The conductor told him he must move to a car for black people. Plessy wouldn't leave. He was then *forced* to leave the "white" car and arrested.

Why was this important? It was the start of a famous civil rights case. Plessy's arrest was a test of the Jim Crow laws in the South. It started this way:

In the 1880's, Southern states began passing Jim Crow railroad laws. These laws said that railroads had to carry Negroes in "separate but equal" cars. Negroes could not sit in the same cars as whites. They were to have their own, segregated cars. Tennessee passed the first such law in 1881. Louisiana did the same in 1890.

The black people of Louisiana decided to fight this law. They collected money and hired a New York lawyer, Albion Tourgee (toor-ZHAY). Tourgee had been an officer in the Union army. After the Civil War, he went South. There he helped black citizens to obtain their rights. He was, in the eyes of most white

Southerners, a carpetbagger. Now he was being asked to test a law that black people hated.

Testing the law. The arrest of Homer Plessy was arranged on purpose. It was to test the law. The courts in Louisiana said the law was all right. Then Tourgee took the case to the U.S. Supreme Court, the highest court in the land.

Tourgee told the Supreme Court that the Jim Crow law was against the Constitution. It went against the 13th and 14th Amendments. The 13th Amendment ended slavery. The 14th said that every person born in the U.S. is a citizen of the U.S. It also said that every citizen has the right to "life, liberty, and property." Tourgee argued that Jim Crow laws took away black people's *civil rights* (their rights as citizens). Such laws also made it seem as if black Americans were still slaves in some ways.

On May 18, 1896, the Supreme Court came out with its decision. It ruled in favor of the Jim Crow railroad law. It said that separate cars for blacks and whites were not against the law so long as the cars were *equal*. "Separate but

355

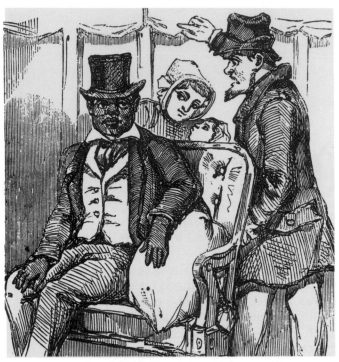

A black man is barred from a railway car in Philadelphia — proof of "Jim Crow" in the North.

equal" things for blacks and whites should not make black people feel inferior, the Court said. The Court pointed out that whites did not feel inferior because they were separated from blacks.

Disagreeing with the Court.
Only one Supreme Court Justice supported Tourgee. He was John Marshall Harlan, a Southerner who had once owned slaves. Justice Harlan said: "Our Constitution is color-blind. . . . All citizens are equal before the law."

Harlan also said that the law regards humans as humans and takes no account of their color. Civil rights, in other words, could not be taken from a person because of his or her color.

This case became known as *Plessy v. Ferguson.* It became very famous because it set an example. It left the legal door wide open for more Jim Crow laws. Soon some Southern states were passing many of them. Black people were kept separate on streetcars and in hospitals and prisons. They were even expected to use separate drinking fountains.

Not until May 17, 1954, was the "separate but equal" idea struck down. On that day, the Supreme Court ruled the opposite of what it had ruled in 1896. And this time all nine Justices were in agreement. One of the Justices on the Supreme Court that day was John Marshall Harlan. He was a grandson of the Justice Harlan who had ruled in favor of Homer Plessy.

A Second Look. . . .

1. *What law did Homer Plessy break? Why did Albion Tourgee think this law was against the Constitution? When was Tourgee's opinion shown to be correct in the eyes of the law?*

2. *In 1863 Abraham Lincoln signed the Emancipation Proclamation, freeing slaves in the Confederacy. Within 40 years, however, black people were forced to accept the idea of "separate but equal." Do you think that freedom under the idea of "separate but equal" was better than no freedom at all? Explain.*

3. *Imagine that the case of* Plessy v. Ferguson *is being decided today. Pretend that you are one of the Supreme Court Justices overturning the Louisiana law. Prepare a one-minute opinion in favor of Plessy. Your opinion should state why you think the Louisiana law was unconstitutional. Be ready to read your opinion aloud in class.*

356

Chapter 35

Voice of Black Patience

He was born a slave in Virginia a few years before the Civil War. He lived in a cabin and slept on rags on a dirt floor. He worked long hours and often went hungry. Yet this boy became famous as a teacher and a leader of the black struggle for a better life. He advised Presidents of the United States. He dined at the White House with President Theodore Roosevelt. Queen Victoria of England invited him to Windsor Castle.

Who was he? He was Booker T. Washington, the man who built Alabama's Tuskegee Institute into a great trade school and technical college.

Washington was nine years old when a Union soldier told him he was free. His family then moved to a mining town in West Virginia. When he was 10, he went to work in the mines. He wanted to go to school, but his stepfather would not let him. The family needed the money he earned. Finally he was allowed to go to school, but had to work in the mines before and after school. He did this for five years.

Then Washington heard about Hampton Institute, a trade school for black students in Virginia. He would be able to work there to pay for his studies. Hampton was 500 miles (800 kilometers) away, and Washington walked almost the whole distance to get there. "When I finally saw Hampton," he said, "I thought I was in heaven."

Washington worked his way through Hampton as a janitor. After graduation, he became a teacher. Soon he got his big chance. A principal was needed for a new school for blacks in Tuskegee, Alabama. In 1881 Washington got the job.

Practical needs. Before starting, Washington traveled around in Alabama. He saw black people living in poverty almost everywhere. He saw black farmers who knew nothing about better farming methods. He saw blacks who had no job skills. Washington decided that his school should not teach subjects such as Latin, Greek, and law. Instead, it should teach practical things such as farming, shoemaking, and carpentry. Washington believed that black Americans had to have job skills before they could start working their way up.

Washington's school turned out to be an old run-down church with one small side building for a classroom. The roof leaked. When it rained, a student had to hold an umbrella over Washington's head — indoors.

Soon Washington borrowed money to buy a farm. He had his students make bricks. From these, they put up their own buildings. Then they made their own tables, benches, and chairs. They were learning useful skills all the time they were working. Washington also taught his students to save money and

357

open bank accounts. He was sure that money, power, and civil rights went together — or that they *would* go together some day.

"Go-slow" stand. But Washington also taught his students to go slow in asking for civil rights. He believed that the time was not "ripe" for protest. During Reconstruction, black people had won seats in Congress and state legislatures. This was "starting at the top," Washington said, and it had failed. Now Washington urged black people to build from the bottom up. "No race can prosper," he said, "till it learns there is as much dignity in tilling a field as in writing a poem."

Some black leaders did not like Washington's ideas. They said that lands, houses, and money in the bank were not worth as much as self-respect. They said that lands, houses, and money would not bring black people true freedom. Washington, they said, *should* tell blacks to speak out for equal rights and justice — without delay.

But many black people agreed with Washington's ideas. So did most whites. To them, Washington's plan seemed like a good way for whites and blacks in the South to live in peace.

They liked Washington because he didn't "rock the boat."

Washington died in 1915. The Tuskegee Institute he left behind was a training center known all over the world. It had more than 100 buildings and some 1,500 students. Even people who didn't agree with Washington had to admit that he was a great leader. Today Booker Washington is still honored by blacks and whites as one of the most remarkable Americans who ever lived.

A Second Look. . . .

1. *Booker T. Washington urged black people to go slow in asking for civil rights. Why? How did he think blacks would finally win equality with whites?*

2. *Which education is more valued in America today: (a) an education that stresses skills such as carpentry, bricklaying, and plumbing? (b) an education that stresses history, science, and literature? Or do you think both are equally valued? Why? Do you agree that Booker T. Washington's ideas about educating black people were the right ones at the time? Why or why not?*

3. *Organize a class debate to argue for and against this statement: "Booker T. Washington should have fought harder for the rights of black Americans." Each debate team should prepare at least two arguments to support its position.*

Booker T. Washington in 1894.

Chapter 36

Voice of Black Protest

"This book is dangerous for the Negro to read. It will only excite discontent. And it will fill his imagination with things that should not be upon his mind."

These words were written by a Southern white editor in 1903. He was talking about a new book called *The Souls of Black Folk*. The editor was right on one point. This book was dynamite. What did it say? Its message was this:

Be proud you are black. Stand up for your rights. Protest against Jim Crow. Demand equality.

These were "dangerous" ideas in 1903. Ever since the end of Reconstruction, blacks had been told to give in to white people. Booker T. Washington had been telling blacks to work hard and make money. This way, he said, the whites would come to respect black people. The time wasn't ripe yet, Washington and others were saying, to fight for equal rights.

But now here was a book telling blacks to *protest*. It was not enough to make money, it said. Blacks must fight for their *manhood*. Young blacks, especially, read the book and held their heads higher. It was the start of the modern protest movement.

Who was the man who wrote this book? His name was William E.B. Du Bois (doo-BOYS). For many years he was the leading voice of black protest in the U.S. He spoke for the blacks of Africa too. He was proud of African history and culture. Some day, he said, the African peoples would free themselves from European colonial rule.

"Great veil." William E.B. Du Bois was born in a small town in Massachusetts in 1868. It was less than three years after the end of the Civil War. Du Bois was of mixed ancestry — French, Dutch, and African — and his parents had always been free. They were poor, but they were proud people. Most of Du Bois' friends were white and well off. But he soon learned that he was "different." A white girl insulted him in school. "Then it dawned on me," he said later, "that I was different from the others, shut out from their world by a great veil."

Du Bois was the top student in his high school. A friendly white minister raised money to send him to college. Du Bois didn't go to a white college. Instead, he went to Fisk, a black school in Nashville, Tennessee. He had never known many blacks at home. Now, at Fisk, he was thrilled by the beauty of the people he met. But he also saw how blacks were victims of discrimination (the act of treating people differently, usually because of their membership in a particular group). He felt their suffering very deeply.

Du Bois later studied at Harvard University in Massachusetts and then in

THE CRISIS

A RECORD OF THE DARKER RACES

Volume One   NOVEMBER, 1910   Number One

Edited by W. E. BURGHARDT DU BOIS, with the co-operation of Oswald Garrison Villard, J. Max Barber, Charles Edward Russell, Kelly Miller, W. S. Braithwaite and M. D. Maclean.

CONTENTS

Germany. He earned a Ph.D. degree in history in 1895. This made him *Dr.* Du Bois. Even so, no white college would give him a teaching job. Du Bois began teaching at a small black college instead.

In 1896 Du Bois took a job teaching history at Atlanta University in Georgia. He also studied the living conditions of blacks in the South. He wrote several books about them. Each book showed that when blacks were given a fair chance, they were the equals of whites.

"We must not flinch." Then Du Bois wrote *The Souls of Black Folk.* The book burst like a bombshell among blacks. It started Du Bois' career as leader of a black protest movement. In 1905 Du Bois called for a meeting of leading black citizens to take action. They met at Niagara Falls and formed the Niagara Movement. The following year the protest group met again and sent out an *Address to the Country.* It said: "We will not be satisfied to take one bit less than our full manhood rights. We want the right to vote and we want it now. We want discrimination to end. We want our children educated. Courage, brothers! We must not flinch. Above are the everlasting stars."

In 1909 the Niagara Movement helped bring other groups together to form one large organization. The following year it took a name: the National Association for the Advancement of Colored People (NAACP). From the first, the NAACP set out to obtain equal rights for black people. Du Bois became the editor of its monthly magazine, *The Crisis.* The magazine's message was always the same:

W.E.B. Du Bois helped found the NAACP and edited its monthly magazine, The Crisis.

Be proud that you are black.

After World War I, Du Bois also organized meetings of African peoples. These meetings demanded freedom for the blacks of Africa. Du Bois saw many African colonies become nations after World War II. Du Bois was honored by the leaders of these nations.

But at home after World War II, Du Bois more and more lost faith in the black protest movement. And he lost many of his followers too. Some of them felt that his ideas had become too extreme. Others didn't like the way he spoke out in favor of the Soviet Union. Then in 1961, at the age of 93, Du Bois joined the Communist Party of the United States.

Finally he was invited to live and work in the nation of Ghana, in Africa. Du Bois accepted the invitation. Du Bois died in Ghana in 1963. He was buried with great honors near the spot where one of his great-grandfathers had been sent to America in chains.

A Second Look. . . .

1. Who was W.E.B. Du Bois? What were some of the ideas he expressed in his writings? What were the goals of his Niagara Movement?

2. Du Bois was impatient to obtain equal rights for black people. In your opinion, was he right to be impatient? Was he right to demand equality now?

3. Compare the life of W.E.B. Du Bois and the life of Booker T. Washington. Write an essay of 100 words in which you answer these three questions: (a) In what ways were Washington and Du Bois alike? (b) In what ways were they different? (c) Which person do you admire more — and why?

Chapter 37

Crusader for Women's Rights

Young Susan B. Anthony was puzzled by what she saw at her father's cotton mill. She noticed that the most able worker at the mill was a tall woman, Sally Ann Hyatt. This woman understood the weaving machines better than her boss. Elijah. Whenever a machine broke, Elijah had to ask Sally Ann to fix it.

One day Susan discussed the matter with her father. "If Sally Ann knows more about weaving than Elijah," Susan asked, "then why don't you make her overseer [boss]?"

"It would never do," her father answered. "It would never do to have a woman overseer in the mill."

An answer like this did not satisfy young Susan Anthony. She had a very independent mind. Why, she wondered, should not women and men be treated equally? For the rest of her life, Susan B. Anthony would ask this question. She would always come up with the same answers. Giving men more privileges than women was wrong.

Susan B. Anthony grew up in Massachusetts and New York in the 1830's. At this time, many parents believed that education was for their sons, not their daughters. But Susan was lucky. Her father, Daniel Anthony, wanted her to get an education. For a year, he sent Susan and another daughter to a Quaker school in Philadelphia.

When Susan was in her late teens, her father met with misfortune. He fell into debt and lost his cotton mill. The family sold almost everything they owned and moved to a farm in Rochester, New York. Susan took a job teaching school to help pay off family debts.

Temperance worker. While teaching, she became interested in several social causes. One of them was the drive to stamp out heavy drinking. This was known as the *temperance* movement. Anthony began to travel to temperance meetings around the state. Once, in 1851, she spent the night with a family in the small town of Seneca Falls, New York. There she met one of the town's most active women, Elizabeth Cady Stanton. The two women soon became fast friends.

Stanton had already helped to start the first modern women's rights movement. In July 1848, she had called together 100 people — men and women — in Seneca Falls, New York. Those attending the meeting approved a declaration of independence for women. It was much like the Declaration written in 1776. But it did not complain about British tyranny. Instead, it complained about the tyranny of a world run almost entirely by men.

In New York, women were not allowed to vote. As soon as they were married, they were forced to give all their money and property to their husbands. As wage earners, they were almost always paid much less than men for doing the same work. They were kept out of most colleges. They were kept from becoming doctors or lawyers. They were often kept out of business and politics as well.

Campaigner for a cause. These were some of the things Elizabeth Cady Stanton had protested. Now Stanton and Anthony worked together to gain fairer treatment for women in New York. First of all, they tried to change state laws concerning married women. They drew up a petition explaining why the current laws were unfair. In the middle of winter, 1854, Anthony traveled from town to town to get people to sign her petition. Her hands and legs almost froze in the cold weather.

People were not used to the idea of a woman making speeches about politics. Many of the men in Anthony's audiences only wanted to heckle and sneer at her. One man, however, was deeply impressed. He asked Anthony to marry him. But of course, he said, she would have to give up her speaking tour. Anthony refused. She thought her work was too important to give up.

For a long time, New York lawmakers ignored her petition. But by 1860, they had passed laws that gave married

Susan B. Anthony (right) and Elizabeth Cady Stanton led the fight for women's rights in the second half of the 19th century.

363

women new rights. For the first time, married women in New York could make contracts and buy and sell property. For the first time, they could spend their own wages instead of turning them over to their husbands.

Social organizer. One battle was won. But the next great battle took the rest of Susan B. Anthony's life. It was the battle to give all women in the U.S. the right to vote. After the Civil War, the 15th Amendment to the Constitution gave black citizens the vote. Anthony wondered why *women* — black women as well as white women — were not mentioned in this amendment. She was bitterly angry about this. In 1869 she and her friend, Elizabeth Cady Stanton, started a new organization. They called it the National Woman Suffrage Association. Its one purpose was to give American women the right to vote.

Anthony took the lead in this movement herself. While reading the newspaper one day in 1872, she decided to act. The newspaper said: "Now register! ... If you were not permitted to vote, you would fight for the right, undergo all privations [hardships] for it, face death for it. ..." Anthony agreed. She walked to a barbershop where her male neighbors were registering (signing up) to vote. She insisted on being allowed to register as well.

The men protested that women were not allowed to register by New York law. But Anthony had her way. Then on election day, 1872, she cast the first ballot of her life. She was overjoyed. Several days later, she was arrested for breaking the election law. At her trial, Anthony argued with the judge about the meaning of the law and the Constitution. The judge fined her $100. She said that she would never pay it — and she never did.

Susan B. Anthony was now famous. Even men were beginning to admire her courage. Her speeches for women's suffrage drew large crowds. As she grew older, she became even better loved and respected. Younger women rallied around her in growing numbers. They too went out and made speeches and handed out petitions. They called their leader "Aunt Susan."

Susan B. Anthony worked for women's rights for almost 60 years. She died in 1906, 14 years before all American women won the vote. But she knew that the movement she had started was growing. She told the younger women that they could not fail to get the vote. "Failure is impossible," she said. And so it proved to be.

A Second Look. . . .

1. *When Susan B. Anthony was growing up, what rights did men have that women did not have? What changes in the laws did Susan B. Anthony fight for?*

2. *Susan B. Anthony thought that it was wrong for men to have more opportunities than women. Do you agree or disagree? What is the situation today? Do men still have more opportunities than women for good jobs? What facts would you need to answer this question?*

3. *Follow up the above questions with a research project. Using the reference room of your local library, find out how many people in today's labor force are women. Find the average income of female workers and compare this with the average income of male workers. Report your findings in class and discuss.*

Looking Back: Those Sometimes Forgotten

	A	**B**	**C**	**D**	**E**	**F**
January 1855	January 1865	January 1875	January 1885	January 1895	January 1905	January 1915

Putting Events in Order

Chapters 31 through 37 have described some events in the history of certain ethnic groups and the women's movement. Ten events of this period are listed here. Your job is to match each event to the correct period shown on the timeline above. On a piece of paper, number from **1** to **10**. After each number, write the letter of the 10-year period within which the event occurred.

1. Susan B. Anthony is arrested for voting in a New York election.

2. A meeting of leading black citizens takes place at Niagara Falls, New York.

3. The U.S. government orders the Nez Perce Indians to move to a reservation in Idaho.

4. New York lawmakers change state laws to allow women to make contracts and buy and sell property.

5. The U.S. Supreme Court decides that "separate but equal" railroad cars are constitutional.

6. Booker T. Washington is appointed to be principal of the Tuskegee Institute in Alabama.

7. The National Association for the Advancement of Colored People (NAACP) is formed.

8. A law passed by Congress bars most immigration from China.

9. Mary Antin leaves Poland and enters the United States.

10. The population of "Little China" in San Francisco reaches 47,000.

Interpreting a Source

On July 16, 1870, some New Yorkers listened to a speech by a chief of the Teton Sioux Nation — Red Cloud. This old Sioux chief had traveled from his home on the Great Plains to plead for peace and fair treatment. Part of Red Cloud's speech is reprinted on the next page.

My brethren and my friends who are here before me this day, God Almighty has made us all. And He is here to bless what I have to say to you today. The Good Spirit made us both. He gave you lands and He gave us lands. He gave us these lands; you came in here, and we respected you as brothers. God Almighty made you but made you all white and clothed you. When He made us He made us with red skins and poor; now you have come.

When you first came we were very many, and you were few. Now you are many, and we are getting very few, and we are poor. You do not know who appears before you today to speak. I am a representative of the original American race, the first people of this continent. We are good and not bad. The reports that you hear concerning us are all on one side. . . . You are here told that we are traders and thieves, and it is not so. We have given you nearly all our lands. And if we had any more land to give we would be very glad to give it. We have nothing more. We are driven into a very little land. And we want you now, as our dear friends, to help us with the government of the United States.

The Great Father made us poor and ignorant — made you rich and wise and more skillful in these things that we know nothing about. The Great Father, the Good Father in Heaven, made you all to eat tame food — made us to eat wild food — gives us the wild food. You ask anybody who has gone through our country to California; ask those who have settled there and in Utah, and you will find that we have treated them always well. You have children; we have children. You want to raise your children and make them happy and prosperous; we want to raise [ours] and make them happy and prosperous. We ask you to help us to do it. . . .

Colonel Fitzpatrick of the government said we must all go to farm, and some of the people went to Fort Laramie and were badly treated. I only want to do that which is peaceful, and the Great Fathers know it, and also the Great Father who made us both. I came to Washington to see the Great Father in order to have peace and in order to have peace continue. That is all we want, and that is the reason why we are here now.

1. *What does Red Cloud say is the major difference between his people and white people?*

2. *To whom do you think Red Cloud is referring when he speaks of Washington?*

3. *Do you trust what Red Cloud is saying? Does it sound as if he sincerely wants peace?*

4. *Can you find any evidence in this speech that Red Cloud holds prejudices about white people? If so, what are the prejudices? Where is the evidence? Did white people in 1870 probably hold prejudices about the Sioux? If so, what do you think they were?*

Sharpening Your Skills

Immigration to the United States between 1860 and 1920 had several effects. One of them was to speed up the growth of U.S. cities. The graph and the chart on the opposite page show some details of that growth. Study them carefully. Then answer the questions on the opposite page.

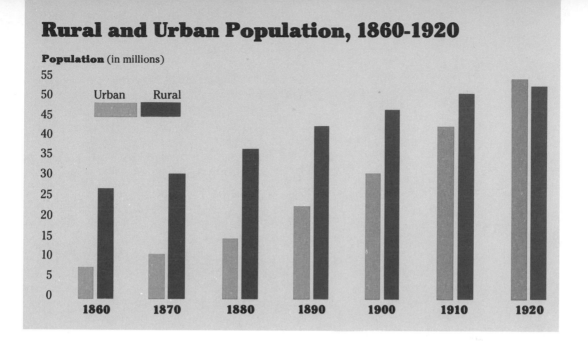

Rural and Urban Population, 1860-1920

Population (in millions)

Urban   Rural

1860 1870 1880 1890 1900 1910 1920

1. About how many Americans lived in cities in 1860? About how many lived in rural areas? About how many lived in cities and rural areas in 1920?

2. Which group grew faster between 1860 and 1920 — (a) Americans who lived in cities, or (b) Americans who lived in rural areas?

3. In which type of urban area did the population grow fastest between 1900 and 1910 — (a) large city, (b) medium-sized city, or (c) small city?

4. Which accounted most heavily for the growth of small cities — (a) immigration, (b) natural increase, or (c) rural migration?

5. Which accounted most heavily for the growth of medium-sized cities?

6. To judge from the chart, where would you guess most newcomers to the U.S. settled — in large cities, medium-sized cities, or small cities?

Increase in U.S. Population, 1900-1910

	Large Cities (500,000 or more population)	Medium-Sized Cities (25,000 to 500,000 population)	Small Cities (2,500 to 25,000 population)	Total-U.S.
Total urban gain	2,581,000	4,701,000	3,731,000	11,013,000
Gain from immigration[1]	74.9%	36.1%	28.2%	42.3%
Gain from natural increase[2]	30.5%	23.1%	24.5%	25.3%
Gain from rural migration[3]	−5.4%	40.8%	47.3%	32.4%

[1] *Immigration,* in this sense, means movement into the U.S. from foreign countries.
[2] *Natural increase,* in this sense, means births.
[3] *Rural migration* means movement from farming areas to cities.

Book Three

Coming of Age

369

1 INTO THE 20th CENTURY

Looking Ahead: The "Good Years"

The United States went to war with Spain in 1898. In only four months the Americans defeated the Spanish troops in Cuba. Commodore George Dewey destroyed the Spanish fleet in Manila Bay in the Philippines. The war with Spain was a turning point in American history. It showed that the U.S. had become a world power (a nation powerful enough to affect the rest of the world by its actions). Americans began to take a larger interest in world affairs. In 1900 the U.S. got involved in a full-scale uprising in China. In 1904 it began building the Panama Canal.

This new role as a world power reflected changing times. The America of 1900 was very different from the America of 100 years earlier. How did it differ? In several important ways:

Size. In 1800 the United States was very young. It had only 16 states and fewer than six million people. Almost all Americans in those days were country people. They were trying to push the frontier westward. But few settlers had yet reached the Mississippi River.

By 1900 the United States was no longer a new nation. It had been independent for 124 years. It stretched across a continent from ocean to ocean. With 45 states and 76 million people, it was a giant among nations. The frontier had nearly vanished too. Much of the nation's land had now been settled.

Output. The United States had also grown into a giant of industry. It produced more steel than any other nation. It sent its factory products to countries all over the world. And the United States was a farming giant. Its farms

"You're not the only rooster in South America," says Europe in this 1901 U.S. cartoon. "I was aware of that when I cooped you up," replies Uncle Sam. Notice that the European powers are "penned in" by the Monroe Doctrine of 1823.

produced so much food that there was plenty left over to sell to other nations.

Growth of cities. The U.S. was becoming an urban nation. In 1800 only about one out of every 10 Americans had lived in cities. By 1900 four out of 10 lived in them. More and more people from the country were moving to cities every day.

The United States in 1900 was a very rich country. But it had its problems too. The great wealth of the nation was not spread evenly. Some people were very wealthy. They seemed to be getting richer all the time. But then there were millions of farmers and working people. They put in long hours for very little money. It was hard for them to make ends meet.

Many people depended on factory wages for a living. These wages were very low. And for the many women and

U.S. Population Density, 1800

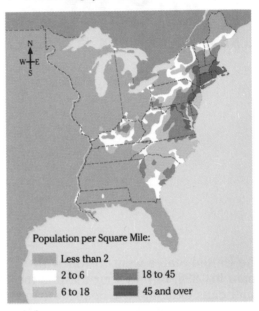

Population per Square Mile:

Less than 2
2 to 6   18 to 45
6 to 18   45 and over

U.S. Population Density, 1900

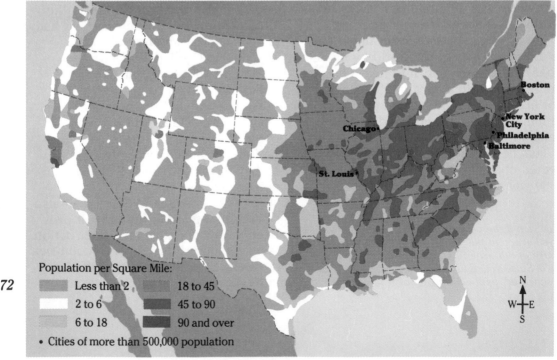

Population per Square Mile:

Less than 2   18 to 45
2 to 6   45 to 90
6 to 18   90 and over
• Cities of more than 500,000 population

372

children who worked in mines and factories, the pay was even less. When business was bad, factories could fire their workers or shut down for a while. When that happened, many families went hungry. The government provided no welfare in those days. There was little help for a person who lost his or her job or got hurt. In 1900 there were few laws to see that workers were protected. There were no laws to see that they got a decent wage, either.

Many business owners saw nothing wrong in this. "Business is business," they thought. They kept wages low so that they could make as much profit as possible. They believed that life was a struggle for everyone. Some people were bound to get rich and come out on top. Anyone who did not get rich had not worked hard enough or well enough. That, at least, was the way many of these

Mrs. George Gould, daughter-in-law of a banker, posed for a portrait wearing a $500,000 necklace (below). But in 1900, few could afford such trappings. Millions lived in shabby rooms, surrounded by despair. The woman above was pictured by a famed photographer, Lewis Hine.

373

374

business leaders looked at the world.

A new form of business — called a *trust* — had come to control whole industries. Trusts were giant businesses which were made up of several companies. They were run by a common group of managers known as *trustees.* Trusts were a danger partly because they could charge high prices and get away with it. They had no competition to hold their prices down.

In government there were dangers of another kind. Some states and large cities were controlled by corrupt bosses. Often these bosses gave more thought to their own power than to the people they governed. Some of them took bribes. Others stole from public funds. Still others rigged elections so that their candidates were sure to win.

What was the United States to do about such problems? How could it rescue its poor, clean up its politics, and move forward in the most democratic way? This question concerned more and more Americans at the turn of the 20th century. Those it concerned most were people called *progressives.* Progressives belonged to many different political groups. Generally, though, they shared the faith that American life could be improved by making reforms in government.

They went about their jobs as reformers in a variety of ways. Progressive journalists, called *muckrakers,* wrote articles about injustice and corruption. Progressive business leaders

In 1893 Chicago celebrated the 400th anniversary of Columbus' arrival in America with a huge fair. The fair was called the Columbian Exposition. *Its posters (left) showed the sense of self-confidence that was common around the turn of the century.*

tried to restore fair competition in the marketplace. Progressive politicians tried to clean up government on the state and city level.

Some of the reforms came from the top. In 1901 the U.S. got its first progressive President, Theodore Roosevelt. Roosevelt thought of the White House as a "bully pulpit." From this "pulpit" he delivered many "sermons" on how to make the U.S. a better place. In 1912 another progressive, Woodrow Wilson, was elected President. Wilson carried out many of the ideas Roosevelt had mentioned in his "sermons."

All through the Progressive Era, changes were made by passing new laws. Some helped make government more honest and effective. Some protected the public from dishonest businesses. Some made it illegal to restrain trade, as certain large trusts had done. Many states also passed laws to protect working people, especially women and children.

These first years of the 20th century have been called the "good years." And what was so good about them? The U.S. was at peace, but it had been so for most of the 19th century. Businesses were growing, but this was nothing new. These years were "good" because they were years of national self-confidence. People were sure they could fix anything that went wrong. Not all of them agreed on what was "wrong" or the right way to fix it. But most people believed in their ability to make things work.

America at the turn of the century was bustling and energetic. It was full of pride and full of change. America had come of age and was about to make its mark on the world.

Chapter 1

War with Spain

It was February 15, 1898. In the harbor of Havana, Cuba, the U.S. battleship *Maine* was at anchor. Cuba was then a Spanish colony struggling for its independence. The *Maine* was there on a "friendly visit." All seemed calm. A bugle had just blown "Taps." The time was 9:40 P.M.

A second later there was a tremendous explosion. The *Maine* blew up! All the lights went out. Fires roared. Shells popped like firecrackers. The screams of wounded and dying men were heard everywhere. Some sailors jumped overboard — and were attacked by sharks. Within minutes the wreck of the *Maine* sank into the mud. Two hundred sixty men were killed.

The *Maine* had been blown up by a mine. That was clear. The question was, Who did it? No one knew the answer then, and it is still a mystery today. But angry Americans blamed the Spanish. Huge newspaper headlines warned: "Remember the *Maine!*"

Many Americans wanted a war with Spain. They wanted to free the Cuban people from Spanish rule. For years Cuban rebels had been fighting the Spanish. Many had died or been thrown into prison camps. Americans, remembering their own war for independence, wanted to help the Cubans. After all, Cuba was only 90 miles (about 145 kilometers) from the U.S. coast.

At this time two big-city newspapers were competing heavily for readers. One was the New York *Journal,* owned by William Randolph Hearst. The other was Joseph Pulitzer's New York *World.* Both papers sided with the rebels in Cuba. They found that reporting of horror stories from Cuba improved their sales. So the two papers outdid one another in printing sensational stories about Cuba. When there were no stories to report, reporters were told to make them up. These methods came to be known as *yellow journalism.*

At one point, Hearst sent a well-known artist, Frederic Remington, to Cuba. Remington was supposed to draw sketches of the fighting for Hearst's paper. But Remington did not find any fighting, and he wired Hearst to tell him so. Hearst is said to have shot back a quick response: "You furnish the pictures, and I'll furnish the war."

Such journalism further stirred support among many Americans for the Cuban rebels. There were other reasons too for wanting a war. Some Americans who did business in Cuba wanted to make the island part of the United States. Some generals and admirals wanted the U.S. to have Army and Navy bases in Cuba. They thought that control of the island was necessary to the safety of the U.S.

Finally, on April 25, 1898, Congress declared war on Spain. President Wil-

To this day no one knows why the Maine *exploded. But in 1898, some papers tried to build their sales by offering "causes" of their own making.*

863,956
WORLDS CIRCULATED YESTERDAY

VOL. XXXVIII. NO. 13,330.

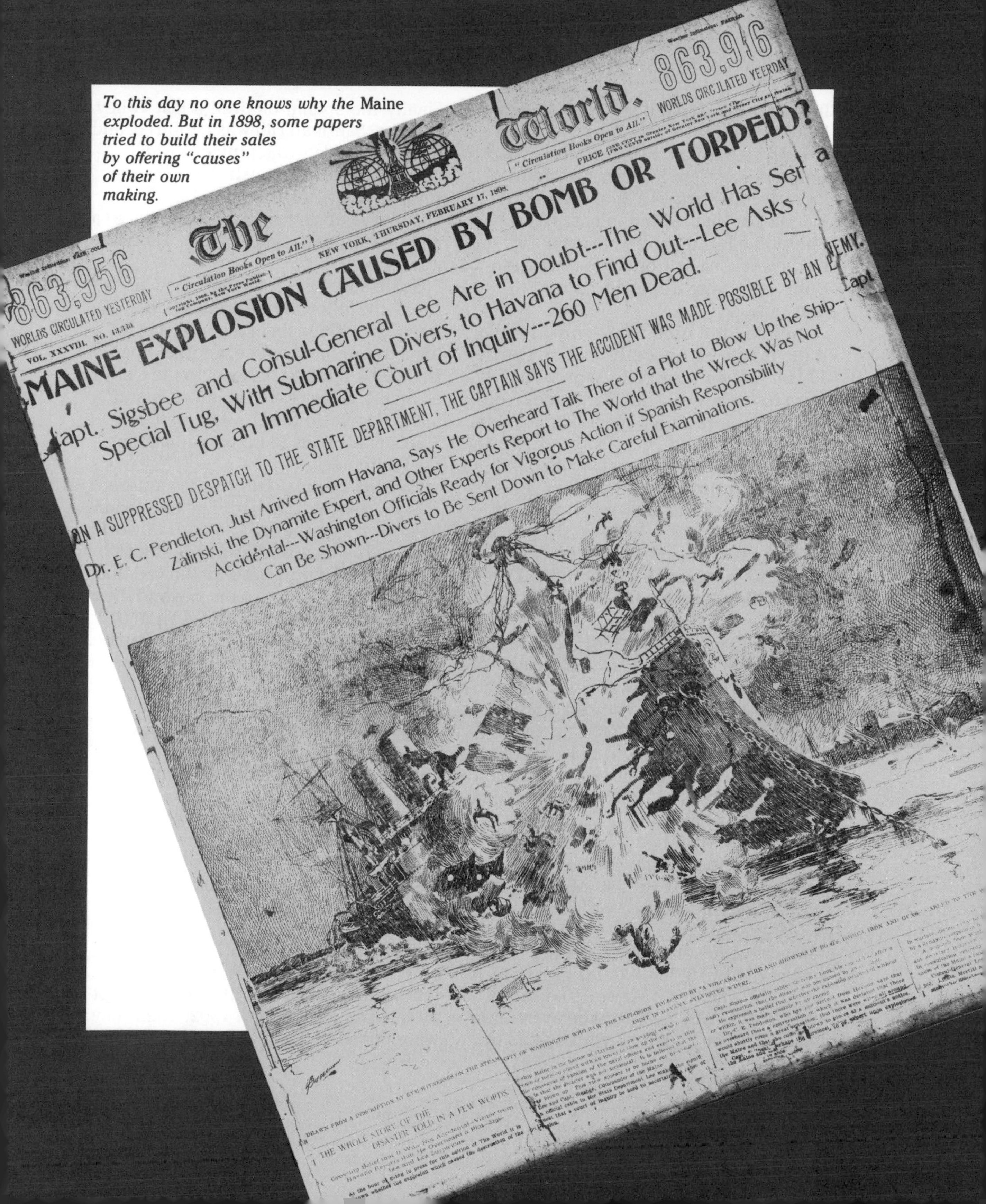

The World.

"Circulation Books Open to All."

NEW YORK, THURSDAY, FEBRUARY 17, 1898.

PRICE ONE CENT in Greater New York and Jersey City. TWO CENTS outside of Greater New York and Jersey City.

863,956
WORLDS CIRCULATED YESTERDAY

MAINE EXPLOSION CAUSED BY BOMB OR TORPEDO?

Capt. Sigsbee and Consul-General Lee Are in Doubt---The World Has Sent a Special Tug, With Submarine Divers, to Havana to Find Out---Lee Asks for an Immediate Court of Inquiry---260 Men Dead.

IN A SUPPRESSED DESPATCH TO THE STATE DEPARTMENT, THE CAPTAIN SAYS THE ACCIDENT WAS MADE POSSIBLE BY AN ENEMY.

Dr. E. C. Pendleton, Just Arrived from Havana, Says He Overheard Talk There of a Plot to Blow Up the Ship---Capt. Zalinski, the Dynamite Expert, and Other Experts Report to The World that the Wreck Was Not Accidental---Washington Officials Ready for Vigorous Action if Spanish Responsibility Can Be Shown---Divers to Be Sent Down to Make Careful Examinations.

DRAWN FROM A DESCRIPTION BY EYE WITNESSES ON THE STEAMSHIP CITY OF WASHINGTON WHO SAW THE EXPLOSION FOLLOWED BY "A VOLCANO OF FIRE AND SHOWERS OF BODIES, BEAMS, IRON AND GUNS HURLED TO THE..."

THE WHOLE STORY OF THE DISASTER TOLD IN A FEW WORDS.

liam McKinley called for 125,000 men to fight.

Early in May, a U.S. fleet under Commodore George Dewey won a big victory. It destroyed a Spanish fleet at Manila Bay, in the Philippines. The Philippine Islands were in East Asia, half a world away from Cuba. But like Cuba, they were a Spanish colony at that time.

Landing the American Army in Cuba took longer. Two months passed before 17,000 troops were put ashore. They were not ready for war. Their rifles were old. They wore heavy woolen uniforms in the jungle heat. Their food was often unfit to eat. Men became ill from bad water and from diseases such as yellow fever and malaria. Yet the Army fought bravely.

Rough Riders. With the Army was a special group of *cavalry* (soldiers who usually fight on horseback). These were the "Rough Riders." Many of them were cowboys from the Western states. Colonel Teddy Roosevelt was the leader of the Rough Riders. He was eager to fight and win victories and make a name for himself.

Roosevelt and his Rough Riders became heroes in the battles of Kettle Hill and San Juan Hill. Atop San Juan Hill, a Spanish army was dug in. It was protected by a blockhouse, or fort. The Americans looked like a ribbon of blue as they moved up the hill on foot. The top roared and flashed with fire.

Many Americans fell, sinking into the tall grass. But others charged on bravely, moving higher and higher toward the Spanish position. The fire of the Spanish riflemen became even more fierce. But the blue line crept up and up.

Finally the Spaniards fired a last volley and fled. San Juan Hill was captured, and the Spanish flag was pulled down.

Soon another Spanish fleet was destroyed at nearby Santiago Bay. Then Spain gave up and signed an *armistice* (a temporary peace agreement). The war was over.

Spain and the U.S. signed a peace treaty the following December. The treaty gave Cuba its independence. It turned over Puerto Rico, another Spanish island in the Caribbean, to the United States. It also gave Guam, an island in the Pacific, to the U.S. The United States paid Spain 20 million dollars for the Philippines.

Broad reach. Europe was amazed at how fast the U.S. had defeated Spain. It showed that the U.S. was now a world power. The old frontier inside the U.S. was gone. And now the war showed that Americans could reach out beyond their continent — into the Caribbean and thousands of miles away into the Pacific.

Many Americans were also surprised at the result of the war. Some liked the idea of being a "power." Others did not. They thought that the U.S. now looked too much like the old empire-building nations of Europe. They said that this was wrong for the United States. They said it went against everything the U.S. had stood for in history. There was a great argument about the peace treaty. Some people said that the U.S. had gone to war just to get hold of some colonies for itself.

What did the United States finally do with its "empire"? All in all, it made a fairly good record over the years. It kept its troops in Cuba until 1902. Then they were pulled out, and Cuba became inde-

Central America and the Caribbean, 1898

pendent. This pleased most Americans. "After all," they said, "Cuban freedom was what the war was fought for in the first place." They were also proud that Americans were able to wipe out yellow fever on the island.

The U.S. signed an agreement with Cuba in 1903. The agreement gave the U.S. a lease on the naval base at Guantanamo (gwan-TAHN-uh-moe) Bay. This lease was signed again in 1934. The U.S. still holds this base today.

The United States has also held on to the island of Guam. Today Guam is an important Pacific base for two military branches — the Navy and the Air Force.

U.S. troops in the Philippines put down a revolt after the Spanish left. Many Filipinos did not want Americans to run their country. They thought that the Americans would govern them the same way the Spanish had. But in 1934 Congress promised independence to the Philippines. This promise was kept. The Philippines became independent on July 4, 1946. This was the 170th birthday of the United States.

Puerto Rico remained a U.S. Territory until 1952. Since then it has been a Commonwealth with close ties to the United States. Puerto Rico has its own constitution and its own government. All Puerto Ricans are citizens of Puerto Rico *and* the United States. But they don't vote in U.S. elections unless they have moved to one of the 50 states.

A Second Look. . . .

1. What reasons can you give for the U.S. decision to go to war with Spain?

2. The U.S. had once been a group of British colonies. In the Declaration of Independence, Americans had expressed a strong belief in the idea of self-government. Why, then, do you suppose that in the 1890's many Americans showed so much interest in gaining colonies? Did the desire for colonies conflict with the belief in self-government? Why or why not?

3. Pretend you are a news reporter covering the Maine *incident for the New York* Journal *or the New York* World. *Write a sensational story concerning the event. Then write a separate note to your editor. In the note explain which details are true and which may possibly be false.*

When Americans arrived in Japan in 1853, their fleet fascinated the Japanese. Woodblock print was made by a local artist. In box at top right he included notes on the ship's size and the arms it carried.

Chapter 2

The U.S. in the Pacific

The United States had become a world power in 1898. It defeated Spain and gained overseas possessions. America had always been close to Europe. Most Americans' ancestors had come from there. Europeans were still coming to America by the millions. But the U.S. now had ties to the nations of the Pacific too.

American contact with East Asia went back to 1784. In that year a small merchant ship sailed into the harbor of Canton, China. The *Empress of China,* as it was called, had sailed all the way from New York. It brought a cargo of cotton, hardware, and furs. It returned to New York with its hold full of tea, spices, and silks.

The voyage was a great success. The China trade grew more important. There was a great demand for Chinese goods. Some Americans grew wealthy from this trade.

China was a weak country. Many

countries were eager to trade with it. But China's government was not much interested in trading with them. The European powers, especially Britain, took advantage of China's weakness. In 1839 Britain went to war with China. The British won easily. They forced China to grant them favorable trading rights.

The United States did not follow the British example. But Americans wanted to share in the wealth. In 1844 the Chinese agreed to give the U.S. certain trading rights.

Trade with Japan. The United States also wanted to trade with China's neighbor, Japan. But the Japanese did not want to have any contact with the more modern West. In 1853 the U.S. made a bold move. Commodore Matthew C. Perry sailed into Tokyo Bay with a fleet of ships. The Japanese ordered Perry to leave. Perry demanded to see a high-ranking official. For six tense days, Perry waited. Finally the Japanese gave in. They received Perry and exchanged gifts. When Perry returned the next year, the Japanese signed a treaty. Now the U.S. had trade with Japan too.

Perry's bold move inspired Japan to become more modern. By 1894 it had grown much stronger. Like the Western powers, the Japanese were now interested in trading with China. But they followed the British example and went to war. In 1895 Japan won a great victory over the Chinese.

The Japanese triumph worried the European powers. They didn't want Japan taking over China. They hurried to make their own demands. Each country had special military and trading rights in China. These were called *spheres of influence*. The U.S. did not have a sphere of influence. Secretary of State John Hay worried that the U.S. might get shut out of China. He also feared that the European powers and Japan might start a war among themselves.

Hay decided to act. In September 1899 he sent notes to Britain, Germany, Russia, Italy, France, and Japan. He asked these powers to agree to an *Open Door Policy* in China. Businesses of all countries should have equal rights, Hay said. China should not be carved up. It should remain independent. Its land should not be under foreign control.

The other countries were slow to reply. They wanted all they could get. This didn't stop Hay. He simply announced that all countries had agreed to the Open Door Policy.

But Hay's efforts came too late to avoid violence. Patriotic Chinese were tired of seeing their rulers give in to foreigners. Most of the trade agreements were unfair to China. Finally a group of Chinese rebelled. Westerners called them the *Boxers*. Their goal was to kill all foreigners or chase them out of China forever.

Most Americans and Europeans in China lived in Peking, the capital. They were housed in walled-in areas of several buildings called compounds. The Westerners' compounds were in a separate district of the city. Foreigners had little contact with the Chinese. Maybe this was why the Americans and Europeans failed to notice the signs of trouble. Normally the Chinese were respectful to foreigners. But now some of them became less friendly. Some referred to Europeans as "foreign devils." As the situation grew more serious, the British ambassador called for help.   *381*

An international brigade of marines arrived. They were Russian, French, Italian, British, and American. Surely, the Europeans thought, this show of force would put a stop to trouble. But this was not a simple mob scene. It was a full-scale uprising.

Rebellion in China. On June 20, 1900, all the foreigners and some Chinese Christians took refuge in the British compound. And not a moment too soon. A force of 20,000 Chinese troops attacked the compound. For 55 days, 480 men held off the Chinese troops. More than 200 people in the compound were killed or wounded.

One American leader in the siege was a clergyman. The Reverend Frank D. Gamewell had been an engineer before joining the ministry. He took charge of the defense of the compound. Gamewell turned the compound into a fortress. He built new walls. He reinforced the existing walls. He organized the women to sew sandbags. Pedaling around the compound on his bicycle, Gamewell seemed to be everywhere. And it was the strength of his defenses that saved the day.

Finally, as food was running out, a relief force fought its way into Peking. This force was made up of soldiers from several countries, including 2,500 Americans. With its arrival, the 55-day siege was lifted at last. Then the rebellion was stamped out.

Now it was the diplomats' turn again. The European powers insisted the Chinese pay a heavy fine. John Hay saw to it that the relief armies left China. China remained intact. The United States later returned half of its fine to China. This money was used to set up a fund to bring Chinese students to the U.S.

For the time being, the U.S. had guaranteed the Open Door. It had been able to do so because none of the

Japan and European powers fought one another for the "right" to do business in China. Japan's role was especially resented. This U.S. cartoon asks: "What about China's rights in China?"

In 1900 a group known in the West as Boxers tried to rid China of foreigners. This Chinese print takes the Boxers' side. It shows them using sabers, bayonets, cannons, and dynamite against outsiders.

A Second Look. . . .

1. What was the Open Door Policy? Which U.S. official first put it into effect? How did it serve U.S. interests?

2. In 1853 Japan did not have the scientific know-how of the West. But it did have its own customs and its own way of doing things. How would you compare the Japanese of 1853 to the Americans of 1800? Do their situations seem similar in any way? Do you believe Americans of 1853 had reason to think themselves superior to the Japanese just because their nation was stronger? Explain. Is it fair to say that one way of life is "better" than another? Why or why not?

3. Not all Chinese people supported the Boxer Rebellion. But most people in the large cities were tired of Westerners who meddled in Chinese affairs. Pretend you are a Peking merchant. Write a letter to relatives in the country telling them about the rebellion. Explain your feelings about Westerners and your hopes for the future of China.

foreign powers in China trusted the others very much. The U.S. could not yet rival the British or the French in East Asia. But it had made plain its future interest in the area.

383

One of the major tasks in building a canal across Panama was the construction of locks to raise and lower ships. This lock — 41 feet (12.3 meters) deep — is shown in 1910, while the canal was being built.

Chapter 3

"Making the Dirt Fly"

John F. Stevens stood on deck as his ship edged to the dock at Colón (kuh-LOAN), Panama. It was a hot, sticky July day in 1905. Stevens had come to Panama to direct the building of the Panama Canal. He was acting under orders from President Theodore Roosevelt to "make the dirt fly."

From the moment Stevens arrived, he saw that there was more to his job than moving dirt. As he stepped ashore, 384 moving dirt. As he stepped ashore,

workers rushed up the gangplank past him. They were eager to leave the country. Looking around, Stevens saw why. On the dock among the outgoing freight were long wooden boxes — coffins. The Canal Zone had been hit by a disease called yellow fever.

Stevens knew he had his work cut out for him. He also knew that the world would be watching his ditch-digging task with interest. Once completed, the

Panama Canal would shorten the journey between the east and west coasts of North and South America. It would save 8,000 miles (12,800 kilometers) on the ocean passage between New York and San Francisco.

The Spanish-American War had made Americans aware of the problems of defending two coasts. During the war, the battleship *Oregon* had left California to join the fleet in Cuba. Its progress was reported every day in the newspapers. In 68 days the *Oregon* raced around the tip of South America to Cuba. It was a new speed record. But wars could be won or lost in two months. Many Americans began calling for a shortcut across the continent by sea.

After the war the U.S. had an even greater need for a shortcut. Puerto Rico, Hawaii, and the Philippines were now possessions of the United States. U.S. defense posts stretched halfway around the world. Getting from one area to another became a problem.

Building a canal across Panama was not a new idea. A French company had attempted it in the 1880's. Panama was the narrowest stretch of land between the Atlantic and Pacific Oceans in the entire Western Hemisphere. But the engineering challenge was great. The French company ran out of money and gave up.

Bargaining with Colombia.

President Roosevelt was eager for a canal across Panama, which was then part of the Republic of Colombia. U.S. Secretary of State John Hay worked out a treaty with Colombia in January 1903. Colombia agreed to sell a strip of land six miles wide to the U.S. The Canal Zone, as this land was called, would run from the Atlantic to the Pacific Ocean. It would be completely under U.S. control.

But then Colombia's senate stalled. Many Colombians opposed the treaty because it gave away control of their land. Meanwhile many Panamanians were unhappy under Colombian rule. In November 1903 some of them rebelled. President Roosevelt was furious at Colombia for stalling. U.S. troops were landed in Panama to aid the rebels. Their revolution was successful. Then the U.S. quickly signed a treaty with the new Republic of Panama.

The actual building of the canal began in 1904. There were many problems. Panama was a tropical country. The heat was smothering. Worst of all was the dreaded yellow fever. Yellow fever had been a killer in the Spanish-American War. Dr. Walter Reed had discovered that it was carried by certain mosquitoes. His assistant in Cuba was Dr. William Gorgas. Now Gorgas came to Panama to wipe out yellow fever.

Gorgas' plan was to get rid of the mosquitoes that caused the disease. Mosquitoes bred mostly in swamps and still water. Gorgas decided on a complete clean-up program. He was given a team of workers to perform this job. The men drained swamps. They hunted down water containers, then junked and burned them. They moved workers from their homes. Then they sealed up the cracks, cleaned out dirt, and sprayed the houses with great care.

Gorgas was successful. Slowly yellow fever was overcome. It took about a year to make the Canal Zone safe from the disease. But once it was safe, workers were eager to work on the canal.

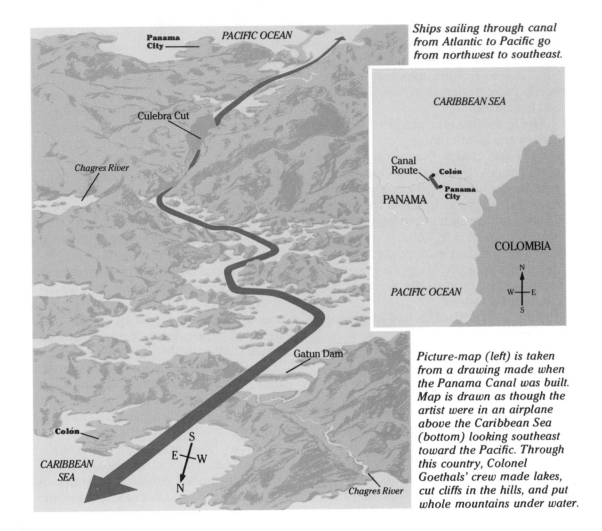

Ships sailing through canal from Atlantic to Pacific go from northwest to southeast.

Picture-map (left) is taken from a drawing made when the Panama Canal was built. Map is drawn as though the artist were in an airplane above the Caribbean Sea (bottom) looking southeast toward the Pacific. Through this country, Colonel Goethals' crew made lakes, cut cliffs in the hills, and put whole mountains under water.

Planning the canal. Now Stevens turned his attention to the plan for the canal. One plan was to dig a big ditch at sea level from the Atlantic Ocean to the Pacific. Another plan was to use locks along with the sea level ditch. Locks are devices for raising and lowering ships. They use pumps and gates to change the level of the water.

Stevens decided to build locks in the 386 canal. He could make use of a major

river — the Chagres (CHAHG-rays). He would build a dam in the river to make a large lake in the hills. This would make the overall route shorter. In 1906 Stevens went to Washington to present his plan to Congress. His ideas were accepted. But Stevens was tired from the

Landslides took place often along the part of the canal called Culebra Cut *(right). When they did, dirt would have to be dredged out again.*

hard work. He resigned his position.

Colonel George W. Goethals (GOH-thahlz) replaced Stevens in Panama. At first the workers were afraid of Goethals. They thought he would make them obey Army rules. But Goethals proved to be a good administrator. He took part of each day to listen to workers' complaints. He showed an ability to organize that won their respect.

Goethals was also a brilliant engineer. And he needed all his genius to handle the many problems in building the canal. The most frequent problem was landslides. Digging at the base of the hills caused dirt from the top to slide into the ditch. Building the locks was also a difficult job. Concrete was poured. Millions of tons of dirt were moved. At last, on April 1, 1914, canal workers carefully guided an old boat from the Atlantic Ocean to the Pacific. The canal system worked.

Canal workers practiced with larger ships in the weeks ahead.

Then on August 15, 1914, the Panama Canal was officially opened to traffic. The opening ceremonies were brief. World War I had just started in Europe. The Panama Canal became an important part of America's defenses in that war. And it remains one of the greatest engineering jobs of all time.

A Second Look. . . .

1. *Why did the Spanish-American War make the building of a canal across Panama seem vital to many Americans? Name three problems John Stevens and Colonel George Goethals faced in building the canal.*

2. *When Panamanians rebelled against Colombia in 1903, the U.S. went to the aid of the rebels. What reason did the U.S. have for doing so? Do you think the U.S. was right in aiding the rebels? Why or why not?*

3. *On a piece of paper, trace a map of North and South America. Include the islands of Cuba and Puerto Rico in the Caribbean Sea. Then draw the route of the battleship* Oregon *as it traveled to Cuba in 1898. How much shorter a trip would the* Oregon *have had if it could have traveled through the Panama Canal? See for yourself by also drawing in that route.*

Chapter 4

The Big Mitt Ledger

In 1902 a scandal was brewing in Minneapolis, Minnesota. The mayor and the chief of police had quietly slipped out of town. A grand jury was looking into their conduct in office. What the grand jury found shook the city to its roots.

The mayor, Dr. Amos Alonzo Ames, and his brother, the police chief, had "invited" criminals into Minneapolis. They had set up gambling, burglary, and other rackets supervised by the police! The rackets were run by the chief of detectives, a well-known gambler. The crooks were organized into groups just like a regular business.

The job of a grand jury is to decide whether there is reason to hold a trial. The leader of this grand jury was a courageous citizen named Hovey C. Clarke. The other members of the grand jury thought the "Ames gang," as it was known, was too strong to take on. But Clarke knew something had to be done. He led a complete investigation.

The grand jury turned up a great deal of information on the Ames gang. Most amazing was a book called the "Big Mitt Ledger." It was the record of money taken from people in crooked card games. The Big Mitt was the crook who raked in the money. The grand jury was surprised. Crooks rarely kept written records of their crimes. This was important evidence.

Soon a magazine reporter from New York by the name of Lincoln Steffens arrived in Minneapolis. Steffens was an expert at revealing city corruption. Clarke was eager to talk with Steffens. He showed the reporter the "Big Mitt Ledger." Some important information was missing. Steffens agreed to find the criminals who kept the book and ask them to explain it. But the two criminals were hiding from the law and their fellow crooks. Would they talk to Steffens and let him keep the book?

Detective story. Steffens found Billy Edwards and "Cheerful Charlie" Howard in a house in a run-down part of town. He knocked on the door. No answer. But when he held the book up to the window, the crooks decided to let him in. Edwards and Howard were glad to see Steffens. The Ames gang had cheated them. Now they were eager to get back at the gang. They "spilled the beans," telling Steffens everything.

They had been "invited" to Minneapolis by the police, they said. They had found "suckers" for their poker games. Then they had cheated these players with marked decks. A police detective had stood by to protect the crooks if there were any problems. The crooks had shared their profits with the mayor and his gang.

Steffens was a good reporter. He gained the crooks' confidence and took down all the information. When Steffens got up to leave, Edwards and Howard had the book. They all shook hands. Then Steffens reached for the book. To his surprise, they let him have it.

Steffens returned the book to Clarke. Thanks to the "Big Mitt Ledger," some members of the Ames gang were put on trial. The gang was broken up, and a new mayor was elected. But few members of the gang ever went to jail. Corruption and crime were hard to root out.

Lincoln Steffens was a very careful reporter. He made sure he had the facts before writing his story. He was one of a group of reporters who came to be called *muckrakers*. These reporters looked into corruption in business and government. Like detectives, they investigated their stories. They created a new kind of reporting — *investigative reporting*.

"The Shame of Minneapolis" was published in *McClure's Magazine* in 1903. *McClure's* was a leading journal of muckraking. Other famous muckrakers who wrote for *McClure's* were Ida Tarbell and Ray Stannard Baker. Tarbell wrote a series of articles on a big business company called the Standard Oil Trust. Baker exposed the corrupt practices of railroads.

Pattern of boss rule. As for Lincoln Steffens, he was very busy. After reporting on Minneapolis, he reported on several other cities in America. Steffens found a pattern in big cities run by political bosses. The bosses rigged elections to make sure they controlled the city government. Then, said Steffens, they stole the city blind. Steffens thought that the main source of corruption in government was *privilege*. That is, people used their money or power to get spe-

In 1906 a Puck *magazine cartoon made muckraking a laughing matter. It pictured Lincoln Steffens (on horse) and his boss, S. S. McClure (lower left), as crusaders battling against evil.*

389

cial favors. But these favors could only come at the public's expense. Government must be restored to the control of the people, Steffens wrote.

Steffens was a progressive. Progressives wanted to reform government and business. They wanted government to work better and be less corrupt. They also thought that government should help regulate business. It was government's role, they argued, to protect the public's interest.

This was a new idea. Before the progressives came along, most people had thought government should do as little as possible. They had believed that business could take care of itself. But America had changed. The growth of industry and large cities had changed the face of the nation. Progressives worked to make government more modern.

Many progressive reforms are part of government today. One is the secret ballot. In the old way of voting, a voter was given a colored ballot. The color of the ballot a voter was given depended on the party the voter chose. Anyone watching could see which party a voter was choosing. Bosses could check to make sure people voted the "right" way. With the secret ballot, a voter could make the choice in private.

Another progressive reform was the 17th Amendment to the U.S. Constitution. This amendment provided for the direct election of U.S. Senators by the people. Before this, Senators had been elected by their state legislatures. The legislatures were often controlled by state bosses who chose their own friends for the Senate. The 17th Amendment provided for a more democratic method of electing U.S. Senators.

The reformers' greatest contribution, though, was making people more aware of government. Progressives reminded the nation that in a democracy people must care about government. If they don't, corruption will surely grow. From the progressive movement came voter-education projects and citizenship programs in schools. In fact, the movement aroused concern for "good government" all across the nation.

A Second Look. . . .

1. *Who was the "Big Mitt"? What was the "Big Mitt Ledger"? In what way did it help to arouse concern for "good government" in Minneapolis?*

2. *What is meant by the term* public interest? *How did progressives believe that the public interest could best be protected? What was new about this belief? Which of the following groups seem to you to do the most to protect the public interest today: (a) political leaders, (b) newspapers, (c) TV news commentators, (d) civic groups such as the League of Women Voters? Why?*

3. *Scandals in government still occur. Do you know of any which have been uncovered recently in your town, city, or state? If so, you may want to look closely into the events surrounding the scandal. Using old newspapers or local magazines, try to find out what really happened. Then report on the scandal to the class. In your report, try to make certain you do* not *include charges that have not been proved in court. After your report, the class may want to consider these questions: Why do some successful people violate the public trust? Only for greed? Or are there other reasons?*

Chapter 5

"Reform in a Derby"

Newspaper editor William Allen White had a gift for making up catch-phrases. And few of his phrases were more fitting than the one he applied to President Theodore (Teddy) Roosevelt. "Teddy," White once wrote, "was reform in a derby." In White's day, derby hats were signs of wealth. What White meant was that Roosevelt was a well-to-do man who was not simply concerned with getting richer. He wanted to change things and make life better for everyone. White added that Roosevelt's was the "most fashionable derby you ever saw."

Teddy Roosevelt had come from a New York family of moderate wealth. He was also a man of high spirits and enormous energy. Yet it wasn't always this way with Teddy. As a boy, he had been weak and skinny, and sick much of the time. When Teddy was 12, his father bought him a punching bag and other gym equipment. Teddy began building up his body. By the time he entered Harvard College, he had grown quite strong.

Teddy went into politics in 1881. He ran for the New York State Assembly as a Republican from New York City—and won. In those days, crooked "bosses" ran both the Republican and Democratic parties in New York. But Teddy soon

Theodore Roosevelt was a bully speaker in a whistle-stop campaign. He would ride a train, blow the whistle, make a speech, and move on.

Theodore Roosevelt's adventures in Cuba made him an instant folk hero. Someone began making dolls showing "Teddy" as a Rough Rider.

showed the bosses they couldn't push *him* around. He became well known for his honesty, and for his fight against slum conditions in New York City.

Then, on February 14, 1884, the world almost came to an end for Roosevelt. His wife died after giving birth to a baby girl. The same day his mother died of an illness. Roosevelt wrote in his diary, "My life has now been lived out." He went to live on his ranch in the Dakota Territory. He tried to forget his grief. He "broke" wild horses and shot bears.

The blizzards of 1886-1887 killed most of Teddy's cattle. After this, he went back into government work. For a while, he was police commissioner of New York City. He fought hard against policemen who were crooked or did not do their jobs.

Rise to fame. When the Spanish-American War began, Teddy was Assistant Secretary of the Navy. But he didn't want to sit at a desk when he could be fighting in Cuba. Teddy quit his Navy job and formed an outfit of cavalry (horse soldiers). Cowboys, college boys, and some policemen joined Teddy's outfit. They were known as the Rough Riders. Teddy and the Rough Riders became heroes in the U.S. There were stories about them in most of the nation's newspapers.

Teddy's fame as a war hero helped him in politics. He was soon elected governor of New York and then Vice-President of the United States. But he was not Vice-President for long. On September 6, 1901, President William McKinley was shot by an assassin. McKinley died a few days later. At 42, Theodore Roosevelt became the youngest President in the history of the United States. He soon became the most popular man in the country too. In 1904, after he had served out McKinley's term, he ran for election to a second term as President. He won the election hands down.

As President, Roosevelt lost little time in making changes. In 1902, only six months after taking office, he first hit out at giant business trusts. Trusts were powerful enough to charge high prices and get away with it. Many Americans feared that trusts had become too powerful. In 1890 Congress had passed the Sherman Antitrust Act to control their growth. Now Roosevelt moved to enforce this law.

He had government lawyers file a law suit against a railroad trust, the Northern Securities Company. He charged that the company had violated the Sherman Antitrust Act. The President's move was very popular. People called him the "Trust-Buster." In the next seven years, the U.S. government brought suit against 43 other large companies.

Business v. labor. Busting trusts was only the beginning. Roosevelt also made efforts to control big business in other ways. In the past, some Presidents had tended to side with big business in its dealings with labor unions. Unlike these Presidents, Roosevelt accepted the rights of both business *and* labor. Yet in at least one famous case, Roosevelt did not take either side. Instead he thought the

rights of the general public came first.

In the fall of 1902, the nation's coal miners went on strike. The strike threatened to leave homes, schools, and hospitals in many parts of the country without any heat. Roosevelt tried to bring both sides to an agreement. He had no success. So then he took direct action. He said he would send the Army to operate the coal fields if the two sides could not agree. As a result of Roosevelt's warning, the strike was settled. For the first time, the federal government had stepped into a labor dispute to get both sides to work out an agreement.

Roosevelt carried out many other reforms in the interest of the general pub-

Congress passed the Sherman Antitrust Act in 1890. But by 1903 there were more than 300 giant trusts. John D. Rockefeller's Standard Oil Trust was one of the biggest. The magazine Puck *saw this many-armed monster gobbling up everything — from steel companies to the Capitol. Not even the White House was safe.*

lic. He got Congress to pass laws against the selling of dangerous or fake drugs and impure food. He also did much to save U.S. forests from businesses that threatened to destroy them. He created five new national parks. He set up more than 50 wildlife preserves. He added millions of extra acres to forest reserves. In fact he did more to conserve America's wilderness areas than any President before him.

Roosevelt's ideas came to be called the *Square Deal*. They were progressive ideas but not very radical ones. Roosevelt stayed popular partly because he kept his reforms in line with the wishes of the voters. Yet some critics charged that he was not reformer enough.

Third-party fight. Roosevelt did not run again for President in 1908. Four years later, in 1912, Republican reformers wanted him back in the White House. Roosevelt tried to regain leadership of the Republican party. But this time he had a fight on his hands. Regular Republicans favored President William Howard Taft to run on their ticket. Roosevelt supporters collided with the Taft forces at the Republican convention in 1912. Taft was chosen as the party candidate. Roosevelt supporters walked out of the convention.

They then formed a third party — the Progressive party. In the campaign, the Progressives had to fight not only Taft but also the Democratic candidate, Woodrow Wilson. Roosevelt put up a good fight as usual. He got more votes than Taft, but not as many as Wilson. Wilson became the new President. Roosevelt's defeat ended the most active part of his political career.

In the first years of this century, Roosevelt had shown Americans that they could make reform work. He had also widened the powers of the President. He had used his position as leader to call the people's attention to problems at home and abroad. For this reason, he is often called "the first modern President."

A Second Look. . . .

1. *As President, Theodore Roosevelt was famous for a number of reforms. Can you name three of them?*

2. *Roosevelt was an American hero. People admired him for his energy, determination, and toughness. What is it about some people that make them heroes or heroines? Who are your heroes or heroines? Why do you admire these people?*

3. *In the 19th century, people had been used to a seemingly unlimited supply of timber, coal, water, and oil. When something was used up, there always seemed to be more of it somewhere else. Theodore Roosevelt was the first President to show Americans that this might not always be true. He did much for the conservation of natural resources such as forests.*

Conservation is even more important in our own time than it was in Roosevelt's. More and more, energy and water are in short supply. Yet despite the moves to conserve energy, there is still a lot of waste today. Make a list of things that are used just once and then thrown away. Explore the ways they could be reused. One of these ways is "recycling." Why do you think recycling has been slow to catch on? What can you do to learn about recycling and teach others?

At the turn of the century, many women worked long hours in dark and dreary sweatshops.

Chapter 6

Arguing for Social Justice

Curt Muller called his business the Lace House Laundry. He ran it from a white frame building on a busy street in Portland, Oregon. Muller was a successful businessman. He had several employees, mostly women. They did the washing and ironing, waited on customers, and performed odd jobs.

Muller was a hard worker and a model citizen. He expected a lot from his employees too. He put them to work 12 hours a day, but this was nothing unusual. Around the turn of the century, most people worked at least 60 hours a week.

Then in 1905 one of Muller's women employees took him to court. She charged him with breaking a new state law which said that women could work only 10 hours a day. Muller did not deny the charge. Instead he challenged the law. His attorney claimed that the law

Lowest-paid people in a tobacco plant were often the women and children who stripped stems from tobacco leaves (above). Many worked 13 hours a day. Few earned more than nine cents an hour.

got in the way of an employer's freedom to hire and fire employees. Therefore, the attorney said, the law was unconstitutional.

When one court rejected Muller's argument, he took it to a higher court. In 1907 he took it to the highest court of all — the U.S. Supreme Court. Muller's case tested whether state lawmakers could set rules to govern the hours women worked. In the end it became a turning point in the movement for social justice in the United States.

The seeds of that movement had been planted late in the 19th century. When Americans looked around them, many thought they saw injustices that needed correcting. There was the misery of life in city slums. There was the threat of giant trusts, now so powerful that they were hard to control. And there was the helplessness of millions of women and young people who worked long hours for very little pay.

Long hours, low pay. The problems of women and children workers seemed most immediate. Women workers almost always made less money than men. Young people usually earned even less than women. Partly because young people could be hired so cheaply, they were put to work in mills and coal mines at an early age. In 1900 nearly two million young people between the ages of 10 and 15 were working full-time in the U.S. Few of them had any chance for schooling. For most of them, life was a steady round of work. Often the work ended in injury, illness, or early death.

Women workers were usually found in offices, mills, and small businesses. In the clothing industry, they spent their days in factories called *sweatshops*. Most sweatshops were located in dark, crowded tenements. Few women who worked in them could buy the clothes they made. Most of these women could barely afford to pay their grocers' bills and rent.

What could be done to help such people? Not all progressives agreed that something *should* be done. Some progressives were owners of businesses themselves. They tended to think first of the business costs of raising wages and reducing hours. Some of them thought that workers could best be helped by helping themselves.

Others, however, were sure that help was needed. They turned to government as the only place where great help could be found. Many of these progressives were women — social workers, housewives, and others. They supported laws that protected children and limited working hours. They formed groups such as the National Consumers' League to fight for such laws. Between 1900 and 1905, they partly succeeded. Several states passed "hours laws." One of these states was Oregon.

The trouble was that these laws sometimes failed to get past the courts. Each time an hours law came before a court, the judge or judges had two things to consider. One was the well-being of the workers. The other was the employer's freedom to run a business any way he or she saw fit. Quite often the courts put themselves on the side of the employers. They usually did so by ruling that no citizen could be denied his or her property without *due process* of law. (Due process is an orderly set of rules for bringing a lawsuit or a person accused of a crime to trial.)

Coal miners weren't often paid enough to support their families. So their children had to help out. Nine-year-olds with backs bent from crouching in mine shafts were a common sight in coal country.

Louis D. Brandeis

Vital test. The case of Curt Muller and his laundry workers promised to be a vital test of the hours laws. The case was known as *Muller v. Oregon.* The state of Oregon asked the National Consumers' League to help prepare a defense of the law. The League's secretary was a driving, single-minded woman named Florence Kelley. Kelley was a fighter. She went out to hire the best lawyer in the land.

She turned to a Boston attorney, Louis D. Brandeis (BRAN-dies). In a way, Brandeis seemed an unusual choice. He had made a name for himself by defending businesses, not attacking them. The son of a Jewish merchant from Kentucky, Brandeis had a special genius for the law. He had made his way through Harvard Law School in only two years. By the time he had turned 40, he had become one of the best-paid lawyers in the land. But making money from large legal fees was not enough for Brandeis. He had a rest-

397

less mind and a passion for reform. He quickly accepted the case.

Brandeis' challenge was to convince the Supreme Court that long hours were unsafe. He asked Florence Kelley to find all the facts she could about the effects of tiredness on accident rates. There wasn't much time. The case would go to court in three weeks. Kelley and her assistant, Josephine Goldmark, rounded up the facts Brandeis needed. He gave them careful study. Three weeks later he was ready to go before the Court.

Lengthy brief. A lawyer's formal argument is called a *brief*. Most briefs present legal arguments and past court decisions in similar cases. But Brandeis' brief in *Muller v. Oregon* was different. It spent only two pages on legal arguments and earlier decisions. As the Justices listened to Brandeis read his brief, they were a little stunned. Surely he did not mean to rest his case on such a skimpy argument. But Brandeis read on, and it was clear that he did not. His brief continued for more than 100 pages. All the rest of it presented *facts* showing that long hours were harmful for women workers.

The Court was swayed by Brandeis' argument. Five weeks later, in February 1908, it announced a decision upholding the Oregon law. The Justices admitted the need for facts in ruling on laws of this kind. Curt Muller was fined $10 for breaking the law. Now he would have to shorten the workday of his women workers. The case was closed.

But the Supreme Court had opened the door for social reform. Between 1909 and 1917, 39 states passed new hours laws or strengthened old ones. Brandeis kept at the work he had so ably begun. In the months after the Muller decision, he sent briefs on other labor laws to 14 different courts.

Brandeis believed in a "living law" that would keep pace with the new century. In 1916 he got his greatest chance to put his beliefs into practice. President Woodrow Wilson named him to be a Justice of the Supreme Court, the first Jew to be so honored. The choice also honored the movement for social justice which Brandeis had served so well.

A Second Look. . . .

1. *What were the issues involved in* Muller v. Oregon? *How was the case "a turning point in the movement for social justice in the United States"?*

2. *Progressives introduced a new idea to government. They said it was the job of government to protect the public interest. Think about the ways government influences your life. What effect does the government have on the school you attend, the housing you live in, and the food you eat? Is government control always helpful? If not, why not? When is it most helpful?*

3. *In* Muller v. Oregon, *Louis Brandeis used facts to support his legal arguments. His basic methods are still used in debates of all kinds. To understand them better, you and your classmates might undertake a research project. First choose a subject of current controversy. One example is capital punishment. Another is noise pollution. Take one side of that controversy and find out what arguments are generally used to support it. Then find as many facts as you can to back up each argument. Each of you should report your findings to the class.*

Looking Back:
Into the 20th Century

Putting Events in Order

Chapters One through Six have shown some of the changes that took place in the United States at the beginning of the 20th century. Ten events of this period are listed here. Your job is to match each event to the correct period shown on the timeline above. On a piece of paper, number from **1** to **10.** After each number, write the letter of the four-year period within which the event occurred.

1. Construction begins on the Panama Canal.
2. The U.S. Supreme Court decides the case of *Muller v. Oregon.*
3. Woodrow Wilson is elected President.
4. Theodore Roosevelt settles a coal strike.
5. The United States defeats Spain in the Spanish-American War.
6. The Panama Canal is opened to traffic.

7. John Hay announces the Open Door Policy.
8. The Boxer Rebellion takes place in China.
9. Theodore Roosevelt becomes President.
10. Lincoln Steffens publishes "The Shame of Minneapolis" in *McClure's Magazine.*

Interpreting a Source

The progressive movement continued under President Woodrow Wilson. During Wilson's first term as President (1913-1917), many reform laws were passed. The passage below is adapted from a speech Wilson made while running for President in the election of 1912.

We have come to a very different age from any that came before us. In this new age we find that our laws are often out of date. They were passed for another age which nobody now living

399

remembers. Our laws that apply to employers and employees are especially impossible. The employer is now generally a corporation or a huge company of some kind. The employee is one of hundreds or of thousands brought together to work. He no longer works for a master whom he knows personally. Now he is hired by agents who work for the corporation. Workingmen are gathered together in great numbers to work in giant factories. They generally use dangerous and powerful machinery. They have no control over its safety.

New rules must be written with regard to the workers' duties and their rights, their duties to their employers and their duties to one another. Rules must be written for their protection, for their payment when injured, for their support when disabled.

We must not match power against weakness. The employer is generally, in our day, as I have said, a powerful group. Yet the workingman, when dealing with his employer, is still, under our present law, an individual.

We used to think differently in the old-fashioned days when life was very simple. We thought that all government had to do was put on a policeman's uniform and say, "Now don't anybody hurt anybody else." We used to say that the ideal of government was for every man to be left alone. He should not be interfered with except when he interfered with somebody else. But we are coming to realize that life is much more complicated now. And new approaches are necessary. The law has to step in and create conditions under which we can live decently.

In North Carolina, many 10-year-olds such as this girl were put to work as spinners in cotton mills. By 1909 fast-moving machinery was sometimes more than children could handle. Accidents were common.

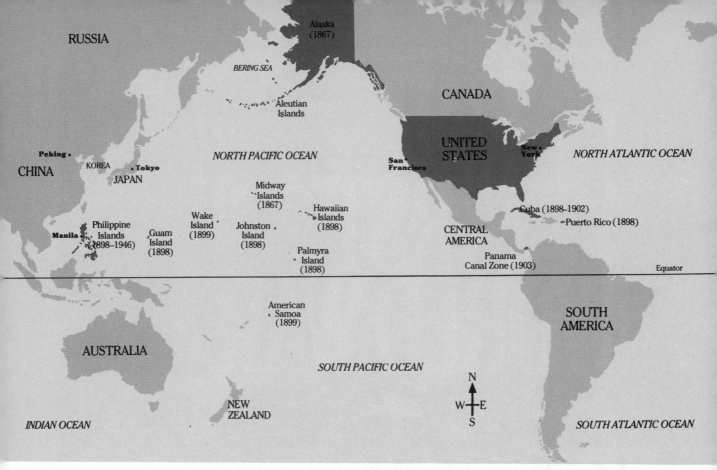

United States and Possessions, 1867-1903

1. By 1912 the old relationship between employer and employee had changed in a number of ways. Name two changes mentioned by Wilson.

2. How does Wilson propose to change the laws to fit the changing times?

3. Why does Wilson warn Americans not to "match power against weakness"? What does he mean?

4. Does Wilson seem to take the side of the employer or the employee in his proposals? Why? Is it possible that his proposals really benefit both sides in some ways? If so, explain the ways in which they do.

Sharpening Your Skills

By 1903 the U.S. held possessions stretching halfway around the globe. Exactly where were these areas? Find out by studying the map shown above.

1. Which of the areas shown became U.S. possessions in 1898?

2. Which of the U.S. possessions shown were *not* islands?

3. Two areas which were possessions in 1903 are now states of the U.S. Which areas are these?

4. What possession of the U.S. in 1903 is now an independent country?

401

2 THE FIRST WORLD WAR

Looking Ahead: An End to Innocence

Many Americans had entered the new century full of hope. These were the "good years," and they lasted into the century's second decade. As the summer of 1914 began, there appeared no way of spoiling the mood. Woodrow Wilson was in the White House. The U.S. was at peace. And there seemed little reason to be worried by events happening far away.

Then, on July 28, 1914, this mood was shaken by one word: war.

Some leaders of Europe had thought a war was coming. They said it would not last longer than six weeks. For many the war promised to be a glorious event. It was a time to be brave and dashing, a time to wear fine, colored uniforms and ride horses into battle.

But the "short, glorious" war turned out to be neither short nor glorious. It

World War I, the first "modern" war, raged for four years, left troops dazed and out of hope.

lasted four bloody years. It took more than eight million lives. It cost 337 *billion* dollars. The peace treaty that finally ended it did nothing to end the hatred that had caused it. In some ways the treaty led directly to World War II, which was even longer and bloodier.

What were the causes of World War I?

An arms race. In 1914 Europe was divided into two armed camps. Britain, France, and Russia were in one camp. Germany and Austria-Hungary were in the other. The rivalry between the two camps had been growing for years. Each country had built up its army and navy to prepare for war. Nations in each camp had made secret agreements with one another. Each had agreed to go to war if its ally was attacked.

Nationalism. Strong national pride — a sort of super-patriotism — led some people of Europe to look down on, and dislike, others. This super-patriotism was often an outlet for people

403

bored with their lives. For such people war was a kind of escape. They became eager to prove that their nations were better than their rivals' nations.

The desire for colonies. Britain and France had many colonies in Africa and Asia. Germany had few colonies and wanted more. It had become a nation as recently as 1871. Now Germany wanted a "place in the sun." Britain and France feared that Germany's desire for more colonies would interfere with their own empires.

No way to keep peace. In 1914 there was no organization such as the United Nations to help keep peace. If a crisis arose, it seemed as if war would be the only way to settle it.

Europe was a powder keg. All it needed was a spark to make it explode. The killing of Archduke Francis Ferdinand of Austria-Hungary on June 28, 1914, provided that spark. Within a few weeks, most of Europe was at war.

In the United States, the war excited great interest. But President Wilson was at first determined to keep the U.S. out of the fighting. Wilson was a very high-minded man. He thought the U.S. should remain above the conflict.

Yet this was not to be. Both sides in the fighting carried on a propaganda war in the U.S. The aim was to win Americans over to one camp or the other. British agents, for example, tried to make Americans believe that Germany was entirely in the wrong. German agents tried to make Americans believe the same thing about the British.

In 1915 a German submarine sank a British liner, the *Lusitania,* off the coast of Ireland. More than 100 Americans went down with the ship. This event turned many Americans against Germany. The U.S. drifted toward war.

German submarines kept up their attacks on British and French ships in the Atlantic Ocean. Then, in March 1917, the Germans sank two U.S. ships. A few days later, Woodrow Wilson went before Congress. He asked for a declaration of war against Germany. He got it.

America soon became a beehive of activity. Congress set up a program for drafting men into the military services. Army camps began turning raw recruits into a trained fighting force. Congress also gave the President sweeping wartime powers. It allowed him to control the prices paid for many goods. It permitted him to take over entire industries to move the war effort ahead.

For the U.S., the war lasted only a year-and-a-half. None of the fighting took place on American soil. Far fewer American troops were killed in the conflict than French or British troops. Yet the war brought great changes to America. It uprooted many people and altered their daily lives.

Some who bore the brunt of the war effort were Americans of German descent. Sadly, the campaign against Germany rubbed off on German-Americans too. Schools stopped teaching the German language. People with German names were hooted at in the streets. Some of them lost their jobs.

The war ended in 1918. The U.S. was one of the victors. But by this time, the conflict had shattered the hopeful mood that had existed at the turn of the century. The U.S. was less innocent in 1918 than it had been in 1910. It was a little older and wiser, and nothing seemed as simple to fix as it had before the war.

Chapter 7

Murder at Sarajevo

Archduke Francis Ferdinand of Austria-Hungary was on a goodwill tour. He and his wife, Sophie, were visiting the town of Sarajevo (sahr-uh-YEH-voe). This was a city in Austria-Hungary near its border with the small nation of Serbia. The year was 1914.

On the morning of June 28, the archduke and his wife took a drive through the streets. It was a holiday, and many flags were flying. People lined the streets to watch the archduke pass. No one knew that seven young men in the crowds were waiting to kill him.

These young men were Serbians. Serbia is now part of Yugoslavia. But in those days many Serbian people were ruled by Austria-Hungary. This made some patriotic Serbians hate the Austro-Hungarians because they wanted all Serbians to live together under one flag. So the seven young Serbians plotted to kill the archduke — for Serbia. They spread out along the streets of Sarajevo. They were armed with pistols and bombs. The streets were not well guarded.

Grim welcome. The archduke's car passed the first Serbian plotter. The Serbian lost his nerve and did nothing. But the second plotter threw his bomb at the archduke. The archduke raised his arm and knocked the bomb into the street, where it exploded and wounded about a

Archduke Francis Ferdinand of Austria-Hungary and his wife Sophie begin their last auto ride in Sarajevo in 1914. Serbian plotters shot them, lighting the spark that set off World War I.

dozen people. Quickly the archduke's car sped past three more plotters, who did nothing.

Finally the car stopped at the City Hall. The archduke was very angry. He shouted at the mayor: "I came for a visit and I get bombs. Mr. Mayor, what do you say?" The mayor did not understand what had happened. He made a speech welcoming the archduke. Then the archduke calmed down and smiled.

The archduke then said he wanted to visit the hospital. He wanted to see the people who had been wounded by the bomb explosion. He begged his wife not to go with him. It was too dangerous. But she said, "No, I must go with you." Along the way, their car passed the sixth plotter. He did not make a move.

Then the archduke's driver made a mistake. He turned the car into the wrong street. He stopped to turn around. Five feet away was the seventh Serbian plotter. He drew his gun and fired twice. One bullet hit the archduke in the neck. The other hit Sophie in the stomach.

The car sped back. Blood began pouring from the archduke's mouth. Then Sophie fell forward. Both were soon dead.

Point of no return. This was the spark that set off World War I. Austria-Hungary wanted revenge. On July 28, 1914, it declared war on Serbia. Russia had already said it would help Serbia if war broke out. Germany had said it would help Austria-Hungary. Armies began to move, and it was too late to stop. When France backed Russia, German armies marched into neutral Belgium to attack France. Then Britain joined in with the French and Russians. By August 4, all the great nations of

Europe were at war except Italy. Britain, France, and Russia were on one side. (Italy joined them later.) Germany and Austria-Hungary were on the other. Both sides thought they would win a quick, easy victory. They were wrong.

What did the United States do when World War I broke out? Many Americans leaned toward the Allies — Britain, France, and Russia. But few people wanted to get into the war. President Wilson said the U.S. must stay neutral — not take sides. Most Americans agreed.

But in 1915 a German submarine sank the *Lusitania,* killing many Americans. Then it began to look as if America might have to get into the war.

A Second Look. . . .

1. *Why did a group of Serbians assassinate Archduke Francis Ferdinand and his wife in 1914? How did the assassination lead to a wider war?*

2. *Serbian nationalists wanted all Serbians to live together under one flag. Do you think the Serbians' goal was a fair one? Why or why not? Was this a good enough reason for the Serbians to plan a killing? Explain your answer.*

3. *World War I might not have taken place if Europe had not had its system of alliances. To understand the two main alliances of 1914 more fully, you might want to prepare a bulletin-board display on them. Your display should name the main alliances and list the member-nations in each. You can obtain such information from most encyclopedias. Map-makers might draw a wall map with color codes showing the member-nations in each alliance. The wall map should identify Sarajevo and the major capitals of the nations involved.*

Chapter 8

The U-Boat and the Lusitania

The captain of the German U-boat (submarine) was worried. He had good reason to be worried too. In those days a submarine was like a dangerous toy. Any warship could sink it easily. The submarine was slow, and it had little armor. A single hit from even a small gun could sink it. Any large ship could ram it and crush it like an egg.

The captain was worried, and he was tired. His men were tired too. The date was May 7, 1915, and Europe was at war. For two months the captain and his crew had been sailing off the English coast. They had sunk a few British ships, but they were only small ones. Now they were off the coast of Ireland, and they wanted to go home.

Then the captain saw a large ship in his periscope. Here was the prize he had been waiting for. He got ready to fire a torpedo.

What ship did the captain see? It was the British liner *Lusitania*. It was the largest and fastest passenger ship in the world. Inside, it was like a palace.

German warning. The *Lusitania* had sailed from New York on May 1. That morning Germany had printed a warning in U.S. newspapers, saying that the German navy would sink British ships, even passenger ships. It warned Americans not to travel on British ships.

Despite the warning, 179 Americans sailed on the *Lusitania*. Altogether, more than 1,900 people were on the ship. Also, just as the Germans had thought, there were war supplies on board. Though having such supplies was against the law for passenger ships, the *Lusitania* carried 4,000 cases of bullets.

The captain of the *Lusitania* was given special orders. He was told not to take the usual route to England. He was also told to steer the ship in a zig-zag direction. If he saw an enemy submarine, he

German notice ran in New York papers on day Lusitania *sailed.*

NOTICE!

TRAVELLERS intending to embark on the Atlantic voyage are reminded that a state of war exists between Germany and her allies and Great Britain and her allies; that the zone of war includes the waters adjacent to the British Isles; that, in accordance with formal notice given by the Imperial German Government, vessels flying the flag of Great Britain, or of any of her allies, are liable to destruction in those waters and that travellers sailing in the war zone on ships of Great Britain or her allies do so at their own risk.

IMPERIAL GERMAN EMBASSY

WASHINGTON, D. C., APRIL 22, 1915.

407

was to ram it. But the captain did not want to scare his passengers. So he took the usual route and did not zigzag. The skies were sunny, and the sea was smooth. Everyone was having a good time.

On May 7, about lunch time, the *Lusitania* neared the coast of Ireland. So did the German submarine *U-20*. The German captain gave the *Lusitania* no warning. (International law said he was supposed to.) He ordered the torpedoman to fire. There was a great explosion. The *Lusitania* began to sink.

Ten minutes later, the liner went under. Nearly 1,200 people went down with the *Lusitania*. Many were women and children. More than 100 were Americans.

The submarine captain went home to Germany. There he was given a medal. The German people had reason to reward him. Just then they were suffering from a British blockade of German ships. The blockade was aimed at starving Germany into defeat. It had brought widespread suffering. Most Germans, then, saw the attack on the *Lusitania* as a proper response to this blockade.

U.S. reaction. Most Americans took a different view of the attack. Some called it "murder." These people were boiling with anger. They wanted the U.S. to declare war on Germany at once.

But Woodrow Wilson tried to hold the U.S. on a neutral course. Wilson was a strong-minded leader. He had a clear, almost religious sense of duty. He rarely shrank from action. But his Christian faith and sense of history made him realize what an awful price the war would bring. Besides, Wilson had no heart for war. He said, "There is such a thing as a man being too proud to fight."

Even so, Wilson was very angry over the loss of American lives. He sent very

"A grave crisis is at hand," said The New York Times *when the* Lusitania *was sunk. But the crisis was slow to worsen. The U.S. did not declare war against Germany until 1917, two years after the sinking.*

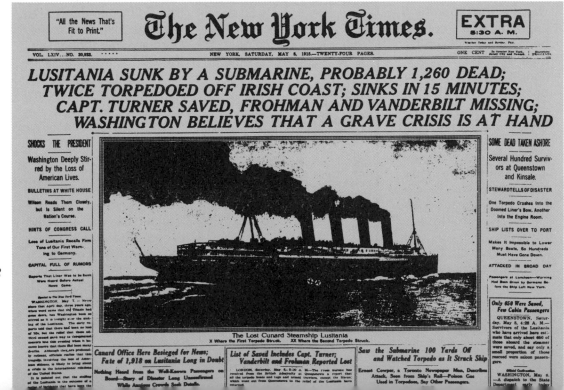

strong letters to the German government. In the summer of 1915, German leaders reached a temporary agreement with him. They said they would not sink peaceful, unarmed passenger ships without warning. But these leaders kept asking the U.S. to persuade the British and French to give up their blockades.

In 1916 Woodrow Wilson was again elected President. Many people voted for him because "he kept us out of war." But in 1917 Germany broke its promise. U-boats again began to sink passenger ships without warning. Now there was little hope that the U.S. could remain neutral. The German kaiser (KIE-zur; emperor) said, "If Wilson wants war, then let him have it."

A Second Look. . . .

1. *The captain of the* Lusitania *was given special orders. What were the orders he was given? Why were they given? Why did he disobey them?*

2. *On May 1, 1915, Germany had printed a warning in U.S. newspapers. The warning said that the German navy would sink British passenger ships. Do you think this was enough warning? If you had been planning to sail on the* Lusitania, *would the warning have made a difference in your plans? Explain.*

"U-boats out!" exclaims this German poster. Though Americans thought U-boat warfare sneaky, Germans thought it quite heroic.

3. *Pretend that you are (a) a German-American sailor, or (b) an American related to someone who went down with the* Lusitania. *The time is May 15, 1915. Prepare a speech to a local gathering stating your views on neutrality. In your speech, give at least two reasons for thinking as you do.*

Chapter 9
The U.S. Declares War

It was April 2, 1917. President Woodrow Wilson looked pale and sad. He had just asked Congress to declare war on Germany. Only the year before, Wilson had been re-elected, partly because he had kept the nation out of war. Now the man who had "kept us out of war" felt that the U.S. had to go to war.

What made Wilson change his mind about entering World War I?

After the *Lusitania* was sunk, Germany made a promise. It said its submarines would not attack passenger ships without warning. Yet as time went on, the U.S. looked more and more likely to enter the war on the Allied side. The Germans believed that their submarines could win the war before the U.S. could get any troops to France to fight with the Allies. So, early in 1917, the kaiser gave his submarine captains new orders. They were to sink without warning *all* ships going to Britain — even American ships.

President Wilson was shocked. On February 3, he ordered the German ambassador to go home. He warned Germany that if American ships were sunk, he would take further steps.

That same month, the United States got hold of a secret German message. The message had been sent by the Ger-

In April 1917, Woodrow Wilson told Congress that world must be "safe for democracy." It meant war.

410

I WANT YOU
FOR U.S. ARMY
NEAREST RECRUITING STATION

man foreign minister, Arthur Zimmermann. It was meant for the German ambassador in Mexico. The message said that Germany hoped the United States would not enter the war. But *if it did,* Germany wanted Mexico to make war on the United States. Germany offered Texas, New Mexico, and Arizona to the Mexicans in return — that is, if Germany won the war.

The message made President Wilson even more angry. And the submarine news was getting worse all the time. Germany was sinking 23 Allied ships a week! At this rate, it would win the war. Then, on March 16, two U.S. ships were sunk by German submarines. All over the United States, angry citizens held parades. They carried banners saying, "Kill the kaiser!" and "On to Berlin!"

Wilson acts. On April 2, President Wilson asked Congress to declare war. He said, "The world must be made safe for democracy. Its peace must be founded on . . . liberty." Even so, the American people did not see it as a war to save democracy — yet. They were too angry. They were still upset with Germany for overrunning neutral Belgium in 1914. They also wanted to settle the score with the Germans for sinking U.S. ships and offering United States land to Mexico.

Anti-German feeling ran high for other reasons too. Americans were tied to Britain by language. They remembered that France had helped America during the Revolutionary War. Many Americans also had business ties with Britain and

"At last a perfect soldier!" says an Army medical examiner in this cartoon from The Masses, *a magazine that was against the war.*

France, and they did not want to see the Germans win. Also British propaganda made it look as if the Germans were very cruel fighters. News reports said that German soldiers were killing helpless women and children in Belgium and France. Americans were shocked by these reports. By 1917 most Americans were ready to go to war with Germany.

Congress votes. Congress cheered President Wilson's speech. So did the crowds in Washington's streets. Still Wilson was an unhappy man. He said, "My message of today was a message of death for our young men. How strange it seems to cheer that."

On April 6, Congress voted to declare war on Germany. But the United States was not prepared for war. It had fewer

When the U.S. went to war, its Army was small. Posters such as this one by James Montgomery Flagg urged people to join the Army and fight.

413

than 200,000 men in its Army, and very few of them were ready for action. Besides, the Army's guns were too old to be used in Europe.

Early in May, General John J. Pershing was put in command of the Army. A few days later, Congress passed a draft act. This law said that any man between 21 and 31 years of age could be drafted into the armed forces. Critics of the law said that some men would refuse to obey it. These critics thought there would be rioting in the streets.

On June 5, more than nine million men signed up for the draft. There were no riots as some people had expected. The day was more like a holiday than anything else. Everywhere people sang, "Johnny Get Your Gun."

The United States had already begun building Army camps. Factories now began to work day and night to turn out guns and other war supplies. America was sure it would win the war. Its Navy destroyers were already sinking German submarines. Early in June, General Pershing and about 160 officers and men reached France. By the end of 1917, more than half a million men would be in uniform. The Yanks were coming! And American power would help bring victory to the Allies in Europe.

A Second Look. . . .

1. *Woodrow Wilson won reelection in 1916. He had hoped to keep America out of war. Yet only months after the start of his second term, Wilson asked Congress for a declaration of war. What made him change his mind?*

2. *This chapter and the previous one mention several reasons why the U.S.*

414 *entered World War I. Which of these reasons seem most important to you? Which of the events described would have moved you the most? Why?*

3. *Pretend you are a 21-year-old U.S. citizen. Suppose that your parents have been born in Germany and still keep in touch with relatives in the "old country." It is the summer of 1917, and you are now required to sign up for the draft. Next you will be asked to fight against Germany. This means you will be fighting against your own family since you have cousins in the German army. What are your alternatives? What would you do in the situation? Once you have reached a decision, write a letter to a German cousin explaining what you will do and why.*

Even before 1917, Girl Scouts collected peach stones to help the British. The stones were burned and made into charcoal for gas masks.

Chapter 10

The Yanks Over There

The war looked hopeless on the battlefields of France. Millions of young soldiers had died fighting between 1914 and 1917. But neither side was winning. Their armies were dug into trenches to escape the murderous machine-gun fire.

These trenches stretched for hundreds of miles. Often they were filled with water and rats. The torn and muddy ground between them was called "no man's land." For months at a time, the front lines never changed more than a few miles either way.

Then, in 1917, the United States joined the Allies. The Germans knew they had to win before a large American Army faced them. In March 1918 and again in May, the Germans attacked. These attacks carried the Germans to less than 40 miles (64 kilometers) from Paris. The war seemed lost. The Allies thought Paris would fall.

Bound for victory. Finally the French commander called on the Americans for help. General John J. Pershing rushed 30,000 men to the front. French soldiers, falling back to Paris, shouted, "The war is finished!" The Americans shouted back, "It is *not* finished!"

At Château-Thierry (sha-toe-tyeh-REE), a French officer told the U.S. troops to retreat. "Retreat, nothing!" a Marine officer answered. "We just got here!" The American soldiers — called *Yanks* or *doughboys* — attacked instead. Their attack stopped the Germans cold. Then the doughboys drove the Germans out of Belleau (beh-LOW) Wood. Their daring and bravery gave the Allies new heart. A French leader visited them. "I have come to see the brave Americans who saved Paris," he said.

Now it was the Allies' turn to attack. The Americans were ordered to clear the Germans out of the Argonne (ar-GAHN) Forest. This was a difficult job. The Germans had machine-gun nests everywhere.

Lost in a forest. The attack into the forest began on September 16, 1918. The shooting sounded like the end of the world. On the fourth day, 700 Yanks from New York's 77th Division were completely surrounded by the Germans. These men became known as the Lost Battalion. They dug in, forming a rough circle. German rifle and machine-gun bullets tore into the dirt. Cries of "Surrender, Americans!" came from the woods. The American major in charge sent a message to his men: "Our job is to hold this position at all costs."

At night the men of the Lost Battalion were pounded by mortar shells. The cries of the wounded were terrible. First-aid bandages were used up. Then bandages were taken from the dead.

In the morning, the American major sent a message by carrier pigeon asking

for help. He prayed the message would get through. About the same time, the Germans sent a captured American soldier through the lines with a note. It asked the American major to surrender. The major refused. Then the Germans charged. Some of them used flame-throwers. The Lost Battalion fired rapidly and beat back the attack. The major again sent a message by pigeon asking for help. Cruel "help" came. American gunners made a mistake. Their cannons pounded the Lost Battalion instead of the Germans.

Later the Germans inched closer. They bombed the Americans with hand grenades. "Surrender!" they called.

Posters such as British one below showed soldiers as knights in shining armor. But things were not so glorious in the muddy Argonne Forest (left).

417

But the Americans would not give up.

After five days, the Lost Battalion was at last rescued. Only 194 of its 700 men walked out alive.

The U.S. Army finally drove the Germans out of the Argonne Forest. The cost was very high. The Americans suffered more than 100,000 dead and wounded. But now the Germans were finished. They could not face the two million fresh American troops now in France, waiting for action. In a few weeks, Germany would have to give up. At last World War I would be over.

A Second Look. . . .

1. *What was* trench warfare? *What role did the machine gun play in it? What was "no man's land"? How did the Lost Battalion help the Allies to victory?*

2. *Some events in history can be used for a guessing game called "what-might-have-been." What might have happened in World War I if there had been no Lost Battalion? What if the U.S. had never entered the war? Would the other Allies have gone on to victory by themselves? Would it have taken them longer to win? Explain your answers.*

3. *Pretend that you are the mother or father of a U.S. soldier who has been killed in the Argonne Forest. You are writing the commanding officer of the Lost Battalion to thank him for informing you of your son's death. Try to describe what your son meant to you. Then explain whether or not the U.S. victory in the war has eased your grief.*

New weapons made World War I a deadly game of terror. Warplanes struck from the skies (top). "Tanks" hit from the ground (center). Ugly masks were used to avoid effects of poison gas (below).

New Yorkers streamed into the streets to celebrate on November 11, 1918. George Luks painted the scene.

Chapter 11

The Peace That Failed

It was 11 o'clock in the morning on the 11th day of the 11th month, 1918. All over the battlefields of France, the guns fell silent. World War I was over at last. More than eight million people throughout the world had lost their lives. Germany had agreed to an armistice, and both sides had stopped fighting. The kaiser had fled to Holland.

In Allied countries, people went wild with joy. At the front, soldiers laughed, cried, and cheered. American and German soldiers mixed. The Yanks traded cigarettes for pistols and bayonets. Then they played children's games such as blindman's buff.

Here in the United States, happy crowds poured into the streets. They waved flags and paraded while bands played. They sang songs such as "Over There" and "Pack Up Your Troubles." Soldiers in uniform were kissed and cheered. Never had the end of a war brought such happiness.

Now a peace treaty had to be made. Early in December, President Woodrow Wilson sailed for Paris. In Europe crowds cheered him as a great hero. Flowers were thrown in his path. Banners said, "Hail the champion of the rights of man!"

Losing the peace. But at the peace talks, Wilson ran into trouble. Wilson wanted a fair peace that would make a better world. He called it "peace without victory." He did not want to punish

419

Germany too harshly. He did not want any German lands for the United States. Wilson told the world about his peace plans in a speech in January 1918. These peace plans quickly became known as the "Fourteen Points." They were so fair that even many Germans were in favor of them.

But the other Allied leaders were against some of Wilson's peace plans. They wanted to blame Germany for all the death and damage of the war. They wanted to make Germany pay for it. They wanted to make Germany so weak it could never make war again. And they wanted to take some German land in Europe and all German colonies overseas. The French leader said, "Wilson annoys me with his Fourteen Points."

Wilson and the other Allied leaders had many arguments. "The peace talks make a noise like a riot in a parrot house," one reporter said.

One of Wilson's Fourteen Points was a plan for an organization to prevent fu-

Victorious veterans were given heroes' welcomes when they returned to their own neighborhoods.

ture wars. It was to be called the *League of Nations.* In the League, nations would talk over their problems peacefully, instead of going to war. (It was something like the United Nations, set up after World War II.) Of all his plans for peace, Wilson fought hardest for the League. But to get the Allies to accept the League, Wilson had to give up many of his other Points.

As a result, the peace treaty was very cruel to Germany. It said that Germany was to blame for the war. It took away part of Germany's land. Germany lost towns and cities, rich coal mines and factories and farmlands. Germany had to give the Allies coal, cattle, railroad cars, ships, and money. Germany also lost all of its colonies.

At first the Germans would not sign the treaty. They said it was a double-cross, for it went against Wilson's Fourteen Points. If they had known that the peace treaty was going to be like this, they said, they would not have stopped fighting. But later they gave in. They had to, because they had already turned over all their warships and arms to the Allies.

The treaty was signed in the Palace of Versailles (vair-SY) near Paris. The Germans agreed to it on June 28, 1919. This caused much bitter feeling in Germany. Many people today believe the treaty helped cause World War II.

Losing the League. Wilson went home to the United States. He asked the U.S. Senate to vote for the treaty and make the United States a member of the League of Nations. (The League was part of the treaty.) "Dare we turn down the League and break the heart of the world?" he asked.

Woodrow Wilson ended his Presidency crippled by a stroke and haunted by defeat. His dreams of a better world had faded. His hand was so unsteady that his wife had to help him sign his papers.

Still he traveled west by train, making speeches for the League. The farther west he went, the larger were the crowds that cheered him.

He went all the way to California. Then he turned around and headed east. In mid-September, he gave a speech at Pueblo, Colorado. With tears running down his cheeks, he begged people to support the League. He said it was the best hope of preventing future wars.

After the speech in Pueblo, Wilson collapsed. He was rushed back to Washington, D.C., a very sick man. Back in the White House, Wilson had a stroke. Soon after, the treaty was voted down in the U.S. Senate. Wilson's dream of a League of Nations, with the United States as a member, was gone. He died four years later, a broken man.

But many Senators were against the treaty because they were against the League of Nations. They believed the United States should not mix in Europe's business. Wilson grew more and more worried. In the summer of 1919, he decided to go to the American people for help.

The man with the iron-gray hair and the shy smile planned a trip around the country. He had never liked the glad-handing and back-slapping of politics. Nor was he in the best of health.

A Second Look. . . .

1. *Why were many U.S. Senators against the League of Nations? What did President Wilson do to fight for it? Was he successful?*

2. *Wilson wanted a peace treaty that gave advantage to no one. France and Britain wanted a treaty that punished Germany for its part in the war. How can you account for the differences in these views? Could geography have played a part? Why?*

3. *Two soldiers meet on a street in a German city in early July of 1919. One is German. The other is American. The German soldier has just returned home after four years of fighting. He has seen his friends killed and his nation defeated. Now he has learned the final terms of the peace treaty, and he discusses it with the American. Create a conversation between the two.*

421

Looking Back: The First World War

	A	B	C	D	E	F	
January 1, 1914	January 1, 1915	January 1, 1916	January 1, 1917	January 1, 1918	January 1, 1919	January 1, 1920

Putting Events in Order

Chapters Seven through 11 have described American action in World War I. Ten events of this period are listed here. Your job is to match each event to the correct period shown on the timeline above. On a piece of paper, number from **1** to **10**. After each number, write the letter of the year in which the event occurred.

1. The liner *Lusitania* is torpedoed off the coast of Ireland.
2. The United States declares war on Germany.
3. Germany agrees to an armistice.
4. A peace treaty is signed at Versailles outside Paris.
5. Archduke Francis Ferdinand of Austria and his wife Sophie are assassinated in Sarajevo.
6. The Lost Battalion is surrounded by German troops.
7. Congress passes a draft act.
8. President Wilson announces his Fourteen Points for peace.
9. World War I begins.
10. Woodrow Wilson is re-elected President.

Interpreting a Source

In 1917 President Woodrow Wilson decided that U.S. entry into World War I was necessary. Not all Americans agreed with him. One who did not was U.S. Senator George Norris, Republican from Nebraska. This passage is adapted from a speech Norris made in April 1917.

We ought to remember the advice of the Father of Our Country and keep out of entangling alliances. Let Europe bear its burdens as we have borne ours. In the greatest war of our history, . . . we were engaged in solving an American problem. We settled the question of human slavery and washed our flag clean by the sacrifice of human blood. It was a great problem and a great burden but we solved it ourselves. Never once did any European nation undertake to settle the great question. We solved it, and history has rendered a . . . verdict that we solved it right. The troubles of Europe ought to be settled by Europe, and wherever our sympathies may lie, . . . we ought to remain absolutely neutral. We ought to permit them to settle their questions without our interference.

1. *In this passage, Senator Norris compares the war in Europe to the U.S. Civil War. How does he do so?*

2. *Why does Norris believe that the U.S. should stay out of World War I?*

Sharpening Your Skills

The heaviest fighting of World War I took place in France and Belgium. This map shows where that fighting occurred. Study the map carefully. Then answer the questions below.

1. In what year were German soldiers closest to Paris?

2. True or false? At the signing of the armistice, Allied armies were deep inside Germany.

3. Using a piece of string and the scale of miles, determine the following: From late 1914 to July 1918, the Western front moved (a) about 25 miles (40 kilometers), (b) about 500 miles (800 kilometers), or (c) about 1,000 miles (1,600 kilometers)?

Europe's Western Front, 1918

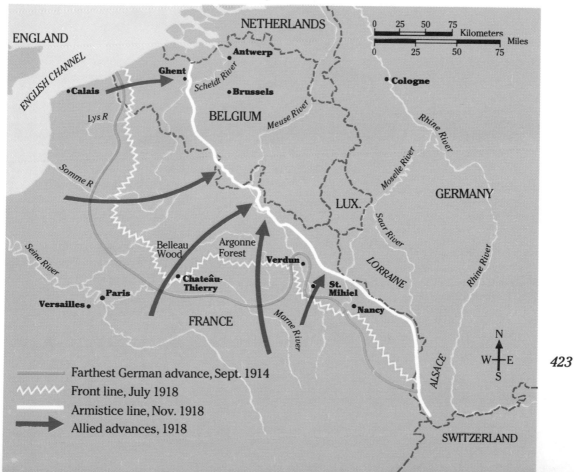

Farthest German advance, Sept. 1914
Front line, July 1918
Armistice line, Nov. 1918
Allied advances, 1918

423

3 RISING INTOLERANCE

THE LAND OF OPPORTUNITY

VICIOUS ALIENS

DEPORTATION

Looking Ahead:
A Time of Fear and Panic

One evening soon after the end of World War I, a New Yorker was strolling up Lexington Avenue. As he neared the corner of 58th Street, he suddenly saw a crowd. He paused and asked someone what was going on. "Hey, fellows, here's another of the Reds!" a sailor shouted from the crowd. With that, several men jumped the stroller. They ripped off his tie and knocked him to the ground.

The crowd could not have been more mistaken. The stroller worked as a broker on Wall Street selling stocks and bonds. He was not a Red (Communist) at all. He was one of the first people wrongly thought to be a Communist after World War I. But he would not be the last. Many others were about to be called into question in a national panic known as the "Red Scare."

The Red Scare took place in the U.S. in

Cartoon against immigration (left) was drawn during mood of intolerance after World War I.

the five years following World War I. It came soon after one of the major revolutions of this century — in Russia. Russia had suffered greatly during World War I. From 1914 to 1917, more than six million Russian soldiers had been killed or wounded. Russia itself was close to collapse. In March 1917 a revolution broke out. The Russian emperor was imprisoned. A democratic government took control.

Six months after the first revolution, another one occurred. This time radicals known as *Bolsheviks* (BOL-shuh-vicks) took power. The Bolsheviks were Communists. That is, they urged that all business and land should be owned and controlled by the government. They seized factories, mills, and business firms. They put the Russian emperor and his family to death.

The violence in Russia went still further. A bloody civil war soon broke out between the Bolsheviks (Reds)

425

and the anti-Bolsheviks (Whites). Many Russians began fleeing their country. The nation was in great confusion. U.S. newspapers printed shocking stories of what was happening there.

Cause for alarm. The stories continued long after the end of World War I. They alarmed millions of Americans. For a year-and-a-half, Americans had whipped up their anger against Germany. They had strained their energies in the war effort — and their patience as well. Now every morning it seemed there was some new horror story from Russia. If a Red revolution could break out there, some people asked, what was to prevent one here at home?

There was another reason for the question. For in 1919 the United States was in a restless mood. Millions of soldiers were leaving the Army and looking for work. Many of them remained jobless and unhappy. At the same time, some U.S. businesses were going through a downturn. And many workers were demanding higher pay. In 1919 U.S. businesses were hit with more than 3,600 strikes. To some Americans, further trouble did not seem far away.

Many people blamed the strikes on radicals. To some, "Communist" and "Red" became dirty words. Other people were just as afraid of *anarchists* (people who are against all forms of government). But the fear was not simply a fear of people with strange ideas. It was, first and foremost, a fear of revolution.

Dangers from within. Strikes were not the only cause of fear. Race riots broke out in some northern cities. The homes of several national leaders were bombed. Americans had just finished fighting a war to make the world "safe for democracy." Now some people worried that they faced another struggle to make America safe for itself.

In fact, the danger was not that serious. It was true that some radicals were active in the labor movement. Yet they were only a tiny part of the movement as a whole. Communists and anarchists could cause trouble. But the two groups did not share the same ideas or goals. Even if they had, there were not enough of them in the U.S. in 1919 to bring on a major revolution like the one in Russia. Even so, fears of a "Red menace" kept on

Nikolai Lenin led Bolshevik Revolution in Russia.

building. They led, in the end, to a series of "Red raids." In these raids, the U.S. government rounded up and jailed thousands of people accused of being anarchists or Communists. Less than half of those arrested were Communists. Many were no more radical than the stockbroker who had been beaten up in New York.

Fears of outsiders. Many other unnecessary fears troubled the United States in the 1920's. Some Americans seemed to distrust anything foreign. They feared people whose race, religion, or nationality was different from their own. This led to a dislike of immigrants because many came from southern or eastern Europe. "America must be kept American," people said. Con-

Hooded members of the Ku Klux Klan first rode in the South after the Civil War. They used their symbols of terror — burning crosses — to keep blacks "in their place." After World War I, the Klan sprang up elsewhere. Men wearing bedsheets spread terror from Oklahoma (left) to New York.

gress passed a law that closed the door to most immigration from southern or eastern Europe. This law lasted 31 years.

Sometimes it was hard to see where fear of outsiders ended and justice began. This was especially true in the most famous murder trial of the period. In 1920 two Italians, Nicola Sacco (NICK-oh-luh SACK-oh) and Bartolomeo Vanzetti (bar-toe-lo-MEE-oh van-ZET-ee), were arrested and charged with murder. Both were anarchists. Neither had a good alibi. As the case continued, some Americans became convinced that the two men were guilty. But others were just as convinced that the two were innocent victims of the Red Scare.

The first five years after World War I were, then, a time of rising intolerance. That is, these years were a period when some Americans were not willing to share their rights with others. It is not pleasant to look back on some of the events of this period. But they all happened. They are a part of our history.

Many labor unions barred foreigners. But members of the International Ladies Garment Workers Union spoke their minds in Russian, Italian, Yiddish.

Chapter 12
Red Scare

During World War I, Americans had worried that Germany might gain control of Europe. After the war ended, new fears bubbled to the surface in the U.S. The greatest of these fears concerned communism. Many Americans thought that Communists might take over the U.S. government by revolution.

A Communist revolution had overthrown the government of Russia in 1917. This happened during World War I, when the Russian people were fighting hard against the Germans. Because of this revolution, Russia pulled out of the war. It stopped helping the Allies.

The Communists urged that all business and land should be owned and controlled by the government. They said

The Red Scare took place against a backdrop of great unrest. In the summer of 1919, rioting between whites and blacks rocked Chicago (left). In the fall of 1920, a bomb exploded on Wall Street in New York City, killing at least 30 (right). Some said that Communists or anarchists were behind such trouble.

they wanted to take over the government of every country. "Workers of the world, unite! Revolt against your bosses!" they said. "Bosses" not only meant leaders of industry. It also meant heads of government around the world.

In March of 1919, Communist leaders of several nations met in Russia. They called for a Communist victory all across the globe. Later that year, the Communist Party of America was set up. Right away it began telling workers to fight for a revolution. It stirred up trouble between workers and bosses in many large industries.

Labor unrest. Just at this point, the U.S. was having more than its usual share of troubles, anyway. Many of these troubles were labor disputes. In Boston the police struck for higher wages. In Seattle there was a general strike — workers from many unions walked out all at once. A strike by the steelworkers in Pittsburgh went on for months, and bitter fighting broke out. Many Americans believed that Communists and anarchists were somehow mixed up in all the strikes that took place.

Race riots. America was also troubled by racial unrest. The black populations of several Northern cities had grown by leaps and bounds during World War I. After the war there were race riots in some of these cities. The worst riot of all took place in Chicago in the summer of 1919. It lasted six days and took 38 lives. Some people believed that Communists were behind the riots.

Bomb scares. Bombs were a third cause of the panic. One day a postmaster checked some strange packages in his post office. They were addressed to some of the biggest names in U.S. busi-ness and banking. He discovered that the packages held bombs. Some bombs were not found in time. One went off in Wall Street in New York City and killed at least 30 people. Who could have sent the bombs — or planted them? To many Americans it looked as if the bomb scare was the work of Communists or anarchists.

Even without all these troubles, there was a lot of hate in the air. Some of it had started during the war years. Then most Americans had been against anything German. But after the war, feelings turned against anyone who seemed "different." This meant not only Communists and anarchists. It also meant blacks, Jews, Asian Americans, and Roman Catholics. Before long, some people began to say that anybody they did not like was a Communist.

Late in 1919 and early in 1920, the U.S. Attorney General, A. Mitchell Palmer, led a series of raids. He wanted to hunt out the Reds. Palmer's raiders went into immigrant neighborhoods all over the country. They arrested more than 6,000 people. Many of those arrested were U.S. citizens. Very few were Communists. And even if they had been radicals, it was not against the law to be a Communist or an anarchist.

The country seemed to be going crazy with fear. Many immigrants were afraid to speak out. Other Americans began to be afraid of saying the "wrong" thing. They thought they would be suspected too. In New York, members of the Socialist party elected to the state legislature were not allowed to take their seats. The right of free speech was in danger.

The Red Scare ground on for many

429

months. One third of those arrested by Palmer's men were finally released. The government simply had no case against them. Many others were turned over to state officials and tried in state courts. In the end, the federal government took action against only a few hundred who were *aliens* (citizens of foreign countries). They were *deported* — sent back to the countries they had come from.

Slowly Americans began to come to their senses. They saw that it was unfair to suspect a person of being a Communist just because he or she was different. A few Communists did hope someday to take over the U.S. government. But in the early 1920's, Communists and other radicals had not succeeded in taking over anything at all.

It also became clear that most union leaders were not Communists. They were only trying to hold onto gains they had made during the war years. And now prices were going up. Working people needed better wages just to keep up with the cost of food and rent. So the unions were fighting for better pay.

Some Americans even spoke out against the raids themselves. During the raids and jailings, the civil rights of many people had been taken away. A number of leading lawyers took note of this. They called attention to the importance of civil rights. They believed that the raids had put free speech in danger.

By the end of 1920, the Red Scare had passed its peak. But some of the things which had helped cause it remained. There was still much prejudice against immigrants and members of minority groups. These feelings continued to cause hardships throughout the 1920's.

A Second Look. . . .

1. *What was the Red Scare? Why were people so worried about communism? Why did some lawyers believe that the Palmer raids put the right of free speech in danger?*

2. *Some Americans believed that Communists were behind several of the strikes of 1919. Why should this have caused so much fear? Were the fears sound ones? Explain. What are some labels people use today to brand those they dislike? What do these labels really mean? Is the use of such labels really fair? Why or why not?*

3. *Imagine you are a U.S. newspaper editor in 1919. Write an editorial for your paper either defending the Palmer raids or attacking them.*

During the Red Scare, one cartoonist drew up a list of famous people who might be barred from the U.S. Moral turpitude *means lacking in moral values. How many of the names can you identify?*

Chapter 13

Immigrants Not Wanted

Give me your tired, your poor,
Your huddled masses yearning to breathe
free.

These words are part of a poem written
on the Statue of Liberty. They welcome
immigrants to the United States. Emma
Lazarus, the woman who wrote this
famous poem, was a native-born American citizen. She was Jewish, so she was
also a member of a minority group. She
was proud that America welcomed most
immigrants from minority groups.

For more than a century, the U.S. had
opened its arms to people arriving here
from Europe. Millions had come here to
find freedom and a better life. They
worked in factories, mines, fields, and
forests. They helped build our cities,
railroads, dams, and canals.

For some years, Asian immigrants had
been fewer in number and less welcome.
The reason had to do with racial prejudice — and jobs. In the 1870's the
Chinese had begun to compete with
whites for jobs in California. White
workers had tried to put a stop to the
competition with a new rallying cry:
"The Chinese must go!" In 1882 Congress
had passed the Chinese Exclusion Act.
This and later laws had stopped Chinese
immigration completely. In 1908 the
U.S. State Department had reached
an agreement with the government
of Japan. This agreement all but

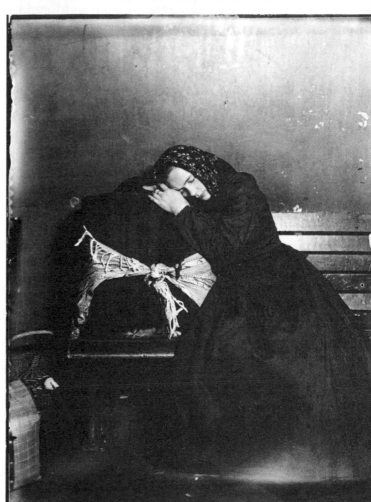

The United States did not open its doors to all
who knocked. Some immigrants had to wait for
months on Ellis Island in New York harbor before
being admitted. Photographer Lewis Hine pictured
this East European woman as she waited her turn. 431

ended Japanese immigration as well.

Still Europeans kept on coming. Between 1901 and 1914, about one million immigrants a year arrived in the United States. Some were from Britain, France, and Germany. But most came from southern and eastern Europe — mainly from Italy, Poland, and Russia.

Closing the door. After the war, immigration to the U.S. again began to grow. In 1921 Congress passed a new immigration law. For the first time, limits were placed on how many people could come to the U.S. from each country. The new law was aimed mostly against people from eastern and southern Europe. It meant to cut down on the number of Italians, Greeks, Poles, and Slavs coming to America.

What did the law say? It said that a country could send to the United States only a tiny percent of the number of its people living here in 1910. This was called the *quota system*. It worked in favor of the countries of northern Europe. This was because these countries had sent huge numbers of immigrants to the U.S. when America was young. The countries of eastern and southern

Europe were a different story. The quota system worked against them because they had sent far fewer immigrants to the U.S. before 1910.

Why did the United States decide to limit immigration in 1921?

First, many people in the U.S. did not like "foreigners." They forgot that their own ancestors had also been foreigners at one time.

Second, many Americans, whose ancestors came from northern Europe, believed that people from eastern and southern Europe were not as "good" as they were.

Third, some people feared that many of the immigrants from eastern and southern Europe might be "Reds" or anarchists or criminals.

Fourth, large numbers of American workers were afraid that immigrants would take their jobs away. Immigrants, they said, would work longer hours for less money.

Holding the line. The quota system was used for the next 44 years. A new immigration bill came before Congress in 1952. This bill would allow some 2,000 Asians to enter the U.S. each year.

This Puck *cartoon says that* all *Americans, no matter how opposed to foreigners, have immigrant roots.*

But it would do little to change the unfair quota system. President Harry Truman vetoed the bill. "The idea behind this law," he said, "is that Americans with English or Irish names are better people than Americans with Italian or Greek or Polish names. Such an idea is unworthy of our ideals." But Congress passed the bill over Truman's veto.

As the years went by, more and more people spoke out against this law. Americans began to understand that quotas based on nationality were really unfair. President John F. Kennedy asked for a fairer system. So did President Lyndon Johnson.

Finally in 1965 Congress passed a new immigration law. It did away with the quota system. The new law favors relatives of American citizens and people with skills needed here. It does not matter what country they come from. The new law allows 170,000 immigrants a year from outside the Western Hemisphere. It allows 120,000 people a year from the Western Hemisphere.

Was the U.S. growing overcrowded by 1921? The Literary Digest *saw immigration quotas as "the only way to handle" Europe's teeming masses.*

A Second Look. . . .

1. What was the quota system? When was it first put into effect? How was it unfair to people from southern and eastern Europe?

*2. Debate over immigration has continued in the U.S. in recent years. In the 1970's millions of people from other nations of the Western Hemisphere entered the U.S. illegally. Most came in search of higher-paying jobs. What do you think the U.S. should do about these immigrants? Should it crack down on those who came here illegally? If so, what problems does the U.S. face with other governments? Should the U.S. govern-*ment allow more foreigners to enter the country legally? If so, what problems might we make for our own work force? In 1977 President Jimmy Carter proposed that people who entered the U.S. illegally before 1970 should be allowed to stay on a permanent basis. Does this seem fair to you? Why or why not?*

3. Most of us have roots on another continent. How far back can you trace your ancestry? Ask your parents about your family. Make a list of as many relatives as you can. Find out where they were born, where they lived, and what kind of work they did.

433

Chapter 14

The Shoemaker and the Fish Peddler

On August 23, 1927, two men died in the electric chair. They had been found guilty of murder. But many people believed they were innocent. These people said that the two men were executed because they were foreigners and anarchists. Their death divided all America. To this day, men and women still argue the case.

This is what happened:

On April 15, 1920, five gunmen held up a shoe factory in South Braintree, Massachusetts, about 20 miles south of Boston. The paymaster and his guard were killed. The gunmen got away with nearly $16,000.

Soon after, police arrested two Italian immigrants for the crime. One was Nicola Sacco, a shoe worker. The other was Bartolomeo Vanzetti, a fish peddler. Both men were anarchists, who opposed all forms of government. At this time, the U.S. was in the middle of the Red Scare. Federal agents and police were rounding up people accused of being anarchists and Communists.

Running against the tide. Both Sacco and Vanzetti said they were against war and the use of force. They had never been in trouble before. But there were some things that people held against them: Both men had anarchist leaflets attacking the whole idea of government. Both men had dodged the draft in World War I. Both men carried guns. They said that the guns were to protect them against people who hated anarchists.

One of their guns was identified as the

Bartolomeo Vanzetti (left) and Nicola Sacco, 1920.

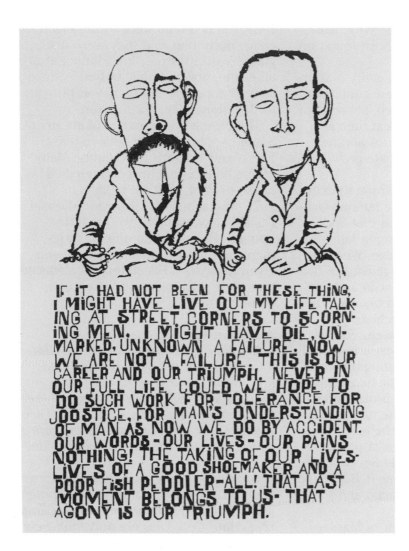

IF IT HAD NOT BEEN FOR THESE THING, I MIGHT HAVE LIVE OUT MY LIFE TALKING AT STREET CORNERS TO SCORNING MEN. I MIGHT HAVE DIE, UNMARKED, UNKNOWN, A FAILURE. NOW WE ARE NOT A FAILURE. THIS IS OUR CAREER AND OUR TRIUMPH. NEVER IN OUR FULL LIFE COULD WE HOPE TO DO SUCH WORK FOR TOLERANCE, FOR JOOSTICE, FOR MAN'S ONDERSTANDING OF MAN AS NOW WE DO BY ACCIDENT. OUR WORDS—OUR LIVES—OUR PAINS NOTHING! THE TAKING OF OUR LIVES—LIVES OF A GOOD SHOEMAKER AND A POOR FISH PEDDLER—ALL! THAT LAST MOMENT BELONGS TO US—THAT AGONY IS OUR TRIUMPH.

Debate over the trial of Sacco and Vanzetti lived on long after the trial itself had ended. To many people, the trial was a warning that in times of trouble the U.S. system of justice could easily err. In 1958 artist Ben Shahn made this print as a comment on another, later Red Scare. The drawing is based on the photo on the opposite page. The words are from the last statement of Bartolomeo Vanzetti as he went to the electric chair. Feelings about the trial run high even today. Historians still argue heatedly over it. Were Sacco and Vanzetti guilty or innocent? Were they found guilty on evidence or because Americans wanted easy answers in an uneasy, fear-ridden time?

same gun carried by the guard killed at South Braintree. The other gun was similar to the one used to kill the guard. Neither Sacco nor Vanzetti had a good alibi. Vanzetti could not remember where he had gone with his pushcart on April 15. Sacco had gone to the Italian consul in Boston. But there were times during the day that Sacco could not account for.

At the trial, jurors were given some good reasons for thinking the two men were guilty. But they were also given some good reasons for doubt. Several witnesses said they saw Sacco and Vanzetti at the scene of the murder. Other witnesses were sure Sacco and Vanzetti were not the men.

There were other questions: Five men had taken part in the holdup. Where were the other three men? Why hadn't any of the stolen money been found on either Sacco or Vanzetti?

The jury found the men guilty of murder and robbery. They were sentenced to die. After the trial ended, lawyers for the two men tried to appeal the case (take it to a higher court for another hearing). As they did, debate grew and grew.

The sentence seemed wrong to many people. Among them were famous writers and lawyers. They said that Sacco and Vanzetti had not gotten a fair trial. They claimed that the judge, Webster Thayer, was prejudiced against the two men. They thought that Sacco and Vanzetti were being punished because they were foreigners and anarchists.

Studying the evidence. For six years, lawyers fought to get a new trial for Sacco and Vanzetti. During this time, a gangster confessed to the two killings. He was part of a gang of professional robbers. When arrested he had $2,800 on him. Many policemen believed the holdup and murders were "a professional job." They said that Sacco and Vanzetti couldn't have done it. But Judge Thayer would not give Sacco and Vanzetti a new trial.

Meanwhile the governor of Massachusetts chose three important men to study the case. Two of these men were college presidents. The third was a famous lawyer. These men were to review the evidence and decide whether or not to recommend a new trial. In the end, they said a new trial was not necessary.

All over the world, people protested against the death sentence for Sacco and Vanzetti. But finally, on August 23, 1927, the two men went to the electric chair. Both men said they were not guilty. Vanzetti said, "I am innocent of all crime, not only this, but all." Sacco said, "I am never guilty, never, not yesterday, nor today, nor forever."

The case is still a matter of argument. Some people honestly believe that Sacco and Vanzetti were guilty. Many others believe that the two men died because of their political beliefs. In 1977 Massachusetts Governor Michael Dukakis gave support to this latter opinion. He issued an official statement that the two men had not been given a fair trial. His statement also said that their guilt had never been completely proved.

A Second Look. . . .

1. *Who were Nicola Sacco and Bartolomeo Vanzetti? What country had they come from? Give at least two reasons why some people believed the two men were innocent. Give at least two reasons why others thought they were guilty. What was the final outcome of the case?*

2. *Many people thought that Sacco and Vanzetti were on trial for their political beliefs and national origins, not for a real crime. Could this possibly have been true? Why or why not?*

3. *Putting a person to death for a crime is called* capital punishment. *It is as hotly debated today as it was in 1927, when Sacco and Vanzetti were executed. Using newspapers, almanacs, and other research material, find out the current status of capital punishment in your state. Under what circumstances, if any, is it used? Do you think your state law is a fair one? Why or why not?*

Looking Back: Rising Intolerance

A	B	C	D	
January 1, 1916	January 1, 1919	January 1, 1922	January 1, 1925	January 1, 1928

Putting Events in Order

Chapters 12 through 14 have described some events in the United States after World War I. Ten of these events are listed here. Your job is to match each event to the correct period shown on the timeline above. On a piece of paper, number from **1** to **10**. After each number, write the letter of the three-year period within which the event occurred.

1. Police in Boston go on strike.

2. Communists take power in Russia after a revolution.

3. Five gunmen hold up a shoe factory in South Braintree, Massachusetts, killing two people.

4. The Communist Party of America is organized.

5. A riot in Chicago takes 38 lives.

6. Communist leaders of several nations meet in Russia.

7. Nicola Sacco and Bartolomeo Vanzetti are executed.

8. Congress passes an immigration law establishing a quota system.

9. U.S. Attorney General A. Mitchell Palmer leads a series of "Red raids."

10. A general strike occurs in Seattle.

Interpreting a Source

Many Americans spoke out against deporting aliens in the early 1920's. One of them was Kansas newspaper editor William Allen White. This passage is adapted from his editorial in The Emporia *(Kansas)* Gazette *of January 8, 1920.*

The attorney general seems to be seeing red. He is rounding up every manner of radical in the country. Every man who hopes for a better world is in danger of deportation by the attorney general. The whole business is un-American. There are certain fundamental rules which should govern in the treason cases.

437

First, it should be agreed that a man should believe what he chooses.

Second, it should be agreed that when he preaches violence he is disturbing the peace and should be put in jail....

Third, he should be allowed to say what he pleases so long as he advocates[1] ... constitutional methods of procedure.[2] Just because a man does not believe this government is good, is no reason why he should be deported. Abraham Lincoln did not believe this government was all right 75 years ago. He advocated change, but he advocated constitutional means. And he had a war with those who advocated force. Ten years ago [Theodore] Roosevelt advocated great changes in our American life.... Most of the changes he advocated have been made, but they were made in the regular legal way. He preached no force. And if a man desires to preach any doctrine under the shining sun, and advocate the realization of his vision by lawful, orderly, constitutional means — let him alone. If he is Socialist [or] anarchist, ... and merely preaches his creed[3] and does not preach violence, he can do no harm. For the folly of his doctrine will be its answer.

The deportation business is going to make martyrs[4] of a lot of idiots whose cause is not worth it.

People from many parts of the world came to Ellis Island. There they waited, staring at the New York City skyline, hoping for a chance to stay.

1. *When does White believe people should be allowed to say what they please? When does he believe they should be jailed for what they say?*

2. *Why do you suppose White believes deportation will "make martyrs of a lot of idiots"? Why would they help their cause by being martyrs?*

3. *How does White use Abraham Lincoln and Theodore Roosevelt to make his point? Do you think they are good examples? Do you think an average U.S. citizen can bring about change? If so, how?*

---

[1]*To advocate* is to recommend in public.

[2]*Constitutional methods of procedure* are those legal methods given support by the U.S. Constitution. Voting is one example of such methods.

[3]A *creed* is a set of principles or beliefs on any subject.

[4]*Martyrs* are people who suffer torture or death for the sake of their principles.

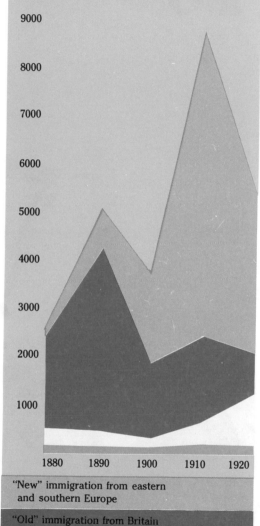

Changing Patterns of Immigration, 1880-1920

Figures show total immigration for each decade in thousands. From 1901 to 1910, for example, immigration of all groups was about 8,800,000.

9000
8000
7000
6000
5000
4000
3000
2000
1000

1880   1890   1900   1910   1920

"New" immigration from eastern and southern Europe

"Old" immigration from Britain and northern Europe

Immigration from elsewhere in the Americas

Immigration from Asia

Sharpening Your Skills

During the early 19th century, most immigrants to the United States came from northern and western Europe. Then in the 1880's thousands of people from southern and eastern Europe began arriving. Historians called the first group "old" immigrants and the second "new." Using both the graph and the pie chart, answer the questions.

1. In what decade did "old" immigration reach its high point?

2. In what decade did "new" immiation reach a peak?

3. At the beginning of which decade did "new" immigration become larger than "old" immigration?

4. Of the European immigrants, which group was larger by 1925, the "old" or the "new"?

5. What total percentage of immigrants were European by that year?

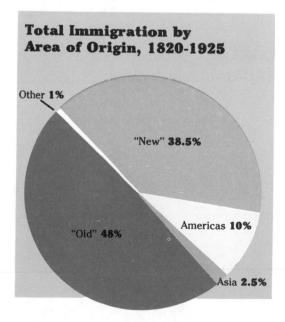

Total Immigration by Area of Origin, 1820-1925

Other **1%**

"New" **38.5%**

"Old" **48%**

Americas **10%**

Asia **2.5%**

439

4 BOOM TO BUST

Looking Ahead: A 10-Year Spree

A family sits at the dinner table. The mother and father are dressed in the formal clothes of 1920. But their teenage daughter is not. The daughter has much shorter hair than her mother does. She wears makeup and has painted her lips in a bright Cupid's bow. Her skirt is an inch or two above the knees. Her stockings are rolled down below them.

The teenager does not think of herself as unusual. She is dressed in the bold new style of most "flappers" (young women) of her age. Yet her dress sets her apart from her parents. And she talks in phrases they find hard to understand.

This sort of scene took place again and again in the 1920's. In one home after another, earlier ideas of dress and speech had been swept away by changing times. There was a new accent on youth and a new style to go with it. The nation seemed caught in a whirlwind of social change.

World War I was over. Woodrow Wilson's dream of bringing the U.S. into the League of Nations was dead. Now the idea of struggling for a better world seemed too much for many Americans. They wanted to forget the cares of the past and just have fun.

During the 1920's they went on a spree. They danced new fast dances — the Charleston and the Black Bottom. They set aside classical music and listened to jazz. People sat on flagpoles. They swallowed live goldfish. They held contests to see who could dance the longest. One craze seemed to follow another in this "time of wonderful nonsense."

Flappers were in fashion, and the Charleston was the rage during the "Roaring Twenties." Writer F. Scott Fitzgerald called the period "The Jazz Age." Cartoon at left appeared on a magazine cover in 1926. It was drawn by John Held, Jr., a leading cartoonist of the times.

441

Flappers shown above came from Harlem, a section of New York City. To older people in the 1920's, the flappers' bobbed hair (below) and short skirts suggested youth in revolt.

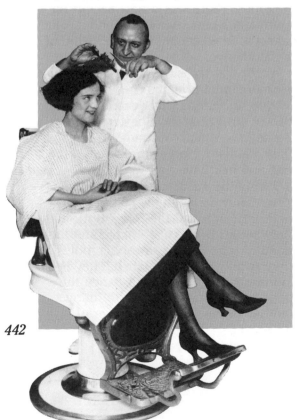

The age of the horse-and-buggy had nearly ended. Trucks had begun replacing horse-drawn wagons during World War I. After the war, autos started rolling out of production plants in greater and greater numbers. The most popular auto of the period was Henry Ford's Model T. Young people in high schools bought Model T's secondhand. Then they painted them bright colors and wrote slogans on them such as "Oh you kid!," "Joe sent me," and "23 Skiddoo."

Autos redrew the map of America. New highways sprang up. So did billboards, filling stations, and garages. A trip that once took an hour by horse-and-buggy now took only a few minutes by car. Farm people who lived a few miles from town could go there for an evening and be home in time for bed. Young people who once dated in their homes could now go out on dates in cars. Parents wondered what the younger generation was up to.

The age that gave us inexpensive autos also gave us many other social changes. Here are some of them:

Prohibition. The 18th Amendment to the U.S. Constitution went into effect in January 1920. It banned the sale of liquor in the United States. It also prohibited Americans from manufacturing or transporting liquor. The amendment had been passed because many people thought of drinking as an evil. But Prohibition, as the "dry" spell was called, did not put a stop to drinking.

"Speakeasies" replaced neighborhood taverns. Speakeasies were illegal bars where liquor was served. They became very popular places. Gangsters often took control of them, and then went on to control the liquor trade itself.

People got liquor from dealers called *bootleggers*. Much of this liquor was made in illegal stills or was smuggled in from Canada or Cuba. Every day millions of people broke the law by drinking such liquor in speakeasies. The more they broke the law, the less respect they had for it.

Women's suffrage. The 19th Amendment took effect the same year as the 18th. The 19th gave all women 21 years old and over the vote. Leaders of the women's movement had been fighting for suffrage (voting rights) for many years. Now they were overjoyed.

In the next 10 years, women enjoyed more freedom than they had ever known. Some of them threw out the petticoats and corsets that had been standard dress for years. Others began going to beauty parlors, another rage of the 1920's. Flappers went there to have their hair "bobbed" (cut short).

Growth of communications. Some of the greatest changes of the 1920's took place in communications. By the middle of the decade, many U.S. homes had radios. Later the first "talkies" — motion pictures with sound — came to local theaters. Advertising became bolder. Magazines such as the *Saturday Evening Post* became very popular. And in 1923 a young man by the name of Henry Luce started a magazine called *Time*. *Time* was the first weekly magazine given over mainly to reporting the news. It led to the rise of other magazines such as *Newsweek* and *Look*.

The 1920's was a time of great heroes. There were aviators such as Charles A. Lindbergh and explorers such as Admiral Richard E. Byrd. In sports there were heroes such as Babe Ruth, swimmer Gertrude Ederle, and boxer Jack Dempsey. People "flipped" over movie stars such as Rudolph Valentino, Greta Garbo, and Douglas Fairbanks. Valentino died in 1926 at the age of 31. Thousands screamed, fainted, and cried at his funeral.

The 1920's was also a great time for big business. Many people made money by buying and selling stocks (shares of ownership) in the nation's large businesses. Some government officials made money less honestly. When one "deal" was discovered it led to one of the worst scandals in U.S. history.

In some ways, the 1920's looked like a good time for black Americans. In New York City's Harlem and Chicago's South Side, many black writers, artists, singers, and poets became famous. Some people said that the "race problem" would be over in a few years. But it turned out these people were wrong.

The end of the "Roaring Twenties" came in October 1929. That month the price of stocks came crashing down, and the nation went from boom to bust. Thousands of wealthy people were "wiped out." Hard times set in. Many people looked back on the 1920's as a childish, stupid time. But many others said it was a great time to be alive.

"Shipwreck" Kelly sat on a flagpole for 23 days and seven hours — a record-breaking stunt!

Chapter 15

Winning Votes for Women

Washington, D.C., was swarming with women from many parts of the nation. They had come to the Capitol Building for their "big day." So had several Congressmen who had taken some risks in getting there. One arrived with a broken arm. Another staggered in straight from a hospital bed. A third was brought in on a stretcher.

It was January 10, 1918, and the hubbub was over women's suffrage. The U.S. House of Representatives was deciding whether or not to grant all women 21 and over the vote. Women in several states already had voting rights. But laws differed from state to state. Now many women wanted to amend the U.S. Constitution to allow for women's suffrage all across the nation.

The vote on women's suffrage had been a long time coming. Women had first demanded the vote in the years before the Civil War. These demands had grown sharper late in the 19th century. Some suffragists, such as Susan B. Anthony, became nationally known.

Yet many Americans still balked at the idea of women's suffrage. Some political leaders were against it, for they feared that their parties might lose power. Most saloon-keepers were against it, for they thought women would try to pass laws against liquor. And a great many people — women as well as men — were against it simply because it meant change.

Wyoming's stand. The first crack in the solid front against women's suffrage came from the West. In 1889 Wyoming Territory applied for statehood. Women had voted in Wyoming for 20 years. Congress debated Wyoming's application. Wyoming's delegate wired home that the territory might have to give up women's suffrage in order to enter the Union. Wyoming's lawmakers wired back: "We will remain out of the Union a hundred years rather than come in without the women." Wyoming entered in 1890 — with the women.

One by one other states began to yield. Women's suffrage picked up added support during the progressive years. A new generation of suffragists with new ideas joined the movement. They staged parades, picketed the White

Cartoon says that winning votes for women was only part of a larger movement for full equality.

IN CONGRESS. JULY 4, 1776.

The unanimous Declaration of the thirteen united States of America.

We hold these truths to be self-evident that all men **and women** are created equal,

PAUL STAHR

Women's Suffrage Before 1920

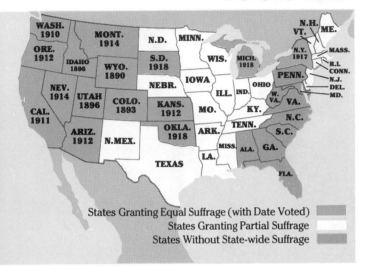

WASH. 1910
ORE. 1912
IDAHO 1896
NEV. 1914
CAL. 1911
ARIZ. 1912
MONT. 1914
WYO. 1890
UTAH 1896
N.MEX.
N.D.
S.D. 1918
NEBR.
COLO. 1893
KANS. 1912
OKLA. 1918
TEXAS
MINN.
IOWA
MO.
ARK.
LA.
WIS.
ILL.
IND.
KY.
TENN.
MISS.
ALA.
MICH. 1918
OHIO
W. VA.
VA.
N.C.
S.C.
GA.
FLA.
N.H.
VT.
ME.
N.Y. 1917
MASS.
R.I.
CONN.
N.J.
DEL.
MD.
PENN.

States Granting Equal Suffrage (with Date Voted)
States Granting Partial Suffrage
States Without State-wide Suffrage

House, went to prison, and held hunger strikes.

Their first success on a national level came on January 10, 1918. The House passed the 19th Amendment, and the women who looked on were overjoyed. But the Senate rejected the amendment a few months later. Suffragists noted which Senators voted against it. The women worked against their re-election. In 1919 a newly elected Congress considered the matter again. This time, the amendment passed both houses.

Now the amendment had to be ratified (approved) by three fourths of the states. Thirty-five states ratified it right away. Then the issue came to a vote in Tennessee. If Tennessee approved the amendment, it would become law.

Representatives from both sides tried to persuade Tennessee lawmakers to vote their way. By the day the vote was scheduled, the suffragists lacked two

446

votes to win. They had not counted on support from the youngest member of the Tennessee legislature. He was a man named Harry Burn.

Mother's advice. Burn knew that political leaders in his area opposed the amendment. He said he would vote in favor of it only if his vote was needed to get the amendment passed. But Harrry Burn's mother was a strong suffragist. "I have been watching to see how you stood, but have noticed nothing yet," she wrote her son. "Don't forget to ... [vote for] ratification."

When the roll of names was called, Harry Burn followed his mother's advice. "Yes," he said, tying the vote. For a few moments the issue stood in doubt. Then another lawmaker, Banks Turner, changed his stand. He also voted in favor of suffrage. Tennessee became the 36th state to ratify the amendment.

The 19th Amendment became part of the U.S. Constitution on August 26, 1920. The right to vote had been won by 26 million women then of voting age. Many of them cast their first votes in a Presidential election the next November.

In 1916 the Women's Congressional Union for Equal Suffrage stormed the U.S. Capitol.

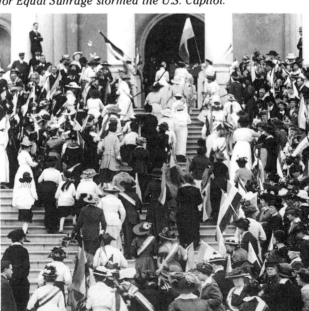

Most women favored the winning candidate, Republican Warren G. Harding of Ohio.

Fears of great changes at the polls soon proved groundless. In the next few years, it became clear that women tended to vote the same way as men. Still, the 19th Amendment had made women the equals of men at the polls. And it had prompted many women to take a more active role in the world at large.

A Second Look. . . .

1. *Name three reasons why some people opposed women's suffrage. In what ways did women show their support for suffrage during the progressive years? When did the 19th Amendment become law?*

2. *The 19th Amendment won voting rights for women. But it did not win them rights of any other kind. In recent years women have protested that they still are not treated equally with men. Can you think of any ways in which inequality exists? Should such inequality be ended? How do you think you would answer this question if you were a member of the opposite sex?*

3. *Women made great contributions to U.S. history in the first 40 years of this century. Choose one of the following women: Marian Anderson, Pearl Buck, Amelia Earhart, Frances Perkins, or Margaret Sanger. Using library sources, find out all you can about this woman's life. Then write a one-page report discussing her main achievements.*

Life, *a humor magazine of the 1920's, didn't have much sympathy for women's suffrage. Some men really did think their lives would be ruined if women got the vote. In the end, though, the American male survived.*

Chapter 16

The Wets and the Drys

On January 16, 1920, the United States went "dry." The making, selling, or transporting of liquor was prohibited by law. The new law, the 18th Amendment, was called *Prohibition*.

"A splendid experiment," some people said. Others groaned.

Prohibition lasted 14 years. People argued about it all during that time. Those in favor of Prohibition were called "Drys." Those against it were called "Wets."

Prohibition probably did cut down on drinking and drunkenness. But it did not succeed in ending all use of liquor in the United States. A joke of those times was, "Prohibition is a darn sight better than no liquor at all." True, the saloons were gone. But a new kind of bar called a speakeasy soon took their place.

Sometimes these illegal bars were found in dark alleys or on side streets.

Sometimes they were out in the country. But they were not very secret. If you wanted to know where a speakeasy was, all you had to do was ask around.

Sometimes speakeasies were raided by the police. Then people were often arrested. Or owners might pay off the raiders to let their places stay open. Payoffs and bribes made Prohibition hard to enforce. A *bribe* is a gift made or promised to persuade someone to act dishonestly. Payoffs and bribes also raised the costs of running speakeasies. This made speakeasies expensive places to go to for a drink.

Speakeasy customers were mostly people with lots of money. Women drank too, which was almost unheard of in saloon days. But in the speakeasy, drinking was taken as a sign of women's "freedom." Working men and the poor

Prohibition was the result of a long battle against the bottle. Saloons closed, but speakeasies opened.

CLOSE THE SALOONS

complained about speakeasies — they could no longer get a cheap drink or a nickel beer.

New sources. Some of the liquor was homemade. "Bathtub gin" wasn't just a joke. Illegal stills — small "factories" for making liquor — sprang up in basements, backyards, and barns. Some of the "bootleg" (illegal) drinks put up in these stills were very harmful. They could poison or kill people who drank too much.

Smugglers, called *rumrunners,* sneaked liquor into the country from Canada and the West Indies. They charged a high price for the risks they took. Some big-time smugglers made millions of dollars.

Soon the liquor business came under the control of gangsters and the "rackets." They began to carve out "territories" where only one gang sold all the liquor. Gangsters also owned most of the speakeasies. If one gang got in another's way, there would be trouble. The gangsters settled their troubles with submachine guns and bombs. Gang wars broke out in some cities. In Chicago more than 500 gang murders took place in the 1920's.

About half a million people were arrested for breaking the Prohibition laws during the 1920's. But most of these were common citizens caught in speakeasy raids, or small-time still operators. Big-time gangsters and criminal leaders were hardly ever touched, except by other gangsters.

New controversy. The Wets pointed out all these things and said that Prohibition should be ended. "This is a law that is good for bootleggers [sellers of illegal liquor]," they said.

Speakeasy owners operated outside the law. Some screened customers by using secret passwords.

"We can't enforce a law that nobody wants."

The Drys said the law *could* be enforced. And they believed it *should* be enforced more strongly. If the law cracked down, they said, rumrunners wouldn't risk getting caught. The stills would go out of business. Then there would be no liquor for the gangsters to get mixed up in. The speakeasies would close. It was as simple as that, or so the Drys believed.

But the Drys were slowly losing ground. People were getting more and more disgusted with the crime that Prohibition encouraged.

In the election of 1932, the Democrats promised to support repeal of the Pro-   *449*

hibition amendment. They said they hoped to make the country "wet" again. One reason to get rid of Prohibition was that the country was in a Depression that began in 1929. Almost 13 million workers were out of jobs. People needed jobs. The liquor industry would provide work for some, the Democrats said. The government would put a tax on liquor. This would provide money for assisting people without jobs. These arguments helped the Democrats win the election.

In February 1933 Congress passed the 21st Amendment. It took a new amendment to repeal the old one. This new amendment gave authority for controlling the sale of liquor back to the states. By December, three fourths of the states had ratified (approved) the new

"Drys" campaigned for Prohibition with buttons such as the one at right. After U.S. went "dry," some people made their own "booze" in home stills (above); others drank in speakeasies (shown below after police raid).

VOTE "DRY" FOR "MY" SAKE

amendment. Some local areas would remain "dry" for many years. But on a national basis Prohibition was dead.

A Second Look. . . .

1. *What was Prohibition? How did it help to encourage the growth of the rackets? How did speakeasies play a part in Prohibition? Why were they illegal? Why were they expensive places to go for a night out?*

2. *Drys considered Prohibition a "splendid experiment." Wets thought it encouraged disrespect for the law. How would you explain these different points of view? Which view is closer to your own? Why? What do you think would happen if Prohibition laws were passed today? Would people break these laws as often now as they did in the 1920's? What reasons can you give for answering as you do?*

3. *Since the end of Prohibition, many states have changed their laws on the sale of liquor. Today liquor can be bought and sold in most U.S. communities. But some communities ban the sale of liquor in restaurants. Others control the sale of liquor by putting a heavy tax on it. Using sources in your school or local library, try to find out state and local regulations governing the sale of liquor in your area. If necessary, write to your state liquor authority for information. Then report your findings to the class.*

Prohibition took a drubbing in many newspapers. Cartoon at top right appeared amid the Great Depression and was titled "No Slump Here." It showed a bootlegger reading a tape used to record stock prices. Sum on tape is amount bootleggers took in each year. Cartoon at right pictured "Mr. Prohibition" as a mean-spirited man.

451

Chapter 17

The Tin Lizzie

It shook, rattled, banged, and groaned. It wasn't pretty, either. It looked like a black box sitting on high, skinny wheels. But it could do almost anything, and go almost anywhere. And it was cheap.

What was it? It was the Model-T car — better known as the Tin Lizzie. It was the king of the road for nearly 20 years. And it changed the American way of life forever.

The man who had the idea for the Tin Lizzie was a Detroit mechanic named Henry Ford. Ford had been born on a farm near Dearborn, Michigan, in 1863. As a boy, Ford loved big steam engines. When he was 12, he saw one that really

Henry Ford didn't invent the horseless carriage. But he began mass-producing it with the Model T.

excited him. It was on wheels, but it wasn't pulled by horses. It had a chain connecting the engine to the rear wheels. It could go about 10 miles an hour under its own power. Ford saw that it was heavy and clumsy, but the steam engine gave him a great idea. It started him on his dream of building a better engine. It prompted him to build a "horseless" carriage — an auto that would run on gasoline.

At 16, Ford quit the farm and left school. He got a job as a mechanic in Detroit for $2.50 a week. He could fix almost anything within 30 minutes. At night he made money fixing watches. There wasn't a watch he couldn't repair.

Ford's horseless carriage.
By this time, many inventors and mechanics were working on horseless carriages. Ford was one of them. He worked at home at night. At first he tried to make a better steam engine to use in an auto. But in December 1893 he began working on a gasoline engine. When he finished it, the little engine made a popping noise — and ran. Now Ford was ready to put an engine into a car.

The car took more than two years to build. Friends helped him. The engine he finally used had two cylinders. It had about three horsepower. The car weighed only 500 pounds (225 kilograms). At last, on June 4, 1896, it was ready for a trial run. Ford and his friends pushed the car into the street. One friend rode ahead on a bicycle to warn all horses and buggies away. That morning Ford made only a short run. But the car worked, and many people were soon talking about it. It was a "sign of the future," some said.

Ford went on to make other cars, some of them for racing. In 1903 he formed his own company, the Ford Motor Company. Some auto-makers believed that cars would always be luxury items. But Ford wanted to make a car that would be simple, tough, and cheap. He wanted everyone to be able to buy a car. So Ford came up with the Model T. The first ones came out in 1908. The Model T remained the company's only model until 1927.

Ford's Model T. It was quite a car. You had to crank it to start it; there was no starter to turn the engine over. Once it got going, it jittered and clanked. But it usually ran — and ran and ran. The Tin Lizzie was light. It was only 100 inches (254 centimeters) long and could turn within a 12-foot (360-centimeter) circle. It was high enough off the ground to clear ruts, large stones, and even tree stumps. Because it was so light, it could pull itself out of sand and mud. (And that was important in those days of dirt roads.) The car was strong and rarely tired. A farmer could use his Model-T engine to pump water, saw wood, and run machinery.

Hardly anything could go wrong with it. If something did, you could fix it with a few simple tools. New parts were cheap. A new fender cost $2.50. A new muffler was $1.25. You could order a Model T part by part and put it together yourself. Many people did.

"A sudden plunge, yet an undamaged Ford," reads the caption on this photo, probably taken for use in an ad. Well, maybe. But driving was certainly an adventure when many roads were cart tracks.

The Model T was plain. It came in one color — black — and had few gadgets. But stores sold hundreds of gadgets you could put on it yourself.

People liked to make jokes about the Tin Lizzie. There was a story about an old lady who saved all her old tomato cans. She sent them to the Ford factory. Soon she got a letter from the factory. It said, "Your shipment arrived. We are making it up today and will send you one new Model T. We are also returning eight cans left over." Henry Ford loved such jokes. They helped advertise his car.

Ford's assembly line. The Model T was gobbled up by the public. Eleven thousand Model T's were sold in

453

As more and more autos rolled off assembly lines, Americans built more and more highways to make driving easier. Above, artist Winsor McCay predicts these highways will unite all regions of the U.S.

1908. They cost $850 each. Other cars cost almost three times more. Then Ford put the assembly-line system of making cars into use. Each car was put together as it moved along an overhead chain. Each worker did one special job on the car. This made it possible to turn out cars much faster and cheaper. In 1924 Ford turned out 1.6 million Model T's. This was more than half the new cars on the road. And you could buy one for less than $300!

On June 4, 1924, the 10 millionth Model T rolled off the assembly line. There were big celebrations. The car was driven from New York to San Francisco. Brass bands welcomed the car in almost every town. And more than five million Model T's would still be made.

What finally happened to the Model T? It went out of style. The Model-T body style never changed. By 1926 the flashy-looking Chevrolet outsold it. Then Ford shut down his factories. Next year he came out with a new car — the fancier Model A.

But the Model T had done its job. Partly because of it, new concrete roads were built everywhere in the U.S. It became easier for farmers to visit towns and cities. City people were able to drive to the country. The Model T had put America on wheels.

A Second Look. . . .

1. *What is an assembly line? How did the assembly line allow Henry Ford to reduce the price of the Model T by more than half?*

2. *For many years the auto has been considered a force for progress in America. Only lately has it come under serious attack. Critics believe that it burns too much precious gas. They also say it pollutes the air. Defenders of the auto point out that it has given Americans freedom. That is, autos allow us to come and go wherever and whenever we like. How important do you think such freedom is to us? Do you believe it outweighs the drawbacks of the auto? How do you think you would answer this question if you were a Detroit automaker? A woman lawyer who gets to and from her work by car? An oil driller? A housewife interested in ecology? The President of the United States?*

3. *This chapter points out a few ways in which the auto has changed American life. It isn't hard to think of others. Make a list of five changes the auto has brought to the United States.*

Chapter 18

America's New Toy

In 1922 Americans went mad over a wonderful new toy. It was called *radio,* and it seemed as though everyone wanted to buy a set. The trouble was there weren't enough to go around. People visited the homes of friends lucky enough to have radios. To hear these radios, they had to use earphones. People took turns listening. They were amazed. Imagine hearing voices and music that came from the air!

How did it all begin? An Italian inventor, Guglielmo Marconi (gool-YELL-mo mar-COE-nee) made the first radio in 1895. But Marconi's radio could only send Morse-code messages. It could not send voices or music. On the radio the code is made up of many dots that stand for letters. It sounds very much like static.

Five years later, the first human voice was sent by radio. Soon there were thousands of amateur radio operators. They were called "hams." They talked to each other by radio.

Disc jockey. In 1920 Dr. Frank Conrad set up an amateur radio station. He operated it above his garage in Pittsburgh, Pennsylvania. Soon Dr. Conrad got a pleasant surprise. Many nearby "hams" were picking up his broadcasts. After a while, Dr. Conrad got tired of talking to these "hams." So he began playing records for them to give himself a rest. More and more people began listening to his broadcasts. They asked for

Using "hi ho" as his trademark, Rudy Vallee sang his way to stardom in early radio. Here he stands before a microphone (left) with his band and another famous "voice," announcer Graham McNamee.

baseball and football scores too. Before long, a Pittsburgh store advertised radio sets that could pick up Dr. Conrad's broadcasts.

Dr. Conrad worked for the Westinghouse Company. The company thought that radio could mushroom into a big thing. It decided to build a station that would make regular radio broadcasts — as a business. The station, which was a little box-shaped room, was built on the roof of the Westinghouse factory in East Pittsburgh. Its call letters were KDKA.

On the night of November 2, 1920, KDKA made the first regular radio broadcast in America. It broadcast the results of the election for President of the United States held that day. It announced that Warren G. Harding was the winner. About 500 people heard the broadcast. They were excited about hearing the news "from the sky." Major stories were printed about the broadcast in the newspapers. Before long almost everyone *had* to have a radio.

"Live" music. KDKA began broadcasting music by a "live" band. The band played from a tent set up on the roof. KDKA also broadcast church services and speeches. The next summer another station was set up. It broadcast an important boxing match between Jack Dempsey and Georges Carpentier (CAR-pen-tyay) of France.

The fight took place in Jersey City, New Jersey, on July 2, 1921. During the fight, the radio transmitter (sender) got hot and began to smoke. At the end of the fight, the transmitter melted completely. But 200,000 people heard the fight. Radio was a success. Soon stations began springing up in many parts of the U.S.

In 1922 Ed Wynn, a famous comedian, was about to broadcast from a studio. But Wynn couldn't work without an audience. The announcer rounded up electricians, scrubwomen, and telephone operators. They became the first studio audience. Soon they were laughing at

Radio made great changes in the everyday lives of most Americans. Now a farm couple could listen to the big city without stirring from their chairs (below). Millions heard the same programs at the same time.

456

Wynn's jokes. And Wynn was able to go on with the show.

Within a few years, radio became a big business. Business people formed companies called *networks* to broadcast shows coast-to-coast. Everyone listened to the news reports, popular singers, and comedy shows that were on every week. And everyone in the country heard the same news and entertainment at just about the same time.

Radio was part of the new *mass media* that became more highly developed in the twenties. The mass media are means of public communications — newspapers, magazines, radio, and TV. The mass media do more than entertain us. They inform us and shape our view of the world.

A Second Look. . . .

1. *Who invented radio? Could the first radios send voices or music? Where was the first radio station located? What sort of program did it produce?*

2. *Today people are more influenced by TV than radio. But the effect is much the same. In what ways do you think radio and TV influence you? Do you watch TV newscasts regularly? If so, how do they affect your views? Is this influence a good one? Why or why not?*

3. *As a research project in oral history, talk to people who remember the early days of radio. Find out what kinds of programs were presented and how radio of those days differed from radio today. How often did people listen to the radio? Where did they listen? What sorts of programs were most popular? Be sure to ask people in what ways radio was important in their lives. Then write a report on your findings.*

As radio networks increased regular broadcasts, a new type of entertainer appeared — the radio celebrity. And along with celebrities came fan magazines to make stars even better-known. Who was behind that golden voice? Radio Stars magazine would tell all. Cover drawing for the November 1932 issue was of comic Ed Wynn.

457

Chapter 19

Harlem Renaissance

Oh, to be in Harlem again after two years away. The deep-dyed color, the thickness, the closeness of it. The noises of Harlem, the sugared laughter. The honey-talk on its streets. And all night long, ragtime and "blues" playing somewhere . . . singing somewhere, dancing somewhere! . . .

This is what Claude McKay wrote in his book *Home to Harlem*. McKay's story is about Harlem in New York City. Harlem was the capital of black America during the early 1920's. The twenties were a "roaring" time, and Harlem was a "with-it" place.

Ragtime and blues were the musical styles of the twenties. They had started out as Dixieland in New Orleans. Then they came north and found a second home in Chicago during World War I.

From Chicago the blues went to Harlem. There they found a third home. Bessie Smith gained fame singing them. King Oliver, Louis Armstrong, Duke Ellington, and others made their names playing the blues. Many great musicians flocked to Harlem. Soon the whole nation was listening to this new sound. It combined sounds of Africa and America and of city and farm into a sweet blue

Singers such as Bessie Smith (left) created the jazz that made Harlem clubs famous in the 1920's. But blacks were often refused a chance to listen.

music that told stories of love and deep sadness.

Black literature. But there was more going on in Harlem than the sweet blue notes played and sung by the great artists of jazz. To Harlem came black writers from all over the country. They wrote novels. They wrote short stories and autobiographies (stories of their own lives). They wrote plays too. But most of all, they wrote poetry. Poems and more poems. They poured themselves into their work.

At first the work of some black writers was printed in a magazine called *The Crisis*. Then book publishers took notice. The publishers thought these writers were important. They had something to say.

Soon writers such as Langston Hughes, James Weldon Johnson, Claude McKay, and Countee Cullen became famous. Their success brought more black writers to Harlem. Never before and not again till the 1960's was so much written by black Americans or about them.

What did they write about? Themselves, mostly. They were telling their readers what it meant to be black. Some of their stories and poems were full of joy and hope. Some were very funny. Others were filled with sadness and anger. They wrote stories about the unfair treatment of black people. They pro-

459

tested against poverty. Sometimes they blasted whites.

There was a lot of pride and soul in these works. Pride in being black.

While all this was going on uptown in Harlem, changes were taking place in white New York. Black people were appearing on the stage in important roles. There were all-black plays and musicals.

Black theater. Black actors were cheered and applauded for their work on the stage. Among them was Paul Robeson, a former All-America football player. He won fame for his starring performance in *Othello,* a play by William Shakespeare. He was also a concert singer.

Black writing. Black music. Black acting. Black entertainers. Some called this

Actor-singer Paul Robeson (shown, top left, in Othello) was barred from many U.S. stages because he was black. Poet Langston Hughes (left) wrote about people scarred by such discrimination. Both men rode to fame in a rebirth of black culture that was centered in Harlem (below) in the 1920's.

time the *Harlem Renaissance,* although some of it took place outside Harlem. Renaissance is a French word that means "rebirth." It usually refers to a time in history when Europe had a great rebirth of writing and art.

The Harlem Renaissance was also a wild time. It was part of an age, the 1920's. Many people remember Harlem and the South Side of Chicago for the singers and the nightclubs and good times in the speakeasies.

But it wasn't all fun. Only a few black people read the poems, stories, and plays of the black writers and poets. Most could not afford to buy books. Some Harlem nightclubs were Jim Crow spots, for whites only. Blacks could play their jazz there. But they couldn't sit at the tables to hear it. They could act on the stage. But sometimes they couldn't get in to see the play.

That was one reason for the sadness and anger of black writers. They were "telling it like it was."

A Second Look. . . .

1. *What was the Harlem Renaissance? Where did it take place? Who were some of the famous people in it?*

2. *The Harlem Renaissance was a special time in U.S. history. Why do you suppose it took place when and where it* did? *Why did black artists sometimes perform for whites only? Why was this a cause of sadness and anger among many blacks? Would such a situation have made you angry if you had been in their place? Why or why not?*

3. *The Harlem Renaissance was black people writing, singing, and playing music about their lives. Their books and articles and phonograph records are the best documents of the era. Your class might want to organize a Harlem Renaissance Day. You and your classmates could read passages from Langston Hughes or Claude McKay, or listen to the music of Bessie Smith, Duke Ellington, and Louis Armstrong.*

Louis Armstrong and his trumpet in mid-1920's.

Chapter 20

Oil Scandal

In 1923 the Republican party (sometimes called the GOP for "Grand Old Party") was stunned by news of a Wyoming "teapot" in a tempest.

In the twenties Americans talked a lot about Tin Lizzies. They also talked about an issue with an even more unusual name. The name was that of a rock formation about 50 miles (80 kilometers) north of Casper, Wyoming. Over many centuries, the wind had pushed the rock into a shape that resembled a teapot. Beneath the "teapot" was a valuable "dome" of oil. So the rock was known as *Teapot Dome.*

Teapot Dome was more than just an oil field. It was the name used to describe one of the worst scandals in American history. The scandal shook the country to its roots. And in the end it stained an era of American politics.

How did the scandal come about?

In 1920 Warren G. Harding was elected President of the United States. Harding was an Ohio Republican. He had served as U.S. Senator from his state. He was neither a brilliant thinker nor a great man of action. But he was an honest man. He might have gone down in history as a better President had he not made several mistakes.

Most of his mistakes were in choosing men to fill top government jobs. Some of his choices were both able and honest. But Harding also put some of his political friends in important posts. One of these men was Albert B. Fall. Fall had been a U.S. Senator from New Mexico. Fall wore Western clothes and had a

large mustache. He looked like a movie sheriff. Harding made him Secretary of the Interior in his Cabinet.

In this job, Fall soon took charge of government oil fields. The government had owned several fields since 1910. They were set aside to supply the Navy with oil in case of war. One of the fields was Teapot Dome. Another was Elk Hills in California.

Fall's leases. In 1922 Fall made a secret deal with two rich oilmen. He gave them the right — called a *lease* — to pump oil out of the fields and sell it. Elk Hills was leased to Edward L. Doheny. Teapot Dome was leased to Harry Sinclair. Why were the deals so secret? Partly because U.S. officials did not want other nations to know what was being done in the nation's defense.

There was no law against leasing these fields to oil companies. But the deals made by Fall were "steals." Under them, Doheny and Sinclair could have made 100 million dollars each. And the government would have gotten very little in return. Fall was bribed (given money) to make these deals.

News of the deals soon leaked out. In 1923 a Senate committee began looking into them. Senator Thomas J. Walsh, Democrat of Montana, was put in charge of the committee. One day a newsman from New Mexico came to Walsh's committee. He said that in 1920 Fall was practically "broke." He had been unable to pay the taxes on his cattle ranch for eight years. Yet now he was buying land worth $124,000. And he was paying off all his debts — often with brand new $100 bills.

Walsh's questions. Senator Walsh wanted to know where this money was coming from. Doheny rushed to Washington to save Fall's neck. He said that he had "loaned" Fall $100,000 in cash. He had sent the money to him in a little black bag. Wasn't this a lot of money to carry around in a bag? Walsh wanted to know. "Not to me," said Doheny. "No more than $25 or $50 to the ordinary man."

Then Walsh began looking into Fall's deal with Harry Sinclair. Sinclair's secretary had said that he had turned over $68,000 to the manager of Fall's ranch. But Walsh kept digging. It was finally proved that Sinclair had given Fall more than $300,000!

All three men — Fall, Doheny, and Sinclair — were put on trial for bribery. The two millionaire oilmen were found not guilty. But Fall was found guilty, fined $100,000, and sent to prison for a year. He was the first member of the U.S. Cabinet ever to go to jail. Sinclair later went to jail for refusing to answer questions on the stand. He got a nine-month sentence. In addition, Sinclair had to re-

turn 12 million dollars to the government. Doheny had to return almost 35 million dollars.

Teapot Dome was not the only scandal of the Harding years. One high official was caught stealing public money and resigned. Another was accused of taking money in return for pardoning prisoners. As Harding got word of such deals, he grew gloomier and gloomier. "I can take care of my enemies all right," he told newspaper editor William Allen White. "But my . . . friends . . . keep me walking the floor nights."

In the summer of 1923, Harding traveled to the West to make some speeches. He had been having trouble breathing for several months. In San Francisco he became ill and died. His Vice-President, Calvin Coolidge of Massachusetts, succeeded him in office. Some of Harding's followers believed that he had died of a broken heart.

A Second Look. . . .

1. *What was Teapot Dome? How did it become linked to scandal in the U.S. government? Who were the people involved in this scandal? What was wrong about what they did?*

2. *Name one reason why the Teapot Dome leases were kept secret. Does it seem like an honest reason to you? Are there ever valid reasons for secrecy in government? If so, what are they?*

3. *You are the judge sentencing Albert Fall for his misdeeds in the Teapot Dome scandal. For the first time in American history, a U.S. Cabinet officer is going to jail. Write a brief speech, expressing the meaning of this fact. Be sure to talk of the importance of trust in government.*

463

Chapter 21

The Babe

He was the greatest home-run hitter of his time. He was called "the Babe," or "the Bambino." His real name was George Herman Ruth.

The Babe didn't *look* like a ballplayer. The Babe was fat. And he was top heavy — he had skinny legs. One sportswriter said he had a belly like Santa Claus. Yet he could hit the ball a mile — and the fans loved him for it. The Babe didn't like to bunt or get a base on balls. He swung for the fences. When he missed, his body twisted up like a pretzel. Each time the Babe came to bat, the fans roared. They expected him to hit a home run.

In 1927 Ruth set the record for home runs in a 154-game season. He did it on the next-to-last day of the season. The date was September 30. The place was Yankee Stadium in New York City. The pitcher for the Washington Senators was Tom Zachary.

The Babe had already hit 59 home runs, tying his old record, set in 1921. Now Babe waited for the pitch, swinging his bat a little. Zachary's pitch came in. The Babe swung. *Crack!* It was the special sound Babe Ruth made when he connected. The ball sailed far over the right-field fence. Seconds later the Babe came trotting around the bases. He tipped his hat to the cheering fans. Sixty home runs in one season! It was a record that was not topped until base-ball officials made the season longer.

"Bad kid." Babe Ruth was born February 6, 1895, in Baltimore, Maryland. He came from a very poor family. As a boy, Babe played "hookey" and ran around in the streets. "I was a bad kid," he later said. When he was seven, his parents put him into St. Mary's Industrial School. It was for orphans and "bad kids." Babe lived there for 12 years.

At St. Mary's, Brother Gilbert got the Babe interested in baseball. Soon Ruth was the pitching and batting star of his team. At 19 he was signed by the minor league Baltimore Orioles. "You mean you'll *pay* me to play baseball?" Babe asked. "Sure," said Jack Dunn, manager of the Orioles. "Six hundred dollars a year to start."

Great hitter. When Ruth came to the Orioles, a coach said, "Here's Jack Dunn's newest babe." After that, Ruth became known as "the Babe." Soon he was sold to the Boston Red Sox of the American League. Ruth was a fine pitcher, winning more than 20 games a year. But by 1918 he was also playing the outfield. In 1919 he hit 29 homers, more than anyone had ever hit before.

Then the Red Sox sold the Babe to the New York Yankees for $125,000. The Yankees wanted Babe's bat in the

The Babe ate too much and drank too much. Yet there was power in his swing, magic in his name.

lineup every day. So Ruth gave up pitching completely and played only the outfield. In his first year with the Yankees, he hit 54 home runs. Ruth helped the Yankees win their first seven pennants. With Ruth and other great players such as Lou Gehrig, the Yankees became known as "Murderers' Row." And the new Yankee Stadium was called "the house that Ruth built." Baseball was becoming a big business. Ruth's salary climbed to $80,000 a year — the highest in that sport. It was more than the President of the

The Yankees'
fortunes improved
when they got Babe Ruth
from Boston and changed him
from a pitcher into a slugger.

United States was making at the time.

Off the field, the Babe ate and drank like a giant. And he loved kids. He was never too busy to visit a sick boy in a hospital. He'd give the boy a bat and a baseball, which he signed. Then he'd promise to hit a home run that afternoon. Usually he did.

The Babe retired as a player in 1935. His greatest disappointment was that he never became manager of the Yankees. When he died of cancer in 1948, he left behind a magic name and a long list of records. His greatest record was hitting 714 major league home runs. This record went unbroken until 1974, when Henry Aaron finally passed it. In 1969 sports fans across the nation were asked to pick the greatest baseball player of all time. They chose the Babe.

A Second Look. . . .

1. *What was Babe Ruth famous for? How did he get the name "Babe"?*

2. *Babe Ruth was once criticized for making more money as a baseball player than Herbert Hoover was earning as President of the U.S. "Why not?" the Babe replied. "After all, I had a better year than he had." What does this story say about American society? Does the U.S. reward its heroes from the sports or entertainment worlds with too much fame and money? Why or why not?*

3. *The twenties were known as the Golden Age of Sports. Each sport had great heroes who helped to make their sport more popular. Using biographies and encyclopedia material, write a report on one of the following: Bill Tilden, Red Grange, Jim Thorpe, Gertrude Ederle, Bobby Jones.*

Chapter 22

"Lucky Lindy"

For hundreds of years, humans had dreamed of flying. Some thought they could fly by putting wings on their arms and feet. They jumped off high places and flapped their wings as hard as they could. It always ended sadly.

By the 1800's people were able to "fly" in balloons. Balloons were lighter than air. They could go up, but they needed the wind to move them along. Then came airships, or "blimps." These were lighter than air too. In fact, they were cigar-shaped balloons with motors on their bellies. They were better than balloons, but they were slow.

An airplane is heavier than air. Partly for this reason, inventors took longer trying to figure out ways to make airplanes work. Two Americans, Wilbur and Orville Wright, finally made the breakthrough. At Kitty Hawk, North Carolina, on December 17, 1903, the Wright brothers got their plane into the air four times with a man aboard.

The newspapers didn't say much about the Wright brothers' airplane. They didn't think it was very important. But a lot of daring young men and women heard about it anyway. And they got excited about flying. Soon they too were building airplanes and flying them. These daredevils risked their lives almost every day to set new records or win flying contests.

Then came World War I. Flying got a big boost from the war. The planes of those days were usually made of wood, canvas, and wire. They were slow and had little power. Later models were faster and more powerful. Some even flew as fast as 100 miles (160 kilometers) an hour. They were safer too. It wasn't long before some people were talking about flying the Atlantic Ocean.

After the war, several pilots tried flying the Atlantic in stages. Some of them succeeded, and some did not. In 1919 a New York City hotel owner put up a prize of $25,000 for the first nonstop flight between New York and Paris. Six men died trying to get that prize.

"The Spirit of St. Louis." In May 1927 three more planes were ready for a crack at the prize. They were at Roosevelt Field, Long Island. Two of them were big, powerful planes. The third was a small, silver-colored plane called *The Spirit of St. Louis.* It had a single engine. There was no radio and no fancy instrument for finding one's way — only a compass.

The pilot of this plane was a 25-year-old airmail flier named Charles A. Lindbergh. Lindbergh was tall, slim, and handsome. Reporters called him "Lindy." He meant to make the trip across the Atlantic alone. (The other two planes carried more than one man.)

On the morning of May 20, only *The Spirit of St. Louis* was ready to go. But

When Charles A. Lindbergh edged the nose of The Spirit of St. Louis *onto a French runway on May 21, 1927, it was Lucky Lindy's luckiest day.*

would it ever get off the ground? It was overloaded with gasoline. The runway was wet and muddy from rain. And the wind was blowing in the wrong direction. Still this was Lindbergh's big chance to beat the other two planes. He decided to take it.

Lindbergh slipped into his flying suit and put on his helmet and goggles. Then he climbed into the cockpit. As the engine roared, someone shouted, "Good luck, kid!"

At first the plane moved slowly. Some men had to push it to get it moving.

Soon it gathered speed, but it wouldn't lift off the ground. It looked as if *The Spirit of St. Louis* would crash. But at the last minute, the little plane rose into the air. It cleared some telephone wires at the end of the runway by just 20 feet (600 centimeters).

Ice over the Atlantic. Hours later Lindbergh was far out over the Atlantic, flying through heavy clouds. The air grew cold. Lindbergh put his bare hand out the cockpit window. It was stung by pieces of ice. Now Lindbergh knew he was in serious danger. If ice formed on his wings, it would drag his plane down into the sea. He had to reach clear air at once! Carefully Lindbergh turned the plane until he reached open sky. Then he flew around the clouds to get back on course. The small silver plane flew on.

One thousand miles (1,600 kilometers) from Paris, Lindbergh faced another danger — sleepiness. The night before his takeoff, he had been too busy and excited to sleep. Now, at noon on May 21, he found it hard to stay awake. Sleep was winning out. But to fall asleep could mean death. Lindbergh shook his head and stamped his feet. It was no use. Finally he forced his head out the cockpit window. He let a blast of cold air rush into his lungs. The shock made him feel fresh again.

Now wide awake, Lindbergh saw a fishing fleet below him. He knew land was near, but he wasn't sure of his direction. He dove his plane down a few feet over the boats. "Which way is Ireland?" Lindbergh shouted. Only one man appeared, but he didn't answer. An hour later, however, Lindbergh reached the coast of Ireland, exactly where he had planned. Then he headed toward France.

At Le Bourget (luh bouhr-ZHAY) airfield outside Paris, a huge crowd began to gather. Night fell. Then, at 10:18 P.M., the sound of a motor was heard over the airfield. Search lights picked up Lindbergh's plane overhead.

Four minutes later, after 33$\frac{1}{2}$ hours in the air, the plane landed in the darkness. A mob of people rushed toward *The Spirit of St. Louis.* They lifted Lindbergh over their heads and shouted his name. The next day the man who had flown the Atlantic nonstop, alone, was a world hero. Back home "Lucky Lindy" got a welcome never seen before.

A Second Look. . . .

1. *What made Charles A. Lindbergh a hero to millions of people? What was significant about his journey?*

2. *Lindbergh was a special hero in an age of heroes. In the twenties, flying excited people. While the automobile was changing Americans' daily lives, the airplane stood as a sign of the future. How has the airplane changed the way people live today? Has it had more or less of an effect than the auto? Give reasons for your answer.*

3. *The first successful airplane flight was made by the Wright brothers in 1903. Using the* Guinness Book of World Records *in your school or local library, make an outline of the significant "firsts" in aviation since 1903. Include the dates when these events occurred.*

After Lindbergh returned from his historic flight in 1927, he made the traditional ride up Broadway in New York. More people showered more ticker tape on him than on any other hero of the time. This welcome was not matched until 1969, when astronauts returned from the moon.

Looking Back: Boom to Bust

	A	B	C	D	
1919	1922	1925	1928	1931

Putting Events in Order

Chapters 15 through 22 have shown how America lived in the 1920's. Ten events in this decade are listed here. Your job is to match each event to the correct period shown on the timeline above. On a piece of paper, number from **1** to **10.** After each number, write the letter of the three-year period in which the event occurred.

1. The 19th Amendment is ratified.
2. KDKA makes the first regular radio broadcast in the United States.
3. Charles A. Lindbergh flies the Atlantic.
4. America goes "dry."
5. Word of secret deals involving members of the President's Cabinet becomes public.
6. Babe Ruth sets a home-run record for a 154-game season.
7. Warren G. Harding is elected President of the United States.
8. The Chevrolet outsells the Model T.
9. Stock prices come tumbling down in a stock market crash.
10. The 10 millionth Model-T Ford rolls off the assembly line.

Interpreting a Source

One poet of the Harlem Renaissance was Langston Hughes. His poem, "Mother to Son" (opposite page), was included in his first book of poetry, The Weary Blues, *in 1926. Read it carefully. Then answer the questions below.*

1. *What does Hughes mean by a "crystal stair"? What does he mean by "tacks" and "splinters"?*
2. *What does the poem say about the lives of black Americans in the 1920's?*
3. *How would you describe the poem — as one of sorrow, of joy, of protest, of hope? Give reasons for your answer.*
4. *Would a black American be likely to write such a poem today? Explain.*

Mother to Son

Well, son, I'll tell you
Life for me ain't been no crystal stair.
It's had tacks in it,
And splinters,
And boards torn up,
And places with no carpet on the floor —
Bare.
But all the time
I'se been a-climbin' on,
And reachin' landin's,
And turnin' corners,
And sometimes goin' in the dark
Where there ain't been no light.
So boy, don't you turn back.
Don't you set down on the steps
'Cause you find it's kinder hard.
Don't you fall now —
For I'se still goin', honey.
I'se still climbin'
And life for me ain't been no crystal stair.

Sharpening Your Skills

During the 1920's, autos became an important part of American life. This chart indicates how widespread auto ownership became. Study it carefully. Then answer the questions.

1. How many autos were registered in the U.S. in 1910? How many autos were registered in 1970?

2. How many more autos were registered in 1970 than in 1910?

3. In which decade did the greatest growth in numbers of autos registered take place?

4. In which decade did the greatest growth in numbers of trucks registered take place?

5. Which has grown the most between 1910 and 1970 — the registration of autos, buses, or trucks?

Motor Vehicle Registrations, 1910 to 1970
(in thousands)

Year	Autos	Buses	Trucks	Total
1910	458.3	—	10.1	468.4
1920	8,131.5	—	1,107.6	9,239.1
1930	23,034.7	40.5	3,674.5	26,749.7
1940	27,465.8	101.1	4,886.2	32,453.2
1950	40,339.0	223.6	8,598.9	49,161.5
1960	61,682.3	272.1	11,914.2	73,868.6
1970	89,279.8	379.0	18,748.4	108,407.2

471

5 THE GREAT DEPRESSION

Looking Ahead: The Lean Years

Tuesday, September 3, 1929, was uncomfortably hot in most of the northeastern U.S. It was the day after Labor Day, but the heat made it feel like July. Even so the crowds on Wall Street in New York City seemed especially happy. Wall Street was the home of the New York Stock Exchange. The exchange was the leading market for the buying and selling of stocks, or shares, in various U.S. businesses. On September 3, prices on the exchange had hit a new high.

The "Big Bull Market," people called it. It seemed as if everyone with money in stocks was getting rich. But in the next few weeks the market started to do strange things. Sharp nosedives in stock prices were followed by equally sharp

When rains stopped coming to Midwestern prairies in the 1930's, rich topsoil simply blew away. As one observer put it, wheat became thin "like the stubble on an old man's chin." Alexandre Hogue's painting (left) catches the spirit of the lean years when dreams had a way of turning into dust.

recoveries. Then in October the market began to decline rapidly. There were more sellers than buyers. Quickly the mood changed from uneasiness to doubt.

When the market opened on Tuesday, October 29, 1929, the dam broke. Doubt gave way to panic. Nearly everyone wanted to sell his or her stocks. But there were few buyers. In one day, billions of dollars worth of stocks were wiped out. One newspaper headline said: "Wall Street Lays an Egg."

The stock market crash set off a chain reaction. It led to the Great Depression, the worst economic crisis in U.S. history. In the next four years, business came almost to a standstill. Many businesses could not sell their products because people had less money to buy them. Factories closed, and some businesses failed. By 1932 almost 13 million people — about one out of every four U.S. workers — were out of jobs.

473

Hunger and heartache. The Depression was a disaster for most Americans. Many people were so poor that they went hungry. It was not uncommon to find people going through garbage to find a few scraps of food. Many people lost their homes because they couldn't pay for them. Thousands drifted around the country looking for jobs that did not exist. The mood was summed up in a popular song of the period. It was called "Brother, Can You Spare a Dime?"

In the Midwest farmers faced disaster. Low farm prices during the 1920's had left many of them near ruin. Then in the 1930's a severe drought hit the Midwest. Good farm and grazing land turned into a desert of dust. The "Dust Bowl," as it was called, was the final blow for many small farmers. They ran out of money and lost their farms.

When the Depression began, Republican Herbert Hoover was President. Many people blamed Hoover for the hard times. Hoover had little control over the events that had caused the Depression. But Hoover did not manage to end the hard times once they had begun.

The year 1932 was the worst of the Depression. It was also an election year. The Republicans chose Hoover to run again. The Democrats chose Franklin D. Roosevelt, governor of New York. Roosevelt promised the American people a *New Deal.* He was not sure of what he would do if elected. But he knew
474 something different had to be done.

New Deal. Roosevelt won the election easily. He took office in the darkest hour of the Depression. In his first 100 days as President, Roosevelt sent 15 major bills to Congress. These bills laid the basis for the New Deal he had promised.

The New Deal was an effort to rescue the American economy. Unlike Hoover, Roosevelt believed that only the federal government could get America back to work again. At first he tried to provide relief from the worst hardships of the Depression. Not all of his plans were successful. But they gave the American people hope.

Roosevelt was a strong President who excited strong feelings. Some Americans said he was destroying the business system he was trying to save. But millions of Americans loved him and his wife, Eleanor. Mrs. Roosevelt emerged as a public figure in her own right.

The New Deal did not bring an end to the Depression overnight. Roosevelt sent Congress a new set of plans in 1935. His first plans had mainly been *relief* efforts. These new plans were primarily for *reform.* One of them — Social Security — would provide most workers

The Depression brought a new problem for working people in a land of opportunity — mass unemployment.

WORK-is-WHAT-I WANT-AND-NOT-CHARITY WHO-WILL-HELP-ME-GET-A-JOB-7-YEARS-IN-DETROIT. NO-MONEY SENT-AWAY-FURNISH-BEST-OF-REFERENCES PHONE RANDOLPH 8381 ROOM #59.

In the 1930's, some people became desperate for money. One way of getting it was to enter a dance marathon. In these cruel events, spectators paid to watch couples dance until they dropped. Winners were those who danced the longest. They picked up a few dollars, perhaps enough to pay their rent.

with money when they retired after the age of 65. Another extended labor's right to form unions and bargain with employers as a group.

Roosevelt ran for the Presidency again in 1936 — and won. In fact, he was re-elected by the greatest landslide of votes ever given a candidate for President to that date. By the time he started his second term in 1937, business had begun to pick up. A marked recovery had taken place.

Victory for labor. The business upturn brought labor unions onto the attack. Earlier, unions had watched helplessly while wages were slashed to the bone. Now the New Deal had given unions the right to *collective bargaining.* This is the right to bargain for employees as a group. Union membership soared. In Michigan, auto workers staged a new kind of strike, known as a *sit-down.* It lasted several weeks, but it worked. A large auto company, General Motors, agreed to bargain with labor leaders.

The business upswing continued until the fall of 1937. Then business activity took another slide. Many business people said that the New Deal had been a flop. But Franklin Roosevelt shrugged off such complaints. He carried on with his reforms.

Some of the New Deal reforms worked. Some of them did not. When they didn't work, new ideas were brought forth to replace the old ones that had failed. Above all, the New Deal was proof that the U.S. was alive and growing. In the years ahead, the nation would grow stronger than it had ever been before.

Chapter 23
Wall Street Lays an Egg

The year was 1928, an election year. It was a year of great prosperity for most people. The Republican candidate for President was Herbert Hoover. In his speeches Hoover promised that Americans were going to have great times. Most Americans thought he was right.

"A chicken in every pot, a car in every garage." This is what the Republican campaign slogan of 1928 promised all Americans. Business was booming, and everybody wanted to keep it that way. So Hoover and the Republicans won the election easily.

Many people — both the rich and some who were not so rich — were making money by buying stocks. When a person buys a share of stock in a company, he or she owns part of the business. If the company makes money, the stockholder stands a good chance of making money too. When business is very good, many people want shares in the companies that make money. So the prices of these stocks go up. Anyone who bought shares before prices went up can then sell them at a profit.

High road to riches? In the late 1920's, it seemed as if anybody could get rich by buying and selling stocks. Some of America's richest people said so. "Just let a man save $15 a week," one of them wrote. "If he puts it into good stocks, he will have at least $80,000 in 20

During the 1920's, many people were persuaded to buy stocks. As early as 1921, a cartoonist for Life magazine showed stockbrokers as anglers fishing for victims (above). Such criticism was mostly forgotten though — until 1929. When the stock market crashed, anglers and fish alike milled about in Wall Street (opposite). It was too late for criticism. Everything was gloom.

years. His income will be around $400 a month. Anyone can not only *be* rich, but *ought* to be rich!"

In the summer of 1929, people all over the country were buying stocks. You didn't need much cash. You bought "on margin" — made a small down payment. How could you lose? Stocks were going up, up, up. Some people thought the stock market would go on booming forever.

There were stories like this: A barber down the street made $50,000 on General Motors. A taxi driver made $100,000 from a "tip" on U.S. Steel. A beauty-parlor operator watched her $100 grow into a fortune on Wall Street. Of course, most Americans did not have money in stocks. Not many of those who did made a "killing" in the market. And most of the lucky people who made a "killing" did not see their gains in real dollars. The gains were all tied up in stocks.

The big risk in buying and selling stocks is that their value can go down as well as up. And until you sell a stock and get some real money for it, you aren't really rich — except on paper.

A few people said, "Stock prices are much too high. They're going to take a fall. And when this happens a lot of people are going to be hurt." But hardly anyone listened. Only a handful of people sold their stocks early.

In September the stock market started to rumble. The first great break came on Thursday, October 24, 1929. That morning thousands of shares of stock were put on sale. But no one was ready to buy at the price that was asked. So the price went down. Finally the stock sold, but at low prices. This was a sign of trouble.

Now panic swept over the stock mar-

ket. Everyone wanted to sell stocks at once, before prices went down farther. But no one wanted to buy. This sent prices tumbling even lower. People went wild. They ran, shouted, cursed, and pushed, trying to sell their stocks. Extra policemen were rushed to the stock market to keep order. Within three hours, stocks lost more than 11 billion dollars of their value. But then a group of bankers pooled their money and began to *buy* stocks. This stopped the fall in prices. Some people thought the worst was over. But it was yet to come.

Low road to despair. Tuesday, October 29, 1929, was "Black Tuesday" — the day of the big crash. Tens of thousands of shares of stock were put on sale for whatever they could bring. But there were no buyers! Prices fell, fell, fell, wiping out millionaires and barbers alike. Stocks that once sold for $48 a share were now offered for one dollar. Even the best stocks dropped as much as $60 a share.

In all, stocks lost 40 billion dollars of their value. Nothing like it had ever happened before. No one could understand it. People were in a daze. One thing that made the stock market crash so bad was that the people who bought shares "on margin" now had to pay up in cash. But most did not have the cash. They had thought their down payment was safe, but now it was lost too.

October 29 was like a nightmare. One man who had been worth 85 million dollars in stocks was now completely broke. One company lost the 100 million dollars it had invested in the stock market. Grocery clerks, window cleaners, and others who had bought stocks on credit now lost all their savings. A few people couldn't take it. They jumped from skyscraper windows. A few others went home, put their heads in their ovens, and turned on the gas.

By November the stock market had fallen even farther. Millions of Americans had gone from riches to rags. It was good-bye to everything, the end of the dream of riches. The Great Depression was beginning to set in. America would suffer terribly in the years to come.

A Second Look. . . .

1. *How did people get rich in the stock market? Was their wealth real? Why or why not? What was meant by buying stocks "on margin"? Why did this practice make the stock market crash much worse?*

2. *Some historians have found a lesson in the crash. They believe that many people who bought stocks in the 1920's did so out of greed. Does this belief seem fair to you? Can you think of any other motives for owning stocks? If so, what are they? Do you think greed ever plays a part in business affairs? How might it do so? There are obvious reasons why anyone might enjoy "hitting the jackpot." Can you think of reasons why "hitting the jackpot" might be damaging to a person? Explain your answer.*

3. *The New York Stock Exchange is still alive and well. You and your classmates might find it interesting to study some stocks bought and sold on the exchange and take note of their worth. Using your local paper or* The Wall Street Journal, *pick out several stocks. Chart their performance over a period of several weeks. At the end of this period, take a vote to see which of the stocks seem most worth buying.*

478

This Margaret Bourke-White photo of flood victims in Louisville, Kentucky, came to be a symbol of the Depression. Amid the "World's Highest Standard of Living," one out of four workers couldn't work.

Chapter 24

Breadlines and Debts

In millions of U.S. homes, frightened people were asking:

How will we pay the rent?

Where will we get money for food?

How will we buy shoes for the children?

What will become of us?

It was 1932 — the worst year of the Depression. There was misery almost everywhere. It had started with the stock market crash of October 1929. Then factories, mines, steel mills, and banks had begun shutting down. Many people had lost their savings overnight. By 1932 almost 13 million workers — one out of every four — were jobless.

In 1933 some dairy owners dumped milk rather than sell it at a loss. They hoped to lower the milk supply and bring prices to a higher level.

What had caused the Depression? Some experts thought it had come about because too many Americans had borrowed too much money. Others said it had taken place because wealth was not spread evenly enough. There were many other ways of explaining the crisis. But explaining the crisis did not solve it.

Looking for work. People stood in line all night hoping to get jobs. Usually it was the same story — no jobs. A Depression joke went like this:

One high school graduate asks another, "What are you going to do now that you have a diploma?"

The other answers, "Join the army."

"The army?" asks the first.

"Yeah — the army of the unemployed."

Both skilled and unskilled workers lost their jobs. They lived on their savings while they looked for work.

Then they borrowed — from friends, family, or banks. Some men stood on street corners selling apples for pennies. Others stood in "breadlines" waiting for a free handout of bread and soup. Lawyers took jobs as salespeople at $15 a week. Teachers took jobs as taxi drivers. Pay was very low. Some factory workers made less than 10 cents an hour.

"We owe the landlord, the grocer — everybody," one jobless steelworker said. "My kids can't go to school. They don't have shoes."

The suffering was terrible. In one school, a teacher asked a little girl, "What's wrong with you?"

"I'm just hungry," the girl said.

"You may go home and eat," the teacher said.

"I can't," the child answered. "Today it's my sister's turn to eat."

Tens of thousands of people lost their

Herbert Hoover

480

homes. Half of the country's farmers lost their farms. This happened because home-owners and farmers could not pay the banks the money they had borrowed to pay for their property. In towns and cities, storekeepers went out of business. Many people weren't buying anything. They had no money.

Living on hope. Many farmers became tenant farmers, paying rent for the farms they had once owned. Some farmers and their families packed up their things in old trucks and cars and headed for California. They hoped to find work picking fruit there. These families were called "Okies," because many of them came from Oklahoma. Some had lost their farms to banks. Some lost them to the terrible dust storms that hit the Midwest in the 1930's.

Other farmers struggled to keep their farms. But it was an uphill battle. Farm prices dropped so low that farmers *lost* money on the food they produced. In some areas they destroyed crops and killed livestock rather than sell them at a loss. They were trying to decrease supplies. By doing so, they hoped to bring prices up to a fair level.

Another group badly hurt by the Depression were black Americans. Black workers had often found it hard to join labor unions. Now joining became even harder. Jobs were limited. White workers wanted these jobs for themselves. In many cases they kept black people out of their unions to keep them from competing for jobs. Without jobs, black workers had no money. In the larger U.S. cities, vast numbers of them had to go on relief.

About two million men and boys roamed the country looking for work.

Between 1930 and 1933, 5,000 U.S. banks failed. People with savings in these banks could not collect. This cartoon by John T. McCutcheon of The Chicago Tribune *won a major prize in 1932.*

They lived in shack towns called "Hoovervilles" after President Herbert Hoover. These shantytowns were usually on the edges of large cities. The towns had no streets, lights, or sewers. The shanties were made of boxes, pieces of tin, wood, and cardboard. They had no furniture, water, or heat. Men burned scraps of wood to keep warm. They dug into garbage cans for bits of food.

Asking for help. In 1932, 15,000 veterans of World War I marched on Washington, D.C. They wanted to be paid a bonus that was promised them for 1945. This "Bonus Army" brought their wives and children with them. They camped in tents and huts on empty lots. The veterans were ordered out. Many wouldn't go.

President Herbert Hoover then called out troops. The troops drove the veter-

481

ans out with tanks and tear-gas bombs. Then they set fire to the veterans' huts and tents. Many people were angry with President Hoover for what happened.

President Hoover believed business would come out of the Depression by itself. He was against most forms of U.S. government relief — money or jobs — for the unemployed. He believed that such programs should be left to the states or local communities. Hoover did approve a program of federal loans to local governments to provide jobs for the jobless. He also gave federal help to farmers and some businesses. But he thought the Depression would soon end by itself.

Instead conditions grew worse. Many people blamed President Hoover for the Depression, or for not doing enough about it. And they began to look to another man, Franklin D. Roosevelt, for help.

A Second Look. . . .

1. What was the Great Depression? Give three reasons why it is still looked upon as a time of terrible suffering.

2. Many people still blame Herbert Hoover for the Depression. Do you think such blame is fair? Why or why not? Should any one man or woman ever be thought of as solely responsible for great events such as depression or war? Explain your answer.

3. The material in this chapter provides a good starting point for another oral history project. Using a tape recorder, if possible, interview people in your community who lived through this period. Some questions you might want to ask: How were you and your family affected by the Depression? Where did you live? How well? What is your most vivid memory of these years? Was anything about this period enjoyable? If so, what?

In 1932 veterans of World War I came to Washington, D.C., to ask for help. They were told to leave, but they wouldn't go. Herbert Hoover then called out troops, who used tear gas on the veterans.

Chapter 25

The New Deal

He promised the American people a "New Deal." He said he would help the "forgotten man" — the jobless worker, the poor farmer. He gave hope to the frightened, hungry Americans of the Great Depression. People believed that Franklin Delano Roosevelt was the friend of the common man. In November 1932 they elected him President over Herbert Hoover. Soon Roosevelt was being called "FDR."

On March 4, 1933, FDR was sworn in as President. It was a cold, raw day. Sleet fell on the watching crowds. But FDR's voice was full of hope and courage. He said he had a "firm belief" that "the only thing we have to fear is fear itself."

Did he mean it? Was he really as sure as he sounded? Many people wondered about the new President. The Depression was so widespread that there was talk of revolution in the air.

In the four months since FDR's election, hundreds of banks had closed. People who had money in these banks had lost all their savings. In some cities cash was disappearing. Paper money called *scrip* was issued in place of it. Some people even turned to the barter system. That is, they swapped one thing for another — say, potatoes for corn meal — since the supply of money was so short.

The bank crisis only made the Depression worse. In March 1933 one out of every four workers still remained jobless. Certainly, many people said, there was more to fear than fear itself. The very foundations of the American system seemed to be collapsing.

FDR promised quick action — and he gave it. He began by bringing new people into government — college professors and bright young lawyers. Newspaper reporters quickly named them FDR's "Brain Trust." After the election, FDR and his Brain Trust sat down to plan the New Deal.

Great experiment. The New Deal was more of an experiment than a plan. "Take a method and try it," FDR said. "If it fails, admit it frankly and try another. But above all, try something." The first task of the New Deal, as FDR saw it, was to get America back to work again. The vicious cycle of depression and unemployment had to be broken. If people had jobs that paid them enough money, they would buy things. This would produce more jobs. Factories and mills would reopen to meet the increased demand for more goods.

FDR realized that aid to business alone would not help enough. Only the federal government could get people back to work. Therefore it was up to the government to create as many jobs as possible.

FDR explained his ideas to the American people in radio speeches he called

Peter
Arno

"fireside chats." He spelled his ideas out to Congress in special messages. Most of the major laws of the New Deal were passed in two spurts. Each spurt was about 100 days long. The first, in 1933, was the most dramatic. FDR called Congress into special session. The Brain Trust worked around the clock preparing bills for Congress. And just as fast as they prepared the bills, Congress passed them into law.

Fifteen major laws were passed in the first 100 days. They included:

The Emergency Banking Act. This was the first New Deal bill sent to Congress. It pledged government support to banks and helped them get their affairs in order. Soon after the law was passed, people were putting their money back in banks. A later law insured bank savings up to $10,000.

The Civilian Conservation Corps Act. Congress took only eight days to create this act. The corps, known as the CCC, gave unemployed young men healthy outdoor work. They planted trees, built dams and bridges, and helped prevent forest fires and floods. The corps gave many of its members their only chance to eat three meals a day.

The Agricultural Adjustment Act. This law gave help to farmers. It paid them *not* to plant crops on part of their land. This cut down farm output. As the supply of farm products dwindled, farm prices rose to a fairer level.

Hoover and Roosevelt did not think much of each other. Peter Arno, cartoonist for The New Yorker, *drew them on the way to Roosevelt's swearing-in — Roosevelt all smiles, Hoover full of distrust. The magazine did not use the drawing. It chose not to focus on FDR because of threats made on his life.*

Editorial writers and cartoonists had a field day with Roosevelt's programs. Some said that New Deal programs were so many and so confusing that the government could not juggle them (above). To millions, however, Roosevelt seemed a savior. Many Americans hung his picture on their walls.

The National Industrial Recovery Act. This was the most sweeping law passed in the first 100 days of the New Deal. It set up the National Recovery Administration (NRA). The NRA was to bring businesses together in one great effort to provide jobs and raise wages. One part of this program helped each industry to draw up a "code of fair practices." The act also guaranteed labor's right to form unions. And it set up the Public Works Administration to give people jobs.

The U.S. Supreme Court later declared the NRA to be against the Constitution. Among other things, the Court said that the President had no authority to approve business codes. But FDR saved parts of the NRA in the second 100 days in 1935. The Works Progress Administration (WPA) extended the public works program. Hundreds of schools, hospitals, and post offices were built around the country. Writers, artists, actors, and teachers were also given jobs with the WPA.

Two other major laws came out of the second 100 days. One was the *Wagner Act*. This act extended labor's right to form unions. It also set up the National Labor Relations Board to rule on union questions. The other law was the *Social Security Act*. Social Security gave workers an income when they retired at the age of 65. It also paid unemployed workers while they looked for jobs.

The New Deal had many critics. Some of them said that FDR's programs were against the Constitution. Others said these programs interfered too much with private business. Still others said that the New Deal simply did not put an end to the Depression. As an experiment, these people claimed, it had failed.

Just how successful was the New Deal? There is no doubt that it did help to ease the worst suffering of the Depression between 1933 and 1937. Then, in 1938, many businesses went into another slump. They did not pull out of it completely until World War II in the 1940's.

Even so, the New Deal brought hope to millions. People slowly got used to the idea of government's doing some jobs private businesses had once done. The New Deal helped America survive one of its worst periods in history. And it helped Americans adapt to changing times.

A Second Look. . . .

1. *What did FDR do to get jobless workers back to work? How did his ideas differ from those of Herbert Hoover?*

2. *In the first part of this book, you have read about the progressive movement of the early 1900's. This movement has often been compared to the New Deal. Like progressives, New Dealers were willing to use government to meet human needs. What, then, was really* new *about the New Deal? How did it go beyond the changes of the Progressive Era? Do you think FDR's distant cousin, Theodore Roosevelt, would have agreed with him about the need to experiment? Why or why not?*

3. *The New Deal may seem to have happened a long time ago. But many of its programs still play a large part in our daily lives. Study the chapter carefully. Then make a list of three ways in which laws passed during the New Deal still affect the nation today.*

Chapter 26

First Lady

On a train late at night, a group of reporters sat talking with Eleanor Roosevelt. The reporters had spent the whole day with the new First Lady. They had arisen at six in the morning. They had traveled 300 miles (480 kilometers) and watched Mrs. Roosevelt make 14 speeches along the way. Then, at the end of the day, they had boarded the train for the trip back to Washington. Now some of them were bone-weary.

At 11 P.M. Mrs. Roosevelt stood up as if to say that the session was ended for the night. One reporter said, "Thank you very much, Mrs. Roosevelt, for such a good story. I'm not surprised, though, that

you should want to get some rest at last."

Mrs. Roosevelt smiled. "Oh," she said quickly, "I'm not going to bed yet. I think I'll do a magazine piece before I turn in. I'm not really tired."

Eleanor Roosevelt was a woman of great energy. When she became First Lady, people did not know at first what to make of her. President's wives had usually been expected to be hostesses. They were supposed to take care of social life at the White House — and very little else. Many people still thought women belonged at home with their children. They disapproved of women being involved in public life.

But Eleanor Roosevelt was different. She had been forced into public life long before her husband became President. In 1921 FDR had been paralyzed by polio. For a time, he could no longer go to most political meetings himself.

Mrs. Roosevelt had always been shy and nervous with large groups. But she overcame her fears. She went to the meetings in place of her husband. She acted as his eyes and ears.

Eleanor Roosevelt was a very public First Lady.

She continued doing so as First Lady. She traveled around the country. She talked to people and heard their problems. She also wrote magazine articles and a daily newspaper column. She gave radio talks that were very popular. The country had never seen anything like her.

Remembering the forgotten.

Eleanor Roosevelt took on many projects as First Lady. But her special interest seemed to be people who had been forgotten: poor people, old people, black people, and others. The 1930's were not a time of improving race relations. Still, Eleanor Roosevelt wanted to help all the people she could. She invited blacks to the White House. She spoke out forcefully for equal rights.

Eleanor and Franklin Roosevelt shake hands with well-wishers from a train in Nebraska in 1935.

Many people criticized her for this. But others praised her, and she became a friend to black people.

In 1933 unemployed veterans of World War I returned to Washington. They set up a camp as the Bonus Army of 1932 had done (see Chapter 24). The veterans were angry. They said they would not leave until the government gave them help. President Roosevelt did not want to use force against them as President Hoover had.

One day Mrs. Roosevelt visited the veterans' camp alone. The muddy camp was made up of rough huts and tents. Mrs. Roosevelt ate with the veterans and listened to their stories. She sang World War I songs with them, and they cheered her. Then they agreed to go home peacefully, knowing that President Roosevelt would do his best for them.

Mrs. Roosevelt also took great interest in young people. She was worried over the effect the Depression was having on them. High school graduates couldn't find jobs or afford college. Mrs. Roosevelt thought they should be given part-time work so that they could stay in school. She worked closely with FDR's advisers to develop such a program. Millions of students were helped.

Working for women's equality.

Mrs. Roosevelt wanted women to be treated as the equals of men. It upset her that the government hired women only as clerks and typists. She urged FDR to name women to more important jobs — and he did. He asked Frances Perkins to serve as Secretary of Labor. She was the first woman to hold a Cabinet post.

Eleanor Roosevelt never seemed to rest. She was usually traveling and meeting with people. She visited poor farmers in the Great Plains. She went to the mines and met with coal miners. She visited prisons, factories, orphan homes, schools, and hospitals. In World War II, she visited thousands of American soldiers overseas. As a joke, a Washington newspaper once ran a headline that read: "Mrs. Roosevelt Spends Night at the White House."

After President Roosevelt died in 1945, his wife continued her career of speaking and writing. President Harry Truman named her as a U.S. delegate to the United Nations. There she chaired a group interested in human rights. She worked hard for peace and the freedom of all peoples. She died in 1962.

Throughout her travels, Eleanor Roosevelt brought concern and understanding to the people she visited. She tried to show the importance of human dignity everywhere she went. She had some critics. She was a woman in what was then a man's world. Her pioneering role was resented by some. But even many of her critics respected her. Some of her friends called her "First Lady of the World."

"But it would make such a nice scoop if you'd only tell me, Franklin," says Mrs. Roosevelt in this cartoon. Her newspaper column, "My Day," was read from coast to coast. Here she wonders if her husband will seek a third term.

A Second Look. . . .

1. *What made Eleanor Roosevelt such an unusual First Lady? How was she different from most earlier Presidents' wives?*

2. *Eleanor Roosevelt was called the "First Lady of the World." She inspired millions of people. But some critics disliked the idea of a woman having so much influence on national affairs. If Mrs. Roosevelt were still the First Lady, do you think she would be criticized the same way now? Or are women leaders more accepted today? Why do you suppose no women have ever been elected President of the U.S.? Would you like to see this happen? Do you think it ever will? Explain your answers.*

3. *The nation's First Lady does not hold elected office. Yet her importance is sometimes greater than that of leaders we elect. Using magazine articles and biographies, research the activities of one of the other First Ladies of this century. In your report, compare your subject's importance to that of Mrs. Roosevelt.*

489

Chapter 27

Dust Bowl

"Okies." The name was hissed at them at the California border. It sounded like a dirty word, and the newcomers were surprised.

They had come to California to find work. They had heard that the state was covered with grape vines, vegetable farms, and fruit trees. They had heard that the growers needed pickers to pick their crops. Pickers were needed for oranges, for strawberries, for grapes, for almost anything you could name. And picking meant pay. Not very much pay, but at least enough to live on. Without it they would starve.

They had driven their old trucks and Tin Lizzies more than 1,000 miles (1,600 kilometers) to escape the dust storms and their dried-out farms. They needed these jobs in California that they had come so far to get. But now some of them were told, "Okie, go back where you came from."

The Okies were mainly families from Oklahoma in the mid-1930's. Many came from the other states of the Great Plains, but all were called Okies. The Great Plains stretch down from the Dakotas in the north to Texas in the south. Only 10 years before, these states had been major producers of the nation's grain. What had gone wrong?

During World War I, food prices shot up. To take advantage of the high prices, farmers planted on lands that usually didn't get much rain. Ranchers let their cattle and sheep graze over more and more acres. As luck would have it, rainfall was a little heavier than usual. More and more grain grew, and so more and more cattle grazed. Prices stayed pretty high even after the war was over.

But the plowing and the grazing ripped off the sod (the top layer of grass that protects the soil). The farmers and ranchers never bothered to plant new grass on the places they had

Dust storms of the 1930's turned daylight to darkness in towns and cities of the Great Plains.

Dorothea Lange photographed this 32-year-old woman in California's fields. Lange described her subject: "She said they had been living on frozen vegetables . . . and birds that the children killed."

used. This kind of thing had been going on for years. During the "good times" of high prices, it got much worse.

Dry wells. Then around 1921 prices began to go down again. In the early 1930's, rainfall went down too. By the time FDR took office, there had been little or no rain on the Great Plains for a year-and-a-half. The wells and water holes were drying up. The grain and grass were turning brown. As the winds blew over the dry land, they picked up the soil in giant clouds of dust. There was no sod to hold it down.

Crops were ruined. The farmers couldn't pay off the banks for the money they had borrowed for new equipment and more land during the good years. So banks began taking over the farms.

People kept saying that if they could hold out for a while, things would get better again. The rains would come back. But the rain didn't come back. The drought went on. It continued, year after year, all through the thirties. The land was becoming powdery.

Dust storms were common in this dry area without trees. Usually a dust storm lasted a few hours. But the dust storms of the 1930's were something else. They lasted for days. Farmers and ranchers had to go inside to get away from blowing dust and sand. They had to stuff rags into the openings and cracks of their houses.

Some days the dust got so bad it blotted out the sun, turning day into night. Dust and sand from the Great Plains were blown all the way to the Eastern states. Once, the dust of Kansas partly blocked the sun in Massachusetts.

Sometimes farmers found dust and
492   sand piled up to their windows like

snowdrifts. Farmers couldn't plant in this dust. And if they did there was no rain to water their crops.

More and more farmers went broke and began leaving their homes. Between 1934 and 1939, some 350,000 people left their farms. They headed west in strange, sad lines of old, battered cars and trucks, mattresses on top, pots and pans clanging on the sides, suitcases strapped to the back. To many of these migrants (travelers), California seemed like a promised land.

Cardboard houses. For most, California turned out to be something less than that. It was a place where the whole family went into the fields — if there was work. If not too many pickers showed up, they might make 45 cents an hour. Many of these families lived in the fields. Their houses were made of tin sheets or cardboard boxes. Water for

Center of Dust Bowl

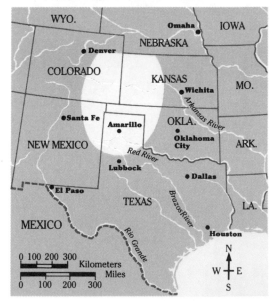

cooking and drinking came from a nearby ditch.

When the picking of one crop was done, the Okie families would move on to the next. They traveled in their old trucks or cars. Or else they walked to the next job, if they could find one.

In 1937 the U.S. government took action. The Farm Security Agency — called "FSA" for short — was set up. The FSA tried to help the migrant workers and also the small farmers who had not left the Dust Bowl area. FSA money built new, cleaner, and healthier migrant-worker camps. The FSA also bought up empty land in the Dust Bowl and turned it into forests and pasture. FSA agents taught farmers to plant grass to hold down the soil, and trees and shrubs to hold back the wind.

The FSA did much to help the victims of the Dust Bowl. But the Depression was still on. The problems of the people who had lost their lands were never fully solved in the fields. In 1940 war production opened thousands of new jobs. Soon the migrants were leaving the fields and going to the cities for work.

YEARS OF DUST

RESETTLEMENT ADMINISTRATION
Rescues Victims
Restores Land to Proper Use

Artist Ben Shahn painted this scene in 1936 for the U.S. Resettlement Administration, later to become part of New Deal's Farm Security Agency.

A Second Look. . . .

1. *What were the causes of the Dust Bowl? How did this natural disaster make things worse for already troubled farmers?*

2. *During the thirties, farm prices were so low that farmers lost money harvesting their crops. Yet millions of people did not get enough to eat. Farm prices did not rise until farmers produced less food. How can you explain this? Can you think of any possible solutions to such a problem?*

3. *The drought of the 1930's was a* natural disaster of a major sort. Other local disasters have also had an effect on U.S. history. To study them, organize a committee of three classmates. Each of you should do library research on one of the following: The Johnstown (Pennsylvania) Flood of 1889 or 1977, the Galveston (Texas) Flood of 1900, the San Francisco Earthquake of 1906. What caused each disaster? How far did each disaster area extend? How many people were killed? What long-term effects, if any, did each disaster have on U.S. history? Report your findings to the class.

Chapter 28

Hollywood's Dream Factory

Fred Astaire and Ginger Rogers

Not all the people who crossed the border into California in the 1930's were farm-workers. Some were people looking for work in a growing industry. The industry was film-making. It had taken root between 1910 and 1920 along the dusty streets of a California town called Hollywood. Now, in the gloom of the Depression, Hollywood and its movies seemed to shine.

Hundreds of films were being turned out each year by the big studios. These films were being sent to theaters all over the nation. In the 1930's, movies cost 25 cents for adults, and 10 cents for children. More than 100 million Americans were going to the movies every week.

The lines before ticket booths were nearly as much a sign of the Depression as breadlines. In a world filled with hardships, movies meant a holiday from care. They were a chance to escape, to forget the hard times. They were also a chance to have some fun.

Movie palaces. The first giant movie theater had been built in New York City in 1915. More of these theaters soon went up in other big cities across the land. Such theaters were almost as great an attraction as the films they showed. Some were like palaces. Others looked like temples of a religious sort. They had plush seats and walls lined with imitation gold. Ceilings were two or three stories high.

In front of these palaces stood doormen in frock coats and white gloves. They opened car doors, greeted people, and showed them to ticket booths. Once inside the theaters, people were met by ushers in uniforms with brass buttons and gold braid. The ushers led the way to vacant seats with their flashlights.

These sorts of theaters once inspired a magazine cartoon. It showed a child in a picture-palace lobby, asking, "Mama, does God live here?"

Audiences sat in the big, dark theaters and looked up at a world of make-believe on the silver screen. They saw movies about people who seemed larger than life. Rich people. Beautiful people.

Charming people. Brave people. People no one in the audience had ever met. People one would hardly meet in real life.

The movies of the 1930's had child stars, monster stars, musical stars, and romantic stars. They also had "tough-guy" stars who acted in gangster movies. Most gangster movies were set during Prohibition. All were meant to show that "crime does not pay." In the early 1930's, audiences were held spellbound by these films. They loved to listen to the colorful "tough-guy" talk.

The first and most popular gangster film was *Little Caesar.* Its main character, Little Caesar, was boss of a big-city gang. In one scene from this film, the gang is talking about one of its members.

"Eddie's turned yellow. He's goin' to rat on us."

"He can't get away with that."

"I just seen Eddie goin' into the church."

"Get Eddie," says Little Caesar.

The scene cuts suddenly to the outside of a church with Eddie coming down the steps. A long, black car swings into view. There is a burst of machine-

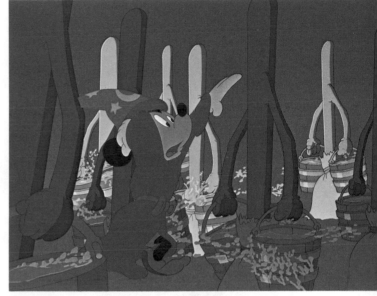

Cartoon characters were stars of Fantasia.

gun fire. Eddie lies sprawling on the steps. The next scene is Eddie's funeral.

Full-length "talkies." *Little Caesar* was made in 1930. It was one of the first feature films to make use of a new effect — sound. Feature films made before 1927 were silent. The actors and actresses "talked" through printed titles between scenes. Then came a film called *The Jazz Singer,* the first full-length "talkie" in motion-picture history. Other film-makers rushed to turn out movies with sound.

The "talkies" added a new element to the movies. Voices and sound effects made the stories seem more real. But the talkies also caused problems in the industry. It was very expensive for movie studios to convert to sound.

Some popular silent film stars were a failure in the talkies. In silent films all an actor or actress had to do was act, not

Edward G. Robinson (left) as a gangland thug.

495

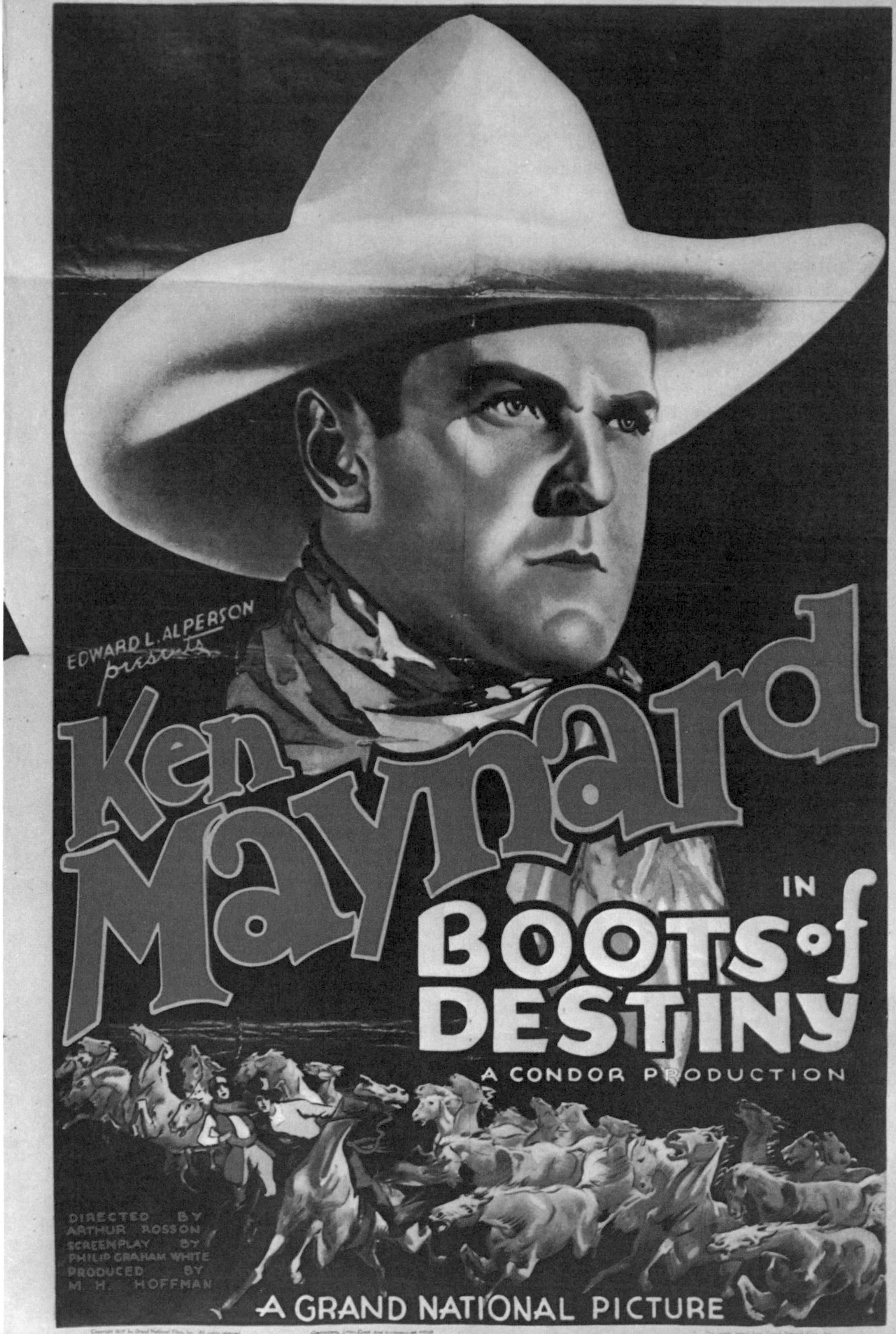
EDWARD L. ALPERSON
presents
Ken Maynard
IN
BOOTS of DESTINY
A CONDOR PRODUCTION
DIRECTED BY
ARTHUR ROSSON
SCREENPLAY BY
PHILIP GRAHAM WHITE
PRODUCED BY
M. H. HOFFMAN
A GRAND NATIONAL PICTURE

talk. In the talkies, voices became much more important. New stars rose to fame overnight.

Star system. Some of these stars were "tough guys" such as James Cagney and Edward G. Robinson. Some were song-and-dance people such as Ruby Keeler and Dick Powell. A few had also been successful in silent films. The comedian Charlie Chaplin was an example. Two of the new stars weren't people at all. One was King Kong, a mechanical ape. Another was Mickey Mouse, a cartoon creation of Walt Disney.

Movie producers found out that a popular star could insure a film's success. The "star system" led to a new industry of fan magazines and gossip writers. Movie-goers were eager to know more about their favorite stars. The stars' fantastic wealth and glamorous lives seemed too good to be true.

Hollywood did open new doors to millions. The movies taught Americans about faraway places, about manners and morals, about how and how not to behave. But in the dark days of the Depression, Hollywood was mostly the nation's dream factory. Just as the Midwest grew wheat, and the South produced tobacco, so Hollywood supplied the U.S. — and the world — with dreams.

A Second Look. . . .

1. In what way did the talkies create a crisis in the film industry? Who was affected? Why?

2. People went to the movies in the 1930's mainly to be entertained. Yet while they were enjoying themselves,

Films of yesteryear were advertised in colorful posters. Few films or posters outlived their day.

they were also drawing ideas and values from the films they saw. We do the same while watching TV today. Think about a TV program you enjoy. Does it have a star you like? What is it about the looks, manner, and behavior of the star that attracts you? Do you want to be like that person? Why? What do you think your choice of heroes or heroines says about you as a person?

3. Many films of the 1930's turn up from time to time on TV. You and your classmates might enjoy reviewing these film classics as "historians." At the start of each week, go through a TV listing. Select those films made in the 1930's, and assign two students to review each. In watching the film, the reviewers should look for scenes that seem to be influenced by the times in which the film was made. The reviewers can write a one-page review explaining how these scenes fit the 1930's. Reviews can then be posted on the class bulletin board.

A mechanical ape for a movie star? Yes, indeed. King Kong first became a celebrity in the 1930's

Chapter 29

Fiorello

"I'm going to throw the crooks and bums out of City Hall. I'm going to make my city clean again. I'm going to see that New York does what it is supposed to do — serve the people. And this means *all* the people. No pregnant mother will go without medical care. No child will go without milk. No family will go without a roof. And I mean what I say!"

It was Fiorello LaGuardia (fee-or-ELL-oh lah-GWAHR-dee-ah), the "Little Flower," speaking. He was running for mayor of New York City in 1933. New Yorkers were still upset by a scandal in the old government of Tammany Hall (the name New Yorkers gave to the ruling committee of the Democratic party in their city). Many New Yorkers liked LaGuardia because he promised to bring back honest government. It was also the middle of the Depression. Many people were out of work. LaGuardia's promises to help poor people made him even more popular.

Fusion candidate. LaGuardia had been a Republican Congressman. Now he was backed by a new reform party called the Fusion party. He was running against the power of Tammany Hall. Reporters asked LaGuardia if he could beat Tammany running on a Fusion ticket. LaGuardia shot back, "I could beat those bums running on a *laundry* ticket!"

The Tammany machine put up a tough fight. It was also a dirty one. Tammany hoodlums broke up Fusion meetings. Fusion posters were torn down. Fusion speakers were shouted at. City workers were told they would be fired if they helped LaGuardia's campaign.

LaGuardia and his Fusion friends fought back in their own way. They sang "Who's Afraid of the Big Bad Wolf?" (This song came from a Walt Disney cartoon movie.) Tough Golden Gloves boxers from LaGuardia's home section battled Tammany hoodlums.

Reform victory. On election day, Tammany "stole" thousands of votes. But LaGuardia won anyway. His supporters went wild with happiness. There were parades and dancing in the streets that night. The people had voted a new deal in New York City to match FDR's New Deal for the U.S.

LaGuardia's victory in the 1933 election was his greatest triumph in a lifetime of battles. Many of the battles were fought against injustice, poverty, crime, and corruption. The story began in New York City in 1882, the year LaGuardia was born. His mother had come from a Jewish family in Austria. His father was an Italian musician.

LaGuardia became a lawyer, then entered politics. People knew him as the "Little Flower" — the meaning of "Fiorello" in Italian. He was elected to Congress as a Republican in 1916. The next year he quit Congress to become a flier in World War I. At 35 he was old to be a flier. But he won many medals and became a hero.

Workers' friend. When the war ended, he went back to politics. He served in Congress from 1923 to 1933. The people of his district were mainly poor Italians and Jews. LaGuardia made speeches to them in Italian and Yiddish. (He spoke other languages too.) In Congress he was known as a friend of the working man and the poor.

After 1933 Fiorello LaGuardia became one of New York City's greatest mayors. The people re-elected him twice. He wiped out hundreds of acres of slums. He replaced them with good, low-rent houses. He also built parks, playgrounds, beaches, parkways, hospitals, and schools. A hard worker, LaGuardia needed three secretaries to keep up with him. Yet he cut his own salary!

LaGuardia was full of life. He was short and pudgy, but he wore big

Comics would not be kept from children while Fiorello LaGuardia was mayor. During a newspaper strike, he read comics over the radio.

Western-style hats. He loved to chase after fire engines in his car. At a fire he always wore a fireman's hat. He led police raids on gamblers. On a big construction job, he would operate the power shovel. He liked to lead bands, waving his arms about. During a newspaper strike, LaGuardia read, over the radio, comics from the papers to children. Reading *Dick Tracy,* he asked, "Why can't *our* detectives look like Dick Tracy?"

LaGuardia stepped down as mayor in 1945. He died two years later. He was mourned not only by the people of New York, whom he served so well, but by people all over the world.

A Second Look. . . .

1. What did Fiorello LaGuardia accomplish as mayor of New York City?

2. Fiorello LaGuardia gave New Yorkers hope. His energy and colorful style helped people through the hard times of the Depression. It has been said that political leaders are often as important for what they stand for as for what they do in office. Do you agree or disagree? Why?

3. New York City named an airport after Fiorello LaGuardia. Many towns and cities have named places and buildings for other famous people. Some of the heroes and heroines so honored have been national ones such as George Washington or Abraham Lincoln. But local people have been honored too. As a research project, make a list of buildings, schools, parks, and other places in your area that are named for local people. Find out who these people were and what they did to be so honored by the community.

499

Chapter 30
Sit-Down Strikers

When they tie the can to a union man,
  Sit down! Sit down!
When the speed-up comes, just twiddle your thumbs,
  Sit down! Sit down!
When the bosses won't talk, don't take a walk,
  Sit down! Sit down!

This is a song that thousands of workers were singing in 1937. They were taking part in a new kind of strike — the sit-down. Usually workers walked out of a factory to go on strike. But these workers would *not* leave the factories when they went on strike. Instead they just sat down at their work benches. They stayed inside the factories until the strikes were settled. This way strikebreakers could not be brought in to take their jobs.

Sit-down strikes made big headlines in the 1930's. Here is the story of one of

In 1937 workers at a General Motors plant in Michigan pioneered a new tactic — the sit-down strike.

the largest and most famous sit-down strikes in the history of the American labor movement:

Workers at the General Motors factories in Flint, Michigan, were angry. They earned only about $1,000 a year. And there was a speed-up on the assembly line. Workers had to do their jobs very quickly. It put them under a great strain. This line takes your guts out, some workers said.

Union strength. Soon the workers began to join a new union, the United Automobile Workers. But officers of General Motors would not meet with the union. In January 1937 the union called a strike. This strike was something new. The workers just put away their tools and sat down where they worked.

At night they slept on the floors of new cars. Food was passed to them through the factory windows. The workers kept good order. They had their own "policemen" inside. These men carefully guarded the company's property. No drinking was allowed. Even smoking was cut down.

General Motors officers said the workers had no right to stay on company property. The union officers said: "What more sacred right is there than the right of a man to his job? This means the right to support his family and to feed his children."

General Motors shut off the heat in its factories. It was winter, and the men were cold. But they wouldn't leave. Police tried to rush into one factory. Workers drove them back with flying soda bottles, coffee mugs, iron bolts, and door hinges. The police came back with tear-gas bombs. The workers drove them back again with fire hoses.

Court order. The strike dragged on for weeks. Finally a court ordered the strikers to leave the factories. They had to get out by three o'clock on February 3. The National Guard was called in to back up the court order. But the workers said they would not leave. Then Michigan's Governor Frank Murphy ordered General Motors and the union to hold peace talks. Meanwhile the workers expected another attack. Outside the factories, thousands of union workers and relatives were ready to help fight it off. There were many women among them.

Three o'clock — zero hour — came on February 3. But there was no battle. Governor Murphy would not order the National Guard to attack. He did not want any blood spilled. President

Most common labor tactic of 1930's was "taking a walk" — going out on strike. Picketers below are from Congress of Industrial Organizations (CIO).

Roosevelt also asked for a peaceful end to the strike. A week later the end came. General Motors agreed to bargain with the leaders of the United Automobile Workers. The company also agreed in advance to make changes in the assembly line. This was a great victory for the auto union.

A Second Look. . . .

1. Why did workers at General Motors go on strike in 1937? What were their goals and how did they achieve them?

2. The idea of sitting down on the job was a new one in 1937. The sit-down strike ended in a victory for the auto union. Yet it was not very popular with the American people. Why do you suppose it wasn't? Should labor leaders think about public reactions to their strikes? Or should the welfare of their workers be their only thought? Explain.

3. You and your classmates might enjoy taking part in a "collective bargaining" session for yourselves. Before beginning, the class should be divided into two groups. One group will represent management — that is, employers. The other will represent labor — that is, employees.

Now imagine that the employees at your plant are earning $4.20 an hour. They are working a 35-hour week. The labor union wants a shorter work week and a raise in pay. The labor committee gets together for the purpose of agreeing on demands. The management group knows it will have to raise pay slightly. But it doesn't want to go too far. The management committee meets to agree on its position.

Then the two groups meet together. The labor group attempts to persuade management why its demands should be met. Management attempts to "hold the line." Some final questions for class discussion: Which committee has won the most? Has labor's ability to bargain collectively given it more strength than a single employee would have had alone? If so, why?

Not all labor disputes were peaceful. In 1937 steel leaders fought CIO attempts to organize workers. Result was a "Memorial Day Massacre" that took the lives of 10 workers in South Chicago.

Looking Back:
The Great Depression

A	B	C	D	
January 1, 1931	January 1, 1933	January 1, 1935	January 1, 1937	January 1, 1939

Putting Events in Order

Chapters 23 through 30 have described events in the United States in the 1930's. Ten events from this period are listed here. Your job is to match each event to the correct period shown on the timeline above. On a piece of paper, number from **1** to **10.** After each number, write the letter of the period within which the event occurred.

1. The Farm Security Agency is set up to help migrant workers and small farmers in the Dust Bowl.

2. Franklin Roosevelt defeats Herbert Hoover in a Presidential election.

3. The United Auto Workers stage a sit-down strike against General Motors.

4. FDR is re-elected President in a landslide.

5. Fiorello LaGuardia is elected mayor of New York City.

6. Congress passes the Social Security Act.

7. The business upswing following the New Deal comes to an end.

8. Fifteen major bills are sent to Congress in the first 100 days of the New Deal.

9. Business hits rock bottom in the worst year of the Depression.

10. Congress passes the Emergency Banking Act.

Interpreting a Source

In his book, Hard Times, *Studs Terkel has recorded the thoughts of many people who lived through the Depression. Virginia Durr lived in Alabama. Here is how she recalled these years to Terkel.*

Oh, no, the Depression was not a romantic time. It was a time of terrible suffering. The contradictions were so obvious that it didn't take a very bright person to realize something was terribly wrong.

503

Have you ever seen a child with rickets[1]? Shaking as with palsy[2]. No proteins, no milk. And the companies pouring milk into gutters. People with nothing to wear, and they were plowing up cotton. People with nothing to eat, and they killed the pigs. If that wasn't the craziest system in the world, could you imagine anything more idiotic? This was just insane.

And people blamed themselves, not the system. They felt they had been at fault: ... "if we hadn't bought that old radio" ... "if we hadn't bought that old secondhand car." ...

People who were independent, who thought they were masters and mistresses of their lives, were all of a sudden dependent on others. Relatives or relief. People of pride went into shock or sanitoriums. My mother was one....

[1]*Rickets* is a childhood disease. It is marked by a softening of the bones and, sometimes, crooked growth.

[2]*Palsy* is the loss of power to control movement of the limbs or other parts of the body.

Above all, the Depression was a time of fear and desperation. It left its scars in cities, towns, and villages, and among workers on the nation's farms (below). Some of the scars were slow to heal.

The Depression affected people in two different ways. The great majority reacted by thinking money is the most important thing in the world. Get yours. And get it for your children. Nothing else matters. Not having that stark terror come at you again. . . .

And there was a small number of people who felt the whole system was lousy. You have to change it. The kids come along and they want to change it too. But they don't seem to know what to put in its place. I'm not so sure I know, either. I do think it has to be responsive[3] to people's needs. And it has to be done by democratic means, if possible. Whether it's possible or not — the power of money is such today, I just don't know. Some of the kids call me a relic[4] of the thirties. Well, I am.

1. *What was there about the Depression that Virginia Durr found "idiotic" and "insane"? What does she mean by "relatives or relief"?*

2. *What is the "stark terror" that Durr refers to?*

3. *Why were milk, cotton, and livestock destroyed when people were in great need of them? Does this suggest that money came ahead of human needs? Why or why not?*

4. *Whom does Durr hold responsible for the Depression — its victims or the system? Why?*

5. *Is she hopeful of changing the system? What kinds of changes does she seem to want? Do you agree with her? Why or why not?*

---

[3] *Responsive* means giving response or answering.

[4] A *relic* is an object or idea from the past that no longer has practical use.

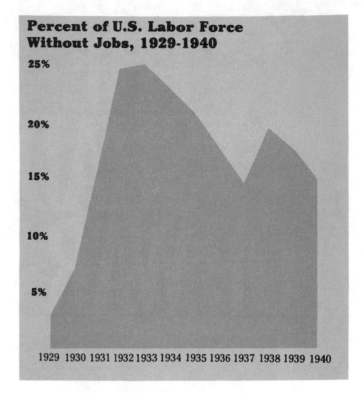

Percent of U.S. Labor Force Without Jobs, 1929-1940

25%
20%
15%
10%
5%

1929 1930 1931 1932 1933 1934 1935 1936 1937 1938 1939 1940

Sharpening Your Skills

During the Great Depression, millions of workers lost their jobs. This graph shows the percentage of the U.S. labor force that was out of work. Study the graph carefully. Then answer the questions.

1. About what percent of the total U.S. labor force was out of work in 1930?

2. About what percent of this force was out of work in 1932?

3. To judge from this chart, what was the worst year of the Depression?

4. After reading this chart, do you think the New Deal was successful in getting people back to work? Why or why not?

6 THE SHADOWS OF WAR

Looking Ahead: Distant Voices, Distant Threats

By the summer of 1938, more and more Americans were getting their news from the radio. Every evening millions of families gathered around their loudspeakers to learn what had happened that day. Often news reports were beamed direct from world capitals. "We take you now to Berlin," a newsman would say, followed by a pause as radio signals jumped the Atlantic Ocean. Then another, more distant voice would crackle through the airwaves.

Such newscasts were fresh proof of how small the world had become. In the summer of 1938 they were also proof of how troublesome world events could be. The news from Berlin was nothing to take lightly that summer. Europe was trembling on the brink of war. And as World War I had already shown, a con-

Adolf Hitler used the old German city of Nuremberg (left) as the sinister scene for Nazi rallies, told Germans they would rule the world.

flict in Europe could threaten peace around the world.

What was the latest crisis? And how had it begun?

The story went all the way back to the Treaty of Versailles in 1919. The treaty had forced Germany to give up large amounts of territory and to pay heavy damages for its role in the war. It had also said that Germany was to blame for starting the war in the first place. Most Germans had found this hard to accept.

Worthless money. After the war many Germans could not find work. Their country's wealth had been used up. To make matters worse, Germany suffered from inflation. (*Inflation* is the process by which the prices of goods and services go up.) The same amount of money bought less and less. People with savings were ruined. Their money was worthless.

Germans felt angry and helpless to do anything about the situation. Some of

The German economy went haywire in the 1920's. Extreme inflation made money nearly worthless. Here a German housewife lights her stove with it.

them believed that their government was too weak to improve things. At this point, Germany was politically divided. In election after election, no party won enough votes to provide the confident leadership Germany needed.

Inflation was followed by depression — the same Great Depression that had gripped the U.S. Depression sent prices skidding downward. But it also threw large numbers of workers out of jobs. In Germany many people began to look for extreme answers. Some Germans gave strong support to the Communist party. Others turned to the opposite extreme. They joined a party led by a former army corporal. His name was Adolf Hitler. The party he led was the National Socialist party, or Nazi party, for short.

Pride and prejudice. Hitler and the Nazis did not rise to power because of any noble ideas. Their main appeal was to German pride, which had been rubbed raw by the events of 15 years.

They also appealed to the prejudices of many Germans. They looked down upon almost everyone but the people of northern Europe as inferior. They preached hatred of all who opposed them, especially Jews. They blamed the Jews for Germany's defeat in World War I.

Hitler's Nazi party was a movement of the *right*. In politics, a right-wing movement is a strongly conservative one. Rightists are people who oppose most political change. Outside the U.S., rightists often favor such forms of government as monarchies or military dictatorships. (A political movement of the *left*, by contrast, is one that is strongly liberal or radical. Leftists stand for political ideas tending to change, reform, or overthrow things as they are. Outside the U.S., the term *left* usually refers to Communists or other followers of the German thinker, Karl Marx.)

Nazis paraded this Jewish man and non-Jewish woman through Nuremberg. The signs they wore said that they had offended "racial purity."

Rise to power. The Nazis got their chance at power in 1933. On January 30, Adolf Hitler was named chancellor, the head man of Germany's government. On March 5, the day after FDR took office in the U.S., the German people went to the polls. They gave nearly half their vote to the Nazi party. Before the month was out, Hitler had become dictator of Germany. He banned all other political parties. He gave himself the title "Der Führer" (dair FYUR-uhr), the leader. Then he began jailing and killing those who disagreed with him.

Germany was not alone in being ruled by dictators at this time. In Italy the dictator Benito Mussolini (beh-NEET-oh moo-suh-LEE-nee) had taken power in 1922. In the Soviet Union, a Communist

This 1933 cartoon portrayed Hitler as a bad joke on Germany. Later in the decade, it became clear that the Nazis were not a laughing matter at all.

Cartoon makes fun of isolationists who didn't want the U.S. to get involved in Europe.

dictator, Josef Stalin, had taken control a few years later. Stalin was especially ruthless. He killed hundreds of Soviet citizens without trial. He put millions to work in forced labor camps.

But it was Hitler who made it his special goal to wipe out all Jewish influence in his country's life. He took away the German citizenship of Jews. He forbade Jews to marry non-Jews. And this was only a beginning. Between 1935 and 1945, he directed the most enormous crime in human history. Under his leadership, the Nazis murdered about six million European Jews.

As Hitler became more powerful, he began to look beyond Germany's borders. In speech after speech, he called for a German empire that would rule the entire world. At

509

the same time, he began re-arming Germany. In 1936 German forces took back the Rhineland, an area west of the Rhine River. These lands had been given up by Germany following World War I. No democratic government in Western Europe wanted to get involved. All of them looked the other way.

Empire-building. So in March of 1938 Hitler became still bolder. This time he sent German troops to invade Austria and take it over. Britain, France, and the Soviet Union protested. But they took no action.

By the summer of 1938, then, the stage was set for still another of Hitler's daring acts. This time his target was the Sudetenland (soo-DAY-ten-land). The Sudetenland was an area of Czechoslovakia near the German border. About three million German-speaking people lived there.

In September Hitler announced his plan to seize the Sudetenland on October 1. He would go through with this plan, he said, unless the area was given to him peacefully. His threat brought Europe to the brink of war.

Americans did not watch these events with any pleasure. Yet they were in no mood to fight another war. Many of them now believed that the U.S. had been drawn into World War I by mistake. They thought that the U.S. should isolate itself — that is, stay clear of all agreements with foreign governments. These people were called *isolationists*.

Not all Americans were isolationists. A few went to Spain to fight against right-wing forces there. Others tried to help Germans and Italians escape from their homelands and come to the U.S. But most Americans seemed less actively concerned with events overseas.

The world *was* growing smaller, of course. In the end there was no retreat from the kind of trouble Hitler was stirring up in Europe. By 1940 Americans such as historian Ralph Barton Perry were sounding the call to arms. "If democracy be the great and good thing we believe it to be," Perry wrote, "we should expect its cost to be high." By that time, the costs of defending democracy in Europe were already mounting. They would soon begin to mount in the U.S. as well.

Nazi Germany on the March, 1935-1939

510

Chapter 31

Rise of a Dictator

As a boy in Austria, Adolf Hitler had not been strong enough to do hard labor. Later he had tried designing gift cards without any great success. During World War I, he had fought for Germany as an obscure corporal. Only after the war did Hitler discover his greatest talent — his voice.

He found it while making political speeches in the early 1920's. His speeches were in support of the National Socialist party — or Nazi party, for short. There was fire in his eyes as he promised to make Germany strong again. Germans, he said, were the master race.

His message was quite simple. The German army had not really been beaten in World War I, he claimed. Instead, he shouted, Germany had lost the war because it had been "stabbed in the back" by traitors and Jews. Germany must rebuild its army. It must win back the territory it had lost in World War I.

Hitler's message was both false and foolish. Yet it appealed to many Germans. Just then Germany was in a bad way. People were without jobs and were hungry. Hitler promised them jobs — and greatness. In 1923 he and his party tried to take power. But the police fired on them and sent them running.

Then Hitler was put in jail. There he wrote a book called *Mein Kampf* (mine kahmpf) which means "my struggle." It told of his plans to conquer much of Europe. Lands lost in World War I would be retaken. Germany would grab "living space" from Russia and other east European countries. And the Jews would be dealt with harshly. Hitler believed they were to blame for most of the evils of the world.

Hitler built up the Nazi party when he got out of prison. He won the support of many generals and businessmen who believed that the Nazis would save Germany from a Communist take-over.

Party in power. The worldwide Depression of the 1930's gave Hitler his big chance. Again many Germans were out of work and hungry. Hitler's promises of jobs and German greatness sounded better than ever.

In 1932 the Nazi party got four votes out of every 10. Early in 1933, Hitler became the German chancellor. Within a few months he got special laws passed that took away most of the German people's civil rights. The laws placed all the power in the hands of Hitler and the Nazi party. So Hitler became dictator. He soon began to rule Germany with an iron fist.

Hitler hated democracy, the Christian religion, and anything that wasn't German. His secret police shot or jailed all who spoke out against him. Labor unions and all political parties except the Nazis were outlawed. Books the

Nazis didn't like were burned. Jews were driven from their jobs and businesses. Many fled to other countries.

"Tomorrow the world." In 1934 Hitler began to prepare Germany for war. "Conquest is not only a right, but a duty," he told the German people. Today, Hitler bragged, the Nazis rule Germany. Tomorrow, the dictator promised, Germans would rule the world.

Hitler built the German army and air force into a powerful war machine. Factories turned out guns day and night. Of course, almost everyone was at work or in the army. Many Germans thought Hitler was a great man.

In 1936 Hitler sent troops into Germany's Rhineland. This action was against the Treaty of Versailles. The treaty said that there should be no German soldiers in the land west of the Rhine River. But Britain and France did nothing. This made Hitler bolder. Soon he grabbed Austria as well.

How did people in the United States take all this? At first they were not worried about it. The United States had enough problems of its own. It was too busy fighting the Depression at home to worry about Hitler over in Europe. Besides, many Americans felt they had no business in Europe's affairs. "Let Europe stew in its own juice," these people said. "Let's

World War I had wiped out the old German empire. To many Germans, the empire had been Germany itself. Hitler promised to rebuild the empire, known in German as the Reich *(pronounced "rike"). Nazi poster below says "Germany lives!" Armband and flags bear swastikas, the Nazi symbol.*

Es lebe Deutschland!

512

avoid doing anything that might get us involved in a war again," other people warned.

Congress felt the same way. It passed a series of Neutrality Acts in the 1930's. These acts were meant to keep the U.S. out of war. They forbade trade with either side in a war. But in 1937 President Roosevelt began to warn the American people of the danger from abroad. Few paid much attention to these warnings. Wasn't the United States protected by two oceans? The best course was to stay neutral, most Americans believed.

A Second Look. . . .

1. *What did Adolf Hitler say to make many Germans follow him? What did he say that caused some Germans to fear him?*

2. *A scapegoat is a person who takes the blame for others. What people did Adolf Hitler use as scapegoats in the 1930's? Why do people sometimes use someone else as an excuse for their own fail-*

ings? Give reasons for your answer.

3. *Imagine that your class is the U.S. Senate in the 1930's. Organize two committees. One committee should present arguments in favor of keeping the U.S. neutral. The other should present arguments against neutrality. After the debate, all "members of the Senate" should vote on the question.*

Hitler promised an empire to last a thousand years. But he sacrificed many Germans to build it. In this 1935 U.S. cartoon, he is shown using people to load his cannon. He looks warily out across Germany's borders with revenge in his eyes. His followers blindly give him the Nazi salute.

513

Chapter 32

The Brown Bomber

Joe Louis — the "Brown Bomber" — was enraged. In 1936 the boxer had been knocked out by Max Schmeling (SHMAY-ling), the German fighter. That was bad enough. But now the Nazis were bragging about it. It was, they said, a victory for Germany and the "master race."

Adolf Hitler had told the German people they were "supermen." All other people were inferior. Hitler especially looked down on black athletes from the U.S. Now Schmeling too was beginning to sound like a Nazi. He called Louis "black fellow" and "stupid amateur."

Louis couldn't wait to get even. "Get me Schmeling," he told his managers. "I want Schmeling." Finally the fight was set for the night of June 22, 1938. Louis trained harder than he ever had before. His muscles were like steel springs. A reporter asked him how long the fight would last. Louis held up one finger. "One round," he said.

More than 70,000 fans packed New York's Yankee Stadium for the fight. Millions more listened to it on the radio. At the bell, Louis tore into Schmeling. Three lefts and a right drove Schmeling back into the ropes. Louis kept hammering away. Schmeling looked sick. He couldn't move. His legs turned to jelly. Down he went for a count of three.

Schmeling got up, and Louis swarmed over him again. A right and a left sent Schmeling down again. Schmeling got to his feet, and Louis knocked him down a third time. Schmeling's handlers threw a towel into the ring (a sign they wanted to stop the fight). The referee threw it back. Now Schmeling was hanging on the ropes, helpless. Then the referee stopped the fight. "If I hadn't," he said later, "Joe would have killed him."

The Brown Bomber had gotten even in two minutes and four seconds of the first round!

Hard beginnings. Joe Louis Barrow (his real name) was born on May 13, 1914. His father was a poor Alabama tenant farmer, who died when Joe was four. Soon Joe was helping his mother, brothers, and sisters pick cotton. Joe's mother remarried, and the family moved to Detroit. Joe was then 10 years old. He hadn't gone to school much. In Detroit he was put in a class with younger kids. Joe didn't like that.

When the Depression came, Joe's stepfather lost his job. Joe had to go to work after school. He delivered ice. He would carry a 50-pound (23-kilogram) block of ice up four flights of stairs. Then another — and another. It was hard work, but it made Joe big and strong.

When Joe was 18, he heard that an amateur fight club paid fighters with food. Joe had hungry brothers and sisters at home, so he signed up for a fight. He was knocked down six times in the first two rounds. He went home aching

Two fights between Joe Louis (facing camera) and Max Schmeling made political history.

heavyweight title. He kept the title for 12 years. He defended it 25 times. He won 20 of his title fights by knockouts.

Boxing was good to Louis, and Louis was good for boxing. He had millions of fans, black and white. Louis often spoke of black Americans as "my people," and to them he was a special hero. "If I ever let my people down," he once said, "I want to die." He never let them down.

A Second Look. . . .

1. *What made Joe Louis such a special heavyweight champion? What was important about his defeat of Max Schmeling?*

2. *Many people say that sports in America are too competitive. They argue that the main purpose should not be winning but playing. Many other people repeat the words of Vince Lombardi, the famous football coach: "Winning isn't everything. It's the only thing." What's your view? Why do you take the position you do?*

3. *Many sports fans love statistics. For these fans, facts seem to take on a magical power. Choose one sport. Using an almanac or other source, make a list of several key facts in that sport over your lifetime: team champions, individual champions, individual records. Are sports statistics easier to remember than historical facts? If so, why?*

Joe Louis

and swore never to box again. He gave his mother the seven dollars worth of food he got. A little later he quit school and took a factory job.

Coming on strong. Soon Joe met a professional boxer. He gave Joe some lessons and talked him into entering the Golden Gloves. In 1934 he won the Golden Gloves light-heavyweight title. Then he became a pro. He won his first three pro fights by knockouts. Sportswriters began calling him the "Brown Bomber." He became the golden boy of boxing.

Louis came to New York and knocked out the giant Primo Carnera. Soon he was earning $250,000 a fight. In 1937 he knocked out Jim Braddock and won the

Chapter 33
The New Immigrants

By the time he was 40, Albert Einstein had done work that would win him the famed Nobel Prize.

Albert Einstein stood in front of his house, surrounded by suitcases. The world-famous scientist and his wife Elsa were about to leave Germany for a trip to the United States. Einstein seemed lost in thought as he gazed off into the distance and smoked his pipe. Finally he turned to Elsa and said, "Before you leave this time, take a good look at your house."

"Why?" Elsa asked.

"You will never see it again," was the reply.

In the fall of 1932, Germany was still a democratic country. But Einstein knew that the Nazis would soon be in power. He feared that the Nazis meant trouble for all Jews such as himself. And he was right.

Soon after Hitler took control in Germany, the Nazis began attacking Jews. Einstein was high on Hitler's "hate list." While the scientist was in America, the Nazis searched his German home for weapons. They found a bread knife in the kitchen and considered it a "dangerous weapon." The Nazis claimed the mild-mannered scientist was the leader of a "criminal gang."

Einstein never returned to Germany. At first he lived in Belgium. Then in 1933 he moved to Princeton, New Jersey, to

Although Adolf Hitler couldn't possibly have understood Einstein's work, he dismissed it as "Jewish physics." Nazi cartoon above shows the scientist being swept from his "ivory tower."

continue his scientific work. Einstein was famous for discoveries he had made about the structure of the universe. His discoveries were the most important work in science in 300 years.

Albert Einstein was one of the first Jews to leave Germany because of Hitler. He was followed by thousands more. In 1933 Hitler barred Jews from the universities as a first step in his attack on this group. This prompted a great many Jews to look for a way of escape. But finding another home was a problem. There was a Depression all over the world. Few foreign countries wanted outsiders, no matter where they came from or why.

In the U.S. and Britain, many people worked hard to help these new refugees.

To do so, Americans not only had to find ways around their own immigration laws. They also had to overcome prejudice against Jews and foreigners in general. Jewish groups and others helped people leave Germany and find new homes. U.S. college professors donated part of their salaries to hire foreign teachers.

Not all the refugees who came to the U.S. in the 1930's were Jewish. Some were Italians who were at odds with Mussolini. Others were non-Jewish Germans who disliked Hitler and simply wanted to get away from the Nazis. But most of these immigrants did share one thing in common. They were *political* refugees — people who had left their homelands for political reasons. And many were highly educated people — scientists, doctors, thinkers, and artists. Some were already well known when they arrived in the U.S. Others achieved fame afterward.

Who were these people? Here are three of the many who left their mark on American history:

Enrico Fermi (n-REE-koe FAIR-me). Fermi was one of the best-known refugees at the time he arrived. He came to

Enrico Fermi

517

the U.S. from Italy in 1939, a year after winning the world-famous Nobel Prize for physics. In the U.S. Fermi discovered how to make controlled atomic energy. Other refugee scientists helped him in his work. Then they joined with U.S. scientists to work on a top-secret military project. The *Manhattan Project,* as it was called, built the first atomic bombs which were used to end World War II.

Erik H. Erikson. Unlike Fermi, Erickson was just beginning his career when he came to the U.S. in 1933. Erikson had been raised as a Jew in Germany. Before he left Europe, Erikson had studied to be a psychiatrist (si-KI-a-trist). Psychiatry is the branch of medicine that deals with mental health.

In the U.S. Erikson became Boston's first child psychiatrist. He studied how children learn and change. His work with children led him to find a new use for psychiatry. Up to this time, psychiatry had been used mostly to treat the mentally sick. Erikson discovered ways to use it to help better understand healthy people. His ideas brought important changes in medicine and education.

Erik H. Erikson

518

Rudolf Serkin

Rudolf Serkin. When Serkin came to the U.S. in 1936, he was already a well-known pianist. He was born in Czechoslovakia of Jewish parents in 1903. At age 12, Serkin gave his first concert. His playing of the German masters — Bach, Beethoven (BAY-toe-ven), and Brahms — made him a great success in the U.S. In 1950 Serkin started the Marlboro Music School and Festival in Vermont. Every summer young musicians came to the school to live and make music with older people such as Serkin. In 1964 Serkin received the Presidential Medal of Freedom for his services to music and education.

Still other immigrants were social thinkers, or business or religious leaders. In all fields the new immigrants helped change the way people saw the world. Through their teaching and writing, their ideas reached millions. In time these ideas became an important part of American life.

There was another, sadder side to the story of immigration in the 1930's. Millions of Jews without money or influence found they could not leave Germany. As Hitler took over more countries, more people's lives were endangered. Only government action could have saved most of the millions of people who were threatened by Hitler. But the U.S. government did not want millions of people coming to America. The immigration laws sharply limited the number of people who could enter the U.S. Britain and France also refused to help on a massive scale. The millions left behind died in Hitler's gas chambers.

Reasons for limits. Today historians give several reasons for the U.S. government's policy. First, Americans of the 1930's did not realize how dangerous Hitler was. Few people seriously believed he would carry out a campaign of terror against all the Jews in Europe.

Second, Nazi Germany was not the only country to be troubled by anti-Semitism (prejudice against Jews). Some of it existed in the U.S. as well.

Third, the U.S. was in the midst of the Depression. Millions of Americans were out of work. For this reason, the U.S. government was not eager to allow large numbers of immigrants to enter. A larger wave of immigration would have made joblessness even worse.

Fourth, the 1930's were a period of isolationism. Many Americans thought the U.S. entry into World War I had been a mistake. Now they wanted no part of Europe or its problems. America was better off minding its own business, they believed.

In spite of U.S. immigration laws, about 100,000 refugees from Nazism did find their way to U.S. shores in this period. And in America they found freedom. Many of the new immigrants became U.S. citizens. Some of them fought in the U.S. armed forces during World War II. Others served in the government as experts on Hitler and Germany. After the war they continued to enrich American life as had immigrants before them.

A Second Look. . . .

1. What did most European immigrants of the 1930's have in common? What were some of their achievements? Give at least two reasons why the U.S. government refused to allow more of them to enter this country.

2. Do you think the U.S. should take in political refugees? What are the reasons for doing so? What are the reasons for turning large numbers of political refugees away? Can the U.S. afford to do so, as it did in the 1930's? Can it afford not to? Explain your answers.

3. Pretend you are an American of the 1930's. You have followed events in Nazi Germany, and they worry you. You have also studied U.S. immigration laws enough to have an opinion about them. Write a letter to the editor of your local newspaper. In the letter, you should either (a) defend U.S. immigration policy, or (b) criticize it for not allowing more Europeans to enter the U.S. Argue for one of these two positions as clearly as you can.

Chapter 34

Peace for Our Time

England. It was September 30, 1938. A huge crowd had gathered at an airport near London. They were waiting for a plane from Munich (MEW-nick), Germany. As the plane slowed to a stop, the crowd began to cheer loudly.

The door of the plane opened. There stood Neville Chamberlain, the British prime minister. In his hand was a piece of paper. He held it up for the crowd to see. Then the prime minister stepped to some microphones. "I think that it is peace for our time!" he said.

More cheers: "Good old Neville!"

France. Another crowd had gathered at an airport in Paris. When the plane came in, the Parisians rushed up to it even before it had stopped. Then Edouard Daladier (ED-wahr duh-LAHD-yay), the French premier, appeared. Crowds began dancing and cheering.

Daladier turned to a man at his side. "The fools," he said. "They don't know what they are cheering."

Czechoslovakia. There were crowds in the cities of Czechoslovakia too that day. These crowds were not cheering. Some people had tears running down their faces. September 30, 1938, was a sad day for the people of

Czechoslovakia, especially for the country's Jewish citizens.

Why were the crowds in London and Paris so happy? They believed that their leaders had saved them from a war with Nazi Germany. They thought Chamber-

In 1938 Hitler had been given the Sudetenland, part of Czechoslovakia. But he wanted the entire country. On March 15, 1939, Nazi troops entered Prague, the Czech captial. Czech citizens could not do anything but shake their fists and cry.

520

lain and Daladier had made a "deal" with Adolf Hitler. It wasn't just a deal. It was a bargain, so they thought.

The price of this "bargain" was some land that belonged to Czechoslovakia. It was called the *Sudetenland*. Hitler had wanted this land for a long time. He gave many warlike speeches about it at Nazi party meetings in Germany. "The people of the Sudetenland are Germans!" he screamed. "The Sudetenland must be turned over to Germany!" And if it weren't, he warned, Germany would go to war for it.

Fears of war. By the summer of 1938, people all over Europe were sure that a war would break out any moment. People were very scared.

The British and the French wanted to prevent war. So on September 29, 1938, Chamberlain and Daladier flew to Munich, Germany. They had a meeting with Hitler. All Europe held its breath for the outcome. Benito Mussolini, the Italian dictator, also went to Munich. He was Hitler's ally, and he backed everything Hitler said.

Hitler told the British and French that,

if they gave the Sudetenland to Germany, there would be no war. He also said that this would be his final demand for territory. He would ask for nothing more. Chamberlain and Daladier argued for hours. Finally they gave in. Early in the morning of September 30, they agreed to let Hitler take over the Sudetenland. In other words, they decided to *appease* Hitler (satisfy him to keep him at peace). Ever since, their policy has been known as one of *appeasement*.

No defense. Now Czechoslovakia was doomed. The Sudetenland was made up of many mountains. The mountains were vital to Czechoslovakia's defense. Without the Sudetenland, the Czechs could not hope to hold their country together against an outside force.

There was cheering in London and Paris. Most people in these cities thought that peace had been saved. The price of peace was not too high, many English and French people said. Besides, they were not ready for war. Neither England nor France had a large army or air force. Neither country was as powerful as Nazi Germany in 1938.

Many Americans also breathed a sigh of relief. To be sure, Czechoslovakia had been a small democracy. Its government had been on good terms with the U.S. Now thousands of Czech-Americans wept over the loss of their former homeland. Some other Americans worried all the more about the threat of war. But most Americans were relieved that the peace had been saved — at least for a little while.

The Czechs and Slovaks, on the other hand, believed that the price of peace was *much* too high. To keep Hitler quiet, they said, England and France had sold them down the river. England and France would see how wrong they had been. There was no way of stopping a man like Hitler from making more demands.

It turned out the Czechs and Slovaks were right. The English and the French *were* wrong. In a few months, German armies marched in and took over most of the rest of Czechoslovakia.

By that time, Hitler was looking for more land. Germany was more powerful than ever. The leaders of France and Britain had made a terrible mistake. World War II was the proof of it.

A Second Look. . . .

1. *What did Hitler gain in the Munich Pact in 1938? What did Britain and France gain? Who lost? Why?*

2. *The U.S. was not involved in the Munich Pact. At the time the U.S. was still following a policy of isolation. Some people say that, if the U.S. had shown some muscle, Hitler could have been stopped before World War II broke out. When, in your view, should the United States get involved in world affairs? Only when its self-interest is at stake? Or, in some cases, to help other people? Was American interest threatened by Hitler? If so, how?*

3. *Imagine that four people have met on the streets of Washington D.C. The first is British, the second is French, the third is German, and the fourth is Czech. The date is September 30, 1938. The four have just gotten word of the Munich Pact. Create a conversation in which each gives his or her opinion of what has happened.*

Looking Back: The Shadows of War

	A		B		C		D	
January 1, 1931		January 1, 1933		January 1, 1935		January 1, 1937		January 1, 1939

Putting Events in Order

Chapters 31 through 34 have described events in the days leading up to World War II. Ten events from this period are listed here. Your job is to match each event to the correct period shown on the timeline above. On a piece of paper, number from **1** to **10**. After each number, write the letter of the period in which the event occurred.

1. Joe Louis knocks out Max Schmeling in the first round.
2. Adolf Hitler takes control of Austria.
3. Adolf Hitler invades the Rhineland.
4. Albert Einstein comes to the U.S.
5. Adolf Hitler becomes chancellor of Germany.
6. Joe Louis wins the Golden Gloves light-heavyweight title.
7. Enrico Fermi wins the Nobel Prize.
8. Franklin Roosevelt first warns Americans of the dangers from abroad.
9. Adolf Hitler bars Jews from German universities.
10. Britain and France sign the Munich Pact with Adolf Hitler.

"Peace for our time," said British prime minister Neville Chamberlain, as he held up a copy of the agreement he had signed with Hitler in Munich.

Interpreting a Source

In 1937 Franklin Roosevelt went on a political tour of the nation. Like many other Americans, he was growing more and more alarmed by world lawlessness. Germany had seized the Rhineland. Italy had attacked the African country of Ethiopia (ee-thee-OH-pee-uh). For a brief time, Roosevelt seemed to consider taking action against "aggressor" nations — those nations which attacked others. During this period, he made the following speech in Chicago.

The present reign of terror and ... lawlessness began a few years ago.

It began through ... interference in the internal affairs[1] of other nations or the invasion of ... territory in violation of treaties, and has now reached a stage where the very foundations of civilization are seriously threatened.

The landmarks and traditions which have marked the progress of civilization

... are being wiped away. Without a declaration of war and without warning or justification[2] of any kind, civilians ... are being ruthlessly murdered with bombs from the air. In times of so-called peace, ships are being attacked and sunk by submarines without cause or notice. Nations are fomenting[3] and taking sides in civil warfare in nations that have never done them any harm. Nations claiming freedom for themselves deny it to others. Innocent peoples and nations are being cruelly sacrificed to a greed for power and supremacy[4] which is devoid[5] of all sense of justice and humane consideration....

If those things come to pass in other parts of the world, let no one imagine that America will escape....

If those days are not to come to pass, ... then the peace-loving nations must ... uphold laws and principles on which alone peace can rest secure....

---

[1]*Internal affairs* are those affairs within a country. The opposite of internal affairs is *external affairs* — those affairs affecting a nation's foreign policy.

[2]*Justification* means "a good reason."
[3]*To foment* something is to promote its growth and development, or to arouse or stir it up.
[4]*Supremacy* is the highest authority or power.
[5]To be *devoid* of something is to be completely without it.

Leaders of four European nations met at Munich in 1938. They are (left to right) Neville Chamberlain of Britain, Edouard Daladier of France, Adolf Hitler of Germany, and Benito Mussolini of Italy.

It seems . . . that the epidemic of world lawlessness is spreading. When an epidemic of physical disease starts to spread, the community . . . joins in a quarantine[6] of the patients in order to protect the health of the community against the spread of the disease. . . .

War is a contagion,[7] whether it be declared or undeclared. It can engulf[8] states and peoples remote from the original scene of hostilities. We are determined to keep out of war, yet we cannot insure ourselves against the disastrous effects of war and the dangers of involvement. We are adopting such measures as will minimize[9] our risk of involvement. But we cannot have complete protection in a world of disorder in which confidence and security have broken down. . . .

1. *Roosevelt gives several examples of how "traditions" which meant progress are being "wiped away." What are two of the examples he cites?*

2. *What does Roosevelt say peace-loving nations should do to prevent further lawlessness?*

3. *Does Roosevelt seem to be proposing that the U.S. be less neutral? Why or why not? What does he mean by the use of the term "quarantine"? Can nations be quarantined for their acts? If so, how might such a quarantine be carried out?*

---

[6]A *quarantine* is a keeping of a person away from other people because he or she has a disease which others could catch.

[7]A *contagion* is a spreading of a disease by contact.

[8]*To engulf* is to swallow up.

[9]*To minimize* is to reduce to the smallest amount possible. To minimize a risk is to make it much less.

Consultation.

Sharpening Your Skills

This cartoon appeared in the Louisville, Kentucky, *Courier Journal* in the late 1930's. Study it carefully. Then answer the questions.

1. What five nations are shown in the cartoon?

2. Why are four of them shown in an operating room?

3. Why is Czechoslovakia the "patient"?

4. What is the significance of the swords the "surgeons" hold?

5. What event in the 1930's does the cartoon refer to?

525

Book Four

4

Yesterday, Today, Tomorrow

1 THE U.S. IN WORLD WAR II

Looking Ahead: Allies Against the Axis

Headlights glared against the wet pavement. Cars inched along the busy street. Shouts and laughter rang out in the cool autumn evening. Another workday was ending at a large U.S. factory.

This was no ordinary daytime rush hour. It was midnight in Seattle, Washington, in November 1941. The aircraft factories of the Boeing Corporation were working around the clock. So were plants of other companies in places such as Santa Monica, California, and East Hartford, Connecticut. Workers were making weapons for a war they hoped would never come to the United States.

Far across the Pacific Ocean, a struggle for power was raging in China. Across the Atlantic Ocean in Europe, a

The grim meaning of World War II was often written in its rubble. Left, Rotterdam in the Netherlands, an hour after a Nazi bombing raid left the city in ruins in May of 1940.

similar struggle was under way. In 1941 these wars still seemed distant. Yet they were moving closer to the United States with almost every passing day.

What had started all this? In Europe the causes went back to the end of World War I in 1918. After the war, many Germans were out of work. They were hungry and angry. Some were ready to follow anyone who would give them back what they had lost in the war. Millions of Germans began to listen to a man with fire in his voice. His name was Adolf Hitler. He promised to make Germany a great nation again.

Restless mood. In 1933 Hitler and his National Socialist (Nazi) party took power in Germany. Hitler was a dictator who believed in using force. Soon the Nazis rebuilt the German army, navy, and air force. Threatening war, they took control of neighboring countries — first Austria, then parts of Czechoslovakia.

Germany was not the only country

Americans cheered new recruits marching off to war. These men were joining the Navy in Macon, Georgia.

grabbing land in the 1930's. Italian dictator Benito Mussolini also talked of greatness for his people. He marched armies into Ethiopia in Africa and Albania in Eastern Europe. He promised Italians an empire as great as that of ancient Rome.

In Asia, meanwhile, an old rivalry had long been brewing between China and Japan. Japan had won victories against China in 1895, and against Russia in 1905. Those victories had given the Japanese a new feeling of confidence. Military leaders had become a powerful force in Japanese life.

In 1931 Japanese troops attacked Manchuria (man-CHOO-ree-uh), a part of China. Before long, they took control of the region. This attack led to further fighting between China and Japan. The fighting continued, off and on, throughout the 1930's.

Lightning war. The shooting war in Europe began on September 1, 1939. On that day, Nazi Germany attacked Poland. Two days later, Britain and France declared war on Germany. In Poland, German dive bombers and tanks smashed all opposition. German armies rolled quickly across the Polish plains. The Nazis surprised the Poles with this new form of warfare. They called it *blitzkrieg* (BLITZ-kreeg) — "lightning war."

Germany, Italy, and Japan formed a war partnership known as the *Axis*. In 1940 and 1941, the Axis grew in strength. Germany and Italy took control of much of Europe. They also gained a foothold in North Africa. Japan was on the march in the Pacific.

In June 1941, Hitler attacked the Soviet Union. This later turned out to have been one of his greatest mistakes. The Soviet Union joined Britain, Canada,

Australia, and other nations in a fight to the finish against Germany. These nations became known as the *Allies*.

Sneak attack. Many Americans believed that the U.S. should also join the Allies. But some said that the U.S. had no business getting into other people's wars. On December 7, 1941, Japan settled the matter. Japanese warplanes attacked the U.S. naval base at Pearl Harbor, Hawaii. The next day, the U.S. declared war on Japan. Three days later, Germany and Italy declared war on the U.S.

At first the U.S. suffered some military setbacks. By the end of 1942, however, the U.S. and Britain had begun to push the Japanese back in the Pacific. The Soviets began to beat back Hitler's armies in Eastern Europe. The British did the same in North Africa.

Allied troops invaded Italy in 1943. The next year other Allied forces crossed the English Channel from Britain. The invasion of Nazi-held France was one of the greatest military operations in history. It spelled the beginning of the end for the Nazis. In less than a year, Allied armies were in Germany, and Hitler was dead.

Franklin Roosevelt did not live to see the end of the war. He died suddenly in April 1945, a few months after being elected to a fourth Presidential term. Vice-President Harry Truman followed FDR as President. Truman's first major decision was to use the atomic bomb against Japan. The bomb ended the war in the Pacific. But it began a new and possibly deadly time in human history. The period became known by a word used to describe atomic energy. It was called the *Nuclear Age*.

At war's end, most of the Allies were exhausted, and the Axis was in ruins. The United States had become the most powerful nation in the world. But the U.S. could no longer think of returning to the ways of its isolated past. The world had become too small.

The cartoon below appeared in 1944, when the war was nearly over. Allied leaders Roosevelt (left), Churchill (right), and Stalin (behind Churchill) look very pleased with their game. The Axis chiefs — Hitler (center), Mussolini (wiping his head), and Japanese Emperor Hirohito — aren't exactly smiling.

531

Chapter 1

Blitzkrieg

The Polish farmer bent to grab a handful of soil from his field. As he did, he heard a sound on the road behind him. Motors! And clanking like moving tractor treads. Whose tractor was this? Where was it going? And why?

The farmer turned to get a glimpse of the tractor. He soon saw that it was not a tractor at all but a German tank. Then came another tank, and another. The farmer hurried toward his house. Oddly, the first thought to cross his mind was the date. It was his son's fourth birthday — September 1, 1939.

The tanks were part of a new kind of war. The Germans called it *blitzkrieg*. Blitzkrieg meant speed and surprise — armies that traveled fast, sudden death from the skies. Nazi bomber planes led the way. They smashed Polish cities and towns. *Stuka* "dive bombers" swooped low and gunned soldiers and ordinary people alike.

On the ground, German tanks and motorcycles raced along Polish roads. Nazi troops, taking orders by radio and telephone, spread fire and death. Polish soldiers fought back bravely, but their guns were old. The Polish army was not prepared for such a war.

Britain and France declared war on Germany on September 3. But they were not much help to Poland. The Germans wrecked the Polish army within a week. Then Soviet armies moved in and grabbed eastern Poland. The Poles gave up on September 28. Germany and the Soviet Union divided Poland between them.

Military build-up. To most Americans, the war still seemed a long way off. They weren't in any danger — or so they thought. Still, President Roosevelt was worried. He was sure that Germany, Italy, and Japan planned to take over all of Europe and Asia. He did not want the U.S. to sit back and let this happen. "When you see a rattlesnake getting ready to strike," he said, "you do not wait till he has struck before you crush him."

Slowly, the President persuaded Congress to help Hitler's enemies. First, Britain and France were allowed to buy U.S. guns. Then the President asked for — and got — money to start building thousands of warplanes.

In June 1940, the Nazis crushed France. Britain stood almost alone. If it were beaten, the U.S. would be without any friendly nations in Western Europe. In September, the President sent Britain 50 old destroyers to help its fleet. In return, Britain gave the U.S. the right to lease naval bases in the Caribbean and part of Canada.

The U.S. also began beefing up the size of its Army and Navy. Under a 1940 law, all men between the ages of 21 and 35 were required to sign up as candidates for military service. Then certain of these men were chosen by lot from the larger group and *drafted* (called into the armed forces). This was the first peacetime draft in U.S. history. President Roosevelt approved it because he believed the country had to be ready to defend itself.

Lend-Lease. In the meantime, Britain was being pounded by German bombers at home. German tanks were overrunning the British in North Africa. Roosevelt knew that Britain had to have more weapons. But he also knew that the British did not have money to pay for them. Roosevelt suggested to Congress that the U.S. lend or lease weapons to Britain. He suggested that Britain could pay for the weapons later. Congress agreed to this Lend-Lease idea in March 1941. The U.S. was soon speeding weapons to the defense of Britain.

In the fall of 1940, Roosevelt ran for

The Nazi blitz broke homes and hearts. At right, a Belgian mother flees from German bombs. Below, a Frenchman cries as French flags come down. Flags were often removed before the Nazis came. The French knew they couldn't stop the blitz.

President for the third time. His Republican opponent, Wendell Willkie, was also "for Britain and against Hitler." But some Republicans said that Roosevelt was leading the country into war. Some Democrats said that Republicans wanted to ignore Hitler. Willkie worked hard, but Roosevelt won easily. He was the first President to be elected for a third term. (He is still the only President ever to have served more than two terms.)

By 1941 U.S. factories were busy day and night turning out all kinds of guns and other war materials. Our aim, the President said, was to give Britain all help "short of war." Millions of Americans agreed, including Kansas editor William Allen White. Americans, said White, must show that we are "not too blind or too timid to help those who are fighting tyranny abroad."

A Second Look. . . .

1. *What actions did the United States take in 1940-1941 to prepare for war? What did FDR do to help Britain? Why did Britain need help?*

2. *Britain is an island almost 3,000 miles (5,000 kilometers) across the Atlantic Ocean. Why should Americans have cared what happened to Britain in 1940? Couldn't the U.S. have just "sat this one out"? Explain your answers in as much detail as possible.*

3. *President Roosevelt's stand on war between 1939 and 1941 was somewhat similar to the stand taken by President Wilson between 1914 and 1917. How much do you recall of Wilson's stand? Make a list of the similarities between the two Presidents on this subject. Then make a list of the differences between them. Which President do you think was stronger in his stand? Why?*

Hitler made a point of following his troops into captured capitals. In October 1939, he reviewed soldiers from a victory stand in Warsaw, Poland. His photographer, Hugo Jaeger, recorded the scene.

Chapter 2

"This Is No Drill"

General Hideki Tojo (hih-DECK-ee TOE-joe) was carrying out a plan. It was to take over most of Asia. Tojo was one of the proud military men who ran Japan. These men thought Japan had a special right to rule Asia. Besides, Japan needed oil, tin, and rubber for its many factories. There was a large supply of such materials in the lands to the south and west of Japan.

The plan to rule Asia had begun long before Tojo became premier (head of government) in 1941. It had started a full 10 years earlier. In September 1931, Japanese armies had marched into Manchuria. In less than four months, they had taken complete control of it. This attack had set off a long war between Japan and China. By the end of 1940, Japan held sway over much of China. Japanese armies had also marched into the French colony of Indochina and occupied it.

Embargo on iron. U.S. leaders had grown more and more concerned. It seemed clear to many of them that the Japanese had to be prevented from grabbing more land. In 1940 the U.S. had stopped selling scrap iron to Japan. In 1941 it had stopped selling the Japanese oil. Such a ban on commerce and trade is called an *embargo*. These U.S. embargoes set back Japanese plans.

In November 1941, the U.S. was hav-ing peace talks with the Japanese. The talks were going badly. The Japanese wanted a free hand in China. The United States wanted them to get out of China. Neither side would give in.

General Tojo secretly set November 25 as the last day for a peaceful agreement. After that, he planned to bomb Pearl Harbor, Hawaii. Pearl Harbor was the chief U.S. Navy base in the Pacific. By smashing the U.S. fleet, Japan could grab what it wanted in Asia before the United States could hit back.

On November 26, a large Japanese fleet sailed secretly toward Pearl Harbor. A few days later, the Japanese admiral got a message. It said, "Climb Mount Nitaka." This was a code meaning, "Attack Pearl Harbor." In Washington, D.C., the Japanese ambassador and his helpers were still holding "peace" talks.

"Blips" on a screen. The date for the Japanese attack was set for Sunday, December 7, 1941. That Sunday morning the weather over Hawaii was clear. Two U.S. Army privates were watching their radar screen. This new equipment was supposed to spot planes from far away.

At 7:02 A.M., the men noticed a "blip" on the screen. This little spot on the screen meant that planes were coming near. The men phoned their command post. The only man on duty there was new at his job. He said, "Don't worry."

535

The blips were probably U.S. planes.

At 7:55 the first Japanese planes attacked. They dropped bundles of bombs. U.S. warships lying at anchor along "Battleship Row" in Pearl Harbor were easy targets. So were the planes neatly lined up on the airfields. Minutes later a Navy loudspeaker blared: "Air raid, Pearl Harbor. *This is no drill.*"

Not everyone could hear the announcement. A few guessed that it was a Japanese attack. But others thought U.S. planes were bombing the place by mistake. Still others thought it was a "practice" raid.

Finally, the men on the ships realized that this really was not a drill. The Japanese were bombing them. Sailors climbed up ladders, trying to reach their battle stations. On some ships, they found the ammunition boxes locked. On shore there was great confusion too. But many men fought bravely against the attackers.

A base on fire. By 10 A.M., it was all over. The last of the Japanese planes had left. The great U.S. base at Pearl Harbor was a burning wreck. When the smoke cleared, the Japanese attack had left 2,400 people dead and 1,200 wounded. The Japanese had sunk 18 ships, including six big battleships. The enemy had destroyed 188 U.S. planes.

In just two hours, most of the U.S. Pacific fleet was put out of action. Half the planes in Hawaii had been destroyed. The Japanese had caught the U.S. off guard.

The next day, President Roosevelt called Congress together and reported

Smoke and flames pour from a U.S. battleship after the Japanese attack on Pearl Harbor.

Pearl Harbor dashed all doubts about U.S. entry into the war. As cartoonist Daniel Bishop predicted, the attack rallied the U.S. to fight.

the great damage done by the Japanese sneak attack. He asked Congress to declare war on Japan. Within 40 minutes the voting was over. The United States was now in World War II until the end.

A Second Look. . . .

1. *Why was the Japanese attack on Pearl Harbor considered such a disaster? What was the extent of the damage done in the attack?*

2. *In 1940 and 1941, the United States stopped selling scrap iron and oil to Japan. What was the purpose of this embargo? How might the embargo be considered a cause of the Pearl Harbor attack? In the light of this attack, do you think the embargo was a good idea? Why or why not?*

3. *December 7, 1941, was a day few Americans now past 50 have forgotten. Talk to people in your community who recall learning of Pearl Harbor. Find out where they were when they first heard the news. What were their thoughts and feelings? Write an essay based on your interviews.*

Chapter 3

The Home Front

In the 1940's, most local movie theaters ran newsreels along with their features. Newsreels recorded news events of the recent past. And by 1942 many newsreel scenes from the home front were familiar. There were soldiers and sailors kissing their wives, mothers, and sweethearts good-bye. There were women in Army, Navy, and Air Force uniforms or working in overalls in war factories. There were young people collecting aluminum pots and pans for the war drive.

Most Americans at home did not suffer much. There were air-raid drills and blackouts, but U.S. towns and cities were never bombed. Many goods and foods were hard to get, but few Americans went hungry. Taxes were higher, but people were working hard and earning good pay.

Americans took pride in the way they helped win the war. Millions of people pitched in. Airplane factories were built in cornfields. Soon the U.S. was making 5,000 planes a month. Shipyards sprang up almost overnight. Some ships were built in just six weeks.

"Arsenal of democracy." Factories almost everywhere started to make war goods. Automobile factories turned out tanks — 86,000 of them. Typewriter factories made machine guns. Vacuum cleaner factories made shells and bullets. A flood of war goods

538

poured out of these factories. There was enough for our armies and for our allies too. Some people compared the United States to an *arsenal* (a workshop and storehouse for guns and ammunition). The U.S. was called the "arsenal of democracy."

Americans paid for these war goods with higher taxes and by buying war bonds. War bonds were certificates issued by the U.S. government to raise money for the war effort. The govern-

Most of America's industrial power went into the war effort. These women assembled airplane engines in a factory kept open round-the-clock.

ment promised to repay the buyer, with interest, over a given time. Americans also had to put up with empty store shelves. It was hard to get such things as hairpins, nylon stockings, cigarettes, and alarm clocks. If people complained, storekeepers had an answer: "Don't you know there's a war on?"

Many foods were *rationed* (strictly limited). Under the rationing program, each U.S. family received a fixed amount of such food. Housewives needed ration stamps to buy meat, butter, sugar, coffee, and canned goods. Many people grew food in "victory gardens." These gardens soon turned out 40 percent of the nation's fresh vegetables. Ration stamps were also needed to buy gasoline and shoes. There were no new cars, tires, or refrigerators.

"Black markets." The government "froze" wages and prices — wages and prices could not be raised. Most Americans did all they could to cooperate, but some people cheated. They *hoarded* (stored up) goods and foods that were hard to get. *Black markets* were places where you could buy rationed or hard-to-get items such as meat, tires, or cigarettes. Black-market buyers paid high prices — prices higher than the stores charged.

About six million women went to work in offices and factories. They performed such jobs as hammering rivets in planes and ships. About 200,000 women joined the armed forces. Children also did their part. They collected pots, pans, and tin cans for scrap metal.

There was a sadder side to the war on the home front, however. This sad story concerned the treatment of one of the

World War II was fought overseas. Yet this poster tried to persuade Americans that the distant fighting could come close to home.

smallest U.S. minority groups. Early in 1942, prejudice against Japanese Americans began to grow. Anti-Asian groups spread fears that Japanese spies would blow up oil refineries or do other damage. Could most people of Japanese descent be trusted? Without any solid evidence to support their case, these anti-Asian groups said, "No!"

Such groups called for the imprisonment of everyone of Japanese descent. They urged that such a program include American-born citizens and foreign-born aliens alike. As pressure grew, some high-ranking military leaders joined in the call. On February 19, 1942, President Roosevelt gave in to these pressures. He signed an order permitting the setting up of "military areas" within the U.S. Military leaders could remove people from these areas as they saw fit.

"Relocation" program. The military acted quickly. It removed all Japanese Americans who lived in California, Oregon, the western part of Washington, and the southern part of Arizona. More than 110,000 people were rounded up, about 70,000 of them U.S. citizens. They became prisoners in two main stages. First, they were moved to assembly centers — temporary dwellings built mostly at racetracks and fairgrounds. Then they were sent to one of 10 specially built "relocation centers" in wilderness areas of the West.

This program was known as *internment*. The move wrenched families from their homes, their friends, even their household pets. It also forced them to sell or store their belongings, often at great cost. Yet, in almost every instance, the Japanese accepted the move peacefully. Some simply said, "It cannot be helped."

The move was difficult, but camp life was even harder. Each relocation center differed, of course, but most had several things in common. All were lined with

The tags on these Americans showed that they were bound for internment camps. Few Americans of German or Italian descent were confined by the U.S. government during the war.

tar-paper barracks and encircled by heavy barbed wire and watchtowers. The wire was meant to keep Japanese Americans in and other people out.

Life in the camps caused many Japanese Americans to ask some searching questions. Why had this happened to *them?* After all, German and Italian Americans had not been victims of mass imprisonment. Were the Japanese more dangerous? If so, why hadn't most Japanese Americans who lived in Hawaii been put into camps?

Many people in the camps decided they must prove their loyalty to the U.S. in whatever way they could. As soon as it became possible, hundreds of men signed up for military service. Many went to Europe to fight in the 442nd Regimental Combat Team.

Honored unit. The famed 442nd was made up entirely of Japanese Americans from Hawaii and the mainland. Battling its way through Italy and eastern France, it saw some of the heaviest fighting of the war. By war's end, it had become one of the most decorated units in U.S. military history. When it came time to honor these soldiers, however, their relatives rarely attended. Most remained confined in relocation camps.

Many people stayed in the centers for more than two years. When the war ended in 1945, a few Japanese Americans asked to be sent to Japan. But most returned to the West Coast — to towns and villages that had been home, to neighbors who had once been friends. These people were betting on the future, and the odds were about to turn in their favor.

Over the next few years, prejudice against them would begin to fade. As the fame of the 442nd spread, many Americans would realize that loyalty could not be measured by the color of one's skin. The U.S. government would also make up for some of the damage done by internment. It would repay Japanese Americans for some of their property losses.

The internment program had cost U.S. taxpayers more than one quarter of a *billion* dollars. It had cost Japanese Americans millions more in losses never recovered. Much more painful was the human cost — the two-and-a-half years of hardship borne by Japanese Americans themselves. Historians now agree that little or nothing would have been lost by leaving these people at liberty throughout the war.

A Second Look. . . .

1. What changes did the war make in people's daily lives — especially the lives of U.S. women? Name three of these changes.

2. During World War II, some people hoarded goods and foods that were hard to get. Why do you suppose such hoarding was considered cheating in wartime?

3. Pretend that you are a 21-year-old U.S. citizen of Japanese descent. It is September 1942, and you are living in a relocation center. You have just finished reading an editorial from a West Coast newspaper. The editorial suggests that the U.S. has gone to war to fight for democracy. You owe a letter to a friend stationed with the U.S. Army in London. You want to explain your feelings without making your friend feel bitter toward the U.S. government. What will you say?

Allied troops poured onto the beaches of northern France during the D-Day invasion. Meanwhile, German guns blasted the beaches from nearby cliffs. The invasion was the beginning of the end of the war.

Chapter 4

End of the Nazis

In the spring of 1944, England was an armed fort. Airfields were packed with fighter planes and bombers. Harbors were filled with warships and freighters to carry supplies. Nearly three million

Allied soldiers were waiting to climb onto ships and planes. The ships and planes would take the soldiers to France. Their invasion of France would be called *D-Day* (Debarkation Day).

Debarkation means "to put ashore."

The Nazis knew an invasion was coming. Their best general, Marshal Erwin Rommel, had been chosen to throw it back. He had turned the beaches of France into death traps. The waters along the shore were filled with mines and iron fences. Barbed wire was strung along the beaches. Machine-gun nests were built on the cliffs above. Hitler boasted that "no power in the world can drive us out."

It was up to General Dwight D. ("Ike") Eisenhower, the Allied Commander, to name the invasion day. Ike decided that the best days would be June 5, 6, or 7, when the tides would be favorable. For a week before the invasion, Allied planes bombed roads, bridges, and airfields in France. They also smashed at German guns on the coast.

On the night of June 5, 1944, the Allied invasion fleet sailed for Normandy, France. In it were 4,000 ships of all sizes. They carried 175,000 men and thousands of tanks, trucks, and jeeps. Overhead, thousands of Allied planes covered them.

Normandy landing. On the morning of June 6, the invasion fleet reached the beaches of Normandy. The Germans had expected the Allies to land somewhere else. Allied planes bombed and machine-gunned the German defenders. Six big battleships fired on the German forts. Guns from dozens of destroyers smashed at German defenses. Then the landing boats went in.

Many German cannons and machine guns had not been knocked out. They opened fire with a roar. Many landing boats were hit. Some still kept coming on. Sometimes the Allied soldiers jumped into the water too soon and drowned. But thousands of soldiers made it to the beaches.

On the beaches, Allied soldiers were hit by a storm of fire. At one beach, called Omaha, U.S. soldiers ran into a top German outfit. The Americans were machine-gunned as they jumped into the water. Many were killed. Others were wounded and drowned. Some were hit along the water's edge.

Yet the Allies finally took Omaha Beach and other beaches. By the night of June 6, they occupied about 80 miles (130 kilometers) of the French coast. Nearly 155,000 Allied soldiers were in France. Slowly they began to move inland. The final push toward Germany was getting underway.

Rhine crossing. The Germans did not give ground easily. Every mile inland from the beaches was bought with Allied blood. But by July, Allied tanks had broken through German lines. In August, Paris was freed after four years of Nazi rule. In October, Allied forces crossed the Rhine River into Germany itself.

Germany had been at war on two fronts, east and west, since 1941. In that year, Germany had attacked the Soviet Union by surprise. At first, German armies had driven deep into Soviet territory. Then the Soviets had begun a counterattack. By the end of 1944, Soviet armies were rolling steadily westward.

The Nazis were being pounded on two sides at once. By February 1945, both the Allies and the Soviets were fighting inside Germany. German armies were on the edge of complete collapse. The Allies were headed toward the German capital, Berlin.

543

Along the way, soldiers came upon sights too terrible to believe. These were the Nazi death camps. Here millions of people had been tortured and killed by the Nazis. Some had been starved to death. Some had been beaten to death. Many had been killed with poison gas. Who were these people? Some were lame, feeble, or retarded. They were outcasts among Nazis who thought of

As Allied armies drove deeper into Germany, they stumbled upon scenes like this one at Nordhausen. In such death camps, Nazis killed people they thought to be of "inferior races" — mainly Jews.

Germans as being a "master race." Other victims were prisoners of war. Still others were Hitler's political opponents. But nearly half — several million men, women, and children — were Jews.

The Nazis usually burned the bodies of their victims in ovens. But in some camps they did not have time to destroy the "evidence." Allied soldiers found bodies piled up like logs of wood. In other camps, the bodies were buried in giant graves. Some of the prisoners were still alive when Allied soldiers arrived. Many cried when they were finally saved from the Nazis.

Fall of Berlin. On April 25, 1945, Soviet armies cut off Berlin from the rest of Germany. Hitler himself took charge of German soldiers in the city. Some were 12 and 13 years old, but Hitler ordered them to fight to the end. There was bitter fighting from street to street and house to house. But by May 2 the Soviets had taken the city.

As the Allies drew closer, Hitler moved to an underground fort. By April 30, he knew Germany was beaten. He did not want to be captured, so he put a pistol to his head and shot himself to death.

One week later, on May 7, 1945, Germany gave up. The next day, May 8, was celebrated as *V-E Day* — for Victory in Europe. All over the free world, people cheered until they lost their voices. Many cried with joy.

What happened to the top Nazi leaders? Some followed Hitler's example and killed themselves. The Allies rounded up others and put them on trial as war criminals. The trials began in November 1945 in Nuremberg, Germany, before a

Allied bombers leveled many German cities in the final days of the war. This is Munich in 1944.

watchful world. The Nazi defendants claimed they were guilty of no crimes. They had merely "followed orders."

But the French, British, Soviet, and U.S. judges did not think this was a good excuse. They found many Nazis guilty of "crimes against humanity." Murder could not be justified by "following orders," the Allies said. Every person was responsible for his or her own actions.

Eleven top Nazis were sentenced to death. Seven were sent to prison. Three were freed. Later, more than 80,000 Germans were found guilty of war crimes. Very few served long sentences — not even those convicted of murdering many people. Today some Nazi war criminals are still hiding in other countries, including the U.S.

A Second Look. . . .

1. *What was D-Day? When and where did it take place? How did Adolf Hitler meet his end in the closing days of World War II? What happened to other Nazi leaders after the war was over?*

2. *The Nazis who went on trial for "crimes against humanity" claimed they were "not guilty." They said they were just "following orders." Is a person who does something wrong while following orders less wrong than someone who does the same thing on his or her own? Explain.*

3. *At the end of World War II, the Allies included the U.S., Britain, Canada, France, China, and the Soviet Union. The enemies of the Allies included Germany, Italy, and Japan. Where do those nine countries stand today? Make three lists, one for those countries allied with the U.S., one for those allied against the U.S., and one for neutrals. How do you explain the membership in each group? What, if anything, does this say about alliances? Why?*

545

Chapter 5

FDR's Last Days

President Franklin Roosevelt was tired, very tired. He had been President of the United States for 12 years. Now he was beginning his fourth term in office. No other President had ever served that long. Since the U.S. entry into World War II, Roosevelt had managed to rest very little. He had worked into the night, every night, to get his job done. His doctors had warned him to take it easy. But the President had found this impossible to do.

In January 1945, Roosevelt had traveled half way around the world to Yalta in the Soviet Union. There he had met with Britain's Prime Minister Winston Churchill and Soviet dictator Josef Stalin. The three leaders had planned the final victory over Germany and Japan. They had also planned a meeting in San Francisco to set up the United Nations.

The 14,000-mile (22,500-kilometer) trip was hard on FDR. When he got back to the U.S., people were shocked by his appearance. He looked pale and thin. He seemed older than his 63 years. When he spoke to Congress about his trip, he sat in a chair. It was easier, he said, than standing with a 10-pound ($4\frac{1}{2}$-kilogram) brace around his legs. (Roosevelt's legs had been paralyzed by polio when he was a young man.)

The President's doctor ordered him to take a rest. He agreed to go to Warm Springs, Georgia, for a month of spring vacation. Warm Springs was a treatment center for polio. The President had often gone there in the past to relax and exercise his body. He had spent many hours in a pool. Walking was difficult and painful for him. But swimming was easier, good exercise, and fun.

The vacation at Warm Springs seemed to have a good effect. After a few days, a rosy color came back to FDR's cheeks. On Thursday, April 12, the President planned to spend an easy day. He would read some official papers and pose for a painting. Roosevelt felt happy. The war news that day was good. One U.S. Army unit was only 57 miles (92 kilometers) from Berlin.

Sudden headache. Near one o'clock, Roosevelt was finishing his work in his cottage. Lunch was set on a tray before him. The artist was busy painting. Suddenly FDR put his hand to his head. He was in pain. "I have a terrific headache," he said. Then he fainted. He never spoke again.

Doctors rushed to the President's side. But there was nothing they could do. At 3:35 in the afternoon, FDR was dead. The cause of his death was a stroke, or cerebral hemorrhage (bleeding in the brain).

At about 4:50 that afternoon, the news of FDR's death was flashed to the world. At first, people couldn't believe it. "No, it can't be," they said. Then, as the truth sank in, millions of men and women cried. Aboard a ship, a sailor said, "It's like someone dying in your own family."

Sad telegram. Mrs. Roosevelt sent a telegram to her four sons in the armed forces. It said: "Pa slept away this afternoon. He did his job to the end as he would want you to do."

Then she broke the news to Vice-President Harry Truman. At first he was too overcome to speak. Finally, he turned to Mrs. Roosevelt and asked,

In January 1945, President Franklin Roosevelt (center, front row) met with Winston Churchill (left) and Josef Stalin (right) at Yalta.

"Is there anything I can do for you?"

"Is there anything *we* can do for *you?*" she replied. "For *you* are the one in trouble now."

Within two hours, Truman had been sworn in as the nation's 33rd President.

Republican Senator Robert Taft spoke for millions when he said, "Franklin Delano Roosevelt died a hero of the war, for he worked himself to death in the service of the American people."

A younger member of Congress, Democrat Lyndon B. Johnson, mopped his eyes. FDR, he said, "was the one person I ever knew, anywhere, who was never afraid."

But perhaps the American people said it best. As their President's body was carried by train from Warm Springs to Washington, D.C., thousands of them stood by the railroad tracks and wept.

A Second Look. . . .

1. *How old was Franklin D. Roosevelt when he died? Where was he and why? How long had he been President?*

2. *FDR was a popular President. To many Americans he was like a father through the hard times of the Depression and World War II. Is there a public figure who is important to you? How is this person important in your life? What values, hopes, and style does he or she represent?*

3. *Some people say, "The times make the man." They mean that events sometimes bring out the best in even ordinary people. What events in Roosevelt's time brought out the best in him? What did he do about these events? Write a 50-word essay telling (a) why the times brought out the best in him, or (b) why the times did not.*

547

Chapter 6

A-Bomb

At seven o'clock on the morning of August 6, 1945, the people of Hiroshima (hear-uh-SHE-muh), Japan, were getting up for a new day. Some of them were eating breakfast. Others were on their way to work. Japan was still at war with the United States and its allies. But people were doing the same things they did on any day.

Just then air-raid sirens sounded. The people of Hiroshima were not surprised. The warning sounded every morning when a U.S. weather plane flew over. So far, Hiroshima had been lucky. Almost every other large Japanese city had been hit hard by air raids. Hiroshima, with 245,000 people, had not been bombed at all. The people were beginning to wonder how long their luck would last.

At eight o'clock, the all-clear signal sounded. Japanese radar men had spotted three U.S. planes flying toward Hiroshima. But they did not believe it was a bombing raid. Raids were usually carried out by many planes.

Darkness after dawn. Suddenly, at 8:15, a blinding flash of light cut across the sky. It was much brighter than sunlight. The center of this great ball of light was hotter than the surface of the sun. A great column of heat and dust began to climb miles into the sky. Clouds of smoke and dust turned the day into darkness.

548   What had happened? A U.S. plane, the

Enola Gay, had dropped an atomic bomb on the city.

Such a bomb had been in the planning stage in the U.S. for four years. Scientists had begun developing it in 1941. From the beginning, their work had been top secret. After 1943 it had been carried out in a unit known by its code name, the *Manhattan Project.*

Harry Truman knew nothing of the Manhattan Project when he became President in April 1945. When he first learned of it, he just sat and stared into space. The bomb would have more power than 20,000 tons (18,000 metric tons) of TNT. It would have more than 2,000 times the power of the biggest dynamite bomb used so far in World War II. Yet, like it or not, Truman did not interfere with the project. He and his top advisers hoped that the use of the bomb might shorten the war.

Split in the skies. In mid-July, the bomb was tested in the desert near Alamogordo, New Mexico. One observer described the test. "It was as though the earth had opened and the skies had split," he wrote. The test was a success. A few days later, Truman gave a temporary go-ahead to plans for using the bomb on Japan. But before the bombing actually took place, the Allies made one last try to end the war.

Late in July, the U.S., Britain, and China offered Japan new peace terms.

Under these terms, Allied troops would occupy Japan. War criminals would be punished. But Japan would not be enslaved or destroyed. Japan was told that its only other choice was "prompt and utter destruction." Even so, Japan would not surrender.

Japan's refusal sealed its fate. To top-level U.S. officials, the use of the bomb seemed less costly than trying to invade Japan's home islands. A month earlier, the U.S. had driven the Japanese from the island of Okinawa (oh-kee-NAH-wah). In the fighting, 11,260 U.S. soldiers and sailors had lost their lives. The Japanese had lost a staggering 100,000 men. Now fighting in Japan's home islands promised to be even bloodier. No one could predict how long it would take to win a victory.

And so the U.S. used the bomb on Hiroshima. In the center of the city, almost every building was knocked down.

The temperature was so hot that steel bubbled away as if it were boiling water. Farther out, trees were burned black. Burned-out streetcars and autos filled the streets. Even houses on the far edge of the city were badly damaged.

Burials from the blast. Thousands of people were buried alive in the ruins. Some lucky ones were able to dig themselves out. Fire broke out all over. The people who had lived through the blast began to run away from the blazing city. They were shocked and dazed. Many of them bled from their heads, chests, and backs. Some sat or lay down in the streets, vomited, and waited to die.

Soon the wounded began to crowd into hospitals. For many there was no hope. Many doctors had been killed, the hospitals wrecked. In one hospital, patients died by the hundreds.

About two weeks after the blast,

War in the Pacific, 1941-1945

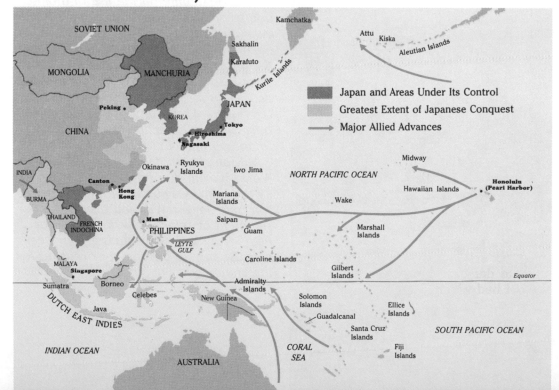

thousands of people suddenly became sick. Their hair began to fall out. They became weak with fever. Soon their gums bled, and red spots appeared on their skin. Old wounds opened up or did not heal. These people were suffering from a new disease — radiation sickness. Many died. In all, between 70,000 and 80,000 people died from the blast or its effects. About the same number were wounded.

The Japanese kept on fighting after August 6. But U.S. leaders were more determined than ever to bring the war to an end. On August 9, another atomic bomb was dropped by the U.S. on the city of Nagasaki (nah-guh-SAH-kee). This city was also largely destroyed. On August 10, President Truman warned that more A-bombs would be dropped unless the Japanese surrendered.

On August 14, the Emperor of Japan said his country would give up. After six years of fighting, World War II was over at last.

Some people said it was wrong to drop atomic bombs on cities where many civilians lived. The U.S. should have found another way of ending the war, these people believed. Others said that it was necessary to drop the bombs. If they had not been used, the war might have lasted at least another year.

Today people in the U.S. and other countries still argue over whether the U.S. should have used the bomb on Japan. And all the world's people hope that the two bombs dropped on Japan are the last ever to be used.

A tiled fireplace survived the atomic attack on Hiroshima. More than 70,000 Japanese did not.

A Second Look. . . .

1. *What effects did the atomic bombing have on Hiroshima? What effect did the two bombings have on World War II?*

2. *The debate on the use of atomic bombs on Japan continues. Some people even claim that it was a "war crime" to have dropped the bombs. Others point to the thousands of lives that would have been lost in an invasion of Japan. What do you think? What other choices did the U.S. have? Would any of these choices have been as effective as the bombings in ending the war? Why or why not?*

3. *Imagine that you are a U.S. pilot in World War II. You have been chosen to fly the* Enola Gay *on its atomic-bombing run over Japan. Will you accept the assignment or reject it? Write a one- or two-paragraph essay stating your decision. Be sure to include your reasons for the choice you have made.*

Looking Back:
The U.S. in World War II

	A	B	C	D	
January 1, 1939		January 1, 1941	January 1, 1943	January 1, 1945	January 1, 1947

Putting Events in Order

Chapters One through Six have covered the history of World War II. Ten events from this period are listed here. Your job is to match each event to the correct period shown on the timeline. On a piece of paper, number from **1** to **10.** After each number, write the letter of the two-year period within which the event occurred.

1. Japanese airplanes attack the U.S. base at Pearl Harbor, Hawaii.

2. German armies invade Poland.

3. Franklin Roosevelt signs an order allowing "military areas" to be set up within the U.S.

4. An atomic bomb is dropped on Hiroshima, Japan.

5. Wendell Willkie runs for President.

6. Franklin Roosevelt dies at the age of 63.

7. Allies launch a D-Day invasion of Normandy.

8. Franklin Roosevelt sends Britain 50 old U.S. destroyers.

9. Germany attacks the Soviet Union.

10. World War II comes to an end.

Interpreting a Source

One of the best-known reporters of World War II was radio broadcaster Edward R. Murrow. Murrow became famous for his reports on the bombing of London and other British cities by Nazi Germany in 1940 and 1941. During the war, he also traveled to other parts of the world to report on the fighting at firsthand. When the war was formally ended on September 2, 1945, Murrow was back in London. Here is his report of that date.

And now there is peace. The papers have been signed. The last enemy has given up — unconditionally.[1] There is a

---

[1]To give up *unconditionally* is to surrender without any "ifs" or "buts."

551

silence you can almost hear. Not even the distant echo of guns or the rumble of bombers going out with a belly full of bombs.... There are white crosses and scrap iron, scattered round the world, and already some of the place names that will appear in the history books are fading from memory.... Six years is a long time — and it was more than twice as long for the Chinese.

Today is so much like that Sunday six years ago today [when war began in Europe]. There is sun; the streets are empty. There is just enough breeze to fill the sails of small boats on the Thames [River]. People are sitting in deck chairs in the parks. People *and* chairs are shabbier than they were six years ago. It is a long time, long enough for nations to disappear and be recreated. Long enough ... for a way to be found that may destroy humanity.

But there is a fundamental difference between the atmosphere[2] today and six years ago. Then the assumption[3] was that this war was just taking up where the last one left off.... Few, if any, foresaw what the price of victory would be. I doubt that any single individual can grasp it now.... Those who thought this would be an old-fashioned war when it started six years ago do not believe that peace can be made in the old-fashioned mold. It will require daring ... and the constant knowledge that victory is no guarantee of peace.

We seem to be in a condition where there are few fixed, firm standards, so many of the old landmarks have been destroyed. There is even confusion about the meaning of familiar words.... Democracy is used to defend policies pursued in [the capitals of several Eastern European countries]. It is clear that the word has a different meaning in different parts of the world but is still found useful as a slogan. Maybe we should start by redefining the word and settle for a written constitution, freedom of speech, a secret ballot, and no secret police.

1. *How does Murrow describe the city of London on September 2, 1945?*

2. *What does he mean by "white crosses and scrap iron"?*

3. *What does he mean by saying that six years is "long enough ... for a way to be found that may destroy humanity"? What does he mean by "victory is no guarantee of peace"?*

4. *Why, at the end of World War II, might it have occurred to some people that the world needed to redefine "democracy"? Do you agree that the four terms Murrow uses in his definition sum up the idea of democracy? If so, why? If not, what other terms come to mind?*

Sharpening Your Skills

After D-Day, the Allies freed France and Belgium from German control within seven months. The map on the next page shows the routes taken by the U.S., British, Canadian, and French armies in their drive toward Germany. Study the map carefully. Then answer the questions below.

1. On what day in 1944 was St. Malo freed? Which forces freed it?

---

[2]*Atmosphere,* in this sense, means surrounding influence or mood.

[3]An *assumption* is something taken for granted.

2. On what day was Paris retaken? About how many weeks went by between the taking of St. Malo and the taking of Paris?

3. Name three rivers crossed by U.S. forces.

4. True or false? The port of Calais was in the area of the D-Day landing.

5. True or false? The French army had a big role in freeing Paris.

War in Western Europe, 1944

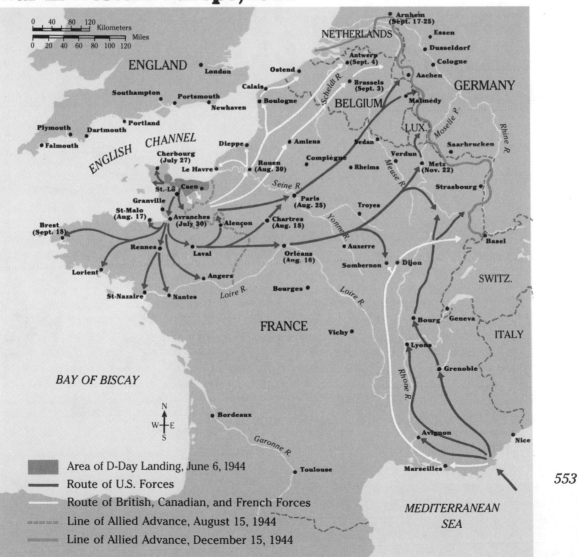

Area of D-Day Landing, June 6, 1944
Route of U.S. Forces
Route of British, Canadian, and French Forces
Line of Allied Advance, August 15, 1944
Line of Allied Advance, December 15, 1944

2 WAR COLD AND HOT

Looking Ahead: Rivalry for World Power

The audience at the San Francisco Opera House rose to its feet. Applause and cheers filled the hall. But no opera singers were taking bows onstage. The cheers were meant for something else.

During World War II, the Allies had laid plans for a world organization. Now, in 1945, diplomats from 50 countries had just approved the Charter of the United Nations. They hoped their charter would pave the way for a just peace. They hoped the U.N. would help nations settle differences with words rather than guns.

Americans had much to be happy for on this pleasant June day in 1945. The war with Germany was over. In the Pacific, the Japanese were being pushed back. The U.S. was now the strongest

In 1948 the German people of West Berlin looked for help from the skies. The Soviet Union had clamped a blockade on the city. For 321 days, the U.S. and Britain delivered supplies by air.

and richest country in the world. Its factories and cities had come through the war unharmed. Peace was in sight.

No one could know, in June 1945, how difficult it would be to keep this peace. Only a few months after the war, the U.S. began quarreling with a new "enemy," the Soviet Union. The two countries had entered into the *Cold War*.

In this "war," Soviet and U.S. troops did not shoot at each other. Their "war" was one of words, threats, and other actions. Both nations took part in an *arms race* — a race to see which could build the most powerful weapons. Both nations kept large peacetime armies. Both nations worked to win the support of governments in Europe, Africa, and Asia. In short, both nations became rivals around the world.

How did the Cold War begin?

Even during World War II, the U.S. and the Soviet Union had not completely trusted each other. The two countries had very different ways of life. The Soviet way was *communism,* a system in which most land and businesses are owned and controlled by government. The U.S. system was *capitalism,* in which most land and businesses are owned and controlled by private individuals or companies. The Soviet government was run by a dictator, Josef Stalin. The U.S. government was chosen freely by the people.

Yalta Conference. By February 1945, Soviet armies had driven the Nazis out of Eastern Europe. That month President Roosevelt met with British and Soviet leaders at Yalta, as we have seen. There, the "Big Three" agreed to allow the peoples of Eastern Europe to elect their own governments. But when the war ended a few months later, Soviet armies stayed in Eastern Europe. Free elections were not held.

U.S. leaders were very upset. The United States wanted these countries to have freely elected governments.

American eagle and Russian bear scowl at each other in this prize-winning 1946 cartoon by Bruce Russell: "Time To Bridge That Gulch."

556

U.S. leaders thought such governments would be friendlier to the U.S. But the Soviet Union had suffered badly in two world wars. It wanted to be sure that its neighbors would not soon threaten it again. To insure this, Soviet leaders saw to it that these countries had Communist governments. The Soviets believed that Communist governments would be friendlier to the Soviet Union.

"Iron curtain." In the late 1940's, then, Soviet armies stayed in Eastern Europe. Their purpose was to keep it under Soviet control. By 1946 disagreement between the U.S. and the Soviet Union was growing serious. That spring, British leader Winston Churchill visited Westminster College in Fulton, Missouri. He gave a speech that would be remembered for many years. Churchill said that the Soviet Union had lowered an "iron curtain" over Eastern Europe. The "curtain" had shut off Eastern Europe from the West.

Later in 1946, the situation got worse. The Soviet Union threatened to take some of Turkey's land. In Greece, meanwhile, Communists and non-Communists were fighting a fierce civil war against one another. President Truman decided to "get tough" with the Soviet Union. He went before Congress in 1947 to ask for money to help Greece and Turkey. He said that the United States must be ready "to help free peoples" to remain safe from the threats of dictators.

Truman's plan to aid Greece and Turkey became known as the *Truman Doctrine.* It was part of a larger policy to

In Korea, U.S. troops had to fight snows and icy temperatures as well as North Koreans.

contain (stop) the spread of communism throughout the free world. This policy was soon being called *containment.* Another part of the policy was hammered out later in 1947. It was a program of aid to war-shattered Western Europe. This idea was named the *Marshall Plan* after then-Secretary of State George Marshall.

Berlin airlift. The next major area of dispute was Germany. At the end of World War II, Germany had been divided among the four main Allies — the U.S., the Soviet Union, Britain, and France. Berlin was in the middle of the Soviet zone. But because it had been the capital city of Germany, it too had been divided among the four Allies.

In 1948 the U.S., Britain, and France wanted to make Germany a united country again. But the Soviets did not like the plan. They showed their anger by cutting off all road and train traffic into Berlin. The Soviets hoped to starve the Western Allies out of Berlin. But for 321 days the U.S. and Britain supplied Berlin by air. The Berlin airlift showed the Soviets that the Allies meant business. Finally the Soviets lifted the blockade.

In 1949 the Cold War grew still colder. After a long civil war, Communists took control of East Asia's largest country, China. Soon afterward, the Soviet Union tested its first atomic bomb. Both events were jarring to most Americans. Some wondered where Communists would strike next.

McCarthy Era. By 1950 fear of communism had reached a peak. To some Americans it seemed that the very safety of the U.S. was at stake. One U.S. Senator thought the problem had begun at home. There were Communist

"traitors" in the U.S. government, claimed Senator Joseph McCarthy, Republican from Wisconsin. He believed these traitors were doing everything they could to hurt the United States. McCarthy gave little proof for his charges. But many people believed him.

The Cold War did turn "hot" twice in Asia. In 1950 the armies of Communist North Korea invaded non-Communist South Korea. U.S. troops went to the rescue of the South. Later in the 1950's, war broke out in South Vietnam. This time the U.S. gave aid to the South Vietnamese government.

In Korea and Vietnam, the U.S. was practicing containment. Yet U.S. troops did not fight Soviet troops in either war. Both the U.S. and the Soviet Union had become *atomic powers.* That is, both had the ability to destroy each other with atomic bombs. The thought of war between two atomic powers was worrisome indeed.

Then, in 1962, such a war almost came about. The Soviet Union built sites for launching atomic missiles in Cuba, 90 miles (about 145 kilometers) from the U.S. coast. Soviet ships sailed toward Cuba, carrying the missiles themselves. President John F. Kennedy ordered a naval blockade of Cuba. His order brought the U.S. close to war. Finally, however, he worked out an agreement with Soviet leaders. The danger passed.

The Cold War taught Americans to think in terms of jet bombers and guided missiles. It taught them the names of small countries and far-off lands. Above all, it taught Americans what it meant to be a world power. For the U.S. was now the leader of the non-Communist world.

Chapter 7

A Plan for Europe

In 1947 Europe was in deep trouble. World War II had lasted nearly six years. It had caused terrible damage and suffering. Two years after the war was over,

After World War II, the U.S. sent non-Communist Europe billions of dollars in aid. As New York Herald Tribune *cartoonist Talburt saw it, the U.S. and Europe would sink or swim together.*

many European cities were still in ruins. Factories — those left standing — badly needed repairs. Railroads and bridges were still torn up.

The people of Europe — winners and losers alike — were in bad shape. Millions of Europeans were still without homes, jobs, money, or food. They had just gone through a very cold winter without enough fuel to keep warm. Many thousands had caught the killer disease, tuberculosis. Now, in the spring of 1947, lack of rain was threatening crops. Many people were losing hope. Something had to be done to save them from hunger and disease.

From the U.S. point of view, there was another danger — the Soviet Union. Soviet armies had taken over most of Eastern Europe in the last months of World War II. They had helped Communist parties in those countries to take control of their governments.

Communist threat. In Western Europe, hunger and lack of work caused some people to turn to communism. They believed that communism would solve their problems. Already there were large Communist parties in Italy and France. Some people thought Communists might have a 50-50 chance of winning the elections in Italy. Then the Italians might become allies of the Soviet Union. The United States did not want this to happen.

559

President Harry Truman turned to his Secretary of State, George Marshall, for assistance. Marshall had been the top U.S. general in World War II. Truman called him "the greatest living American." Truman asked Marshall and his advisers to come up with a plan to help Europeans fight hunger and find work.

George Marshall made public the first broad outlines of his plan in June 1947. His idea was to help Europe help itself. Each European country would have to draw up its own plan for rebuilding. The U.S. would give it the cash to get started. His plan, Marshall said, was aimed against hunger and poverty.

"Capitalist trick." Many European countries met at Paris to talk over Marshall's idea. Most countries liked it, but the Soviet Union would have nothing to do with Marshall's plan. The Soviet Union also forced other Communist countries to refuse to take part in the plan. Stalin called it a "capitalist trick." He said that the plan was aimed at making capitalism stronger. And he did not want that.

President Truman asked Congress for money to make the Marshall Plan work. He asked for 17 billion dollars to help European countries that were not ruled by Communists. It would be spent over four years.

In Congress the Marshall Plan ran into trouble. Some members of Congress were against it because, they said, it was a "give-away." The United States, they said, would go broke paying for it.

Then, in February 1948, Czechoslovakia went Communist. It had been one of the last non-Communist nations in Eastern Europe. This made Congress — and many other Americans —

angry. The need for a policy of containment seemed clear. Opposition to the Marshall Plan melted. In April the Marshall Plan became law.

Soon U.S. aid was pouring into Western Europe. Factories, dams, railroads, and bridges were rebuilt. New factories went up everywhere. In less than three years, Western Europe's factories were turning out much more than they had before World War II. And there was also much more food than before. People had jobs again and were eating regularly. Hope had come back to the people of Western Europe.

A Second Look. . . .

1. *What was the Marshall Plan? Whom was it meant to help? How successful was it?*

2. *The U.S. backed the Marshall Plan for human and political reasons. In the 1950's and 1960's, such foreign aid programs became the subject of a debate. Some people said that the U.S. should continue helping countries that were on our side. They said we should do this even if the countries were run by dictators. Other people disagreed. They said we should not help dictators — even if they were on our side. What do you think? Give reasons for answering the questions as you have.*

3. *There are many countries in the world today that need help. They do not all have the same problems. Make a list of governments you think the U.S. should help. Pick two countries from the list. Go to the library. Find out what problems these countries have today. Then write your own "plan" for helping each country.*

Chapter 8

Patriot or Fraud?

In 1949 Americans had some great shocks. First, Communist armies won a civil war in China. Communists came to power in that large country. Then the Soviet Union exploded an atomic bomb. No one in the U.S. had believed the Soviets would have atomic weapons so soon. Communists seemed to be getting stronger around the world.

Some Americans were frightened.

They worried that the U.S. might be losing the Cold War. There was also concern that Communist spies had found their way into the U.S. government. Some people even thought that Communists would try to take over the U.S. itself.

While such fears were rising, a Senator from Wisconsin, Joseph McCarthy, was beginning to make headlines. For

In 1954 Senator Joseph McCarthy (standing) tangled with a lawyer for the Army, Joseph Welch (seated), on national television. McCarthy accused a member of Welch's law firm of having Communist ties. "Have you no sense of decency, sir?" Welch replied, and spectators in the hearing room applauded the lawyer.

the next five years, McCarthy turned fear of communism into a national argument. He said he could prove that Communists were really plotting to take over the U.S. government. He said that many secret Communists held important government jobs. Even worse, he said, many government leaders were in favor of Communist ideas.

Storm center. To millions of Americans, McCarthy became a great patriot. He seemed to be a hero fighting the battle against communism. But others said he was a fraud, using fear just to get power for himself. One writer said, "He wanted power to make Presidents jump when he cracked the whip."

Many people who favored Senator McCarthy said that anyone against him was a friend of the Communists. Other people said this wasn't so. They argued: "McCarthy is a dangerous man because he accuses people but doesn't prove anything. Just because we are against the Senator doesn't mean that we are Communists or are for Communists."

So the argument raged. As it did, Joseph McCarthy became steadily more powerful. Many people admired him. Many others found him frightening. Few people in U.S. history had been more controversial.

Who was Joseph McCarthy? Before World War II, he had been an attorney and then a judge in Wisconsin. During the war, he had served with the U.S. Marines in the South Pacific. Returning home, he had been elected Senator from Wisconsin as a Republican in 1946. In the Senate, he had not made much news at first.

Reports and denials. Then, in February 1950, McCarthy made a speech at Wheeling, West Virginia. A local newspaper reported him as saying that there were 205 known Communists in

Shoemaker of the Chicago Daily News *titled his cartoon "Rude Awakening."*

the U.S. State Department. McCarthy later denied he had made this charge. Then he claimed that the number was 57. He offered no proof. He simply said he had a list.

Within weeks, McCarthy had become famous. His speeches made bold headlines in the newspapers. For a time, it seemed that many Americans' hopes and fears had come to rest on the Senator from Wisconsin. Clearly he was saying what many Americans thought to be true.

President Truman denied what McCarthy had said. A group of U.S. Senators said McCarthy's list was a fake. No one knew for sure. McCarthy grew still bolder. He accused Presidents Roosevelt and Truman of "20 years of treason" — selling out to the Soviets and Communist China.

The fact is that McCarthy could not prove most of his charges. Yet many Americans believed what he had to say. In his home state of Wisconsin, McCarthy had strong support — and also strong opposition. But when elections came in 1952, McCarthy won another Senate term.

He kept swinging. Government leaders were afraid to oppose him even when they believed he was wrong. Because of his charges, thousands of people lost their jobs. Some of these people were ruined.

Clash with the Army. Then McCarthy went too far for some of his own supporters. He criticized President Eisenhower's handling of foreign policy. He also began an investigation into the U.S. Army. At one point, an Army general, Ralph W. Zwicker, appeared before McCarthy's committee. Zwicker refused to give McCarthy certain information because it was a military secret. McCarthy exploded. He told Zwicker he did not have "the brains of a five-year-old child."

McCarthy went on to accuse the Army itself of protecting Communists. The stage for this war of words was the Army-McCarthy hearings of 1954. They were shown on television across the nation. For the first time, millions of Americans saw McCarthy in action. Many viewers did not like what they saw.

A few months later, the U.S. Senate voted to condemn McCarthy strongly for his conduct. After this, McCarthy caused less and less of a stir. But in the eyes of many Americans he had already done a terrible harm. President Dwight Eisenhower later said: "No one was safe from reckless charges. . . . The cost was often tragic."

A Second Look. . . .

1. *What great shocks hit Americans in 1949? How did Senator Joseph McCarthy use these shocks to build his career?*

2. *The years between 1949 and 1954 have been called the McCarthy Era. In some ways, these years were similar to the years following World War I. How much do you recall of what you have learned of the Red Scare of 1919-1921? What events took place in that period? What do you think the McCarthy Era has in common with those years? Why?*

3. *Millions of people saw the Army-McCarthy hearings on TV. Their opinions were shaped by what they saw. Interview people in your community who watched these hearings. Ask them what they remember most about the events they witnessed. Write your findings in a report.* 563

Chapter 9

War in Korea

Orange flames lit up the Korean sky on June 25, 1950. Loud explosions shook the ground. What was happening? Korea had been divided between North and South since the end of World War II. North Korea had become Communist. South Korea (the Republic of Korea) was anti-Communist. The government of North Korea wanted to unite the country by force. Now the army of Communist North Korea was attacking South Korea, using Soviet tanks and guns.

President Harry Truman heard the news at his home in Independence, Missouri. He boarded his plane, the *Independence,* and flew back to Washington, D.C. For most of the flight, Truman remained alone. He wanted time to consider what had happened — and what might happen next.

Less than a year earlier, Communists had come to power in mainland China. This development had shaken many Americans. Some members of Congress had criticized Truman for being "soft" on communism. They had urged a "get-tough" policy in Asia.

Korea was not very important to the defense of the U.S. And although the government of South Korea was not

Communist, it was not democratic either. Yet the Republic of Korea had been established by the United Nations. If North Korea succeeded in its attack, the U.N. would suffer a serious blow. And if President Truman did nothing to stop the attack, the Soviets might try to take over other countries.

Taking action. Truman had to consider all these facts as he flew east. Once back in Washington, he summoned his main advisers. The next day, he ordered U.S. planes and Navy ships to help South Korea. But he still said nothing about sending soldiers.

The Security Council of the United Nations had already called for an end to the fighting. Now Truman's aides put pressure on the Council to go still further. The Security Council passed a U.S. resolution. It called on U.N. member-nations to help South Korea.

General Douglas MacArthur said U.S. troops would be needed to save South Korea. General MacArthur, a World War II hero, was U.S. commander in Japan. Truman learned of MacArthur's warning shortly before five A.M. on Friday, June 30. By noon he had made up his mind. He ordered General MacArthur to send U.S. troops to help South Korea. Later, other members of the United Nations sent small forces. Although the army was made up mostly of U.S. soldiers, it was called the U.N. army.

Fighting raged for three years among the hump-backed hills and thatched-hut villages of North and South Korea. Left, U.S. troops search huts for Chinese soldiers, supposed to be in hiding.

Punishing the enemy. The Korean War was a seesaw fight. At first the North Koreans drove far into South Korea. But around Pusan (POO-sahn), U.S. and South Korean forces held the line (see map on this page). Now General MacArthur came up with a daring plan. United Nations troops landed at Inchon (IN-chahn), far to the north. The North Korean army was caught in a trap. Many of its soldiers gave up. The U.N. forces then raced north to the 38th parallel, the line dividing North and South Korea. President Truman ordered MacArthur to cross the 38th parallel to destroy the North Korean army.

Communist China had warned that it would not sit by if North Korea was invaded. But the U.N. forces drove into North Korea. By November 21, some reached the Yalu (YAH-loo) River. The Yalu River is the border between Communist China and North Korea. Chinese troops had already begun to help the North Koreans. On November 26, the Chinese and North Koreans began a major attack. In bitter cold weather, they drove the U.N. forces back into South Korea. Many U.S. soldiers were killed or wounded, or frozen by the cold. There wasn't enough food or medicine. There was terrible suffering.

Feuding over policy. General MacArthur wanted to bomb bases inside China. President Truman and his advisers were against this. They were afraid this action might lead to a third world war. They thought that if the U.S. bombed China, the Soviet Union, China's ally, would probably attack the U.S.

But MacArthur argued hard for bombing China. He wanted to win completely in Korea. "There is no substitute for victory," he said. Finally, on April 11, 1951, Truman fired MacArthur for openly disagreeing with him. Many people in the U.S. were angry with Truman. But as President, Truman was Commander-in-Chief of the U.S. armed forces. And he believed it was his duty to keep control over the military.

Meanwhile U.S. troops began pushing north again. By June 1951, the battle line was a few miles north of the 38th parallel. Then the war became a standoff — neither side could win a major victory. Men fought and died for a few hills.

Reaching a truce. By the early summer of 1951, all the big nations were ready for a truce in Korea. Peace talks soon began. But the talks dragged on for two years. The fighting did not stop until July 27, 1953.

Korea, 1950-1953

- - - - Farthest North Korean Advance, September 10, 1950
—— United Nations Landing, September 15, 1950
- - - - Farthest United Nations Advance, November 24, 1950

Tumen R.

N
W + E
S

CHINA (MANCHURIA)

Yalu R.

SEA OF JAPAN

NORTH KOREA
Pyongyang • • Wonsan
• Tongchon

———1953 Cease-Fire Line

Panmunjom •

CHINA

• Seoul
Inchon •

SOUTH KOREA

YELLOW SEA

Pusan •

KOREA STRAIT

JAPAN

0 50 100 150 200
Kilometers
Miles
0 50 100 150 200

Harry Truman (left) met Douglas MacArthur on Wake Island in the Pacific in October 1950 to discuss U.S. military plans. Six months later, Truman dismissed MacArthur from U.N. command.

Even then there was no final peace for Korea. Soldiers continued to stand guard along the "no man's land" that separated the North from the South. From time to time, shooting still broke out along the border. U.S. ground troops remained in South Korea to guard against any future attack.

In 1977 President Jimmy Carter set forth plans for removing these troops. By doing so, he hoped to avoid getting the U.S. involved in another ground war in Asia. Carter and his advisers hoped to have all U.S. ground troops out of South Korea by 1982. But U.S. planes would remain at South Korean bases. Other forms of U.S. aid to South Korea would also continue.

The Korean War caused many deaths and great damage. More than a million civilian men, women, and children of Korea were killed. Several million lost their homes. The armed forces also lost heavily. The U.S. alone had more than 33,000 dead and more than 100,000 wounded. Neither side could say it had won the war. But the U.S. had halted a Communist take-over in Korea without bringing on a third world war.

A Second Look. . . .

1. *Why did U.S. troops fight a war in Korea? Whom were they fighting? What were the results of this war?*

2. *The U.S. Constitution makes the President Commander-in-Chief of the armed forces. This means that generals and admirals must take orders from a civilian, the President. How was this idea tested in Korea? Should a President have the right to tell a general when to stop fighting a war? Or how to fight it? Why or why not?*

3. *There has been no peace settlement in Korea. Instead, there is only a temporary cease-fire. Using the research materials in your library, write a report on the truce in Korea. Has it been broken? How long do you think it can last? Summarize your findings in a one-page report.*

Many Americans recalled Douglas MacArthur's leadership in World War II. When Truman dismissed MacArthur, there was a loud outcry.

567

Chapter 10

Build-up in Vietnam

The press release was brief. It said: "Lieutenant-General John W. O'Daniel ... assumed charge of the organization and training of the South Vietnamese army today."

It was February 1955. Spring training for the 1955 baseball season was getting under way. The Soviet Union had a new leader, Nikita Khrushchev (kroosh-CHAWF). These were the main stories in the newspapers. Few people paid any attention to the item from Vietnam.

Yet the item was significant. It marked the start of a direct U.S. role in the fortunes of Vietnam. Over the next 20 years, this role grew and grew. In one way or another, the Vietnam War would affect the life of every American.

Why Vietnam? What was there about this country far off in Southeast Asia that could so greatly affect the United States?

Before World War II, Vietnam had been an obscure French colony. Japan had seized it during the war. After Japan's defeat in World War II, France had wanted its colony back. The Vietnamese had wanted their independence. The result was war.

Guerrilla fighting. A Vietnamese named Ho Chi Minh (hoe chee MIN) led the war against France. Ho was a Communist. But both Communist and non-Communist Vietnamese fought alongside Ho. Both groups were fighting 568 for an independent Vietnam.

At first it seemed that the war would be short. France was a powerful country with the latest weapons. The Vietnamese were poor. They had old weapons and no air force. But they fought a different kind of war from the kind the French were used to fighting. Vietnamese peasants took care of their farms during the day. At night they became soldiers. They made hit-and-run raids on the French-controlled towns and cities. Europeans and Americans called these fighters *guerrillas*. (The word *guerrilla* comes from the Spanish language. In Spanish, the word means "little war.")

The French were slowly losing. This worried some U.S. leaders. They saw communism, even in far-off Vietnam, as a threat to the United States. Many

Vietnamese leader Ho Chi Minh

Americans believed that the Soviet Union controlled communism all over the world. To these Americans, Vietnam was another battle in the Cold War. President Truman wanted to keep communism from spreading. He sent weapons to the French. Soon the U.S. was paying for most of the French war effort.

Uneasy peace. Yet U.S. aid did not win the war for France. In 1954 the Vietnamese defeated the French. The two sides signed a peace agreement. Vietnam became independent. But it was divided into two countries. North Vietnam had a Communist government led by Ho Chi Minh. In South Vietnam, a non-Communist government took power. Its leader was named Ngo Dinh Diem (no dinn ZEE-um).

Part of the peace agreement called for an election to be held in 1956 to unify Vietnam. Now Diem refused to hold the election. He said the Communists could not be trusted to run a fair election. Ho Chi Minh said Diem had canceled the election because he knew that Ho would win.

Soon guerrillas began attacking the South Vietnamese government. These guerrillas belonged to a group known as the *Viet Cong* (v'yet KONG). The Viet Cong was led by Communists and helped by North Vietnam. President Eisenhower was concerned. He did not want South Vietnam to become Communist. If this happened, Eisenhower said, then other nations of Asia would become Communist. Eisenhower ordered U.S. aid and advisers sent to South Vietnam. At the same time, he assured Americans that the U.S. would not fight a war there. He hoped U.S. aid would

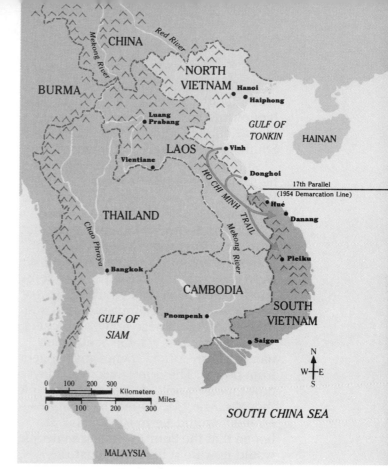

Indochina in the 1960's

help South Vietnam to win the civil war.

Civil war. But President Eisenhower's hopes did not come true. The South Vietnamese government was not winning the war. Its leaders faced growing criticism. They used U.S. aid to build up their own power. More and more South Vietnamese lost faith in their government. Many of them now supported the Viet Cong.

By the time President Kennedy took office in 1961, the civil war in South Vietnam was growing more fierce. There were 685 U.S. military advisers in South Vietnam at the time. They were helping 569 train the South Vietnamese army. The U.S. was also spending millions of dollars on the war effort. Even so, President Kennedy's advisers told him that South Vietnam needed still more help.

So Kennedy decided to send more help. He ordered 8,000 U.S. soldiers to Vietnam. They were not supposed to go into combat. Their job was still merely to help the South Vietnamese army. But now U.S. pilots were flying South Vietnamese troops into battle. U.S. troops were directing the battle plans of some South Vietnamese troops. The U.S. was getting more deeply involved. And still the South Vietnamese army kept losing.

In November 1963, the South Vietnamese army forced Diem's government from power. The army took over. Maybe now the war would go differently, people thought. The U.S. hoped the new government would be more popular. It hoped that the South Vietnamese people would now fight harder against the Viet Cong. Yet this did not happen.

Slowly but surely, the war grew. North Vietnam sent troops to fight alongside the Viet Cong. The U.S. began sending combat soldiers. But U.S. troops fought in support of a government that many Vietnamese opposed. In the 1960's, the U.S. was slipping into a war without victory.

A Second Look. . . .

1. *How did the war start in Vietnam? How and why did the United States get involved in the war?*

2. *The Vietnam War was different from other wars the U.S. fought in the 20th century. Why? How would you compare the Vietnam War to the American Revolution? In what ways do the two wars seem similar? In what ways do they seem different?*

3. *Before the Vietnam War was over, it had divided Americans into two groups: those who were against it and those who were for it. If you had been of voting age during the war, which side do you think you would have been on? Write a one-page essay stating your opinion. Be sure to give your reasons for holding it.*

570

South Vietnamese stormed the palace of Ngo Dinh Diem in 1963. Diem was finally forced from power.

Chapter 11

Crisis in Cuba

Eighteen Soviet ships steamed toward Cuba. Six Soviet submarines sailed with them. U.S. Navy ships rushed to stop them from reaching Cuba. Soviet leader Nikita Khrushchev said his submarines would sink any U.S. ship that tried to stop his ships. The U.S. was ready to sink his submarines, if necessary.

The year was 1962. A showdown was taking place between the United States and the Soviet Union. In many ways, it was the most frightening showdown of the Cold War. If shooting started, it would probably mean the use of nuclear weapons. People everywhere were afraid that this would happen.

Why was this showdown taking place? What was so vital about the island of Cuba to bring the world to the edge of nuclear war?

The story began in the late 1950's. At that time, Cuba was under the thumb of a right-wing dictator, Fulgencio Batista (ful-HEN-see-oh bah-TEE-stuh). A Cuban named Fidel Castro (fee-DELL KASS-troh) led a revolt against Batista. At first Castro and his rebel force had some support from the U.S.

In 1959 Castro came to power. Soon after, he began to ally Cuba with the Soviet Union. His moves were very alarming to many people in the United States. Unlike Korea and Vietnam, Cuba was not a distant land. It was a Caribbean island, only 90 miles (about 145 kilometers) off the Florida coast.

The United States did not take direct military action against Castro. However, the U.S. did put a temporary embargo on the purchase of Cuban sugar. The U.S. government also gave aid to a group of anti-Castro Cubans who had left their country. These Cubans were organized into a military force to overthrow the Castro government.

Flawed invasion. President John Kennedy learned about this force in January 1961. He went ahead with a plan to allow these Cubans to invade their own country. The invaders planned to link up with other anti-Castro Cubans at home. Then they hoped to drive the Castro government from power.

The invasion took place on April 17, 1961. The invaders landed on a Cuban beach at the Bay of Pigs. The plan was a complete failure. Most of the invaders were killed or captured. President Kennedy later admitted that the invasion had failed because of bad planning. He took the blame himself for what had happened at the Bay of Pigs.

A few months later, Fidel Castro announced that he was a Communist and would be one "until the day I die." His ties to the Soviet Union grew more and more firm. In 1962 the Soviets began to send many missiles and planes to Cuba. It also sent men to show the Cubans how to use this equipment.

Nikita Khrushchev said that the missiles and planes were meant only to defend Cuba. He said that the missiles were the kind that could only shoot down planes flying overhead.

Missile build-up. U.S. spy planes flying over Cuba had not spotted any *nuclear* missiles. Even so, President Kennedy was taking no chances. He kept the spy flights going. In October, photographs made by a U.S. spy plane clearly showed nuclear missiles being set up by soldiers. These missiles would be able to reach as far as St. Louis or Dallas. The atomic warheads they could carry were much more powerful than the atomic bomb dropped on Hiroshima in 1945.

Cuban premier Fidel Castro (right) said he needed Soviet missiles for defense. But Castro's plan threatened the U.S. Below, a U.S. ship trails a Soviet ship carrying missiles to Cuba.

President Kennedy believed he had to act fast. In a few days, the missiles would be completely set up. He asked his advisers what ideas they had. There were several different ideas:

1. The U.S. should do nothing. After all, *we* had missiles set up in Turkey near the Soviet Union.

2. We should meet with Soviet leaders and "talk it over."

3. We should blow up the missiles with air attacks.

4. We should invade Cuba and drive out Castro.

5. We should blockade Cuba — send the U.S. Navy to stop any more ships from reaching it.

President Kennedy believed that action was needed. On the one hand, there was no time to meet with Soviet leaders. On the other hand, air attacks or an invasion of Cuba might lead to a nuclear war. A blockade was dangerous too, but not *as* dangerous. A blockade would give both sides time to "cool it." Finally President Kennedy decided to blockade Cuba.

Solemn suspense. On October 22, 1962, the President told the American people about the Soviet missiles. He said he was sending U.S. Navy ships to blockade Cuba until the missiles were taken away. There was a chance this would lead to nuclear war. But, Kennedy said, he was sure the American people would rather take that chance than do nothing.

In the Soviet Union, Nikita Khrushchev made warlike statements. He said that he would not let U.S. ships stop Soviet ships. Soviet submarines were ready for action. Now the question was: Would Soviet ships try to force their way through the U.S. Navy? The whole world waited nervously for the answer.

Finally good news came. Soviet ships heading for Cuba had stopped, then turned back. People breathed a little easier. Yet there was still the danger of the missiles already in Cuba. The U.S. was getting ready to invade Cuba, if necessary, to get the missiles out of Cuban hands.

Then Khrushchev sent President Kennedy a letter. It said that the Soviet Union would take back its missiles if the U.S. promised not to invade Cuba. Kennedy agreed. The Soviets took their missiles out of Cuba. Kennedy called off the blockade. It was a great moment for President Kennedy and the United States. But Kennedy did not want to make Khrushchev look bad. If this happened, the Soviets might make trouble somewhere else in order to look good. So Kennedy did not call Khrushchev's retreat a victory. Instead he said that Khrushchev had helped keep the peace.

The awful danger of a nuclear war was over. Afterward, the U.S. and the Soviet Union put aside some of their differences. A treaty was signed between them that stopped the testing of nuclear weapons, except underground. Many other nations later signed this treaty. John Kennedy called it an important "first step" toward world peace.

A Second Look. . . .

1. What set off the crisis in Cuba in 1962? How was the Soviet Union involved in it?

2. The Cuban missile crisis stirred great fears of a nuclear war. Try to put

yourself in the position of a student as old as yourself in 1962. You are sitting in class when the bell starts clanging as if for a fire drill. Your teacher tells you it is an air-raid drill. You have heard about U.S. and Soviet ships off the coast of Cuba. Someone nearby whispers, "This is no drill. This is it." What thoughts and feelings come to mind in this situation? Why?

3. As a follow-up to the previous question, you and your classmates may want to interview teachers, parents, and neighbors, who lived through those October days in 1962. Ask them to recall their thoughts and feelings about the future of the world. How did their experience change their way of thinking? Write a report on your findings.

Nikita Khrushchev was in a friendly mood when he munched on a hot dog in the U.S. in 1959 (above). After the missile crisis, there was a friendlier mood once more. In the 1962 Herblock cartoon below, John Kennedy says to Khrushchev: "Let's get a lock for this thing."

NUCLEAR WAR

Looking Back: War Cold and Hot

| A | B | C | D |

1945   1950   1955   1960   1965

Putting Events in Order

Chapters Seven through 11 have described some events of the Cold War. Ten of these events are listed here. Your job is to match each event to the correct period shown on the timeline. On a piece of paper, number from **1** to **10.** After each number, write the letter of the five-year period in which the event occurred.

1. The Western Allies airlift supplies into West Berlin.

2. Senator Joseph McCarthy accuses the U.S. Army of protecting Communists.

3. Harry Truman fires Douglas MacArthur.

4. Fidel Castro comes to power in Cuba.

5. The Soviet Union explodes its first atomic bomb.

6. President Kennedy sends U.S. soldiers to Vietnam.

7. The U.S. and the Soviet Union have a showdown over missiles in Cuba.

8. Vietnamese defeat the French in a war for independence.

9. George Marshall announces his plan to help Western Europe.

10. Fighting ends in Korea.

Interpreting a Source

The tensions of the Cold War were not only felt overseas. Some of them came much closer to home. More and more Americans worried about "living with the bomb." The bomb, in this case, was the atomic bomb.

The U.S. had dropped atomic bombs on Hiroshima and Nagasaki in 1945. The Soviet Union had exploded one in 1949. Now people around the world talked of "nuclear terror" — which was perhaps greatest in the cities. In the event of war, it was thought that cities would be the first target of a nuclear attack.

One day in the early 1950's, writer E.B. White was leafing through the New York Daily News. *His eye fell on a regular* News *column — the "Inquiring*

575

Fotographer." The *"fotographer"* had stopped six people and asked them what they would like to buy if they could afford it. Five of the six had fairly routine answers to the question. But one answer was not standard. White wrote about it in The New Yorker *magazine:*

When the question was put to [Private Andrew L.] Trano [of the Bronx, New York], he replied, "A home in the country for my father and mother.

Americans talked about bomb shelters all through the 1950's. By 1961 cartoonist Bill Mauldin figured that even pets would soon have shelters.

There they would be free from any fear of atom bombs. I'd provide a cellar built of lead, too, in case of an accidental bombing or a near-miss. Please print this, because my folks are in bad shape and it might cheer them up."

We have been thinking about this couple in the Bronx who are in bad shape from fear of atom bombs, and about their dream home in the country with its cellar built of lead. The subject of New York as a target for bombs is not much discussed, it seems to us, except indirectly, through casual news items about air-raid shelters and schoolroom instruction in how to dodge when a light is seen in the sky.

Roughly, the city divides into three groups: first, those who, because of lack of money, have no choice whether they will move out of range; second, those who enjoy the luxury of free choice and have decided to leave; and third, those who are free to go but prefer to remain. The first and third groups are very large, the second is very small.

Private Trano's answer to the *News* illustrates not only the demoralization[1] of fear but the futility[2] of flight. For he no sooner gets his parents into the country than he builds them a lead cellar, so their fears can be perpetuated[3] in an atmosphere of peril and apprehension[4]
....

We would not try to argue that it is sensible of human beings to continue living in a big city during the atomic age,

---

[1] To *demoralize* is to weaken the morale (spirit) of a person or persons. *Demoralization* is the state of being demoralized.
[2] *Futility,* in this sense, means uselessness.
[3] To *perpetuate* is to make permanent.
[4] *Apprehension* is fear of what may happen.

but we are fairly sure of one thing: the lead cellar of Private Trano indicates that if fear is part of a person's baggage, it doesn't make much difference where he dwells; he will carry his bomb with him. The only way to dwell in cities these days, whether it be wise or foolish, is in the conviction[5] that the city itself is a monument of one's own making, to which each shall be faithful in his fashion.

1. *What are the three groups into which White divides the city? According to White, which of these groups is smallest?*

2. *What does White mean by suggesting that a fearful person "will carry his bomb with him"?*

3. *What does he mean by saying that "the city itself is a monument of one's own making"?*

4. *Do you agree with White? Why or why not?*

Sharpening Your Skills

The cartoon at right was drawn in 1945 by Jay N. ("Ding") Darling of *The Des Moines* (Iowa) *Register*. It was titled: "Eventually, Why Not Now?" Study the cartoon carefully. Then answer the questions below:

1. What does the man shown in the cartoon represent?

2. What does the globe represent?

3. How does Darling believe future atomic destruction can be prevented?

4. Is the cartoon's message still important today? Explain.

[5] A *conviction,* in this sense, is a strong belief.

3 POST-WAR AMERICA

Looking Ahead: A Period of Plenty

A man hails a cab on a New York City street on a spring evening in 1946. The cab driver stops. The man puts his bags in the trunk and gets into the cab.

"Where to, buddy?" the driver asks.

"Grand Central Station," the man replies.

At the station, the man calls to a porter in a red cap for help with his bags.

"What train?" the redcap asks.

"The *20th Century Limited* to Chicago," the man answers.

Once on board the train, the man takes out a schedule. He reads it: Chicago, St. Louis, Kansas City, Denver, Salt Lake City, San Francisco. He is a businessman going on a long trip.

The man is back on the job after four years in the Army. But he is still traveling much as he did before the war. He

America of the 1950's was remade for the automobile. Car washes sprang up overnight, and a new word — freeway — entered the language.

rides the same trains and stays in the same hotels. All the hotels are in the hearts of cities. The businessman's clients come to see him at his hotel, or he takes a trolley car or taxi to see them in their stores. At night he may go to a movie or a stage show. Before going to sleep, he may listen to some music on the radio in his hotel room.

In the years right after the war, the businessman's routine remained pretty much the same. In the next 15 years, though, U.S. life changed a great deal. These changes took place slowly. Yet they affected the way Americans lived.

Hotels v. motels. By 1960 the same businessman might live in one of the new suburbs that had sprung up around big cities. For a trip of any great distance, he would most likely drive to the airport and take a plane. On arrival he would probably rent a car and drive to his lodgings. They might be in one of the new motels built next to a freeway on the outskirts of town. He would drive to see his clients. In the evening, he might go to a drive-in movie. He might watch television in his room before going to sleep at night.

The changes in the businessman's routine show some of the new directions in U.S. life between 1945 and 1960. During these years, the U.S. took the form we see today. New highways and airports were built. People took long journeys by car, bus, or airplane — and less and less by train. Trains still carried some commuters to and from the cities. And of course trains still carried freight. But now they had rivals even for that. Trucks were carrying more freight.

Cities v. suburbs. The cities continued to grow. But many people were leaving their old neighborhoods and moving to the suburbs. The suburbs had a somewhat different style of life. People needed cars to get almost everywhere. Shopping centers with big parking lots were built along main roads. As people moved to the suburbs, city life began to change. Many people came into the city to work or shop. They would go home to the suburbs at night. "Rush-hour" traffic jams became common in many areas.

The United States economy grew faster than ever. Many people became wealthier than they had ever hoped to be. They bought new appliances such as washing machines. They also bought another new product — television sets.

Between 1945 and 1960, the nation was led by two Presidents. The first was Harry Truman, a Democrat who served from 1945 to 1953. During the Truman years, the U.S. began the switch from a war economy to a peacetime one. Millions of soldiers returned home and looked for jobs. Factories which had once made tanks now turned to making autos. Amid these changes, Truman had to keep things running smoothly. This sometimes meant holding a lid on prices. It also meant preventing costly strikes.

President Truman also had political troubles. As a Democrat, he disagreed with the Republican-controlled Congress on many issues. In 1948 he had to fight hard to win the Presidential nomination of his own party. Few experts gave him much chance of winning the election. But Truman showed great determination. In the end, he scored a major upset.

The second President of the period was Dwight D. Eisenhower. In 1953 he became the first Republican President in 20 years. This World War II hero was one of the nation's best-known figures. Eisenhower's patient leadership healed some serious divisions in the U.S. In the middle 1950's, the nation entered a period of peace and plenty.

Call to courage. Some writers of the period thought they saw a drawback to all this wealth. They said that Americans had grown too smug (satisfied with themselves). One critic, Walter Lippmann, said the U.S. seemed to be losing its "national purpose." Americans had become too "defensive," Lippmann wrote. They wanted to hold on to what they had. They were losing the courage to reach for a better world, Lippmann believed.

Other critics pointed out that the wealth of the fifties wasn't shared by all Americans. Millions of Americans still lived in poverty. Many black Americans still did not have full legal rights in many parts of the U.S. Yet the post-war period saw the beginnings of a new movement to gain full equality for black Americans. Jackie Robinson became the first black player in major league baseball. Soon many black athletes won fame in major professional sports. But the barriers were slow to come down for most blacks. Some people wondered if full equality would ever come.

Our businessman, though satisfied with his profits, might also have had questions about the future. How long would it take before all the cars and trucks would lead to impossible traffic jams and pollution? Were America's most scenic areas being ruined by all the new roads? What would happen to the cities with so many people moving away to the suburbs? Were Americans too concerned with making money? Were they becoming too "soft"?

These questions had just begun to form in the late 1950's. In the 1960's, they would become national issues.

Artists stirred controversy in post-war America. Charlie "Bird" Parker (above) helped to invent a new kind of jazz called be-bop. *To some, it sounded too fast and rough. But Parker's skill made him a hero to his fans. Jackson Pollock poured and splashed paint on his huge canvases (below). Some critics laughed. Others felt this style, called* abstract expressionism, *showed the rhythm and power of modern American life.*

Chapter 12

"I Will Win the Election"

Harry Truman's friends knew he was a fighter. Still, they were worried about him on April 12, 1945. President Franklin Roosevelt had just died. Suddenly Vice-President Truman had become President. Could he handle the job?

The U.S. faced many difficult problems. World War II was still under way in Europe and the Pacific. Important plans for the coming peace were being drawn up by the Allies. No wonder Harry Truman told reporters on his first day as President: "Boys, if you ever pray, pray for me now."

Truman met his decisions head-on. Others could "pass the buck," he said, but he could not. He put a sign on his desk: "The Buck Stops Here." He wanted everyone in the Executive Branch of the U.S. government to know he was the boss.

In his first years as President, Truman showed his leadership in many ways. Here are some examples:

The atomic bomb. Truman had not even known of plans for building an atomic bomb when he became President. Yet it was he who made the final decision to drop atomic bombs on two Japanese cities in August 1945 (see Chapter Six).

Peace. In his first months as President, Truman played an important part in setting up the peace. He met with Winston Churchill and Josef Stalin in the German town of Potsdam to plan the future of Europe. Later, when the Cold War broke out, Truman put the Marshall Plan into action (see Chapter Seven).

The economy. When World War II ended, U.S. industries faced new problems. They had to switch from making tanks and guns to making cars and refrigerators. The switch was not an easy one. President Truman had to make sure it took place as quickly and smoothly as possible.

Strikes. During the war, the U.S. government had controlled wages and prices. When the war ended, government controls ended too. Prices rose faster than wages. Labor unions grew unhappy. Many workers went out on strike to get more pay. Truman helped to settle one major strike and used tough talk to prevent another.

In spite of Truman's action on these problems, some Americans questioned his ability. Critics called him "the little man from Missouri." They thought he was not "big" enough to be President. Now it was 1948 — an election year. Truman's party, the Democratic party, was badly split.

Some Democrats were in favor of Henry A. Wallace, a former Vice-President. Wallace had formed a third party, the Progressive party, and was running for President. He believed that Truman's Cold War actions might get

"Are you sure you didn't miss anything?" Harry Truman asks after his first year in office. How many words in Herblock's cartoon can you define?

Ready for battle. Harry Truman refused to give up. He made a speech with fight in it. "I will win this election and make those Republicans like it," he said. The Democrats cheered him wildly for the first time.

The Republicans had already chosen their candidate. He was Thomas E. Dewey, governor of New York. Dewey had become famous as a fighter of organized crime. All the polls said Dewey would win. And four out of five newspapers were on Dewey's side.

But Truman didn't quit. He rode across the country making speeches from the back of his own special train. As he left on the cross-country trip, one political leader told him to "go out there and mow 'em down." Truman answered: "I'll mow 'em down, ... and I'll give 'em hell." The remark became a key slogan in the campaign.

All across the nation, Truman talked of how he had continued Franklin Roosevelt's New Deal. He attacked Dewey and the Republicans for not helping "the little guy." Everywhere his train went, the crowds got bigger. Truman's simple, down-to-earth speeches were winning friends.

Ready for victory. On election night, Republicans prepared for victory parties. One expert was so certain of a Dewey victory that he had stopped taking polls weeks before the election. When Truman went to sleep, he was ahead. But the experts were still predicting a Dewey victory. *The Chicago Tribune* even came out with a big headline: DEWEY DEFEATS TRUMAN.

At four in the morning, a Secret Service man woke Truman up. He told Truman to turn on the radio, and Tru-

the U.S. into a shooting war with the Soviet Union.

Many Democrats in the South were also against Truman. Truman had called for strong civil-rights laws to end Jim Crow. One woman from the South complained about this. Truman pulled a copy of the U.S. Constitution from his pocket and read her the Bill of Rights!

The Democrats chose Truman to run for President on their ticket. But they did it with very little spirit. Almost all of them were sure he would lose. Some Southern Democrats walked out of the convention. They formed their own party, the Dixiecrats. They chose Strom Thurmond, governor of South Carolina, as their candidate for President.

man did. An announcer said, "Truman is two million votes ahead!" Soon it was all over. Truman had won the election! It was the greatest upset in U.S. election history.

Senator Arthur Vandenberg, a Republican from Michigan, summed up Truman's startling victory: "Everyone had counted him out. But he came out fighting and won the battle. That's the kind of courage Americans admire."

Courage, of course, wasn't the only reason why Truman won. The U.S. had been strongly Democratic ever since 1932. To many people, Truman seemed to be following in Franklin Roosevelt's footsteps.

A Second Look. . . .

1. *Who were Harry Truman's opponents in the election of 1948? What political parties did they represent? Why did "the experts" expect Truman to lose?*

2. *Truman risked defeat by coming out with a strong civil-rights stand in 1948. Even so, Truman did what he thought was right. In your opinion, do political leaders usually do what they think is right? Or do they more often do what they think will get them elected? Give reasons for your answers.*

3. *During his campaign for re-election, President Truman showed an ability for plain speaking. Pretend you are one of his speechwriters at the end of the campaign. It is the morning after election day, 1948. Truman is the winner by an upset. You must write his victory speech, using words he would probably use. What will you say?*

The Chicago Tribune *was too sure of itself on election night.*

Chapter 13

Breakthrough in Brooklyn

Thousands of fans crowded into Shibe Park, Philadelphia. They had come to see the Brooklyn Dodgers play the Philadelphia Phillies. It was the last day of the 1951 baseball season. The Dodgers had to win to tie for the pennant.

In the 14th inning, with the score tied, Jackie Robinson came up to the plate. His face glistened with sweat. He held the bat high, waving it threateningly at the pitcher. The pitcher delivered a fastball right over the plate. Robinson's bat came around in a clear, powerful motion. *Whack!* The ball took off in an arc toward left field. It was gone — a home run! The Dodgers held the Phillies in the bottom of the 14th and won the game.

Jackie Robinson wasn't just a home-run hitter. He was one of the most exciting all-around players of his day. From 1947 to 1956, he was a triple threat to any ball club that played against the Dodgers. He hit, ran the bases, and fielded with a style all his own.

Breaking a barrier. But Jackie Robinson had a more important claim to fame. He was the first black man to play major league baseball. Before Robinson, blacks had not been allowed to play in the major leagues. They had played for much less money in a black league in smaller cities.

The man who gave Jackie Robinson his chance was Branch Rickey, the Dodgers' general manager. Rickey was famous for his shrewd judgment of baseball talent. He had two goals: to make the Dodgers the best team in baseball, and to break the color barrier.

In 1946 Rickey sensed the time was right for breaking the barrier. During World War II, blacks had fought bravely in defense of their country. After the war, more and more Americans realized that blacks were not treated fairly in the U.S. Also, in the 1930's and 1940's, two great black athletes had made Americans feel proud. The two athletes were boxing champ Joe Louis and Olympic track star Jesse Owens.

Jack Roosevelt Robinson — the man who would make baseball history — was born in Georgia in 1919. He was the youngest of five children. When Jackie was still a baby, his father left the family. Jackie's mother moved the family to Pasadena, California. There she cleaned houses and washed clothes to support her children.

Jackie was a gifted athlete even as a child. He was coached and encouraged by his older brother, Mack. In high school, Jackie starred in football, basketball, track, and baseball. Later he became a star in all four at the University of California at Los Angeles (UCLA).

Robinson decided on a career in professional sports. But he never dreamed of playing baseball in the major

leagues. After getting out of the Army in 1945, he signed to play with the Kansas City Monarchs. The Monarchs belonged to the Negro American Baseball League.

Branch Rickey had been following Robinson's career for years. Rickey was a careful man. He could see that the first black player would have a difficult time. Such a player would be insulted and threatened. So Rickey knew that the man he was looking for would have to have more than talent on the playing field. He would have to have character and courage.

Battling with a bat. Rickey sent for Robinson. Rickey told him he would play for the Montreal Royals, the Dodgers' top minor league team. "But first there are several things you have to understand," Rickey said. "I know you've always fought for your rights and for the rights of Negroes. You've spoken up, and I admire you for it. But now you'll have to fight that battle with your bat and glove. A lot of players will be against you and a lot of fans too.... You will not fight back, do you understand?"

Jackie Robinson was both a powerful slugger and a master of the stolen base. Before Robinson broke the color barrier in major league baseball, black athletes were limited to playing in the Negro American Baseball League. Many players in the black league were just as good as white major leaguers.

586

Robinson was confused. "Do you want a ballplayer who is afraid to fight back?" he asked.

"I want a ballplayer who has the guts *not* to fight back," Rickey answered.

Robinson understood. He and Rickey became friends from that day on. In 1947 Rickey brought Robinson up to the big leagues to play with the Dodgers. Some of the Dodgers said they would refuse to play with Robinson on the team. Other teams in the league objected to a black in a major league uniform. But Branch Rickey would have none of it.

Jackie Robinson opened the season at first base for the Dodgers. He helped to make the Dodgers winners. Robinson quickly developed into a clutch hitter and sure fielder. His base-running made pitchers' hair turn gray. Robinson would take a big lead off first base. Bouncing on the balls of his feet, he would dare the pitcher to try to pick him off. His smart base-running often confused pitchers. Then they would make a bad pitch to the next batter. And whoosh, Robinson would bring another run home for the Dodgers.

Becoming a champ. Robinson's success on the field won the respect of his teammates. They began to stick up for him when opposing players jeered him. In 1947 the Dodgers became the National League champions. Robinson was voted Rookie of the Year.

In 1949 the Brooklyn team came back to win the pennant once again. Jackie Robinson won the National League batting championship with a .342 average. He was voted the league's Most Valuable Player. By this time, Robinson was no longer the only black player in the major leagues. He had two black teammates,

catcher Roy Campanella and pitcher Don Newcombe.

Jackie Robinson retired from baseball in 1956. He had helped the Dodgers win six National League pennants. He had shattered the "color barrier" in baseball. By 1956 there were many black players in the major leagues. Willie Mays of the New York Giants was a superstar. In Milwaukee batting champ Henry Aaron was beginning his career.

In 1962 Jackie Robinson was elected to baseball's Hall of Fame. He had been a great baseball champion. But more important, he had been a great champion for black Americans. By breaking the color barrier in major league baseball, he had helped to break color barriers of other kinds.

A Second Look. . . .

1. *Why was Jackie Robinson's joining the Brooklyn Dodgers an important event?*

2. *Robinson has written that when he first joined the Dodgers he felt like an outsider. Some of his teammates wouldn't even talk to him. Why do people sometimes feel like "insiders" or "outsiders"? Have you ever felt like an outsider? How did you handle the situation? Why did you feel the way you did?*

3. *In the past quarter century, black Americans have made important contributions to a great many fields. Choose one of the following people: Ralph Bunche; Lorraine Hansberry; Daniel James, Jr.; Judith Jamison; Thurgood Marshall; Leontyne Price; Carl Rowan; or Andrew Young. Using library sources, find out all you can about this person's life. Then write a one-page report on his or her main achievements.*

The car became a sign of power in America. The fancier one's car, the more admired one would be. Drawing shows a "Rocket Engine" Oldsmobile, said to combine power, "glamor," and "effortless ease."

Chapter 14

Affluent Americans

A cold March wind blew across the Long Island, New York, potato fields. The slate gray sky promised snow before nightfall. Yet on this uncomfortable day in 1949, more than a thousand people waited in lines outside a small building. Some had been there for four days.

William J. Levitt was about to open his sales offices for new homes. Thousands of home-hungry people were eager to buy. After World War II, the U.S. had a housing shortage. Few homes had been built during the war. Young married couples now had to live with parents. Many lived in old Army camps.

Levitt was the first builder of cheap, mass-produced houses on large tracts (areas) of land. He bought a tract, marked out lots, and started building homes. In Levittown, Long Island, he put up 17,500 houses. They looked very much alike. But this didn't bother most of the people who bought them. Buyers were happy just to have a home of their own at last.

The housing boom that built new suburbs was part of a larger boom taking place across the U.S. The causes for this exploding growth went back to World War II. The war had made jobs for almost everybody. Good jobs had put money in people's pockets. But while the war was on, there were many things people could not buy. The U.S. was making ships and planes instead of houses, cars, or refrigerators. So people worked overtime and saved their money.

Spending spree. When World War II ended, Americans wanted to buy all the things they couldn't get during the war. Now they could use their savings. Many people went on a spending spree.

589

They bought some goods as fast as factories could make them. The factories hired more workers and stepped up production. The economy grew and grew. Americans had never been so well off — so *affluent*.

Returning veterans shared in this affluence. A new law, the "G.I. Bill of Rights," gave veterans advantages that earlier veterans had not had. The government paid for the education or job training of these returning veterans. In many cases, it gave them monthly living allowances while they went to school. It helped them get loans for homes, farms, or businesses.

The auto once again became part of the changing scene. In many suburbs, people could get around only in cars. Builders put up new shopping centers along highways. People had to drive to work or to the store. Many families bought two cars. Workers laid down new

Life in sprawling housing developments such as the one at Lakewood, California (below), called for cars and more cars. Many Americans visited car lots to buy something once thought to be out of the question — a second family car.

roads to help handle the increase in traffic. Trucks began to lure some of the freight away from trains.

"Baby boom." The economy wasn't the only thing growing in the post-war years. The number of people living in the U.S. soared. Millions of soldiers returned from the war, got married, and had children. The country had a "baby boom." Thousands of new schools had to be built in the 1950's to educate the new Americans.

The babies of the 1940's grew into young people. A new word — *teenager* — was made up to describe them. Teenagers had their own culture, language, and heroes. Their music took on

a restless beat that annoyed many adults. A young Southern singer named Elvis Presley swung his hips and tossed his head. His teenage fans screamed with delight. Rock 'n' roll music swept the country. Teenagers had money to spend now, and many of them spent it on rock 'n' roll records.

Americans spent more than ever in those years. And they also *borrowed* more. Credit cards and "buy now, pay later" plans became popular. Thrift had long been considered a virtue.

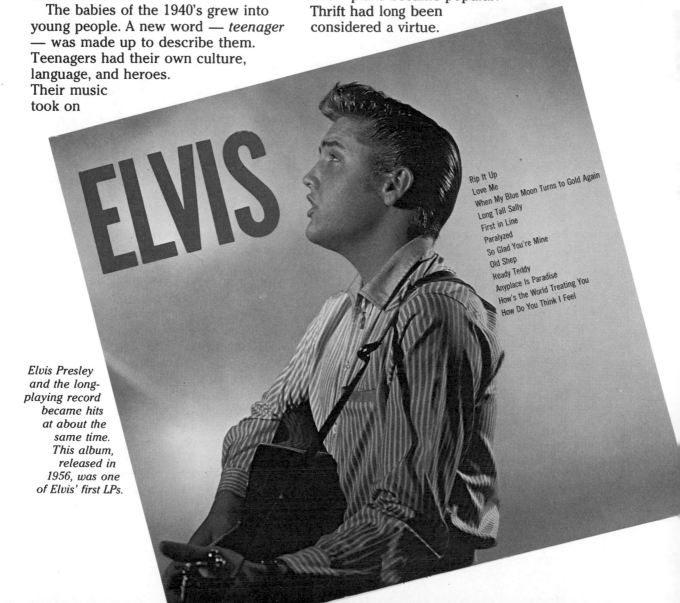

Elvis Presley and the long-playing record became hits at about the same time. This album, released in 1956, was one of Elvis' first LPs.

This early ad for a color TV set shows the square lines and wood paneling popular in early 1950's.

But now people were encouraged to go into debt. By 1970 Americans owed more than 92 *billion* dollars.

To many, the new affluence seemed like the "American dream" come true. But others pointed to some disturbing clouds on the horizon:

Poverty. The economic boom did not include everyone. Millions of poor people in the U.S. did not share in the wealth. Many — but by no means all — were blacks or members of other minority groups. Some of these poor people were jammed into city slums. Others lived in country shacks. Wherever they lived, their lives were scarred by poverty and despair. They were proof that the gap between the poor and the rest of the nation had grown larger in the post-war years.

Urban decay. U.S. cities developed troubles. Many people were moving from the cities to the suburbs. Buildings decayed and good neighborhoods slowly turned to slums. Meanwhile the costs of running cities rose higher and higher. City governments had to raise taxes to meet their budgets. Some of these governments tried to cut back on services such as garbage pickups and street cleaning. But this only hastened the spread of the slums.

Social worries. Even in the suburbs, all was not well. Critics charged that suburban people tended to act, dress, and think alike. In both cities and smaller places, *juvenile delinquency* (law-breaking by young people) was on the rise. Some experts worried about family life. More people got married than ever before. Yet more of these marriages were ending in divorce.

But while experts studied such problems, most Americans went on living, working, and buying. The U.S. was changing faster than ever before. For some, the changes were troubling. For others, the changes were part of the routine. Many Americans just hoped the changes would be good for them.

A Second Look. . . .

1. *Describe three ways in which the United States changed in the years after World War II. What was the main cause of each change?*

2. *Today many people still have difficulty accepting the role of young people in the U.S. They wish for the "good old days" when young people "knew their place" and "behaved themselves." What do you think? Is a separate "teen culture" good for the U.S. or not? What are its advantages? What are its drawbacks? Do you think you would answer differently if you had children of your own? Explain.*

3. *During the late 1950's and early 1960's, the nation's highway system greatly aided auto and truck transportation in the U.S. Yet many critics say that, as gas and oil grow scarcer, Americans may regret building so many of these roads. Obtain a road map of your region as it exists today. Then, using your school or public library, obtain a map of approximately the same area before 1955. What major highways have been added in the past 20 years or so? Make a list of them. Do any of them seem unnecessary? Place a check mark next to those which do. Do you see a need for any additional highways now? Make a separate list of the highways you would build by indicating which areas they would link. Who would stand to benefit from your new roads? Who might be opposed?*

Not all Americans were affluent. Below, an alley in Atlanta before slum clearance went into effect.

Chapter 15

The Coming of TV

Milton Berle first stumbled into U.S. living rooms in 1948. Every Tuesday night, he made a point of doing everything wrong. He wore funny clothes. He twisted his mouth into strange shapes. He had pies thrown in his face. And for what? Strictly for laughs.

Berle was a stand-up comic. In his skits, he was usually the brunt of the jokes. But Berle had the last laugh. He and a few other comics did something earlier entertainers could not have done. These show people of the late 1940's played a large part in making TV-watching a national habit.

Berle's show was called *The Texaco Star Theatre.* When it began, few Americans had TV sets. TV screens were still quite small. All that viewers could see were greenish pictures that flickered. TV networks did not broadcast many shows. At night, most people went to movies, read, or listened to radio.

Then came Berle and other stars of early TV. Some of their shows were sudden hits. People with TV sets would invite friends over to watch such programs. More and more Americans wanted to have sets of their own. More and more of them saved their money and made down payments.

In 1947 only about 14,000 U.S. homes had sets. In 1948 about 190,000 sets were sold. TV screens kept getting larger. TV pictures kept getting clearer.

And Americans kept on buying sets. By 1953, five years later, 20 *million* sets had been sold.

Television led to a revolution in U.S. buying habits. And it led to a revolution in other ways as well. Television brought events and entertainment into homes from far-off places. It changed the way people lived. It changed how they thought. It even influenced the way they voted.

Whirling disk. How did television begin? In 1884 a German scientist named Paul Nipkow (NIP-koe) performed an experiment. He made a whirling disk with holes in it. This disk was able to scan moving images. The light from various parts of the images fell on a chemical cell. This was a crude form of TV camera. A lamp that looked like a headlight reproduced the images. The "headlight" was an early form of a TV picture tube. The images on the lamp were only flickering shadows. Even so, they made a moving picture.

This invention paved the way for the development of TV. Yet scientists still had to find a way to send moving pictures over long distances. In 1925 U.S. inventor Charles Francis Jenkins made a discovery. He sent a picture over a distance in much the same way that radio waves are sent. Soon after, the first TV sets were built.

The first models were very expensive.

594

Though few people could afford a TV set, many were curious about the device. Hundreds crowded into the RCA Building in New York City in 1939. They went to watch the first televised sportscast. It was a college baseball game between Columbia and Princeton. The show wasn't like today's sports-casts. Only one camera was set up — at the third-base line. When the ball was hit, the camera had to hunt all over the field for it. A sportscaster later recalled: "We got so we were praying for all the batters to strike out. That was *one* thing we knew the cameras could record."

TV dinners. A few years after World War II, television started to catch on. TV sets were produced more inexpensively. A few shows such as Milton Berle's became sudden hits. In 1948 sales of TV sets skyrocketed. The television revolution had begun.

People hurried home from school or work to watch "the tube." They went out at night less often, so other businesses were affected. Pre-cooked "TV dinners" went on the market. Restaurant sales took a dip. Movie houses started closing because fewer people went to them. Libraries and book stores reported a drop in business. Even juke box profits were down. Huge numbers of Americans were home, watching TV.

Funnyman Milton Berle was one reason why many Americans of the 1950's spent evenings at home.

Before the 1950's, radio networks had carried many dramas and variety shows. Once TV caught on, the audience for these shows faded. Many radio stations started playing rock music for teenagers. Other stations produced more talk shows.

TV programs were paid for by advertising. Advertisers knew that large numbers of people watched TV commercials. So commercials were beamed to mass audiences. One lipstick company hit the jackpot. It started advertising on TV in 1950. By 1952 it was selling 90 times as many cosmetics as it had two years before.

Millions of Americans watched sports on TV. Many of these people became fans of pro football. Before television, there were only a few pro football teams. Then TV started showing the pro games. Soon football was challenging baseball as the favorite U.S. sport.

"Global village." TV news informed people about national and local events. It covered political speeches and conventions. It showed what was going on across town — and around the world. By doing so, television turned the world into a kind of "global village." That is, it made the world appear even smaller than it had already come to seem.

595

The rules of political campaigns began to change. How candidates looked sometimes seemed as important as what they said. TV's political importance was shown in the 1952 Presidential election campaign. The Republican candidate, General Dwight D. ("Ike") Eisenhower, made 50 campaign ads for TV. His Democratic opponent, Illinois governor Adlai Stevenson, decided not to make TV campaign ads. Stevenson said they would make him feel he was being sold "like breakfast food."

Stevenson's campaign managers did schedule some of his speeches on network TV. But in order to carry one speech, the network had to cancel a popular show, *I Love Lucy*. Stevenson got angry letters with messages such as "I Love Lucy, I Like Ike — Drop Dead." Eisenhower won the election, and his TV campaign probably helped.

From the beginning, television had led to heated arguments. Some people called TV an "idiot box" and said most programs were silly. Others said that TV news was too powerful — and sometimes unfair. Yet TV was also praised as educational. Viewers said it had shown them parts of the world and its people they would not normally have seen.

Whatever the case, the hubbub proved again how much television had changed life in U.S. living rooms.

In I Love Lucy, *Lucille Ball (center) got into a new scrape every week. Helping her into or out of it were Desi Arnaz (left) and Vivian Vance.*

A Second Look. . . .

1. How did television change American habits? Name three ways in which it did.

2. Critics still charge that TV entertainment shows give a false image of the world. They say that TV comedies and dramas lack depth and meaning. They charge that characters on such programs are too shallow to be real. Do you agree with such criticism? How would you defend the shows you watch? Illustrate your points with examples from these programs.

3. Many people watch television because it takes little concentration. Pick an evening and watch three hours of prime-time TV. But instead of just watching, pretend you are a newspaper critic of TV. Take notes on each show: the major characters, purpose, setting, outcome. Write a review of one of the shows from your notes.

Chapter 16

President Ike

His blue eyes twinkled when he smiled. His warm grin put people at ease. On looks alone, some people said, Dwight David Eisenhower could be elected President. In 1952 he *was* elected President — but not simply on his looks. His career as a military man had won him the respect of the country.

Eisenhower had been born on October 14, 1890. He got the nickname "Ike" while he was growing up in Abilene, Kansas. His parents were poor. His father worked in a creamery, a place where butter and cheese are made. His mother grew fruits and vegetables, which she sold to people in town. She raised Ike and his five brothers strictly and taught them to work hard.

After finishing high school, Eisenhower attended the U.S. Military Academy at West Point, New York. He was graduated from West Point in 1915, in the top third of his class. He became an Army officer, and, in time, a general. During World War II, Eisenhower was named top commander of the Allied armies that would invade France.

At the end of the war, Ike was a great hero to millions of Americans. His friends suggested that he run for President. Ike ruled out this idea in 1948. But in 1952 he changed his mind. He became the Republican candidate against Adlai Stevenson, the Democratic nominee.

At first, experts thought the election would be close. Stevenson was a thoughtful speaker with a fine sense of humor. At the time, the U.S. was fighting a war in Korea. The war had dragged on since 1950. During the election campaign, Eisenhower pulled a surprise. If he were elected, he said, he would go to Korea to help end the war.

Eisenhower won the election easily. In December 1952, he went to Korea. The war did not end overnight. But in the summer of 1953 a truce was signed. The fighting came to a halt.

Political restraint. Meanwhile people wondered what Eisenhower would do about problems at home. He was the first Republican President in 20 years. Presidents Roosevelt and Truman had worked hard to promote the programs they favored. Many of those programs had become law. Would Eisenhower now try to get rid of them?

Eisenhower disliked some of the programs. But he did not believe it was the President's job to twist Congress' arm to change them. He had a strong belief in the balance of power among the three branches of government. As President, he stated his ideas and proposed some new laws. Then he simply let Congress debate them. His restraint surprised many people.

Eisenhower was humble, frank, and quietly confident. He actively asked for other people's opinions on important is-

597

sues. This President's strength, said one reporter, was his ability to get people to work together toward common goals.

The United States continued to grow and change under Eisenhower's leadership. Some of the change was physical. The nation began a massive 20-year program of road-building. These roads had a new name: *interstate highways.* Two new states, Alaska and Hawaii, were added to the Union. They came in eight months apart in 1959. Now there were 50 stars in the U.S. flag.

Diplomatic upset. When Eisenhower entered the White House, the Cold War with the Soviet Union was at its coldest. Eisenhower spoke often of the need for world peace. Soviet leaders too were thinking about peace. The Soviet dictator Stalin died in 1953. Soon Soviet leaders began using a new word — *coexistence.* It meant different systems of government living in peace.

In 1959 Soviet leader Nikita Khrushchev came to the United States. He inspected cornfields in Iowa. He talked face-to-face with Eisenhower. The Cold War seemed to be thawing. The "Big Four" — the U.S., the Soviet Union, Britain, and France — made plans for a conference in 1960. The purpose of the meeting was to discuss world peace. Soon after the meeting, Eisenhower was to visit the Soviet Union. But in May 1960, this plan fell apart.

Just before the meeting, the Soviets shot down a U-2 spy plane over their territory. It was a U.S. plane. At first, Eisenhower denied that the plane was on a spying mission. It was a weather plane that had strayed off course, U.S. officials said. But the Soviets had captured the pilot, Francis Gary Powers.

Powers confessed he was on a spy mission. Khrushchev was angry. He took back his invitation to Eisenhower. The crisis became known as the U-2 incident. It was a great setback for Eisenhower.

Military concern. At the end of his second term in 1961, Eisenhower was 70 years old. He was the oldest U.S. President ever. He had not run for election to a third term. But he did not just withdraw quietly. He made a farewell speech on TV that raised some disturbing questions.

For the first time in history, the President declared, the U.S. was keeping a large peacetime military force. The federal government was constantly spending money to buy newer and better military equipment. One result was the growth of a large arms industry. Companies all across the country made weapons and parts for the military. These companies employed many people.

Eisenhower called this "the military-industrial complex." He said it was necessary. The nation had to maintain a strong defense. But he warned the nation to be careful. It must not let the military-industrial complex get too much power.

Eisenhower did not spell out just what he meant. But over the next few years, other people took up his warning. They made these further points:

Jobs. It was unwise, they said, to have too many jobs depend on military spending. If peace should suddenly "break out," many people would lose their jobs.

Influence. Many companies do all or most of their business with the mili-

As President, he is Commander-in-Chief of the armed forces. Military leaders take orders from him. Some people worried that, if the military became too strong, it might try to give orders to the President.

Eisenhower knew that the nation's founders had tried to create a government of checks and balances. He did not want the system to get out of balance. "We must never let the weight [of the military-industrial complex] endanger our liberties," he warned. "We should take nothing for granted."

A Second Look. . . .

1. When was Dwight Eisenhower elected President? Name two changes that took place while he was in office.

2. In the U-2 incident, the United States was caught spying on the Soviet Union. Spying in peacetime is a troublesome issue. Many say it is against the spirit of democracy. But others say it is necessary to protect the safety of the U.S. Do you think the United States should spy on other countries? If so, why? Does spying conflict, in your mind, with the rules of democracy? Why or why not?

3. In Eisenhower's last speech as President, he warned the nation to keep the power of two groups in balance with the rest of the nation. What two groups was Eisenhower talking about? How had they achieved great influence? Was their influence good or bad for the U.S.? Write a one-paragraph essay answering these questions in your own words. Then imagine that you are (a) a U.S. Army general, or (b) a worker in an aircraft factory. Write another paragraph explaining how you believe one of these two people might answer the questions.

Dwight Eisenhower was a confident campaigner. Here he is shown aboard the Eisenhower Special *in Denver, Colorado, as the 1952 campaign begins.*

tary. Often these companies are major employers and have great national influence. Some people feared that they might use this influence to push for unwise military spending.

Civilian rule. Our system of government depends upon rule by civilians. The President is a civilian. He is elected by the voters and is responsible to them.

Looking Back: Post-War America

A	B	C	D	
January 1, 1945	January 1, 1950	January 1, 1955	January 1, 1960	January 1, 1965

Putting Events in Order

Chapters 12 through 16 have described some events in the United States in the period following World War II. Ten events from this period are listed here. Your job is to match each event to the correct period shown on the timeline. On a piece of paper, number from **1** to **10**. After each number, write the letter of the five-year period within which the event occurred.

1. Dwight Eisenhower is elected President of the United States.

2. Harry Truman meets with Winston Churchill and Josef Stalin at the Potsdam Conference.

3. Harry Truman defeats Thomas E. Dewey in a Presidential election campaign.

4. Nikita Khrushchev visits the United States.

5. Jackie Robinson wins the Rookie of the Year award.

6. Dwight Eisenhower warns of the dangers of letting the "military-industrial complex" become too powerful.

7. William J. Levitt opens a sales office for new homes on Long Island.

8. For the first time, television plays an important role in a Presidential election campaign.

9. Dwight Eisenhower makes a trip to Korea.

10. A U-2 spy plane is shot down over the Soviet Union.

Interpreting a Source

In 1959 American Airlines began flying jet passenger planes between one coast of the U.S. and the other. The first flight went from New York to Los Angeles. U.S. poet Carl Sandburg was among the passengers on this flight. Here is his account of the journey.

You remember back to many years ago when you talked in Dayton, Ohio, with Orville Wright, and how he told you, "The faster you go, the less power you need." You remember how he described that first precarious[1] air adventure at Kitty Hawk. And now you're witness to man's latest daring and intelligence, an airplane that moves as fast as the arc of the sun and is itself longer than the distance of Orville Wright's first flight....

Man wants to know. Man has been called "the improbable animal." You never know what he's going to do next. He has performed so many wonders ... that he has forgotten who made the first wheel or who first dared dream that man could fly.

You can repeat it: Man wants to know. This hunger and thirst is irrepressible.[2] Will man get to the moon? Of course man will get to the moon, and he will [circle] it, and report what he may see, hear, touch, taste. One daring visionary[3] sees man at a time when, a million years from now, the planet Earth will no longer support the human race. But having found, by trips to the planet Venus, that he can live there, man moves there....

You have a right to ... thoughts like these when you are riding at nearly 600 miles [960 kilometers] an hour, four miles [nearly 6$\frac{1}{2}$ kilometers] above the Earth, with the only sense of movement that of the wind brushing past the surfaces of the airship. You look out of the window at the waves of dark and light clouds looking like ocean shore lines, and you feel as if you are floating away

in this pleasantly moving room....

By now the moving room you are in has passed over Charleston, West Virginia, and Louisville, Kentucky, and you saw nothing of the lights of those cities, nor did you glimpse the wide Mississippi River as you passed four miles above it. Next you have passed over Amarillo, Texas, and soon afterward you are invited into the cockpit, where you sit in back of Captain Hamilton Smith, and he says it is Albuquerque, New Mexico, ahead — squares and circles of light, long streaks of light leading out as though they are roads....

You search for words to describe the

The Wright brothers seemed like strange birds when they made their first flight in 1903. By the 1950's, though, anyone could fly from coast to coast. Cartoon is by Jay N. ("Ding") Darling.

---

[1]*Precarious* means risky or uncertain.

[2]*Irrepressible* means uncontrollable or not able to be kept down.

[3]A *visionary,* in this sense, is someone with a great imagination.

speed of this flight: You are whisked and streaked, you are zipped and flicked, you are sped, hurtled, flashed, shuttled from an ocean on one side of the continent to an ocean on the opposite side in less time than it takes the sun to trace a 90-degree arc across the sky. Far back and across the ages, man has had his folk tales and legends of flying. The Greeks had the myth about Icarus, who flew too near the sun. His wings melted and he took a fall. The Arabians had their flying carpet; you made a wish and it took you where you wanted to go. Wishes paid your fare, while modern airlines require dollars. But as your pleasant, warm room moves at 10 miles [16 kilometers] a minute through weather that is 40 degrees below [minus 40 degrees Celsius] outside, you can be glad you are not riding an ancient Arabian carpet.

In this trip from New York to Los Angeles, the plane is fighting a 100-mile [160-kilometer] -an-hour head wind, which makes it an hour late in arriving.... As you feel the huge ship setting down with its 112 passengers and glimpse the throng of welcoming people, you think suddenly of a passage from a book about Lincoln, which tells of the relays of ponies and men that rushed the President's first inaugural address west from St. Jo [St. Joseph], Missouri. It took them seven days and 17 hours to reach Sacramento, California, bearing his plea for the east and west coasts, the Great Lakes and the Gulf, the Rio Grande and the Penobscot, to belong to one common country.

You have just [crossed] a distance twice this far, and in infinitely[4] less time,

Jet passenger planes brought a magic touch to flying. This 1959 National Airlines ad made the totally impossible seem only offbeat.

NEW MAGIC CARPET
for the whole family. Last December, when National inaugurated the first jet flights in the U.S.A., you filled our big Boeing 707's every day. Now, National offers twice as many pure jet flights between the North and Florida—eight flights daily—with more to come later this season. But we know that you want more than speed or choice of departures. So you'll find extra measures of National's famous comfort and personalized service on all our flights. National serves 15 states and 39 cities on the Atlantic Seaboard, all Florida, Cuba, the Gulf Coast and Texas. Also, through-plane service from Florida to the West Coast and South America in cooperation with other leading airlines.

NATIONAL LEADS IN IDEAS THAT BENEFIT YOU
AIRLINE OF THE STARS

---

[4]*Infinitely,* in this sense, means vastly or immensely.

Electoral Vote, 1948

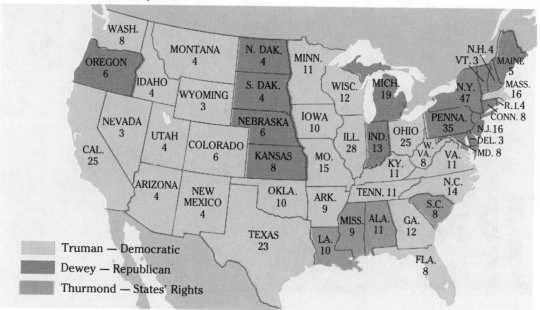

WASH.
8

OREGON
6

MONTANA
4

IDAHO
4

WYOMING
3

N. DAK.
4

S. DAK.
4

MINN.
11

NEVADA
3

UTAH
4

COLORADO
6

NEBRASKA
6

IOWA
10

WISC.
12

MICH.
19

CAL.
25

ARIZONA
4

NEW
MEXICO
4

KANSAS
8

MO.
15

ILL.
28

IND.
13

OHIO
25

W.
VA.
8

KY.
11

OKLA.
10

ARK.
9

TENN. 11

VA.
11

N.C.
14

TEXAS
23

LA.
10

MISS.
9

ALA.
11

GA.
12

S.C.
8

FLA.
8

N.H. 4
VT. 3
MAINE
5

N.Y.
47

MASS.
16

R.I.4
CONN. 8

PENNA.
35

N.J. 16

DEL. 3

MD. 8

Truman — Democratic

Dewey — Republican

Thurmond — States' Rights

and you feel very hopeful, somehow, that this narrowing of the distance between states and rivers, between countries and the people in them, will cement still further the common country that Lincoln saw as the destiny of America.

1. *How does Sandburg describe the plane he has taken?*
2. *What seems "improbable" about human beings? Why does Sandburg use the term?*
3. *What does the Greek legend of Icarus have to do with air travel? Why does Sandburg mention it?*
4. *How does Sandburg relate his journey to that of the Pony Express in Lincoln's time? Do you believe that jet travel has "cemented" the country further? Why or why not?*

Sharpening Your Skills

This map shows the electoral vote by states in the Presidential election of 1948. Although the Progressive party candidate, Henry Wallace, won more than a million popular votes, he won no electoral votes at all. Study the map carefully. Then answer the questions.

1. Which state had the most electoral votes in 1948? Which of the four candidates won this state?
2. True or false? Harry Truman won most of the electoral votes in the West.
3. True or false? Thomas Dewey won almost all of the electoral votes in the Northeast.
4. In what part of the U.S. did Strom Thurmond have most success? Where was Thomas Dewey most successful?

TOWARD EQUAL JUSTICE

Looking Ahead: "Second Reconstruction"

We shall overcome,
  we shall overcome,
We shall overcome some day.
Oh, deep in my heart, I do believe,
We shall overcome some day.

These words were sung in churches. They were sung on the streets of the nation's capital. They were sung in jail cells. All across the nation in the late 1950's and the 1960's, the song could be heard. What did it mean?

"We Shall Overcome" was a theme song of a movement that demanded equal justice for black people. This campaign was called the *civil-rights movement*. Many people were moved to tears by the song. Others became so angry that they wanted to hit the people

The high tide of the civil-rights movement of the 1960's was reached on August 28, 1963. Some 250,000 Americans, blacks and whites together, staged a peaceful "March on Washington" (left).

who sang it. Sometimes they did hit the singers. But the singers kept right on. "The Lord will see us through," they sang. "We shall overcome some day."

Blacks had been freed from slavery for almost a hundred years. But in most places they were still mistreated. Often they were segregated from whites. They didn't have the rights and opportunities of most white people.

Customs and laws. In the North, blacks were segregated by custom. In most states, laws did not require blacks to live in separate neighborhoods. But custom did. In most states, laws did not require blacks to attend separate schools. But most schools served separate neighborhoods. In many black neighborhoods, only blacks were in the schools. Few blacks were able to attend college. Few blacks could get good jobs. And in hard times, blacks were the first to lose their jobs. They were "last hired, first fired."

In much of the South, blacks were segregated by law. Laws required separate schools for blacks and whites. Laws required blacks to stay away from white swimming pools. Laws required blacks to drink only at water fountains set aside for them. Laws required blacks to sit at the back of buses. Laws permitted voting practices such as *poll taxes* (special taxes paid as a requirement for voting). Such practices kept most blacks from voting.

Some white people believed that such treatment of blacks was right. They thought white people were better than black people. Such an attitude is called *racism*.

Laughter and silence. Other whites didn't think much about blacks at all. If they did, many thought about them as objects of humor. A popular radio program was called *Amos 'n Andy*. In it, two white men imitated the voices of black men and women. The blacks were bumbling, scheming, and silly. Whites laughed at the show, but most blacks didn't. They were angry at the way the program treated blacks.

But the times were changing. In 1952 a black writer jarred the minds of book-buying Americans. His name was Ralph Ellison. In his novel, *Invisible Man*, he described his experience of life in the U.S. He told of being jostled on the streets by whites as they walked by. The whites didn't even turn to look at him. They just kept walking, as if he were invisible. Ellison said many whites thought they could ignore blacks altogether.

The civil-rights movement showed white Americans that they couldn't ignore black Americans. But it didn't start all of a sudden. In the 1930's, black

606

Virginia-born Robert Gwathmey spoke for working people in his paintings. In "Poll Tax Country" (above), he showed political leaders reaching for power as farm workers go about their chores.

people had fought in the courts to try to win their rights. They didn't make much headway. Then World War II came. Many black Americans fought — and died — for their country. Yet black veterans came home to segregation. Many blacks made up their minds to change this. And some whites were determined to help them.

Rulings and protests. The spark needed to light the fires of change came in May 1954. The U.S. Supreme Court ruled that segregated schools were illegal. The idea of segregated schools violated the Constitution, the Justices said. Segregation of other kinds was soon questioned by people who had not questioned it before.

One of the most dramatic protests of the period came in Montgomery, Alabama. Rosa Parks, a black woman, refused to give up her seat on a bus to a white person. She was arrested for breaking a Montgomery law. Her arrest sparked a year-long campaign to end segregation on buses in Montgomery. That protest introduced a new leader of Southern blacks, Dr. Martin Luther King.

King was a young minister in Montgomery. He helped organize the protest there. He taught his followers the ways of peaceful protest. In Montgomery, and later in other Southern towns and cities, black people broke laws they considered unjust. They were put in jail. But they kept on with their struggle for equal rights.

The civil-rights movement began to win legal victories. It also began to change people's feelings. In the early 1960's, many young people, both black and white, flocked to the Deep South to work in the movement. They helped people sign up to vote. They helped elect blacks to some local offices. These were the first blacks to hold such offices in the South in more than 75 years.

One historian, C. Vann Woodward, said it was as if the nation were repeating its own history. He coined a phrase for the 1950's and 1960's. He called the period a *Second Reconstruction*.

Rights and roles. The civil-rights movement inspired other groups of Americans to make their own claims for equal treatment. In California, a campaign began to organize farm workers into a union. The workers were poorly paid. Many were Mexican Americans, just like the man who wanted them in a union. His name was Cesar Chavez (SAY-sar CHAH-vess). His goal was to win rights for all Mexican Americans.

Women also began to speak out about unfair treatment. Some called for liberation — freedom from the old roles they had played for so long. They named their campaign the *women's liberation movement*. It revived issues first raised by the women's suffrage movement at the turn of the century. A new word entered the American language. It was *sexism* — discrimination based on a person's sex.

Efforts to win equal justice were helped by the U.S. Supreme Court. Under the leadership of Chief Justice Earl Warren, the Court made rulings against many types of discrimination. Other national leaders gave further help. In 1965 President Johnson spoke to Congress in support of the civil-rights movement's goals. "It is not just Negroes," he said, "but really it is all of us who must overcome the crippling legacy of . . . injustice. And we shall overcome."

Civil-rights workers were thrilled to hear the words of their song from the President's lips. Still, few people in the movement were completely satisfied. They thought there was still a long way to go before Americans had truly equal opportunities.

607

Before 1954, black students and white students went to separate schools in many U.S. communities. Students in the classroom shown here attended an all-black school in West Memphis, Arkansas, in 1949.

Chapter 17

"Separate Is Not Equal"

In 1954 U.S. Chief Justice Earl Warren left Washington, D.C., for a few days of vacation. The Supreme Court had been working hard hearing evidence in a very important case. Now the Justices had decided to take a rest. Warren had always wanted to see some Civil War monuments. He thought that

the best way to see them was by car.

Warren and his driver headed south. They stopped in the evening in a small Southern town. Warren asked his driver to leave him at the hotel and said good night. He assumed that the driver would want to go to a cheaper hotel. Yet when Warren met the driver the next morning, it was obvious that he had spent the night in the car.

"What happened?" Warren asked. "Didn't you get to a hotel?"

"Well, Mr. Chief Justice, I couldn't find a place that would take me," the driver answered.

Then it hit Warren. The driver was black. In this town, as in so many towns across the nation, blacks could not stay in the same hotel as whites. Some towns did not have any hotels for blacks. In such places, black visitors could find no place to spend the night.

Warren was overcome with embarrassment. He went back to work with new energy. As it happened, the case the Court was hearing also dealt with segregation. It centered on discrimination in public schools. (*Discrimination,* in this sense, means treating people differently because of their membership in a particular group.)

Many years earlier, the Court had given legal support to segregation. The Court had taken its stand in 1896 in the case of *Plessy v. Ferguson.* It had ruled that separate passenger cars for blacks and whites were legal on trains so long as the cars were equal. "Separate but equal" had become the law of the land.

Civil-rights groups had begun challenging this decision in the courts in the 1930's. The group leading the attack was the National Association for the Advancement of Colored People (NAACP). The NAACP won several court suits. But the Court did not overturn the decision in the Plessy case.

Segregation had continued. And it had continued to anger most black Americans. One of them was Oliver Brown, a railroad worker in Topeka, Kansas.

Brown had a young daughter named Linda. Linda Brown traveled about a mile to and from elementary school every day. Yet there was a public elementary school only a few blocks from her house. Why couldn't she go there?

Anger in Topeka. One day in 1950, when Linda was seven, Brown tried to have his daughter enrolled at the nearby school. He was turned away. The school accepted only white students, he was told. Outraged, Brown decided to sue the Topeka Board of Education. He wanted to force the Board to allow Linda to go to the school close to her home.

Brown filed his suit in the U.S. District Court for Kansas. He lost the case, but he did not give up. He took his appeal all the way to the U.S. Supreme Court. There the case was combined with four others attacking segregation in the nation's public schools.

The case became known as *Brown v. Board of Education of Topeka, Kansas.* It opened before the Supreme Court in Washington, D.C., in 1952 and went on for many months. It was a difficult case. The Justices studied it with great care. This was the case Earl Warren returned to after his 1954 vacation in the South.

Brown's attack on segregation was argued by a skilled team of NAACP lawyers. Heading the team was a Baltimore-born attorney, Thurgood Marshall. Marshall was later to become the first black man ever to sit on the U.S. Supreme Court. Another important person in the case was Dr. Kenneth B. Clark. Clark was a black professor at the City College of New York. He supplied facts to show that all-black schools were damaging to black children.

609

Ruling in Washington. At 12:52 on the afternoon of May 17, 1954, Earl Warren began reading the Court's opinion in the case. It was Warren's first major opinion as Chief Justice. He read it with a cool and steady voice. He did not give away the Court's verdict immediately. Twenty minutes went by. Still the news reporters could not be sure which way the Court had ruled.

Then they got their answer. All nine Justices had agreed that segregation in the nation's public schools was against the Constitution. Separate schools for blacks and whites could never be equal, the Court said. Segregation denied black people "equal protection of the laws." And equal protection had been guaranteed by the 14th Amendment.

This ruling overturned the 1896 "separate but equal" decision. "Separate is *not* equal," the Court now said. The Court's decision was limited to equal schooling. But it challenged the basis of all forms of racial segregation in the United States.

The reaction came swiftly. In the nation's black communities, there was a sense of thanksgiving. Black people hoped that the decision would end the unfair treatment they had faced for many years. Many white people — in the North, South, East, and West — also rejoiced. One Ohio newspaper praised the Court for acting "as the conscience of a nation."

In the South, white people were mixed in their opinions. The governor of Virginia said the decision called for "cool heads, calm study, and sound judgment." But some other Southerners were neither cool nor calm about the Court's ruling. They were furious.

Questions of public education had usually been decided by state and local government, they said. They thought the Court's opinion showed no respect for states' rights. These Southerners did not see the decision as one which touched the entire nation. Instead, they saw it as an attack on the Southern way of life.

Crisis in Little Rock. In some states, leaders took steps to fight the decision. They closed all public schools rather than bring an end to segregation. In certain areas, white people joined together in white citizens' councils. The councils often used threats to stop people from trying to make changes in the schools.

One showdown came in Little Rock, Arkansas, in 1957. Nine black students were to attend the city's all-white Central High School. To prevent this, Arkansas governor Orval Faubus called out the state's National Guard. President Eisenhower then sent federal troops into the city to get the teenagers into the school. Faubus finally backed down.

Eisenhower showed that he meant to back up the Court. Many people in the South realized that a new way of life had arrived. Opposition to the Brown ruling slowly faded. In one Southern city after another, black students peacefully entered schools formerly reserved for whites.

Few cases in the history of the U.S. Supreme Court had affected so many people. Few decisions had touched more basic values. A few weeks after the decision, one of the Justices, Stanley Reed, commented on the case. "If it was not the most important decision in the history of the Court," he said, "it was very close."

A Second Look. . . .

1. *What was decided by the Brown case? In what ways did the Supreme Court decision differ from earlier decisions concerning segregation?*

2. *Why were most black people pleased by the decision in* Brown v. Board of Education? *Why did some white people oppose it? What do you think you would have thought of it in 1954? What are your thoughts on segregation in general? Explain them.*

3. *The Supreme Court decision in the Brown case was an important event in the civil-rights movement. In the past 25 years, the Court has made other civil-rights decisions. Use research sources to look up some of these decisions. Find one that has or could have a direct impact on your life. Write an essay describing how the decision affects you or could affect you.*

Showdown over segregation took place at Little Rock Central High School in September 1957. Federal troops moved in with bayonets to allow nine black students to attend the school.

Chapter 18

Bus Ride to Equality

Rosa Parks began a decade of black protest by refusing to give up a seat on a bus. Above, Mrs. Parks on the day the bus protest ended in 1956.

Rosa Parks was tired. It had been a warm December day in Montgomery, Alabama. Christmas shoppers at her department store had kept her busy all day long. At closing time, the 42-year-old black seamstress headed for her bus stop on Cleveland Avenue. Her feet hurt.

Along Cleveland Avenue, auto headlights glared in the thickening darkness. Through the maze of traffic rolled the bus which would take Mrs. Parks home. When it reached her curb, she paid her fare and boarded by the rear door. Then she carefully took a seat in the fifth row.

Like most Southern cities (and many Northern ones) in 1955, Montgomery had laws segregating blacks and whites on city buses. Black people sat in the rear. White people sat in the front. Halfway up the aisle was a no man's land. Black people could sit in this section if the white section was not full. This was where Rosa Parks sat to rest her weary feet on the night of December 1, 1955.

For a few blocks, the trip was quite routine. The bus left Court Square, groaning off in the direction of the Empire Theater. All the seats in the white section were filled now. At the Empire Theater stop, six white people boarded the bus. Following bus company direction, the driver asked four of the blacks to give up their seats. Three of them stood. Rosa Parks gently but firmly refused.

Again the driver asked her to give up her seat. Again Mrs. Parks said no. Her manner was quiet, but her voice was as solid as steel. The driver pulled the emergency brake and went to look for the police. Minutes later, he was back with two policemen. They ordered Mrs. Parks off the bus. They took her to the city police station. Her fingerprints were taken. She was put in jail.

Mrs. Parks had not planned on trouble. Her simple protest had taken only a few minutes to make. It involved no news reporters, no popping flashbulbs, no drama of any kind. It had been a lonely act of courage. But it marked the start of a series of protests across the nation lasting more than a decade.

Organizing. News of Rosa Parks' arrest traveled quickly through Montgomery. Black leaders in the city called a meeting at the Dexter Avenue Baptist Church. They were tired of having to board buses by the rear door. They were tired of being told to sit in certain places. They were tired of having to stand when told to stand. They were tired of segregation — tired and ready for a protest of their own.

Most of the people who rode buses in Montgomery were black. What would happen, black leaders asked, if Montgomery's blacks simply refused to ride buses for one day? What would happen, in other words, if black people *boycotted* the buses? Surely such a boycott would show that Montgomery's blacks stood against the city's bus laws.

Committees were set up to convince black people to take part in a boycott. Leaflets were printed to spread the word. Rosa Parks, just out of jail, worked all weekend to tell people of the boycott.

After Rosa Parks' arrest, Montgomery's black people decided not to ride city buses. Many commuters walked to work, even in the rain.

It was scheduled to take place on Monday, December 5.

That Monday, Montgomery's buses rattled through the streets almost empty. Seventeen thousand black people walked to work or got there some other way. That night another meeting was held in the Dexter Avenue Baptist Church. This meeting decided to keep the boycott going.

The church's young minister, Dr. Martin Luther King, Jr., addressed the group. "For many years, we have shown amazing patience," he said. "We have sometimes given our white brothers the feeling that we liked the way we were being treated. But we come here tonight to be saved from that patience that makes us patient with anything less than freedom and justice."

Protesting. Dr. King was new to Montgomery. He had been a minister there for less than a year. Yet he now took leadership of the boycott.

613

Montgomery's black people formed car pools. When necessary, they walked to their jobs. A few of them even rode mules. And they vowed to keep the boycott going until bus seating was no longer segregated.

At first, officials of the bus company did not think the boycott would last long. They met with black leaders, but the two sides could not agree. Bus company officials said the ideas of black leaders were illegal. The talks broke down.

The boycott continued through the winter and into the spring of 1956. Both Dr. King and Mrs. Parks were arrested. King's home was bombed. Still, Montgomery's black citizens kept up their protests. Then the matter of bus seating in Montgomery came before the federal courts.

In June 1956, the U.S. District Court ruled that segregated seating on buses was against the Constitution. But the city of Montgomery appealed the decision to the U.S. Supreme Court. In November the Supreme Court upheld the District Court decision. On December 21, 1956 — more than a year after the boycott began — Dr. King rode the first *de*segregated bus in Montgomery.

By this time, the Montgomery bus boycott had attracted nationwide attention. Many Americans were impressed by the dignity the bus boycotters had shown. Dr. Martin Luther King, Jr., had become known far beyond Montgomery's city limits. He had emerged as a leader of black Southerners in their struggle for civil rights.

The Montgomery protest inspired others. Bus boycotts were organized in several Southern cities. Black people

went to jail to make their views known. New methods of protest were put into practice in many places. Here are a few of them:

Sit-ins. In 1960 four black college students walked into a five-and-ten-cent store in Greensboro, North Carolina. They sat down at the lunch counter and ordered coffee. The waitress reminded them that blacks were not served at "white" lunch counters in Greensboro. The students were polite but firm. They said they would stay until they were served.

They stayed in the store until it closed that evening. The next day they returned. Their method was known as a *sit-in*. It had first been used by labor unions in the 1930's. The Greensboro sit-in soon drew national attention.

As leader of Montgomery's black community, Dr. Martin Luther King was arrested several times. Here his wife, Coretta, is an eyewitness.

Sit-ins spread to other cities — and often worked. Slowly, lunch rooms, restaurants, and other public places were opened to black people.

Freedom Rides. In 1961 a leading civil-rights group, the Congress of Racial Equality (CORE), tried another tactic. It sent teams of bus riders, both blacks and whites, on journeys through the South. These people became known as *Freedom Riders.* They challenged segregation on buses, in restaurants, and in other public places.

Some white Southerners resented these Freedom Riders. They said that Northerners had no business stirring up trouble in the South. Yet the Freedom Riders called attention to their goals. The U.S. Justice Department put pressure on companies which carried passengers between states. It urged them to ban segregation in terminals run for their use. Air, rail, and bus lines agreed to do so.

Voter-registration drives. In 1959 a federal commission made a disturbing report to the nation. It said that large numbers of black people were being denied the right to vote. Most civil-rights groups agreed. Without voting rights, these groups asked, how could black people have an equal role in a democracy?

One summer in the early 1960's, a young black leader, Robert Moses, made a trip through Mississippi. He became convinced of the need to *register* (sign up) black voters there. Moses believed that voter registration was the road to political power for all poor people, whites as well as blacks. He got a voter-registration drive going in Mississippi in 1964. The idea quickly spread.

Some local people resented Moses' drive. A number of Moses' workers were hurt. A few were killed. But the drive did succeed in registering many blacks. The cause of voter registration was also aided by passage of the 24th Amendment to the U.S. Constitution. This amendment banned the use of poll taxes in federal elections. It became law in 1964.

The civil-rights campaign touched the conscience of the nation. Prejudice remained in many parts of the country, North as well as South. Yet people were working to end this prejudice. Equal justice no longer seemed impossible to win.

A Second Look. . . .

1. Why was Rosa Parks arrested? What law had she violated? How was this law finally overturned?

2. How would you have felt if you had been Rosa Parks on the night of December 1, 1955? Would you have refused to stand for the bus driver? Would you have gone to jail for your rights? Would you have helped to organize a bus boycott? Explain your answers.

3. Pretend that you are a white Montgomery merchant. You are proud of the city, even though you believe that bus segregation is unfair. It is late December of 1955, and the bus boycott is under way. You agree with the goal of the boycott. Yet your business is suffering because fewer black people are coming downtown to shop. Write a letter to the editor of the local newspaper suggesting a way to end the boycott. As you write, remember that most city leaders are opposed to the boycott. Also keep your personal views and business needs heavily in mind.

Chapter 19

"I Have a Dream...."

An angry crowd milled around the bombed house. Some people yelled threats at city officials checking on the damage. The house belonged to the Reverend Martin Luther King. Inside, Dr. King was trying to find out what had happened. Outside, violence hung like a thick cloud in the cool night air.

The date was January 30, 1956. The Montgomery bus boycott was still underway, and King had gone to a boycott meeting. While he was away, someone had planted a bomb on his porch. King's wife and daughter, who had been in the house, were unharmed. But the crowd of angry blacks was in no mood to listen to pleas for calm.

Martin Luther King came out on the porch. He looked at the angry people on his front lawn. He knew some were ready to tear the city apart. But his face showed sadness, not anger or fear.

"We must meet hate with love," he said. "We must meet violence with nonviolence. Leave peacefully. And don't worry about me. If I am stopped, this movement will not stop, because God is with the movement."

The crowd grew silent. Martin Luther King's house had been damaged. His family could have been killed. Yet he stood there talking of love and forgiveness. A man's voice broke the silence: "God bless you," he cried. "Amen!" said others.

Martin Luther King was a leader. He proved it during the year-long bus boycott in Montgomery. The boycott was the start of the civil-rights movement of the 1950's and 1960's. And that January night King gave the movement one of its most basic ideas.

Putting ideas into action. King believed that black people should resist laws they thought unjust. If necessary, he thought they should disobey such laws. But King also said that they should be ready to accept punishment for breaking such laws. In some cases, they should even go to jail.

King called for *nonviolent* (peaceful) resistance. He did not believe in angry threats. He did not believe in fighting back when attacked. He thought the civil-rights movement should try to end injustice by appealing to the conscience of the nation.

King drew his ideas from several sources. He learned love for one's enemies from the deep Christian heritage of American blacks. He learned about nonviolent resistance from the writings of a 19th-century American, Henry David Thoreau (thor-OH). Thoreau had written about resistance to laws dealing with slavery. Now King used Thoreau's ideas to fight racial injustice.

King had also studied the life of Mohandas Gandhi (mo-HAHN-dus GON-dee). Gandhi had led India's struggle for independence in the 1930's and 1940's. Under Gandhi's leadership, millions of Indians had refused to buy British goods. Many had refused to pay British taxes. These were forms of nonviolent protest. From Gandhi, King had learned how to build a movement based on such ideas.

Martin Luther King's political and religious training had begun in his youth. His father was the minister of a leading black church in Atlanta, Georgia. The King family was fairly well-off. Young Martin did not know poverty as a boy. But he did know the personal meaning of segregation firsthand.

Putting faith to a test. At Morehouse College in Atlanta, King trained to become a minister. After being graduated from Morehouse, he continued his studies in Massachusetts and Pennsylvania. But he wanted to do more than care for souls. He felt it was his duty to do something to end segregation and poverty too.

King did all he could. As a result of the Montgomery boycott, he became the best known civil-rights leader in the nation. He used his fame to wage an endless campaign against segregation. From 1956 to 1964, King was arrested 29 times for protesting the unfair treatment of his people.

The year 1963 was a special one for black Americans. It was the 100th anniversary of the Emancipation Proclamation, the first step toward ending slavery. Yet 100 years after freedom, black people still suffered from injus-

Demonstrators in the "March on Washington" in 1963 showed their feelings in the songs they sang.

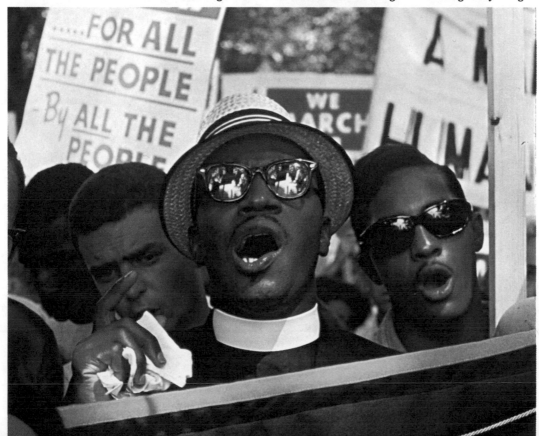

tices. In Washington, D.C., President John F. Kennedy spoke out against unfair treatment of blacks. He sent an important civil-rights bill to Congress. But Congress delayed acting on the bill. Civil-rights leaders thought it was time to put pressure on Congress. They planned a big demonstration in the nation's capital.

The "March on Washington" took place on August 28, 1963. It was a hot, clear summer day. Marchers came in car pools, buses, trains, and planes. They poured into Washington all morning long like a flood. By noon 250,000 people wound around the reflecting pool in front of the Lincoln Memorial. Wealthy merchants marched beside poor farmers. Northerners marched beside Southerners. Blacks marched beside whites.

Putting hope before despair. Millions of people watched the march live on television. Stars of the entertainment world performed. Then, after several speeches, Martin Luther King was introduced. He spoke of how black people had carried in their hearts the hope of full equality. Now was the time, he said, for America to fulfill the promises of democracy.

"I have a dream," he said, "that one day on the red hills of Georgia the sons of former slaves and the sons of former slave-owners will be able to sit down together at the table of brotherhood. . . .

"I have a dream that my four little children will one day live in a nation where they will not be judged by the

Although the "March on Washington" had been proposed by other black leaders, the day belonged, above all, to Martin Luther King.

619

color of their skin but by the content of their character.

"I have a dream. . . ." Over and over again he chanted his dream for America. The crowd listened breathlessly to the rolling words. King ended the speech with the hope that one day all Americans would know the meaning of an old slave song:

Free at last!
Free at last!
Thank God Almighty,
We are free at last!

For a moment there was silence. Some people wept openly. Others were too moved to respond. Then the silence was replaced by thunderous applause.

The next year, King was awarded a high honor, the Nobel Peace Prize, for his civil-rights work. But he did not rest on his honors. He continued to lead the struggle for civil rights. Beginning in 1965, new leaders with different ideas challenged King's leadership of the movement. Some of these new leaders were young Northerners. They were impatient with King's calls for nonviolence. They were angry and defiant. "Black power" was their rallying cry.

But King stood behind the idea of nonviolence. He kept on expanding his activities. He began to speak out against U.S. fighting in Vietnam. Many people criticized him for his views. They said he should limit his work to civil rights. Others supported King. If the U.S. left Vietnam, they said, the government would have more money to spend on civil-rights programs at home.

In 1968 King again broadened his concern. He organized a *Poor People's*
620

Campaign to attack poverty. He went to Memphis, Tennessee, to support a sanitation workers' strike there. On April 4, he was killed by an assassin's bullet. He was 39 years old.

Black communities across America exploded in rage that night. In Washington, D.C., the flames from black neighborhoods could be seen from the White House. In Kansas City, Missouri, National Guard troops moved in to end rioting that took six lives.

Many people found a bitter truth in Martin Luther King's murder. They said it proved that love and forgiveness were useless against hatred. But others remembered his dream. For them, the fulfillment of that dream remained as the work of all Americans.

A Second Look. . . .

1. *Who was Dr. Martin Luther King? How did he become a leader of the civil-rights movement in the 1950's? Why was 1963 a special year to black Americans? How did King mark the occasion?*

2. *What did King mean by* nonviolent resistance? *Is there ever a time when violence is proper? If so, when? If not, why not?*

3. *Martin Luther King made an impact on all Americans. Whether they loved him or hated him, people knew who he was. As a project in oral history, interview people who remember Martin Luther King. Use a tape recorder, if possible, to capture their thoughts. Ask them what they remember about the man and his accomplishments. Did they admire him? What were their feelings about his death? Write up your interviews and submit them as reports to share with your classmates.*

Beaming broadly, a member of the United Farm Workers shows off a box of union grapes. Before its label went on such boxes, the union waged a long strike and boycott against grape-growers.

Chapter 20

La Causa

"Viva la causa!" (Long live the cause!)

The cries in Spanish filled the hot, dusty hall. Mexican-American farm workers in Delano (deh-LAY-no), California, were voting to strike against the large grape-growers. A stocky, dark-haired man called for order. Cesar Chavez looked out at the thousand people assembled before him.

For three years, he had tried to get people to join his National Farm Workers Association. To do so, he had traveled up and down California's Central Valley. Wherever he had gone, he had asked the mostly Mexican-American farm workers if they liked their working conditions. Their answer had been, "No!" Now, in 1965, the time had come for action.

The grape strike that began in 1965 was known as *La Causa* (COW-suh), the cause of the farm workers. It soon turned into a national civil-rights issue. Its leader, Cesar Chavez, was concerned with the economic issues that faced farm workers. But he was also concerned with the unity and dignity of Mexican Americans as a whole.

Dusty harvest. Chavez had grown up on a small farm near Yuma (YOO-muh), Arizona. As a boy, he had worked in the fields with his family at harvest time. At an early age, Chavez had learned how to cut grapes and pick vegetables. But when he was 10 years old, the Chavez family had lost its farm in the Depression. The family had packed its belongings into an old car and joined other farmers heading for California.

The family soon learned the hard and uncertain life of farm laborers. The Chavezes traveled around the fertile California valleys looking for work. They lived in shacks or sometimes in their car. Even the best work was hard "stoop labor" for very low wages.

When he was 15, Chavez left school to work in the fields. He was then living in a run-down slum in San Jose (san ho-ZAY) in the northern part of the state. The slum was called *Sal Si Puedes* (PWAY-dace), a Spanish term meaning "get out if you can." The name was a sort of challenge to Chavez. He was determined to get out.

One day he met a man named Fred Ross. Ross worked for the Community Services Organization (CSO). The CSO was a private agency that tried to help farm workers and other poor people. Ross was looking for someone to help him organize farm workers to fight for their rights. Chavez took a job with the CSO. In his next 10 years with the group, he learned what it took to be a union organizer.

Many of the larger farms in California's Central Valley were owned by wealthy people. Few of these people had been born to wealth. Most had worked for it, and some had worked hard. They used Mexican-American workers to harvest the crops they grew. When

Borrowing an idea from black protesters, farm workers marched to show their strength. Their cry was "Huelga," a Spanish word for "strike."

the harvest was over on one farm, these workers would move on to another. They were known as *migrants* (workers who move from place to place).

Bitter fruits. These workers almost always received low pay. Yet there was not much they could do to improve it. They were specifically left out of federal laws giving workers the right to form unions. So most attempts by farm workers to improve their lives had been wasted efforts.

Chavez believed that the only way for farm workers to help themselves was to form a union. In 1962 he moved with his wife and eight children to Delano. With a few trusted friends, he began to build the National Farm Workers Association.

Chavez continued his organizing for three years. Then, in 1965, came the strike against the large grape-growers. To the cheering crowd, Chavez set down one hard-and-fast rule: The strikers had to be nonviolent. As he put it, "No union movement is worth the life of a single grower or his child or a single worker or his child."

The strike started slowly. The growers argued that, if farm workers went into the union, prices would be pushed so high that they could not make a profit. The growers had many people on their side. Among them were most leaders of local government. The union, on the other hand, had little money and even less power.

But this was *La Causa.* It was a struggle for self-respect of an entire people. It was being led by a man who seemed able to persuade his followers to do almost anything. Chavez' leadership did not come from his looks or speaking voice. His power came from within. It

Cesar Chavez

sprang from his firmness, gentleness, and tireless energy.

The farm workers organized committees to run the strike. A community kitchen made sure that no one went hungry. Other labor unions and community groups pledged support for *La Causa.* College students, housewives, and clergymen came to Delano to help with the strike.

Fertile soil. But the strike could not be won with such support alone. Chavez believed he needed to be strong-minded. At one point, he led a group of farm workers on a 300-mile (480-kilometer) march to Sacramento, the state capital. His key tactic in the strike — and the most controversial one — was a boycott. Strike leaders fanned out across the country, urging people not to buy wine or grapes. More than one of Chavez' opponents hotly termed this tactic "illegal." Still the farm workers kept up the plea for a boycott. Slowly wine and grape sales began to fall.

At first the growers had thought of Chavez as a mere troublemaker. Now some of them began to take a more serious second look. Chavez was accused of being power-hungry. His critics claimed he would destroy the very workers he was trying to save.

Yet some growers feared that their business would suffer badly if the boycott continued. One by one they began talks with the union. In 1966 the United Farm Workers, as the union was now called, signed its first contract with some growers.

Cooler climate. Other growers kept on refusing to talk with Chavez. Tension grew. For a time, it seemed that violence might flare up. Chavez believed that time was on the side of the farm workers. What they needed was courage and an example to follow. Chavez gave them both. As a devout Roman Catholic, he took up an old religious practice. He went on a *fast* (a period of going without food).

Chavez fasted for 24 days. During this time he lived on nothing but plain water. Union members came to visit him from all over the state. "I guess one time I thought about becoming a priest," he said later. "But I did this instead, and I'm happy to [have been] a part of it." At the

624

end of the fast, a thanksgiving feast was held. The farm workers cheered their leader. *La Causa* went on.

The major breakthrough came in July 1970. The largest grape-growers in the Central Valley agreed to a contract with the union. One grower spoke for the others. "We are happy that peace has come to this valley," he said. He looked forward to working out future agreements with the union.

The contract was a real victory for Cesar Chavez. But time was not standing still. That same summer Chavez began organizing lettuce workers. His work in the fields of California continued into the next decade.

A Second Look. . . .

1. *When and where did the National Farm Workers Association begin its strike against the grape-growers? What was the outcome of the strike?*

2. *As one strike method, the farm workers used a boycott. Do you think the boycott was fair? Why or why not? How did the farm workers' boycott differ from the boycott against Montgomery buses in 1955-1956? How were the two boycotts similar?*

3. *To find out more about the role of labor unions, you may want to carry out a class project. First ask a representative from a local or regional labor union to talk to the class about how the union organizes. Ask this person how the union tries to gain new members and win recognition. Then ask a personnel officer of a large business to talk to the class about dealing with unions. Ask this person how unions affect his or her business. Does his or her company welcome unions? Why or why not?*

Chapter 21

Women on the March

The problem lay buried, unspoken, for many years in the minds of American women. It was a strange stirring, ... a yearning that women suffered in the middle of the 20th century in the United States. Each suburban wife struggled with it alone. As she made the beds, shopped for groceries, ... ate peanut butter sandwiches with her children, ... she was afraid to ask even of herself the silent question — "Is this all?"

So began a book about women in America. Its title was *The Feminine Mystique.* Its author was a New York City magazine editor, Betty Friedan. When the book first appeared in 1963, it was a sudden hit. It claimed that many women in the United States were suffering from "a problem that has no name."

U.S. women had been encouraged to think only in terms of being wives and mothers, Friedan argued. They had

This scene appeared in Life *Magazine in 1947. The magazine explained that the average U.S. housewife with three children made 35 beds, cleaned 750 dishes, washed 400 pieces of silver, cooked 175 pounds of food, and handled 250 pieces of laundry — each week. In 1947 few women saw reason to object to this routine.*

been discouraged from using their own skills for their own purposes in their own ways. Many women were not contributing enough of real value to American life, Friedan said. Some of them had grown unhappy with themselves as a result.

Seedbed for reform. Friedan's book started many women thinking. The more they thought, the more some of them concluded that Friedan was right. Some of Friedan's readers *did* feel trapped in a round of washing, ironing, cooking, and cleaning. Some of them felt empty or useless or just plain bored.

Within a year, others were making similar comments about American women. Some took their ideas from the civil-rights movement of the 1960's. This movement had raised the issue of racial discrimination. Many women in the movement started to think about their own civil rights. Some of them believed they were the victims of discrimination based on sex.

Men generally held better jobs than women did, these people noted. Men were often paid more than women for the same jobs. Men had a better chance to get into professional schools. Men even found it easier to take out bank loans or obtain credit cards.

Many working women wanted the same rights as men. Some other women wanted to be *liberated* (freed) from roles they did not like. These women became *feminists* — supporters of equal rights for women. They organized, demonstrated, and wrote books to make their voices heard. Their demands set off a debate in the U.S. that still continues. It is a debate that focuses on some of the basic ideas of U.S. society.

To some people, the women's liberation movement seemed brand new. But its roots went back to the women's suffrage movement of the early 1900's. Supporters of women's suffrage had raised many of the same complaints. They had hoped things would change once women won the right to vote. Then, they thought, women could use their voting power to end discrimination because of sex.

In 1920 the 19th Amendment to the Constitution became law. It gave all women 21 years old and older the right to vote. As the years passed, more women than ever before went to college and held good jobs. But many women complained that they were still not treated as equals. It was still a "man's world," some of them felt.

Complaints over treatment. Feminist writers pointed out how, from early childhood, boys and girls were treated differently. Boys were often given footballs and toy guns to play with. They were encouraged to be tough, brave, and strong. Girls were given dolls. They were told to act "feminine." Girls learned that good little girls didn't make demands. If they did, people would think they were pushy.

What all this amounted to, said feminists, was something called *sex stereotyping*. This meant that people thought of all girls in the same simple terms. Girls were weak and passive. They wanted only to be wives and mothers. Boys were seen in equally simple terms. Only boys were different. They were strong, smart, aggressive. They were cut out to be doctors or political leaders.

These were the stereotypes. But they

Both men and women went on the march in New York City in 1978 to show their support for the Equal Rights Amendment (ERA). The marchers included author Betty Friedan, sixth from left in front row.

were untrue. They did not apply to everyone, said the feminists. Some girls and women were strong, smart, and aggressive. Some boys and men were weak and passive. The stereotypes, said the feminists, did not reflect nature. They reflected only the ideas of our society — *man*-made ideas.

Feminists called these ideas *sexist,* because they favored one sex over the other. These people pointed out examples of such ideas in books. Children's books, they said, almost always showed men as doctors and women as nurses. No wonder, said the feminists, that young people believed that nursing was a woman's job. No wonder they thought being a doctor was a job only for a man. Feminists argued that TV and movies also presented sexist ideas. In fact, these people saw sexism almost everywhere.

Some feminists turned to the law for help. They fought for rules against discrimination based on sex. One such rule was made part of the Civil Rights Act of 1964. The law allowed some women to sue their employers to obtain better working conditions or higher pay. But feminists said such laws were not enough.

Call for an amendment. The feminists helped to revive an old idea. It involved amending the U.S. Constitution. The proposal was called the *Equal Rights Amendment,* or *ERA.* Its goal: to guarantee equal rights for women. The ERA had first been proposed in 1923. But Congress didn't pass it then. Finally, in 1972, Congress passed the amendment. But this didn't make the amendment official. It still had to be approved by three fourths (or 38) of the state legislatures within seven years.

The ERA caused great controversy. It   *627*

was brought up in one state legislature after another. Those for and against the ERA battled it out. Some states passed the ERA at first, but later reversed their action. The battles dragged on for years.

Feminists argued that the ERA was very important. They said that women, although they outnumbered men, made up the largest "minority group" in the U.S. Only the ERA would give women full equality with men, the feminists argued.

But many others feared women would not benefit from the ERA. Many of these opponents were women. They feared women might lose special "protections" they now had under the law. Women might be forced to work long hours, or do hard labor, or be drafted into the Army, the opponents said.

Call for more tradition. Opponents of the ERA were a new type of woman activist. They called themselves *grassroots women*. Many of them liked the traditional women's roles. They feared that feminists wanted to make women just like men. Some of them baked cookies and cakes to take to state legislators. They tied pink ribbons around their gifts. They firmly believed that a woman's place was in the home. If women didn't rear the children, who would? they asked. They formed organizations with long titles. One was called "Women Who Want To Be Women." Another was known as "Happiness of Womanhood."

"No women in history have ever enjoyed such privileges, luxuries, and freedom as American women," said one anti-ERA document. Feminists are "a tiny minority of dissatisfied ... women," the document went on. The opponents

of the ERA were against women's liberation. They saw no need to be "liberated."

All the while, women were taking on new roles in society. More women were accepted into medical schools and law schools. Women moved up in the business and sports worlds. Billie Jean King became a world-class tennis player. She led the drive for equal rewards for female champions. Racetracks hired women jockeys. Girls played Little League baseball alongside boys. Some girls played on boys' soccer teams.

Obviously, there was no single women's movement. Women disagreed among themselves on many issues. Some people felt threatened by changes in the roles of women. Others were pleased. Many people believed, though, that the feminist movement was one more part of the drive for equal justice.

A Second Look. . . .

1. *In what ways do feminists believe women have been victims of discrimination? What steps did feminists take to combat such discrimination? What word did they use to describe it?*

2. *Do you agree that women have been victims of discrimination in U.S. history? Explain your answer. Do you think that women need to be liberated? Why or why not?*

3. *Feminists focused attention on how people thought of themselves. Women talked of their feelings as women. Men too began to think of how they saw the world and themselves. Think about yourself. What is it you like about being male or female? Make a list of the things you like, and compare your list with those of other class members. Which members of the class have the longest lists — boys or girls? Why?*

Looking Back: Toward Equal Justice

Putting Events in Order

Chapters 17 through 21 have described the struggle of black Americans and other groups for equal justice in the 1950's and 1960's. Ten events from this struggle are listed here. Your job is to match each event to the correct period shown on the timeline. On a piece of paper, number from **1** to **10.** After each number, write the letter of the four-year period in which the event occurred.

1. Federal troops are sent to Little Rock, Arkansas, to guard black students attending Central High School.

2. The U.S. Supreme Court rules school segregation unconstitutional.

3. Dr. Martin Luther King is assassinated.

4. A strike against grape-growers gets under way in California.

5. Civil-rights workers stage a "March on Washington."

6. Oliver Brown files suit against the Board of Education in Topeka, Kansas.

7. Congress passes the Equal Rights Amendment and sends it to the state legislatures for ratification.

8. Black students sit in at lunch counters in Greensboro, North Carolina.

9. Thousands boycott segregated buses in Montgomery, Alabama.

10. Cesar Chavez starts the National Farm Workers Association.

Interpreting a Source

In 1957 a federal court ordered nine black students admitted to Central High School in Little Rock, Arkansas. Governor Orval Faubus refused to carry out the court order. He called out the Arkansas National Guard to prevent the students from entering the school. One of the black students, Elizabeth Eckford, recounts that day in the selection on the next page. Read it carefully and then answer the questions that follow. Refer back to Chapter 17 for the outcome of the showdown at Little Rock.

629

The crowd was quiet. I guess they were waiting to see what was going to happen. When I was able to steady my knees, I walked up to the guard who had let the white students in. He too didn't move. When I tried to squeeze past him, he raised his bayonet. And then the other guards closed in, and they raised their bayonets.

They glared at me with a mean look. I was very frightened and didn't know what to do. I turned around and the crowd came toward me.

They moved closer and closer. Somebody started yelling, "Lynch her! Lynch her!"

I tried to see a friendly face somewhere in the mob — someone who maybe would help. I looked into the face of an old woman and it seemed a kind face. But when I looked at her again, she spat on me.

They came closer, shouting, "No [black girl] is going to get in our school. Get out of here!"

I turned back to the guards, but their faces told me I wouldn't get help from them. Then I looked down the block and saw a bench at the bus stop. I thought, "If I can only get there, I will be safe."

When I finally got there, I don't think I could have gone another step. I sat down, and the mob crowded up and began shouting all over again. Someone hollered, "Drag her over to this tree! Let's take care of [her]." Just then a white man sat down beside me, put his arm around me, and patted my shoulder. He raised my chin and said, "Don't let them see you cry."

Then, a white lady — she was very nice — she came over to me on the bench. She spoke to me but I don't re-member now what she said. She put me on the bus and sat next to me.... The next thing I remember I was standing in front of the School for the Blind where Mother works....

Mother was standing at the window with her head bowed, but she must have sensed I was there because she turned around. She looked as if she had been crying, and I wanted to tell her I was all right. But I couldn't speak. She put her arms around me, and I cried.

1. *Why did the guards refuse to allow Elizabeth Eckford to enter Central High School?*

2. *How did the crowd react to the girl? Why do you suppose the crowd reacted this way?*

3. *Put yourself in Eckford's position. How would you have felt? What would you have done?*

4. *Imagine that you are a member of the crowd. Write two paragraphs describing your thoughts as you watch Elizabeth Eckford try to enter Central High School.*

Sharpening Your Skills

A *metropolitan area* is made up of a large central city and the suburbs which surround it. What do the graphs on the next page tell you about the nation's metropolitan areas? Study the graphs carefully. Then answer the questions.

1. What percentage of black Americans lived in inner cities in 1950?

2. What percentage of white Americans lived in inner cities in 1950?

3. True or false? Between 1950 and 1969, white Americans more often moved to cities than to suburban areas.

4. True or false? Between 1950 and 1969, black Americans more often moved to cities than to suburbs.

5. True or false? In 1969 most black Americans lived in the suburbs or outside metropolitan areas.

6. What do the circle graphs tell you about the movement of black Americans in the 1950's and 1960's?

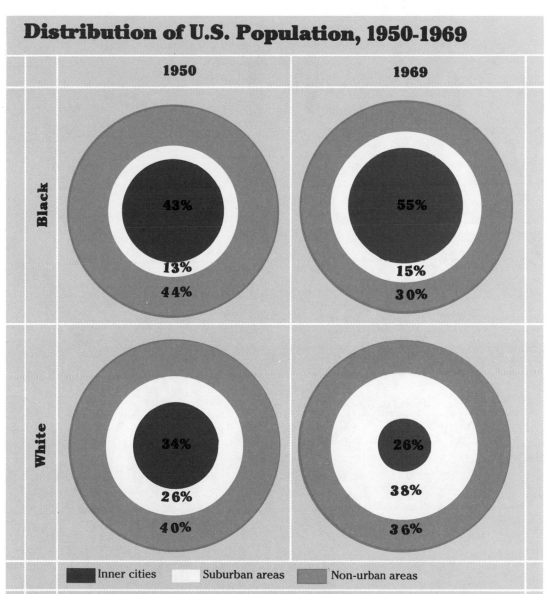

Distribution of U.S. Population, 1950-1969

	1950	1969
Black	43% / 13% / 44%	55% / 15% / 30%
White	34% / 26% / 40%	26% / 38% / 36%

Inner cities   Suburban areas   Non-urban areas

5 THE ANGRY YEARS

Looking Ahead:
Life and Death in the 1960's

On election day, 1960, a man with reddish hair played touch football on a Massachusetts beach. He liked football almost as much as he liked politics. His name was John F. Kennedy. The next morning, Kennedy learned that he had been elected President of the United States. He had beaten the Republican candidate, Richard Nixon, by only a few thousand votes.

In Texas that morning, another leader also celebrated victory. He was Lyndon B. Johnson, the Democratic candidate for Vice-President.

The election of Kennedy and Johnson started a new period in U.S. history. It was a time of excitement and high hopes. But it was to be scarred by anger and violence. Kennedy could not have

The burdens of world leadership increased in the 1960's, as the U.S. role in Vietnam grew. The war divided Americans deeply and led to protests such as this one in Boston in 1969.

known in 1960 that he had only three years to live. He could not have known that Johnson and Nixon would both follow him as President.

Who were these three men who would soon be Presidents in difficult times? Here, briefly, is each man's life story:

John F. Kennedy. In his high school yearbook, Kennedy was named "most likely to succeed." He went to Harvard College and then joined the U.S. Navy during World War II. He was given command of a crew aboard a PT (for Patrol Torpedo) boat. His job was to patrol the sea and torpedo enemy ships. When the Japanese attacked and sank his boat, he and other survivors swam three miles (about five kilometers) to the nearest island. He was later awarded a medal for his bravery.

After the war, Kennedy entered politics. His father, a millionaire, helped him with his campaigns. John Kennedy never lost an election. Three times he was

633

elected to the U.S. House of Representatives. Twice he was elected to the U.S. Senate. Outside Massachusetts he was best known for the books he wrote. His *Profiles in Courage,* a biography of U.S. Senators, won a prize. People liked to call Kennedy by different nicknames — "JFK" or "Jack." At 43 he was the youngest person ever to be elected President. (Theodore Roosevelt became President at 42, when William McKinley died. But Roosevelt was 46 when he won the next election.)

Lyndon B. Johnson. Politics was in Johnson's blood. Both of his grandfathers had been in the Texas state legislature. When Lyndon was born on a Texas farm, one grandfather said, "A United States Senator was born today." The Johnson family was poor. Lyndon had to work as a janitor to pay for his college education at Southwest Texas State Teachers College. He was elected to Congress in 1936.

Johnson enjoyed power. For many years, he was the Democratic leader of the Senate. He had almost as much power as the President. In 1960 Johnson tried to get the Democrats to nominate him for President. Kennedy beat him. Johnson disliked being Vice-President because this job gave him little power.

Richard M. Nixon. Like Johnson, Nixon was born on a farm. His was a farm in California. Like Kennedy, he served in the Navy in World War II. A graduate of Duke University Law School, Nixon ran for Congress from California in 1946. He scored an upset victory over an opponent he accused of being "soft on communism."

In 1950 Nixon won a seat in the U.S. Senate. Two years later, he was the Republican choice for Vice-President. He served in this post under President Dwight D. Eisenhower for eight years. When Kennedy defeated Nixon in 1960, many thought that Nixon's political career was over. Nixon did not give up. He kept

John F. Kennedy as he became President in 1961.

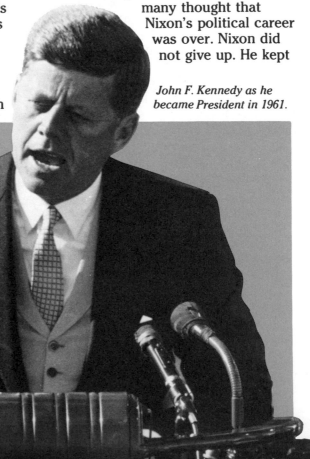

634

All through the 1960's, Vietnam was the scene of terror. Both sides in the war killed and wounded innocent people. Above, refugees flee from rocket attack in South Vietnam in 1968.

telling people, "I am not a quitter." In 1968 Nixon had a second chance to run for President. This time he won.

These were the three men who led the United States through the 1960's. Each had his own vision of a better world. For Kennedy, it was a world where young people could make a difference in improving life. For Johnson, it was a world where poverty could be ended. For Nixon, it was a world where people could — and should — rely less on government and more on themselves.

Often, however, the visions grew dim. So many problems kept getting in the way. One problem was a costly and confusing war in Vietnam. Another problem was the revolt of some young people against older values and ideas. A third problem was the growing anger of blacks. Why was each problem so painful and difficult to solve?

Vietnam. The war in Vietnam was different from any other war in U.S. history. It was not like World War II, for example, when Japan attacked Pearl Harbor and Congress then declared war. In the case of Vietnam, by contrast, few Americans knew when the fighting really began. President Eisenhower gave military aid to South Vietnam's government. President Kennedy gave a little more. President Johnson gave a lot more. And suddenly people realized that U.S. troops were fighting and dying in a far-off Asian country.

635

One top TV series of the 1960's was Mission: Impossible. *It introduced an imaginary "spy team," including actor Greg Morris (above). The team operated in a world where power knew no limits. Its members traveled the globe, toppling "wicked" governments without getting caught.*

At first most Americans supported the U.S. role in Vietnam. This role was necessary, they thought, to prevent the spread of communism in Asia. But before long, critics began speaking out. It seemed to some of them as if the U.S. Constitution were being ignored. After all, Congress had not declared war against the Vietnamese rebels. Some critics also thought that the United States was acting like a bully. A few Americans even started cheering for the rebels and their backers in North Vietnam. This behavior upset many people even more than the war itself.

Revolt of youth. Boys in high school used to crop their hair short. That was the fashion in the 1950's. But in the 1960's, many boys let their hair grow over their ears and even down their backs. Parents were bewildered. Students on college campuses rioted against the Vietnam War. They threw rocks and smashed windows. Parents were dismayed. Young people went around saying, "Make love, not war." Parents were appalled. Adults wondered what was wrong with youth. Youths wondered what was wrong with adults. The two age groups seemed to be drifting farther apart. There was a great gap between the generations. People called it the *generation gap.*

Anger of many blacks. Every summer from 1964 to 1967, riots broke out in black neighborhoods. In cities across the country, rioters looted stores and set buildings on fire. The police tried to keep order. At times, innocent people died. These riots stunned Lyndon Johnson. He had done more than any other President to win blacks their civil rights. Yet black people were not satisfied. They had never been angrier than in the 1960's. Why? Few whites could understand it.

Many Americans thought they were living in a revolution. Youth was revolting against the old ways. Blacks were demanding full equality. People were being killed by the thousands in Vietnam. In 1963 President Kennedy was killed by an assassin. In 1968 his brother, Robert Kennedy, was shot and killed. Martin Luther King was also killed that year. The 1960's were angry, confusing years.

Chapter 22

The Youngest President

John F. Kennedy was the youngest person — and the first Roman Catholic — ever to be elected President. He was likeable, charming, and intelligent. But would he make a good President? Some people feared that he was too young to handle one of the world's biggest jobs.

John Kennedy himself had few doubts about his ability. His father, Joseph Kennedy, once warned him about the problems he would face. He said the world's problems in 1960 were worse than at any time in history. John Kennedy answered: "Dad, for 2,000 years, every generation, or most generations, have been faced with the most terrible problems ever seen. They all have been solved by humans with God's help. If they can do it, why can't we?"

It was in this spirit that John Kennedy took the oath of office on January 20, 1961. The day did not begin well. During the opening prayer, a short circuit in the sound system caused smoke to rise from the speaker's stand. Then an 86-year-old American poet, Robert Frost, was bothered by the glare of the sun. He could not read the poem he had written for the occasion. But Kennedy did not seem worried as he rose to make a speech. The words that he spoke were bold and stirring.

He announced that a "new generation of Americans" had now come to power. He asked this new generation to dedi- cate itself to an old ideal — freedom throughout the world. The dangers to freedom were great, he said. This was why he needed the help of all Americans, young and old. "And so, my fellow Americans," he said, "ask not what your country can do for you. Ask what you can do for your country."

Kennedy's speech lasted only 14

John Kennedy first won a seat in Congress at the age of 29. The year was 1946, and Kennedy said he was a leader of "the new generation."

637

minutes. But newspaper editors called it one of the finest speeches ever made by a U.S. President. Kennedy seemed to promise a new beginning for the United States. He called his program the *New Frontier.*

Creative ideas. The young President brought to the White House a team of people to help him. They were much like himself. They were bright. They had new ideas about how to run the government. They were willing to work day and night to get Kennedy's New Frontier moving. One of the most powerful members of the team was the President's younger brother, Robert Kennedy. "Bobby," as people called him, was John Kennedy's Attorney General.

The Kennedy brothers eagerly plunged into their work. The President amazed people by his habit of reading five newspapers while eating his breakfast. He spoke almost as fast as he read. A writer once followed the President through one complete day. He reported that Kennedy "did everything today ex-cept shinny up the Washington Monument."

John Kennedy believed there were many young people with energy like his own. Talented Americans, he thought, could share their skills with people in foreign countries. For example, they could teach African villagers how to make their drinking water safer. The goal was to improve people's lives. This would help make the world more peaceful. Kennedy wanted Americans to be volunteers for the cause of peace. He asked Congress to create what he called a *Peace Corps.*

Congress approved the program in 1961. Kennedy's brother-in-law, Sargent Shriver, ran it. By 1963 about 5,000 Americans — mostly young people — were working in remote villages in Africa, Asia, and South America. The volunteers saw firsthand the joys and heartbreaks of the villagers. The villagers, in turn, discovered a new kind of American. These were not tourists or people who traveled overseas to make

The Peace Corps gave Americans such as Joan Dillard (below) the chance to put their training to use in foreign lands. At the age of 27, Dillard taught English to children in a small town in North Borneo.

money. They were human beings like the villagers, living much as the villagers lived, sharing the same day-to-day problems and pleasures.

John Kennedy and his young team moved fast to try to meet the world's challenges. But the challenges came very rapidly. When Kennedy became President in 1961, there was trouble in Cuba, trouble in Germany, trouble in Southeast Asia. New troubles soon flared up in all three places.

Faulty strategy. The young President caused some of his own problems. His first major decision was to send a band of Cuban exiles to overthrow Fidel Castro's Communist government in Cuba. His military advisers assured him that the attack would succeed. Instead, 1,400 invaders were quickly surrounded by Castro's defending army. Many were slaughtered on a beach in Cuba's Bay of Pigs in April 1961. Why? Partly because of bad planning by the U.S. government, Kennedy admitted. This made people ask if Kennedy was too "green."

Kennedy worried about what people thought. He believed the shrewd Soviet leader, Nikita Khrushchev, might try to take advantage of any weakness. In the summer of 1961, Khrushchev suddenly focused world attention on Germany's former capital, Berlin. He demanded changes that would give the U.S. less voice in Berlin's affairs. Kennedy said no. He sent U.S. troops to West Berlin over a road held by the German Communists. Khrushchev backed down. The next year, the Soviets secretly shipped missiles into Cuba (see Chapter 11). Again Kennedy took strong action. And again, Khrushchev backed down. He ordered the missiles pulled out.

But there was still more to worry about in Southeast Asia. Kennedy wanted to stop Communist-led rebels from overthrowing the government of South Vietnam. For a while, he thought he was succeeding. U.S. advisers helped the government fight the rebels. But South Vietnam's president, Ngo Dinh Diem, treated his opponents in a cruel way. A group of generals revolted against Diem and shot him to death. Kennedy received the news with mixed feelings. He was glad that new leaders had come to power in South Vietnam. He hoped that they could fight the rebels better than Diem. At the same time, he was shocked by Diem's brutal murder.

Grim climax. It was now November 1963. The young President had spent about a thousand days in his new job. He had made some mistakes. He thought he had also made some progress. He hoped to do a lot more in the future to bring about the New Frontier. But first he had to be re-elected.

He therefore flew to Texas to begin campaigning for the 1964 election. His wife, Jacqueline, went with him. They sat side by side in a black car that drove slowly down a street in Dallas. They waved to crowds of cheering people on either side of the street.

Their car passed an old red-brick building that was used for storing school books. A man with a gun was waiting there. A shot rang out; then another; then a third. John Kennedy slumped down in the seat of the car. His wife cradled his head in her arms, crying, "Jack! Jack!" Within an hour, the President was pronounced dead.

For the next three days, television and radio devoted almost full time to the tragedy. Solemn music replaced ads. Bulletins told that a suspect had been captured. His name was Lee Harvey Oswald. His motive was unknown. Then someone shot Oswald in full view of TV watchers. The nation was numb with shock. The emotion-charged events turned John Kennedy into a hero for many people who had not thought of him as one before. They would miss the young President in the difficult years ahead.

A Second Look. . . .

1. What were three of the problems that Kennedy faced as President? How did he deal with these problems?

2. One of a President's key roles is as a maker of foreign policy. How would you rate Kennedy's performance in this respect? Would you say he was: (a) one of the greatest Presidents? (b) a good President who made a few mistakes? (c) a fair President who did not accomplish much? Base your opinion on evidence in this book.

3. Anybody who lived in 1963 probably still remembers the day that Kennedy was shot. Ask two adults (perhaps your parents) about their memories of November 22, 1963. Who told them the news of Kennedy's assassination? What was their reaction? Either tape your interviews or take written notes. Then report your findings to the class.

The flag-draped coffin of the fallen President is taken to be buried on a Virginia hillside.

Chapter 23

LBJ's "Great Society"

Lyndon B. Johnson placed one hand on a Bible and raised the other in the air. He could hardly believe what was happening. Only two-and-a-half hours before, he was helping President John Kennedy campaign in Dallas. Johnson was Vice-President then. Now in the President's airplane, *Air Force One,* he was being sworn in as the nation's 36th President. Next to him stood Mrs. Kennedy, her pink suit stained with blood. In the corridor was her dead husband's coffin.

So began the Presidency of Lyndon Johnson. It was a sad start. Yet there were to be months of great achievement before a new ordeal closed in.

Johnson was nine years older than Kennedy. He had once suffered a heart attack. But fears about his health did not slow him down. He worked as hard as Kennedy — perhaps even harder. In his first month in office, he was lucky to get five hours of sleep a night. He said he wanted to carry out Kennedy's plans.

Civil-rights law. Johnson and Robert Kennedy together fought for a new civil-rights law. It was a law that John Kennedy had proposed to Congress shortly before he was killed. Its main purpose was to protect blacks in the South from discrimination in hotels and restaurants. Up to this time, there had been no federal law against such discrimination. A restaurant owner could refuse to serve meals to blacks. A hotel owner could refuse to rent them rooms. In the North, some states had laws against discrimination. But in the South, the laws of some states required that whites and blacks be kept separate. The new law would make such discrimination illegal in all states.

Some members of Congress were opposed to the new law. But Johnson was a master at dealing with Congress. He was much better at it than Kennedy had been. Also, Kennedy's death had changed the thinking of many Americans. They now wanted Kennedy's program to pass because Kennedy himself would have wanted it. Congress debated the bill for months. At last both houses passed it. Johnson signed the Civil Rights Act into law on July 2, 1964.

"War on poverty." In January 1964, he announced a "war on poverty." He said that 35 million poor people in the United States needed government help. They needed training to hold skilled jobs. Their children needed better education. Johnson traveled to many parts of the country to explain why the poor needed such help. He proposed a law to provide it. Congress enacted Johnson's program in the summer of 1964.

The President, however, was not satisfied. Poor people, he thought, needed still more help. Blacks needed more protection. Schools needed more money. Old people needed help paying doctors'

In the 1960's, Pat Oliphant of The Denver Post *pictured the many faces of President Johnson.*

bills. Young people needed help finding jobs. Americans, Johnson said, could soon hope to live in a *Great Society.* In such a society, there would be no poverty, no injustice, no ugliness. But to build the Great Society, Congress would need to create many new government programs. Also, Johnson would need a strong victory in the 1964 election.

Most Democrats believed that Americans wanted these programs. Democrats chose Lyndon Johnson as their Presidential candidate on Johnson's birthday, August 27. They held a birthday party for the President — with a cake 10 feet (three meters) long. But many Republicans opposed Johnson's program. Their candidate for President, Barry Goldwater, claimed this program would cost too much money.

Johnson campaigned hard. He traveled 60,000 miles (about 95,000 kilometers), shaking hands and making speeches. He shook voters' hands so much that his own hand became swollen. Johnson wanted to win the election by a bigger margin than any President in history. And he did. On election day, 1964, he received slightly more than six out of every 10 votes cast. He won more votes than any President before him.

It was the kind of victory Johnson 642 needed to get his Great Society ideas

through Congress. In 1965 he asked Congress for one law after another. In the past, Congress had rejected some of these ideas over and over again. Now Johnson invited members of Congress to the White House to talk. He knew what to say to get their support.

In one way or another, Johnson persuaded Congress to create the following programs:

Medicare. This program gave health insurance to people 65 years old and over. It paid their hospital bills and most of their doctors' bills. For the first time, most elderly people did not have to worry about using up all their savings

One LBJ victory was passage of the Civil Rights Act of 1964. Below, the President gives Dr. Martin Luther King a pen he used to sign it into law.

. . . He drew LBJ as (left to right) Soldier, Preacher, Policeman, Liberal, Crusader, and Devil.

to pay for expensive medical care.

Voting rights. This law protected black citizens and others whose right to vote was blocked by unfair state laws. State officials could no longer stop an adult citizen from voting because of failure to pass a *literacy test* (a test to determine if a voter can read or write). Federal officials could now go into state polling places and protect blacks as they registered to vote. In Alabama, many black people were free to vote for the first time in their lives. One elderly woman said: "I'm going to vote now. I'm going to vote because I haven't been able to in my 67 years."

Aid to education. This law gave one billion dollars in aid to schools. Most of the money went to improve the education of children from poor families. Of all his Great Society programs, Johnson was proudest of this one. He remembered, as a young man, teaching Mexican-American students in a poor farming region in Texas. He invited some of his former students to be present when he signed the education bill. He also asked a former teacher of his, "Miss Katie," to witness the signing. He offered her the pen he used to sign the bill. But she said it wasn't her pen, and she wouldn't take it.

Lyndon Johnson signed into law a total of 89 major acts of Congress in 1965. He brought more changes to government than any President since Franklin Roosevelt. And yet his Great Society was on shaky ground. It had already cost large sums of money. Many whites resented what they thought was special treatment of blacks. Now the simmering war in Vietnam was about to reach a boil. The war would cost the U.S. more and more money. Prices and taxes would rise. And many Americans would turn their anger against Lyndon Johnson.

A Second Look. . . .

1. *Which groups benefited most from Lyndon Johnson's programs? Which specific programs helped each of the groups identified? Why?*

2. *Suppose you were a U.S. Senator in 1964 and 1965. Would you have voted for or against the following: (a) the Civil Rights Act of 1964, (b) the act creating Medicare in 1965, (c) the 1965 act providing federal aid to education? Give reasons for each decision.*

3. *Write an essay giving your idea of what a great society is. State whether you think America is a "great society" today. If so, explain why you think so. If not, explain what changes would make America a "great society."*

643

Police clash with antiwar demonstrators during the 1968 Democratic convention in Chicago.

Chapter 24

The Tragedy of Vietnam

"Hey, hey, go away! Hey, hey, go away!"

A crowd of people were shouting at police officers on a street in Chicago. It was early in the evening, August 28, 1968. Democratic leaders were meeting in Chicago to select a candidate for President. People on the street wanted to get closer to the place where the meeting was taking place. They wanted to show their anger over the war in Vietnam. But the police blocked their way. "Hey, hey, go away," the mob chanted.

The police felt angry, threatened. Glass bottles flew at them. Bags of gar-

bage landed at their feet and splattered on the pavement. Suddenly the police started swinging their billy clubs and charged into the mob. People got hurt. Some tried to run for safety. The police chased them, hit them, and dragged them into police wagons.

Millions of TV viewers that night had their sets tuned to the Democratic convention. The picture on their screens kept switching from the convention itself to the bloody street fighting outside. It seemed like madness. It was just one more example of the kind of thing that

644

kept appearing on TV in 1968. One more example of the nation's anguish over the war in Vietnam.

Two views. Many people were bitter and confused about the war. Why can't we end it? they asked. Who got us into it in the first place? they wanted to know. The answer to the second question was complex. Dwight Eisenhower had sent arms and advisers when he was President. Then John Kennedy had sent more arms, more advisers, and some noncombat troops. Lyndon Johnson had gone still further. He said he was carrying out promises made to South Vietnam by former Presidents.

Johnson had first taken his stand in November 1963. He had said the U.S. had a duty to protect South Vietnam. He had claimed that North Vietnam had no business sending troops to help the rebels in South Vietnam. He had called North Vietnam an *aggressor* nation (one which had attacked first). Aggressors must be stopped, Johnson believed, or freedom everywhere would be in danger.

But others saw the matter differently. They argued that the war had begun as a *civil war* within South Vietnam. To them, the U.S. had no business getting involved. They said the U.S. should leave the future of Vietnam to the Vietnamese.

Escalation. At first Johnson ignored these critics. After his landslide election victory in 1964, he moved to strengthen U.S. aid. Now Army generals advised him that the Viet Cong rebels and their North Vietnamese allies could be beaten. But the U.S. would have to strike at military targets in North Vietnam. In 1965 Johnson ordered U.S. planes to drop bombs over North Vietnam. At the same time, he ordered more U.S. troops into South Vietnam.

How many U.S. troops were needed? Under Kennedy in 1963, there had been about 15,000. By 1965 the generals were saying 100,000 would probably be enough. By 1968 there were almost 550,000 U.S. soldiers in Vietnam. News reporters gave a name to this military buildup. They called it *escalation.*

Reporters also wrote about something called a *credibility gap.* They meant that there was a gap between what the U.S. government said and what many U.S. citizens believed. It was a confusing time. The U.S. government would announce a "major victory" in Vietnam. Then news reporters would go to the battle site. They would report that U.S. troops had suffered heavy losses. They would make the same battle sound like a defeat. Whom should the public believe?

Tet offensive. In February 1968, public doubts about the war grew. This was the time of the Vietnamese New Year, called *Tet.* The Viet Cong had smuggled guns and bombs into every major city of South Vietnam. Rebels had hid in the homes of friends. Just as Tet began, the rebels attacked. In many places, there was terrible fighting and loss of life. Americans were shocked to hear about this *Tet offensive,* as it was called. By this time, millions of tons of U.S. bombs had been dropped. Yet the rebels were still strong — very strong. More than 20,000 U.S. troops had been killed.

Growing numbers of people wanted an end to the war. Lyndon Johnson was criticized from two sides. Some people said he should get the war over by using more bombs — or more powerful ones. *645*

The U.S. could win if it tried harder, these people argued. These people were called *hawks*. Others thought the U.S. could not win the war. They argued that the U.S. should get out and let the Vietnamese settle their own problems. These people were called *doves*.

Johnson tried to please both sides. He stepped up the bombing to please the hawks. He helped to start peace talks to please the doves. Still the war dragged on, seemingly without end. Johnson grew more and more frustrated.

Mounting criticism. So did U.S. citizens. They wanted a way out. Some of them turned to one of the war's strongest critics, Eugene McCarthy. McCarthy was a Democratic Senator from Minnesota. He decided to challenge Johnson for the Democratic nomination for President. McCarthy entered Democratic *primaries* in several states. (*Primaries* are elections within a political party, held to help decide the candidates for a main election.) Experts said McCarthy had no chance at all.

Even so, McCarthy stayed on the attack. He made speeches calling the war in Vietnam wrong, immoral. Thousands of college students backed him and worked for him. Because of them, McCarthy almost beat the old pro, Lyndon Johnson, in the New Hampshire primary. The experts were amazed.

After McCarthy's surprise showing in New Hampshire, other war critics also entered the race. One of them was Robert Kennedy, who had become a Democratic Senator from New York. He had split with Johnson over the war. Now Kennedy was challenging Johnson directly.

646   Lyndon Johnson worried about what

In Vietnam, death could wait in hiding behind the next tree. Most U.S. troops fought bravely, but with a constant sense of fear. Many hoped only to get through the war, and then get home.

was happening. He could see that the nation was dividing into two angry groups — hawks and doves. He believed that much of the controversy centered on himself. So he made a surprising decision. On March 31, 1968, he went on TV. He began with a routine talk about the war. Then he announced his surprise. He would not run for re-election. TV viewers could hardly believe it. Can he mean it? they wondered. Johnson did mean it — every word.

Political violence. One writer called 1968 "the year that everything went wrong." First there was the Tet offensive. Then the turmoil over the Presidential election campaign. In April, Martin Luther King was shot to death. In June, shots rang out again. This time the victim was Robert Kennedy. He had just won California's Democratic primary. It looked as if he might win the Democratic nomination for President.

Now, on June 5, he crumpled to the floor of a hotel kitchen in Los Angeles. Within a few hours, he was dead. Vice-President Hubert Humphrey became the leading Democratic candidate for President.

Next came the Democratic convention in Chicago. Inside the convention hall, there were battles of words between supporters of McCarthy and supporters of Humphrey. Outside, on Chicago's streets, there were battles between antiwar demonstrators and police. Injured young people staggered into McCarthy's hotel room. Hotel sheets were torn into rags to bandage their bleeding heads.

Hubert Humphrey won the Democratic nomination. But the feuding Democrats were still deeply divided. They could not unite behind Humphrey. He had been too close to Lyndon Johnson. Neither the hawks nor the doves were happy. Everyone wanted to know how much longer the war would last. In 1968 there was no clear answer.

A Second Look. . . .

1. What reasons did Lyndon Johnson give for escalating the war in Vietnam? Why did some Americans reject Johnson's arguments?

2. If you had been following the news in the 1960's, which one or two events would have concerned you the most: (a) Lyndon Johnson's decision to bomb North Vietnam, (b) the Tet offensive, (c) Johnson's decision not to run for re-election, (d) the assassination of Robert Kennedy, (e) the assassination of Dr. Martin Luther King, or (f) telecasts of mass arrests in Chicago, 1968? Make a list of your choices in order of your concern. Be prepared to give reasons for your answer.

3. Suppose that you are an adviser to President Johnson in 1968. Johnson has asked you to write down your ideas about ending the war in Vietnam. On a piece of paper, state two ways of ending the war. Then explain which of these two ways you believe is better and why.

As the fighting went on, millions of Vietnamese were caught in the cross fire. This woman had just found her husband's body buried in a mass grave. Photo was one of the most famous of the war.

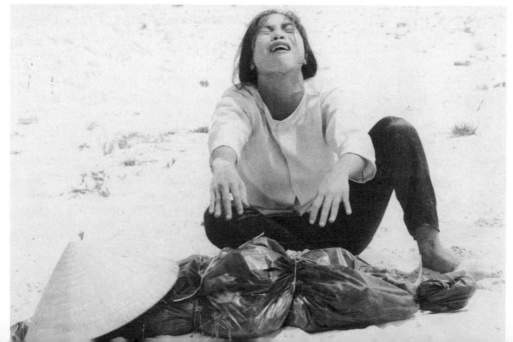

647

Chapter 25

Trouble in the Streets

Sunday, July 23, 1967, was to have been a day off for patrolman Ronald August. August worked for the Detroit police force. At seven A.M. a telephone call awakened him. Go to the police station at once, the caller said. There is big trouble in Detroit.

Soon the patrolman was in a paddy wagon moving through riot-torn streets. "Gee," he remembered later, "it looked like everything was burning. There were people swarming everywhere." Many of the people were looters. They had broken into stores and stolen things. Some

National Guard troops keep watch on a Detroit street during the "long, hot summer" of 1967.

were carrying whiskey; some, tape recorders; others, cameras or TV sets. Even, August recalled, "little six-year-olds with wagons full of brand-new underwear, socks, and shoes. Carrying everything out."

The riot lasted five days. Forty-three people died. An estimated 2,000 were injured. Fire destroyed some 2,000 stores and homes. The riot was the most destructive one in the U.S. in the 1960's.

The National Guard went into action. U.S. Army troops moved into Detroit streets. Michigan's governor George Romney toured the city. He saw block after block with nothing but ruined stores and apartments. "It looked like a city that had been bombed," he said.

Detroit wasn't the decade's first flare-up. In 1964 rioting had ripped through Harlem in New York City. In 1965 a part of Los Angeles called Watts had been torn up. In 1966 there had been riots in Cleveland and Chicago. Early in July 1967, riots had broken out in Newark, New Jersey. The nation was on edge. Were law and order crumbling away?

The riots all had one thing in common: They hit black neighborhoods hardest. Most — but not all — of the rioters were black. This led some people to call the incidents "race riots." But the riots of the 1960's did not pit race against race. They pitted rioters against property — stores that were looted, buildings that were burned. And they pitted citizens against police.

The Detroit riot started when police raided a party being held by about 80 blacks. It was a "welcome-home" party for two veterans just back from Vietnam. But it was an illegal party. It was being held in a club that had stayed open into the early-morning hours, after closing time. Police began to arrest party-goers. Someone threw a bottle. It broke the window of a police car. The riot had begun.

Death by accident. At first police did nothing to stop looting. They were under orders not to shoot. Detroit's leaders considered the black area a powder keg. They feared that police shooting might touch off a real war between blacks and police. "If we had started shooting," Detroit's police commissioner said, "not one of our policemen would have come out alive."

Some of the rioters set fire to buildings. As the riot spread, police reported gunshots being fired by people on rooftops. Many police officers were scared. So were young soldiers called up to control the crowds. On one street, a youth lit a cigarette in his apartment house. A nervous soldier saw a sudden flash of light and fired. A bullet ripped through the apartment window and killed a little girl, four years old. Many other innocent people were also killed by accident. Most reports of snipers on rooftops later turned out to have been false.

By the end of the week, order had been restored. But many questions remained. Why would people purposely burn down neighborhoods in which they lived? Why was there such hatred be-

"These weren't damaged in the riots — they went to pieces years before," says the photographer's friend in this 1967 Herblock cartoon. The drawing first appeared in The Washington Post.

tween police and citizens? Why was racial trouble hitting hardest in the North, not the South?

Many white people had assumed that all was well for blacks in the North. Hadn't the civil-rights movement broken down old barriers? Hadn't President Johnson declared war on poverty? Indeed, for many blacks, there had been progress. In Detroit, particularly, many blacks had well-paying jobs in auto factories.

Defeat by circumstance. But reporters covering the slums brought back another story. They found angry young men and women who were unable to get jobs. These youths had seen on TV and in the movies how other Americans lived. They wanted a share of this good   *649* life. Yet they had limited education and few job skills. They were unfamiliar with the customs of the business world. They took up a bold swagger and slangy speech that set them apart. Many of these youths had nothing but scorn for white society. In fact, they were calling the violence in the cities "revolution," rather than riots.

Some people began to talk of such blacks as part of a separate *class* of Americans. (A *class* is a division of the social order, usually based on wealth and social standing. Usual examples are the upper class, middle class, and lower class.) These blacks became known as members of an *underclass*. This term meant a group of people locked into poverty from one generation to the next. People who feel beaten. People with no hope. People who are very hostile toward the community they live in.

After the Detroit riot, President Johnson asked a group of experts to study the causes of urban rioting in general. He called this group the *National Advisory Commission on Civil Disorders*. It reached these conclusions:

First, nobody planned the riots. No group of blacks plotted in secret to stir up trouble.

Second, there was not just one cause for the riots, but many. Distrust of police was one important cause. Unemployment among blacks was another.

Third, there was not just one solution to the problem, but many. Most of the cities affected by the rioting needed to do a better job of training police officers. Most of them needed more black officers. Two million new jobs were needed, especially for black youths. More money was needed for schools

and housing in black neighborhoods.

Above all, the commission said, whites would have to change their attitudes toward blacks. Whites had long treated black people unfairly, the commission argued. This treatment is called *racism*. The commission said that "white racism" had been a major cause of the rioting.

The nation was sharply divided over the commission's report. Some applauded the stark statement against racism. Others were angry. They felt that the riots resulted from a breakdown of law and order. The police had been too soft, they said. Police officers should have cracked down on the looting as soon as it began.

The riots left their scars. A decade later, gaping shells of buildings still remained in some places. But the riots also started many people thinking about some hard questions. Just how *could* blacks and whites work out their problems with each other? And what lay ahead if they didn't?

A Second Look. . . .

1. *What event touched off the riot in Detroit? What were two general causes of the rioting?*

2. *How did each of the following groups suffer during the riots in Detroit? (a) Looters. (b) Police and soldiers. (c) White store-owners. (d) Black families who lived in riot-torn neighborhoods. Explain.*

3. *Imagine that it is mid-August of 1967 in Detroit. A person from a riot-torn neighborhood meets a police officer on a street. The two strike up a conversation about the causes of the riots. What will they say?*

"Do your own thing" was the advice offered by hippies in the 1960's. These San Francisco hippies did their thing by living in a rainbow-colored bus and traveling around the city giving "concerts."

Chapter 26

The Now Generation

In 1967 a runaway girl sat in a pizza parlor in Haight-Ashbury (hate ASH-buh-ree), a section of San Francisco. On the wall, brightly colored magic mushrooms danced across a mural. Outside, other young people strolled past. Their rumpled clothes and dreamy eyes looked odd to many people in 1967. But to the runaway, these young people were part of a big family.

"If I went home," she was saying, "I'd have food and fine clothes. But I'd have to give up and be somebody I'm not.

When I grew up, there wasn't a name for it. The word *hippie* didn't exist. But I knew I wasn't the same as the [other] kids. . . . I knew there was something wrong with the society I was living in. But I couldn't put my finger on it. I only found out when I got here."

Haight-Ashbury was a community of hippies. Above all, it was a community of runaways. Teenagers running away from their parents. People in their twenties running away from rules and regulations. People in their thirties

651

running away from boring jobs. They all came together in places such as Haight-Ashbury.

What has happened to our children? parents asked. Why are there so many runaways? What are they trying to escape?

The runaway girl was giving some of the answers. She was trying to explain her friends. They didn't want wealth — although many had money and didn't mind spending it. They didn't want nine-to-five jobs. They didn't want to have to smile when they felt like screaming. These young people rejected the "straight" world of their parents. They called themselves "freaks," and that's what they seemed to be — misfits in somebody else's world.

"Freaking out." What they wanted, hippies said, was to enjoy life — *now.* Most adults, they said, were out of touch with life. Adults worked and sacrificed for *future* happiness. You can't enjoy life that way, hippies said. Instead, you can know the joy of life only by being aware of your feelings NOW ... this very second.

What frightened many parents were the methods some hippies used in order to enjoy life now. The most common method was drugs. Marijuana. LSD. Speed. Uppers. Downers. The young people borrowed an advertising slogan

Rock stars of the 1960's used electronics to create a new music. One writer claimed that Jimi Hendrix (above) "could make an electric guitar sing or even talk in a million different voices." The Beatles used clever electronics on their 1967 album, Sgt. Pepper's Lonely Hearts Club Band. *Photo below is from the album jacket.*

used by a chemical company: "Better living through chemistry." Young hippies giggled and popped a pill. Older people were horrified.

Many hippies had their moments of horror too. When they used drugs, they talked about "taking a trip." But some trips were frightening. Instead of pleasant visions, there were nightmares. Like a war zone, Haight-Ashbury had a place for casualties. It was called the Free Clinic. A sign on the door in the morning said: "Bum trippers and emergencies only. No doctors until four P.M."

In its heyday, Haight-Ashbury had several thousand hippies. Similar communities could be found in other big cities. There were hippie groups on ranches and farms. But most young people weren't hippies — even if they looked that way to adults. They might wear their hair long, if they were boys. Or wear jeans instead of dresses, if they were girls. But they weren't hippies. They hadn't completely rejected the adult world.

Playing by older rules. To the contrary, most young people accepted adult rules — and did so proudly. Instead of trying to escape from the world, many threw themselves into it. They took part in clean-up projects in city slums. They helped raise money for worthy charities. They handed out leaflets for political candidates they favored. And in many cases they did these things with their parents' support.

Yet young rebels attracted more attention in the newspapers and on TV. Many of these young people criticized their parents for not living up to their own ideals. Was it decent, they asked, to kill people in Vietnam? Was it decent to push blacks around, as whites had done for so long? Adult life, these rebels said, was too often an empty lie — a sham.

All this made many adults very angry. Nothing like this had happened when *they* were young. Oh, of course, sometimes they too had defied their parents. Sometimes they had used drugs — alcohol mostly. But they had soon settled down. Many of them had gone off to fight in World War II. After that, they had gotten jobs. They had worked hard to save their money so their children would have a good life. And now *this*.

"Ripping the war." Certainly the young generation was not marching off to war like the last one had. The Vietnam War did not bring Americans together in a common cause. Instead, it divided them. Some young people did go off to fight. Others stayed home — and in school — hoping they would not be called. Still others went to Canada, Sweden, and other countries to avoid the draft. Young people were among the war's most outspoken critics.

Some of these critics were as hostile to the hippies as many adults were. They thought the hippies were wasting their lives. Young people should work to improve the world, they said, not drop out of it. Because they called for sweeping changes, these youths were known as *radicals*.

The radicals came in all varieties. Some were violent. They set bombs in public buildings to protest the war. Others were peaceful. They folded their arms and sang when the police moved in to arrest them. Some called themselves Communists. They waved red flags and talked of revolution. Others cared nothing about communism. They

653

thought *any* government that used force to get its way was wrong. These people simply thought *both* sides in the Vietnam War too brutal.

Many radicals blamed the war on the *Establishment.* But what did they mean by the term? To them, the Establishment was a group of powerful individuals who ran the U.S. Its members were not just Presidents and U.S. Senators. They were also business leaders, college professors, scientists, editors, and others. In short, a ruling class. The radicals argued that democracy in the U.S. was only skin deep. They said the important decisions were made behind the scenes, by the Establishment.

Young people were only part of the antiwar movement. Many adults — including some members of the Establishment — also disliked the war. Nor did all the nation's young people stand against the war. Polls showed that only a minority of them did. Yet those who did were quite outspoken. They made the antiwar movement seem part of the generation gap.

Learning to cope. What had caused this gap between the generations? Some Americans thought they saw an answer in the way parents had raised their children. Parents had given their children too much, these people said. American parents had not been strict enough in their standards. They had become too easy, too "permissive" in raising children. This permissiveness had led to muddled thinking among young people, these critics claimed.

One scholar, Margaret Mead, had another explanation. She presented it in a book, *Culture and Commitment.* Why were youths so different from their parents? Because, Mead said, the world they were growing up in was so different from the world their parents knew. For thousands of years, parents had been able to teach children how to cope with life. They had taught them how to raise crops, build homes, and rear children of their own. But now, for the first time in history, the world was changing too fast. The old skills weren't needed. The old values didn't always fit. Children saw that their parents' generation no longer knew how to cope. "The young do not know what must be done," said Mead, "but they feel that there must be a better way."

In her book, Mead quoted the words of a 15-year-old boy. He wrote: "Sometimes I walk down a deserted beach listening to the waves and birds and I hear them forever calling and forever crying. And sometimes we [young people] feel that way but everyone goes on with his own little routine, afraid to stop and listen.... The answer lies out there somewhere. We need to search for it."

A Second Look. . . .

1. *What was the generation gap? Why were adults concerned about it?*

2. *In your opinion, does a generation gap still exist today between adults and youth? Explain your answer.*

3. *Rock and folk music of the 1960's is still around today. Hold a 15-minute music festival in your classroom. Bring to class albums that feature stars from the 1960's — the Beatles, Joan Baez, Led Zeppelin, Janis Joplin, the Grateful Dead, and others. After listening, discuss how this music expresses the idea of living now.*

Chapter 27

More War, More Grief

In 1969 the United States had a new President — Richard Nixon. Nixon had defeated the Democratic candidate, Hubert Humphrey, in the election of 1968. Nixon had promised to bring Americans together again. He had promised to put "an honorable end" to the war in Vietnam.

Nixon tried. He announced a policy that he called *Vietnamization*. This meant turning over the defense of South Vietnam to the South Vietnamese government and army. Nixon planned to pull U.S. troops out of Vietnam slowly. In two or three years, he said, the South Vietnamese would be fighting mostly on their own. They would no longer have much help from the U.S.

Antiwar protests. But many Americans could not wait two or three years. They wanted peace now. Some of them plastered this message — "Peace Now!" — on the bumpers of their cars. Students showed that they were against the war by wearing black armbands to school. (Black armbands are often worn at funerals as signs of grief.) Special days were set aside for demonstrating against the war. More than a million people took part in the first such day on October 15, 1969. Whole families went to church together wearing black armbands. They carried candles and listened to speeches calling for peace.

Richard Nixon argued that he was doing everything he could to make peace. He called the demonstrators a small minority. He asked for support from "the great silent majority of my fellow Americans." Some people made signs to show their support of the

North Vietnam was a stubborn enemy. U. S. planes bombed this bridge more than 200 times. Each time the North Vietnamese patched it up again.

President. One sign said: "God Save America from Traitors." Another sign said: "America, Love It or Leave It." Instead of black armbands, supporters of Nixon wore armbands with red, white, and blue stripes.

More and more people began talking about a "silent majority." It was true that most Americans were not demonstrating about the war on one side or the other. But this didn't mean that they had no thoughts about the war. Opinion polls showed that most people didn't want to lose the war. But they wanted it to end.

Richard Nixon did not want to lose either. He could not send more troops to Vietnam as Lyndon Johnson had done. Public opinion was against this. Instead, Nixon hoped to crush North Vietnam with bombing attacks. Wave after wave of U.S. planes flew over Hanoi (hah-NOY), North Vietnam's capital. They dropped more bombs on this city than had been dropped on the German city of Berlin in World War II. Their targets were military bases and fuel tanks. Still, some bombs missed the targets and hit homes and hospitals. Hundreds of civilians — men, women, and children — were killed.

Paris peace talks. Nixon hoped that these bombings would make North Vietnam give up. But he was disappointed. U.S. diplomats and North Vietnamese diplomats met together in Paris, France. For four years, off and on, they sat across a table and talked about terms of peace. Neither side was willing to back down. The Paris peace talks dragged on and on — and so did the war.

Meanwhile, Viet Cong and North Vietnamese forces had been using trails in neighboring Cambodia for moving supplies. Early in 1970, U.S. and South Vietnamese forces crossed into Cambodia. They marched over jungle trails seeking to destroy Viet Cong camps. In the end, however, the invasion made many Americans angry. On more than 100 college campuses across the nation, students went on strike. They refused to attend classes until the invasion of Cambodia ended.

On May 2, an antiwar protest at Kent State University in Ohio ended in the burning down of a school building. The

A young woman screams in horror at the killing of a Kent State University student. The death occurred in 1970, when troops shot into a crowd of antiwar protesters. Four students died.

656

governor of Ohio ordered the National Guard to the campus. Two days later, there was another demonstration. A few Kent State students threw rocks at the soldiers. Apparently panicking, the soldiers opened fire without warning. Sixty-one bullets ripped into the crowd of students. Four students fell to the ground, dead. The news shocked the nation. Angry protests swept other college campuses. The Senate voted to deny the President money to keep the invasion of Cambodia going.

Not all the anger was on the nation's campuses. Many people who supported Nixon were angry at college rioters. They agreed with the President when he called the rioters "bums." In New York, a group of construction workers wearing hard hats charged into a line of student demonstrators. They beat the students up, as police looked on. The nation was becoming more divided every day.

Election of 1972. The Democratic party was divided too. It needed a strong candidate to run against President Nixon in the 1972 Presidential election. But the Democrats fought among themselves. George McGovern, a Senator from South Dakota, won the Democratic nomination. He said that the U.S. should withdraw from Vietnam. But many leading Democrats refused to support him. They thought he talked too much like the student radicals. Many Democrats voted for Nixon. So Nixon won, with 60.7 percent of the popular vote. He collected 520 electoral votes. This was the second largest electoral-vote victory in U.S. history. (The largest had been Franklin Roosevelt's in 1936.)

President Nixon had been bringing U.S. troops home from Vietnam. This was one reason many people voted for him. In 1968 there had been 550,000 U.S. troops in Vietnam. By election time, 1972, fewer than 50,000 of them were left. The South Vietnamese government was taking over the fighting. This was Vietnamization.

Richard Nixon and his successor, Gerald Ford, hoped that Vietnamization would do two things. They said it would get the U.S. out of the war. They also hoped that it would lead to a victory for South Vietnam's government. Only the first happened. In April 1975, South Vietnam's army fell apart. It lost the war. A Communist government took over in the South. Vietnam became one country again.

The war was over. But the arguments went on. Could the U.S. and South Vietnam have won by fighting harder, bombing more? Why had the U.S. stayed in the war so long? Was it all worth it — or was the war just one ghastly mistake?

A Second Look. . . .

1. *How did Richard Nixon and Gerald Ford try to end the war in Vietnam? In what way did they succeed? In what way did they fail?*

2. *Imagine that you were a high school student in 1969. Would you have supported the U.S. role in the Vietnam War or opposed it? Or would you have been neutral? Why?*

3. *Review the three chapters in this book on Vietnam (Chapters 10, 24, and 27). Notice that five Presidents gave U.S. aid to South Vietnam's government. Which of these Presidents do you think was* most *responsible for the U.S. part in the war? Write a one-page essay explaining your answer.*

Looking Back: The Angry Years

	A	B	C	D	E
1958	1962	1966	1970	1974	1978

Putting Events in Order

Chapters 22 through 27 have covered events in recent history. Ten events of the period are listed here. Your job is to match each event to the correct period shown on the timeline above. On a piece of paper, number from **1** to **10.** After each number, write the letter of the four-year period within which the event occurred. There may be an event that occurred during several periods. In that case, write the letter **S.**

1. National Guard troops are sent to stop rioting in a black neighborhood in Detroit.

2. John F. Kennedy is assassinated in Dallas.

3. More than a million people take part in a demonstration against the Vietnam War.

4. The U.S. gives military aid to the government of South Vietnam.

5. South Vietnam's government collapses. Vietnam becomes one country under a Communist government.

6. Richard Nixon serves as Vice-President under Dwight D. Eisenhower.

7. An invasion of Cuba at the Bay of Pigs ends in failure.

8. Rioting breaks out as a national political party holds its convention.

9. Lyndon Johnson is elected President by a huge margin.

10. Richard Nixon begins serving a second term as President.

Interpreting a Source

One of the most popular folk singers of the 1960's was a young man from Minnesota, Bob Dylan. And one of his most popular songs was this.

Blowin' in the Wind

How many roads must a man walk down
Before you call him a man?
How many seas must a white dove sail
Before she sleeps in the sand?
How many times must the cannonballs fly
Before they're forever banned?
The answer, my friend, is blowin' in the wind,
The answer is blowin' in the wind.

How many times must a man look up
Before he can see the sky
How many ears must one man have
Before he can hear people cry?
How many deaths will it take till he knows
That too many people have died?
The answer, my friend, is blowin' in the wind,
The answer is blowin' in the wind.

How many years can a mountain exist
Before it's washed to the sea?
How many years can some people exist
Before they're allowed to be free?
How many times can a man turn his head
Pretending he just doesn't see?
The answer, my friend, is blowin' in the wind,
The answer is blowin' in the wind.

1. *"Blowin' in the Wind" has been de-scribed as a song of protest. Name at least two things you believe it is protest-ing. Be as specific as you can.*

2. *Would a songwriter still have cause to make such protests today? Why or why not? Do you think a writer would still be likely to express himself or herself in this way? Explain.*

3. *Does anything about this song seem dated? If so, what is it?*

4. *What is there about the song, if anything, that seems timeless? Explain.*

Sharpening Your Skills

In 1968 *Fortune Magazine* asked three groups of young people about their views on Vietnam and other issues. The young people were all between the ages of 18 and 24. One group had not gone to college. A second group had gone to college for practical reasons — getting training for a career. A third group had gone to college with no career goals in mind. They just wanted to attend college to learn about life. As you can see from the tables shown here, each group reacted differently to the same set of questions. Study the three tables carefully. Then answer the questions at right.

1. Which group is *most* likely to support the idea of going to war? Which group is *least* likely to support the idea of going to war? (Compare especially the responses in Table Two.)

2. On one point in Table One, all three groups come very close to sharing the same attitude. What point is this?

3. Compare the attitudes of Groups A and C on the issue of law and order (Table Three). Write a statement pointing out the differences between the two groups on this issue.

4. Which of the three groups do you think gave most support to Presidents Johnson and Nixon? Which group probably criticized these Presidents the most? Explain your answers.

Survey of Young People's Opinions, 1968

	Group A No college	Group B College for practical reasons	Group C College to learn about life
TABLE ONE: *Which of the following phrases describe your personal feelings about the war?*			
Sympathy for our boys	78%	75%	76%
Patriotism	46%	37%	22%
Strong support for the U.S. position	46%	26%	14%
Feeling of helplessness	31%	31%	54%
Disgust with our government	30%	40%	54%
Anger at our government	20%	24%	31%
Anger at opponents of the war	19%	11%	6%
Sympathy for the Viet Cong	11%	8%	21%

	Group A	Group B	Group C
TABLE TWO: *Aside from the particular issues of the Vietnam War, which of these values do you believe are always worth fighting for?*			
Protecting our national interest	73%	65%	40%
Containing the Communists	68%	59%	28%
Counteracting aggression[1]	65%	75%	50%
Fighting for our honor	64%	44%	20%
Maintaining our position of power in the world	54%	46%	22%
Protecting allies	53%	51%	37%
Keeping a commitment[2]	30%	24%	14%
TABLE THREE: *Which of the following social changes would you welcome?*			
More emphasis on law and order	91%	78%	39%
More emphasis on combating crime	88%	95%	70%
More respect for authority	87%	73%	41%
More emphasis on work being meaningful in its own right	85%	78%	88%
More emphasis on self-expression[3]	69%	68%	90%
More freedom to debate and disagree openly	68%	73%	92%
More freedom for the individual to do whatever he wants, provided he doesn't hurt others	65%	69%	84%
More acceptance of other people's peculiarities	60%	75%	93%
Less emphasis on status — on "keeping up with the Joneses"	57%	75%	80%
Less emphasis on money	57%	53%	80%
More emphasis on private enterprise	42%	55%	36%
More emphasis on the arts	42%	55%	84%
More vigorous but nonviolent protests by blacks and other minority groups	35%	41%	64%

[1]*Aggression,* in this sense, means the making of an attack on the rights or territory of another without good reason.

[2]A *commitment* is a promise.

[3]*Self-expression,* in this sense, means the freedom to express oneself as one wishes.

6 YESTERDAY, TODAY, TOMORROW

Looking Ahead: Searching for New Values

One day in 1972, Bob Light and his wife Lee moved to a farm. He was 30 years old. She was 28. Up to then, they had had no farm experience. Bob had worked with his father in a machinery business in New Jersey. But Bob and Lee had been saving money and making plans. They had bought a farm at the end of a dirt lane overlooking the Winooski (wuh-NOO-skee) River in Vermont. The farm had a 150-year-old house and a broken-down barn. They wanted to fix it up, then grow and sell vegetables. Why, one might ask, would anyone leave a comfortable home for such a life?

"What we want is self-sufficiency," said Bob. "To make and produce as much as we can so we have to have as few dollars as possible. We don't want to support the factories belching out smoke."

Could city people be happy picking tomatoes in Vermont? In the 1970's, many tried to find out.

Bob and Lee were going "back to the land." Other Americans were also on the move in the 1970's. In fact, census-takers discovered a startling thing. After 1970 nonurban areas were growing faster than large cities were. People were moving away from the cities for many reasons. Some were finding jobs in industries that had also moved out of the cities. Some were searching for smaller and more peaceful suburbs. Still others were looking for a place where they could retire.

But many were actively seeking to go "back to the land." City-bred men and women suddenly wanted to grow their own food. They wanted to raise animals. They wanted to get more exercise, breathe clean air, and make things with their hands. They wanted to depend more on themselves and less on others. That is, they wanted to become more self-sufficient, like Bob and Lee.

In many ways, the back-to-the-landers

663

were expressing the concerns of the whole nation in the 1970's. Such people were a small minority, of course. They did not have all the answers — or even most of them. But they were ready for new challenges. And they were responding to the same things that other Americans were thinking about. For example:

Self-sufficiency. Bob and Lee wanted to grow their own food and not depend on others. Many Americans were wrestling with the question of self-sufficiency. In 1973 Arab oil-producing nations suddenly cut off supplies of oil to the U.S. Americans realized with a jolt how much they depended on the outside world. The U.S. imported one third of the energy it needed to keep factories humming and homes warm. What could be done? President Nixon ordered an effort to increase U.S. oil and coal production. He made self-sufficiency in energy a national goal.

Pollution. Bob and Lee didn't want to buy factory-made goods. They felt that factories polluted the air with their smoke. Many other Americans began worrying about pollution in the 1970's. But they didn't want to do away with factories. They wanted to find ways to operate factories without making so much pollution.

The back-to-the-landers shunned much of what we think of as progress. They went back to burning wood to heat their homes. They farmed with animals or small tractors instead of the giant farm machines of the 1970's. They coped with insects and weeds without using chemicals. They grew their own food instead of buying it in cans and bottles and plastic wrappings.

To most people, this seemed crazy.

You can't turn the clock back, they said. Progress is here to stay. Humans have walked on the moon. Scientists will find answers to the problems that progress brings. But the questions raised by the back-to-the-landers were also being asked by others. How long can we afford to use scarce fuels such as natural gas and oil? What are chemicals doing to our land and our bodies? Where will we put all the garbage produced by modern ways of living?

Leaders. Many back-to-the-landers questioned their political leaders. Some felt they could no longer trust their government. U.S. policy toward Vietnam in the 1960's had brought on some of the distrust. More questions arose in the 1970's. From 1972 to 1974, a growing scandal haunted President Nixon's White House. Some of his closest advisers were accused of crimes. Many people said Nixon himself was a criminal. Nixon's troubles grew out of an affair called *Watergate*. The Watergate affair was a troubled time for the whole nation.

World tensions. The back-to-the-landers had lived all or most of their lives in the nuclear age. So had millions of other Americans. They could not remember a time when the atomic bomb did not exist. The U.S. and the Soviet Union maintained a "balance of terror." Each was so powerful that it could devastate the other. According to leaders of the two nations, no country would start a war that it knew might destroy the winner and loser alike. This was supposed to make all-out war impossible. But did it really? Was the balance of terror so shaky that it might one day collapse?

Old neighborhoods took on a new look in the 1970's, as city people worked together to improve their lives. Above, teenagers paint a mural of their own design on a New York building in 1975. The mural, "Women Hold Up Half the Sky," was part of a Cityarts Workshop project on the Lower East Side. Through such projects, young people expressed pride in their ethnic backgrounds and in their nation.

No one could be sure. There were many causes of world tensions, people said. But maybe something could be done to ease those tensions. This is what the leaders of the U.S. and some Communist countries thought in the 1970's. They signed agreements that marked a truce in the Cold War. These agreements were just a beginning. But many people hoped that, step by step, the nations of the world might find a way to turn that truce into lasting peace.

The future. On July 4, 1976, the United States entered its third century. Where was it headed? The back-to-the-landers offered one answer — a return to small-scale, human values. Others said we could not go back — we must go forward. They predicted that today's big cities and large businesses would not quickly disappear. They said ways could be found to maintain human values even in large-scale undertakings. They saw the future as a challenge to make old values fit new needs.

Chapter 28

One Giant Leap

It was early Sunday evening on the West Coast of the U.S. On the East Coast, it was late Sunday night, July 20, 1969. In Europe it was the small hours of Monday morning. In Asia the sun was already up. Wherever they were, about 500 million people were doing the same thing. They were watching the most spectacular TV show in history.

The image on TV sets was ghost-like. There was U.S. Astronaut Neil Armstrong coming out of his spaceship. Slowly he lowered himself down the nine-step ladder. As his foot touched ground, Armstrong's voice buzzed across 240,000 miles (390,000 kilometers) of space:

"That's one small step for a man, one giant leap for mankind."

Humans had landed on the moon.

For thousands of years, people had dreamed of exploring beyond Earth. But these dreams had always seemed fanciful — until human beings learned to fly. Then scientists began to invent new ways of flying faster and farther. In 1957 the Soviet Union put an object into orbit around the Earth. The object was known as an artificial *satellite*. The Space Age had begun.

President Eisenhower started a program to catch up with the Soviets in space. President Kennedy decided to try to beat them to the moon. In May 1961, Kennedy told Congress that the U.S.

should put an astronaut on the moon before 1970. That was only nine years away.

Congress liked Kennedy's idea. The race to the moon was on. About 400,000 Americans worked in the space program. It cost more than 24 *billion* dollars.

Around the Earth. Many space flights were made, some with astronauts, some without. In 1962 John Glenn became the first U.S. astronaut to orbit Earth in space. In the U.S., astronauts such as Glenn were heroes. Television brought the space flights into American living rooms. Gradually the U.S. caught up with the Soviets.

The last moon practice flight, Apollo 10, took place in May 1969. Two astronauts flew to within nine miles (about 14 kilometers) of the moon. Everything went well. The stage was set for Apollo 11, the moon landing.

The moon flight was set to blast off from Cape Kennedy, Florida, on Wednesday, July 16, 1969. Nearly a million people crowded nearby beaches to see it. On the launching pad, the huge rocket and spaceship looked like a tall white candle. It was as high as a 36-story building.

At 6:45 A.M., the three astronauts — Neil Armstrong, Edwin Aldrin, and Michael Collins — stepped into the spaceship. The door was shut and sealed behind them. During the long countdown, ground crews checked out all equipment. Then a worker pressed a button in the control room. Orange flames and dark smoke shot from under the rocket. A roar like thunder filled the air. Apollo 11 lifted off the ground. Within minutes it was out of sight.

To the moon. On Saturday, July 19, Apollo 11 neared the moon and went into orbit around it. The next day, Armstrong and Aldrin entered the machine that would take them to the moon's surface. It was called a Lunar Module (LM). The LM looked like a big bug with four legs. Collins remained in the command ship *Columbia* in orbit around the moon.

The actual landing on the moon was the most dangerous part of the trip. The

The Space Age reached its high point in 1969, when two U.S. astronauts landed on the surface of the moon. Below, Edwin Aldrin takes his moon walk. Behind him is Apollo 11's Lunar Module, the Eagle.

moon's surface has many large craters (holes). It also has many large rocks. If the LM had hit a rock or fallen into a crater, it could have been the end for the astronauts. On the way down, they saw that they were headed for a crater. But Armstrong took over the controls from the automatic pilot. He steered the LM to a safe landing. At 4:17 P.M. on July 20, Armstrong radioed a message back to Earth: "The Eagle has landed."

On Earth millions of people shouted with joy.

Six hours later, Armstrong and Aldrin stepped on the moon. They set up a U.S. flag. They picked up rocks and sand to take back to Earth for study by scientists. The astronauts spent 21 hours on the moon. Their space suits protected them from the extreme heat and cold. It was 234 degrees Fahrenheit (112 degrees Celsius) in the sunlight and 279 below zero (minus 73 degrees Celsius) in the shade. The space suits also gave them oxygen and water.

The next day, Armstrong and Aldrin climbed back into the LM and took off from the moon's surface. They rejoined the *Columbia.* Then the long trip home began. From 175,000 miles (280,000 kilometers) out in space, the astronauts sent back a television picture of Earth. On Thursday, July 24, they splashed down safely in the Pacific Ocean.

Far into space. Five more flights went to the moon. Then the space program began exploring farther reaches of space with unmanned rockets.

By the 1970's, more and more people were becoming critical of the space program. They said it was wrong for the United States to spend so much money exploring space. The U.S. should take care of its problems on Earth, they said. Poverty, disease, injustice — these were the problems that needed attention, not outer space.

The space program's defenders pointed out its benefits. Humankind gained knowledge about the universe and the creation of Earth. And much of the research done for the space program helped improve life on Earth. Out of this research came devices such as pocket calculators and tiny cells that produce energy from the sun.

But just about everyone agreed that the moon landings were a great achievement. Humans had walked where no mortal had ever set foot before. These courageous explorers had taken human thoughts and feelings to the vast darkness of space.

A Second Look. . . .

1. *What was the purpose of the Apollo program? Which Presidents were first to see the need for such a program?*

2. *Some critics have said that money spent on the Apollo program should have been used to end poverty, disease, and injustice. Do you agree? How would more money help solve such problems? Would money alone solve them? What else might be necessary? Do you think it was a good idea or a bad idea to use the money for the Apollo program?*

3. *People have dreamed of traveling beyond Earth for centuries. The space-shuttle program, which followed the Apollo program, could make that dream a reality for some people. Write an essay for an imaginary contest in which the first prize is an all-expenses-paid trip to the moon. Explain why you want to go there, and what you hope to see.*

Chapter 29

Saving the Environment

January is usually a windy month in Santa Barbara, California. The breeze blowing in from the Pacific smells like salt. But on January 31, 1969, the breeze had a strange odor. Some surfers on the beach were the first to notice the smell. Was it oil? The ocean began turning black. It *was* oil. The oil stuck to their surfboards. Soon the beaches began to darken.

Later in the day, Santa Barbara residents found the cause of the trouble. An oil well, six miles off-shore, had blown

"We need offshore drilling so that you people can drive your cars to the beaches and enjoy them," says an agent for oil companies in this 1969 Conrad cartoon for The Los Angeles Times.

out. Thousands of gallons of oil were spilling into the Pacific. For days the oil floated up to the beaches, turning them black. Birds covered with oil couldn't fly. Their feathers no longer kept them warm. Many lay dying.

The Santa Barbara oil spill wasn't the first accident of its kind in the ocean. But it made Americans more aware of a serious problem — *pollution*.

Pollution had been a threat to humans for centuries. Sewage in water made people sick. Smoke in the air hurt their eyes and lungs. People had long worked to prevent such pollution. But the mid-20th century brought new forms of pollution. It seemed to go hand in hand with progress.

In 1969 scientists were already warning about the new kinds of pollution. Here are some of the things that concerned them:

Air pollution. For years factories had belched smoke into the air. People had burned trash in their yards. Cities had burned it at dumps. This kind of pollution made clouds of black smoke. But other kinds of air pollution were invisible. For example, automobiles pumped harmful gases into the air. One such gas was carbon monoxide. People who breathe in too much carbon monoxide in closed areas can die from it. In open air, carbon monoxide can damage human health. As more and

669

more cars crowded streets and high-ways, such health hazards were growing.

Water pollution. For centuries, some towns and cities had dumped raw sewage into rivers. But other kinds of water pollution were quite modern. Clothes-washing detergents caused soap suds to clog some streams. Phosphates (minerals) in the detergents made water plants grow too fast. The plants used up oxygen in streams and lakes and killed plant and animal life. Factories dumped oil and other wastes into rivers. So many wastes built up in Cleveland's Cuyahoga (kie-uh-HO-guh) River in 1969, for example, that it actually caught fire. The fire was intense enough to damage two railroad trestles.

Nuclear waste. Nuclear energy began producing electricity for some U.S. homes in 1957. But it produced more than electricity. It also produced waste. This waste is radioactive. That is, it gives off dangerous rays. These rays can harm or kill animals and plants. The waste continues to give off such rays for hundreds of years. It is so dangerous that it cannot be touched by human hands. Instead, nuclear waste is picked up by machinery inside thick walls. Then it must be stored in tanks or caves deep in the earth or the oceans. The more power we produce in nuclear plants, the more waste we must get rid of. But where can we put it? What happens if an earthquake releases the waste? What if it spreads to underground water supplies or into the air?

Farm chemicals. In 1962 a writer named Rachel Carson wrote a book called *Silent Spring*. She sounded a warning about a chemical used in farming. It was called *DDT*. DDT killed insects that once caused serious crop damage. The chemical helped farmers get bigger harvests. But DDT didn't just disappear. It remained in the soil and in the cells of animals. When a bird ate a poisoned insect, some of the chemical stayed in the bird's body. If it ate enough DDT, the bird might die or be unable to produce offspring. Will one year come, asked Carson, when no birds are alive to greet the arrival of spring with song? And what happens to humans when they eat animals whose flesh contains chemicals such as DDT?

Industrial chemicals. Many advances in industry depend on new uses of chemistry. One family of chemicals, called *PCB's*, came into wide use in the 1930's. They were put into paint, ink, even hand soaps. PCB's began turning up in rivers, in the soil, in the air. Scientists discovered that PCB's can cause nervous illness and cancer in animals. Many other chemicals besides PCB's were being used in industry. Many people wondered how safe they were.

Life on Earth is very delicate, scientists said. All forms of life depend on other forms of life to survive. We humans depend on plants to produce our food — and even the oxygen we breathe. We depend on birds to control some insects. We depend on bees and other insects to make many of our crops grow. The environment is a complex balance. Anything we do to one part of this balance will upset other parts. If we kill certain insects, many other kinds of animal and plant life will suffer. The balance is so complex that we cannot fully know what changes we may cause.

In the late 1960's, scientists' warnings were beginning to sink in. But what could be done to save the environment?

Some people said the environment must be protected at all costs. These people were known as *environmentalists*. The best way to clean up the environment, they said, was to stop pollution at its source. They wanted strict laws against pollution. If an industry

Earlier in this century, autos helped to shape new cities such as Albuquerque, New Mexico (left). But by the 1970's, cars were proving a mixed blessing even in the cities they helped to shape. Many autos gave off exhaust fumes, which poisoned the air along major city roads.

caused pollution, they said, it should pay to clean it up and prevent it for the future.

Others took issue with the environmentalists. They agreed on one point — that pollution must be cut. But they disagreed on how this should be done, and on who should pay for it. Business leaders argued that tax money should be used to help industries stop polluting. Otherwise, they said, some businesses could not afford pollution controls. They might have to close down. Then workers would lose their jobs.

Moreover, some people argued that not all pollution *could* be stopped. A certain amount of pollution, they said, cannot be avoided in modern life. We must strike a balance between purity of environment and progress, they said.

Some people argued, "People cause pollution, and people can stop it." They urged each individual to examine his or her own life. They stressed, for instance, that people should be more careful about throwing cans away. Find out how you are polluting, they said. Then change your ways.

As the debate went on, the federal government began taking steps against pollution. Congress passed new laws. The government laid down new rules about what could be dumped into rivers and oceans. It ordered pollution controls on cars. It required factories to stop much of the pollution from smokestacks. It banned most uses of DDT. It set up new procedures for testing other chemicals.

Perhaps the most far-reaching action was the *National Environmental Policy Act of 1970*. This act didn't tell anyone to stop doing anything. What it said was:

Look before you leap. The law required a study before any federal project could begin. The study asked: How will this project affect the environment? Will it improve the environment? Will it hurt it? A project didn't have to be abandoned just because it might hurt the environment. But the cost to the environment had to be taken into account.

Public protests were also having an effect. A plan to build another bridge across San Francisco Bay was stopped. Plans for many new shopping centers and highways were abandoned or changed. A proposal to build a post office on a plot of land in Fort Snelling, Minnesota, was dropped. A public park was built there instead.

By 1976 U.S. industry and government were spending some 16 billion dollars a year to control pollution. One estimate was that the total cost of such controls through the early 1980's would reach 500 billion dollars. There was no denying that fighting pollution was costly. But was there any choice?

A Second Look. . . .

1. *What are some different types of pollution? Where do they come from?*

2. *Some environmentalists charge that our modern desire to "conquer nature" causes pollution. Primitive peoples didn't pollute, they argue. Neither did the first Americans. Do you agree? Is it possible to have the comforts of modern life without pollution? Discuss.*

3. *Imagine that you have been hired to look into the environment of your area. What are the sources of pollution? How could pollution be stopped? What government agencies should be told? Write up your findings in a report.*

Burdened by the danger and expense of the arms race, the U.S. and the Soviet Union talked about slowing it down. "Do me a favor — help me drop it," says the U.S. in Oliphant's 1970 cartoon for The Denver Post.

Chapter 30

Time for a Thaw?

Henry Kissinger was sick in bed. At least that is what reporters traveling with President Nixon's top foreign policy adviser were told. No news today, they thought. But they were wrong. Kissinger was not really in a sick bed at all.

Henry Kissinger had slipped away from the press. He was no longer in Pakistan on a trip around the world. Instead, at two o'clock one July morning in 1971, he was in a plane flying over the Himalaya (him-uh-LAY-uh) Mountains. For the first time in 22 years, a high official of the U.S. government was going to China.

The United States and China had been quarreling since 1949. In that year, a long Chinese civil war ended. Communists, led by Mao Tse-tung (MAH-oh dzay-DOONG), took power. A year later, U.S. and Chinese troops were shooting at each other in Korea (see Chapter Nine). After Korea, the U.S. and China exchanged little but threats. Now was the time, Kissinger thought, to patch up the quarrel.

Kissinger was in China only two days. But those two days began a new series of events. The U.S. and China began to patch up their quarrel. This affected U.S. dealings with the Soviet Union. And it led to a thaw in the Cold War.

673

Dangers of war. Richard Nixon had thought about the Cold War for many years. When he became President in 1969, he asked Henry Kissinger to help him guide U.S. foreign policy. Kissinger already had some strong opinions. As a college professor, he had written an important book on nuclear weapons. In it, he had taken a hard line against Communist nations. But he had also stressed the dangers of modern weapons. He had urged the U.S. to find a way to avoid all-out war with the Communist world.

This same theme would be sounded by President Nixon. The goal was called *détente* (day-TAHNT), a French word meaning "relaxation." The idea was to relax the tensions of the Cold War. The plan was to improve U.S. relations with the Soviet Union and China.

There were obstacles to the new plan, though. Soviet and Chinese leaders were suspicious of the United States. They said that the U.S. had been an "international bully." Most Americans, for their part, were suspicious of Communists. For decades, U.S. leaders had been speaking out strongly against communism. Richard Nixon had been one of them. In time, Nixon's stand against communism helped him to sell *détente* to the American people. His supporters said he could be trusted to bargain with Communists.

It took some changes in the Communist world, though, to give Nixon his chance. The Soviet Union and China had been close allies during the early years of the Cold War. Then, during the 1960's, they began to bicker. Mao Tse-tung accused the Soviets of straying from true communism. China and the Soviet Union

674   squabbled over where their nations' boundary ran. By 1969 Soviet and Chinese soldiers were shooting at each other from time to time along their shared border.

Invitation to talk. President Nixon realized that China was ready for a change. He saw a chance to work out new agreements with both China and the Soviet Union. The planning was done in secret. Any change in the relations between superpowers would create a big stir. Kissinger went on his secret trip to China in 1971. For two days, he met with Chinese Premier Chou En-lai (joe en-LIE). The Premier gave Kissinger an invitation for President Nixon to visit China. Then Kissinger flew back to Pakistan. He "recovered" from his illness.

When Kissinger returned home, Nixon went on TV with the dramatic news about China. The news created shock waves around the world. The Soviets were unhappy. Many Americans were bewildered. But many other Americans were delighted about the "opening to China."

Nixon, Kissinger, and other officials flew to China in February 1972. With them went swarms of news reporters. Every word, every gesture was recorded for history. At home, Americans watched on TV as Nixon clinked glasses with Chou En-lai at a glittering banquet. Arm in arm, Nixon and Chou marched from table to table. Six dozen times the glasses clinked as the once-hostile leaders exchanged toasts. Chou and Nixon did not iron out all the differences between their two countries. But they did put stress on the hopes that now united them.

Limit on weapons. The new warmth between the U.S. and China worried the leaders of the Soviet Union. They didn't want China and the U.S. to team up against them. They decided to seek new agreements with the United States too.

Ever since World War II, the U.S. and the Soviet Union had been building bigger and bigger weapons. Neither nation wanted to fall behind the other. Each feared that the other would destroy it if given half a chance. But each year, the arms race became more costly. It drained away money that might have gone for homes or hospitals. It posed a constant threat to peace.

In May 1972, President Nixon traveled to Moscow to confer with Soviet leader Leonid Brezhnev (BRESH-n'yev). It was the first time a U.S. President had visited the Soviet Union in peacetime. The two leaders signed a historic document. It was a treaty aimed at slowing down the arms race. For the first time, it put limits on how many *strategic* (major) weapons each side could have. It was called the *Strategic Arms Limitation Treaty (SALT)*.

The SALT pact didn't stop the arms race. It merely slowed it down. It led, however, to new talks about a possible second treaty, to be called SALT II. And it gave the world a breathing spell by easing Cold War tensions.

Feud over land. There were still many difficulties in the way of *détente*. One continuing trouble spot was the Middle East. At issue in this conflict was a slice of land on the eastern shores of the Mediterranean Sea. This land became known to history as Palestine. In Biblical times, it was the home

Chinese premier Chou En-lai (left) welcomed President Nixon (second from left) on his trip to China. Here the two dine in Shanghai with a local leader, Chang Chun Ciao, and Pat Nixon.

of the Jews. But the Jewish people were driven out of it by waves of conquerors. Arabs moved into Palestine. In time, they came to regard the area as *their* home.

After World War II, the United Nations recommended that Palestine be divided into separate Jewish and Arab nations. The Jews accepted the decision. The Arabs did not. Arab leaders insisted that the U.N. had no right to give away land that Arabs saw as their own.

The Jewish state of Israel was born in 1948. Hardly had it been created when Arab armies attacked it from all sides. Since then the area has often been the scene of bitter fighting. War has been followed by truce, followed by another war. Efforts to reach a lasting settlement have failed.

In the 1950's and early 1960's, the U.S. and the Soviet Union took different sides in the dispute. The Soviet Union backed the Arabs. The United States backed Israel. In recent years, however, the two countries have pursued a similar goal. Both have tried to get the feuding nations to a peace conference. Such efforts have been part of the spirit of *détente.*

Détente brought no new alliances. The United States did not become friends with the Soviet Union or Communist China. Yet the threats of the 1950's and early 1960's seemed to be past. Trouble might flare up at any moment. But many people hoped that a peaceful future was now more likely.

Americans disagreed about other aspects of the Nixon Presidency. But these changes in foreign policy brought wide praise to Nixon and to Henry Kissinger.

A Second Look. . . .

1. *Why did the United States quarrel with China in the 1950's and the early 1960's? What changes made an "opening to China" possible in 1972?*

2. *What is the meaning of* détente? *How has* détente *represented a change in U.S. foreign policy? What are some possible advantages of* détente? *What do you suppose might be some of its drawbacks? Do you favor a policy of* détente? *Why or why not?*

3. *The dispute between Israel and its Arab neighbors has continued ever since 1948. Over the years, it has led to several wars. Using reference works in your school or public library, conduct a research project on this dispute. What are the major differences between the two sides? How many times have they gone to war? When and why? What efforts have been made to reach a lasting settlement? What has been the outcome of those efforts? Write up your findings in a report.*

When Ralph Steadman drew this cartoon in 1971, the SALT talks seemed to be going nowhere. All the two sides exchanged were empty words. But in 1972 there was progress. The SALT pact was signed.

Chapter 31

Watergate

Of course I am not dumb and I will never forget when I heard about this — forced entry and bugging. I thought: What is this? What is the matter with these people? Are they crazy?

The above statement was made by President Nixon on March 21, 1973. He was talking to a member of his White House staff, John Dean. Nobody else was in the President's office on that spring morning in March. But a tape recorder was turned on. It was recording every word the President said.

Nixon and Dean were talking about a scandal that had been making news for almost one whole year. It would continue to make news for another year. Finally the scandal — and the tapes of the President's conversations — would ruin Nixon's career. The name for this scandal was *Watergate.*

The Watergate story is complicated. People still disagree about how deeply the President was involved in it. But these are the basic facts:

Watergate was the name of a fancy hotel, apartment, and office complex in Washington, D.C. In 1972 offices at Watergate were used by the Democrats to run their election campaign against Richard Nixon, the Republican President. At the time, Nixon was hoping to be re-elected to a second term. He was relying on a special committee to plan

his campaign and beat the Democrats. The group was called the *Committee to Re-Elect the President.* It met in an office building across the street from the White House. The head of the committee was John Mitchell. Mitchell had been U.S. Attorney General until February 1972.

Bungled burglary. In January 1972, Mitchell met with a professional spy, Gordon Liddy. Also present at the meeting was John Dean of Nixon's White House staff. Liddy described his plan for spying on the Democrats. He said his plan would cost a million dollars. Mitchell objected that the plan was too expensive. About two months later, Liddy proposed a less costly plan that involved spying on Democrats in Watergate. This time Liddy's plan was approved.

Liddy and another government spy, Howard Hunt, hired two Americans and three Cuban refugees to do the work for them. Late one Friday night in June 1972, the five burglars broke into the Democrats' offices in Watergate. But a night watchman became suspicious and called the police. The burglars were caught in the act of tampering with the Democrats' telephones. On Sunday morning, a Washington newspaper told the story of the break-in.

At first, few people took the matter seriously. Only a tiny group knew then about John Mitchell's meeting with Gordon Liddy. The Democratic candidate for President, George McGovern, blamed the Republicans for planning the burglary. But Mitchell insisted that Liddy and Hunt had acted on their own. Nixon was re-elected by a big vote.

The wheels of the law had been set in motion, however. Even before the election, a federal grand jury had begun an inquiry. Liddy, Hunt, and the burglars were sent to jail. Still, some nagging questions remained.

Secret fund. Did Liddy and Hunt in fact plan the burglary alone? Or were higher-ups involved? Newspaper stories in *The Washington Post* said that Mitchell had used a secret fund of money to pay for the burglary. If this were true, then what about the President himself? As a close friend of Mitchell, could Nixon have known about the burglary beforehand? Could he have tried to cover up Mitchell's guilt after the burglars' arrest? Nixon assured people that nobody in the White House was involved in Watergate. But many people now began to wonder. Was Richard Nixon telling the whole truth? Or was he hiding something?

In 1973 a special Senate committee started to look into Watergate. Its hearings were broadcast on TV. The committee sent for the key members of Nixon's White House staff as witnesses. One of the most important witnesses was boyish-looking John Dean.

Dean told the Senate committee about his meeting with John Mitchell and Gordon Liddy. He told of his own attempts to cover up his guilt and the guilt of others. Dean said Nixon knew about the cover-up efforts as early as the autumn

John Dean tells a Senate committee — and the nation — his version of Watergate.

of 1972. If this were so, then the President was helping to hide a crime. And, by law, this itself was a crime — "obstructing justice."

The President said he first learned about Dean's cover-up in March 1973. Nixon claimed to be trying to get to the bottom of things. Who was lying — Dean or the President?

Hidden recorders. Next the Senate committee learned something even more surprising. A witness revealed that the President had hidden tape recorders in the White House. Nixon had wanted a record for history. He had taped his conversations with almost everyone. There were hundreds of tapes of the President's past meetings and phone conversations. By listening to these tapes, the committee might at last know the full truth.

But the President refused to give up the tapes. The U.S. Constitution, he said, had created three equal branches of government — the Executive, the Legislative, and the Judicial. Congress was part of the Legislative Branch. It could not tell the Executive Branch what to do.

Many members of Congress rejected Nixon's argument. They said that the Constitution made the three branches of government equal but not independent. If the President knew something about a crime, they argued, it was his duty to say so. If he refused, it was Congress' duty to find out the truth. To do this, the Congressional committee had a right to the tapes. This was the law, these people argued, and not even the President was above the law.

Now the battle lines were drawn. Nixon's own lawyers were firm. Congress has only one power over the President, they argued. It is spelled out in the Constitution. First, the House of Representatives must *impeach* (accuse) the President of "high crimes and misdemeanors." Then the Senate must decide whether the President is guilty of the House's charges against him. If two thirds of the Senators find him guilty, the President must leave office.

Impeachment is a most serious matter. Only one President had ever been impeached — Andrew Johnson in 1868. He had not been found guilty. But now talk of impeachment began to spread. Some members of Congress demanded it. Newspaper editorials said Nixon should resign to prevent impeachment. Opinion polls showed that a majority of Americans distrusted their President. What was he to do?

A Second Look. . . .

1. *Who was responsible for planning the Watergate burglary? If Nixon did not plan it, why did the burglary cause him such trouble?*

2. *In your judgment, what was the worst part about the Watergate scandal: (a) The burglary itself? (b) The fact that it was not taken seriously until after the election of 1972? (c) Richard Nixon's failure to tell people the complete truth about Watergate? (d) The way John Dean testified against his former friend and boss, Richard Nixon? What, if anything, was wrong about each?*

3. *Some people said that the Republicans were unfairly accused in the attempt to "bug"' the Democrats' offices. Write an essay telling what you think. Is it "part of the game" to use every means possible to win an election? Do you think the Democrats have used their own "dirty tricks"? What, if anything, makes Watergate different from other "tricks"?*

Television gave close coverage to the Senate hearings on Watergate. As they continued, some people compared them to other "shows." Cartoon is by Mike Peters of The Dayton Daily News.

Chapter 32

A President Resigns

It was Sunday evening, April 29, 1974. Richard Nixon was calm as he faced the TV cameras. Beside him on a table were 38 notebooks. They contained the transcripts (typed records) of many of his White House tapes. Nixon pointed to the notebooks and said that everyone could now read them. "I want there to be no question remaining," he declared, "about the fact that the President has nothing to hide."

Nixon was going part way to meet Congress' demands. He was releasing only transcripts — not the tapes themselves. The transcripts, he said, had been edited to remove bad language. But Nixon said they contained all the important parts of his conversations. He asked Americans to judge for themselves whether he was telling the truth about Watergate.

Up to this time, Nixon had thought he could fight off impeachment. He thought it was a party issue. He thought Democrats would vote against him, but that Republicans would stand by him. The Democrats alone did not have enough votes to remove him from office.

Since January 1974, a committee of the House had been meeting to decide whether Nixon should be impeached. There were 21 Democrats on this committee and 17 Republicans. Only one Republican had been expected to vote for impeachment. But now Republican committee members read the transcripts of Nixon's tapes over and over. Six of them concluded that the President deserved to be impeached.

Court order. There was still worse news for Nixon. The Supreme Court ruled that he would have to surrender 64 more of his tapes. It said he had no right to keep this evidence from being used in a court trial. Nixon had appointed four of the Supreme Court Justices. In a sense, then, they owed their jobs to him. Yet three of

President Nixon as he appeared on television on April 29, 1974.

these men agreed with five other Justices on the point. Now Nixon had to give in or else openly defy the law. He turned over the tapes.

The President had had good reason to be worried. One of the tapes recorded a meeting between himself and a close adviser, H. R. Haldeman (HALL-duh-man). This meeting had occurred in June 1972, only one week after the Watergate burglary. Haldeman had told Nixon that leading Republicans had paid for the burglary. Haldeman had said that the Federal Bureau of Investigation (FBI) was working on the case. He had warned that the FBI might soon find out who was involved. Nixon had then told Haldeman to make the FBI drop its work on the case. In other words, Nixon was part of the cover-up of the Watergate burglary almost from the beginning.

Listening to this tape of the Haldeman meeting, President Nixon's lawyers were shocked. His Republican friends in Congress were even more shocked. They realized now that he had been misleading them all along. Republican Senators came to see Nixon in the White House. They told him that the House would certainly impeach him. But there was at least one way Nixon could stop this from happening. He could resign immediately. And this, finally, was what Richard Nixon decided to do.

Family ordeal. On August 7, 1974, the President gathered his family about him. He told them of his decision. At noon on Friday, August 9, he would resign. The President wanted one last photograph taken of himself and his family in the White House. He linked arms with his wife, Pat, and his two daughters, Tricia and Julie. He told them

Did Nixon get a "fair trial"? Cartoonist Hy Rosen thought not (below). But another cartoonist, Robert Pryor, believed that Nixon had caught himself in a web made from tape recordings of his conversations with aides.

681

to smile, even though they all felt like crying. They smiled, and the picture was taken. Then Julie burst into tears. Her father tried to comfort her.

No President in U.S. history had ever resigned before. No President had ever been forced to leave office before his term ended. For the Nixon family, and for the nation, it was a tragic time.

On August 9, Richard Nixon and his family flew home to California. A new family prepared to move into the White House. It was the family of the new President, Gerald Ford.

Only a year before, Ford had been a Republican Congressman from Michigan. Then Nixon chose him to be Vice-President. It was not an election year. But Nixon's first Vice-President, Spiro Agnew, had resigned in October 1973. Agnew had been accused of taking part in a bribery scandal. He had been found guilty of tax evasion. Ford became Vice-President when Congress approved him. And this put Ford in line to take over when Nixon resigned.

Presidential pardon. Americans seemed relieved to have Gerald Ford as their President. He was not controversial, as Richard Nixon had been. He seemed honest and straightforward, somebody you could trust. Ford wanted to end the nation's anguish over Watergate. Many people expected to see Richard Nixon face trial for the crime of "obstructing justice."

Then President Ford made a surprise announcement. He said he was pardoning Richard Nixon for any illegal acts that he might have committed as President. He said Nixon had suffered enough punishment. Nixon was now a sick man. There was no point making him suffer through a trial. The nation, Ford said, must forget Watergate and get on with its other business.

Some Americans accepted Ford's decision. Some even praised Ford for showing mercy. But other Americans wondered: What kind of justice is this? Other people had gone to jail for crimes less serious than those Nixon was accused of. Why should a former President get special treatment?

After a while, the anger died down. Some Americans even congratulated themselves about the Watergate affair. After all, hadn't the nation proved that a President must also obey the law? The Constitution still worked. The U.S. system of government had been tested to the utmost by the Watergate scandal. And it had survived the test.

A Second Look. . . .

1. Nixon might have been impeached by the House for certain actions. What illegal acts was he accused of? Why was he not impeached?

2. If a President is guilty of a crime, should he be sent to jail? Should he be pardoned instead? Or does it all depend on what kind of crime the President commits? Explain your answers.

3. Your opinion of recent Presidents is based on many different sources. This book is only one source for your opinion. Some others are: (a) conversations with family and friends, (b) television programs, (c) movies, (d) books, (e) magazines, and (f) newspapers. Which sources have been most important in forming your opinion of Richard Nixon as a President? Why? You might compare several sources on Watergate by reading passages from them aloud.

682

Chapter 33

Heading South

Al Massey wanted to get away from the Northern city where he lived. The weather was cold, he said, and the people weren't very friendly. To make matters worse, Massey complained, the crime rate was soaring. Going outside one's house, he claimed, "was almost like taking your life in your own hands."

Massey was a young businessman. In 1975 he heard of a job opening in Atlanta, Georgia. He welcomed the chance to move there with his family. In Atlanta he found what he wanted. Neighbors were friendly, business was good, and his family didn't miss the North — not even its winter sports. Now his daughter went ice skating on an indoor rink.

Massey was one of many thousands of people moving south in the 1970's. At the start of the decade, the South was gaining one million people each year. This meant that the South was growing

Retired people, heading for palm trees and golf courses, joined the movement from city to "sunbelt."

10 times as fast as the Northeast. Why were people leaving the North? Some were moving for business reasons. That is, the companies they worked for were heading south. Others were simply seeking warm weather, low taxes, and a more relaxed life. Many said they found these things in the "new South."

The term *new South* dated back at least to 1886. It had been used by an Atlanta newspaperman, Henry Grady, only 21 years after the Civil War. Grady was looking ahead to a brighter future. He believed the South could move forward — if more industries moved in. Industries, he said, would bring the South more jobs and money.

Sense of defeat. Some industries did grow in these years. In the 1870's and 1880's, Birmingham, Alabama, became a center for steel production. In the early 1900's, Texas became a center for the oil industry. Yet most Southern industries were based on farm products. And the South continued to rely on farming for most of its income.

Some Southerners were still struggling to get over feelings of defeat after the Civil War. This conflict had wounded Southern pride. As a Mississippi woman said, "Losing the Civil War made us think we were never as good as anyone else."

Many Southerners also tried to separate themselves from national politics. They distrusted the federal government. They feared Congress would pass laws they didn't want to follow. Some said Congress might try to strike down segregation laws. Most of these laws (though by no means all of them) existed in the South. Some Southerners, both blacks and whites, felt that the laws

were unfair. But many white Southerners wanted the laws to stay.

So, half a century after Henry Grady had talked about a new South, the region was still slow to change. By now it stood in marked contrast to the heavily industrial Northeast. In 1941 a historian, W. J. Cash, wrote: "The South is another land, sharply [different] from the rest of America."

Winds of change. Then came World War II. Some defense industries settled in the South. Some oil and gas companies moved their main offices there. After the war, these industries kept on growing. They brought more people and more money into the region. Other industries followed.

The South's warm weather also spurred its growth. After the war, more people headed south on their vacations. Some parts of the region became tourist spots. When people retired, many moved to warmer areas such as Florida, Georgia, and the Carolinas. Retirement centers also sprang up in warm-weather areas of the West — mainly in Arizona and Southern California.

In the early 1960's, the South became a hub for a brand new industry. The region played a key part in the U.S. exploration of space. Missiles were developed in Huntsville, Alabama. They were launched from Cape Canaveral, Florida. Manned spacecraft were controlled from Houston, Texas.

Meanwhile, other changes were sweeping the nation. Some of them further narrowed the gap between North and South. One was the fading out of segregation — something Southerners themselves had helped to end. Another was a growing suspicion of the federal

As the South grew, its cities shot skyward. Dallas, once a market for buffalo hides, became a banking center for the Southwest.

government, brought about partly by the Vietnam War and Watergate. Many Southerners had long held such suspicions. Now distrust seemed to be growing in other parts of the country too.

Lures for business. Still more industries began to take a second look at the South. They saw features that might help them make more money. Taxes were low in many parts of the South. Land was available at low cost. Some business leaders also liked the fact that the South had fewer labor unions than other regions. To some of these leaders, the weakness of labor unions was a main attraction.

There were several reasons why unions were weak in the South. For one thing, the South had long been a farming region. It had had few industries to unionize. For another thing, Southern factory workers had expected their employers to take care of them. They had not usually seen a need for unions.

The weakness of unions in the South disturbed union members in other areas. Yet this weakness was welcomed by many Southern business leaders. It meant that they would be less threatened by strikes and other labor troubles. It also meant cheaper labor costs.

As business boomed, other changes came. In cities such as Atlanta and Houston, new buildings rose higher and higher. An airport built between Fort Worth and Dallas covered an area larger than Manhattan Island in New York. With more money to spend, Southern cities began to give more support to local art and theater groups.

For some Southerners, the growth of "skyscraper cities" was a mixed bless-

685

ing. These people thought of their region as something special. Now, they said, their cities were beginning to look exactly like cities everywhere else. In the midst of all the growth, the South was losing its Southern charm. Southerners who held this view questioned whether growth meant progress or not.

Shift in power. Growth did mean one thing: new political power. One sign of this new power came in 1976. Voters elected a Southerner, Jimmy Carter, as President of the United States. It was the first time a resident of the Deep South had been elected President since 1848. Carter, a peanut farmer, had been governor of Georgia from 1971 to 1974. When he entered the race for President, he was unknown to most Americans. But voters didn't mind that he was a new face in national politics. After Watergate, in fact, many voters distrusted well-known leaders.

Jimmy Carter campaigns outside a church in his hometown, Plains, Georgia, before being named Democratic candidate for President in 1976.

Carter campaigned on his lack of experience in national politics. He talked about Southern ideals such as honesty, cooperation, and respect. Yet he also had views many Southerners didn't agree with. He said the Civil Rights Act of 1964 was the "best thing" that had happened to the South.

Carter, a white Southerner, had appealed to white Northerners and Southerners. He had also appealed to blacks. Four out of five black voters cast ballots for Carter. Some called this a sign that the gap between black and white Southerners was closing.

In his address upon taking office, Carter looked to the future. He said he hoped people would say of the 1970's that Americans "had torn down the barriers that separated those of different race and region."

A Second Look. . . .

1. *What reasons can you give for the growth of the South? Name at least two reasons.*

2. *In what ways have Northerners and Southerners become more alike? What are the advantages to such a development? What are its drawbacks? Give reasons for your answers.*

3. *On a map of the United States, find 35° latitude. Make a list of 10 major cities which fall to the south of this line. Then choose one of these cities. Using an encyclopedia, look up the city's history. Write a research report on when and how the city was founded. Indicate the city's location and explain how this location affected its growth. Also list the city's largest ethnic minorities. Explain, if you can, how at least one of these groups happened to settle there.*

Chapter 34

Crisis in Energy

The line of cars stretched for several blocks. Drivers sat behind the wheels reading newspapers or talking with friends. Exhaust smoke formed small, white clouds in the winter air. This scene was repeated all across the U.S. in the winter of 1974. People were waiting to buy gasoline. Service stations often ran out. They put signs out front: NO GASOLINE TODAY.

What was going on?

In the fall of 1973, fighting had broken out in the Middle East. Israel had battled Egypt and Syria in a short but bloody war. The United States had sent arms and ammunition to Israel. Egypt, Syria, and their Arab allies had not been able to keep U.S. aid from reaching Israel. But they had vowed to punish the United States for taking sides against them.

Most of the world's known oil supplies were located in the Arab nations. The U.S. had been buying oil from the Arabs since the 1950's. The U.S. was using more oil than it could produce itself. If the Arabs made good their threat, it would mean trouble for the U.S.

As cold weather was settling in over much of the U.S., the Arabs united to show their power. They refused to sell the United States any oil. Their refusal caused immediate shortages in the U.S. Motorists were shocked to find some local service stations closed.

This wasn't the only surprise. The price of gasoline shot up. The shortage of fuel forced many factories and offices to close. The economy took a nose dive. There hadn't been so many people out of work since the Great Depression.

The Arab embargo lasted until March 1974. In the spring, the long lines disappeared from U.S. service stations. But the price of gasoline did not come down. Many layoffs ended, although the economy was slow to recover. Americans became familiar with a new term — *energy crisis.*

"Bigger is better." Americans had never really had to worry about energy before. The United States was a rich land with abundant supplies of coal, natural gas, and oil. The U.S. was also a growing country. "Bigger is better," many people said. And there had always seemed to be cheap supplies of energy to fuel that growth.

The use of energy was growing at a rapid rate. Between 1950 and 1970, energy use in the U.S. doubled. The number of large, "gas-guzzling" cars rose. New appliances such as home freezers and clothes dryers burned up more and more electricity. Air conditioners took an especially heavy load.

Few people worried about the growth in demand for energy. After all, people said, growth was what had made America strong. But during this period, the nation had outgrown its own ability to produce oil. The United States had had to import foreign oil. Now the Arab embargo made Americans aware of just how much they depended on that foreign oil.

After the embargo, there was a lot of talk about the energy crisis. But much of it was confusing. Some people claimed the oil companies had withheld oil to get higher prices for it. This was a "phony" crisis, these people claimed. U.S. oil companies denied the charges. But they also said they needed the higher prices to pay for finding more oil.

President Nixon worked out a plan to tackle the energy crisis. It was designed to make the United States independent of foreign oil by 1980. One step was to lower the speed limit on the nation's highways. This alone would save a lot of gasoline. But the heart of the plan was to increase energy production within the U.S.

"Wasteful nation." In 1976 Jimmy Carter made the energy crisis an issue in his campaign for President. If elected, Carter promised to send Congress a major energy plan. Once in office, Carter wasted no time. First, he created a new Department of Energy. He named James Schlesinger (SHLESS-in-jer) as his Secretary of Energy.

Four months after taking office, Carter sent his energy plan to Congress. He also addressed the nation on TV two times in one week. "Ours is the most wasteful nation on Earth," he said. "We waste more energy than we import."

Unless we stopped waste, Carter declared, we would have to spend more and more money to import oil. The time might come when the oil would run out. This would mean no gasoline for cars,

no oil for heat, no power for machinery. He asked people to work together to avoid such a crisis. He told them it was almost like wartime — it was *that* serious.

Carter's plan had three basic parts:

Conservation. Carter said the nation needed to find ways of using less fuel. Many homes, he pointed out, had little *insulation* (material used to prevent the passage of heat). In winter, heat seeped out through the walls and roof. In summer, heat seeped in. Heaters and air conditioners used more fuel than necessary. Carter proposed that the government reward people who added insulation to their homes. He also suggested a higher tax on gasoline. This would make gasoline more expensive. Then people would use less. He wanted to put stiff taxes on large, gas-guzzling cars. Then people would buy smaller cars that get more miles to a gallon of gasoline, he said.

Exploration. The second part of Carter's plan encouraged U.S. industry to search for new supplies of oil and gas. Under the plan, the government would reward oil and gas companies with certain tax breaks for doing so.

Sources. Our most abundant energy source is coal, Carter said. The U.S. should start using more coal and less oil, he believed. Many factories could burn coal instead of oil or gas. They must be encouraged to make the switch. By 1985, Carter declared, the U.S. should increase its coal production by two thirds. It should also make more use of nuclear power.

In addition, Carter said that the U.S. should seek new sources of power — sources that cannot be used up. One

Rooftop solar panels can collect sunlight and use it to heat buildings. These "collectors" will heat a government center in New Mexico.

such source might be *solar energy* (energy from the sun's rays). Scientists said that solar energy could be used for heating homes and water. It could even be used to produce electricity. Another source of energy might be the wind. Giant windmills could be used to make electricity. But scientists needed to know more about solar and wind energy before they could make these sources practical. Carter's plan called for money to develop this know-how.

The Carter plan immediately ran into trouble. Some members of Congress disagreed with parts of the plan. So did many others, including oil and gas companies. Auto-makers did not like the tax on big cars. Consumer groups were against higher gasoline prices. Environmentalists were worried that the mining and burning of coal would create more

pollution. They argued that nuclear energy was harmful. They pointed out that it produced radioactive wastes that were hard to get rid of safely. They also said that accidents in nuclear plants could cause dangerous rays to be released.

This was U.S. politics at work. The question was now in the open. People knew that some changes had to be made in the American way of life. Now they were arguing over how sweeping the changes should be. And about who should pay for them.

Thoughtful Americans did agree on one thing, however. The days of cheap, plentiful energy were over. From now on, big cars and big growth rates would mean bigger bills, one way or another. Big did not mean better anymore.

A Second Look. . . .

1. *Why did the Arab nations refuse to sell oil to the United States in 1973? What was one lasting effect of the embargo?*

2. *Americans reacted differently to President Carter's ideas on energy. What do you think of them? Why? What, if anything, are you doing to conserve energy? Explain.*

3. *Some people have suggested that the best way to cut down on the use of gasoline would be to limit the amount a person could buy. Such a system was used in the U.S. during World War II. This system was called* rationing. *Talk to someone who remembers gasoline rationing. Find out how it worked, and what the person thought about it. Does he or she think rationing would work now? Have each class member report. Then add up the number of answers for and against rationing.*

689

Chapter 35

Old and Still Young

No one had ever seen a birthday party quite like this one. Red, white, and blue were the colors of the day. Some people wore red, white, and blue pants. Others had red, white, and blue sneakers. One man even sported a red, white, and blue beard.

It was July 4, 1976. The United States was 200 years old. It was a day for young and old to celebrate, all across the land.

In Philadelphia, people stood in line for hours to see the original Declaration of Independence. One woman came in an 18th-century gown. At 12:45 P.M. on July 4, the famous document was read aloud. Some listeners wept with emotion.

In New York, six million people lined the Hudson River. They gazed in wonder as hundreds of sailing boats moved past in a spectacular parade.

In Baltimore, bombs fell again on historic Fort McHenry. They were make-believe bombs, this time. They were re-enacting the 1814 battle during which Francis Scott Key wrote "The Star-Spangled Banner." By dawn's early light, 30,000 people were there to watch.

Small towns and villages also whooped it up. In Greenville, Ohio, the local Bicentennial queen led a parade down Broadway to the fairgrounds. Fifteen thousand people turned out to watch the pie-eating and beard-judging contests. The greased-pig contest had to be called off, though. No one had brought a pig.

Two hundred years old! This seemed like a long time. Yet most Americans thought of the U.S. as being a young nation. And in some ways it was. Compared to the much older countries of Europe, Africa, and Asia, the U.S. was indeed young. Its people were youthful in spirit. In fact, almost half the people in the U.S. were under the age of 25.

Youthful spirit marked many of the 1976 events. Still, the grand holiday had

its serious side too. Countless newspaper articles and TV shows told of the ways the United States had grown and changed in 200 years. Here are some of them:

Land. The United States started as a small strip of land along the Atlantic Coast. In 1976 it stretched across the continent. It reached out to Alaska in the north and Hawaii in the west. It also included many outlying territories. Some of these were off the Southeastern Coast, such as Puerto Rico and the Virgin Islands. Some were off the West Coast, such as Guam, Wake, Midway, and American Samoa.

People. In 1776 there were fewer than four million Americans. In 1976 there were more than 215 million. This made the U.S. the fourth-largest country in the world.

But there were more changes than just the *number* of people. In 1776 most Americans had their roots in Northern Europe. Three out of four were British. Most were Protestant. Though there were many Indians, most Americans did not count them as part of the U.S. Though there were many blacks, most were slaves. Some blacks did play important parts in the young nation. On the whole, though, the country was run by white males of British origin.

In 1976 there were Americans from just about every part of the world. Almost 50 million — or one out of four — were Roman Catholic. More than six million were Jewish.

Americans of many different backgrounds had a share in running the country. There were Catholic mayors and Jewish mayors, Italian mayors and Polish mayors, black mayors and white mayors. There were U.S. Senators whose ancestors came from Asia and one whose ancestors came from Africa. There was at least one governor of Mexican-American heritage. Even so, not all groups felt that they had a fair share in running the country. Blacks, Indians, Mexican Americans, and others were still struggling to make their voices heard more directly.

Wealth. In 1776 most Americans were farmers or craftspeople. But in the 19th century, the U.S. began to change. Factories sprang up. Cities spread as millions of immigrants came to America from Europe and Asia. The United States grew wealthy. But the wealth was spread unevenly. Some people became rich. Most people had to work very hard for a living.

By 1976 the wealth was spread more widely. Yet millions of Americans were living in slums. And the wealth of industry had created serious problems. Filth poured into many lakes and rivers. Dirty air sometimes made people ill. The nation's founders would have been amazed by some of the problems. Yet they would have been glad to know that Americans were working to put things right.

Power. Americans were strong enough to fight for their independence in 1776. But the U.S. was not a strong country. The big powers of the world were then in Europe. For years the U.S. tried to stay off by itself.

By 1900 the U.S. was becoming a world power. Then it helped win two world wars. In 1945, at the end of World War II, its power looked almost limitless. The U.S. was then the only country with an atomic bomb. Its businesses began spreading around the globe. U.S. culture

— TV shows, for example — followed close behind. U.S. astronauts went farther still — to the moon.

By 1976 people were arguing about the way the U.S. used its power. Some said it used its power fairly. Others said it pushed small countries around. Still others said it had become too friendly with Communist countries such as the Soviet Union and China. But most Americans agreed that the U.S. had great power. They knew that U.S. actions affected the whole world.

One remaining question was: How much of an effect did it have? Many people pointed out that there were limits to U.S. power. By 1976 other countries had gained nuclear weapons. The Vietnam War had shown that military power wasn't everything. Supplies of oil depended partly on the goodwill of other countries. The value of the U.S. dollar depended on how much other countries' money was worth too.

On the nation's 200th birthday, people also thought of the future. They talked about some problems the U.S. might face in the years to come.

Equality. Blacks, women, and other groups were still seeking a more equal share in American life. So were poor people and old people.

Energy and the environment. The U.S. was looking for new sources of energy. At the same time, it was trying to clean up pollution. This, some leaders said, would require changes in the way people lived.

World tensions. The threat of nuclear war still hung over the world. The U.S., the Soviet Union, and at least four other nations had the ability to make nuclear weapons. More nations sought

this ability. A search was on for ways to ease the dangers to world peace.

The United States was now in its third century. What would tomorrow bring? Problems lay ahead, certainly. So did opportunities. The problems and opportunities would surely bring changes in their wake. But then, dealing with change was part of what life in the United States was all about. "It is difficult to be an American," the prizewinning U.S. author Thornton Wilder once said. "Americans are still engaged in inventing what it is to be an American."

A Second Look. . . .

1. *List three ways the United States has changed in the 200 years since the Declaration of Independence.*

2. *Some people say that the nation's growth must be slowed down to save the environment. Others say that growth is the only way to assure jobs for all. Which do you think is more important — more jobs or a cleaner environment? Do you believe that the two goals are really in conflict? Discuss.*

3. *Pretend it is New Year's Eve, 2000. You are waiting for the century to begin. In your diary, write a one-page description of what life is like on the eve of the 21st century. Think about the things that would concern you: work, fashion, transportation, recreation. Try to imagine what you and the world will be like by the year 2000.*

"What do you think endures?" American poet Walt Whitman once asked. "Do you think the greatest city endures?" Ernst Haas' photo of a reflection in a shop window (right) seems to be asking the same question. Whitman gave an answer to his question: "The greatest city is that which has the greatest men and women."

Looking Back: Yesterday, Today, Tomorrow

	A	B	C	D	E
	July 1, 1968	July 1, 1970	July 1, 1972	July 1, 1974	July 1, 1976	July 1, 1978

Putting Events in Order

Chapters 28 through 35 have described recent events in American history. Ten events of this period are listed here. Your job is to match each event to the correct period shown on the timeline. On a piece of paper, number from **1** to **10**. After each number, write the letter of the two-year period within which the event occurred. There may be an event that occurred during several periods, not just one. In that case, write letter **S.**

1. Richard Nixon visits China.

2. Oil blackens the beaches of Santa Barbara, California.

3. Richard Nixon resigns as President.

4. Neil Armstrong and Edwin Aldrin walk on the moon.

5. Arab nations place an embargo on oil to the U.S.

6. Burglars break into Democratic party headquarters in Washington, D.C.

7. President Jimmy Carter submits his energy plan to Congress.

8. The Senate begins holding special hearings on Watergate.

9. The United States is 200 years old.

10. The population of the South grows much faster than the population of the Northeast.

Interpreting a Source

The year 1976 was a special one for a North Texas woman named Mattie White. As the U.S. celebrated its 200th birthday, White turned 100. She had made her home in or near the prairie town of McKinney for all 100 years. Here is what she told Newsweek *reporters in 1976:*

The country is very different from ... when it was all prairie with the native grasses and wildflowers. That was before the days of the oil wells. You could see it when we went down and played in the pasture and got our feet all oily. When we got home, we had to have a bath first thing before we went in....

I come from very poor people. My

father came out here from Tennessee in [18]51 with his wife and one baby and five Negroes.... It wasn't too long till the Negroes were free. My father provided for his — he bought each one a small farm, 50 acres [20 hectares], I think. Maybe 60. That left him with the responsibility of a family, and there was a bunch of us by then. Eight of us, all hungry at the same time....

The farm had to supply everything. Of course, we all worked in the fields. We made long furrows with little hand plows.... In one end we put in sweet potatoes, and at the other end turnips, and put white potatoes under the house.... And everybody had a bunch of hogs, because that's what we lived on. Hog meat. Good and greasy.

My father passed away before I remember. My mother, when she came from Tennessee, brought one Negro woman to be her maid. This old Negro ... stayed with my mother. I really didn't know too much from my mother about what I was going to wear or when I was going to have a bath. I didn't have to mind my mother but I had to mind that Negro....

The most important thing in those early times was making a living. For amusement — well, everybody went to church Sunday morning, whether you wanted to or not.... And then in the summer you had camp meetings.[1] Everybody stretched a tent around.... The preachers came from all around the country, and we always had something good to eat because the women always

[1]*Camp meetings* are religious gatherings held outdoors or in a tent and often lasting several days. They were much more common earlier in this century than they are today.

Mattie White at 100

695

brought their best food to the camp. They always said that the men came to trade cattle and farm instruments; the women came to talk about their babies and trade recipes; the young people came to court, and the children came to play. And they stayed a week and had the best time ever....

Then we moved back to McKinney, and I've been here ever since. I never married. Nobody ever asked me. In the early days, you know, we didn't know much about doctors, and little babies weren't very well taken care of, and most of them didn't live through the second summer. And I always said I knew my husband died in the second summer.

I lived with my mother, who was an invalid, until she passed away, and then I went to work. And you know, in those days it was not the same for women to work downtown, out in the public.... Working downtown in the public was not the thing for first-class women to do.

But it never bothered me any, because I worked for some very fine men. It was a dry-goods store,[2] and I had charge of the piece goods.[3] We bought from Dallas. We went in Model T's, and we got over the ground pretty good — just about as good as any new Cadillac. I got paid $12.50 a week.... While I was working that way, I built a house. A frame house, seven rooms — a good-size house. And it was nice inside. All pretty. And I paid for it on $12.50 a week.

McKinney has changed a great deal, of course, but not as much as other towns around. In fact, we kind of like it to stay the way it is. We are not so strong on all this progress. We like it because we all know each other.... You know what ruined the country? The first world war. The bigwigs in Washington sent all the damn Yankees south and all the Southern people north, and we haven't gotten it straightened out yet.

In the early days, we were more of a friend to each other. The thing is now in America, everybody is looking out for himself. Everybody seems to be living off the government. I'm doing it, and all the rest of the poor people like me are snatching and grabbing and telling stories to get more.

But I don't think the country's in a real bad way. We've had bad days and good days before.... What's the point of moaning and looking back? Look *forward*. Why, just think of the things that's going to happen in the next hundred years. Oh, I'd love to see it.

1. *Name three changes Mattie White has seen in her lifetime. What is her reaction to these changes? Does she seem to like change or not?*

2. *What does she mean by saying that "we were more of a friend to each other" in the old days? Based on what you now know of U.S. history, do you think she is right? Why or why not?*

3. *Imagine that you are living in the 2060's and have just turned 100 years old. Write a one-page essay looking back on your life. What changes have taken place during your lifetime? Do you think they are changes for the better? Are you proud to be an American? Why or why not?*

---

[2]*Dry goods* are clothing and similar items of trade. A *dry-goods store* is one which sells such items.

[3]*Piece goods* are fabrics made or sold in standard lengths.

Shifts in U.S. Population, 1970-1975

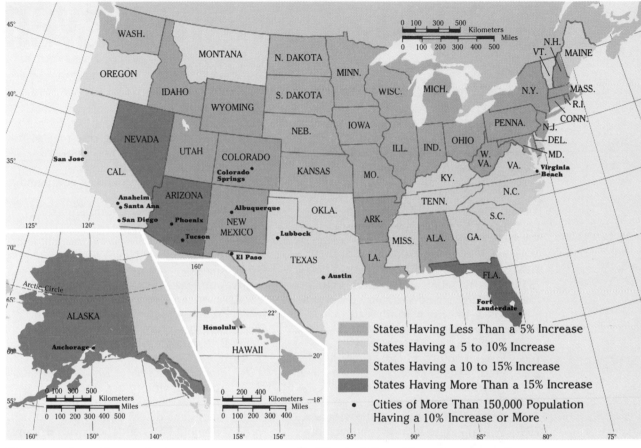

States Having Less Than a 5% Increase

States Having a 5 to 10% Increase

States Having a 10 to 15% Increase

States Having More Than a 15% Increase

• Cities of More Than 150,000 Population Having a 10% Increase or More

Sharpening Your Skills

The map on this page shows some shifts in the U.S. population between 1970 and 1975. Study the map, then answer the questions.

1. Which state grew the most between 1970 and 1975: Connecticut, Massachusetts, New Hampshire, Rhode Island, or Vermont?

2. Which grew the least: Alabama, Florida, Georgia, Mississippi, or South Carolina?

3. Most of the cities shown on the map are located in the South or Southwest. Which is farthest north?

4. Consider the following events: (a) In 1971 an earthquake struck southern California, taking 62 lives and causing billions of dollars in property damage. (b) In 1968 oil was discovered in a part of Alaska facing the Arctic Ocean. (c) In 1977 a flash flood took the lives of 68 people in Johnstown, Pennsylvania. Which event do you think had an effect on the growth pattern shown on the map? Why?

Chronology of Key Events

Pre-Colonial and Colonial America

20,000 B.C., Start of Indian civilizations in America (date approximate).
4 B.C., Birth of Christ.

900 A.D., Golden Age of Mayas ends.
1492, Columbus "discovers" America.
1497-1498, John Cabot explores North America.
1500, Aztec civilization flourishes.
1519-1522, Magellan's crew circles globe.
1540-1542, Francisco Vásquez de Coronado explores American Southwest.
1565, Spain sets up St. Augustine.
1607, British arrive at Jamestown.
1608, French colony of Quebec founded.
1619, First black people reach Jamestown.
1620, Mayflower lands at Plymouth.
1630, Puritans found Massachusetts Bay.
1636, Roger Williams founds Providence.
1681, William Penn founds Pennsylvania.
1732, James Oglethorpe and others found colony of Georgia.
1754, Start of French and Indian War.

Background to Revolution

1759, British victory at Quebec.
1763, French and Indian War ends.
1764, British Parliament passes Sugar Act.
1765, Parliament passes Stamp Act.
1766, Stamp Act repealed.
1766, Parliament passes Declaratory Act.
1768, British troops sent to Boston.
1769, Father Serra builds San Diego mission.
1770, Boston Massacre takes place.
1772, Committees of correspondence formed.

1773, Boston tea party.
1774, First Continental Congress meets.
1775, Battle of Lexington and Concord.
1775, Battle of Bunker Hill.
1775, George Washington takes command of Continental Army.
1776, Thomas Paine's *Common Sense* appears in Philadelphia.
1776, Declaration of Independence signed.
1776, British capture New York.
1776, American victory at Trenton.
1777, American victory at Princeton.
1777, American victory at Saratoga.
1778, French-American alliance formed.
1778, British capture Savannah, Georgia.
1780, British capture Charleston, South Carolina.
1780, American victory at King's Mountain.
1781, American victory at Cowpens.
1781, Articles of Confederation take effect.
1781, Americans defeat British at Yorktown.
1783, Treaty of Paris ends war with Britain.

A Nation Is Formed

1785, U.S. Congress sets up coinage system.
1786, Shays' Rebellion.
1787, Northwest Ordinance passed.
1787, Constitutional Convention meets.
1788, U.S. Constitution ratified.
1789, U.S. Constitution takes effect.
1789, George Washington becomes first President of the United States.
1791, Bill of Rights takes effect.
1791, Vermont enters Union.
1792, Kentucky enters Union.
1793, Eli Whitney invents cotton gin.
1794, Whiskey Rebellion put down.

1795, Jay's Treaty ratified by U.S. Senate.
1796, Tennessee enters Union.
1796, Washington delivers farewell address.
1797, John Adams becomes second President.
1798, Alien and Sedition Acts passed.
1798, Kentucky Resolutions.
1801, John Marshall becomes Chief Justice.
1801, House of Representatives decides Presidential election.
1801, Thomas Jefferson becomes third President.

Federalists and Democratic-Republicans

1803, Ohio enters Union.
1803, *Marbury v. Madison.*
1803, Louisiana Purchase expands size of the U.S.
1804, Twelfth Amendment ratified.
1804-1806, Lewis and Clark expedition.
1805-1807, Zebulon Pike expeditions.
1807, U.S. ship *Chesapeake* attacked.
1807, Robert Fulton perfects steamboat.
1807, Embargo Act.
1808, Further importation of slaves to U.S. banned.
1809, Embargo Act repealed.
1809, James Madison becomes fourth President.
1811, Battle of Tippecanoe.
1811, National Road is begun.
1812-1814, U.S. and Britain fight War of 1812.
1814, Battle of Bladensburg.
1814, British burn Washington, D.C.
1814, Francis Scott Key writes "The Star-Spangled Banner."
1814, Treaty of Ghent ends War of 1812.
1815, Battle of New Orleans.
1816, Indiana enters Union.
1817, James Monroe becomes fifth President.
1817, Mississippi enters Union.
1818, Illinois enters Union.
1818, Andrew Jackson invades Florida.
1819, *McCulloch v. Maryland.*
1819, Alabama enters Union.
1819, Treaty gives East Florida to U.S.
1820, Missouri Compromise.

1820, Maine enters Union.
1821, Missouri enters Union.
1821, U.S. settlers start colony in Texas.
1823, Monroe Doctrine issued.
1824, *Gibbons v. Ogden.*
1825, John Quincy Adams becomes sixth President.
1828, Tariff of Abominations passed.
1829, Andrew Jackson becomes seventh President.

Jacksonian Democracy

1831, First issue of *The Liberator.*
1831, Nat Turner leads slave uprising.
1832, Congress passes Tariff of 1832.
1832, Ordinance of Nullification.
1832, Jackson refuses to renew charter for Bank of the United States.
1833, Congress passes lower tariff.
1833, Congress passes Force Act.
1836, Texas declares independence from Mexico.
1836, Arkansas enters Union.
1837, Martin Van Buren becomes eighth President.
1837, Michigan enters Union.
1837, Period of economic depression begins.
1837, Horace Mann begins school reform.
1841, William Henry Harrison becomes ninth President; Jacksonian Era ends.

Years of Expansion

1841, President William Henry Harrison dies in office; John Tyler becomes 10th President.
1845, Annexation of Texas.
1845, Florida enters Union.
1845, James K. Polk becomes 11th President.
1846, U.S. and Britain sign treaty settling Oregon border.
1846, Iowa enters Union.
1846, U.S. declares war on Mexico.
1846, U.S. settlers in California declare independence from Mexico.
1847, U.S. wins the Battle of Buena Vista.

1848, Discovery of gold in California.

1848, Mexican Cession adds all of California, Nevada, Utah, and parts of other territories to U.S.

1848, Seneca Falls convention.

1848, Wisconsin enters Union.

1849, Zachary Taylor becomes 12th President.

1849, California Gold Rush.

1849, Francis Parkman's *The Oregon Trail* is published.

1850, Compromise of 1850.

1850, California enters Union.

1850, Zachary Taylor dies in office; Millard Fillmore becomes 13th President.

A House Divided

1851, Harriet Beecher Stowe writes *Uncle Tom's Cabin.*

1853, Franklin Pierce becomes 14th President.

1853, Gadsden Purchase.

1854, Commodore Matthew Perry "opens" Japan to trade with the U.S.

1854, Kansas-Nebraska Act passed.

1854, Republican party formed.

1856, Fighting breaks out in Kansas.

1856, Attack on Senator Charles Sumner in U.S. Senate.

1857, James Buchanan becomes 15th President.

1857, Dred Scott decision.

1858, Lincoln-Douglas debates.

1858, Minnesota enters Union.

1859, John Brown's raid on Harpers Ferry.

1859, Edwin L. Drake drills first oil well near Titusville, Pennsylvania.

1859, Oregon enters Union.

1860, South Carolina secedes.

1861, Kansas enters Union.

1861, Confederate States of America formed.

1861, Abraham Lincoln becomes 16th President.

1861, Firing on Fort Sumter; Civil War begins.

1861, First Battle of Bull Run.

1862, Seven days' campaign against Richmond.

1862, Battle of Antietam.

1863, Emancipation Proclamation issued.

1863, Siege of Vicksburg, Mississippi.

1863, Battle of Gettysburg.

1863, West Virginia enters Union.

1863, Lincoln delivers Gettysburg Address.

1864, Union armies occupy Atlanta and Savannah, Georgia.

1864, Nevada enters Union.

1865, Freedmen's Bureau created.

1865, Lee surrenders to Grant, ending Civil War.

1865, Abraham Lincoln assassinated; Andrew Johnson becomes 17th President.

The Nation Reunites

1865-1877, Reconstruction Era.

1865, Thirteenth Amendment ratified, ending slavery.

1866, Radical Republicans gain control of Congress.

1866, Ku Klux Klan founded.

1867, Nebraska enters Union.

1867, U.S. purchases Alaska from Russia.

1867, Congressional plan of Reconstruction put into effect.

1867, Tenure of Office Act passed.

1867, "Granger" movement started.

1868, Fourteenth Amendment ratified, insuring black Americans "equal protection of the laws."

1868, President Andrew Johnson impeached by House.

1868, Johnson found not guilty by Senate.

1869, Ulysses S. Grant becomes 18th President.

1869, First transcontinental railroad completed.

1869, Knights of Labor organized.

1869, National Woman Suffrage Association formed.

1870, Fifteenth Amendment ratified, guaranteeing black men the vote.

1872, Susan B. Anthony arrested for breaking election law.

1873, Bessemer process of making steel put into wide use.

1875, San Francisco's "Little China" grows to population of 47,000.

1876, Colorado enters Union.

1876, Centennial Exhibition held.

1876, Alexander Graham Bell invents telephone.

1876, Presidential election disputed.

1877, Rutherford B. Hayes becomes 19th President.

1877, Federal troops withdrawn from South.

1877, Nez Perces attempt escape to Canada.

Creating New Wealth

1877, Thomas A. Edison invents phonograph.

1879, Edison develops electric light bulb.

1880-1890, Immigration to U.S. swells.

1881, Tennessee passes first post-war law segregating black people on trains.

1881, Tuskegee Institute founded.

1881, James Garfield becomes 20th President.

1881, James Garfield assassinated; Chester A. Arthur becomes 21st President.

1882, First electric power station built.

1882, Chinese Exclusion Act.

1882, Standard Oil Trust organized.

1885, Grover Cleveland becomes 22nd President.

1886, American Federation of Labor (AFL) is organized.

1889, Benjamin Harrison becomes 23rd President.

1889, Washington, Montana, North Dakota, and South Dakota enter Union.

1890, Wyoming and Idaho enter Union.

1890, Sherman Antitrust Act passed.

1890, End of the frontier.

1892, Populists form People's party.

1893, Grover Cleveland becomes 24th President.

1893-1897, Economic depression in the U.S.

1893, American Railway Union organized.

1894, Pullman strike.

1895, Guglielmo Marconi develops first radio.

1896, William Jennings Bryan delivers "Cross of Gold" speech.

1896, Utah enters Union.

1896, *Plessy v. Ferguson.*

1897, William McKinley becomes 25th President.

The Progressive Years

1898, U.S.S. *Maine* sinks in Havana harbor.

1898, U.S. victory in Spanish-American War.

1898, Spain signs Treaty of Paris, giving Puerto Rico, the Philippines, Guam to U.S.

1898, U.S. annexes Hawaiian Islands.

1899, John Hay announces Open Door Policy.

1900, Boxer Rebellion in China.

1900, William McKinley re-elected.

1901, William McKinley assassinated; Theodore Roosevelt becomes nation's 26th President.

1902, U.S. gives Cuba its independence.

1902, U.S. government lawyers file suit against Northern Securities Company.

1902, Theodore Roosevelt attempts to settle nationwide coal strike.

1903, Lincoln Steffens' "The Shame of Minneapolis" is published.

1903, U.S. signs lease with Cuba for naval base at Guantanamo Bay.

1903, U.S. acquires Canal Zone in Panama.

1903, Orville and Wilbur Wright make first airplane flight.

1903, Henry Ford forms an auto company.

1904, U.S. construction begins on Panama Canal.

1904, Dr. William Gorgas begins work to wipe out yellow fever in Panama.

1904, Theodore Roosevelt re-elected.

1905, W.E.B. DuBois helps to found Niagara Movement.

1906, Congress passes Pure Food and Drug Act.

1906, Meat Inspection Act passed.

1907, Oklahoma enters Union.

1907-1908, "Gentlemen's Agreement" restricts immigration from Japan to U.S.

1908, Muller v. Oregon.

1908, Henry Ford develops Model T.

1909, William Howard Taft becomes 27th President.

1909, National Association for the Advancement of Colored People (NAACP) formed.

1910-1920, Motion picture industry takes root in Hollywood, California.

1912, New Mexico and Arizona enter Union.

1912, Progressive party formed.

1913, Woodrow Wilson becomes 28th President.

1913, Sixteenth Amendment ("Income Tax" Amendment) ratified.

1913, Seventeenth Amendment ratified, allowing direct election of U.S. Senators.

1914, Panama Canal opened to traffic.

The U.S. and World War I

1914, Archduke Francis Ferdinand and his wife assassinated.

1914, World War I begins.

1915, German submarine sinks *Lusitania.*

1916, Woodrow Wilson re-elected.

1916, Louis Brandeis named to U.S. Supreme Court.

1917, Germany renews submarine warfare.

1917, Zimmermann Note incident.

1917, U.S. enters World War I.

1917, Congress passes Selective Service Act.

1917, Bolshevik Revolution in Russia.

1917, Russia withdraws from the war.

1918, Wilson issues Fourteen Points.

1918, Fighting at Château-Thierry.

1918, Argonne offensive successful.

1918, Armistice ends World War I.

1919, Eighteenth Amendment ("Prohibition" Amendment) ratified.

1919, Chicago race riots.

1919, Boston police strike.

1919, United Mine Workers strike.

1919, U.S. Communist party formed.

1919-1920, "Palmer raids" conducted.

1919, Treaty of Versailles signed, setting up League of Nations.

1919, U.S. Senate rejects treaty.

The "Roaring Twenties"

1920, Harlem Renaissance begins (approx.).

1920, Nineteenth Amendment ("Women's Suffrage" Amendment) ratified.

1920, First regular radio broadcast on KDKA.

1921, Warren Harding becomes 29th President.

1921, First "Quota Law" passed, limiting immigration.

1921, Sacco-Vanzetti trial.

1922, Benito Mussolini takes power in Italy.

1923, Warren Harding dies in office; Calvin Coolidge becomes 30th President.

1923, Teapot Dome oil reserve scandal.

1924, Josef Stalin begins taking power as dictator of Soviet Union.

1924, New Quota Law passed, further limiting immigration.

1924, Ten millionth Model T built.

1927, Charles Lindbergh flies Atlantic.

1927, Babe Ruth sets home-run record.

1927, Sacco and Vanzetti executed.

1927, First talking movie produced.

1929, Herbert Hoover becomes 31st President.

1929, "Black Tuesday" stock market crash marks beginning of Great Depression.

Turmoil of the Thirties

1930, Hoover begins public works program.

1931, Japan invades Manchuria.

1932, "Bonus Army" encampment.

1932, Worst year of the Depression; number of jobless people rises to 13 million.

1933, Adolf Hitler takes office in Germany, begins campaign against German Jews.

1933, Twentieth Amendment is ratified, defines terms of President, Vice-President.

1933, Franklin Roosevelt becomes 32nd President.

1933, Frances Perkins is named Secretary of Labor, becoming first woman Cabinet member.

1933, First "Hundred Days" of New Deal.

1933, Albert Einstein immigrates to U.S.

1933, Fiorello LaGuardia elected mayor of New York City.

1933, Twenty-first Amendment ratified, repealing Prohibition.

1933, U.S. recognizes Soviet Union.

1934, Drought creates Dust Bowl in Midwest.

1934, U.S. promises independence to the Philippines.

1934, Hitler prepares Germany for war.

1935, New Deal's Second "Hundred Days."

1935, U.S. Supreme Court declares National Industrial Recovery Act unconstitutional.

1935-1937, Neutrality Acts passed.

1935, Hitler begins program of mass murder of German Jews.

1936, Roosevelt wins second term.

1936, Agricultural Adjustment Act ruled unconstitutional.

1936, Germany seizes Rhineland.

1937, United Automobile Workers stage a sit-down strike in Michigan.

1937-1938, Business slump in U.S.

1937, Farm Security Agency set up.

1938, Nazi Germany takes control of Austria.

1938, Joe Louis knocks out Max Schmeling.

1938, Munich Pact.

1939, Nazi Germany takes most of Czechoslovakia.

War on Several Continents

1939, Nazi Germany invades Poland; World War II begins in Europe.

1940, Netherlands, Belgium, and France fall to Nazi Germany.

1940, Franklin Roosevelt sends Britain 50 U.S. destroyers.

1940, First peacetime draft in U.S.

1940, Franklin Roosevelt becomes first President to be elected to third term.

1941, Congress passes Lend-Lease Act.

1941, Germany invades Soviet Union.

1941, Japan occupies French Indochina.

1941, Japan attacks U.S. naval base at Pearl Harbor; U.S. enters war.

1942, Internment of Japanese Americans.

1943, Manhattan Project begun.

1943, Allies invade Italy.

1944, D-Day invasion of Normandy.

1944, Allies liberate France and Belgium.

1944, Roosevelt wins a fourth term.

1945, Yalta Conference.

1945, Franklin Roosevelt dies in office; Harry Truman becomes 33rd President.

1945, Allies discover Nazi death camps.

1945, Berlin falls to Allies; Germany surrenders; World War II ends in Europe.

1945, San Francisco Conference drafts charter for United Nations.

1945. First atomic bomb exploded in test at Alamogordo, New Mexico.

1945, Potsdam Conference.

1945, Atomic bombs dropped on Hiroshima and Nagasaki, Japan.

1945, Japan surrenders to end World War II.

Peace, Plenty, and Cold War

1945, War crimes trials open in Germany.

1946, Philippines gain independence from U.S.

1946, Most wage and price controls ended.

1947, Truman Doctrine announced.

1947, Marshall Plan proclaimed.

1947, Jackie Robinson joins Brooklyn Dodgers.

1948, Communists take power in Czechoslovakia.

1948, New nation of Israel created.

1948-1949, Berlin airlift.

1948, U.S. sales of television sets begin to skyrocket.

1949, Soviets explode atomic bomb.

1949, Communist armies win civil war in mainland China.

1950, Senator Joseph McCarthy makes charges of Communist influence in U.S. State Department.

1950, North Korea attacks South Korea; U.N. troops go to aid of South Korea.

1951, Twenty-second Amendment ratified, setting two-term limit on Presidency.

1951, Truman-MacArthur controversy.

1952, U.S. tests hydrogen bomb.

1953, Dwight Eisenhower becomes 34th President

1953, Korean armistice signed.

1953-1954, Army-McCarthy hearings.

1954, Brown v. Board of Education.

1954, Vietnam gains independence from France and is divided into two parts.

1955, First U.S military advisers sent to Vietnam.

1955-1956, Montgomery bus boycott.

1956, Congress passes Highway Act of 1956, providing for interstate road network.

1957, School crisis in Little Rock, Arkansas.

1957, Soviet Union puts artificial satellite in orbit around Earth.

1959, Fidel Castro comes to power in Cuba.

1959, Soviet leader Nikita Khrushchev visits U.S.

1960, Sit-in in Greensboro, North Carolina.

1960, U-2 spy plane incident; Soviet Union cancels "Big Four" Conference.

1961, Eisenhower delivers speech on military-industrial complex.

1961, John F. Kennedy becomes 35th President.

Burdens of World Leadership

1961, Peace Corps established.

1961, Twenty-third Amendment ratified, allowing District of Columbia to vote in Presidential elections.

1961, Bay of Pigs invasion.

1961, Kennedy commits U.S. combat troops to aid of South Vietnam.

1962, U.S. astronaut orbits Earth.

1962, Cuban missile crisis.

1963, Limited Nuclear Test Ban Treaty.

1963, Betty Friedan's *The Feminine Mystique* is published.

1963, "March on Washington."

1963, John Kennedy assassinated; Lyndon Johnson becomes 36th President.

1964, Twenty-fourth Amendment ratified, banning poll tax in national elections.

1964, Civil Rights Act passed.

1964, Economic Opportunity Act passed as part of "war on poverty."

1964-1968, Rioting in urban ghettoes.

1964, Johnson wins Presidential election.

1965, Medicare established.

704 *1965,* Voting Rights Act passed.

1965, California grape strike begins.

1965, Escalation in South Vietnam.

1965, Congress ends quota system of limiting immigration.

1967, Twenty-fifth Amendment ratified, providing for Presidential succession.

1968, Tet offensive in Vietnam War.

1968, Martin Luther King assassinated.

1968, Vietnam peace talks begin in Paris.

1968, Robert Kennedy assassinated.

1968, Antiwar demonstrations at Democratic convention in Chicago.

Yesterday Becomes Today

1969, Richard Nixon becomes 37th President.

1969, Santa Barbara, California, oil spill.

1969, Vietnamization plan put into effect; U.S. troop withdrawals begin.

1969, U.S. astronauts land on the moon.

1969, Nationwide antiwar demonstration.

1970, National Environmental Policy Act.

1970, U.S., South Vietnamese forces enter Cambodia to destroy Viet Cong camps.

1970, Four students killed in antiwar protest at Kent State University.

1971, Twenty-sixth Amendment ratified, giving 18-year-olds the vote.

1972, Nixon visits mainland China.

1972, SALT agreement signed.

1972, Watergate break-in.

1972, Nixon wins a second term.

1973-1974, Senate hearings on Watergate.

1973, Vice-President Spiro Agnew resigns.

1973-1974, Arab oil embargo.

1973, Congress approves Gerald Ford as new Vice-President, replacing Agnew.

1974, Supreme Court rules Richard Nixon must surrender tapes.

1974, Nixon resigns as President; Gerald Ford becomes 38th President.

1974, Ford grants pardon to Richard Nixon.

1975, South Vietnam falls to Communists.

1976, U.S. celebrates Bicentennial.

1977, Jimmy Carter becomes 39th President.

1977, Department of Energy created.

Glossary

abolitionist. Supporter of an early 19th-century movement against slavery. Abolitionists wanted to put an immediate end to slavery.

aliens. People living in a country who are not citizens of that country.

alliance. An association or agreement between countries to promote their shared interests.

ambassadors. Officials who represent their governments in a foreign country.

ambush. A trap by which hidden persons attack an enemy by surprise.

amendments. Additions or changes to a bill, law, or constitution.

anarchists. People who believe in *anarchism,* the idea that every government is evil and unnecessary. Anarchists propose to do away with all government. Some anarchists have called for peaceful change. Others have called for revolution.

annex. To add to. Politically, to make a territory part of a nation.

anti-Semitism. Hostility toward, and/or discrimination against, Jews.

appeasement. A word sometimes used to define a nation's foreign policy. To *appease* someone is to satisfy him or her. A policy of *appeasement* is one which buys peace at almost any price.

armistice. A temporary end to fighting, agreed upon by both sides.

arms race. A rivalry between nations in which each tries to build more fighting power than the others.

assassinate. To murder by sudden or secret attack.

assembly line. A system of machines, equipment, and workers for the purpose of making something — a car, for example. In an assembly line, work passes from one operation to another in a direct line.

bail. A sum of money left with a court to guarantee that an accused person will appear for trial. The money is returned if the suspect appears in court for trial.

Black Codes. Laws passed by Southern states after the Civil War to define the legal position of former slaves. In some states, these codes said that blacks could not own land or farm on their own.

black markets. Places where goods are traded illegally. Most goods traded in black markets sell for very high prices.

blacklist. A list of people who are barred from holding jobs in an industry.

blockade. The barring of normal traffic into and out of an area.

boycott. To join together to refuse to deal with a nation, organization, store, or person. Most boycotts are staged to show disapproval or to force new terms.

buy on margin. To purchase shares of stock by making a small down payment. In such a sale, a buyer puts down only a percentage, or *margin,* of the stock's total value.

Cabinet. A group of officials who meet with the President of the United States and help run the Executive Branch of the government. Most Cabinet members head departments of government. The U.S. Constitution does *not* require the President to have a Cabinet. But Cabinets have existed since George Washington's first term.

calculators. Machines used to perform mathematical tasks.

capitalism. An economic system in which most business is carried on by individuals and corporations, rather than by government. Capitalism is often referred to as the *free-enterprise system.*

carpetbaggers. Northerners who went south in the late 1860's to help black people or to go into business. Many Southerners claimed that carpetbaggers took unfair advantage of unsettled conditions.

census. A count of the national population. In the U.S., a census has been taken every 10 years since 1790.

centennial. A 100th anniversary. In 1876 the U.S. celebrated its Centennial. In 1976 the nation celebrated its *Bicentennial.*

cession. Something given to another. In 1847 Mexico signed over to the U.S. land later known as the *Mexican Cession.*

chattel. An item of movable property. A slave was considered chattel and could be sold at will by his or her master.

checks and balances. A system which gives each branch of government some ability to counter the powers of the other branches. Congress checks the power of the President; the Supreme Court checks the power of Congress; etc.

citizen. A person who owes loyalty to a government and is guaranteed the privileges and protection of that government.

civilian. A person who is not a member of the armed services.

coexistence. Living in peace with each other. In the mid-1950's, the term was often applied to relations between the United States and the Soviet Union.

Cold War. A conflict that does not involve the active use of military force. The term is often used to describe the period after World War II when the U.S. and the Soviet Union were competing for power around the world.

communism. A plan for arranging society in such a way that all land and businesses are owned by everyone together. However, none of the world's Communist nations operates under this plan in a pure form. In practice, Communist governments have generally been forms of dictatorship. Under such governments, most business and land have been owned and controlled by the state.

"company town." A community built and controlled by a particular business company. In the 19th century, for example, many workers had to live in company houses and buy their food, clothing, etc., in company-run stores.

compromise. An agreement reached between two or more people or groups in which each side settles for less than it originally wanted.

confederacy. A loosely organized union of people, parties, or states. During the late 18th century, the term referred to the union that existed under the Articles of Confederation. During the 19th century, the term referred to the central government of the 11 Southern states that seceded from the U.S. in 1860 and 1861.

Congress. The lawmaking branch of the U.S. government. Congress is divided into two houses — the House of Representatives and the Senate.

consul. A government officer who protects and supports the businesses and the needs of citizens of his or her nation in a foreign country.

consumers. People who buy or use products and services such as clothing, books, food, electricity, etc.

containment. The policy of trying to stop the spread of communism. In the late 1940's and early 1950's, U.S. leaders hoped that containment would weaken the Communist system.

credit cards. Cards which allow consumers to buy goods and services on a "buy-now, pay-later" basis.

delegates. People selected by a group as representatives to a convention.

democracy. A government in which the supreme power is held by the people.

deport. To send out of the country.

depression. A period in which business is depressed (made less active). In a depression, prices are generally low, and many workers are out of jobs.

détente. A French word meaning the easing of strained relations or tensions between countries. Often used to describe relations between the U.S. and the Soviet Union in the 1970's.

dictator. A ruler with complete power

over the government he or she heads.

diplomats. People skilled at handling problems and relations between nations. Also, government officials who represent their nation in other nations. The management of affairs between nations is known as *diplomacy.*

discrimination. The act of treating people differently, usually because of their membership in a particular group. Discrimination often results in denying people equal rights.

doctrines. Beliefs and teachings of a church, political movement, or other group.

doughboys. Members of the U.S. infantry during World War I.

"doves." Americans of the late 1960's who preferred peaceful settlement of the Vietnam War to a larger U.S. role in the fighting. Opposite of "hawks."

drought. A long spell of dry weather.

due process of law. An orderly set of rules for bringing a lawsuit or person accused of a crime to trial. The Fifth and 14th Amendments to the Constitution guarantee *due process.* They say that no federal or state government may take away a citizen's life, liberty, or property without following fair legal procedures.

editorial. An article which expresses the *opinion* of an editor or owner of a newspaper or magazine.

electoral vote. The vote cast by people specially chosen to elect the President and Vice-President of the U.S. The electoral vote of each state is determined by its population.

electors. People chosen to select the President and the Vice-President of the U.S. Today an elector usually votes for the candidates who receive the most votes in his or her state.

emancipation. Release from slavery.

embargo. A ban on commerce and trade.

emigrant. A person who leaves his or her nation to settle elsewhere.

energy crisis. A term used in the 1970's to describe the shortage of available fuels throughout the world.

environmentalists. People concerned with protecting the human *environment* — especially air, land, food, and water — from pollution.

escalation. An increase in number, intensity, and/or scope of a military program.

"Establishment." A ruling class or controlling group within a society.

Executive Branch. The branch of government responsible for enforcing the laws of the land. In the U.S., the Executive Branch is made up of the President, who is the Chief Executive, and all the departments under the President.

exports. Merchandise sent to a foreign country for purposes of trade.

feminists. Supporters of equal rights for women.

foreign policy. The idea or plan behind a government's dealings with other nations.

fraud. Deceit or trickery.

free-soilers. Followers of a political party active in the elections of 1848 and 1852. Like abolitionists, free-soilers opposed slavery. But unlike them, free-soilers simply wanted to prevent the spread of slavery into the western lands.

Freedmen's Bureau. An agency set up by the U.S. Army in March 1865 to resettle blacks on abandoned lands in the South. The bureau also provided blacks with schools and other benefits.

fugitive. A person who runs away or tries to escape.

gallows. A frame from which criminals are hanged.

general strike. A work stoppage by employees of the main industries of an area. Such strikes may be nationwide, statewide, or citywide. They are usually staged for the purpose of improving working conditions.

generation. All the people born at about the same time. Also, the time it takes, about 30 years, for one group to grow up and have children of its own.

generation gap. Differences in attitudes between one generation and another — for example, between parents and their children.

ghetto. In the U.S., a section of a city in which one religious or ethnic group is dominant. Ghettoes are occupied mainly by poor people.

global village. A term used to describe today's "small" world, in which television and other means of communication have brought places closer together.

grand jury. A group of citizens who decide whether there is enough reason to hold a suspected lawbreaker for trial.

"Grange." A popular name for a farmers' organization formed in 1867. Formally, the group was known as the *Patrons of Husbandry*. Its goal was to improve life for the nation's farmers.

guerrillas. Soldiers who take part in irregular warfare. Guerrillas often carry out hit-and-run raids at unexpected times and places.

"hawks." Supporters of war or warlike policies. Opposite of "doves."

immigrant. A citizen of one country who comes to live permanently in another.

immoral. Wicked or evil.

impeach. To accuse a public official of misconduct in the performance of his or her duty. A vote to impeach always occurs *before* there can be another vote to remove the official from office.

impressment. The act of seizing for public use or forcing into public service. In the early 1800's, the term referred to the British practice of forcing U.S. sailors to serve in the British navy.

industrialism. A stage of economic development in which manufacturing is built to a high level.

inflation. The process by which the prices of goods and services go up. The result is that the same amount of money buys less and less.

international law. A set of rules accepted by many nations. Such rules govern the conduct of these nations toward one another.

internment. The act of confining a person or group, especially in wartime. During World War II, the federal government interned most Japanese Americans living on the U.S. mainland.

investigative reporting. News reporting in which a reporter acts as an investigator. He or she tries to track down all the facts surrounding an event in order to expose the truth.

isolationists. People who believe that their nation should *isolate* itself — that is, not become involved with foreign governments.

Jim Crow. A term used to describe the segregation of blacks and whites in the U.S. Jim Crow laws are no longer constitutional.

Judicial Branch. The branch of government which conducts trials and interprets the law. In the U.S., the Judicial Branch is made up of a system of courts, the highest one being the U.S. Supreme Court.

judicial review. The power of the U.S. Supreme Court to decide whether the acts of Congress and the President are allowed by the U.S. Constitution.

juvenile delinquency. A violation of the law committed by a young person or groups of young people. Also, any behavior on the part of young people that is subject to legal control.

labor unions. Organizations of wage earners. Unions represent workers' interests in dealing with employers.

ledger. A book of accounts showing money paid out and taken in by a business.

Legislative Branch. The branch of government responsible for making laws. In the U.S., the Legislative Branch is made up of the two houses of Congress — the Senate and the House of Representatives.

legislature. The lawmaking body of a government. See also *Legislative Branch*.

Lend-Lease. Supplying goods and services to an ally to aid in a common cause. In Lend-Lease agreements, there is an understanding that payment will be made at a later date.

literacy test. An exam to determine if a person can read or write. Such tests were once used as requirements for voting.

majority. More than half. Also, the number of votes by which one side is elected.

Manifest Destiny. A phrase used by many Americans in the mid-19th century. The phrase expressed the belief that the U.S. would expand from the Atlantic Ocean to the Pacific Ocean.

mass media. All means of communication which reach a large audience. The mass media are now divided into two groups: (1) the *print media* such as newspapers and magazines, and (2) the *electronic media* — radio and television.

migrant workers. Laborers who move from place to place.

militia. Citizens trained and equipped by state governments for local defense.

missiles. Objects such as weapons which are projected to a distant target. *Guided missiles* are those whose course can be changed during flight.

muckrakers. Writers or news reporters who expose misconduct.

nationalism. A feeling of love of and pride in one's country. In the U.S., nationalism has also meant the shifting of power from the states to the federal government.

nativists. Americans of the 19th century who favored the interests of native-born citizens over those of immigrants.

neutral. Not favoring either side in a quarrel, contest, or war.

nonviolent resistance. A form of peaceful protest in which people resist laws and/or customs they oppose.

nuclear weapons. Devices with explosives that can cause tremendous destruction of property and life. Such weapons work either by fission (the atomic bomb) or by fusion (the hydrogen bomb). The explosives (called *warheads*) are usually attached to missiles.

nullify. To make worthless. In law, the act by which a state sets aside a federal law and prevents its enforcement within its boundaries.

oil spill. An overflowing of oil into an ocean or other body of water.

Open Door Policy. The idea that the businesses of all nations should have equal rights within a given country. The U.S. supported such a policy in China in 1899.

pardon. Forgiveness, a release from punishment.

petition. A formal request, usually in writing, for government officials to do some particular thing.

picket. To try to influence opinion on a public matter by carrying signs in a public place. Striking workers sometimes picket to persuade people not to enter a building where a strike is taking place.

plantations. Large farms worked by resident laborers.

political refugees. People who have left a country to escape discrimination or arrest for political reasons.

poll. A survey taken among a sample of the population to measure public opinion of an issue, a candidacy, or a product.

poll tax. A tax of a fixed amount per person, once used in some states as a requirement for voting. The 24th Amendment, ratified in 1964, banned use of the poll tax in national elections.

pollution. Making or being unclean or impure.

popular sovereignty. In U.S. history, the term refers to an idea set forth in the 1850's. The idea was that settlers in Western territories should decide for themselves whether or not to allow slavery.

prejudice. A strong feeling for or against something, formed without any real knowledge or reason. The term is often used to refer to unfair attitudes about racial, ethnic, or religious groups.

primary. An election to choose party candidates for a regular election.

profit. The amount of money gained

from selling goods for more than they cost to produce. In a broader sense, profit can be any kind of benefit or advantage.

progressives. Those who favor gradual reforms of a political or social nature. Also, members of the Progressive party (1912-1916, 1924, and 1948).

propaganda. The spreading of ideas to influence someone else's opinion. Propaganda may take the form of words, pictures, music, or public demonstrations. People who spread propaganda are known as *propagandists.* They may use falsehoods to sway an audience. But not all propaganda is made up of falsehoods. Sometimes it consists of a clear and thorough presentation of the truth.

prospectors. People who explore for gold or other minerals.

psychiatry. The branch of medicine that deals with mental health.

public welfare. The well-being of the community. Also, and more commonly, the payments that governments give to people with low incomes and the system by which these payments are made.

quota system. A plan set forth in the U.S. immigration acts of 1921, 1924, and 1929. Under this system, limits were placed on how many people could come to the U.S. from each country each year.

radicals. People who want rapid and basic changes in governments or laws. Most radicals of the present day are concerned with laws governing economic and social welfare. Radicals are often distinguished from *moderates.* Moderates are people whose political ideas are not extreme.

ratify. To approve or authorize.

ration. To limit very strictly each person's share of a scarce or hard-to-get item.

rebate. A return of part of a payment. After the Civil War, railroads gave rebates to some of their customers.

Reconstruction. The act of building again. In U.S. history, the term refers to the years between 1865 and 1877. During this period, the federal government controlled the Southern states which had formerly belonged to the Confederacy.

recruits. People newly enlisted into military service.

reformers. People who speak for and carry out changes or improvements in an existing system.

register. To sign up for something formally — especially to vote.

relocation. Establishment in a new place.

repeal. To take back, withdraw, or do away with. When a law is repealed, it is no longer a law.

republic. A form of government under which the power resides in voters who elect officials to govern according to law.

reservation. Land set aside by the government for a particular purpose. Indian reservations are special areas set aside for Indian peoples after their homelands were occupied by white settlers.

satellite. A man-made object intended to circle Earth in space.

scrip. Paper money issued for temporary use.

secede. To withdraw from an organized body.

sectionalism. Concern with local or regional interests as opposed to national interests.

sedition. The spreading of ideas to make people unhappy with a government.

segregation. Practice of preventing one racial, ethnic, or class group from mixing with another.

self-sufficiency. The ability to produce what one needs without relying on outside sources.

sit-down strikes. Work stoppages in which employees occupy a factory building in the hope of winning their demands.

sit-in. A form of protest demonstration. In the sit-ins of the 1960's, black Americans occupied seats previously thought to be off-limits to members of minority groups.

slaughterhouse. An establishment

where animals are butchered for market.

social justice. The treatment of all members of a society in a fair way. Also, a movement which began in the late 19th century and called for such treatment.

socialism. An economic system in which government controls all manufacturing, transportation, commerce, and agriculture.

solar energy. Power from the sun.

speakeasies. Places where liquor was sold illegally during Prohibition.

sphere of influence. An area within a nation or territory in which another, more powerful nation has some control over business and/or government.

states' rights. The rights of the states in relation to the rights of the federal government. Believers in states' rights want to limit the powers of the federal government to those specifically listed in the U.S. Constitution. They believe that the states should have the largest possible role in the federal system.

stereotype. A fixed idea, greatly oversimplified, about a particular group. Stereotypes encourage the opinion that all members of a particular group think and act alike.

stock. Shares of ownership in a business company.

strikebreakers. People hired to replace striking workers.

suffrage. The right to vote.

sweatshops. Factories in which workers are employed for long hours at low wages and under unhealthy conditions.

tariff. A tax on goods sent from another country.

temperance. Avoidance of the use of alcoholic beverages. The word is also applied to movements to put an end to heavy drinking.

tenure. Term of holding office.

treason. The attempt to overthrow the government to which one owes loyalty. In the broadest sense, treason is the betrayal of any trust.

truce. A cease-fire or suspension of fighting agreed upon by opposing forces.

trust. A combination of business firms, usually for the purpose of limiting competition.

tyrant. A cruel and unjust ruler.

unanimous. Approved or rejected with the agreement of all.

unconstitutional. Forbidden by the U.S. Constitution. The U.S. Supreme Court makes the final decision as to just what the Constitution permits and what it does not. See also *judicial review*.

underclass. A group of people locked into poverty from one generation to the next with little or no hope of improving their condition.

"Underground Railroad." Organized aid given secretly to slaves before the Civil War. This aid helped runaway slaves to reach the North and Canada.

verdict. A decision handed down in court, usually by a jury.

veto. The President's rejection of a bill passed by Congress. The veto power is the right of a President to prevent or delay bills from becoming law.

Vietnamization. A plan put into effect in 1969 to end U.S. involvement in the Vietnam War. The plan was to turn over the defense of South Vietnam gradually to the South Vietnamese government and army.

wage and price freeze. A government order preventing wages and prices from being increased.

warrant. A document, granted by a court, that permits the police to search a person or his or her property — or to arrest someone. Warrants are granted only when there is evidence of guilt.

writ of mandamus. An order issued by a higher court to force a public official or a lower court to do something that should legally be done.

yellow journalism. News reporting of a sensational sort. One who practices yellow journalism might, for example, report horror stories mainly to improve newspaper sales. *711*

Our Nation's Leaders: Presidents, Vice-Presidents, and Secretaries of State

President	Party	State[1]	Born–Died	Vice-President	Secretary of State
1 George Washington Term: 1789-1797	None	Virginia	1732-1799	John Adams	Thomas Jefferson Edmund Randolph Timothy Pickering
2 John Adams Term: 1797-1801	Fed.	Massachusetts	1735-1826	Thomas Jefferson	Timothy Pickering John Marshall
3 Thomas Jefferson Term: 1801-1809	Rep.[2]	Virginia	1743-1826	Aaron Burr George Clinton	James Madison
4 James Madison Term: 1809-1817	Rep.[2]	Virginia	1751-1836	George Clinton Elbridge Gerry	Robert Smith James Monroe
5 James Monroe Term: 1817-1825	Rep.[2]	Virginia	1758-1831	Daniel D. Tompkins	John Quincy Adams
6 John Quincy Adams Term: 1825-1829	Rep.[2]	Massachusetts	1767-1848	John C. Calhoun	Henry Clay
7 Andrew Jackson Term: 1829-1837	Dem.	Tennessee (South Carolina)	1767-1845	John C. Calhoun Martin Van Buren	Martin Van Buren Edward Livingston Louis McLane John Forsyth
8 Martin Van Buren Term: 1837-1841	Dem.	New York	1782-1862	Richard M. Johnson	John Forsyth
9 William Henry Harrison Term: 1841	Whig	Ohio (Virginia)	1773-1841	John Tyler	Daniel Webster
10 John Tyler Term: 1841-1845	Whig[3]	Virginia	1790-1862	——————	Daniel Webster Abel P. Upshur John C. Calhoun
11 James K. Polk Term: 1845-1849	Dem.	Tennessee (North Carolina)	1795-1849	George M. Dallas	John C. Calhoun James Buchanan
12 Zachary Taylor Term: 1849-1850	Whig	Louisiana (Virginia)	1784-1850	Millard Fillmore	John M. Clayton
13 Millard Fillmore Term: 1850-1853	Whig	New York	1800-1874	——————	Daniel Webster Edward Everett
14 Franklin Pierce Term: 1853-1857	Dem.	New Hampshire	1804-1869	William R. King	William L. Marcy
15 James Buchanan Term: 1857-1861	Dem.	Pennsylvania	1791-1868	John C. Breckinridge	Lewis Cass Jeremiah S. Black
16 Abraham Lincoln Term: 1861-1865	Rep.	Illinois (Kentucky)	1809-1865	Hannibal Hamlin Andrew Johnson	William H. Seward
17 Andrew Johnson Term: 1865-1869	Rep.[4]	Tennessee (North Carolina)	1808-1875	——————	William H. Seward
18 Ulysses S. Grant Term: 1869-1877	Rep.	Illinois (Ohio)	1822-1885	Schuyler Colfax Henry Wilson	Elihu Washburne Hamilton Fish
19 Rutherford B. Hayes Term: 1877-1881	Rep.	Ohio	1822-1893	William A. Wheeler	William M. Evarts
20 James A. Garfield Term: 1881	Rep.	Ohio	1831-1881	Chester A. Arthur	James G. Blaine
21 Chester A. Arthur Term: 1881-1885	Rep.	New York (Vermont)	1829-1886	——————	James G. Blaine Frederick T. Frelinghuysen

President	Party	State[1]	Born–Died	Vice-President	Secretary of State
22 Grover Cleveland Term: 1885-1889	Dem.	New York (New Jersey)	1837-1908	Thomas A. Hendricks	Thomas F. Bayard
23 Benjamin Harrison Term: 1889-1893	Rep.	Indiana (Ohio)	1833-1901	Levi P. Morton	James G. Blaine John W. Foster
24 Grover Cleveland Term: 1893-1897	Dem.	New York (New Jersey)	1837-1908	Adlai E. Stevenson	Walter Q. Gresham Richard Olney
25 William McKinley Term: 1897-1901	Rep.	Ohio	1843-1901	Garret A. Hobart Theodore Roosevelt	John Sherman William R. Day John Hay
26 Theodore Roosevelt Term: 1901-1909	Rep.	New York	1858-1919	_____ Charles Warren Fairbanks	John Hay Elihu Root Robert Bacon
27 William H. Taft Term: 1909-1913	Rep.	Ohio	1857-1930	James S. Sherman	Philander C. Knox
28 Woodrow Wilson Term: 1913-1921	Dem.	New Jersey (Virginia)	1856-1924	Thomas R. Marshall	William Jennings Bryan Robert Lansing Bainbridge Colby
29 Warren G. Harding Term: 1921-1923	Rep.	Ohio	1865-1923	Calvin Coolidge	Charles Evans Hughes
30 Calvin Coolidge Term: 1923-1929	Rep.	Massachusetts (Vermont)	1872-1933	_____ Charles G. Dawes	Charles Evans Hughes Frank B. Kellogg
31 Herbert C. Hoover Term: 1929-1933	Rep.	California (Iowa)	1874-1964	Charles Curtis	Henry L. Stimson
32 Franklin D. Roosevelt Term: 1933-1945	Dem.	New York	1882-1945	John N. Garner Henry A. Wallace Harry S. Truman	Cordell Hull Edward R. Stettinius
33 Harry S. Truman Term: 1945-1953	Dem.	Missouri	1884-1972	_____ Alben W. Barkley	Edward R. Stettinius James F. Byrnes George C. Marshall Dean G. Acheson
34 Dwight D. Eisenhower Term: 1953-1961	Rep.	New York (Texas)	1890-1969	Richard M. Nixon	John Foster Dulles Christian A. Herter
35 John F. Kennedy Term: 1961-1963	Dem.	Massachusetts	1917-1963	Lyndon B. Johnson	Dean Rusk
36 Lyndon B. Johnson Term: 1963-1969	Dem.	Texas	1908-1973	_____ Hubert Humphrey	Dean Rusk
37 Richard M. Nixon Term: 1969-1974	Rep.	New York (California)	1913-	Spiro T. Agnew Gerald R. Ford	William P. Rogers Henry A. Kissinger
38 Gerald R. Ford[5] Term: 1974-1977	Rep.	Michigan (Nebraska)	1913-	Nelson Rockefeller	Henry A. Kissinger
39 Jimmy Carter Term: 1977-	Dem.	Georgia	1924-	Walter F. Mondale	Cyrus Vance

[1]State of residence at time of election. If state of birth is different, it is shown in parentheses.

[2]Jeffersonians called themselves Republicans. Until the Presidency of Andrew Jackson, however, the party was officially called the Democratic-Republican party.

[3]A member of the Democratic party but elected on the Whig ticket.

[4]A member of the Democratic party but elected on the National Union party ticket, which was the name taken by Republicans during the election of 1864.

[5]After charges of wrong-doing caused Spiro Agnew to resign as Vice-President on October 12, 1973, President Nixon nominated Gerald Ford to this office. Ford's appointment was approved by the Senate and House. He was sworn in on December 6, 1973. Nixon, faced with probable impeachment, resigned as President on August 9, 1974. Ford then became the first President to serve without being chosen for either the Presidency or the Vice-Presidency in a national election.

Facts About the 50 States

State	Capital	Largest City	Entry into Union		Area in Square Miles	Area in Square Kilometers	Population		Electoral Votes
			Order	Year			In 1800	In 1976	
Alabama	Montgomery	Birmingham	22	1819	51,609	133,616	1,250	3,665,000	9
Alaska	Juneau	Anchorage	49	1959	586,412	1,518,220	___	382,000	3
Arizona	Phoenix	Phoenix	48	1912	113,909	294,910	___	2,270,000	6
Arkansas	Little Rock	Little Rock	25	1836	53,104	137,486	___	2,109,000	6
California	Sacramento	Los Angeles	31	1850	158,693	410,856	___	21,520,000	45
Colorado	Denver	Denver	38	1876	104,247	269,895	___	2,583,000	7
Connecticut	Hartford	Hartford	5	1788	5,009	12,986	251,002	3,117,000	8
Delaware	Dover	Wilmington	1	1787	2,057	5,326	64,273	582,000	3
Florida	Tallahassee	Jacksonville	27	1845	58,560	151,612	___	8,421,000	17
Georgia	Atlanta	Atlanta	4	1788	58,876	152,430	162,686	4,970,000	12
Hawaii	Honolulu	Honolulu	50	1959	6,450	16,699	___	887,000	4
Idaho	Boise	Boise	43	1890	83,557	216,329	___	831,000	4
Illinois	Springfield	Chicago	21	1818	56,400	146,020	___	11,229,000	26
Indiana	Indianapolis	Indianapolis	19	1816	36,291	93,957	5,641	5,302,000	13
Iowa	Des Moines	Des Moines	29	1846	56,290	145,735	___	2,870,000	8
Kansas	Topeka	Wichita	34	1861	82,264	212,981	___	2,310,000	7
Kentucky	Frankfort	Louisville	15	1792	40,395	104,583	220,995	3,428,000	9
Louisiana	Baton Rouge	New Orleans	18	1812	48,523	125,626	___	3,841,000	10
Maine	Augusta	Portland	23	1820	33,215	86,619	151,719	1,070,000	4
Maryland	Annapolis	Baltimore	7	1788	10,577	27,384	341,548	4,144,000	10
Massachusetts	Boston	Boston	6	1788	8,257	21,377	422,845	5,809,000	14
Michigan	Lansing	Detroit	26	1837	58,216	150,721	___	9,104,000	21
Minnesota	St. Paul	Minneapolis	32	1858	84,068	217,652	___	3,965,000	10
Mississippi	Jackson	Jackson	20	1817	47,716	123,537	8,850	2,354,000	7
Missouri	Jefferson City	St. Louis	24	1821	69,686	180,417	___	4,778,000	12

State	Capital	Largest City	Entry into Union		Area in Square Miles	Area in Square Kilometers	Population		Electoral Votes
			Order	Year			In 1800	In 1976	
Montana	Helena	Billings	41	1889	147,138	380,940	____	753,000	4
Nebraska	Lincoln	Omaha	37	1867	77,227	199,941	____	1,553,000	5
Nevada	Carson City	Las Vegas	36	1864	110,540	286,188	____	610,000	3
New Hampshire	Concord	Manchester	9	1788	9,404	24,088	183,858	822,000	4
New Jersey	Trenton	Newark	3	1787	7,836	20,287	211,149	7,336,000	17
New Mexico	Santa Fe	Albuquerque	47	1912	121,666	314,993	____	1,168,000	4
New York	Albany	New York City	11	1788	49,576	128,352	589,051	18,084,000	41
North Carolina	Raleigh	Charlotte	12	1789	52,586	136,145	478,103	5,469,000	13
North Dakota	Bismarck	Fargo	39	1889	70,665	182,952	____	643,000	3
Ohio	Columbus	Cleveland	17	1803	41,222	106,724	45,365	10,690,000	25
Oklahoma	Oklahoma City	Oklahoma City	46	1907	69,919	181,020	____	2,766,000	8
Oregon	Salem	Portland	33	1859	96,981	251,084	____	2,329,000	6
Pennsylvania	Harrisburg	Philadelphia	2	1787	45,333	117,367	602,365	11,862,000	27
Rhode Island	Providence	Providence	13	1790	1,214	3,143	69,122	927,000	4
South Carolina	Columbia	Columbia	8	1788	31,055	80,401	345,591	2,848,000	8
South Dakota	Pierre	Sioux Falls	40	1889	77,047	199,475	____	686,000	4
Tennessee	Nashville	Memphis	16	1796	42,244	109,370	105,602	4,214,000	10
Texas	Austin	Houston	28	1845	267,339	692,141	____	12,487,000	26
Utah	Salt Lake City	Salt Lake City	45	1896	84,916	219,848	____	1,288,000	4
Vermont	Montpelier	Burlington	14	1791	9,609	24,878	154,465	476,000	3
Virginia	Richmond	Norfolk	10	1788	40,817	105,675	808,200	5,032,000	12
Washington	Olympia	Seattle	42	1889	68,192	176,549	____	3,612,000	9
West Virginia	Charleston	Huntington	35	1863	24,181	62,605	____	1,821,000	6
Wisconsin	Madison	Milwaukee	30	1848	56,154	145,383	____	4,609,000	11
Wyoming	Cheyenne	Cheyenne	44	1890	97,914	253,499	____	390,000	3
District of Columbia					67	173	14,093	702,000	3

Sources: 1800 population source — *The World Almanac* (1977); 1976 figures — Census Bureau Library.

The Declaration of Independence

Preamble
When in the course of human events, it becomes necessary for one people to dissolve the political bands which have connected them with another, and to assume among the powers of the earth the separate and equal station to which the laws of nature and of nature's God entitle them, a decent respect to the opinions of mankind requires that they should declare the causes which impel them to the separation.

New ideas about government
We hold these truths to be self-evident: that all men are created equal, that they are endowed by their Creator with certain unalienable rights, that among these are life, liberty, and the pursuit of happiness.

Basis for government
That to secure these rights, governments are instituted among men, deriving their just powers from the consent of the governed.

"Right to revolt"
That whenever any form of government becomes destructive of these ends, it is the right of the people to alter or to abolish it, and to institute new government, laying its foundation on such principles and organizing its powers in such form, as to them shall seem most likely to effect their safety and happiness. Prudence, indeed, will dictate that governments long established should not be changed for light and transient [temporary] causes; and accordingly all experience has shown, that mankind are more disposed to suffer, while evils are sufferable, than to right themselves by abolishing the forms to which they are accustomed. But when a long train of abuses and usurpations [power plays], pursuing invariably the same object, evinces a design to reduce them under absolute despotism, it is their right, it is their duty, to throw off such government, and to provide new guards for their future security.

716

Causes of separation

Such has been the patient sufferance of these colonies; and such is now the necessity which constrains [forces] them to alter their former systems of government. The history of the present king of Great Britain is a history of repeated injuries and usurpations, all having in direct object the establishment of an absolute tyranny over these states. To prove this, let facts be submitted to a candid world.

Complaints against the king

He has refused his assent to laws, the most wholesome and necessary for the public good.

He has forbidden his governors to pass laws of immediate and pressing importance, unless suspended in their operation till his assent should be obtained; and when so suspended, he has utterly neglected to attend to them.

He has refused to pass other laws for the accommodation of large districts of people, unless those people would relinquish [give up] the right of representation in the legislature, a right inestimable [of the greatest importance] to them and formidable [frightening] to tyrants only.

He has called together legislative bodies at places unusual, uncomfortable, and distant from the depository of their public records, for the sole purpose of fatiguing them into compliance with [obedience to] his measures.

He has dissolved Representative Houses repeatedly, for opposing with manly firmness his invasions on the rights of the people.

He has refused, for a long time after such dissolutions, to cause others to be elected; whereby the legislative powers, incapable of annihilation [destruction], have returned to the people at large for their exercise; the state remaining, in the mean time, exposed to all the dangers of invasion from without and convulsions within.

He has endeavored to prevent the population of these states; for that purpose obstructing the laws of naturalization of foreigners, refusing to pass others to encourage their migration here, and raising the conditions of new appropriations of lands.

He has obstructed the administration of justice, by refusing his assent to laws for establishing judiciary powers.

He has made judges dependent on his will alone, for the tenure [term] of their offices, and the amount and payment of their salaries.

He has erected a multitude of new offices, and sent here swarms of officers to harass our people, and eat out their substance.

He has kept among us, in times of peace, standing armies without the consent of our legislatures.

He has affected to render the military independent of and superior to the civil power.

He has combined with others to subject us to a jurisdiction

foreign to our constitution, and unacknowledged by our laws, giving his assent to their acts of pretended legislation:

For quartering large bodies of armed troops among us;

For protecting them, by mock trial, from punishment of any murders which they should commit on the inhabitants of these states;

For cutting off our trade with all parts of the world;

For imposing taxes on us without our consent;

For depriving us, in many cases, of the benefits of trial by jury;

For transporting us beyond seas, to be tried for pretended offenses;

For abolishing the free system of English laws in a neighboring province, establishing therein an arbitrary government and enlarging its boundaries so as to render it at once an example and fit instrument for introducing the same absolute rule into these colonies;

For taking away our charters, abolishing our most valuable laws, and altering fundamentally the forms of our governments;

For suspending our own legislatures, and declaring themselves invested with power to legislate for us in all cases whatsoever.

He has abdicated [given up authority over] government here, by declaring us out of his protection and waging war against us.

He has plundered our seas, ravaged our coasts, burnt our towns, and destroyed the lives of our people.

He is at this time transporting large armies of foreign mercenaries [hired soldiers] to complete the works of death, desolation, and tyranny already begun with circumstances of cruelty and perfidy scarcely paralleled in the most barbarous ages, and totally unworthy the head of a civilized nation.

He has constrained our fellow citizens, taken captive on the high seas, to bear arms against their country, to become the executioners of their friends and brethren, or to fall themselves by their hands.

He has excited domestic insurrections [uprisings] amongst us, and has endeavored to bring on the inhabitants of our frontiers the merciless Indian savages, whose known rule of warfare, is an undistinguished destruction of all ages, sexes and conditions.[1]

In every stage of these oppressions we have petitioned for redress [remedy] in the most humble terms; our repeated petitions have been answered only by repeated injury. A prince whose character is thus marked by every act which may define a tyrant is unfit to be the ruler of a free people.

Nor have we been wanting in attentions to our British brethren.

Complaints against the king and Parliament

More complaints against the king

Appeals to the British people

-----

[1]This statement was intended as an attack on King George III. It is clearly not an objective description of American Indians.

We have warned them, from time to time, of attempts by their legislature to extend an unwarrantable [unlawful] jurisdiction over us. We have reminded them of the circumstances of our emigration and settlement here. We have appealed to their native justice and magnanimity [kindness]; and we have conjured them, by the ties of our common kindred [ancestry], to disavow these usurpations, which would inevitably interrupt our connections and correspondence. They, too, have been deaf to the voice of justice and of consanguinity [common blood]. We must, therefore, acquiesce in the necessity which denounces our separation, and hold them, as we hold the rest of mankind, enemies in war, in peace, friends.

Declaration of war We, therefore, the representatives of the United States of America, in General Congress assembled, appealing to the Supreme Judge of the world for the rectitude [rightness] of our intentions, do, in the name, and by authority of the good people of these colonies, solemnly publish and declare, that these united colonies are, and of right ought to be, free and independent states; that they are absolved [freed] from all allegiance to the British crown, and that all political connection between them and the state of Great Britain is, and ought to be, totally dissolved; and that as free and independent states, they have full power to levy war, conclude peace, contract alliances, establish commerce, and to do all other acts and things which independent states may of right do. And, for the support of this declaration, with a firm reliance on the protection of Divine Providence, we mutually pledge to each other our lives, our fortunes and our sacred honor.

IN CONGRESS, JULY 4, 1776.

The unanimous Declaration of the thirteen united States of America.

The Constitution of the United States

PREAMBLE. We, the people of the United States, in order to form a more perfect Union, establish justice, insure domestic tranquility, provide for the common defense, promote the general welfare, and secure the blessings of liberty to ourselves and our posterity, do ordain and establish this Constitution for the United States of America.

Legislative Branch

ARTICLE I. Section 1. All legislative powers herein granted shall be vested in a Congress of the United States, which shall consist of a Senate and a House of Representatives.

House of Representatives

Section 2. The House of Representatives shall be composed of members chosen every second year by the people of the several states; and the electors in each state shall have the qualifications requisite for electors of the most numerous branch of the state legislature.

Qualifications for Representatives

No person shall be a Representative who shall not have attained the age of 25 years, and been seven years a citizen of the United States, and who shall not, when elected, be an inhabitant of that state in which he shall be chosen.

How the number of Representatives sent to Congress by each state is to be fixed

Representatives and direct taxes shall be apportioned among the several states which may be included within this Union, according to their respective numbers, which shall be determined by adding to the whole number of free persons, including those bound to service for a term of years, and excluding Indians not taxed, three fifths of all other persons. The actual enumeration shall be made within three years after the first meeting of the Congress of the United States, and within every subsequent term of ten years, in such manner as they shall by law direct. The number of Representatives shall not exceed one for every 30,000, but each state shall have at least one Representative; and until such enumeration shall be made, the state of New Hampshire shall be entitled to choose three, Massachusetts eight, Rhode Island and Providence Plantations one, Connecticut five, New York six, New Jersey four, Pennsylvania eight, Delaware one, Maryland six, Virginia ten, North Carolina five, South Carolina five, and Georgia three.

Vacancies

When vacancies happen in the representation from any state, the executive authority thereof shall issue writs of election to fill such vacancies.

Rules, impeachment

The House of Representatives shall choose their Speaker and other officers; and shall have the sole power of impeachment.

Senate

Section 3. The Senate of the United States shall be composed of two Senators from each state, chosen by the legislature thereof, for six years; and each Senator shall have one vote.

Methods of election to the Senate

Immediately after they shall be assembled, in consequences of the first election, they shall be divided as equally as may be into three classes. The seats of the Senators of the first class shall be vacated at the expiration of the second year, of the second class at the expiration of the fourth year, and of the third class at the expiration of the sixth year, so that one third may be chosen every second year; and if vacancies happen by resignation, or otherwise, during the recess of the legislature of any state, the executive thereof may make temporary appointments until the next meeting of the legislature, which shall then fill such vacancies.

Qualifications for Senators

No person shall be a Senator who shall not have attained the age of 30 years, and been nine years a citizen of the United States, and who shall not, when elected, be an inhabitant of that state for which he shall be chosen.

Vice-President's role

The Vice-President of the United States shall be President of the Senate, but shall have no vote, unless they be equally divided.

The Senate shall choose their other officers, and also a President *Pro Tempore,* in the absence of the Vice-President, or when he shall exercise the office of President of the United States.

Impeachments

The Senate shall have the sole power to try all impeachments. When sitting for that purpose, they shall be on oath or affirmation. When the President of the United States is tried, the Chief Justice shall preside: and no person shall be convicted without the concurrence of two thirds of the members present.

Judgment in cases of impeachment shall not extend further than to removal from office, and disqualification to hold and enjoy any office of honor, trust, or profit, under the United States; but the party convicted shall nevertheless be liable and subject to indictment, trial, judgment, and punishment according to law.

Elections to Congress

Section 4. The times, places, and manner of holding elections for Senators and Representatives, shall be prescribed in each state by the legislature thereof; but the Congress may at any time by law make or alter such regulations, except as to the places of choosing Senators.

The Congress shall assemble at least once in every year, and such meeting shall be on the first Monday in December, unless they shall by law appoint a different day.

Section 5. Each House shall be the judge of the elections, returns, and qualifications of its own members, and a majority of each shall constitute a quorum to do business; but a smaller number may adjourn from day to day, and may be authorized to compel the attendance of absent members, in such manner, and under such penalties, as each House may provide.

Each House may determine the rules of its proceedings, punish its members for disorderly behavior, and, with the concurrence of two thirds, expel a member.

Each House shall keep a journal of its proceedings, and from time to time publish the same, excepting such parts as may, in their judgment, require secrecy; and the yeas and nays of the members of either House on any question, shall, at the desire of one fifth of those present, be entered on the journal.

Neither House, during the session of Congress, shall, without the consent of the other, adjourn for more than three days, nor to any other place than that in which the two Houses shall be sitting.

Section 6. The Senators and Representatives shall receive a compensation for their services, to be ascertained by law, and paid out of the Treasury of the United States. They shall, in all cases, except treason, felony, and breach of the peace, be privileged from arrest during their attendance at the session of their respective Houses, and in going to, and returning from, the same; and for any speech or debate in either House, they shall not be questioned in any other place.

No Senator or Representative shall, during the time for which he was elected, be appointed to any civil office under the authority of the United States, which shall have been created, or the emoluments whereof shall have been increased during such time; and no person holding any office under the United States, shall be a member of either House during his continuance in office.

Section 7. All bills for raising revenue shall originate in the House of Representatives; but the Senate may propose or concur with amendments as on other bills.

Every bill which shall have passed the House of Representatives and the Senate, shall, before it become a law, be presented to the President of the United States; if he approves he shall sign it, but if not he shall return it, with his objections, to that House in which it shall have originated, who shall enter the objections at large on their journal, and proceed to reconsider it. If after such reconsid-

eration two thirds of that House shall agree to pass the bill, it shall be sent, together with the objections, to the other House, by which it shall likewise be reconsidered, and if approved by two thirds of that House, it shall become a law. But in all such cases the votes of both Houses shall be determined by yeas and nays, and the names of the persons voting for and against the bill shall be entered on the journal of each House respectively. If any bill shall not be returned by the President within 10 days (Sundays excepted) after it shall have been presented to him, the same shall be a law in like manner as if he had signed it, unless the Congress by their adjournment prevent its return, in which case it shall not be a law.

President's "pocket veto" power

Every order, resolution, or vote, to which the concurrence of the Senate and House of Representatives may be necessary (except on a question of adjournment), shall be presented to the President of the United States; and before the same shall take effect, shall be approved by him, or being disapproved by him, shall be repassed by two thirds of the Senate and House of Representatives, according to the rules and limitations prescribed in the case of a bill.

Powers of Congress

Section 8. The Congress shall have power:

To lay and collect taxes, duties, imposts, and excises, to pay the debts, and provide for the common defense and general welfare of the United States; but all duties, imposts, and excises shall be uniform throughout the United States;

To borrow money on the credit of the United States;

To regulate commerce with foreign nations, and among the several states, and with the Indian tribes;

To establish a uniform rule of naturalization, and uniform laws on the subject of bankruptcies throughout the United States;

To coin money, regulate the value thereof, and of foreign coin, and fix the standard of weights and measures;

To provide for the punishment of counterfeiting the securities and current coin of the United States;

To establish post offices and post roads;

To promote the progress of science and useful arts, by securing, for limited times, to authors and inventors, the exclusive right to their respective writings and discoveries;

To constitute tribunals inferior to the Supreme Court;

To define and punish piracies and felonies committed on the high seas, and offenses against the law of nations;

To declare war, grant letters of marque and reprisal, and make rules concerning captures on land and water;

To raise and support armies; but no appropriation of money to that use shall be for a longer term than two years;

To provide and maintain a navy;

To make rules for the government and regulation of the land and naval forces;

To provide for calling forth the militia to execute the laws of the

Union, suppress insurrections and repel invasions;

To provide for organizing, arming, and disciplining the militia, and for governing such part of them as may be employed in the service of the United States, reserving to the states respectively, the appointment of the officers, and the authority of training the militia according to the discipline prescribed by Congress;

To exercise exclusive legislation, in all cases whatsoever, over such district (not exceeding 10 miles square) as may, by cession of particular states, and the acceptance of Congress, become the seat of the government of the United States, and to exercise like authority over all places purchased by the consent of the legislature of the state in which the same shall be, for the erection of forts, magazines, arsenals, dockyards, and other needful buildings. And,

"Elastic clause"

To make all laws which shall be necessary and proper for carrying into execution the foregoing powers, and all other powers vested by this Constitution in the government of the United States, or in any department or officer thereof.

Limits on the power of Congress

Section 9. The migration or importation of such persons as any of the states now existing shall think proper to admit, shall not be prohibited by the Congress prior to the year 1808; but a tax or duty may be imposed on such importation, not exceeding 10 dollars for each person.

The privilege of the writ of *habeas corpus* shall not be suspended, unless when in cases of rebellion or invasion the public safety may require it.

No bill of attainder or *ex post facto* law shall be passed.

No capitation, or other direct tax, shall be laid, unless in proportion to the *census* or enumeration herein before directed to be taken.

No tax or duty shall be laid on articles exported from any state. No preference shall be given by any regulation of commerce or revenue to the ports of one state over those of another; nor shall vessels bound to, or from, one state be obliged to enter, clear, or pay duties in another.

No money shall be drawn from the treasury, but in consequence of appropriations made by law; and a regular statement and account of the receipts and expenditures of all public money shall be published from time to time.

No title of nobility shall be granted by the United States; and no person holding any office of profit or trust under them, shall, without the consent of the Congress, accept of any present, emolument, office, or title of any kind whatever, from any king, prince, or foreign state.

Limits on powers of the states

Section 10. No state shall enter into any treaty, alliance, or confederation; grant letters of marque and reprisal; coin money; emit bills of credit; make any thing but gold and silver coin a tender in payment of debts; pass any bill of attainder, *ex post facto* law, or law impairing the obligation of contracts, or grant any title of nobility.

No state shall, without the consent of the Congress, lay any imposts or duties on imports or exports, except what may be absolutely necessary for executing its inspection laws; and the net produce of all duties and imposts, laid by any state on imports or exports, shall be for the use of the Treasury of the United States; and all such laws shall be subject to the revision and control of the Congress. No state shall, without the consent of Congress, lay any duty of tonnage, keep troops, or ships of war, in time of peace, enter into any agreement or compact with another state, or with a foreign power, or engage in war, unless actually invaded, or in such imminent danger as will not admit of delay.

Executive Branch

ARTICLE II. Section 1. The executive power shall be vested in a President of the United States of America. He shall hold his office during the term of four years, and together with the Vice-President, chosen for the same term, be elected as follows:

Election of the President

Each state shall appoint, in such manner as the legislature thereof may direct, a number of electors equal to the whole number of Senators and Representatives to which the state may be entitled in the Congress; but no Senator or Representative, or person holding an office of trust or profit under the United States, shall be appointed an elector.

Electoral system

The electors shall meet in their respective states, and vote by ballot for two persons, of whom one at least shall not be an inhabitant of the same state with themselves. And they shall make a list of all the persons voted for, and of the number of votes for each; which list they shall sign and certify, and transmit sealed to the seat of the government of the United States, directed to the President of the Senate. The President of the Senate shall, in the presence of the Senate and House of Representatives, open all the certificates, and the votes shall then be counted. The person having the greatest number of votes shall be the President, if such number be a majority of the whole number of electors appointed;

Role of the House in Presidential elections

and if there be more than one who have such majority, and have an equal number of votes, then the House of Representatives shall immediately choose by ballot one of them for President; and if no person have a majority, then from the five highest on the list the said House shall in like manner choose the President. But in choosing the President, the votes shall be taken by states, the representation from each state having one vote; a quorum for this purpose shall consist of a member or members from two thirds of the states, and a majority of all the states shall be necessary to a choice. In every case, after the choice of the President, the person

725

having the greatest number of votes of the electors shall be the Vice-President. But if there should remain two or more who have equal votes, the Senate shall choose from them by ballot the Vice-President.

The Congress may determine the time of choosing the electors, and the day on which they shall give their votes; which day shall be the same throughout the United States.

No person except a natural-born citizen, or a citizen of the United States, at the time of the adoption of this Constitution, shall be eligible to the office of President; neither shall any person be eligible to that office who shall not have attained the age of 35 years, and been 14 years a resident within the United States.

In case of the removal of the President from office, or of his death, resignation, or inability to discharge the powers and duties of the said office, the same shall devolve on the Vice-President, and the Congress may by law provide for the case of removal, death, resignation, or inability, both of the President and Vice-President, declaring what officer shall then act as President, and such officer shall act accordingly until the disability be removed, or a President shall be elected.

The President shall at stated times receive for his services a compensation, which shall neither be increased nor diminished during the period for which he shall have been elected, and he shall not receive within that period any other emolument from the United States or any of them.

Before he enter on the execution of his office, he shall take the following oath or affirmation:

"I do solemnly swear (or affirm) that I will faithfully execute the office of President of the United States, and will, to the best of my ability, preserve, protect, and defend the Constitution of the United States."

Section 2. The President shall be Commander-in-Chief of the Army and Navy of the United States, and of the militia of the several states, when called into the actual service of the United States; he may require the opinion, in writing, of the principal officer in each of the executive departments, upon any subject relating to the duties of their respective offices, and he shall have power to grant reprieves and pardons for offenses against the United States, except in cases of impeachment.

He shall have power, by and with the advice and consent of the Senate, to make treaties, provided two thirds of the Senators present concur; and he shall nominate, and by and with the advice and consent of the Senate, shall appoint ambassadors, other public ministers and consuls, judges of the Supreme Court, and all other officers of the United States, whose appointments are not herein otherwise provided for, and which shall be established by law. But the Congress may by law vest the appointment of such inferior officers, as they think proper, in the President alone, in the courts of law, or in the heads of departments.

Vacancies   The President shall have power to fill up all vacancies that may happen during the recess of the Senate, by granting commissions which shall expire at the end of their next session.

Further powers of the President   **Section 3.** He shall, from time to time, give to the Congress information of the state of the Union, and recommend to their consideration such measures as he shall judge necessary and expedient. He may on extraordinary occasions, convene both Houses, or either of them; and in case of disagreement between them, with respect to the time of adjournment, he may adjourn them to such time as he shall think proper. He shall receive ambassadors and other public ministers. He shall take care that the laws be faithfully executed; and shall commission all the officers of the United States.

Impeachment   **Section 4.** The President, Vice-President, and all civil officers of the United States, shall be removed from office on impeachment for, and conviction of, treason, bribery, or other high crimes and misdemeanors.

Judicial Branch   **ARTICLE III. Section 1.** The judicial power of the United States shall be vested in one Supreme Court, and in such inferior courts

Courts and judges   as the Congress may, from time to time, ordain and establish. The judges, both of the Supreme and inferior courts, shall hold their offices during good behavior; and shall, at stated times, receive for their services, a compensation, which shall not be diminished during their continuance in office.

Scope of power of federal courts   **Section 2.** The judicial power shall extend to all cases, in law and equity, arising under this Constitution, the laws of the United States, and treaties made, or which shall be made, under their authority; to all cases affecting ambassadors, other public ministers, and consuls; to all cases of admiralty and maritime jurisdiction; to controversies to which the United States shall be a party; to controversies between two or more states, between a state and citizens of another state, between citizens of different states, between citizens of the same state claiming lands under grants of different states, and between a state, or the citizens thereof, and foreign states, citizens, or subjects.

In all cases affecting ambassadors, other public ministers and consuls, and those in which a state shall be party, the Supreme Court shall have original jurisdiction. In all the other cases before mentioned, the Supreme Court shall have appellate jurisdiction, both as to law and fact, with such exceptions, and under such regulations, as the Congress shall make.

Trial by jury   The trial of all crimes, except in cases of impeachment, shall be by jury; and such trial shall be held in the state where the said crimes shall have been committed; but when not committed within any state, the trial shall be at such place or places as the Congress may by law have directed.

Definition and punishment for treason

Section 3. Treason against the United States, shall consist only in levying war against them, or in adhering to their enemies, giving them aid and comfort. No person shall be convicted of treason unless on the testimony of two witnesses to the same overt act, or on confession in open court.

The Congress shall have power to declare the punishment of treason, but no attainder of treason shall work corruption of blood, or forfeiture, except during the life of the person attainted.

Federal System

ARTICLE IV. Section 1. Full faith and credit shall be given in each state to the public acts, records, and judicial proceedings of every other state. And the Congress may by general laws prescribe the manner in which such acts, records, and proceedings shall be proved, and the effect thereof.

Rights of citizenship

Section 2. The citizens of each state shall be entitled to all privileges and immunities of citizens in the several states.

A person charged in any state with treason, felony, or other crimes, who shall flee from justice, and be found in another state, shall, on demand of the executive authority of the state from which he fled, be delivered up to be removed to the state having jurisdiction of the crime.

No person held to service or labor in one state, under the laws thereof, escaping into another, shall, in consequence of any laws or regulation therein, be discharged from such service or labor, but shall be delivered up on claim of the party to whom such service or labor may be due.

Admission of new states to the Union

Section 3. New states may be admitted by the Congress into this Union; but no new state shall be formed or erected within the jurisdiction of any other state; nor any state be formed by the junction of two or more states or parts of states, without the consent of the legislatures of the states concerned, as well as of the Congress.

Governing U.S. territories

The Congress shall have power to dispose of and make all needful rules and regulations respecting the territory or other property belonging to the United States; and nothing in this Constitution shall be so construed as to prejudice any claims of the United States, or of any particular state.

Protection of the states

Section 4. The United States shall guarantee to every state in this Union a republican form of government, and shall protect each of them against invasion; and on application of the legislature, or of the executive (when the legislature cannot be convened), against domestic violence.

Amendment process

ARTICLE V. The Congress, whenever two thirds of both Houses shall deem it necessary, shall propose amendments to this Constitution, or, on the application of the legislatures of two thirds of the several states, shall call a convention for proposing amendments, which, in either case, shall be valid to all intents and purposes, as part of this Constitution, when ratified by the legislatures of three fourths of the several states, or by conventions in three fourths thereof, as the one or the other mode of ratification may be proposed by the Congress; provided that no amendment, which may be made prior to the year 1808, shall in any manner affect the first and fourth clauses in the ninth section of the first article; and that no state, without its consent, shall be deprived of its equal suffrage in the Senate.

Constitution as supreme law

ARTICLE VI. All debts contracted, and engagements entered into, before the adoption of this Constitution, shall be as valid against the United States, under this Constitution, as under the Confederation.

This Constitution, and the laws of the United States which shall be made in pursuance thereof, and all treaties made, or which shall be made, under the authority of the United States, shall be the supreme law of the land; and the judges, in every state, shall be bound thereby, anything in the constitution or laws of any state to the contrary notwithstanding.

The Senators and Representatives before mentioned, and the members of the several state legislatures, and all executive and judicial officers, both of the United States and of the several states, shall be bound, by oath or affirmation, to support this Constitution; but no religious test shall ever be required as a qualification to any office or public trust under the United States.

Ratification process

ARTICLE VII. The ratification of the conventions of nine states shall be sufficient for the establishment of this Constitution between the states so ratifying the same.

AMENDMENTS

(The first 10 amendments, adopted in 1791, are called the Bill of Rights.)

Basic freedoms

AMENDMENT I. Congress shall make no law respecting an establishment of religion, or prohibiting the free exercise thereof; or abridging the freedom of speech, or of the press; or the right of the people peaceably to assemble, and to petition the government for a redress of grievances.

729

Right to bear arms   **AMENDMENT II.** A well regulated militia being necessary to the security of a free state, the right of the people to keep and bear arms shall not be infringed.

Quartering of soldiers   **AMENDMENT III.** No soldier shall, in time of peace, be quartered in any house without the consent of the owner; nor in time of war, but in a manner to be prescribed by law.

Freedom of persons   **AMENDMENT IV.** The right of the people to be secure in their persons, houses, papers, and effects, against unreasonable searches and seizures, shall not be violated; and no warrants shall issue, but upon probable cause, supported by oath or affirmation, and particularly describing the place to be searched, and the persons or things to be seized.

Rights of people accused of crimes   **AMENDMENT V.** No person shall be held to answer for a capital or otherwise infamous crime, unless on a presentment or indictment of a grand jury, except in cases arising in the land or naval forces, or in the militia, when in actual service, in time of war or public danger; nor shall any person be subject for the same offenses to be twice put in jeopardy of life or limb; nor shall be compelled, in any criminal case, to be a witness against himself; nor be deprived of life, liberty, or property, without due process of law; nor shall private property be taken for public use without just compensation.

Trial by jury   **AMENDMENT VI.** In all criminal prosecutions the accused shall enjoy the right to a speedy and public trial, by an impartial jury of the state and district wherein the crime shall have been committed, which district shall have been previously ascertained by law, and to be informed of the nature and cause of the accusation; to be confronted with the witnesses against him; to have compulsory process for obtaining witnesses in his favor; and to have the assistance of counsel for his defense.

Civil law   **AMENDMENT VII.** In suits at common law, where the value in controversy shall exceed 20 dollars, the right of trial by jury shall be preserved; and no fact tried by a jury shall be otherwise re-examined in any court of the United States than according to the rules of the common law.

Bails, fines, and punishments   **AMENDMENT VIII.** Excessive bail shall not be required, nor excessive fines imposed, nor cruel and unusual punishments inflicted.

Rights of the people **AMENDMENT IX.** The enumeration in the Constitution of certain rights shall not be construed to deny or disparage others retained by the people.

Rights reserved to the states **AMENDMENT X.** The powers not delegated to the United States by the Constitution, nor prohibited by it to the states, are reserved to the states respectively or to the people.

Limits on judicial powers **AMENDMENT XI (1798).** The judicial power of the United States shall not be construed to extend to any suit in law or equity, commenced or prosecuted against one of the United States by citizens of any state, or by citizens or subjects of any foreign state.

Electoral College **AMENDMENT XII (1804).** The electors shall meet in their respective states, and vote by ballot for President and Vice-President, one of whom, at least, shall not be an inhabitant of the same state with themselves; they shall name in their ballots the person voted for as President, and in distinct ballots the person voted for as Vice-President; and they shall make distinct lists of all persons voted for as President, and of all persons voted for as Vice-President, and of the number of votes for each, which list they shall sign and certify, and transmit, sealed, to the seat of the government of the United States, directed to the President of the Senate; the President of the Senate shall, in the presence of the Senate and House of Representatives, open all the certificates, and the votes shall then be counted. The person having the greatest number of votes for President shall be the President, if such number be a majority of the whole number of electors appointed; and if no person have such majority, then from the persons having the highest numbers, not exceeding three, on the list of those voted for as President, the House of Representatives shall choose immediately, by ballot, the President. But in choosing the President, the votes shall be taken by states, the representation from each state having one vote; a quorum for this purpose shall consist of a member or members from two thirds of the states, and a majority of all the states shall be necessary to a choice. And if the House of Representatives shall not choose a President whenever the right of choice shall devolve upon them, before the fourth day of March next following, then the Vice-President shall act as President, as in the case of the death or other constitutional disability of the President.

The person having the greatest number of votes as Vice-President shall be the Vice-President, if such number be a majority of the whole number of electors appointed; and if no person have a majority, then from the two highest numbers on the list the Senate shall choose the Vice-President. A quorum for the purpose shall consist of two thirds of the whole number of Senators, and a majority of the whole number shall be necessary to a choice.

But no person constitutionally ineligible to the office of President shall be eligible to that of Vice-President of the United States.

Slavery ended **AMENDMENT XIII (1865). Section 1.** Neither slavery nor involuntary servitude, except as a punishment for a crime whereof the party shall have been duly convicted, shall exist within the United States, or any place subject to their jurisdiction.

Section 2. Congress shall have power to enforce this article by appropriate legislation.

Citizenship **AMENDMENT XIV (1868). Section 1.** All persons born or naturalized in the United States, and subject to the jurisdiction

Due process of law thereof, are citizens of the United States and of the state wherein they reside. No state shall make or enforce any law which shall abridge the privileges or immunities of citizens of the United States; nor shall any state deprive any person of life, liberty, or property, without due process of law, nor deny to any person within its jurisdiction the equal protection of the laws.

Right to vote **Section 2.** Representatives shall be apportioned among the several states according to their respective numbers, counting the whole number of persons in each state, excluding Indians not taxed. But when the right to vote at any election for the choice of electors for President and Vice-President of the United States, representatives in Congress, the executive and judicial officers of a state, or the members of the legislature thereof, is denied to any of the male inhabitants of such state, being 21 years of age, and citizens of the United States, or in anyway abridged, except for participation in rebellion or other crime, the basis of representation therein shall be reduced in the proportion which the number of such male citizens shall bear to the whole number of male citizens 21 years of age in such state.

Disqualification **Section 3.** No person shall be a Senator or Representative in
for office Congress, or elector of President and Vice-President, or hold any office, civil or military, under the United States, or under any state, who, having previously taken an oath, as a member of Congress, or as an officer of the United States, or as a member of any state legislature, or as an executive or judicial officer of any state, to support the Constitution of the United States, shall have engaged in insurrection or rebellion against the same, or given aid or comfort to the enemies thereof. But Congress may, by a vote of two thirds of each house, remove such disability.

Public debt **Section 4.** The validity of the public debt of the United States, authorized by law, including debts incurred for payment of pensions and bounties for services in suppressing insurrection or rebellion, shall not be questioned. But neither the United States nor any state shall assume or pay any debt or obligation incurred in aid of insurrection or rebellion against the United States, or any claim for the loss or emancipation of any slave; but all such debts, obligations, and claims shall be held illegal and void.

Section 5. The Congress shall have power to enforce, by appropriate legislation, the provisions of this article.

Right to vote **AMENDMENT XV (1870). Section 1.** The right of citizens of the United States to vote shall not be denied or abridged by the United States or by any state on account of race, color, or previous condition of servitude.

Section 2. The Congress shall have power to enforce this article by appropriate legislation.

Income tax **AMENDMENT XVI (1913).** The Congress shall have power to lay and collect taxes on incomes, from whatever source derived, without apportionment among the several states, and without regard to any census or enumeration.

Direct election **AMENDMENT XVII (1913).** The Senate of the United States
of Senators shall be composed of two Senators from each state, elected by the people thereof, for six years; and each Senator shall have one vote. The electors in each state shall have the qualifications requisite for electors of the most numerous branch of the state legislatures.

When vacancies happen in the representation of any state in the Senate, the executive authority of such state shall issue writs of election to fill such vacancies: *Provided,* That the legislature of any state may empower the executive thereof to make temporary appointments until the people fill the vacancies by election as the legislature may direct.

This amendment shall not be so construed as to effect the election or term of any Senator chosen before it becomes valid as part of the Constitution.

Prohibition **AMENDMENT XVIII (1919). Section 1.** After one year from the ratification of this article the manufacture, sale, or transportation of intoxicating liquors within, the importation thereof into, or the exportation thereof from the United States and all territory subject to the jurisdiction thereof for beverage purposes is hereby prohibited.

Section 2. The Congress and the several states shall have concurrent power to enforce this article by appropriate legislation.

Section 3. This article shall be inoperative unless it shall have been ratified as an amendment to the Constitution by the legislatures of the several states, as provided in the Constitution, within seven years from the date of the submission hereof to the states by the Congress.

Women's suffrage **AMENDMENT XIX (1920).** The right of citizens of the United States to vote shall not be denied or abridged by the United States or by any state on account of sex.

Congress shall have power to enforce this article by appropriate legislation.

Terms of office **AMENDMENT XX (1933). Section 1.** The terms of the President and Vice-President shall end at noon on the 20th day of January, and the terms of Senators and Representatives at noon on the 3rd day of January, of the years in which such terms would have ended if this article had not been ratified; and the terms of their successors shall then begin.

Section 2. The Congress shall assemble at least once in every year, and such meeting shall begin at noon on the 3rd day of January, unless they shall by law appoint a different day.

Presidential succession **Section 3.** If, at the time fixed for the beginning of the term of the President, the President-elect shall have died, the Vice-President-elect shall become President. If a President shall not have been chosen before the time fixed for the beginning of his term, or if the President-elect shall have failed to qualify, then the Vice-President elect shall act as President until a President shall have qualified; and the Congress may by law provide for the case wherein neither a President-elect nor a Vice-President-elect shall have qualified, declaring who shall then act as President, or the manner in which one who is to act shall be selected, and such person shall act accordingly until a President or Vice-President shall have qualified.

Section 4. The Congress may by law provide for the case of the death of any of the persons from whom the House of Representatives may choose a President whenever the right of choice shall have devolved upon them, and for the case of the death of any of the persons from whom the Senate may choose a Vice-President whenever the right of choice shall have devolved upon them.

Section 5. Sections 1 and 2 shall take affect on the 15th day of October following the ratification of this article.

Section 6. This article shall be inoperative unless it shall have been ratified as an amendment to the Constitution by the legislatures of three fourths of the several states within seven years from the date of its submission.

Repeal of Prohibition **AMENDMENT XXI (1933). Section 1.** The 18th article of amendment to the Constitution of the United States is hereby repealed.

Section 2. The transportation or importation into any state, territory, or possession of the United States for delivery or use therein of intoxicating liquors, in violation of the laws thereof, is hereby prohibited.

Section 3. This article shall be inoperative unless it shall have been ratified as an amendment to the Constitution by conventions in the several states, as provided in the Constitution, within seven years from the date of the submission hereof to the states by the Congress.

Two-term limit on President

AMENDMENT XXII (1951). No person shall be elected to the office of the President more than twice, and no person who has held the office of President, or acted as President, for more than two years of a term to which some other person was elected President shall be elected to the office of the President more than once. But this article shall not apply to any person holding the office of President when this article was proposed by the Congress, and shall not prevent any person who may be holding the office of President, or acting as President, during the term within which this article becomes operative from holding the office of President or acting as President during the remainder of such term.

Vote given to District of Columbia in Presidential elections

AMENDMENT XXIII (1961). Section 1. The district constituting the seat of government of the United States shall appoint in such manner as the Congress may direct: A number of electors of President and Vice-President equal to the whole number of Senators and Representatives in Congress to which the district would be entitled if it were a state, but in no event more than the least populous state; they shall be in addition to those appointed by the states, but they shall be considered, for the purposes of the election of the President and Vice-President, to be electors appointed by a state; and they shall meet in the district and perform such duties as provided by the 12th article of amendment.

Section 2. The Congress shall have power to enforce this article by appropriate legislation.

Poll tax ended in national elections

AMENDMENT XXIV (1964). Section 1. The right of citizens of the United States to vote in any primary or other election for President or Vice-President, for electors for President or Vice-President, or for Senator or Representatives in Congress, shall not be denied or abridged by the United States or any state by reason of failure to pay any poll tax or other tax.

Section 2. The Congress shall have the power to enforce this article by appropriate legislation.

AMENDMENT XXV (1967). Section 1. In case of the removal of the President from office or his death or resignation, the Vice-President shall become President.

Section 2. Whenever there is a vacancy in the office of the Vice-President, the President shall nominate a Vice-President who shall take office upon confirmation by a majority vote of both houses of Congress.

Section 3. Whenever the President transmits to the President *Pro Tempore* of the Senate and the Speaker of the House of Representatives his written declaration that he is unable to discharge the powers and duties of his office, and until he transmits to them a written declaration to the contrary, such powers and duties shall be discharged by the Vice-President as Acting President.

Section 4. Whenever the Vice-President and a majority of either the principal officers of the executive departments or of such other body as Congress may by law provide, transmit to the President *Pro Tempore* of the Senate and the Speaker of the House of Representatives their written declaration that the President is unable to discharge the powers and duties of his office, the Vice-President shall immediately assume the powers and duties of the office as Acting President.

Thereafter, when the President transmits to the President *Pro Tempore* of the Senate and the Speaker of the House of Representatives his written declaration that no inability exists, he shall resume the powers and duties of his office unless the Vice-President and a majority of either the principal officers of the executive departments or of such other body as Congress may by law provide, transmit within four days to the President *Pro Tempore* of the Senate and the Speaker of the House of Representatives their written declaration that the President is unable to discharge the powers and duties of his office. Thereupon Congress shall decide the issue, assembling within 48 hours for that purpose if not in session. If the Congress, within 21 days after receipt of the latter written declaration, or, if Congress is not in session, within 21 days after Congress is required to assemble, determines by two-thirds vote of both houses that the President is unable to discharge the powers and duties of his office, the Vice-President shall continue to discharge the same as Acting President; otherwise, the President shall resume the powers and duties of his office.

AMENDMENT XXVI (1971). Section 1. The right of citizens of the United States, who are 18 years of age or older, to vote shall not be denied or abridged by the United States or any state on account of age.

Section 2. The Congress shall have power to enforce this article by appropriate legislation.

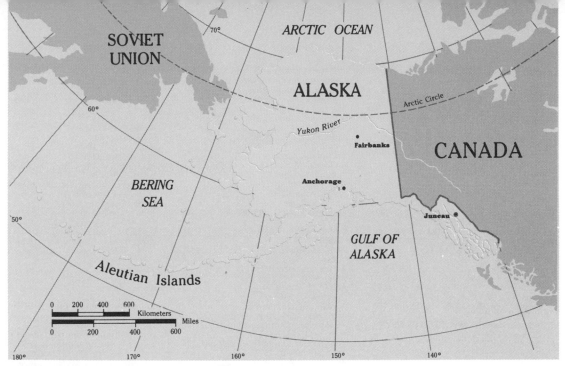

The United States Today

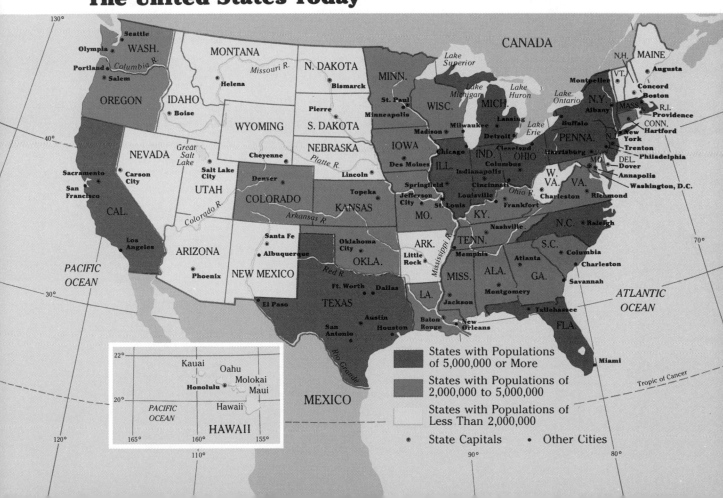

Kauai
Oahu
Molokai
Honolulu • Maui
PACIFIC OCEAN Hawaii
HAWAII

States with Populations of 5,000,000 or More

States with Populations of 2,000,000 to 5,000,000

States with Populations of Less Than 2,000,000

• State Capitals   • Other Cities

Index

741

745

746

Picture Collection (3) • 234, The Metropolitan Museum of Art, Gift of I. N. Phelps Stokes, Edward S. Hawes, Alice Mary Hawes, Marion Augusta Hawes, 1937 • 236, 237, The New York Public Library, Picture Collection (2) • 238, The Cincinnati Art Museum — Purchase • 241, National Portrait Gallery, Smithsonian Institution • 242, Anne S. K. Brown Military Collection, Brown University Library • 244, (top) The Kansas State Historical Society, Topeka; (bottom), *Kansas, Its Interior and Exterior Life,* 1856 by Sara T. L. Robinson • 247, Missouri Historical Society, St. Louis • 248, National Archives • 250, The New York Public Library, Picture Collection • 251, (top) Culver Pictures; (bottom) Courtesy of the Pennsylvania Academy of Fine Arts • 252, Library of Congress • 253, Georgia Historical Society • 254, Library of Congress • 255, Courtesy, Museum of Fine Arts, Boston. Fund: M. and M. Karolik Collection • 256, Chicago Historical Society • 262, Winslow Homer, *In Front of Yorktown,* Yale University Art Gallery. Gift of Samuel R. Betts, B.A. 1875 • 265, Library of Congress • 266, The Metropolitan Museum of Art, Gift of Lyman G. Bloomingdale, 1901 • 268-269, (top) Courtesy, Kennedy Galleries, Inc., New York • 271, Library of Congress • 272, Courtesy of The New-York Historical Society, New York City • 274, The New York Public Library, Picture Collection • 275, CIVIL WAR BATTLE #1542, American School, National Gallery of Art, Washington. Gift of Edgar William and Bernice Chrysler Garbisch • 279, Valentine Museum, Richmond, Virginia • 280, National Archives • 282, The Metropolitan Museum of Art, Gift of Mrs. Frank B. Porter, 1922 • 284, (top) National Archives • 284-285, (bottom) Illinois Central Gulf Railroad • 285, (top) Library of Congress • 287, 290, 293, Library of Congress (3) • 294-295, Culver Pictures • 297, Brown Brothers • 299, The New York Public Library, Picture Collection • 301, U.S. Signal Corps Photo No. 111-B-4138 (Brady Collection) in the National Archives • 308, Culver Pictures • 310, Smithsonian Institution • 311, (top) Culver Pictures; (bottom) Free Library of Philadelphia • 313, Library of Congress • 314, Union Pacific Railroad Museum Collection • 317, The Thomas Gilcrease Institute of American History and Art, Tulsa, Oklahoma • 318, Drake Well Museum, photo American Petroleum Institute • 319, Brown Brothers • 320, 321, Wide World (2) • 322, Thomas Alva Edison Foundation Museum, West Orange, N.J. • 323, The New York Public Library, Picture Collection • 325, Culver Pictures • 327, (top) The Bettmann Archive; (bottom) Library of Congress • 328, Library of Congress • 330, Merkle Press • 333, Library of Congress • 338, The Bettmann Archive • 340, Smithsonian Institution, Photo No. 128 • 341, Oklahoma Historical Society • 343, Photograph by Jacob A. Riis, The Jacob A. Riis Collection, Museum of the City of New York • 344, Sterling and Francine Clark Art Institute, Williamstown, Massachusetts • 345, Montana Historical Society, Helena • 349, (top) Courtesy, The Bancroft Library, University of California, Berkeley; (bottom) Culver Pictures • 350, International Museum of Photography at George Eastman House • 353, Museum of the City of New York; (inset) Dan Nelken • 354, History Division, Los Angeles County Museum of Natural History • 356, Library of Congress • 358, Wide World • 360, (foreground) Brown Brothers • 363, Smithsonian Institution, Photo No. 74-847 • 370, Culver Pictures • 373, (top) International Museum of Photography at George Eastman House; (bottom) Brown Brothers • 374, Chicago Historical Society • 377, Library of Congress • 380, The Carl H. Boehringer Collection • 382, Seibel, Richmond (Va.) *Times-Dispatch* • 383, reproduced by Courtesy of the Trustees of the British Museum • 384, Library of Congress • 387 UPI • 389, *Puck,* February 21, 1906, photo Library of Congress • 391,

UPI • 392, Smithsonian Institution, Photo No. 73633 • 393, The New York Public Library • 395, International Museum of Photography at George Eastman House • 396, Cook Collection, Valentine Museum, Richmond, Va. • 397, (top) Wide World; (bottom) International Museum of Photography at George Eastman House • 400, International Museum of Photography at George Eastman House • 402, National Archives • 405, UPI • 407, Culver Pictures • 408, *The New York Times* © 1915 by The New York Times Company. Reprinted by permission • 409, Imperial War Museum, London • 410-411, UPI • 412, Library of Congress • 413, *The Masses,* July 21, 1916, photo Library of Congress • 414, The Bettmann Archive • 416-417, UPI • 417, (right) Imperial War Museum, London • 418, UPI (3) • 419, George Luks, *Armistice Night.* 1918. Oil on canvas. 37 x 68¾ inches. Collection of Whitney Museum of American Art • 420, UPI • 421, Research Library, Twentieth Century-Fox • 424, Chicago Historical Society • 426, Wide World • 427, (top) UPI; (bottom) ILGWU • 428, UPI (2) • 430, *The Masses,* March 1913, photo Library of Congress • 431, International Museum of Photography at George Eastman House • 432, The New York Public Library, Prints Division • 433, *Literary Digest,* May 7, 1921, photo Library of Congress • 434, UPI • 435, Estate of Ben Shahn, photo New Jersey State Museum • 438, International Museum of Photography at George Eastman House • 440, *Life,* February 18, 1926, photo Library of Congress • 442, (top) Schomburg Center for Research in Black Culture, The New York Public Library, Astor, Lenox, and Tilden Foundations; (bottom) UPI • 443, Brown Brothers • 445, The New York Public Library, Picture Collection • 446, (bottom) UPI • 447, The New York Public Library, Picture Collection • 448, Charles Stelzle, *Why Prohibition!,* 1918, photo The New York Public Library, Picture Collection • 449, Culver Pictures • 450, (top, bottom) Brown Brothers; (middle) Smithsonian Institution • 451, (top) Summers, Cleveland *News,* photo The New York Public Library, Picture Collection; (bottom) The New York Public Library, Prints Division • 452, Ford Motor Company • 453, Library of Congress • 454, Chesler Collection, Florham-Madison Library, Fairleigh Dickinson University • 455, Brown Brothers • 456, Photo World • 457, The New York Public Library, Picture Collection • 458, Rudi Blesh Collection, Courtesy of Columbia Records • 460, (top) The Theatre Guild, photo Alfredo Valente, (bottom left) Schomburg Center for Research in Black Culture, The New York Public Library, Astor, Lenox, and Tilden Foundations; (bottom right) James Van Der Zee Institute • 461, *Metronome Magazine* • 462, Alley, *The Commercial Appeal,* Memphis, Tenn. • 465, International Museum of Photography at George Eastman House • 466, UPI (2) • 472, Dallas Museum of Fine Arts, photo Sandak, Inc. • 474, The Detroit *News* • 475, Culver Pictures • 476, *Life,* September 22, 1921, photo Library of Congress • 477, UPI • 479, Margaret Bourke-White, Time/Life Picture Agency • 480, UPI (2) • 481, Reprinted, courtesy of *The Chicago Tribune* • 482, Wide World • 484, © Copyright 1978, Estate of Peter Arno, photo Franklin D. Roosevelt Library, Hyde Park, New York • 485, (top) Tom Howard, courtesy of *The Columbus (Ohio) Dispatch;* (bottom) Schomburg Center for Research in Black Culture, The New York Public Library, Astor, Lenox, and Tilden Foundations • 487, Wide World • 488, UPI • 489, Jacob Burck, *Chicago Sun-Times,* photo Franklin D. Roosevelt Library, Hyde Park, New York • 490, Farm Security Administration, Photo by Rothstein • 491, Dorothea Lange, Magnum • 493, Estate of Ben Shahn, photo New Jersey State Museum • 494, The Bettmann Archive • 495, (top) © Walt Disney Productions, World Rights Reserved; (bottom) The

Museum of Modern Art/Film Stills Archive • 497, The Museum of Modern Art/Film Stills Archive • 499, 500, UPI (2) • 501, Farm Security Administration, Photo by Rothstein • 502, Wide World • 504, UPI • 506, Hugo Jaeger, *Life* Magazine, © Time Inc. • 508, (top) UPI; (bottom) Keystone • 509, (top) Collection Mrs. Joel Rosen, photo Amon Carter Museum of Western Art; (bottom) Hirschfeld drawing, courtesy of The Margo Feiden Galleries, New York City • 512, U.S. Army • 513, *Life,* June 1935, photo The New York Public Library, Picture Collection • 515, UPI (2) • 516, Wide World • 517, (top) Library of Congress; (bottom) UPI • 518, (top) Columbia Records; (bottom) Olive Pierce Photographer, Copyright © 1978 • 520-521, Czechoslovak News Agency • 523, Wide World • 524, UPI • 525, Page, *The Louisville* (Ky.) *Courier Journal* • 528, Hugo Jaeger, *Life* Magazine, © 1940, Time Inc. • 530, Victor Barron • 531, Franklin D. Roosevelt Library, Hyde Park, New York • 533, UPI (2) • 534, Hugo Jaeger, *Life* Magazine, © 1939, Time Inc. • 536, Wide World • 537, Daniel Bishop, *St. Louis Star-Times* • 538, UPI • 539, National Archives • 540, Dorothea Lange, photo no. 210-GC-160 in the National Archives • 542, Culver Pictures • 544, UPI • 545, Hugo Jaeger, *Life* Magazine, © 1944, Time Inc. • 547, Franklin D. Roosevelt Library, Hyde Park, New York • 550, UPI • 554, German Information Center • 556, Copyright, 1964, *The Los Angeles Times.* Reprinted by permission • 557, UPI • 559, Talburt, *The New York World Journal Tribune* • 561, UPI • 562, Shoemaker, *Chicago Daily News* • 564, UPI • 567, (top) UPI; (bottom) Leo Joseph Roche, Buffalo *Courier Express* • 568, UPI • 570, Wide World • 572, (left) Wide World; (right) Lee Lockwood/Black Star • 574, (top) Wide World; (bottom) "Let's Get a Lock for This Thing," from *Straight Herblock* (Simon & Schuster, 1964) • 576, Copyright © 1961, *The St. Louis Post-Dispatch,* reproduced by courtesy of Bill Mauldin • 577, Copyright 1945, Des Moines Register and Tribune Company. Reprinted by permission • 578, Wayne Miller/Magnum • 581, (top) UPI; (bottom) The Metropolitan Museum of Art, George A. Hearn Fund, 1957 • 583, "Are You Sure You Didn't Miss Anything?," copyright 1946 by Herblock in *The Washington Post* • 584, Wide World • 586, (bottom) UPI • 586-587, Hy Peskin, *Life* Magazine, © 1949, Time Inc. • 589, reproduced by permission of Oldsmobile Division, General Motors Corporation • 590, (top) Elliott Erwitt/Magnum; (bottom) UPI • 591, Factors, Inc. • 592, Admiral Group, Rockwell International • 593, Wide World • 595, UPI • 599, Wide World • 601, Copyright 1903, Des Moines Register and Tribune Company. Reprinted by permission • 602, National Airlines • 604, Flip Schulke/ Black Star • 606, Terry Dintenfass Gallery, New York City, and Hirshhorn Museum and Sculpture Garden, Smithsonian Institution • 608, Edward Clark, *Life* Magazine, © 1949, Time Inc. • 611, (left) Wide World; (right) Burt Glinn/Magnum • 612, UPI • 613, Grey Villet, Time/Life Picture Agency, © 1963, Time Inc. • 621, 622, Bob Fitch/ Black Star (2) • 623, George Ballis/ Black Star • 625, Nina Leen, *Life* Magazine, © 1947, Time Inc. • 627, Ginger Chih/Peter Arnold • 632, Constantine Manos/Magnum • 634, Wide World • 635, Philip Jones Griffiths/ Magnum • 637, Yale Joel, *Life* Magazine, © 1946, Time Inc. • 638, Peace Corps/ACTION • 640, Bob Gomel, *Life* Magazine, © 1963, Time Inc. • 642, (bottom) UPI • 642-643, (top) Pat Oliphant, Copyright *The Denver Post.* Reprinted with permission, Los Angeles Times Syndicate • 644, UPI • 646, Donald McCullin/Magnum • 647, Wide World • 648, UPI • 649, "These Weren't Damaged in the Riots — They Went to Pieces Years Before," from *The Herblock Gallery* (Simon & Schuster, 1968) • 651, Harvey Lloyd/Peter Arnold • 652, (top) Ken Regan/Camera 5; (bottom) Capitol Records • 655, Marc Riboud/Magnum • 656, Copyright, Tarentum, Pa., *Valley News Dispatch* • 662, Constantine Manos/Magnum • 665, Copyright © 1976, Cityarts Workshop, Inc. • 667, NASA • 669, Conrad, Copyright © 1969, *The Los Angeles Times.* Reprinted with permission. • 670-671, Ernst Haas • 673, Pat Oliphant, Copyright © 1970, *The Denver Post.* Reprinted with permission, Los Angeles Times Syndicate • 675, Magnum • 676, Ralph Steadman, photo Amon Carter Museum of Western Art • 678, Mark Godfrey/Magnum • 679, Mike Peters, *Dayton Daily News* • 680, UPI • 681, (top) Robert Pryor; (bottom) Hy Rosen, *The Albany* (N.Y.) *Times-Union* • 683, Burk Uzzle/Magnum • 685, M. C. Magruder/Black Star • 686, Alex Webb/Magnum • 689, UPI • 690, Library of Congress • 693, Ernst Haas • 695, McKinney (Texas) *Courier-Gazette.*

Cover Credit: Washington University Gallery of Art, St. Louis.